EVIDENCE IN CHILD ABUSE AND NEGLECT
SECOND EDITION
VOLUME 2

EVIDENCE IN CHILD ABUSE AND NEGLECT
SECOND EDITION
VOLUME 2

JOHN E.B. MYERS

Professor of Law
University of the Pacific
McGeorge School of Law

Wiley Law Publications

JOHN WILEY & SONS, INC.

New York • Chichester • Brisbane • Toronto • Singapore

In recognition of the importance of preserving what has been
written, it is a policy of John Wiley & Sons, Inc., to have
books of enduring value published in the United States
printed on acid-free paper, and we exert our best efforts
to that end.

Copyright © 1987, 1992 by John Wiley & Sons, Inc.

Previously published as *Child Witness Law and Practice*.

All rights reserved. Published simultaneously in Canada.

Reproduction or translation of any part of this work
beyond that permitted by Section 107 or 108 of the
1976 United States Copyright Act without the permission
of the copyright owner is unlawful. Requests for
permission or further information should be addressed to
the Permissions Department, John Wiley & Sons, Inc.

This publication is designed to provide accurate and
authoritative information in regard to the subject
matter covered. It is sold with the understanding that
the publisher is not engaged in rendering legal, accounting,
or other professional services. If legal advice or other
expert assistance is required, the services of a competent
professional person should be sought. *From a Declaration
of Principles jointly adopted by a Committee of the
American Bar Association and a Committee of Publishers.*

All quoted material from WEINSTEIN'S EVIDENCE is
reprinted with permission from *Weinstein's Evidence* by
J. Weinstein & M. Berger. Copyright © 1992 by Matthew
Bender & Co., Inc. All rights reserved.

John Spencer and Rhona Flin, *The Evidence of Children,* copyright © 1990 by Blackstone Press Limited. Used with permission.

Professor Imwinkelreid's schematic is adapted and reprinted with permission from *Uncharged Misconduct Evidence* (ch. 2, p. 48, 1992), published by Clark Boardman Callaghan, 155 Pfingsten Road, Deerfield, IL 60015. Toll-free 1-800-323-1336. Price $98.00

Certain material is reprinted with permission from LaFave & Isreal, *Criminal Procedure* (West Pub. 1984), Vols. 1 and 2, pages 805 and 366.

Passages are reprinted with permission from C. Wright & K. Graham, *Federal Practice as Procedure* (West Pub. Co. 1978, 1990), Vols. 22, pages 467, 476, 480 and Vol. 27, pages 244, 278, 193, 210.

D. Louisell & C. Mueller, *Federal Evidence.* Reprint permission has been granted by the copyright holder, Lawyers Cooperative Publishing, a division of Thomson Legal Publishing, Inc.

J. Wigmore, *Evidence in Trials at Common Law* (Chadbourn Rev. 1978). Reprinted by permission of Little Brown & Co.

Material from G.S. Goodman & A. Clarke-Steward, "Suggestibility in children's testimony: implications for sexual abuse investigations" In the suggestibility of children's recollections: implications for eyewitness testimony (J. Dores, ed.) Copyright 1991 by the American Psychological Association. Reprinted by permission.

Library of Congress Cataloging-in-Publication Data

ISBN 0-471-55664-5 (set)
      0-471-58352-9 (v. 2)

Printed in the United States of America

10 9 8 7 6 5 4 3 2 1

KF
8950
.M94
1992
v.2

SUMMARY CONTENTS

VOLUME 1

Short Reference List		xxi
Chapter 1	Accusatory Pleadings, Privilege, and Discovery	1
Chapter 2	Testimonial Competence	59
Chapter 3	Physical Child Abuse and Neglect	137
Chapter 4	Child Sexual Abuse	217
Chapter 5	Direct Examination, Cross-Examination, and Impeachment	337

VOLUME 2

Short Reference List		xiii
Chapter 6	Character Evidence and Uncharged Misconduct Evidence	1
Chapter 7	Hearsay	79
Chapter 8	Altering the Courtroom to Accommodate Children	323
Table of Cases		355
Index		417

DETAILED CONTENTS

VOLUME 1

Short Reference List

Chapter 1 Accusatory Pleadings, Privilege, and Discovery

ACCUSATORY PLEADINGS AND CHILDREN'S UNDERSTANDING OF TIME

§ 1.1   Accusatory Pleadings
§ 1.2   Children's Understanding of Time
§ 1.3   —Court Recognition of Time Problems
§ 1.4   —Assessing Sufficiency of Pleadings
§ 1.5   —Protecting Defendants Against Double Jeopardy
§ 1.6   —Necessity for Specific Act and Jury Unanimity
§ 1.7   —Sufficient Evidence
§ 1.8   —Nonspecific Testimony and Defendant's Equal Protection
§ 1.9   Children's Understanding of Legal System
§ 1.10 —Legal Terms
§ 1.11 —Legal Procedures and Personnel

PRIVILEGE AND DISCOVERY

§ 1.12 Privilege
§ 1.13 Defense Discovery in Criminal Litigation
§ 1.14 —*Ritchie* Impact on Discovery of Confidential Records
§ 1.15 —Factors in Considering Confidentiality
§ 1.16 Prosecution Discovery in Criminal Litigation
§ 1.17 State Discovery in Dependency Litigation
§ 1.18 Discovery of Confidential Communications in Custody Litigation
§ 1.19 Discovery in Civil Litigation

Chapter 2 Testimonial Competence

§ 2.1   Overview
§ 2.2   History of Child Competence Law
§ 2.3   Rule 601: Every Person Competent
§ 2.4   —Rule 403: Unfair Prejudice
§ 2.5   —Rule 602: Personal Knowledge

§ 2.6	—Rule 603: Oath or Affirmation
§ 2.7	—Rule 611: Witness Order
§ 2.8	Presumptive Incompetence
§ 2.9	Child Abuse Litigation and Competency
§ 2.10	Capacity to Observe
§ 2.11	Memory
§ 2.12	Capacity to Communicate
§ 2.13	Using an Interpreter
§ 2.14	Differentiating Truth from Falsehood, Fact from Fantasy
§ 2.15	Obligation to Testify Truthfully
§ 2.16	Oath or Affirmation
§ 2.17	Personal Knowledge
§ 2.18	Competency Examinations
§ 2.19	When the Child Must Be Competent: Competence of Hearsay Declarants
§ 2.20	Questions for Competency Examinations
§ 2.21	Excluding Defendant from Competency Examination
§ 2.22	Psychological Evaluations Regarding Competence

Chapter 3	**Physical Child Abuse and Neglect**
§ 3.1	Prevalence of Physical Abuse and Neglect
§ 3.2	Physical Abuse Defined
§ 3.3	Defenses in Physical Abuse Litigation
§ 3.4	Medical Evidence of Physical Abuse
§ 3.5	Battered Child Syndrome
§ 3.6	Expert Qualifications
§ 3.7	Bases for Expert Opinion
§ 3.8	Expert Testimony on Means of Inflicting Injury
§ 3.9	Caretaker's Explanation of Injury
§ 3.10	Bruises
§ 3.11	Head Injury
§ 3.12	Chest and Abdominal Injuries
§ 3.13	Burns
§ 3.14	Fractures
§ 3.15	Munchausen Syndrome by Proxy
§ 3.16	Neglect
§ 3.17	—Medical Neglect
§ 3.18	—Psychological Neglect
§ 3.19	—Nonorganic Failure to Thrive
§ 3.20	—Mentally Retarded Parents
§ 3.21	—Psychiatrically Disabled Parents

DETAILED CONTENTS

	§ 3.22	—Physically Impaired Parents
	§ 3.23	—Drug Abuse as Neglect
	§ 3.24	—General Neglect
	§ 3.25	—Abandonment
	§ 3.26	—Educational Neglect
	§ 3.27	Poisoning and Other Forms of Maltreatment
	§ 3.28	Criminal Intent
	§ 3.29	Methods of Proving Intent
	§ 3.30	Identity of Perpetrator
	§ 3.31	Battering Parent Syndrome
	§ 3.32	Admissibility of Photographs
Chapter 4		**Child Sexual Abuse**
	§ 4.1	Introduction
	§ 4.2	Prevalence and Effects of Child Sexual Abuse
	§ 4.3	Defenses in Child Sexual Abuse Cases
	§ 4.4	—Fabrication Defense
	§ 4.5	—Leading Questions Defense
	§ 4.6	—Misinterpretation Defense
	§ 4.7	—Mistaken Identity Defense
	§ 4.8	—Statutory Language Defenses
	§ 4.9	Admissibility of Expert Testimony
	§ 4.10	Qualifications of Expert Witnesses
	§ 4.11	Bases for Expert Testimony
	§ 4.12	Form of Expert Testimony
	§ 4.13	Testimony on Ultimate Issues
	§ 4.14	Novel Scientific Evidence
	§ 4.15	—Need for Special Rules
	§ 4.16	—Defining Science
	§ 4.17	—Defining Novel Scientific Evidence
	§ 4.18	—*Frye* Test
	§ 4.19	—Relevance Analysis
	§ 4.20	Medical Evidence of Child Sexual Abuse
	§ 4.21	—Medical History
	§ 4.22	—Physical Examination
	§ 4.23	—Nonabusive Explanations for Findings
	§ 4.24	—Sexually Transmitted Disease
	§ 4.25	—Classification of Medical Findings
	§ 4.26	—Genetic Fingerprinting
	§ 4.27	—Colposcope
	§ 4.28	—Admissibility of Medical Testimony

§ 4.29	Psychological Evidence of Child Sexual Abuse
§ 4.30	Expert Testimony as Substantive Evidence
§ 4.31	—Literature Review
§ 4.32	—Significance of Symptoms
§ 4.33	—Child Sexual Abuse Accommodation Syndrome
§ 4.34	—Rape Trauma Syndrome
§ 4.35	—Anatomical Dolls
§ 4.36	—Questionable Techniques for Evaluation
§ 4.37	—Case Law
§ 4.38	—Behavior after Sexual Assault
§ 4.39	Expert Testimony to Rehabilitate Impeached Credibility
§ 4.40	—Delay in Reporting
§ 4.41	—Recantation
§ 4.42	—Inconsistencies
§ 4.43	—Ambivalence Toward Abuser
§ 4.44	—Case Law
§ 4.45	Expert Testimony about Credibility
§ 4.46	Expert Testimony Identifying Perpetrator
§ 4.47	Expert Testimony about Perpetrator Personality Traits or Profile
§ 4.48	—Defining and Describing Paraphilia
§ 4.49	—Psychological Evaluation of Sexual Offenders
§ 4.50	—Profile of "Typical" Child Molester
§ 4.51	Court-Appointed Experts
§ 4.52	Invited Error Doctrine

Chapter 5 Direct Examination, Cross-Examination, and Impeachment

§ 5.1	Introduction

DIRECT EXAMINATION

§ 5.2	Preparing Children to Testify
§ 5.3	Direct and Redirect Examination
§ 5.4	Supporting the Child's Competence
§ 5.5	Establishing Dates and Times
§ 5.6	Explaining Delay in Reporting Abuse
§ 5.7	Use of Leading Questions
§ 5.8	Demonstrative Evidence to Aid Testimony
§ 5.9	Questioning by Court
§ 5.10	Recess to Reduce Stress
§ 5.11	Refreshing Recollection
§ 5.12	—Use of Privileged Material to Refresh Memory
§ 5.13	—Misuse of Recollection Aids

DETAILED CONTENTS

§ 5.14 —Refreshing Recollection Distinguished from Recorded Recollection
§ 5.15 While Child Is Not on Stand
§ 5.16 Court-Ordered Psychological Examinations Regarding Credibility
§ 5.17 Corroboration of Victim's Testimony

IMPEACHMENT AND CROSS-EXAMINATION

§ 5.18 Impeachment Modes
§ 5.19 —Voucher Rule
§ 5.20 Collateral Fact Rule
§ 5.21 Bias
§ 5.22 Cross-Examination of Expert Witnesses
§ 5.23 —Expert's Personal History of Abuse
§ 5.24 Untruthful Character
§ 5.25 Evidence of Conviction
§ 5.26 Contradiction
§ 5.27 Defects in Capacity
§ 5.28 Rape Shield Statutes
§ 5.29 —Source of Semen or Injury: Rule 412(b)(2)(A)
§ 5.30 —Consent: Rule 412(b)(2)(B)
§ 5.31 —Defendant's State of Mind
§ 5.32 —General Impeachment of Credibility
§ 5.33 —Impeachment by Contradiction
§ 5.34 —Prior False Accusations of Abuse
§ 5.35 —Experience as Source of Fantasy or Fabrication
§ 5.36 —Bias or Ulterior Motive
§ 5.37 —Rape Shield as Protection for Defendant

VOLUME 2

Short Reference List

Chapter 6   Character Evidence and Uncharged Misconduct Evidence

CHARACTER EVIDENCE

§ 6.1 Categories of Evidence Reflecting on Character
§ 6.2 Character "in Issue"
§ 6.3 —Criminal Litigation
§ 6.4 —Child Custody Litigation
§ 6.5 —Juvenile Court Dependency Proceedings
§ 6.6 —Proceedings to Terminate Parental Rights
§ 6.7 Conduct in Conformity with Character

DETAILED CONTENTS

§ 6.8	—Defendant's Character: Rule 404(a)(1)	
§ 6.9	—Victim's Character: Rule 404(a)(2)	
§ 6.10	Habit	

UNCHARGED MISCONDUCT EVIDENCE

§ 6.11	Describing Uncharged Misconduct Evidence
§ 6.12	—Distinguishing Uncharged Misconduct Evidence from Character Evidence
§ 6.13	—Recurring Issues
§ 6.14	Motive
§ 6.15	Proof of Intent, Absence of Mistake, or Accident
§ 6.16	—Motive, Plan, or Knowledge
§ 6.17	—Doctrine of Chances
§ 6.18	—Inference from Intent at Time of Uncharged Acts
§ 6.19	Prior Attempts to Commit Charged Offense
§ 6.20	"Entire Picture" of Crime
§ 6.21	Depraved Sexual Propensity
§ 6.22	Plan
§ 6.23	Consciousness of Guilt
§ 6.24	Modus Operandi to Prove Identity
§ 6.25	Opportunity or Capacity
§ 6.26	Proof of Coercion, Force, or Threat

Chapter 7	**Hearsay**
§ 7.1	Introduction

OUT-OF-COURT UTTERANCES

§ 7.2	Hearsay Defined
§ 7.3	—Analyzing Out-of-Court Statements
§ 7.4	Justification for Excluding Hearsay
§ 7.5	Preliminary Rulings on Admissibility
§ 7.6	Verbal Assertions to Prove Other than Matter Asserted
§ 7.7	Written and Drawn Assertions to Prove Other than Matter Asserted
§ 7.8	Nonverbal Assertions to Prove Other than Matter Asserted
§ 7.9	Silence or Inaction as Assertion
§ 7.10	Implied Assertions
§ 7.11	—Verbal and Written Implied Assertions
§ 7.12	—Assertions Implied from Conduct
§ 7.13	Utterances During Sleep
§ 7.14	Verbal Acts and Verbal Parts of Acts
§ 7.15	Assertions to Prove Effect on Listener
§ 7.16	Assertions to Prove Source of Unique Knowledge

DETAILED CONTENTS

EXCEPTIONS TO HEARSAY RULE

§ 7.17	Rationale for Exceptions
§ 7.18	Prior Inconsistent Statements
§ 7.19	—Admissibility Requirements
§ 7.20	—Recurring Issues
§ 7.21	Prior Consistent Statements
§ 7.22	—Admissibility Requirements
§ 7.23	—Fabrication Motivated by Improper Influence, Bias, or Interest
§ 7.24	—Impeachment Through Prior Inconsistent Statements
§ 7.25	—Impeachment Charging Memory Lapse
§ 7.26	Out-of-Court Statements of Identification
§ 7.27	Present Sense Impressions
§ 7.28	Excited Utterances
§ 7.29	—Admissibility Requirements
§ 7.30	—Evaluation Factors
§ 7.31	Fresh Complaint of Rape or Sexual Abuse
§ 7.32	State of Mind
§ 7.33	—Criminal Litigation
§ 7.34	—Civil Litigation
§ 7.35	Diagnosis or Treatment Exception
§ 7.36	—Rationales for Exception
§ 7.37	Past Recollection Recorded
§ 7.38	Business Records
§ 7.39	Public Records
§ 7.40	Learned Treatises
§ 7.41	Proof of Age
§ 7.42	Residual Exception
§ 7.43	—Analysis of Reliability
§ 7.44	—Factors Surrounding Statement
§ 7.45	—Factors Corroborating Statement
§ 7.46	Child Hearsay Exception
§ 7.47	Sufficiency to Support Finding of Fact or Verdict
§ 7.48	Unavailable Hearsay Declarants
§ 7.49	Testimonial Competence of Hearsay Declarants

RIGHT TO CONFRONT ACCUSATORY WITNESSES

§ 7.50	Confrontation Right: Applicability and Elements
§ 7.51	Hearsay and the Confrontation Clause
§ 7.52	—Unavailability Rule
§ 7.53	—Reliability Requirement
§ 7.54	Two-Defendant Trials

§ 7.55	Former Testimony
§ 7.56	Limitations on Cross-Examination
§ 7.57	Applicable Proceedings
§ 7.58	Waiver and Forfeiture of Confrontation Right

Chapter 8 **Altering the Courtroom to Accommodate Children**

§ 8.1	Support Persons
§ 8.2	Sequestering Witnesses
§ 8.3	Altering Courtroom Practices and Configurations
§ 8.4	Defendant's Right to Public Trial
§ 8.5	Right to Attend Criminal Trials
§ 8.6	Right of Access to Court Records
§ 8.7	Video Testimony
§ 8.8	—Confrontation Clause
§ 8.9	—Assistance of Counsel
§ 8.10	—Impartial Jury
§ 8.11	—Compulsory Process Clause
§ 8.12	—Due Process Clause
§ 8.13	—Right to Be Present
§ 8.14	Jury's Perception of Children's Credibility

Table of Cases

Index

SHORT REFERENCE LIST

Short Reference	*Full Reference*
Bays & Chadwick	Bays & Chadwick, *Medical Diagnosis of the Sexually Abused Child,* _____ Child Abuse & Neglect _____ (To publish 1993)
Darro & McCurdy	Darro & McCurdy, Current Trends in Child Abuse Reporting and Fatalities: The Results of the 1990 Annual Fifty State Survey National Comm. for Prevention of Child Abuse, 1991
Enos, Conrath & Byer	Enos, Conrath & Byer, *Forensic Evaluation of the Sexually Abused Child,* 78 Pediatrics 385 (1986)
Flin, Stevenson & Davies	Flin, Stevenson & Davies, *Children's Knowledge of Court Proceedings,* 80 Brit. J. Psychol. 285 (1989)
Giannelli	Giannelli, *The Admissibility of Novel Scientific Evidence:* Frye v. United States, *A Half-Century Later,* 80 Colum. L. Rev. 1197 (1980)
Goodman, Rudy, Bottoms & Aman	Goodman, Rudy, Bottoms & Aman, *Children's Concerns and Memory: Issues of Ecological Validity in the Study of Children's Eyewitness Testimony, in* Knowing and Remembering in Young Children 249 (R. Fivush & J. Hudson eds. 1990)
Graham	M. Graham, Handbook of Federal Evidence (3d ed. 1991)
Graham, *Critique*	Graham, *Prior Consistent Statements: Rule 801(d)(1)(B) of the Federal Rules of Evidence, Critique and Proposal,* 30 Hastings, L.J. 575 (1979)
Imwinkelried	E. Imwinkelried, Uncharged Misconduct Evidence (1984)
LaFave & Israel	W. LaFave & J. Israel, Criminal Procedure (1984)
LaFave & Scott	W. LaFave & A. Scott, Criminal Law (2d ed. 1986)

SHORT REFERENCE LIST

Short Reference	*Full Reference*
Louisell & Mueller	D. Louisell & C. Mueller, Federal Evidence (1979)
McCormick	C. McCormick, McCormick on Evidence (E. Cleary ed., 3d ed. 1984)
MMPI	Minnesota multiphasic personality inventory
Park	Park, *"I Didn't Tell Them Anything About You": Implied Assertions as Hearsay under the Federal Rules of Evidence,* 74 Minn. L. Rev. 783 (1990)
Perkins & Boyce	R. Perkins & R. Boyce, Criminal Law (3d ed. 1982)
PTSD	post-traumatic stress disorder
RTS	rape trauma syndrome
Saywitz, *Children's Conceptions*	Saywitz, *Children's Conceptions of the Legal System: "Court Is a Place to Play Basketball,"* in Perspectives on Children's Testimony 131 (S. Ceci, D. Ross & M. Toglia eds. 1989)
Saywitz, Jaenicke & Camparo	Saywitz, Jaenicke & Camparo, *Children's Knowledge of Legal Terminology,* 14 L. & Hum. Bev. 523 1990)
Schmitt	Schmitt, *The Child with Nonaccidental Trauma,* in The Battered Child 129 (R. Helfer & R. Kempe eds., 4th ed. 1987)
Warren-Leubecker, Tate, Hinton & Ozbek	Warren-Leubecker, Tate, Hinton & Ozbek, *What Do Children Know about the Legal System and When Do They Know It? First Steps Down a Less Traveled Path in Child Witness Research,* in Perspectives on Children's Testimony 158 (S. Ceci, D. Ross & M. Toglia eds. 1989)
Wigmore	J. Wigmore, Evidence in Trials at Common Law (Chadbourn rev. 1978)
Weinsten & Berger	J. Weinstein & M. Berger, Weinstein's Evidence (1987)
Wright & Graham	C. Wright & K. Graham, Federal Practice and Procedure: Evidence (1980)

CHAPTER 6
CHARACTER EVIDENCE AND UNCHARGED MISCONDUCT EVIDENCE

CHARACTER EVIDENCE
§ 6.1   Categories of Evidence Reflecting on Character
§ 6.2   Character "in Issue"
§ 6.3   —Criminal Litigation
§ 6.4   —Child Custody Litigation
§ 6.5   —Juvenile Court Dependency Proceedings
§ 6.6   —Proceedings to Terminate Parental Rights
§ 6.7   Conduct in Conformity with Character
§ 6.8   —Defendant's Character: Rule 404(a)(1)
§ 6.9   —Victim's Character: Rule 404(a)(2)
§ 6.10 Habit

UNCHARGED MISCONDUCT EVIDENCE
§ 6.11 Describing Uncharged Misconduct Evidence
§ 6.12 —Distinguishing Uncharged Misconduct Evidence from Character Evidence
§ 6.13 —Recurring Issues
§ 6.14 Motive
§ 6.15 Proof of Intent, Absence of Mistake, or Accident
§ 6.16 —Motive, Plan, or Knowledge
§ 6.17 —Doctrine of Chances
§ 6.18 —Inference from Intent at Time of Uncharged Acts
§ 6.19 Prior Attempts to Commit Charged Offense
§ 6.20 "Entire Picture" of Crime
§ 6.21 Depraved Sexual Propensity
§ 6.22 Plan

§ 6.23 Consciousness of Guilt
§ 6.24 Modus Operandi to Prove Identity
§ 6.25 Opportunity or Capacity
§ 6.26 Proof of Coercion, Force, or Threat

CHARACTER EVIDENCE

§ 6.1 Categories of Evidence Reflecting on Character

A cardinal principle of American law holds that evidence of a person's character generally is not admissible to prove that the person acted in conformity with character on a particular occasion.[1] The prohibition on character evidence is applicable in civil as well as criminal litigation. The Supreme Court described the rule against character evidence in *Michelson v. United States:*[2]

> Courts that follow the common-law tradition almost unanimously have come to disallow resort by the prosecution to any kind of evidence of a defendant's evil character to establish a probability of his guilt. Not that the law invests the defendant with a presumption of good character, but it simply closes the whole matter of character, disposition and reputation on the prosecution's case-in-chief. The State may not show defendant's prior trouble with the law, specific criminal acts, or ill name among his neighbors, even though such facts might logically be persuasive that he is by propensity a probable perpetrator of the crime.[3]

The principle excluding character evidence is found in Rule 404(a) of the Federal Rules of Evidence, which states, "Evidence of a person's character or a trait of character is not admissible for the purpose of proving action in conformity therewith on a particular occasion . . . ."

---

[1] *See* 2 D. Louisell & C. Mueller, Federal Evidence § 136 (1979) [hereinafter Louisell & Mueller]; 2 J. Weinstein & M. Berger, Weinstein's Evidence ¶ 404[04], at 404–29 (1987) [hereinafter Weinstein & Berger]. *See also* Teitelbaum & Hertz, Evidence II: *Evidence of Other Crimes and Proof of Intent*, 13 N.M. L. Rev. 423, 423–24 (1983), where the authors write:
> [The law] makes inadmissible, with certain exceptions, evidence relevant on the following theory: Defendant committed a wrong in the past; defendant therefore has a propensity or a character trait for committing wrongful acts; therefore defendant is more likely to have engaged in the act for which he is on trial than is someone not known to have this character trait.

[2] 335 U.S. 469 (1948).

[3] *Id.* at 475 (footnotes omitted) (citation omitted).

§ 6.1 CATEGORIES OF CHARACTER EVIDENCE

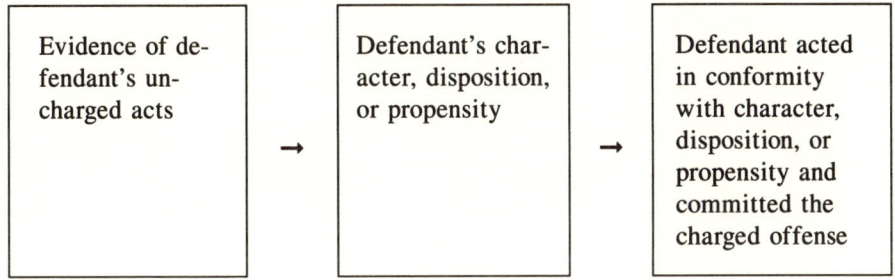

Figure 6–1. Chain of inferences forbidden by Federal Rule of Evidence 404(a).

Imwinkelried employs the schematic in **Figure 6–1** to illustrate the two-step chain of inferences forbidden by Rule 404(a).[4] The arrows represent inferences. With the forbidden chain of inferences, evidence of a person's conduct gives rise to an inference that the person possesses certain traits of character. From this inference of character, a second inference arises that the person probably acted in conformity with the person's character on the relevant occasion.

Evidence of character to prove conduct in conformity therewith is not excluded because it is irrelevant.[5] On the contrary, character evidence may "weigh too much with the jury."[6] Exclusion of character evidence offered by the prosecution is based on two concerns: "(1) that the jury may convict a 'bad man' who deserves to be punished not because he is guilty of the crime charged but because of his prior or subsequent misdeeds; and (2) that the jury will infer that because the accused committed other crimes, he probably committed the crime charged."[7]

With the general principle of Rule 404(a) excluding character evidence as a starting place, it is useful to consider four categories of exceptions to the general principle.[8]

---

[4] E. Imwinkelried, Uncharged Misconduct Evidence (1984).

[5] Michelson v. United States, 335 U.S. 469, 475–76 (1948); Velez v. State, 762 P.2d 1297, 1300 n.5 (Alaska Ct. App. 1988) ("propensity evidence is not excluded because it has too little probative, but because it has too much"); Matthews v. Superior Ct. (People), 201 Cal. App. 3d 385, 247 Cal. Rptr. 226, 231 (1988) ("such evidence is barred not because it lacks probative value but because its prejudicial effect outweighs its probative value"); Montgomery v. State, 810 S.W.2d 372, 377 (Tex. Crim. App. 1990) ("The exclusion of other wrongs evidence under Rule 404 is based, not on its lack of probative value, but rather on its unfair prejudicial effect").

[6] Michelson v. United States, 335 U.S. 469, 476 (1948). *See also* People v. Lewis, 69 N.Y.2d 321, 506 N.E.2d 915, 916–17 514 N.Y.S.2d 205 (1987) (although "evidence of a defendant's prior uncharged crimes may have some probative value, Wigmore contends that such evidence is objectionable because juries attach too much significance to it").

[7] United States v. Phillips, 599 F.2d 134, 136 (6th Cir. 1979). *See also* 2 Louisell & Mueller § 136, at 128–30.

[8] The idea for these categories is drawn from the work of Professor Edward Imwinkelried. *See* E. Imwinkelried, Uncharged Misconduct Evidence (1984).

1. Character in issue
2. Evidence of character admissible to prove conduct in conformity therewith:
   a. Character of accused—Fed. R. Evid. 404(a)(1)
   b. Character of victim—Fed. R. Evid. 404(a)(2)
   c. Untruthful character to impeach—Fed. R. Evid. 404(a)(3); 608(b)
   d. Depraved sexual propensity
3. Uncharged misconduct evidence—Fed. R. Evid. 404(b)
4. Habit—Fed. R. Evid. 406

The first category consists of cases in which a person's character is "in issue" (see § **6.2**). The second category is composed of rules permitting character evidence to prove conduct in conformity therewith on a specified occasion, that is, rules permitting precisely what Rule 404(a) forbids (see § **6.7**). The third category embraces uncharged misconduct evidence (see §§ **6.11** to **6.26**). Uncharged misconduct evidence is the subject of Rule 404(b), which allows evidence reflecting on character to prove matters *other than* conduct in conformity with character, such as motive, intent, or plan.[9] The fourth category is habit (see § **6.10**).

§ 6.2 Character "in Issue"

In certain types of litigation, character is "in issue." The pertinent substantive law makes a person's character an element of a claim or defense. Wigmore wrote that "[s]ubstantive law sometimes makes the rights and liabilities of parties depend in part on the existence or nonexistence of a trait of character."[10] An example of litigation where character is in issue is a personal injury suit alleging that a car owner negligently entrusted the car to a dangerous driver. The driver's character as a danger behind the wheel is in issue because it is an element of the plaintiff's cause of action charging negligent entrustment. Another case where character is in issue is a defamation action in which the defense is truth. Suppose the defendant stated that the plaintiff is "corrupt." In the

---

[9] Fed. R. Evid. 404(b).

[10] 1A J. Wigmore, Evidence in Trials at Common Law § 69.1, at 1457 (1983) [hereinafter Wigmore]. *See also* G. Lilly, An Introduction to the Law of Evidence § 5.3, at 125 (2d ed. 1987) ("The substantive law sometimes makes character a dispositive issue at trial: the existence or nonexistence of a character trait is itself an issue that directly determines the outcome of the case"); C. McCormick, McCormick on Evidence § 187, at 551 (E. Cleary ed., 3d ed. 1984) [hereinafter McCormick] ("A person's character may be a material fact that under the substantive law determines rights and liabilities"); 2 Weinstein & Berger ¶ 404[02], at 404–17 ("A person's possession of a particular trait of character may be a material, consequential fact which under the substantive law determines the rights and liabilities of the parties").

ensuing defamation action, the defense is that the statement is true. The plaintiff's character for corruption is in issue under the substantive law.

§ 6.3 —Criminal Litigation

In criminal litigation, character is seldom in issue as that term is used in this section.[11] Louisell and Mueller explain:

> Since criminal sanctions aim to deter and penalize *misbehavior* . . . and not *condition or status,* it is unsurprising that character is seldom an element in a charge. It is perhaps equally to be expected that character seldom amounts to an element of a defense, and a person who engages in the proscribed behavior (if he also has or entertains the requisite mental condition) may be guilty of a crime even if his general character assures him favored consideration in heaven or the esteem of posterity. And in fact proof of good character is almost always advanced as the basis for an inference that the accused did not engage in the behavior charged. The rarity of cases in which character may be said to be an element of a charge or defense is attested by the obscurity of the solitary example from the criminal sphere cited by the Advisory Committee in its Note to Rule 405—"the chastity of the victim under a statute specifying her chastity as an element of the crime of seduction"![12]

Thus, the defendant's character usually is not an element of the offense, and is not in issue. If, however, the offense includes threats against the victim, the defendant's character for following through on threats may be in issue.[13] When an element of an offense includes prior criminal activity by the defendant, "pretty clearly at least one aspect of the character of the accused is an element in the government's case."[14]

---

[11] In criminal litigation, courts often state that when a defendant offers character witnesses (Rule 404(a)(1)), the defendant's character is in issue. In this book the term *in issue* has a narrower meaning. Character is in issue only when the relevant substantive law makes a person's character an element of a cause of action or defense. *See* 2 Louisell & Mueller § 137 at 135–36.

[12] 2 Louisell & Mueller § 141, at 278–79 (footnotes omitted).

[13] *See* 2 Weinstein & Berger ¶ 404[02], at 404–21 ("Character evidence is customarily received in Hobbs Act prosecutions. Since the government must prove that property was extorted from the victim by threats, the defendant's reputation for violence—when known to the victim—is relevant in ascertaining the victim's fear and its reasonableness").

See also United States v. Billingsley, 474 F.2d 63, 66 (6th Cir.), *cert. denied,* 414 U.S. 819 (1973) (Hobbs Act prosecution; "The reputation of the defendant is admissible not to show that he was a bad man and likely to commit a crime, but to indicate that the threats of the defendant were not idle").

[14] 2 Louisell & Mueller § 141, at 280–81.

With rare exceptions, such as the seduction statute referred to by Louisell and Mueller,[15] the victim's character is not in issue in criminal litigation, including child abuse litigation. When attention shifts from criminal litigation to child abuse and neglect litigation in the civil arena, character frequently is in issue. Parental character is in issue in custody litigation incident to divorce, juvenile court dependency proceedings, and litigation to terminate parental rights.

§ 6.4 —Child Custody Litigation

In child custody and visitation litigation incident to divorce, parental fitness—thus character—is in issue.[16] Wigmore wrote:

> [T]he right of a parent to retain custody of his child may depend on a finding of the fitness of that person as a parent. In these cases, character evidence is of course admissible since what is at issue in the case *is* a character trait, and if the issue is to be resolved on the basis of evidence, evidence of character must be admitted.[17]

§ 6.5 —Juvenile Court Dependency Proceedings

At least four theoretical justifications exist for admitting character evidence at the adjudicatory stage of juvenile court dependency proceedings.

1. Parental character is in issue. Some statutes authorize intervention on proof of parental unfitness. Under such statutes parental character is in issue.

2. Dependency proceedings look to future. It is interesting to contrast criminal child abuse litigation with dependency proceedings in juvenile court. The guilt phase of criminal litigation focuses exclusively on historical facts, that is, on the past. In dependency proceedings, however, historical facts are established not only to prove the past, but to predict the future.[18] The critical issue in juvenile court is the child's future safety.

---

[15] The statute is still on the books in Virginia. *See* Va. Code Ann. § 18.2-68 (Michie 1988).

[16] *See In re* Dorothy I., 162 Cal. App. 3d 1154, 1159, 209 Cal. Rptr. 5, 8 (1984) ("Established law has recognized that the character of a parent is at issue in child custody cases"); Hicks v. Hicks, 249 Cal. App. 2d 964, 58 Cal. Rptr. 63, 65 (1967) (child custody incident to divorce; "Where the character of a witness is in issue (e.g., custody proceedings), specific acts of misconduct are admissible"); Feist v. Feist, 236 Cal. App. 2d 433, 46 Cal. Rptr. 93, 95 (1965) ("Defendant's moral character had a substantial bearing on whether it would be in the best interests of the children to award exclusive custody to her").

[17] 1A Wigmore § 69.1, at 1457.

[18] *See In re* Benjamin D., 227 Cal. App. 3d 1464, 278 Cal. Rptr. 468 (1991); In Interest of Carlita B., 408 S.E.2d 365, 382–83 (W. Va. 1991).

Juvenile court dependency proceedings fall into two categories. First, cases in which the child has already suffered abuse and is threatened with further harm. Second, cases in which the child has not been harmed, but is at risk of harm. Intervention is appropriate in both categories.

In the first category—where the child has already suffered maltreatment—the state's proof has two components: (1) proof that the child was abused, and (2) proof that the child is in danger of further abuse. Proof of each component turns on evidence of historical facts. To prove the first component, however, the evidence is exclusively backward-looking. By contrast, proof of the second component requires evidence that looks forward. Regarding the backward-looking aspect of the evidence, dependency proceedings are indistinguishable from criminal litigation. Evidence is admitted to prove that an act occurred in the past. The forward-looking aspect of the evidence, however, has no analogue in the guilt phase of criminal litigation.

In the second category of cases, the child has yet to suffer harm, and intervention is necessary to forestall threatened harm. Cases in the second category are similar to the second component of cases in the first category. That is, historical facts are advanced to establish the likelihood of future harm.

Both categories of dependency proceedings look to the future welfare of the child, and on this issue evidence of parental character is often highly probative. Pertinent aspects of parental character, including prior acts or threats of abuse, should be admissible on the issue of threatened harm. Wright and Graham explain:

> [T]he general rule [against character evidence] only bars the use of evidence of other crimes, wrongs, or acts, to prove past conduct of the person. [The rule against character evidence] refers to evidence offered to show that the person "acted" in conformity with the posited character. Hence, the rule does not preclude the use of other incidents when the issue is the likelihood that the person will engage in certain conduct in the future.[19]

In dependency proceedings where the state seeks to prove (1) past abuse, and (2) the threat of future harm, an argument can be made that the two issues should be treated sequentially. The state should first be required to prove the former abuse. On this issue the rule against character evidence should apply because the facts to be established occurred in the past. If the state carries its burden of proof on the first issue, so the argument goes, evidence of character then becomes admissible to prove threat of future harm. The argument for sequential ordering of issues has theoretical appeal. In practice, however, such an approach would serve no useful end. The state is nearly always in a position to argue that if it cannot prove former abuse, it must nonetheless be permitted to intervene on the basis of threatened harm. Thus, evidence of character or propensity is admissible in any event.

---

[19] 22 Wright and Graham § 5239, at 467.

3. Child maltreatment as continuing course of conduct.

Many children are subjected to a course of maltreatment extending over months or years. In such cases it is appropriate to allege a continuing course of conduct.[20] Under a continuing course of conduct theory, it is proper to admit all evidence of the perpetrator's conduct during the period of maltreatment,[21] including evidence that reflects on the perpetrator's character.

4. Public policy justifies admission of character evidence.

Character evidence is relevant to prove that a person acted in conformity with character on a specified occasion.[22] Such evidence is excluded because the risk of unfair prejudice is high. A strong argument can be made that in juvenile court dependency proceedings, the rule excluding character evidence should be relaxed. Dependency proceedings are civil, not criminal. The purpose of dependency litigation is not to punish but to protect. The risk of prejudice is low because dependency proceedings are tried to the court, not a jury. Moreover, child abuse is often difficult to prove. The overriding need for relevant evidence justifies admission of character evidence in dependency proceedings.[23]

§ 6.6 —Proceedings to Terminate Parental Rights

Statutory grounds to terminate the parent-child relationship vary.[24] Most statutes authorize termination on a number of grounds, including abandonment, abuse, and neglect. Although grounds for termination differ, a common theme undergirds termination provisions. Termination is proper when the parent-child relationship is irreparably broken and when continuation of the relationship will

---

[20] People v. Keindl, 68 N.Y.2d 410, 502 N.E.2d 577, 582, 509 N.Y.S.2d 790 (1986) (crime of endangering welfare of child is continuing offense).

[21] *See* State v. Hunt, 8 Ariz. App. 514, 447 P.2d 896, 900 (1968) (criminal prosecution for contributing to the dependency or delinquency of a minor; "Since the . . . charge covers a period of time, the State was entitled to put on evidence of other acts which tended to establish that he had contributed to the dependency or delinquency of Tina"); State v. Stevens, 238 N.W.2d 251, 259 (N.D. 1975) (dicta indicating child abuse is a continuing offense); State v. Jones, 735 P.2d 399, 402 (Utah Ct. App. 1987) (dicta); 22 C. Wright & K. Graham, Federal Practice and Procedure: Evidence § 5239, at 452–53 (1978) [hereinafter Wright & Graham] ("where the crime is a continuing offense, as in the case of possession of contraband, proof of possession on some date before or after the one charged in the indictment is permissible"); E. Imwinkelried, Uncharged Misconduct Evidence § 2:10 (1987).

[22] See § **6.1**.

[23] *See In re* Robert P., 61 Cal. App. 3d 310, 316–17, 132 Cal. Rptr. 5, 9 (1976) ("While the fitness of the parent is determined as of the time of hearing and not necessarily determined by prior conduct . . . , the court here was not required to disregard the pattern of the mother's conduct for a substantial period before the hearing").

[24] *See* Hardin & Tazzara, *A Comparison of Model Acts on Parental Rights Termination,* 7 Fam. L. Rep. (BNA) No. 35, at 4025 (1981).

§ 6.6 PARENTAL RIGHTS TERMINATION

harm the child. The decision to terminate parental rights boils down to a question of parental unfitness[25] coupled with potential harm to the child.[26]

Character evidence should be fully admissible in termination proceedings.[27] The four theoretical justifications for admitting character evidence in dependency proceedings apply with equal vitality in termination litigation. Termination proceedings look to the child's treatment in the past, and to what that treatment portends for the future.[28] In *In re M.H.*,[29] the court wrote:

> We look to the child's long-range and immediate interests and consider what the future would hold for the child if returned to the parent. We may obtain insight for this determination from evidence of the parent's past performance, for that performance may be indicative of the quality of the future care that parent is capable of providing . . . . The drastic disregard for the children in the past is a strong indicator of this mother's future conduct and the extreme danger such conduct could hold for these children.[30]

Because termination litigation looks to the future, character evidence is highly probative. Furthermore, under most termination statutes, parental character is directly in issue. Moreover, the acts justifying termination usually constitute a continuing course of conduct. Finally, strong policy arguments justify admission of character evidence in termination cases.

---

[25] *See In re* K.S., 737 P.2d 170 (Utah 1987); Model Statute for Termination of Parental Rights § 12(1) (Nat'l Council of Juvenile & Family Ct. Judges) ("the Court may terminate parental rights when the Court finds the parent unfit or that the conduct of the parent is such as to render him/her unable to properly care for the child and that such conduct or condition is unlikely to change in the foreseeable future").

[26] *In re* M.R., 334 N.W.2d 848, 854 (N.D. 1983) ("Evidence of previous abuse and deprivation may be considered in determining whether deprivation is likely to continue. However, evidence of past abuse and deprivation, is not, by itself, enough to terminate parental rights; there must be a showing of present abuse and deprivation, the conditions and causes of which are likely to continue").

[27] *See In re* W.D.N., II, 443 So. 2d 493 (Fla. Dist. Ct. App. 1984) (termination of parental rights proper when parent had abused other children); *In re* Pasco, 150 Mich. App. 816, 389 N.W.2d 188 (1986) (termination of parental rights proper when state proves a long course of neglect); Asendorf v. M.S.S., 342 N.W.2d 203 (N.D. 1983) (in termination cases is it proper to consider past abuse that is prognostic of future harm); *In re* M.R., 334 N.W.2d 848, 854 (N.D. 1983) ("Evidence of previous abuse and deprivation may be considered in determining whether deprivation is likely to continue").

[28] *See In re* Michael R., 197 Cal. App. 3d 284, 242 Cal. Rptr. 814 (1987); *In re* Cleopatra D., 193 Cal. App. 3d 694, 238 Cal. Rptr. 426 (1987); *In re* Norma M., 77 Cal. App. 3d 110, 143 Cal. Rptr. 412 (1978).

[29] 367 N.W.2d 275 (Iowa Ct. App. 1985).

[30] *Id.* at 278.

Rule 405 of the Federal Rules of Evidence provides that a person's character may be established in two ways.[31] First, when character evidence is admissible, a character witness may testify in the form of reputation or opinion regarding the person's character. Second, when character is "in issue" as that term is used in this book, proof of character may be made either with a character witness or with evidence of specific instances of the person's character.

§ 6.7 Conduct in Conformity with Character

The general principle established by Federal Rule of Evidence 404(a) is that character evidence is inadmissible to prove that a person acted in conformity with character on a specified occasion.[32] To this principle there are four important exceptions. First, Rule 404(a)(1) allows a criminal defendant to offer a character witness to testify about a pertinent trait of the defendant's character that makes it unlikely the defendant committed the charged offense.[33] Second, Rule 404(a)(2) allows a criminal defendant to offer a character witness to testify about a trait of the victim's character that makes it likely the victim acted in a particular way on a specified occasion.[34] Third, Rule 404(a)(3) allows

---

[31] Rule 405 states:

(a) Reputation or opinion. In all cases in which evidence of character or a trait of character of a person is admissible, proof may be made by testimony as to reputation or by testimony in the form of an opinion. On cross-examination [of the character witness], inquiry is allowable into relevant specific instances of conduct.

(b) Specific instances of conduct. In cases in which character or a trait of character of a person is an essential element of a charge, claim, or defense, proof may also be made of specific instances of that person's conduct.

[32] Fed. R. Evid. 404(a) ("Evidence of a person's character or a trait of character is not admissible for the purpose of proving action in conformity therewith on a particular occasion").

[33] Fed. R. Evid. 404(a)(1) ("Evidence of a pertinent trait of character offered by an accused, or by the prosecution to rebut the same"). *See* Michelson v. United States, 335 U.S. 469, 576 (1948) ("He may introduce affirmative testimony that the general estimate of his character is so favorable that the jury may infer that he would not be likely to commit the offense charged"). *See also* 2 Louisell & Mueller §§ 137, 138.

Rule 404(a)(1) creates an exception to Rule 404(a)'s prohibition on character evidence only in criminal litigation. Thus, in civil litigation a defendant cannot offer evidence of good character to prove innocence. In certain types of civil litigation, however, the plaintiff alleges that the defendant committed an act that could be punished criminally. For example, a victim of physical child abuse could sue the perpetrator in tort for damages. In civil cases when the defendant is sued for conduct that is essentially criminal, some courts allow the defendant to offer character evidence under Rule 404(a)(1) to prove innocence. *See, e.g.,* Perrin v. Anderson, 784 F.2d 1040 (10th Cir. 1986) (civil rights action against police officers who shot and killed individual during investigation of car accident).

[34] Fed. R. Evid. 404(a)(2) provides:

Evidence of a pertinent trait of character of the victim of the crime offered by an accused, or by the prosecution to rebut the same, or evidence of a character trait of

§ 6.7 CONDUCT CONFORMING TO CHARACTER

witnesses to be impeached with certain types of character evidence. Use of character evidence to impeach is discussed in **Chapter 5**. Fourth, in sex offense cases some courts allow evidence of the defendant's uncharged sexual misconduct to prove that the defendant has a propensity for sexual deviancy and probably acted in conformity with that propensity to commit the charged offense. This exception to the rule against character evidence is called the *depraved sexual propensity* theory, and is discussed in **§ 6.21**.

When character evidence is offered under Rules 404(a)(1) and 404(a)(2), the evidence is proffered through a character witness. Character witnesses are of two types. First, a character witness may describe a person's reputation in the community for a pertinent trait of character.[35] Second, in many jurisdictions, a character witness may offer the character witness's personal opinion about a pertinent trait of a person's character.[36] Character witnesses may not describe specific instances of a person's conduct.[37]

Character evidence used to impeach under Rule 404(a)(3) may be admitted through a reputation or opinion character witness.[38] More often, however, impeachment occurs during cross-examination of the witness to be impeached. During cross-examination, the impeaching attorney asks the witness about specific instances of the witness's conduct that reflect poorly on the witness's character for truthfulness.[39] See **Chapter 5**.

In jurisdictions where the prosecutor is allowed to offer "depraved sexual propensity" evidence to prove that the defendant acted in conformity with a lustful disposition on a particular occasion, the government's evidence takes the form of specific instances of misconduct. See **§ 6.21**.

---

peacefulness of the victim offered by the prosecution in a homicide case to rebut evidence that the victim was the first aggressor....

See 2 Louisell & Mueller § 139.

The last portion of Rule 404(a)(2) applies in homicide prosecutions when the defendant argues that the victim was the first aggressor. In such cases the prosecution is allowed to offer a character witness to prove that the victim was a peaceful person, and thus probably not the first aggressor. It is difficult to envision child death cases in which the last portion of Rule 404(a)(2) would apply. With the possible exception of older adolescents, the defense in a child homicide case cannot credibly assert that a child was the first aggressor.

[35] *See* Michelson v. United States, 335 U.S. 469 (1948).

[36] At common law the character witness could testify only regarding the defendant's reputation in the community. The character witness was not allowed to offer the witness's own opinion of the defendant's character. Under Rule 405(a), a character witness may testify regarding the defendant's reputation. In addition, a character witness may offer the witness's own opinion about the defendant's character.

[37] *See* Fed. R. Evid 405.

[38] *See* Fed. R. Evid. 608(a).

[39] *See* Fed. R. Evid. 608(b).

§ 6.8 —Defendant's Character: Rule 404(a)(1)

Turning to the first exception to the rule against character evidence, Rule 404(a)(1) provides:

> Evidence of a person's character or a trait of character is not admissible for the purpose of proving action in conformity therewith on a particular occasion, except: Evidence of a pertinent trait of character offered by an accused, or by the prosecution to rebut the same . . . .[40]

To illustrate the first exception, suppose Sam Smith is charged with violent assault. Smith may offer a character witness to testify that he has a reputation in the community as a peaceful person.[41] When the charge is violent assault, peacefulness is a "pertinent trait of character."[42] The theory underlying the

---

[40] Fed. R. Evid. 404(a)(1).

[41] The trial court may limit the number of character witnesses. 2 Louisell & Mueller 137, at 141–42. The foundation for a character witness describing the defendant's reputation in the community is described by Imwinkelried:

1. The witness is a member of the same community (residential, business, or social) as the defendant.
2. The witness has resided there a substantial period of time.
3. The defendant has a reputation for: (a) general, moral, law-abiding character; or (b) a specific, relevant character trait. Federal Rule 404(a)(1) seems to confine the defendant to a relevant specific trait.
4. The witness knows the reputation.
5. The witness states the reputation.

E. Imwinkelried, Evidentiary Foundations 121 (2d ed. 1989). Imwinkelried notes that the foundation is very similar when the character witness describes the witness's personal opinion about the defendant's character. He describes the foundation for the opinion as follows:

1. The witness is personally acquainted with the defendant.
2. The witness knows the defendant well enough to have formed a reliable opinion of the defendant's character.
3. The witness has an opinion of the defendant's character.
4. The witness states his or her opinion.

Id. at 122.

[42] The word *pertinent* in Rule 404(a)(1) means relevant as that term is defined in Rule 401. See 2 Louisell & Mueller § 137, at 141 ("'pertinent trait' means trait which is relevant in the context of the crime charged"). Louisell & Mueller write:

> It seems clear that the intent of Rule 404(a)(1) is to allow the accused to introduce only evidence of a "pertinent trait of his character," and *not* to extend the exception to cover undifferentiated character evidence of the most general sort, such as testimony to the effect that the accused is of "good character" or "good morals." Thus, the Advisory Committee's Note emphasizes the "limitation to pertinent traits of character, rather than character generally," attributing the limit to the "prevailing view." While the "prevailing" (and wiser) strategy may be to present evidence of particular (and pertinent) character traits, we doubt that courts either exclude or *should* exclude

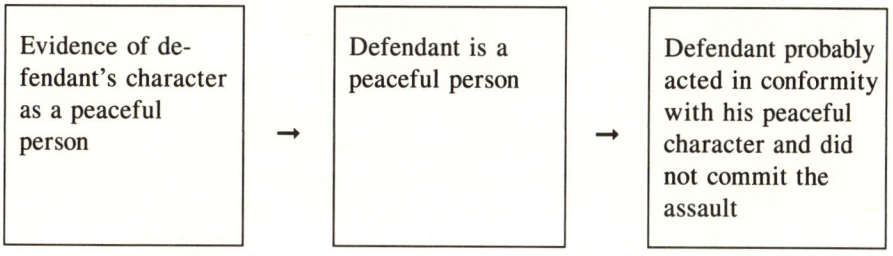

Figure 6–2. Example of chain of inferences permissible for defendant.

character witness's testimony is that peaceful people generally act in conformity with character because it is human nature to do so. Because Smith is a peaceful person, he probably acted in conformity with his character and did not commit the charged assault.[43] Smith's theory of proof involves two inferences. First, from the character witness's testimony the jury infers that Smith is a peaceful person. Second, from this inference, the jury draws the further inference that Smith probably acted in conformity with his peaceful character on the occasion in question and did not commit the assault. Imwinkelried's schematic illustrates the inferences underlying Smith's character evidence in **Figure 6–2**.

When Smith offers a character witness to testify to his peaceful character, he subjects himself to a double-barreled counterattack from the prosecutor.[44] First, the prosecutor may impeach the character witness. Second, during the prosecutor's case-in-rebuttal, the prosecutor may offer a character witness to prove that Smith has a violent character.

It is clear that the defendant invites the prosecutor's counterattack when the defendant puts a character witness on the stand under Rule 404(a)(1). There are times, however, when the defendant makes character a focal point of attention without the assistance of character witnesses.[45] For example, in child abuse litigation, defendants often state or imply, "I'm not the sort of person who would

---

evidence of general "good character" very often; little is to be gained by doing so, and it seems that the defendant should have the choice whether to be more particular or more general. We see no objection, for example, to evidence that defendant is a "law abiding citizen," which would seem at least marginally relevant in any prosecution, even though the phrase imparts little more than the term "good character."

Id. at 138–39 (footnotes omitted).

[43] When a criminal defendant offers a character witness under Rule 404(a)(1), the character witness's testimony constitutes circumstantial evidence of innocence. The character witness's testimony is offered as substantive proof of innocence.

[44] *See* 2 Louisell & Mueller § 138.

[45] *See* State v. Turecek, 456 N.W.2d 219 (Iowa 1990) (defendant did not offer character evidence when she turned to jury and said, "I'm telling the truth").

do that to a child." In many cases such testimony clears the way for the prosecutor's counterattack.[46] Louisell and Mueller write:

> When testimony by the accused goes beyond the facts of the case, and paints not only a picture of innocence but a self-portrait of a person whose background, outlook, personality, or philosophy make him unlikely to have committed the crime charged, it is fair to view his strategy as an effort to adduce character evidence, and to hold that it opens the door to counterattack by the prosecution.[47]

Returning to the assault charge against Smith, recall that he offered a character witness. The character witness, like all witnesses, is subject to impeachment through the traditional modes of impeachment. In addition to normal impeachment, however, character witnesses are subject to a special mode of impeachment—a mode that sometimes devastates defendants. Within the discretion of the trial judge, and subject to Rule 403's exclusion of unfairly prejudicial evidence,[48] the prosecutor is permitted is impeach the character witness by establishing that the character witness: (1) is not a good judge of character, or (2) does not know the defendant's true character. To impeach the *character witness's* credibility, the prosecutor asks the character witness about specific instances of the *defendant's* conduct.[49]

If Smith's character witness testifies on direct that Smith has a reputation in the community for peacefulness, the prosecutor may cross-examine the character witness by asking, "Have you heard that Mr. Smith committed two violent assaults in the past year?" Naturally, the prosecutor must have a good faith belief that Smith actually committed the assaults.[50]

If Smith's character witness offers an opinion of Smith's peaceful character, the form—although not the substance—of the prosecutor's question changes.

---

[46] The prosecutor has at least two theories to support admission of evidence of the defendant's bad character. First, by stating, "I'm not that sort or person," the defendant has acted essentially as a character witness, thus triggering the prosecutor's right under Rule 404(a)(1) to offer rebuttal character evidence. Second, if the defendant's "I'm not that sort" testimony is technically improper, the prosecutor may invoke the invited error doctrine to justify rebuttal character evidence. See **Ch. 4** for discussion of invited error.

[47] 2 Louisell & Mueller § 138, at 159 (footnote omitted).

[48] *See* 2 Louisell & Mueller § 138, at 152.

[49] Cross-examination of the defense character witness is authorized by the last sentence of Rule 405(a), which provides that "[o]n cross-examination [of a character witness], inquiry is allowable into relevant specific instances of conduct." *See* 2 Louisell & Mueller § 138, at 146–47.

When the prosecutor cross-examines the character witness regarding specific instances of the defendant's conduct, the prosecutor must take care to observe the limits of this type of cross-examination. The prosecutor may not use the specific instances of the defendant's conduct to impugn the defendant's character. *See* State v. McCarthy, 589 A.2d 869 (Vt. 1991).

[50] *See* 2 Louisell & Mueller § 138, at 152.

The question is, "Did you know that Mr. Smith committed two violent assaults in the past year?"[51]

Whether the character witness answers yes or no, the *character witness* is impeached. If the character witness says, "No, I had not heard (or I did not know) about any assaults," the character witness is impeached because lack of knowledge regarding Smith's violence indicates the character witness does not know Smith's true reputation. If the character witness says, "Yes, I heard (or I know) about the two other assaults, but I stand by my testimony," the jury is likely to conclude that the character witness has a rather strange standard for measuring peacefulness.[52]

Note that with this mode of impeaching a defense character witness, the prosecutor elicits specific instances of the defendant's conduct that the jury might not otherwise learn of. The theoretical purpose for admitting this information about the defendant is *not* to impeach the defendant, but to impeach the character witness. The danger, of course, is that the jury will not limit its consideration of the information to assessing the character witness's credibility, but will use the information for the improper purpose of concluding that the defendant probably committed the charged offense because the defendant is a bad person.[53]

In addition to impeaching the defendant's character witness, the prosecutor may offer a character witness to rebut the testimony of the defense character witness. As the Court stated in *Michelson v. United States*,[54] "The price a defendant must pay for attempting to prove his good name is to throw open the entire subject which the law has kept closed for his benefit and to make himself vulnerable where the law otherwise shields him."[55]

In physical abuse cases, certain traits of the defendant's character may be "pertinent," and thus admissible by the defendant under Rule 404(a)(1). The court may permit the defendant to offer a character witness to testify that the defendant is a peaceful, nonviolent person. If the defendant is a parent, the court may allow character testimony that the defendant is an affectionate, nurturing parent.

Are there any "pertinent" character traits that a defendant might offer in child sexual abuse litigation? An argument can be made that the answer is no. In *State v. Lebel*,[56] the defendant was charged with sexually abusing his

---

[51] Under traditional practice, the proper cross-examination question for a reputation character witness is, "Have you heard . . . ?" The proper question for an opinion character witness is, "Did you know . . . ?" Since there is no real difference between the questions, many judges do not insist that the cross-examiner use the technically "correct" question.

[52] *See* 2 Louisell & Mueller § 138, at 151.

[53] *See id.* at 152–53.

[54] 335 U.S. 469 (1948).

[55] *Id.* at 479.

[56] 594 A.2d 91 (Me. 1991).

seven-year-old stepson. At trial, the defendant invoked Rule 404(a)(1) to offer a character witness. In an offer of proof, defense counsel established that the character witness had employed the defendant as an ice cream truck driver for nearly 14 years. The character witness "would testify as to [defendant's] responsibility with children and his trustworthiness."[57] The trial court refused to allow the character witness to testify, and the Supreme Judicial Court of Maine affirmed, writing:

> In the past, we have held that Rule 404(a)(1) confines such character evidence to proof of a "specific trait of . . . character, the existence or non-existence of which would be involved in the non-commission or commission of the particular crime charged." *State v. Wells,* 423 A.2d 221 (Me. 1980). The prevailing view, and that emphasized in *Wells,* is that only "pertinent" traits are provable. We do not find that [defendant's] offer of proof attained a level of specificity sufficient to demonstrate that the evidence proffered was pertinent to the case.
>
> In *Wells,* the defendant was a store clerk who was accused of assaulting a patron while at work. There, we held inadmissible testimony from the employer who merely claimed that he had no prior complaint of the defendant's behavior and that the defendant had a good reputation among employees. . . . In the instant case, the testimony that [defendant] purported to offer is similar to that at issue in *Wells.* The court specifically asked [defendant's] attorney to explain what character trait he wanted to prove through [the character witness's] testimony. In response, the attorney replied that he intended to offer evidence of [defendant's] reputation for being responsible or trustworthy with children among those who observed him working as an ice cream truck driver.
>
> We do not find such an offer to have reached the standard of specificity required to show it pertinent. "Rule 404 confines such character evidence to proof of a pertinent trait of the accused, which must be interpreted to mean such specific trait of his character, the existence or non-existence of which would be involved in the non-commission or commission of the particular crime charged. . . ." *Wells,* 423 A.2d at 224. Without some showing that an outward appearance of public responsibility with children "would be involved in the existence or non-existence of the crime," [the character witness's] testimony was inadmissible.[58]

The *Lebel* analysis is persuasive. A public persona of responsible conduct with children says little, if anything, about a person's conduct behind closed doors.

The Washington Court of Appeals' decision in *State v. Jackson*[59] provides further guidance on defense character witnesses in child sexual abuse litigation. In *Jackson,* the defendant was charged with statutory rape of the five-year-old daughter of the woman with whom he lived. The defendant offered

---

[57] *Id.* at 92.
[58] *Id.* at 93.
[59] 46 Wash. App. 360, 730 P.2d 1361 (1986).

§ 6.8 DEFENDANT'S CHARACTER

two character witnesses under Rule 404(a)(1). The character witnesses "would testify to the reputation in the community of [defendant] for not being predisposed to molesting children."[60] The character witnesses would also testify to the defendant's "reputation in the community for not spending an inordinate amount of time in the company of children of ages less than ten . . . ."[61] The trial court rejected the character testimony, and, on this point, the court of appeals affirmed.[62] Characterizing the defendant's proposed character testimony as evidence of reputation for moral decency, the court wrote:

> Whether a person spends an inordinate amount of time with children under ten is not probative here. . . . The crimes of indecent liberties and incest concern sexual activity, which is normally an intimate, private affair not known to the community. One's reputation for sexual activity, or lack thereof, may have no correlation to one's actual sexual conduct. Simply put, one's reputation for moral decency is not pertinent to whether one has committed indecent liberties or incest.[63]

The *Jackson* court also held that "[a] defendant's character trait for truthfulness is not a pertinent trait to the charge of statutory rape."[64]

Despite a credible argument in child sexual abuse cases that there is no pertinent character trait admissible by a defendant under Rule 404(a)(1), there are decisions holding that defense character witnesses may testify that a defendant has a character trait of "sexual morality and decency."[65] In *People v. McAlpin*,[66] the defendant was charged with molesting the daughter of a woman he was dating. The California Supreme Court approved three types of defense character evidence. First, the defendant offered as character witnesses two women whom he had dated previously. The court held that the women should have been permitted to testify that "they observed [defendant's] conduct with their daughters and saw no unusual behavior either by defendant or by their daughters, and that

---

[60] 730 P.2d at 1364.

[61] *Id.*

[62] The court of appeals reversed the conviction on grounds related to improper admission of hearsay.

[63] 730 P.2d at 1364.

[64] *Id.* n.3. *See also* State v. Robinson, 44 Wash. App. 611, 722 P.2d 1379, 1387 (1986) ("'Defendant's character trait for truthfulness is not a trait pertinent to the charge of indecent liberties.' Other traits such as his honesty and truthful reputation make it no less likely he committed the offense of indecent liberties"); State v. Harper, 35 Wash. App. 855, 670 P.2d 296, 299 (1983).

[65] United States v. Hooks, 24 M.J. 713 (A.C.M.R. 1987) (admissibility of good military character in rape case); United States v. Stanley, 15 M.J. 949 (A.F.C.M.R. 1983) (defendant in sex offense case may offer character evidence of good moral character); State v. Blake, 157 Conn. 99, 249 A.2d 232, 234–35 (1968); Thomas v. State, 669 S.W.2d 420, 423–24 (Tex. Ct. App. 1984); State v. Harper, 35 Wash. App. 855, 670 P.2d 296, 299–300 (1983).

[66] 812 P.2d 563, 283 Cal. Rptr. 382 (1991).

it is their opinion, based on those personal perceptions, that defendant is not a person given to lewd conduct with children."[67] The court ruled that such opinion testimony is permissible from lay witnesses.[68] The state argued that the women's testimony was not proper character evidence because character witnesses must confine their testimony to reputation or opinion, and may not describe specific instances of the defendant's conduct.[69] The court rejected the state's argument, writing:

> A fair reading of the offer of proof shows that the women witnesses would not have limited their testimony to specific instances in which defendant had the opportunity to, but did not, molest their daughters. Instead, the witnesses proposed to testify that they observed defendant's behavior with their children throughout the course of their relationship with him, and their opinion that he is not a person given to lewd conduct with children arose from that experience as a whole. Thus viewed, the proffered testimony was intended to prove the relevant character trait not by specific instances of "nonmolestation," but by the witnesses' opinion of that trait based on their long-term observation of defendant's course of consistently normal behavior with their children. The trial court should have allowed such testimony.[70]

In addition to the foregoing character evidence, the *McAlpin* court ruled that a defendant may offer character evidence that he does not have a reputation for being sexually attracted to young girls.[71] Finally, the court held that a defense character witness may testify that the defendant is a person of high moral character.[72]

In *State v. Naylor*,[73] the Maine Supreme Judicial Court ruled that the defendant should have been permitted to offer evidence that he had a character trait for being an excellent father.

As an alternative to character testimony from lay witnesses, the defendant may urge the trial court to allow expert testimony that the defendant does not possess personality traits found in persons who sexually abuse children. Although the California Supreme Court approved such testimony in *People v.*

---

[67] 812 P.2d at 575.

[68] *Id.* ("Because the latter conclusion of the witnesses was based on their direct observation of defendant's behavior with their daughters, it was both a proper subject of lay opinion testimony and relevant to the charge of child molestation").

[69] *Id. See* Cal. Evid. Code § 1102 (West). The Federal Rules are to the same effect. *See* Fed. R. Evid. 405.

[70] 812 P.2d at 575–76 (footnotes omitted).

[71] *Id.* at 576.

[72] *Id.* The court stated that "we construe the word 'moral' in this phrase to refer to *sexual* morality. Thus construed, 'moral character' is a trait that is relevant to a sex offense charge, including the present prosecution for child molesting." *Id.*

[73] 602 A.2d 187 (Me. 1992).

Stoll,[74] the argument is developed in **Chapter 4** that such testimony should be excluded as scientifically unreliable.

§ 6.9 —Victim's Character: Rule 404(a)(2)

The second exception to the rule against character evidence to prove conduct in conformity therewith is articulated in Rule 404(a)(2), which states:

> Evidence of a person's character or a trait of character is not admissible for the purpose of proving action in conformity therewith on a particular occasion, except: Evidence of a pertinent trait of character of the victim of the crime offered by an accused, or by the prosecution to rebut the same . . . .[75]

Rule 404(a)(2) finds its most frequent application in homicide and assault cases when the defense argues that the victim was the first aggressor.[76] Once the defendant introduces evidence of the victim's character, the prosecution may rebut the defendant's evidence with evidence of its own regarding the victim's character. Evidence admissible under Rule 404(a)(2) is supplied by character witnesses who testify in the form of opinion or reputation.[77]

In child abuse litigation, Rule 404(a)(2) finds infrequent application. The defendant in a physical abuse case is seldom, if ever, in a position to argue that a child was the first aggressor, and that the defendant acted in self-defense. Thus, the defendant could not offer a character witness to describe the child's violent character.

In child sexual abuse litigation, Rule 404(a)(2) is seldom available to admit evidence that the victim acted in conformity with some character trait. Inquiry into the victim's sexual experience is usually barred by the rape shield statute.[78] In at least one scenario, however, the rape shield statute does not bar evidence that may reflect a pertinent aspect of the victim's character. A defendant may invoke Rule 404(a)(2) to offer a character witness to testify that the victim has a reputation for making false allegations of sexual abuse.[79]

---

[74] 49 Cal. 3d 1136, 783 P.2d 698, 265 Cal. Rptr. 111 (1989).

[75] Fed. R. Evid. 404(a)(2).

[76] *See* 2 Louisell & Mueller § 139; 2 Weinstein & Berger ¶ 404[06].

[77] *See* Fed. R. Evid. 405. *See also* 2 Louisell & Mueller § 139, at 164–65 ("by virtue of Rules 404 and 405, it seems that proof of the victim's character or disposition must be cast in the form of opinion or reputation").

[78] *See* State v. Kao, 245 Mont. 263, 800 P.2d 714 (1990). See **Ch. 5** for discussion of the rape shield statute.

[79] *See* State v. Kao, 245 Mont. 263, 800 P.2d 714 (1990) (defendant tried unsuccessfully to employ Rule 404(a)(2) to offer evidence that child had been sexually abused by another man; court invoked rape shield statute to reject defendant's evidence).

§ 6.10 Habit

Evidence of a person's character generally is inadmissible to prove the person acted in conformity with character on a specific occasion. By contrast, evidence of a person's habit is admissible to prove that the person acted in conformity with habit on a specific occasion. Rule 406 of the Federal Rules of Evidence states: "Evidence of the habit of a person . . . whether corroborated or not and regardless of the presence of eyewitnesses, is relevant to prove that the conduct of the person . . . on a particular occasion was in conformity with the habit . . . ."

It is not always easy to distinguish character from habit. No one describes the difference more effectively than McCormick:

> Character is a generalized description of a person's disposition, or of the disposition in respect to a general trait, such as honesty, temperance or peacefulness. Habit, in the present context, is more specific. It denotes one's regular response to a repeated situation. If we speak of a character for care, we think of the person's tendency to act prudently in all the varying situations of life—in business, at home, in handling automobiles and in walking across the street. A habit, on the other hand, is the person's regular practice of responding to a particular kind of situation with a specific type of conduct. Thus, a person may be in the habit of bounding down a certain stairway two or three steps at a time, of patronizing a particular pub after each day's work, or of driving his automobile without using a seatbelt. The doing of the habitual act may become semi-automatic, as with a driver who invariably signals before changing lanes.[80]

UNCHARGED MISCONDUCT EVIDENCE

§ 6.11 Describing Uncharged Misconduct Evidence

Uncharged misconduct evidence plays a vital role in child abuse litigation.[81] Uncharged misconduct is admissible to prove: (1) the criminal act (actus reus), (2) the criminal intent (mens rea), and (3) the identity of the perpetrator. The following two sections distinguish uncharged misconduct evidence from character evidence, and discuss several recurring issues regarding uncharged misconduct evidence.

---

[80] McCormick § 195, at 574–75 (footnotes omitted).

[81] For excellent treatment of the entire subject, see E. Imwinkelried, Uncharged Misconduct Evidence (1984); 2 Louisell & Mueller § 140; 22 Wright & Graham §§ 5239–50. Uncharged misconduct evidence goes by other names, including *prior bad acts evidence* and *other acts evidence*.

§ 6.12 —Distinguishing Uncharged Misconduct Evidence from Character Evidence

To clarify the theoretical distinction between uncharged misconduct evidence and character evidence offered to prove that a person acted in conformity with character, it is useful to recall the basic principle of Rule 404(a), which states that evidence of a person's character generally is not admissible to prove that the person acted in conformity with character on a specified occasion. Using Imwinkelried's schematic device, the chain of inferences forbidden by Rule 404(a) is shown in **Figure 6–3**.

There are four exceptions to the general prohibition against character evidence offered to prove conduct in conformity with character:

1. Evidence offered by a criminal defendant regarding the defendant's character: Rule 404(a)(1)[82]
2. Evidence offered by a criminal defendant regarding the victim's character: Rule 404(a)(2)[83]
3. Evidence offered to impeach a witness: Rule 404(a)(3)[84]
4. In some jurisdictions, evidence of the defendant's depraved sexual propensity.[85]

The discussion in the present section is confined to the first two exceptions set forth above. When a criminal defendant offers character evidence under Rule 404(a)(1)[defendant's good character] or Rule 404(a)(2)[victim's character], the evidence is offered as circumstantial proof that the defendant or the victim acted in conformity with character on a specified occasion. The

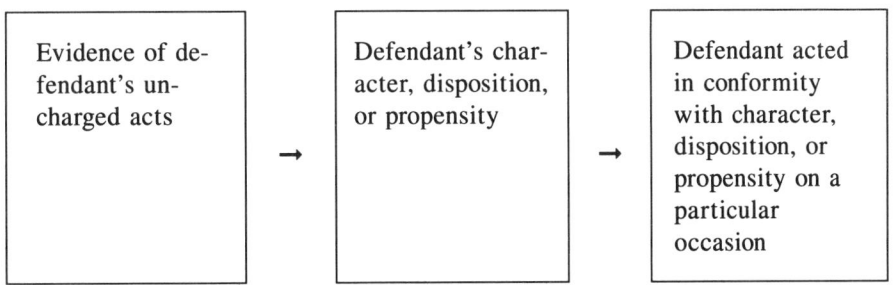

Figure 6–3. Chain of inferences forbidden by Federal Rule of Evidence 404(a).

---

[82] See § **6.8**.
[83] See § **6.9**.
[84] See **Ch. 5**.
[85] See § **6.21**.

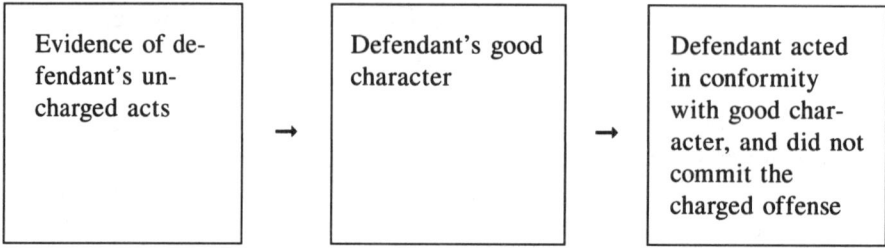

Figure 6–4. Chain of inferences permitted by Federal Rule of Evidence 404(a)(1).

evidence is offered as substantive proof of innocence. Schematically, evidence offered under Rule 404(a)(1) is shown in **Figure 6–4**.

Comparison of **Figures 6–3** and **6–4** reveals that character evidence admitted under Rule 404(a)(1) accomplishes precisely what Rule 404(a) forbids: proof that a person acted in conformity with the person's character on a specific occasion.[86]

In sum, Rule 404(a) states a rule of general application, and Rules 404(a)(1) and 404(a)(2) create exceptions. Where does uncharged misconduct evidence fit into this matrix? Unlike Rules 404(a)(1) and 404(a)(2), uncharged misconduct evidence is *not* an exception to Rule 404(a)'s prohibition of character evidence to prove conduct in conformity with character. Uncharged misconduct evidence is *not* offered to prove that a person acted in conformity with the person's character on a particular occasion; therefore, Rule 404(a) is not offended. Rather, uncharged misconduct evidence is offered to prove such things as "motive, opportunity, intent, preparation, plan, knowledge, identity, or absence of mistake or accident."[87]

§ 6.13 —Recurring Issues

This section discusses several recurring issues related to uncharged misconduct evidence.

Is Rule 404(b) Exhaustive?

Rule 404(b) of the Federal Rules of Evidence states:

> Evidence of other crimes, wrongs, or acts is not admissible to prove the character of a person in order to show action in conformity therewith. It may, however, be

---

[86] Character evidence regarding the victim, offered under Rule 404(a)(2), likewise accomplishes what Rule 404(a) forbids.

[87] Fed. R. Evid. 404(b).

admissible for other purposes, such as proof of motive, opportunity, intent, preparation, plan, knowledge, identity, or absence of mistake or accident.

Rule 404(b) contains a list of purposes for which uncharged misconduct evidence is admissible. Is the list exhaustive? Or is counsel free to offer uncharged misconduct evidence for purposes not listed in Rule 404(b)? By using the words "such as," the drafters made clear that Rule 404(b) does not limit permissible theories of uncharged misconduct evidence to the theories articulated in the rule.[88] Most courts hold that the only limit on uncharged misconduct evidence is relevance, that is, the evidence must be "probative of a material issue other than character."[89] The Supreme Court of Appeals of West Virginia observed in *State v. Edward Charles L.*[90] that Rule 404(b) "is an 'inclusive rule' in which all relevant evidence involving other crimes or acts is admitted at trial unless the sole purpose for the admission is to show criminal disposition."[91] The trial court has considerable discretion to admit or exclude uncharged misconduct evidence, and the court will be reversed only for an abuse of discretion.[92]

Proof of Uncharged Misconduct

Before uncharged misconduct evidence is admitted, the prosecutor must establish that the uncharged act occurred. In addition, under most theories of uncharged misconduct evidence, the prosecutor must establish that the defendant committed

---

[88] *See* State v. Zybach, 308 Or. 96, 775 P.2d 318, 320 (1989), where the court referred to the language of Rule 404(b):

> [T]he listed exceptions are illustrations, not limitations. "[S]uch as" means "[f]or example. Of the stated or implied kind or degree; similar; like." American Heritage Dictionary 1285 (1978). The evidence may be admissible on other than the listed grounds.

See also Montgomery v. State, 810 S.W.2d 372, 377 (Tex. Crim. App. 1990) ("It must also be remembered that the enumerated exceptions to Rule 404(b) . . . are 'neither mutually exclusive nor collectively exhaustive'"); McCormick § 190, at 558.

[89] Huddleston v. United States, 485 U.S. 681, 686 (1988). *See also* United States v. Hadley, 918 F.2d 848, 850 (9th Cir. 1990), *cert. granted,* 112 S. Ct. 1261 (1992) ("Rule 404(b) is an 'inclusionary rule,' under which evidence is inadmissible 'only when it proves nothing but the defendant's criminal propensities'"); People v. Brown, 199 Ill. App. 3d 860, 557 N.E.2d 611, 620 (1990) ("Evidence of other offenses is admissible if it is relevant for any purpose other than to show the propensity to commit crime"); State v. Coffey, 326 N.C. 268, 389 S.E.2d 48 (1990); State v. West, 103 N.C. App. 1, 404 S.E.2d 191, 197 (1991) (Rule 404(b) "is a general rule of inclusion of such evidence"); State v. Zybach, 308 Or. 96, 775 P.2d 318, 320 (1989); Montgomery v. State, 810 S.W.2d 372, 375 (Tex. Crim. App. 1990); Longfellow v. State, 803 P.2d 848, 851 (Wyo. 1990). *But see* Velez v. State, 762 P.2d 1297, 1300 n.5 (Alaska Ct. App. 1988) (Alaska rule is one of exclusion, not inclusion).

[90] 398 S.E.2d 123 (W. Va. 1990).

[91] *Id.* at 129.

[92] People v. Brown, 199 Ill. App. 3d 860, 557 N.E.2d 611, 620 (1990).

the uncharged act.[93] Courts vary on the degree of proof imposed on the prosecutor. Some courts require the uncharged act to be established by a preponderance of the evidence. Other courts require clear and convincing evidence.

In *Huddleston v. United States*,[94] the issue before the Supreme Court was "whether the district court must itself make a preliminary finding that the Government has proved the 'other act' by a preponderance of the evidence before it submits the evidence to the jury."[95] In a unanimous decision, the Court concluded that the trial judge need not make a preliminary finding under Rule 104(a). The Court held that admissibility of uncharged misconduct evidence is governed by Rule 104(b):

> We conclude that a preliminary finding by the court that the Government has proved the act by a preponderance of the evidence is not called for under Rule 104(a). This is not to say, however, that the Government may parade past the jury a litany of potentially prejudicial similar acts that have been established or connected to the defendant only by unsubstantiated innuendo. Evidence is admissible under Rule 404(b) only if it is relevant. . . . In the Rule 404(b) context, similar act evidence is relevant only if the jury can reasonably conclude that the act occurred and that the defendant was the actor. . . .
>
> Such questions of relevance conditioned on a fact are dealt with under Federal Rule of Evidence 104(b). . . . In determining whether the Government has introduced sufficient evidence to meet Rule 104(b), the trial court neither weighs credibility nor makes a finding that the Government has proved the conditional fact by a preponderance of the evidence. The court simply examines all the evidence in the case and decides whether the jury could reasonably find the conditional fact . . . by a preponderance of the evidence.[96]

Huddleston is binding on the federal courts[97] and is likely to influence state courts, with the result that uncharged misconduct evidence will become more readily admissible.

Under Rule 104(b), uncharged acts must be established by admissible evidence.[98] In *United States v. Hadley*,[99] the Ninth Circuit considered a case in

---

[93] The doctrine of chances is the most notable exception to the rule that the prosecutor must prove that the defendant committed the uncharged acts. Under the doctrine of chances, anonymous acts often are admissible. See **§ 6.17** for discussion of the doctrine of chances.

[94] 485 U.S. 681 (1988).

[95] *Id.* at 682. *Huddleston* did not involve a constitutional question. The issue decided by the Court was one of statutory construction.

[96] *Id.* at 689–90 (footnote omitted).

[97] *See* United States v. York, 933 F.2d 1343, 1352 (7th Cir.), *cert. denied*, 112 S. Ct. 321 (1991); United States v. Castillo, 29 M.J. 145, 151 (C.M.A. 1989).

[98] *See* M. Graham, Handbook of Federal Evidence § 104.2, at 44–45 (3d ed. 1991) ("In reaching a determination under Rule 104(b), the court may consider only that evidence which the jury will have before it—evidence admitted under the rules of evidence").

[99] 918 F.2d 851 (9th Cir. 1990); *cert. granted*, 112 S. Ct. 1261 (1992).

which a school teacher sexually abused a student. At trial the prosecutor offered uncharged misconduct testimony from adults who had been abused by the defendant when the witnesses were minors. The Ninth Circuit wrote:

> [W]e hold that sufficient evidence of the prior bad acts existed for a jury to "reasonably conclude that the act[s] occurred and that the defendant was the actor." *Huddleston v. United States,* 485 U.S. 681, 689 (1988). The witnesses testified in detail about the sexual abuse inflicted upon them by [defendant]. This testimony clearly amounted to more than the "unsubstantiated innuendo" that the Supreme Court warned against in *Huddleston.*[100]

Uncharged Misconduct of Third Parties

A criminal defendant has a right to establish that someone else committed the charged offense.[101] To this end, the defendant sometimes offers evidence of a third party's uncharged misconduct to prove that the third party is guilty.[102]

Exclusion of Uncharged Misconduct Evidence under Rule 403

Uncharged misconduct evidence may be excluded under Rule 403 if the probative value of the evidence "is substantially outweighed by the danger of unfair prejudice, confusion of the issues, or misleading the jury, or by considerations of undue delay, waste of time, or needless presentation of cumulative evidence."[103] There is no doubt that uncharged misconduct evidence can unfairly prejudice defendants. The California Supreme Court observed in *People v. Smallwood*[104] that uncharged misconduct is "the most prejudicial evidence imaginable against an accused."[105]

Rule 403 contemplates a balancing process in which the court balances the probative value of evidence against the likelihood of unfair prejudice.[106] The trial judge has great discretion in conducting the required balancing, and the court "will not be overturned on appeal absent a clear abuse of discretion."[107] In

---

[100] *Id.* at 851.

[101] State v. Hayes, 20 Conn. App. 737, 570 A.2d 716 (1990).

[102] *See* State v. Hayes, 20 Conn. App. 737, 570 A.2d 716 (1990); State v. Dean, 589 A.2d 929, 933 (Me. 1991).

[103] Fed. R. Evid. 403. Rule 403 "applies to all forms of evidence: direct and circumstantial, testimonial, documentary, real proof, and demonstrations." 1 Weinstein & Berger ¶ 403[01], at 403–5. *See* United States v. Merriweather, 22 M.J. 657, 660 (A.C.M.R. 1986).

[104] 42 Cal. 3d 415, 722 P.2d 197, 228 Cal. Rptr. 913 (1986).

[105] *Id.* at 429, 722 P.2d at 205, 228 Cal. Rptr. at 922.

[106] *See* Huddleston v. United States, 485 U.S. 681, 691 (1988).

[107] Ballou v. Henri Studios, Inc., 656 F.2d 1147, 1153 (5th Cir. 1981). *See also* United States v. Hadley, 918 F.2d 848, 850 (9th Cir. 1990); *cert. granted,* 112 S. Ct. 1261 (1992).

assessing the probative value of evidence, the trial judge does not consider the credibility or believability of the evidence.[108] As the Fifth Circuit wrote in *Ballou v. Henri Studios, Inc.:*[109] . . . "Rule 403 does not permit exclusion of evidence because the judge does not find it credible. . . . Weighing probative value against unfair prejudice under [Rule] 403 means probative value with respect to a material fact *if the evidence is believed [by the jury], not the degree the court finds it believable.*"[110]

It is important to define when prejudice is "unfair." Evidence that is highly incriminating and damaging to the defendant is not, for that reason, "unfair."[111] Powerful evidence may "prejudice" the defendant in the lay sense of the term, but "unfair prejudice" requires something more than probative force. Weinstein and Berger explain:

> "'[U]nfair prejudice' as used in Rule 403 is not to be equated with testimony simply adverse to the opposing party. Virtually all evidence is prejudicial or it isn't material. The prejudice must be 'unfair.'" The Committee's Notes explain that "unfair prejudice" means an "undue tendency to suggest decision on an improper basis, commonly, though not necessarily, an emotional one." Evidence that appeals to the jury's sympathies, arouses its sense of horror, provokes its instinct to punish, or triggers other mainsprings of human action may cause a jury to base its decision on something other than the established propositions in the case.[112]

The fact that evidence has some tendency to suggest decision on an improper basis is not enough to exclude it under Rule 403. The burden is on the party seeking exclusion to establish that the potential for unfair prejudice *substantially*

---

[108] 22 Wright & Graham § 5214, at 265 ("it seems relatively clear that in the weighing process under Rule 403 the judge cannot consider the credibility of witnesses").

[109] 656 F.2d 1147 (5th Cir. 1981).

[110] *Id.* at 1154.

[111] United States v. York, 933 F.2d 1343, 1353 (7th Cir.), *cert. denied,* 112 S. Ct. 321 (1991); Montgomery v. State, 810 S.W.2d 372, 378 (Tex. Crim. App. 1990). In United States v. Figueroa, 618 F.2d 934, 943 (2d Cir. 1980), the court wrote:

> All evidence introduced against a defendant, if material to an issue in the case, tends to prove guilt, but it is not necessarily prejudicial in any sense that matters to the rules of evidence. . . . Evidence is prejudicial only when it tends to have some adverse effect upon a defendant beyond tending to prove the fact or issue that justified its admission into evidence. . . . The prejudicial effect may be created by the tendency of the evidence to prove some adverse fact not properly in issue or unfairly to excite emotions against the defendant. . . . When material evidence has an additional prejudicial effect, Rule 403 requires the trial court to make a conscientious assessment of whether the probative value of the evidence on a disputed issue in the case is substantially outweighed by the prejudicial tendency of the evidence to have some other adverse effect upon the defendant.

[112] 1 Weinstein and Berger ¶ 403[03], at 403-29 to 403-39.

§ 6.13 RECURRING ISSUES

outweighs the probative value of the evidence. The balance must tip sharply toward unfair prejudice.

When balancing probative value against potential for unfair prejudice, the court considers all relevant factors, including:

Strength of probative value of evidence. The stronger the probative value of an item of evidence, the greater the likelihood the court will conclude that the probative value is not substantially outweighed by unfair prejudice.[113]

Importance of fact to be proven. When evidence is offered on an important issue, the proponent's need for the evidence is often high.

Alternative means of accomplishing same evidential goal. If a fact can be established with evidence that does not carry the potential for unfair prejudice, the court has discretion to require the less prejudicial evidence.

Degree to which fact to be proven is in dispute. When an issue is hotly contested, the need for evidence on point is higher than when an issue is only nominally disputed.

Degree to which jury is likely to follow limiting instruction. In some circumstances the jury may be unwilling or unable to obey an instruction to confine its consideration of evidence to permissible uses. The jury may be so strongly tempted to consider the evidence for an improper purpose that the evidence should be excluded. Thus, evidence which is particularly inflammatory may unfairly prejudice.[114] It is important to recall, however, that jurors are presumed to follow the court's instructions.[115]

Making Uncharged Misconduct Evidence a "Feature of the Trial"

Uncharged misconduct evidence has high potential to unfairly prejudice the defendant. In *Travers v. State*,[116] the Florida Court of Appeal wrote, "The admission of excessive evidence of other crimes to the extent that it becomes a 'feature of the trial,' especially in the absence of a limiting instruction at the

---

[113] *See* United States v. Hadley, 918 F.2d 848, 852 (9th Cir. 1990), *cert. granted*, 112 S. Ct. 1261 (1992) ("The evidence was highly probative on the question of intent, especially in light of the similarity found between the prior acts and the offense charged").

[114] *See* United States v. York, 933 F.2d 1343, 1349 (7th Cir.), *cert. denied*, 112 S. Ct. 321 (1991).

[115] United States v. Hadley, 918 F.2d 848 (9th Cir. 1990), *cert. granted*, 112 S. Ct. 1261 (1992) (potential prejudice of uncharged misconduct evidence on intent "was limited by the instruction given by the district court").

[116] 578 So. 2d 793 (Fla. Dist. Ct. App. 1991).

time such evidence is received, has been recognized as fundamental error requiring reversal."[117]

§ 6.14 Motive

Motive is not an element of a crime.[118] Rather, motive is "[a]n inducement, or that which leads or tempts the mind to indulge in a criminal act."[119] Although motive is not an element, the prosecutor is permitted to prove that the defendant had a motive to commit the charged offense.[120] When identity is disputed, existence of a motive increases the likelihood the defendant is the culprit.[121] Likewise, when the occurrence of the act is disputed, the fact that the defendant was motivated to commit the act increases the probability the act occurred.[122] Finally, evidence of motive may be offered to prove the defendant's intent at the time the act was committed.[123]

Two uncharged misconduct theories are employed to prove motive.[124] First, an uncharged act may give rise to the motive for a charged act. Imwinkelried

---

[117] *Id.* at 797.

[118] 1A J. Wigmore § 118, at 1698; 22 C. Wright & K. Graham § 5240, at 480.

[119] Black's Law Dictionary 914 (5th ed. 1979).

[120] *See, e.g.,* United States v. Bradshaw, 690 F.2d 704 (9th Cir. 1982), *cert. denied,* 463 U.S. 1210 (1983) (proper to receive evidence of uncharged acts of sexual abuse of nine-year-old kidnap victim to prove defendant's motive to kidnap the child); United States v. Rhea, 33 M.J. 413, 422–23 (C.M.A. 1991); United States v. Watkins, 21 M.J. 224 (C.M.A.), *cert. denied,* 476 U.S. 1108 (1986); United States v. Lips, 22 M.J. 679 (A.F.C.M.R. 1986); People v. Phillips, 122 Cal. App. 3d 69, 175 Cal. Rptr. 703 (1981) (proper for state to offer evidence of motive when mother was accused of killing her infant child); Commonwealth v. Scott, 408 Mass. 811, 564 N.E.2d 370 (1990) (felony-murder prosecution; underlying felony was rape; proper to admit uncharged sexual advances on other women to show defendant's sexual frustration and motive to attack victim); W. LaFave & A. Scott, Criminal Law § 3.7, at 227–31 (1986).

[121] E. Imwinkelried, Uncharged Misconduct Evidence § 3:15, at 3-36 (1984) [hereinafter Imwinkelried]; 22 Wright & Graham § 5240, at 480 ("Evidence of motive may be offered to prove that the act was committed, or to prove the identity of the actor, or to prove the requisite mental state").

[122] Imwinkelried § 4:19, at 4-43.

[123] *Id.* § 5:32, at 5-53. See **§ 6.15** for discussion of intent.

[124] Imwinkelried § 3:15, at 3-36. *See also* 22 Wright & Graham § 5240, at 480–81, where the authors write:

> When evidence of other crimes, wrongs, or acts is offered under the motive rationale in Rule 404(b), the relevance of the evidence turns on an analysis of at least two different inferences. First, the act proved must support an inference as to some mental state, such as desire for money, revenge, etc. Second, the mental state shown must be causally related to some other issue in the case, either directly or through appropriate intermediate inferences. As to the first step, it should be noted that the other act can prove the mental state in two ways. First, the other act can be one that caused the mental state;

writes that "[t]he uncharged crime is cause, and the charged act is effect."[125] For example, murder is often committed to silence someone who "knows too much." Thus, in a homicide case, the state may establish motive by proving that the defendant was aware the murder victim witnessed the defendant commit uncharged crimes, and that the victim was about to inform the police.[126] The defendant's knowledge supplies a motive to kill the victim to prevent disclosure of the uncharged crimes.

The second theory using uncharged misconduct to establish motive applies when uncharged and charged acts are products of the same motive. That is, a single motive produces the uncharged and the charged acts. To establish motive for the *charged* act, the state proves the *uncharged* act. Suppose, for example, that the defendant is charged with murder with malice aforethought. The state has evidence that the defendant viciously attacked the victim on a prior occasion. The prior uncharged assault is a product of the defendant's hatred of the victim. The animosity that produced the first attack points to motive to premeditate murder.

The following hypotheticals illustrate the two theories of motive described above.

> *Hypothetical No. 1.* The defendant is charged with physically abusing Sue, his six-year-old stepdaughter. The defense argues the injury was accidental. The prosecutor has evidence that prior to committing the charged offense against Sue, the defendant sexually assaulted Sue's sister, Mary. The defendant then threatened Sue with "a whipping" if she revealed the sexual abuse of Mary. When Sue disclosed the sexual abuse, the defendant attacked her.

In the first hypothetical, the defendant's uncharged misconduct was sexually assaulting Mary and threatening Sue. The uncharged misconduct supplied the motive for the charged act of physical abuse. The fact that the defendant had a reason to attack Sue undercuts the likelihood the injury was accidental. Thus, evidence of the defendant's motive is admissible on the question of intent. The first hypothetical demonstrates the cause-and-effect relationship employed in the first theory of uncharged misconduct to prove motive. Hypothetical number 2 illustrates the second theory of motive.

> *Hypothetical No. 2.* The defendant is charged with incest. The victim is the defendant's 15-year-old daughter. The defendant denies the abuse. The prosecutor offers testimony from the victim's adult sister that when the sister was a minor,

---

for example, a desire for revenge against witnesses produced by a prior conviction. Second, the other act may be offered as another consequence of the same emotion, as when proof that the defendant stole from his wives is offered to show motive for bigamy.

[125] Imwinkelried § 3:15, at 3-36.
[126] *See, e.g.,* United States v. Benton, 637 F.2d 1052 (5th Cir. 1981).

the defendant had sexual intercourse with her. The uncharged abuse of the sister took place years before the charged offense. The prosecutor argues that the prior abuse is evidence of the defendant's motive to commit incest. The uncharged incest is admissible to establish the motive to commit the charged offense.

The facts of the second hypothetical are drawn from *Brown v. State*,[127] where the Wyoming Supreme Court approved admission of the prior uncharged misconduct to establish motive.[128] The court explained:

> Incest involves aberrant sexual behavior—it is a type of sexual deviancy that is difficult to understand. Therefore, a trier of fact might well wonder what would motivate the accused to behave in such bizarre manner. The evidence of prior sexual acts then was probative under the motive exception because of the unusual sexual behavior involved . . . . If the accused had a predilection to deviant sexual practices with young female relatives, it would not be unreasonable for the trier of fact to determine that he had a motive to commit the act complained of by the victim in this case.[129]

The court's analysis is troublesome. The uncharged misconduct does not satisfy the first theory for proof of motive. The prior assault was unrelated to the charged offense, and it is highly unlikely the earlier sexual abuse provided a motive for intercourse with the victim years later.[130]

The *Brown* court appears to rely on the second theory for proving motive. Arguably, the earlier offense was a product of the defendant's motive to commit incest. Proof of motive on the prior occasion increases the likelihood that the defendant was motivated to commit the charged offense. The second theory, however, is not an appropriate vehicle to carry the uncharged misconduct into evidence. The prior incest proves little more than a propensity for deviant

---

[127] 736 P.2d 1110 (Wyo. 1987). For a similar holding, see State v. Jackson, 82 Ohio App. 318, 81 N.E.2d 546 (1948). In *Jackson* the court approved testimony by two other daughters that the defendant assaulted them as proof of the defendant's passion, or more specifically, the defendant's motive to commit incest with the victim. The court pointed out that the evidence was not received to establish the general motive for sexual gratification that is shared by all individuals, but as proof of the defendant's specific motive to gratify his unnatural sexual desires through incest. *See also* State v. Friedrich, 135 Wis. 2d 1, 398 N.W.2d 763 (1987).

[128] The evidence was admitted at trial over the timely objection of defense counsel. 736 P.2d at 1111.

[129] *Id.* at 1113.

[130] *See* State v. Santarelli, 98 Wash. 2d 358, 655 P.2d 697 (1982). In *Santarelli*, the defendant was charged with rape of an adult woman. The trial court permitted the state to offer evidence of an attempted rape by the defendant of another woman that took place some four years earlier. The trial judge admitted the evidence to establish motive and intent. The Washington Supreme Court reversed in an instructive decision. The court wrote, "[I]t is by no means clear how an assault on a woman could be a motive or inducement for the defendant's rape of a different woman almost five years later . . . . [T]he evidence seems to achieve no more than to show a general propensity to rape, precisely forbidden by ER 404(b)." 655 P.2d at 700.

sexual conduct.[131] The dissenting justice in *Brown* recognized this, and wrote that the uncharged misconduct should have been excluded "because its introduction was an attempt to show that the defendant acted in conformity with a criminal character."[132]

The view taken by the dissenting justice in *Brown* is supported by the writing of Lempert and Saltzburg, who criticize the second theory of uncharged misconduct to prove motive, writing:

> There are two different situations in which evidence is admitted under the motive exception. The first is where the existence of another crime provides the motive which explains the criminal behavior with which the defendant is charged . . . .
>
> Other crimes evidence has also been used to suggest the existence of a motive without shedding light on why the defendant should be so motivated. Where the defendant has assaulted a murder victim several times in the past, evidence of other crimes might be allowed in to show that defendant "hated" the victim. Although this connection between other crimes and motive has been suggested by no less an authority than Wigmore,[133] in reality it is but propensity evidence under a different name. All that has been shown is the propensity of the defendant to attack the victim. From this, hate is inferred. From hate, one infers that the defendant attacked the victim on the occasion of the homicide. But the same inference, from previous assaults to the assault charged, could be made without positing the intervening emotion of hate (or jealousy or a sadomasochistic relationship or ***). Perhaps similar crimes perpetrated on the same victim are so probative of other crimes directed against the victim that they should be admitted on the straightforward ground that their relevance in determining who victimized that individual outweighs the associated dangers. We tend to doubt this, but we feel even more strongly that the courts should face the policy issues directly rather than avoid them by applying the mistaken label of motive.
>
> To some extent this has happened in the area of sex crimes . . . . While some courts still admit evidence of prior criminal sex acts with the same person as bearing on motive, others are more frank and state that evidence of a propensity to engage in certain sex acts with the same person is so probative on the issue of whether a given sex act has been engaged in with a given person that it should be admissible despite important reasons for keeping it out.
>
> [When the evidence is admitted to prove "motive," however,] the label is really an excuse for admitting what is analytically propensity evidence.[134]

---

[131] *See* Brown v. State, 736 P.2d 1110 (Wyo. 1987).

[132] 736 P.2d at 1118 (Urbigkit, J., dissenting).

[133] *See* 2 J. Wigmore § 306, at 259 ("To show the hostility towards the deceased of a defendant charged with murder, a former assault by him upon the deceased would be relevant").

[134] R. Lempert & S. Saltzburg, A Modern Approach to Evidence 226–27 & n.71, 229 & n.79 (1982) (the quoted material is a combination of Lempert and Saltzburg's text and footnotes). Professor Imwinkelried observes that the Lempert and Saltzburg view "has merit, but to date no court has embraced this view." Imwinkelried § 3:18, at 3-48.

Despite theoretical arguments against the second theory of motive, courts approve this theory with some regularity in sexual abuse cases.[135]

Rather than characterize the uncharged misconduct in *Brown* as evidence of motive, a more straightforward approach is to adopt the depraved sexual propensity exception to the rule against character evidence (see § **6.21**).

§ 6.15 Proof of Intent, Absence of Mistake, or Accident

Proof of intent is vitally important in child abuse litigation.[136] The prosecution often has special need for uncharged misconduct evidence probative of intent.[137] In *Huddleston v. United States,*[138] the Supreme Court observed that uncharged misconduct evidence "may be critical to the establishment of the truth as to a disputed issue, especially when that issue involves the actor's state of mind and the only means of ascertaining that mental state is by drawing inferences from conduct."[139] In *Boutwell v. State,*[140] the Texas Court of Criminal Appeals wrote:

> [I]n a case where the State's *need* to prove intent is strong because of an otherwise innocent act, extraneous acts are more likely to be more probative than prejudicial. On the other hand, where the circumstances surrounding the offenses are "abundantly supportive of the inference of intent," the necessity for extraneous offenses to prove intent is minimal and the prejudice arising from their admission, comparatively great.[141]

---

[135] Inmon v. State, 585 So. 2d 261 (Ala. Crim. App. 1991).

[136] See **Ch. 3** for discussion of intent in child abuse litigation.

[137] Estelle v. McGuire, 112 S. Ct. 475 (1991); United States v. York, 933 F.2d 1343, 1350 (7th Cir.), *cert. denied,* 112 S. Ct. 321 (1991) ("When the defendant affirmatively denies having the requisite intent by proffering an innocent explanation for his actions, the government is entitled to rebut that argument. 'Evidence of another crime which tends to undermine defendant's innocent explanation for his act will be admitted.' J. Weinstein & M. Berger, Weinstein's Evidence, § 404[12], at 404-84 (1990)"); United States v. Hadley, 918 F.2d 848, 852 (9th Cir. 1990), *cert. granted,* 112 S. Ct. 1261 (1992); People v. Brown, 199 Ill. App. 3d 860, 557 N.E.2d 611, 621 (1990) ("When the defendant pled not guilty, he put the State to its proof, and it was entitled to offer all relevant evidence in its case-in-chief"); Boutwell v. State, 719 S.W.2d 164, 174 (Tex. Crim. App. 1985).

But see Houston v. State, 531 So. 2d 598 (Miss. 1988) (defendant did not claim her child died accidentally; therefore it was error to put on evidence of seven years of defendant's abuse to disprove accident).

[138] 485 U.S. 681 (1988).

[139] *Id.* at 685.

[140] 719 S.W.2d 164 (Tex. Crim. App. 1985).

[141] 719 S.W.2d at 174.

§ 6.17 DOCTRINE OF CHANCES

Intent can be established through five theories of uncharged misconduct evidence:

1. Motive[142]
2. Plan[143]
3. Knowledge[144]
4. Doctrine of chances
5. Inference from intent at time of uncharged acts.

These five uses of uncharged misconduct to prove intent are discussed below.

§ 6.16 —Motive, Plan, or Knowledge

Intent can be inferred from the actor's motive or emotion.[145] For example, evidence that A was furious with B increases the likelihood that A poisoned B intentionally rather than accidentally. A had a motive. Intent also may be inferred from evidence of a plan. Referring again to A and B, suppose that after A's ire was raised, she removed a bottle of arsenic from a locked basement cabinet and hid it in B's room. On the fatal night, A supplied theater tickets to the butler so that A and the victim would be alone in the house. A's plan points toward her intent when she slipped arsenic into B's toddy. Finally, the fact that a person possesses specific knowledge is sometimes probative of intent.[146] If A was a pharmacist, for example, her knowledge of the poisonous qualities of the powder would undercut an assertion of inadvertence.

§ 6.17 —Doctrine of Chances

Many physical abuse cases stand or fall on the prosecutor's ability to overcome a claim of accident. The state must establish deliberateness or willfulness. In this regard, proof of intent frequently rests on the doctrine of chances or probabilities.[147] In his classic description of the doctrine of chances, Wigmore wrote:

> To prove intent, as a generic notion of criminal volition or willfulness, [the] argument . . . is purely from the point of view of the doctrine of chances—

---

[142] See § **6.14**.

[143] See § **6.22**.

[144] Huddleston v. United States, 485 U.S. 681 (1988).

[145] The discussion in this section is modeled after Wigmore. *See* 2 Wigmore § 242, at 45.

[146] Huddleston v. United States, 485 U.S. 681 (1988).

[147] For helpful discussion of the doctrine of chances, see United States v. York, 933 F.2d 1343 (7th Cir.), *cert. denied,* 112 S. Ct. 321 (1991); Imwinkelried § 2:05, at 2-8 to -9.

the instinctive recognition of that logical process which eliminates the element of innocent intent by multiplying instances of the same result until it is perceived that this element cannot explain them all. Without formulating any accurate test, and without attempting by numerous instances to secure absolute certainty of inference, the mind applies this rough and instinctive process of reasoning, namely, that an unusual and abnormal element might perhaps be present in one instance, but that the oftener similar instances occur with similar results, the less likely is the abnormal element likely to be the true explanation of them.

Thus, if A while hunting with B hears the bullet from B's gun whistling past his head, he is willing to accept B's bad aim or B's accidental tripping as a conceivable explanation; but if shortly afterwards the same thing happens again, and if on the third occasion A receives B's bullet in his body, the immediate inference (i.e., as a probability, perhaps not a certainty) is that B shot at A deliberately; because the chances of an inadvertent shooting on three successive similar occasions are extremely small; or (to put it in another way) because inadvertence or accident is only an abnormal or occasional explanation for the discharge of a gun at a given object, and therefore the recurrence of a similar result . . . (here in the shape of an unlawful act) tends (increasingly with each instance) to negative accident or inadvertence or self-defense or good faith or other innocent mental state, and tends to establish (provisionally, at least, though not certainly) the presence of the normal, i.e., criminal, intent accompanying such an act; and the force of each additional instance will vary in each kind of offense according to the probability that the act could be repeated, within a limited time and under given circumstances, with an innocent intent.[148]

Additional insight into the doctrine of chances comes from the New Hampshire Supreme Court's 1876 decision in *State v. Lapage*,[149] where Chief Justice Cushing wrote:

Another class of cases consists of those in which it becomes necessary to show that the act for which the prisoner was indicted was not accidental, e.g., where the prisoner had shot the same person twice within a short time, or where the same person had fired a rick of grain twice, or where several deaths by poison had taken place in the same family, or where children of the same mother had mysteriously died. In such cases it might well happen that a man should shoot another accidentally, but that he should do it twice within a short time would be very unlikely. So, it might easily happen that a man using a gun might fire a rick of barley once by accident, but that he should do it several times in succession would be very improbable.

So, a person might die of accidental poisoning, but that several persons should so die in the same family at different times would be very unlikely.

---

[148] 2 Wigmore § 302, at 241.
[149] 57 N.H. 245 (1876).

§ 6.17   DOCTRINE OF CHANCES

So, that a child should be suffocated in bed by its mother might happen once, but several similar deaths in the same family could not reasonably be accounted for as accidents.[150]

The following hypotheticals illustrate the doctrine of chances to disprove accident or inadvertence.

Hypothetical No. 1. Defendant is accused of murdering his four-year-old son. The boy died of a skull fracture and brain injury. Defendant is charged with inflicting these injuries. The child was rushed to the hospital, where he died. The hospital staff noted that in addition to the fatal head injury, the child had multiple old and new bruises on his face, buttocks, lower back, abdomen, chest, and genitals. Defendant claims that the child was accident prone and that the head injury was accidental. To counter this defense, the state offers proof that the child suffered many soft tissue injuries over an extended period of time. Defendant is not charged with inflicting the soft tissue injuries.

The state's evidence should be received to rebut the defense of accident. It is in the nature of children to suffer minor scrapes and bruises. Furthermore, an occasional accident causes more serious injury. It is highly unlikely, however, that a healthy child will accidentally suffer multiple soft tissue injuries on areas such as the bottom, face, and abdomen over a relatively short period of time.[151] Such repeated injuries probably are the result of human design rather than accident. Evidence of the child's sad history reduces the likelihood that the fatal injury was accidental. Numerous cases approve the doctrine of chances to rebut a claim of accidental injury.[152]

---

[150] *Id.* at 294.

[151] See **Ch. 3**.

[152] Estelle v. McGuire, 112 S. Ct. 475 (1991); United States v. Leight, 818 F.2d 1297 (7th Cir.), *cert. denied,* 489 U.S. 958 (1987); United States v. Harris, 661 F.2d 138 (10th Cir. 1981); United States v. Woods, 484 F.2d 127 (4th Cir. 1973), *cert. denied,* 415 U.S. 979 (1974); United States v. Grady, 481 F.2d 1106 (D.C. Cir. 1973); United States v. Merriweather, 22 M.J. 657, 661 (A.C.M.R. 1986) ("the sheer number of injuries suffered by the victim over a relatively short period of time would have led common persons to conclude that the charged injury was less likely to have been accidental, thus rebutting the inference of possible accident which arose from the testimony elicited by trial defense counsel"); Harvey v. State, 604 P.2d 586 (Alaska 1979) (defendant did not defend on the basis of accident; therefore it was error to admit uncharged misconduct evidence relating to accident); Limber v. State, 264 Ark. 479, 572 S.W.2d 402 (1978); People v. Wade, 43 Cal. 3d 366, 729 P.2d 239, 233 Cal. Rptr. 48 (1987), *cert. denied,* 488 U.S. 900 (1988); People v. Taggart, 621 P.2d 1375 (Colo. 1981); State v. Wilson, 199 Conn. 417, 513 A.2d 620 (1986); State v. Tucker, 181 Conn. 406, 435 A.2d 986 (1980); People v. Brown, 199 Ill. App. 3d 860, 557 N.E.2d 611 (1990); Bludsworth v. State, 98 Nev. 289, 646 P.2d 558 (1982); State v. Stevens, 238 N.W.2d 251 (N.D. 1975); Freeman v. State, 681 P.2d 84 (Okla. Crim. App. 1984); Commonwealth v. Donahue, 519 Pa. 532, 549 A.2d 121 (1988); State v. Holland, 346 N.W.2d 302 (S.D. 1984); State V. Tanner, 675 P.2d 539 (Utah 1983); State v. Mercer, 34 Wash. App. 654, 663 P.2d 857 (1983).

The doctrine of chances does not require proof that the defendant committed the uncharged or the charged acts of abuse. Under the doctrine, the identity of the person or persons committing the uncharged and charged acts is immaterial. Thus, anonymous acts are admissible to prove that a charged act was deliberate.[153] The evidentiary force of the doctrine lies in its ability to prove that the charged act was deliberately caused by *someone*. The doctrine of chances sheds no light on the identity of the perpetrator, and other evidence must be adduced to tie the defendant to the crime. Wigmore explains the admissibility of anonymous acts:

> It will be seen that the strength of the [doctrine of chances] does notrest exclusively on a given person's connection with the prior injurious transactions. It is possible to negative accident or inadvertence, and to infer deliberate human intent, without forming any conclusion as to the personality of the doer. Thus if, one morning after a high wind, A's cellar window is found broken, the pieces lying inside, he may well assume the probability that the force of the wind blew the glass in; but if, on the next morning and the next, he again finds a window broken in the same way, though no high wind prevailed the night before, he gives up the hypothesis of the force of the wind as the explanation, and concludes that a deliberate human effort was the highly probable cause of the breakage, although he can form no notion whatever of the personality of the doer.
>
> Thus it is thus clear that innocent intent—accident, inadvertence, or the like—may be negatived by *anonymous instances* of the previous occurrence of the same or a similar thing . . . .

---

[153] Bludsworth v. State, 98 Nev. 289, 646 P.2d 558 (1982). *Bludsworth* was a murder prosecution for the death of a two-year-old who died of head injuries. The defendant claimed the injuries were accidental. The court stated:

> During the trial, considerable evidence was presented that Eric had sustained numerous bruises, including a bite mark on his scrotum, prior to the day of his fatal injury . . . .
>
> Appellants also erroneously argue that the bite mark evidence and evidence of other bruises were incompetent because there was no prior establishment, by clear and convincing evidence, that either [defendant] was responsible for each of the prior injuries. Admissibility of the bite mark and other bruise evidence does not depend on connecting either defendant to the infliction of the injury. It is independent, relevant circumstantial evidence tending to show that the child was intentionally, rather than accidentally injured on the day in question. Proof that a child has experienced injuries in many purported accidents is evidence that the most recent injury may not have resulted from yet another accident.

646 P.2d at 559. *See also* Estelle v. McGuire, 112 S. Ct. 475 (1991); State v. Mercer, 34 Wash. App. 654, 663 P.2d 857, 860–61 (1983); Imwinkelried § 2:05.

In State v. Stevens, 238 N.W.2d 251 (N.D. 1975), the court excluded evidence of anonymous prior injuries to prove intent. However, this decision can be reconciled with the principle that anonymous acts are admissible under the doctrine of chances to prove intent because the court was particularly troubled by the state offering the evidence to prove not only intent, but also identity. When uncharged misconduct is offered to establish identity, anonymous acts are not admissible. The court implied that if the state had limited the uncharged misconduct to proof of intent, the evidence may have been admissible. *Id.* at 259.

§ 6.17 DOCTRINE OF CHANCES

The only limitation upon this mode of proof is that the defendant's doing of the act in issue must be shown by other evidence at some stage of the trial; and the anonymous instances should not be received until the trial court is satisfied with the amount of evidence introduced or pledged for showing that connection.[154]

Although anonymous acts are admissible under the doctrine of chances, before anonymous acts are received, the state must establish a connection between the defendant and the injured child or children. For example, suppose the defendant is charged with murdering a child. The defense argues the child suffered accidental head injuries. The prosecutor cannot disprove the accident theory with evidence that during the past year five other children in the city suffered head injuries. The other injuries have no connection to the defendant. If, however, the prosecutor establishes that the other victims were all the defendant's children, or were all under the defendant's care, the evidence becomes highly probative on the question of intent. Probative force exists even though the state cannot prove that the defendant inflicted the other injuries.

Hypothetical No. 2. The defendant is the stepmother of the two-year-old victim. On November 16, 1992, the defendant carried the child to a neighbor's home. The child had a large bruise on his head and was unconscious. The defendant told the neighbor that while she was dressing the child, he fell and hit his head on a chair. The child was quickly taken to the hospital, where a subdural hematoma was diagnosed. Emergency surgery was performed, saving the child's life. The government charges the defendant with child abuse. Her defense is accident. The court admits testimony from the surgeon that the injury was probably caused by a blunt, flat instrument.[155] The doctor also testifies that the defendant's explanation is inconsistent with the severity of the injury.[156] The state offers evidence that on November 2, 1992, two weeks *before* the charged act, the child was taken to the hospital suffering multiple bruises about the face and body. The state is unable to establish that the child was in the defendant's exclusive care on November 2nd.[157]

The second hypothetical raises three important issues. First, the admissibility of anonymous acts under the doctrine of chances. Second, the applicability of the doctrine when there is only one uncharged act. Finally, the applicability of the doctrine when uncharged acts are not identical to the charged act. The first issue was addressed in connection with Hypothetical No. 1. The fact that the state cannot establish the identity of the person who caused the November 2nd injuries does not undercut the utility of the doctrine of chances to rebut the defense of accident.

---

[154] 2 Wigmore § 303, at 247–48.

[155] Such expert testimony is admissible in child abuse litigation. See **Ch. 3**.

[156] In many physical abuse cases, parents offer improbable or impossible explanations for a child's injuries. Such explanations are probative of nonaccidental injury. See **Ch. 3**.

[157] Hypothetical No. 2 is based on United States v. Brown, 608 F.2d 551 (5th Cir. 1979).

The second issue is, how often must an event occur to trigger the doctrine of chances? Some authorities state that multiple uncharged acts are required.[158] The better view is that there is no hard and fast rule defining the number of acts needed to trigger the doctrine of chances. The preferred position is articulated by the Oregon Supreme Court in *State v. Johns,*[159] where the court wrote:

[I]s one prior similar incident enough to justify admission . . . ?

We believe no categorical statement can be made one way or the other. Depending upon the circumstances of the case, sometimes one prior similar act will be sufficiently relevant for admissibility and sometimes not. A simple, unremarkable single instance of prior conduct probably will not qualify, but a complex act requiring several steps, particularly premeditated, may well qualify. These decisions must be made case-by-case . . . .[160]

In Hypothetical No. 2 there was only one prior incident of injury to the child. Does this single episode trigger the doctrine of chances? Credible arguments are possible both ways. It seems, however, that the evidence should be received. The type and severity of the child's injuries on the prior occasion point toward child abuse. Multiple bruises over the face and body cannot fairly be described as a "simple unremarkable single instance of prior conduct."[161] Logic and policy support the conclusion that in selected cases a single uncharged event is sufficient to trigger the doctrine of chances.

The third question raised by Hypothetical No. 2 is the degree of similarity required between the charged act and uncharged acts. Authorities agree that the acts must be similar. Wigmore wrote that "prior acts should be similar. Since it is the improbability of a like result being repeated by mere chance that carries probative weight, the essence of this probative effect is the likeness of the

---

[158] *See* 2 Wigmore § 325, at 287–88. Wigmore discusses the doctrine of chances to prove intent in prosecutions for possession of stolen goods.

[T]he recurrence of a like act lessens by each instance the possibility that a given instance could be the result of inadvertence, accident, or other innocent intent. Accordingly, the argument here is that the oftener A is found in possession of stolen goods, the less likely it is that his possession on the occasion charged was innocent. [T]he force of an argument based on the intent theory lies in the multiplication of instances; that a single instance has from this point of view little or no weight . . . .

Id.

It is important to note that Wigmore is not saying the doctrine of chances never comes into play when there is only one similar occurrence. In § 325 Wigmore is discussing possession of stolen property, and in that type of case proof of intent often requires more than a single uncharged episode of possession. In other contexts, however, where there is but a single similar act, Wigmore may have approved use of the doctrine of chances.

See Note, *Admissibility of Evidence of Prior Crimes in Murder Trials,* 25 Ind. L.J. 64, 68 n.23 (1949); Comment, *The Admissibility of Evidence of Extraneous Offenses in Texas Criminal Cases,* 14 S. Tex. L.J. 69, 96 (1973).

[159] 301 Or. 535, 725 P.2d 312 (1986).

[160] 725 P.2d at 324.

[161] *Id.* at 324.

instance."[162] Although similarity is required for the doctrine of chances, the acts do not have to be identical.[163] Imwinkelried observes, "If the acts are similar in material respects, the similarity justifies the admission of the acts to disprove innocent intent."[164]

In Hypothetical No. 2 the charged injury was a blow to the head causing a subdural hematoma. The uncharged injuries also resulted from blows. What is more, the earlier incident included head injuries that were similar to, if less severe than, the charged offense. The facts of Hypothetical No. 2 satisfy the similarity requirement. Thus, the doctrine of chances can be invoked to prove that the victim's injuries were inflicted deliberately.

§ 6.18 —Inference from Intent at Time of Uncharged Acts

There remains for discussion the most controversial theory of uncharged misconduct to prove intent. Under this theory, the defendant's intent when the charged act was committed is established through evidence of the defendant's intent when uncharged acts were committed. Such evidence comes perilously close to violating the rule against character evidence to prove conduct, and raises serious questions of fairness to defendants. Nevertheless, most courts approve uncharged misconduct evidence under this theory.

To understand the problems engendered by establishing the defendant's intent on the charged occasion with evidence of the defendant's intent at other times, it is profitable to review the rule excluding character evidence. The rule disallows the following three-step mode of proof: (1) evidence of the defendant's uncharged misconduct is admitted; (2) an inference regarding the defendant's character is drawn from the uncharged misconduct; and (3) based on the inference of character, a further inference is drawn that the defendant probably acted in conformity with character on a particular occasion.

Wright and Graham describe the forbidden chain of inferences: "The general rule of exclusion applies only when the evidence is offered to prove (1) 'the character of a person'; and (2) 'that he acted in conformity therewith.' Both elements are required."[165] Imwinkelried illustrates the forbidden chain of inferences schematically as shown in **Figure 6–5**.[166]

---

[162] 2 Wigmore § 302, at 245 (emphasis omitted).

[163] United States v. York, 933 F.2d 1343, 1351 (7th Cir.), *cert. denied,* 112 S. Ct. 321 (1991). Contrast the rather flexible similarity requirement of the doctrine of chances with the strict similarity rule imposed when evidence of modus operandi is used to prove identity. See § **6.24** for a discussion of modus operandi.

[164] Imwinkelried § 5:07, at 5-17.

[165] 22 Wright & Graham § 5239, at 459 (footnotes omitted).

[166] Imwinkelried § 2:18, at 2-48 fig. 2–2 (footnotes omitted).

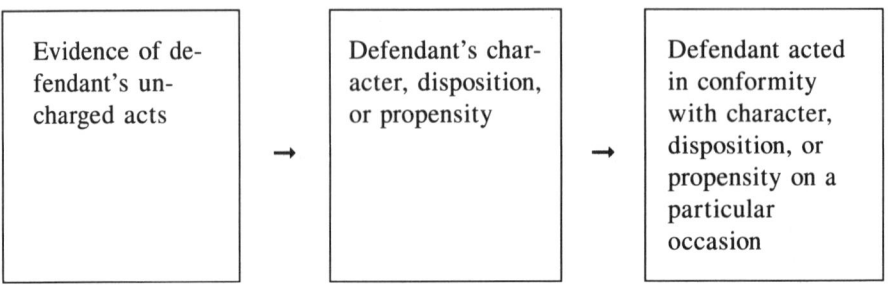

Figure 6–5. Chain of inferences forbidden by Federal Rule of Evidence 404(a).

With the forbidden chain of inferences in mind, the question is, are these inferences at work when the state offers evidence of the defendant's intent at the time uncharged acts were committed to prove intent at the time the charged act was committed? Under the prevailing view, the answer is no because the uncharged misconduct evidence does not rely on the forbidden chain of inferences; that is, when uncharged acts are used to prove intent, the intermediate inference is to the defendant's *intent* at the time uncharged acts were committed, not *character*. Furthermore, under the prevailing view, the ultimate inference is to the defendant's *intent* at the time the charged act was committed, not *conduct* in conformity with *character*. Thus, neither component of the forbidden chain of inferences is implicated when uncharged misconduct is offered to prove intent.[167]

The prevailing view can be illustrated with Imwinkelried's schematic as shown in **Figure 6–6**. In **Figure 6–6**, there is no intermediate inference to character. Nor is there an ultimate inference to conduct conforming to character. Because neither of the forbidden inferences is drawn from the defendant's uncharged misconduct, the rule against propensity evidence is not offended.[168]

The prevailing view is discussed in *State v. Lapage*.[169] In *Lapage* the defendant was charged with murder. The state claimed the murder was committed while the defendant was "perpetrating or attempting to perpetrate a rape."[170] To establish the defendant's intent to rape the victim, the state offered evidence that he raped a different woman some four years earlier. In his argument before

---

[167] *See* United States v. Beechum, 582 F.2d 898, 909–18 (5th Cir. 1978), *cert. denied,* 440 U.S. 920 (1979); 22 Wright & Graham § 5242, at 487 ("The theory upon which evidence of other crimes is admissible on these issues [of intent] under Rule 404(b) is that its use on the mental element of the offense does not require an inference as to the character of the accused or as to his conduct").

[168] Technically, the rule against character evidence would not be violated even if one of the forbidden inferences were raised. The rule is violated *only* when both inferences are drawn from uncharged misconduct. *See* 22 Wright & Graham § 5239, at 459.

[169] 57 N.H. 245 (1876).

[170] *Id.* at 246.

§ 6.18   INTENT IN UNCHARGED ACTS   41

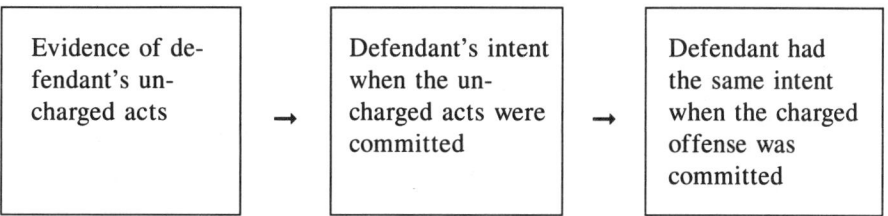

Figure 6–6. Chain of inferences used with theory of intent at time of uncharged misconduct.

the New Hampshire Supreme Court, the attorney general argued that evidence of the uncharged rape was properly admitted at trial. The attorney general put the following hypothetical to the appellate court:

> Suppose the defendant were tried for breaking and entering the store at the north end of Elm Street in Manchester—the most northern of all the stores on that street—with intent to steal: suppose it were proved that he broke and entered that store; that he was arrested as soon as he entered it, and the only question were whether he intended to steal: suppose there were one hundred other stores on that street, and he had broken and entered every one of them, and stolen something in every one of them, beginning at the south end of the street and taking the stores in succession, on his burglarious march from one end of the street to the other: suppose he did all this in one night, and was completing his night's work when arrested: on the question of his intent in entering the one hundred and first store, would anybody think of objecting to evidence of his one hundred larcenies in the other one hundred stores?[171]

Under the prevailing view, it is proper to admit evidence of the 100 uncharged burglaries to prove the defendant's intent when he was arrested in the 101st store. The trier of fact draws an inference of intent from the 100 uncharged acts. Based on this intermediate inference, the ultimate inference is drawn that the defendant intended to steal when he entered the 101st store. The rule against character evidence is not offended because neither of the forbidden inferences is drawn.

The primary difficulty with the attorney general's argument in *Lapage,* and with the prevailing view in general, is that it is very difficult to distinguish evidence of uncharged intent to prove charged intent from inadmissible character evidence.[172] It is not difficult to conceptualize the prevailing view as character evidence. So conceptualized, the chain of inferences is: First, the state proves the defendant's uncharged misconduct. Second, on the basis of the defendant's uncharged misconduct, the jury draws an intermediate inference that

---

[171] *Id.* at 261.

[172] In *Lapage* the New Hampshire Supreme Court held that the uncharged rape was improperly admitted in evidence. The defendant was awarded a new trial. *See* 57 N.H. at 305.

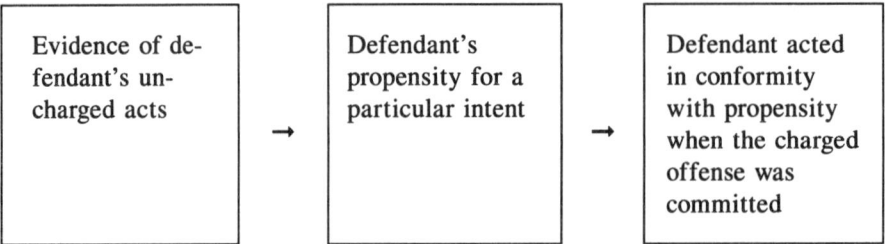

Figure 6–7. Chain of inferences forbidden by Federal Rule of Evidence 404(a) (character/propensity) using uncharged intent to prove charged intent.

the defendant has a propensity to entertain a particular criminal intent. Third, the ultimate inference is drawn that because of the defendant's propensity for a particular criminal intent, the defendant probably entertained that intent when the charged act was committed. This is character evidence.[173]

The argument that proving charged intent with evidence of uncharged intent is actually inadmissible character evidence can be analyzed with Imwinkelried's schematic as shown in **Figure 6–7**.

Consider again the attorney general's burglary hypothetical in *State v. Lapage*. The defendant's intent while he was in the first 100 stores provides some indication of his intent while in the 101st. Indeed, the attorney general was so taken with his hypothetical that he remarked:

> No man on earth would refuse to hear [the evidence], or to consider it unless he were bound by some arbitrary and irrational rule overriding his understanding, and dictating a course at war with his common sense. . . .
>
> . . . .
>
> [I]t is the spontaneous and irreversible judgment of every grade of intellect that has appeared, or is likely to appear, in this state of existence. It is an involuntary and unavoidable perception of the inherent and self-evident relations of conduct and intention; a mental revelation as natural as memory, and as trustworthy and unanswerable as consciousness.[174]

Despite the appeal of the attorney general's argument, it is difficult to escape the conclusion that evidence of the uncharged burglaries is character evidence. The attorney general is arguing that because the defendant is the type of person with a propensity for criminal intent, he probably acted in conformity with that propensity when he entered the 101st store.

---

[173] *See* Teitelbaum & Hertz, *Evidence II: Evidence of Other Crimes as Proof of Intent,* 13 N.M. L. Rev. 423, 427 (1983) (in some cases "it is impossible to distinguish between evidence offered to prove intent and its use as character evidence. . . . [E]vidence of intent based on prior bad acts is sometimes relevant to the charged crime only through an inference about the defendant's character").

[174] 57 N.H. at 268–69.

Since it is possible to conceptualize the prevailing view as inadmissible character evidence, how does the prevailing view survive? The answer lies in the doctrine of limited admissibility,[175] which Wigmore described as follows: "[W]hen an evidentiary fact is offered for one purpose and becomes admissible by satisfying all the rules applicable to it in that capacity, it is not inadmissible because it does not satisfy the rules applicable to it in some other capacity . . . ."[176] Rule 105 of the Federal Rules of Evidence articulates the limited admissibility principle:

> When evidence which is admissible as to one party or for one purpose but not admissible as to another party or for another purpose is admitted, the court, upon request, shall restrict the evidence to its proper scope and instruct the jury accordingly.[177]

If the proponent of evidence can justify admission for one purpose, the evidence is received despite the fact that the evidence would be excluded if offered for another purpose. Evidence of uncharged misconduct to prove intent is admissible because, under one theory, the evidence does not violate the rule against character evidence. The fact that the evidence can be conceptualized as character evidence does not defeat admissibility.[178] A limiting instruction can be given to ensure that the jury does not misuse the evidence.[179] Moreover, the trial court can exclude the evidence if its prejudicial effect substantially outweighs its evidentiary value.

Debate continues over the propriety of admitting evidence of uncharged intent to prove charged intent.[180] The battle lines are clearly drawn in the Fifth Circuit Court of Appeals' decision in *United States v. Beechum*.[181] Mr. Beechum

---

[175] *See* Fed. R. Evid. 105; 1 Wigmore § 13; 1A Wigmore § 215, at 1869 ("the fact that a defendant's acts of misconduct would be inadmissible as showing his bad character does not in the slightest stand in the way of receiving the same acts in evidence if they are evidential for other purposes"); 21 Wright & Graham §§ 5052–5067; 22 Wright & Graham § 5239, at 435–36. *See also* State v. Lapage, 57 N.H. 245, 288 (1876) (any act of a defendant may be put in evidence against him, provided it has any logical and legal tendency to prove any matter that is in issue).

[176] 1 Wigmore § 13, at 694.

[177] Fed. R. Evid. 105.

[178] *See* 22 Wright & Graham § 5239, at 435 ("The other crimes rule is simply a special application of the doctrine of multiple admissibility").

[179] Huddleston v. United States, 485 U.S. 681 (1988).

[180] *See generally* Teitelbaum & Hertz, *Evidence II: Evidence of Other Crimes as Proof of Intent*, 13 N.M. L. Rev. 423 (1983). Teitelbaum and Hertz articulate a strong argument against the prevailing view. *But see* 22 Wright & Graham § 5242, at 368–69 (Supp. 1991), in which Wright and Graham criticize the Teitelbaum and Hertz article.

[181] 582 F.2d 898 (5th Cir. 1978) (en banc), *cert. denied*, 440 U.S. 920 (1979). *See also* United States v. Williams, 816 F.2d 1527 (11th Cir. 1987) (using prevailing view, court holds it proper to prove defendant's intent when he committed charged assault by introducing evidence that he had committed two rapes in past).

was a postal service letter carrier charged with unlawful possession of an 1890 silver dollar that he took from the mail. Beechum's defense was that he lacked criminal intent because he planned to turn in the coin to his supervisor. To establish that Beechum possessed the coin unlawfully, the prosecutor introduced two credit cards found in Beechum's possession when he was arrested. Neither card was issued to Beechum, and neither was signed. The cards had been mailed some months earlier to addresses on Beechum's mail route. The import of the government's uncharged misconduct evidence was that because Beechum intended to steal the credit cards, he probably intended to steal the coin too.

Beechum was convicted. On appeal the conviction was reversed by a panel of the Fifth Circuit.[182] The matter was reheard en banc, and the full court affirmed the conviction and vacated the panel decision. On rehearing, the majority of judges ruled that the government's uncharged misconduct evidence was admissible. Writing for the majority, Judge Tjoflat stated:

> We hold that the credit cards were properly admissible . . . .
>
> * * *
>
> Where the issue addressed is the defendant's intent to commit the offense charged, the relevancy of the extrinsic offense derives from the defendant's indulging himself in the same state of mind in the perpetration of both the extrinsic and charged offenses. The reasoning is that because the defendant had unlawful intent in the extrinsic offense, it is less likely that he had lawful intent in the present offense . . . .
>
> Obviously, the line of reasoning that deems an extrinsic offense relevant to the issue of intent is valid only if an offense was in fact committed and the defendant in fact committed it. Therefore, as a predicate to a determination that the extrinsic offense is relevant, the Government must offer proof demonstrating that the defendant committed the offense . . . .
>
> * * *
>
> Once it is determined that the extrinsic offense requires the same intent as the charged offense and that the jury could find that the defendant committed the extrinsic offense, the evidence satisfies . . . Rule 404(b). The extrinsic offense is relevant (assuming the jury finds the defendant to have committed it) to an issue other than propensity because it lessens the likelihood that the defendant committed the charged offense with innocent intent.[183]

After concluding that the uncharged misconduct evidence was logically relevant, the majority held that the probative value of the evidence was not substantially outweighed by its prejudicial effect.

---

[182] United States v. Beechum, 555 F.2d 487 (5th Cir.), *reh'g granted,* 563 F.2d 782 (5th Cir. 1977), *vacated en banc,* 582 F.2d 898 (5th Cir. 1978), *cert. denied,* 440 U.S. 920 (1979).

[183] 582 F.2d at 905, 911–13.

§ 6.18   INTENT IN UNCHARGED ACTS

In a strident dissent, which was joined by four of his colleagues, Judge Goldberg rejected the majority's analysis.[184] Judge Goldberg wrote:

> [T]he majority thinks [Rule 404(b)] unequivocally allows us to reason that because a defendant displayed an improper intent in the past, he is more likely to have had an evil intent in the act for which he is tried . . . . How this differs from reasoning that the defendant has a "propensity" to act with evil intent is beyond reason . . . . [E]xtrinsic offense evidence submitted allegedly to show intent is really just bad character evidence in sheep's clothing.[185]

When Judge Goldberg wrote that the government's uncharged misconduct evidence was actually character evidence "in sheep's clothing," he was in good company. More than a century earlier, the New Hampshire Supreme Court decided *State v. Lapage*,[186] discussed earlier. In *Lapage* the trial judge permitted the prosecutor to establish the defendant's intent to rape the murder victim by introducing evidence that the defendant raped another woman four years earlier. Lapage was convicted, and on appeal the New Hampshire Supreme Court ruled unanimously that the uncharged misconduct evidence was improperly admitted.[187] Chief Justice Cushing wrote:

> I think it will be found that the courts have always professed to put the admission of [uncharged misconduct] testimony on the ground that there was some logical connection between the crime proposed to be proved other than the tendency to commit one crime as manifested by the tendency to commit the other.
>
> In the case under consideration, I cannot see any such logical connection, between the commission of the rape upon Julienne Rousse and the murder of [the victim], as the law requires. I am unable to see any connection by which from the first crime can be inferred that the [defendant] was attempting the commission of a rape when he committed the murder, if he did it, other than such inference as I understand the law expressly to exclude. Proof of the first crime would show that the [defendant] was a very bad man—would perhaps show a tendency or disposition to commit that particular crime; but it would go no further, and in fact would amount to little more than an attack upon the [defendant's] character, which is inadmissible unless he puts it in issue, and an attack upon his character by showing particular acts, which is also inadmissible.[188]

---

[184] For additional criticism of the Beechum majority, see Teitelbaum & Hertz, *Evidence II: Evidence of Other Crimes as Proof of Intent*, 13 N.M. L. Rev. 423, 429–32 (1983).

[185] 582 F.2d at 920 (Goldberg, J., dissenting).

[186] 57 N.H. 245 (1876).

[187] In *Lapage* the justices wrote separate opinions after the English style.

[188] 57 N.H. at 295–96. In his opinion Justice Ladd wrote:
> Was evidence that the prisoner committed rape upon Julienne Rousse, in Canada, in 1871, legally admissible to show that he committed or attempted to commit rape upon Josie A. Langmaid, at Pembroke, in 1875? . . . The simple naked question is that just stated, namely, Can evidence that he committed rape upon one woman be received

In the final analysis, the Goldberg-Cushing argument has considerable merit.[189] Nevertheless, a large body of case law—including child abuse cases—

> as evidence from which the jury may find that he committed rape upon another?—the two events being entirely independent and distinct—no way connected in time, or place, or circumstances; and we cannot, in my judgment, suffer that question to be changed in form, or to be covered up and disguised by vague and general observations as to the matter of intent, however astute and plausible, without imminent danger of losing our way in a wilderness of fallacy and error . . . .
>
> [I]t is the law, that evidence of the commission of one crime shall not be received to show the commission of another when there is no connection between the two.
>
> *Id.* at 298–300 (Ladd, J.). Justice Smith had this to say:
>
> The charge made by the State is, that this respondent killed the deceased in perpetrating or attempting to perpetrate a rape upon her. As having some tendency to show that he committed or attempted to commit a rape upon Josie Langmaid, the State was permitted to show that four years and more previously he had committed a rape upon Julienne Rousse, in Canada. Had the testimony any such tendency? There was obviously no connection whatever between the two offenses or transactions, either in the persons upon whom the crimes were committed, or in the places where or times when committed. The evidence of Julienne Rousse, at most, would only show that the respondent was depraved enough to commit the crime of rape, or that he possessed a lustful desire in his heart which he on that occasion did not hesitate to gratify by violent means.
>
> * * *
>
> No point is better settled than that the State cannot give evidence of the bad character of the respondent, unless he shall first put his character in question by introducing evidence in support thereof. As the only effect of the State's introducing evidence of another rape by the respondent is that it tended to show that he possessed a disposition to commit that particular crime, a disposition which would incline him to the perpetration of rape whenever the opportunity might occur, how does such testimony differ from that of evidence as to the prisoner's bad character, before he has elected to put it in question, and that too by introducing proof of an isolated fact?
>
> The whole answer to the position, that the evidence of Julienne Rousse was relevant to the issue tried, is, that it does not show or tend to show that the prisoner perpetrated or attempted to perpetrate a rape upon Josie Langmaid. Proof that he committed a rape in Canada, four years previously, upon Julienne Rousse shows what? Not that he then had any design or intent to perpetrate a rape four years afterwards upon another woman whom he had never seen or heard of, or in a place two hundred miles distant where he never had been; not that he had then formed a design to rape and murder women whenever he might have opportunity; not that he had ever before or since committed that crime—but that the defendant had a disposition to commit the crime of rape four years previously.
>
> *Id.* at 302–03 (Smith, J.).

[189] *See* Teitelbaum & Hertz, *Evidence II: Evidence of Other Crimes as Proof of Intent,* 13 N.M. L. Rev. 423 (1983). *See also* People v. Esterline, 159 Ill. App. 3d 164, 512 N.E.2d 358, 361 (1987) (rejecting state's argument that evidence of other alleged acts of indecent liberties indicated defendant's intent to commit charged crime).

accepts the prevailing view,[190] and nothing on the judicial horizon portends a change of course. This comes as no surprise. The prevailing view is supported by defensible logic. What is more, the difficulty of proving intent creates a strong need for the evidence.[191]

When considering evidence offered under the prevailing view, courts are understandably cautious. The line separating such evidence from inadmissible character evidence is elusive at best. Evidence admitted under the prevailing view carries strong potential for unfair prejudice. Jurors may be unable to blind themselves to the fact that the defendant is "a very bad man"[192] deserving punishment, whether guilty of the charged offense or not.

When uncharged misconduct is offered under the prevailing view, the proponent must establish that the defendant committed the uncharged acts.[193] Anonymous acts are not admissible for this purpose because the prevailing view is not based on the doctrine of chances, under which the identity of the actor is immaterial. Rather, the prevailing view is founded on an assumption about human nature; an assumption that posits that when a person possesses a particular trait (criminal intent) on one occasion, the person is likely—not as a matter of chance or probability, but as a matter of human nature—to possess the trait on other occasions as well.

In addition to establishing that the defendant committed the uncharged acts, the prosecutor must show that the uncharged and the charged acts are similar.[194] As the Ninth Circuit stated in *United States v. Hadley*,[195] "[I]f used to prove intent, the prior act must be similar to the offense charged."[196]

The uncharged acts must not be so remote as to rob them of probative value regarding intent at the time the defendant committed the charged offense.[197]

---

[190] *See* Estelle v. McGuire, 112 S. Ct. 475 (1991); United States v. Reynolds, 29 M.J. 105 (C.M.A. 1989); United States v. Saul, 26 M.J. 568 (A.F.C.M.R. 1988); United States v. King, 16 M.J. 990 (A.C.M.R. 1983); Commonwealth v. Scott, 408 Mass. 811, 564 N.E.2d 370 (1990); State v. McKnight, 820 P.2d 1279 (Mont. 1991); State v. Dalphond, 133 N.H. 827, 585 A.2d 317 (1991); People v. Basir, 578 N.Y.S.2d 603 (A.D. 1992); State v. West, 103 N.C. App. 1, 404 S.E.2d 191, 197 (1991) ("Our courts have consistently held that past incidents of mistreatment are admissible to show intent in a child abuse case"); 22 Wright & Graham § 5242, at 369 n.11.

[191] See authorities cited in **note 190**.

[192] State v. Lapage, 57 N.H. 245, 296 (1876).

[193] *See* United States v. Beechum, 582 F.2d 898, 912–13 (5th Cir. 1978), *cert. denied,* 440 U.S. 920 (1979); State v. Wilson, 199 Conn. 417, 513 A.2d 620, 637 (1986).

[194] State v. West, 404 S.E.2d 191, 197 (N.C. Ct. App. 1991).

[195] 918 F.2d 848 (9th Cir. 1990) *cert. granted,* 112 S. Ct. 1261 (1992).

[196] *Id.* at 851.

[197] State v. West, 103 N.C. App. 1, 404 S.E.2d 191, 197 (1991) (four-month lapse of time not too remote); State v. Faircloth, 99 N.C. App. 685, 394 S.E.2d 198 (1990) (28 months not too remote).

Courts reject "an inflexible rule regarding remoteness in the context of Rule 404(b)."[198]

Prevailing View in Child Abuse Litigation

Hypothetical Nos. 3 and 4 illustrate the prevailing view in child abuse litigation.

Hypothetical No. 3. The defendant is charged with physical abuse leading to the death of her young son. While the child was in the defendant's exclusive control, the child suffered a skull fracture and fatal brain injury. The defendant argues the child's injury was accidental. To rebut this defense, the state offers evidence that the defendant physically abused her other two children. One of the uncharged acts of abuse occurred before the charged offense and one after.[199]

The government's uncharged misconduct evidence is admissible under the prevailing view.[200] When the state proves that the defendant committed the uncharged abuse, it is possible to infer the defendant's criminal intent on those occasions. Based on this intermediate inference, the ultimate inference is drawn to the defendant's intent when she injured the deceased child.

Notice that in Hypothetical No. 3 the state could also rely on the doctrine of chances to prove intent. It is possible that one of the defendant's children might suffer serious accidental injury, but when more than one child is afflicted, the likelihood of accident decreases. American courts regularly admit uncharged abuse of other children to disprove a claim of accident.[201]

In Hypothetical No. 3, one of the uncharged acts of abuse occurred after the charged offense. This should not lead to exclusion of the evidence. The temporal relationship between the uncharged misconduct and the charged offense does not undermine the logical relevance of either uncharged act.

---

[198] United States v. Hadley, 918 F.2d 848, 851 (9th Cir. 1990), *cert. granted,* 112 S. Ct. 1261 (1992) (uncharged sexual abuse of another victim 10 years before charged crime not too remote).

[199] The facts of this case are drawn in part from United States v. Leight, 818 F.2d 1297 (7th Cir.), *cert. denied,* 484 U.S. 958 (1987). Factually similar cases include: United States v. Lewis, 837 F.2d 415, 418–19 (9th Cir.), *cert. denied,* 488 U.S. 923 (1988); State v. Ostlund, 416 N.W.2d 755 (Minn. Ct. App. 1987); State v. Lee, 88 Or. App. 556, 746 P.2d 242 (1988).

[200] The uncharged misconduct evidence in this case might also be admissible to prove knowledge. *See* Huddleston v. United States, 485 U.S. 681 (1988).

[201] *See, e.g.,* United States v. Leight, 818 F.2d 1297 (7th Cir.), *cert. denied,* 484 U.S. 958 (1987); United States v. Woods, 484 F.2d 127 (4th Cir. 1973), *cert. denied,* 415 U.S. 979 (1974); Limber v. State, 264 Ark. 479, 572 S.W.2d 402 (1978).

Although there is some authority that uncharged acts must occur before the charged act,[202] the better view predicates admission on logical relevance, not order of occurrence.[203]

> *Hypothetical No. 4.* The defendant is charged with sexual abuse of the eight-year-old daughter of the woman with whom he lives. On May 23, 1992, the daughter was driving with the defendant when she asked if she could steer the car. The daughter got on the defendant's lap and started driving. The defendant put his hands on her legs and then rubbed her genital area. The defendant admits he placed his hands on the girl's thighs, but denies intentional sexual acts, and argues that any touching was innocent and accidental. The prosecutor offers testimony from the victim and her sister that the defendant sexually abused them over an extended period of time prior to the charged acts.[204]

In Hypothetical No. 4 the defendant asserts that if touching occurred, it was accidental. It is certainly possible that when a child is sitting on an adult's lap steering a car, innocent touching could occur. It would be quite natural for the adult to rest his hands on the child's legs while the child steers. From that position the adult could quickly grasp the wheel if the child needed help. Defendant's explanation is plausible. The plausibility of accidental touching is undermined, however, by evidence that the defendant has a history of touching the victim and her sister in the genital area. Accidental touching might occur once or twice, but not a dozen times. The defendant's intent when he committed uncharged assaults indicates his intent when he touched the child in the car. The state's evidence should be received under the prevailing view.

In some sex offense cases the state must prove that the defendant acted with the specific intent to gratify the defendant's sexual desire.[205] Sexual intent can be inferred from the defendant's conduct, including the way the defendant touched the victim.[206] Uncharged misconduct evidence is often admissible to

---

[202] *See* Imwinkelried § 2:11, at 2-32. Indeed, many lawyers use the phrase *prior bad acts* to describe this category of evidence.

[203] *See id.* § 2:11, at 2-3 to -33.

[204] *See id.*

[205] United States v. Hadley, 918 F.2d 848, 851 (9th Cir. 1990), *cert. granted*, 112 S. Ct. 1261 (1992); Inmon v. State, 585 So. 2d 261 (Ala. Crim. App. 1991).

[206] *In re* A.J.H., 210 Ill. App. 3d 65, 568 N.E.2d 964 (1991) (defendant was 13 and was accused of molesting five-year-old child; holding that sexual intent could be inferred from act of touching victim's penis for four or five seconds and telling victim not to tell anyone); People v. Goebel, 161 Ill. App. 3d 113, 514 N.E.2d 60 (1987) (sexual intent inferred when teacher touched nine-year-old student's breast with outstretched hand).

establish the defendant's sexual intent.[207] In *Montgomery v. State*,[208] the defendant was charged with touching the victims' genitals "with the intent to arouse and gratify the sexual desire of the [defendant]."[209] The victims were the defendant's two young daughters. The Texas Court of Criminal Appeals approved testimony that the defendant "had on several occasions paraded around in front of his minor daughters, the complainants, in the nude with an erection."[210] The court also approved evidence that the defendant bathed with the girls, and that he "would ask the children if they had 'washed their slits,' referring to their vaginal area. At other times, appellant would say to the girls, 'You and I were meant for each other'; 'Give me your hot love'; 'My lips were made for kissing'; and 'Press my hot lips.'"[211] The court concluded that this and other evidence was relevant to prove the defendant's "sexual motive if he touched the

---

[207] United States v. Hadley, 918 F.2d 848 (9th Cir. 1990), *cert. granted*, 112 S. Ct. 1261 (1992); United States v. Orsburn, 31 M.J. 182 (C.M.A. 1990), *cert. denied*, 111 S. Ct. 1074 (1991); United States v. Cuellar, 27 M.J. 50 (C.M.A. 1988), *cert. denied*, 493 U.S. 811 (1989); United States v. Herbert, 32 M.J. 707 (A.C.M.R. 1991); Commonwealth v. King, 387 Mass. 464, 441 N.E.2d 248 (1982). *See* State v. Basker, 468 N.W.2d 413, 416–17 (S.D. 1991), where the court wrote:

> The offense of sexual contact with a minor requires proof that the accused touched the breasts, genitalia or anus of the alleged victim with the intent to arouse or gratify the sexual desire of either the accused or the victim. Because the State must prove the touching was done with the intent to arouse or produce sexual gratification, the offense of sexual contact with a minor is a specific intent crime, and evidence of such intent may be proved by other acts evidence. . . .
>
> With respect to the intent requirement of SDCL 22-22-7.1, K.K. testified that when Basker would grab her breasts and buttocks, he would speak of past sexual experiences and tell her jokes with sexual overtones. K.K. noticed his breathing was heavy and she believed him to be sexually aroused. G.D. testified that while staying with K.K. in July 1987, Basker came up from behind her and fondled her breasts and buttocks. She testified that when Basker grabbed her breasts he had a smile on his face, and she believed he was fondling her for his own sexual gratification. Another child who stayed with K.K. in December of 1986, observed that when Basker touched K.K. he would make jokes and had a "smirky" laugh. She described his face as looking "perverted" when he fondled K.K. A fourth child testified that when Basker fondled K.K. he made such comments as "nice butt," "you've grown up pretty good," "you've grown well," and "oh, you've prospered into a nice young woman."
>
> We hold these facts and circumstances are sufficient to allow the jury to infer that Basker grabbed and rubbed K.K.'s and G.D.'s breasts and buttocks with the intent to arouse or gratify some sexual desire.

[208] 810 S.W.2d 372 (Tex. Crim. App. 1990).

[209] *Id.* at 380.

[210] *Id.* at 375.

[211] *Id.* at 380 (footnote omitted).

[children]."[212] The state needed the evidence to refute the assertion that the touching was innocent.[213]

A defendant's possession of pornography is sometimes admissible to establish the defendant's intent.[214] In *State v. Dalphond*,[215] the defendant was charged with sexually abusing his 15-year-old stepdaughter. The New Hampshire Supreme Court approved admission of a pornographic magazine titled *Family Touch*. The magazine dealt largely with incest.

Courts sometimes allow the prosecutor to establish the defendant's intent on the charged occasion with evidence that the defendant sexually abused other children in the past.[216]

§ 6.19 Prior Attempts to Commit Charged Offense

When the defendant's intent is in issue, prior attempts to commit the charged offense may be admissible.[217] The following hypothetical illustrates this use of uncharged misconduct:

> The defendant, a baby-sitter, is charged with molesting his eight-year-old charge. The defendant allegedly rubbed the child's genitals and breasts. The defendant argues that any touching was innocent roughhousing. The prosecutor has evidence that the defendant attempted to molest the victim on previous baby-sitting jobs.

The evidence of prior attempts should be received to prove the intent for the charged crime. The fact that the defendant persisted in his efforts to molest the child undercuts his assertion of innocent intent.[218]

---

[212] *Id.* at 380–81.

[213] *Id.* at 381.

[214] United States v. Orsburn, 31 M.J. 182 (C.M.A. 1990), *cert. denied*, 111 S. Ct. 1074 (1991); United States v. Mann, 26 M.J. 1, 4 (C.M.A.), *cert. denied*, 488 U.S. 824 (1988); United States v. Proctor, 34 M.J. 549 (A.F.C.M.R. 1992); State v. Dalphond, 133 N.H. 827, 585 A.2d 317 (1991).

[215] 585 A.2d 317 (N.H. 1991).

[216] Flanagan v. State, 586 So. 2d 1085 (Fla. Dist. Ct. App. 1991); Potts v. State, 427 So. 2d 822 (Fla. Dist. Ct. App. 1983).

[217] *See* Imwinkelried § 5:11, at 5-22.

[218] *See* Hicks v. Reese, 624 F. Supp. 1116, 1118 (W.D.N.C. 1986) (court held in arson case that it was proper to admit evidence that before fire, defendant solicited another person to burn house because "[t]he testimony simply showed Petitioner's intent to burn his house").
See also Orsini v. State, 281 Ark. 348, 665 S.W.2d 245 (1984), *cert. denied*, 111 S. Ct. 1093 (1991). *Orsini* was a capital felony murder prosecution. On the issue of intent the court held it was proper to admit evidence that before the murder, the defendant and another "planted an explosive in the victim's car which, when detonated, failed to kill her. This incident was probative of their intent to commit the murder. The bombing incident, which

§ 6.20 "Entire Picture" of Crime

Crime does not occur in a vacuum. The prosecutor is allowed to establish the background in which events occurred.[219] Acts of uncharged misconduct are sometimes embedded in that background. Courts admit uncharged misconduct that is inextricably entwined with the charged offense.[220] Wigmore speaks of "other criminal acts that are an inseparable part of the whole deed."[221] McCormick writes of evidence "[t]o complete the story of the crime on trial by placing it in the context of nearby and nearly contemporaneous happenings."[222]

Although it is important for the jury to understand the "entire picture," courts ensure that the "entire picture" theory does not become a free admission ticket for otherwise inadmissible uncharged misconduct. It is not enough that uncharged acts bear a close temporal relationship to the charged offense. Evidence is properly admitted under the entire picture theory only when the evidence is needed for complete understanding of the charged act. Louisell and Mueller write:

> Care must be exercised to assure that prior crimes are not received in evidence merely *because* they precede or follow closely the crime charged; the purpose of this use of such evidence is to complete a picture, not to paint another, and to provide context and meaning to the central events in issue. Other offenses not

---

occurred five weeks before the murder, was not so remote in time that the jury was prevented from connecting the incident to the murder." 665 S.W.2d at 253.

[219] United States v. Alexander, 27 M.J. 834, 837 (A.C.M.R. 1989); United States v. Reece, 21 M.J. 736 (N.M.C.M.R. 1985); Darby v. State, 538 So. 2d 1168 (Miss. 1989); McFee v. State, 511 So. 2d 130, 136 (Miss. 1987); State v. Hall, 108 Or. App. 12, 814 P.2d 172 (1991). Although not an uncharged misconduct case, the Florida Supreme Court's decision in Gillion v. State, 573 So. 2d 810 (Fla. 1991) is pertinent. In *Gillion* the issue was whether a police officer would be permitted to describe the area in which a defendant was arrested. The officer described seeing drug selling activity on the street. The court wrote:

> That information is relevant for the jury to place in context testimony bearing directly on the legal issues of the case. To compel the state to put on its case in a factual vacuum, devoid of such necessary background information, would be a disservice to the fact finder. "[C]onsiderable leeway is allowed even on direct examination for proof of facts that do not bear directly on the purely legal issues, but merely fill in the background of the narrative and give it interest, color, and lifelikeness." McCormick on Evidence § 185, at 541 (3d ed. 1984).

573 So. 2d at 811.

[220] *See, e.g.,* State v. Zihlavsky, 505 So. 2d 761, 763 (La. Ct. App. 1987); State v. Mosby, 450 N.W.2d 629, 633 (Minn. Ct. App. 1990) (prosecutor was allowed to prove that shortly after molestation, defendant attempted to steal a car); State v. Edward Charles L., 398 S.E.2d 123, 131 (W. Va. 1990); 22 Wright & Graham § 5239, at 445–49 (excellent description of the "entire picture" concept).

[221] 1A Wigmore § 218, at 1883.

[222] McCormick § 190, at 558.

§ 6.20 "ENTIRE PICTURE" 53

useful to such ends should be excluded, unless otherwise relevant, no matter how close in time or place.[223]

The following hypothetical raises issues under the entire picture theory.

The defendant is charged with committing fellatio with an adolescent boy named Bill. Bill and another minor, Tom, went to the defendant's trailer on the night in question, where the defendant allegedly showed the boys a pornographic movie. During the movie, the defendant made advances toward both minors. After the movie, he committed fellatio on both and asked them to do the same to him, which they did. Shortly thereafter, the defendant masturbated in front of the minors. The defendant admits that Bill and Tom were in his home, but denies molesting them. In addition to testimony from Bill describing the charged acts, the prosecutor offers testimony from Tom describing the uncharged acts of fellatio with Tom. The state also offers testimony describing the defendant's uncharged masturbation.

The facts of this hypothetical are drawn from the Nevada Supreme Court's decision in *Allan v. State*.[224] The court approved admission of the defendant's uncharged acts of fellatio and masturbation, writing:

The testimony regarding the additional acts of fellatio, as well as the act of masturbation, was admissible as part of the res gestae of the crime charged. Testimony regarding such acts is admissible because the acts complete the story of the crime charged by proving the immediate context of happenings near in time and place.[225]

The *Allan* decision is troublesome.[226] It is true that the uncharged acts share a close temporal relationship with the charged offenses. The uncharged acts are

---

[223] 2 Louisell & Mueller § 140, at 215.

[224] 92 Nev. 318, 549 P.2d 1402 (1976).

[225] 549 P.2d at 1403 (footnote omitted).

[226] For another troublesome case, see State v. Zihlavsky, 505 So. 2d 761 (La. Ct. App. 1987). In *Zihlavsky* the defendant was charged with oral copulation of a minor. In addition to evidence of the sex act, the state was permitted to introduce photographs of the victim measuring his penis with a ruler. The victim testified that the photographs were taken "at a time when oral sexual contact occurred between him and the defendant." *Id.* at 763. The court of appeals upheld the trial judge's decision to admit the photographs. The appellate court wrote:

Generally, the prosecution cannot introduce evidence of other criminal acts of the accused. However, this prohibition does not bar the admission of evidence of other criminal acts which are an inseparable part of the whole deed. . . . Clearly, the circumstances surrounding the taking of the photographs and the photographs themselves were immediate concomitants of or were one continuous transaction with defendant's criminal acts with B.R., and, as such, form part of the res gestae. Such

not, however, inseparable from the charged acts. The jury could understand what happened without evidence of the uncharged misconduct. This is particularly true of the masturbation, which occurred after the charged offense was complete.

Although the uncharged misconduct approved in *Allan* was perhaps unnecessary for full understanding of the charged acts, the *Allan* decision is in line with many decisions. Consider, for example, *Woolridge v. State*,[227] in which the defendant was charged with rape of an 11-year-old child. The prosecutor was permitted to prove that on the night of the rape, the defendant also committed an uncharged act of oral sodomy on the victim. The court wrote that "the sodomy was a part of a series of continuing sexual offenses and was admissible as part of the res gestae of the rape."[228] Other decisions reflect a similarly expansive view of the entire picture theory.[229] Most courts eschew the Latin phrase, *res gestae*,[230] preferring instead terms such as *same transaction, whole story, entire*

---

  evidence was properly admitted despite the fact that it was also evidence pertaining to a separate . . . offense and was prejudicial to defendant.

 Id. (citations omitted).

  It is difficult to accept the *Zihlavsky* court's analysis. The pictures did not show the defendant engaged in the charged sexual contact with the victim. The jury could understand the charged offense without the aid of the photographs. The act of photographing the child is not inseparable from or inextricably entwined with the charged acts, and the potential for unfair prejudice caused by the photographs was high. On balance, it seems that the photographs should not have been admitted as part of the entire picture theory.

[227] 659 P.2d 943 (Okla. Crim. App. 1983).

[228] *Id.* at 946. *See also* Crisp v. State, 667 P.2d 472, 474 (Okla. Crim. App. 1983) (rape of adult; court held it proper to admit evidence of uncharged act of oral sodomy because "[t]he sodomy was part of a series of continuing offenses, and as such, was admissible as part of the res gestae").

[229] Burke v. State, 624 P.2d 1240 (Alaska 1980). *Burke* was a statutory rape case in which the court approved evidence of the defendant's uncharged acts of sexual abuse of the victim. The court stated that such evidence falls within a limited exception to the general rule against propensity evidence. The court wrote that more than one theory justified receipt of such evidence. First, the evidence was justified "as background information to explain [the victim's] testimony in its context." *Id.* at 1250. Second, the uncharged misconduct was admissible "to provide the factfinder with highly probative information of the ongoing relationship between the accused and the victim." *Id.* at 1249.

 See also State v. Tanner, 675 P.2d 539, 548 (Utah 1983) (in murder of three-year-old, state was permitted to offer evidence of prior abuse of victim extending over long period of time to complete story of the crime); Martin v. State, 584 S.W.2d 830, 834 (Tenn. Ct. App. 1979) (incest case); Crozier v. State, 723 P.2d 42, 49–50 (Wyo. 1986) (murder of six-year-old).

[230] The commentators agree that the term *res gestae* should be abandoned. *See* 22 Wright & Graham § 5239, at 447; 1A Wigmore § 218, at 1888 ("It is sometimes said that such acts are provable as a part of the 'res gestae.' But this phrase is unsatisfactory, first because it is obscure and indefinite and needs further definition and translation before either its reason or its scope can be understood, secondly because its very looseness and obscurity lend too many opportunities for its abuse").

§ 6.20 "ENTIRE PICTURE" 55

picture, and *course of conduct.* The Ninth Circuit decision in *United States v. Gibson*[231] captures the flavor of cases in this area. The defendant was charged with interstate kidnapping. The trial court admitted evidence of an uncharged sexual assault on the adult victim that occurred after completion of the crime but while the victim remained in the defendant's control. The Ninth Circuit affirmed, writing:

> [T]he subsequent conduct does tend to present a picture, the whole of which indicates guilt. . . . Proof of the assault characterized the defendant's dominion over the female victim, and the fact that the assault involved sex acts does not alter its relevance. The picture of a kidnapping is not complete unless all of the relationships of the defendant to the victims, from the beginning of the illegal detention to the end of it, are shown. The time sequence of the kidnapping is not continuous if there is some sort of a legal time-out taken during periods while the defendant is committing other crimes against the victim. We believe that the Government is not required to present less than the whole picture; it is not required to present a time sequence with gaps in it. "In evidencing the act charged, it may be necessary to describe an affair which involves a number of acts, one or more others of which will also be crimes. Such proof is receivable, because it is inseparable from the act charged."[232]

A significant amount of otherwise inadmissible uncharged misconduct finds its way into evidence through the entire picture theory.

The entire picture theory is important in sex offense litigation. The theory is used to justify admission of uncharged aspects of the sexual relationship between the victim and the perpetrator.[233] Such evidence is particularly helpful when the perpetrator engages in a course of progressively more intrusive sexual conduct with the child. The perpetrator may begin with seductive talk or brief touching, and progress over weeks or months to sexual intercourse, fellatio, and similarly invasive acts. When the defendant is charged with a single incident of

---

[231] 625 F.2d 887 (9th Cir. 1980).

[232] *Id.* at 888–89 (quoting 2 Wigmore § 306(3)).

[233] *See* People v. Puhl, 211 Ill. App. 3d 457, 570 N.E.2d 447, 458 (1991), where the court wrote:

> There is a well established exception to the rule that evidence of other crimes is generally inadmissible. When prosecuting a sex-related offense upon a child, evidence of prior sexual acts between the defendant and victim is admissible to show the familiar relationship between the parties and to corroborate the victim's testimony as to the act relied upon for conviction.

See also United States v. Castillo, 29 M.J. 145 (C.M.A. 1989); United States v. Clark, 15 M.J. 974 (A.C.M.R. 1983); People v. Esterline, 159 Ill. App. 3d 164, 512 N.E.2d 358, 361 (1987); Commonwealth v. Calcagno, 31 Mass. App. Ct. 25, 574 N.E.2d 420 (1991); State v. Christeson, 780 S.W.2d 119, 123 (Mo. Ct. App. 1989); State v. Edward Charles L., 398 S.E.2d 123, 133 (W. Va. 1990).

invasive sexual contact, the jury sometimes needs information about the entire course of the relationship to fairly evaluate the victim's credibility.[234]

State v. Kristich[235] is an example of the need for evidence regarding the sexual relationship between the victim and the perpetrator. In *Kristich* the defendant was charged with *one* act of sexual intercourse with his 13-year-old stepdaughter. As is typical in sexual abuse, the victim was the only eyewitness. The victim testified that the charged offense occurred during daylight hours on January 12, 1958, at a vacant house the defendant had purchased for the family. The house was undergoing renovation, and the defendant, the victim, and two of the victim's siblings were present in the house cleaning up after the construction workers. While in the house, the defendant took the victim "to an unfurnished bedroom, placed her on a stack of plasterboard, removed part of her clothes and part of his own, indulged in the act of intercourse without further ado, redressed, and proceeded about the work."[236] The victim did not resist. Nor did she tell her mother until she learned she was pregnant. In a credibility contest between the defendant and the 13-year-old victim, the jury might well find the victim's testimony incredible if it were limited to a description of what happened on January 12, 1958. The trial judge allowed the victim to describe acts of sexual intercourse occurring before and after the charged offense, and the Oregon Supreme Court approved, writing:

> This court has repeatedly held that in crimes involving illicit sexual acts evidence of other similar acts between the same persons is admissible.
>
> * * *
>
> In the trial of this case the state elected to prove that the specific act of rape for which defendant was charged occurred within certain hours of the day of

---

[234] *See* United States v. Austin, 32 M.J. 757 (A.C.M.R. 1991); Burke v. State, 624 P.2d 1240 (Alaska 1980); People v. McCarthy, 213 Ill. App. 3d 873, 572 N.E.2d 1219, 1224 (1991) ("In sex-related offenses, evidence of prior acts between the defendant and the complaining witness is admissible to show the familiar relation of the parties and to corroborate the complaining witness' testimony as to the act relied upon for conviction"); Commonwealth v. Calcagno, 31 Mass. App. Ct. 25, 574 N.E.2d 420, 422 (1991); State v. Hall, 108 Or. App. 12, 814 P.2d 172 (1991); Sanderson v. State, 548 S.W.2d 337, 339 (Tenn. Crim. App. 1976); Boutwell v. State, 719 S.W.2d 164 (Tex. Crim. App. 1985); State v. Edward Charles L., 398 S.E.2d 123 (W. Va. 1990).

See also State v. Bridgman, 49 Vt. 202, 210, 24 Am. Rep. 124 (1876). *Bridgman* was a prosecution for adultery. The court wrote:

> The offense charged in this case cannot, ordinarily, be committed till the restraints of natural modesty and the safeguards of common deportment and conventionality have been overcome by gradual approaches, and the relations of the parties have been changed from those usually existing between the sexes, to the most intimate . . . . Thus it appears that the true relation of the parties to each other in this respect, is very material and proper to be shown . . . .

[235] 226 Or. 240, 359 P.2d 1106 (1961).

[236] 359 P.2d at 1108.

January 12, 1958. It was the truth or falsity of that charge which was decisive of guilt or innocence. As the alleged act was described by the victim, she was a willing, if not a cooperative, participant. She testified that in addition to this particular act she had engaged in other acts with defendant as often as once or twice a week for several months before and after the event charged. The course of conduct had its inception by a seductive process during which, so she testified, defendant first fondled her and eventually gained access. . . . There was no evidence of any resistance on her part nor that she ever informed her mother, defendant's wife, until she became pregnant.

* * *

It would have been contrary to all accepted standards of normal conduct for the act to have taken place as an isolated event that had never occurred before. As described by the girl, the act required knowledge of what was expected; understanding and a willingness, if not a desire, to cooperate. Even young girls simply do not so voluntarily surrender to such a relationship unless there has been force or seductive persuasion. The latter does not usually occur while walking from one room to another.

* * *

If the act had been accomplished by force or some coercive process against resistance it perhaps would have been immaterial to the jury's understanding of the case to have limited the evidence to the one act complained of. Forcible rape at a given time and place need not require a background of previous conduct to make the act believable. Here, however, as we have already pointed out, it would have been an unnatural and thus unbelievable story to have described only the particular incident without some background to explain the victim's ready acquiescence. So the state was obliged to show why the act could occur in the manner charged. The evidence was part and parcel of the crime actually charged.[237]

In some cases, the perpetrator's uncharged misconduct against the child or members of the child's family explains the child's behavior, such as delay in reporting abuse.[238] In *State v. Hall*,[239] for example, the defendant was accused of molesting his two granddaughters. The defendant lived with the victims and their mother. In addition to molesting his grandchildren, the defendant had a long-term incestuous relationship with his daughter. The grandchildren did not reveal their abuse until the defendant separated from their mother. The Oregon Court of Appeals approved evidence of the defendant's uncharged incestuous relationship with his daughter, writing:

> The evidence of defendant's relationship with his daughter was relevant for a permissible purpose. The primary issue was the children's credibility.

---

[237] *Id.* at 1108–09.

[238] People v. Gil, 3 Cal. App. 4th 653, 4 Cal. Rptr. 2d 697 (1992); State v. Hall, 108 Or. App. 12, 814 P.2d 172 (1991).

[239] 108 Or. App. 12, 814 P.2d 172 (1991).

Sanatizing the evidence could have unfairly undermined their credibility by painting an artificial picture of events. A victim's relationship to the accused is relevant to explain her conduct. One may react differently to the conduct of a stranger than to that of a friend or relative, and what seems natural in one context may seem absurd in another. In cases involving sexual crimes against children, the relationship is frequently important in explaining the child's delay in reporting the abuse. . . . [The] evidence helps explain why the children did not turn to their mother for help and did not report the crime until after defendant and their mother had separated.[240]

When accurate assessment of the victim's credibility necessitates informing the jury of the entire picture of the sexual relationship between the defendant and the victim, the uncharged sexual activity is relevant, and probative value usually outweighs the potential for unfair prejudice.

§ 6.21 Depraved Sexual Propensity

The basic principle of Federal Rule of Evidence 404(a) is that evidence of a person's character is inadmissible to prove that the person acted in conformity with character on a particular occasion. In sex offense cases a number of courts carve out a limited exception to the rule against character evidence.[241] These courts allow the prosecutor to offer the defendant's uncharged sexual misconduct to prove that the defendant has a propensity to commit sexually deviant acts. The jury is allowed to infer that the defendant probably acted in conformity with this deviant propensity and committed the charged offense. This

---

[240] 814 P.2d at 175 (citations omitted).
[241] Kerr v. Caspari, 956 F.2d 788 (8th Cir. 1992); Burke v. State, 624 P.2d 1240 (Alaska 1980); Velez v. State, 762 P.2d 1297 (Alaska Ct. App. 1988); State v. Treadaway, 116 Ariz. 163, 568 P.2d 1061 (1977); State v. McFarlin, 110 Ariz. 225, 517 P.2d 87 (1973); State v. Cousin, 136 Ariz. 83, 664 P.2d 233 (Ct. App. 1983); Gibbs v. State, 394 So. 2d 231 (Fla. Dist. Ct. App.), *aff'd*, 406 So. 2d 1113 (Fla. 1981); Stine v. State, 199 Ga. App. 898, 406 S.E.2d 292 (1991); Jackson v. State, 198 Ga. App. 447, 402 S.E.2d 279 (1991); Jennette v. State, 197 Ga. App. 580, 398 S.E.2d 734, 737 (1990); Allgire v. State, 575 N.E.2d 600 (Ind. 1991); Brewer v. State, 562 N.E.2d 22 (Ind. 1990); Maynard v. State, 513 N.E.2d 641 (Ind. 1987); Reynolds v. State, 575 N.E.2d 28, 31–32 (Ind. Ct. App. 1991); Bowling v. State, 560 N.E.2d 658 (Ind. 1990); Commonwealth v. King, 387 Mass. 464, 441 N.E.2d 248, 251 (1982); Commonwealth v. Calcagno, 31 Mass. App. Ct. 25, 574 N.E.2d 420 (1991); State v. Reeder, 105 N.C. App. 343, 413 S.E.2d 580 (1992); State v. McKay, 309 Or. 305, 787 P.2d 479 (1990); State v. Tobin, 602 A.2d 528 (R.I. 1992); Montgomery v. State, 810 S.W.2d 372 (Tex. Crim. App. 1990); Boutwell v. State, 719 S.W.2d 164 (Tex. Crim. App. 1985); Crossman v. State, 797 S.W.2d 321 (Tex. Ct. App. 1990); State v. Edward Charles L., 398 S.E.2d 123, 133 (W. Va. 1990) ("collateral acts or crimes may be introduced . . . to show the perpetrator had a lustful disposition towards the victim, a lustful disposition to children generally, or a lustful disposition to specific other children, provided such acts occurred reasonably close in time to the incident(s) giving rise to the indictment").

§ 6.21 DEPRAVED SEXUAL PROPENSITY

Figure 6–8. Limited exception to chain of inferences forbidden by Federal Rule of Evidence 404(a) for evidence of depraved sexual propensity.

theory of proof is referred to here as *depraved sexual propensity* evidence.[242] The theory may be illustrated with Imwinkelried's schematic as shown in **Figure 6–8**.

Note that evidence admitted under the depraved sexual propensity theory directly contravenes the rule against character evidence. Courts approving the depraved sexual propensity theory recognize an outright exception in sex offense cases to Rule 404(a)'s prohibition of character evidence to prove conduct in conformity with character.

Lempert and Saltzburg discuss the depraved sexual propensity theory:

> [M]any courts admit other crimes evidence to show propensity [when] defendant is charged with a sex crime. This use directly contravenes the propensity rule, since the evidence of other crimes is admitted to support the specific inference that the defendant who committed one sex crime probably committed another. In the majority of jurisdictions, however, this exception is tempered by the requirement that the other sex crimes be shown to have occurred with the partner or victim of the crime charged. The theory is that what is being shown is not general propensity to crime but propensity to criminal activity with the same person.[243]

The Oregon Supreme Court's decision in *State v. McKay*[244] illustrates the depraved sexual propensity exception. In *McKay* the defendant was charged with sexual abuse of his stepdaughter. "Before trial, the state moved to allow testimony by the victim about sexual contacts between her and defendant on several occasions, beginning when she was 10 years old and ending when she was about 13. She was 15 when the incident giving rise to this charge occurred."[245] The

---

[242] Some decisions use the term *lustful disposition*.

[243] R. Lempert & S. Saltzburg, A Modern Approach to Evidence 229 (2d ed. 1983) (footnote omitted).

[244] 309 Or. 305, 787 P.2d 479 (1990).

[245] 787 P.2d at 479.

trial court excluded the uncharged misconduct evidence. In concluding that the trial court erred, the court wrote:

> Simply stated, the proffered evidence here was admissible to demonstrate the sexual predisposition this defendant had for this particular victim, that is, to show the sexual inclination of defendant towards the victim, not that he had a character trait or propensity to engage in sexual misconduct generally.
>
> In *State v. Pace,* 187 Or. 498, 507, 212 P.2d 755 (1949), a prosecution for statutory rape, this court held that evidence of other similar criminal acts with the same child is admissible to show the specific sexual predisposition of the defendant towards that child. *State v. Kristich,* 266 Or. 240, 242, 359 P.2d 1106 (1961), stated that "[t]his court has repeatedly held that in crimes involving illicit sexual acts evidence of other similar acts between the same persons is admissible . . . ."[246]

The depraved sexual propensity exception found a home in Alaska. In *Burke v. State*,[247] the Alaska Supreme Court approved admission of uncharged sex acts between the defendant and the victim of the charged offense.[248] The court wrote, "The primary reason given for allowing evidence of prior sexual misconduct is the special exception of lewd disposition. . . . [T]he rationale is to provide the fact finder with highly probative information of the ongoing relationship between the accused and the victim."[249]

In *Soper v. State*,[250] the Alaska Court of Appeals extended *Burke*'s lewd disposition exception to include uncharged sexual assaults on members of the victim's immediate family. In *Bolden v. State*[251] and *Moor v. State*,[252] the Court of Appeals refused to extend the exception further to include uncharged sexual acts "with persons other than the victim and members of her immediate family who, nevertheless, had substantial similarities to the victim, *e.g.*, similar ages or similar relationships to the accused."[253]

Texas courts recognize the depraved sexual propensity exception.[254] In *Boutwell v. State*,[255] the Texas Court of Criminal Appeals wrote that "Texas, like many other states, recognized a very narrow 'exception' to the 'general rule' of

---

[246] *Id.* at 480.

[247] 624 P.2d 1240 (Alaska 1980).

[248] The court found the evidence "akin to proof of motive." *See also* Velez v. State, 762 P.2d 1297, 1301 (Alaska Ct. App. 1988).

[249] 624 P.2d at 1248, 1249 (footnote omitted).

[250] 731 P.2d 587 (Alaska Ct. App. 1987).

[251] 720 P.2d 957 (Alaska Ct. App. 1986).

[252] 709 P.2d 498 (Alaska Ct. App. 1985).

[253] Velez v. State, 762 P.2d 1297, 1301 (Alaska Ct. App. 1988).

[254] *See* Montgomery v. State, 810 S.W.2d 372 (Tex. Crim. App. 1990); Celeste v. State, 805 S.W.2d 579 (Tex. Ct. App. 1991); Crossman v. State, 797 S.W.2d 321 (Tex. Ct. App. 1990).

[255] 719 S.W.2d 164 (Tex. Crim. App. 1985).

nonadmissibility of extraneous offenses . . . permitting the admission of acts which occurred between the minor complainant and the defendant . . . ."[256] In *Celeste v. State*,[257] the Texas Court of Appeals wrote:

> Texas courts recognize an exception to the general rules in the case of sex offenses to permit admission of similar sex offenses by the accused against the minor victim. . . . However, evidence of extraneous acts between a third party and the accused is barred unless admitted to prove a relevant contested issue.[258]

The depraved sexual propensity theory is well developed in Arizona. In *State v. McFarlin*,[259] the Arizona Supreme Court approved propensity evidence, writing that when the charged offense "involves the element of abnormal sex acts such as sodomy, child molesting, lewd and lascivious, etc., there is sufficient basis to accept proof of similar acts near in time to the offense charged as evidence of the accused's propensity to commit such perverted acts."[260] Under Arizona law, a defendant's uncharged sex acts with victims *other* than the victim of the charged offense are admissible.

Under *McFarlin*, three requirements must be satisfied to admit evidence of the defendant's depraved sexual propensity: (1) the uncharged act must be sexually depraved, (2) the uncharged act must be similar to the charged act, and (3) the uncharged act must not be too remote.[261] The Arizona Supreme Court applied this three-part test in *State v. Treadaway*,[262] where the defendant was convicted of sodomizing and murdering a six-year-old child. The defendant entered the victim's home in the middle of the night, and sexually assaulted and asphyxiated him. The defendant, whose palm prints were found on the exterior of the victim's home, acknowledged he looked into windows in the neighborhood, but denied the charged crime. The trial court admitted evidence that three years before the charged offense, the defendant took a 13-year-old boy by the arm, undressed him, and committed fellatio and anilingus on him.

On appeal, the defendant argued that evidence of the three year old sexual assault did not fall within the depraved sexual propensity exception because the prior assault was too remote. The Arizona Supreme Court agreed, reversing the defendant's conviction. The court wrote that a "prior, separate sex offense . . . with a different victim . . . as remote as three years earlier is almost never

---

[256] *Id.* at 174, 175.

[257] 805 S.W.2d 579 (Tex. Ct. App. 1991).

[258] *Id.* at 580–81.

[259] 110 Ariz. 225, 517 P.2d 87 (1973).

[260] 517 P.2d at 90.

[261] Courts in other states have admitted uncharged sex acts occurring years before the charged offense. *See* Jackson v. State, 198 Ga. App. 447, 402 S.E.2d 279, 280 (1991) (five-year lapse of time not too long); Cox v. State, 173 Ga. App. 422, 326 S.E.2d 796 (1985) (defendant's molestation of two other daughters 17 and 22 years earlier not too remote).

[262] 116 Ariz. 163, 568 P.2d 1061 (1977).

admissible and especially not for the purpose of showing only defendant's propensity to commit the crime charged."[263] The court indicated that expert testimony would be useful to determine whether "a prior act three years earlier tends to show a continuing emotional propensity to commit the act charged."[264]

The *Treadaway* court also found that the uncharged and charged acts were not sufficiently similar.[265] The court wrote that "[s]imilarity is . . . a problem because the acts themselves are different and may well involve different psychological and emotional dispositions."[266]

Arizona cases subsequent to *Treadaway* clarify the remoteness and similarity requirements of Arizona's depraved sexual propensity exception. In *State v. Cousin*,[267] the defendant was charged with molesting two children. The prosecutor offered evidence that four to seven years before the charged offenses, the defendant molested another child. The prosecutor supported the uncharged misconduct evidence with expert testimony from a psychiatrist who testified that the uncharged acts "showed an emotional propensity to commit acts of child molestation."[268] On appeal, the defendant objected that the uncharged acts were too remote, but the court of appeals disagreed, largely on the basis of the psychiatrist's testimony linking the uncharged and the charged sex acts.

In *State v. Lopez*,[269] the defendant was charged with committing multiple types of sex acts on a 12-year-old boy whom the defendant hired to sell candy door to door. The state offered testimony from three of the defendant's prior sex offense victims. On appeal, the defendant argued that the acts perpetrated on the victim of the charged offense were not sufficiently similar to the uncharged acts. The court of appeals rejected the defendant's argument, writing:

> An exact replication between the charged acts and the uncharged acts is not required to permit the admission of uncharged acts under the emotional propensity exception. Rather, the exception requires only that the uncharged acts be similar to the charged acts. In this case, the similarities between the uncharged and charged acts were numerous: in each of the uncharged acts, defendant made sexual advances to an adolescent male between the ages of 14 and 16; in each of

---

[263] 568 P.2d at 1064 n.2. The court wrote, "Remoteness in time is clearly a problem because a three year time lapse may leave the prior incident without predictive value." *Id.* at 1065.

[264] *Id.* at 1065.

[265] The court's conclusion that sodomy is not similar to fellatio and anilingus is debatable. All three acts have in common a child victim. Moreover, pedophiles often do not confine their deviant sexual behavior to a single type of sex act. See **Ch. 4**. In Brewer v. State, 562 N.E.2d 22, 25 (Ind. 1990), the Indiana Supreme Court wrote, "[A]cts used to show a depraved sexual instinct need not be identical to the crime for which a defendant is charged. It is sufficient if the same sexual instinct is involved."

[266] 568 P.2d at 1065.

[267] 136 Ariz. 83, 664 P.2d 233 (Ct. App. 1983).

[268] 664 P.2d at 235.

[269] 170 Ariz. 112, 822 P.2d 465 (Ct. App. 1991).

the cases, defendant made promises to procure a woman or girl to have sex with the boy; in each case the victim had been offered or had actually obtained employment with defendant. Finally, two of the other boys suffered a sexual assault while under defendant's supervision. These similarities were sufficient to allow the evidence at trial.[270]

The *Lopez* court correctly concluded that precise similarity between charged and uncharged sex acts is unnecessary.[271] The evidentiary value of depraved sexual propensity evidence lies in its predictive value. Someone with a history of deviant sexual behavior is more likely than someone without such a history to engage in deviant sexual conduct. The predictive value of the evidence lies not so much in the similarity between uncharged and charged acts, as in the deviant nature of the acts.[272] The psychological literature indicates that many paraphiliacs engage in a number of different types of deviant sexual behavior.[273] Thus, the requirement of similarity is considerably less important than the requirement that the charged and uncharged acts constitute deviant sexual behavior.[274]

The defendant in *Lopez* attacked the depraved sexual propensity theory on constitutional grounds, arguing that application of the theory violated his right to equal protection because evidence of uncharged acts admitted in his trial would not be admitted in trials for other offenses. The court of appeals rejected the defendant's constitutional argument, writing:

> Defendant has identified no fundamental right that has been denied to him; neither does he allege that this conduct constitutes denial of equal protection to a suspect class. Accordingly, we analyze his equal protection challenge solely by determining whether there is a rational basis for the rule applied to this type of case. We find such a basis amply expressed in State v. McFarlin, 110 Ariz. 225, 517 P.2d 87 (1973), in which our supreme court held that the usually secret

---

[270] 822 P.2d at 470.

[271] *See* Brewer v. State, 562 N.E.2d 22, 25 (Ind. 1990). *See also* Rodgers v. State, 261 Ga. 33, 401 S.E.2d 735, 736–37 (1991) (defendant charged with oral sodomy on 16-year-old victim; proper to admit evidence that while in jail, defendant attempted to molest one inmate by touching his genitals, and another by offering him a massage and saying that he was homosexual; these acts sufficiently similar); Jackson v. State, 198 Ga. App. 447, 402 S.E.2d 279, 280 (1991) (any sex with young children sufficiently similar); McGowan v. State, 198 Ga. App. 575, 402 S.E.2d 328, 330 (1991) (acts do not have to be identical); Allgire v. State, 575 N.E.2d 600, 604 (Ind. 1991) ("The proffered uncharged acts need not be identical to those charged"); Hodges v. State, 524 N.E.2d 774, 781 (Ind. 1988).

[272] Allgire v. State, 575 N.E.2d 600, 604 (Ind. 1991) ("it is sufficient that the same sexual instinct is involved").

[273] See **Ch. 4**. *See also* Abel, Becker, Mittelman, Cunningham-Rathner, Rouleau & Murphy, *Self-Reported Sex Crimes of Non-Incarcerated Paraphiliacs,* 1 J. Interpersonal Violence 3 (1987); Myers, Bays, Becker, Berliner, Corwin & Saywitz, *Expert Testimony in Child Sexual Abuse Litigation,* 68 Neb. L. Rev. 1, 129 (1989).

[274] Allgire v. State, 575 N.E.2d 600, 604 (Ind. 1991).

nature of the crime and the resultant problems of proof by the prosecution justified an additional, carefully circumscribed exception to the general prohibition of other crime evidence at trial.[275]

A number of courts refuse to recognize an exception for evidence of depraved sexual propensity.[276]

§ 6.22 Plan

Uncharged misconduct establishing the defendant's plan is admissible to prove identity,[277] intent,[278] or the criminal act.[279] On the question of identity, proof that the defendant entertained a plan that included uncharged acts and the charged act increases the likelihood the defendant was the perpetrator. Someone with a plan is likely to carry it out. Thus, evidence of plan is logically relevant to proof of identity.

The state may offer evidence of plan to prove intent. A plan is a product of intent. The fact that the defendant formulated a plan provides insight into the defendant's state of mind during the time the defendant acted in conformity with the plan.[280]

---

[275] State v. Lopez, 170 Ariz. 112, 822 P.2d 465, 471 (Ct. App. 1991).

[276] *See* People v. Thornton, 11 Cal. 3d 738, 523 P.2d 267, 114 Cal. Rptr. 467 (1974), *cert. denied*, 420 U.S. 924 (1975); Lantrip v. Commonwealth, 713 S.W.2d 816, 816–17 (Ky. 1986) ("prior acts are no longer admissible for the purpose of showing lustful inclination").

See also Imwinkelried § 4:18, at 4-50, where the author discusses cases rejecting the depraved sexual propensity exception:

Other jurisdictions will probably reach the same result because of their adoption of the Federal Rules of Evidence. The overwhelming majority of the cases recognizing the special exceptions antedate the Federal Rules. Several commentators assert that it is questionable whether the special exceptions survived the adoption of the rules. To say that the exceptions' survival is questionable is probably an understatement. It is exceedingly difficult to reconcile the exceptions with the clear language of Rule 404(b). The exception seems at odds with the prohibition in the first sentence of Rule 404(b).

(footnotes omitted).

[277] Imwinkelried §§ 3:20 to 3:24, at 3-50 to -64; 22 Wright & Graham § 5244, at 501 ("The plan may serve to identify the perpetrators of the crime") (footnote omitted).

[278] 22 Wright & Graham § 5244, at 502 ("Evidence of other crimes showing a plan may also be relevant on the issue of intent or to disprove mistake or inadvertence") (footnote omitted).

[279] United States v. Munoz, 32 M.J. 359 (C.M.A.), *cert. denied*, 112 S. Ct. 437 (1991); United States v. Ortiz, 33 M.J. 549 (A.C.M.R. 1991); United States v. McDowell, 30 M.J. 796 (A.F.C.M.R. 1990); Matthews v. Superior Ct., 201 Cal. App. 3d 385, 247 Cal. Rptr. 226 (1988) (defendant charged with murdering rape victim; corpus delicti established with evidence of defendant's prior similar rapes of other women); Imwinkelried § 4:20, at 4-44 to -45; 22 Wright & Graham § 5244, at 502 ("evidence of a plan may also be admissible to show the doing of the criminal act") (footnote omitted).

[280] Imwinkelried § 5:33, at 5-54 to -55.

§ 6.22 PLAN

Finally, plan evidence is admissible to establish the criminal act. For example, plan evidence is helpful when the defendant asserts that a child's injuries were accidental. The fact that the defendant had a plan that included maltreatment undercuts the claim of accident.[281]

The plan theory is applicable only when the defendant's plan incorporates the uncharged and the charged acts into *one continuous undertaking*. Imwinkelried captures the essence of this important (and often overlooked) requirement:

> Both [the charged and uncharged] crimes must be part of a common or continuing scheme; the plan must encompass or include both crimes; the crimes must be connected, mutually dependent, and interlocking. All these variations express the same core thought that both crimes must be inspired by the same impulse or purpose. Both crimes must be steps toward the accomplishment of the same final goal. They are different stages of the plan.[282]

The uncharged and charged acts do not have to be similar.[283] When the uncharged and charged acts are similar, it is important to recall that the plan theory has no application unless the acts are part of a single, continuous plan.[284] The theory does not apply to a series of similar but unrelated acts.[285] Thus, it is improper to invoke the plan theory to admit evidence that the defendant molested a series of children unless the molestations were related to each other as steps in a single plan.[286] The fact that the defendant planned each molestation

---

[281] Imwinkelried § 4:20, at 4-44 to -45. See also 22 Wright & Graham § 5244, at 502 n.27, where the authors state:

> It seems doubtful that evidence of a plan would be sufficient by itself to prove the doing of the act since the plan may be abandoned. However, such proof need not be sufficient to prove the act in order to be admissible to support other evidence that the crime was committed.

[282] Imwinkelried § 3:21, at 3-54 (footnotes omitted).

[283] *Id.* § 3:21, at 3-53. *See* Ali v. United States, 520 A.2d 306, 312 (D.C. 1987) ("Completely dissimilar crimes may form part of a true plan or scheme").

[284] For an instructive decision correctly applying the plan theory, see Ali v. United States, 520 A.2d 306 (D.C. 1987).

[285] Imwinkelried writes:

> [I]t is not enough to show mere similarity between the crimes. Standing alone, a series of similar acts does not establish the existence of a true plan. A series of similar robberies could be the result of separate decisions to rob. There must be a permissible inference that both crimes were related to an overall goal in the defendant's mind.

Imwinkelried § 3:22, at 3-58 (footnotes omitted). *See also* People v. Stewart, 181 Cal. App. 3d 300, 226 Cal. Rptr. 252 (1986) (holding that a series of sex offenses against the same victim were not proof of a true plan).

In sex offense cases, courts often admit similar although unrelated sex acts under the plan rubric. *See, e.g.,* State v. Dupay, 405 N.W.2d 444 (Minn. Ct. App. 1987) (approving similar but unrelated acts under a common scheme or plan theory).

[286] Although the uncharged molestations should not be received under the plan theory, they may be admissible on an intent theory (see **§ 6.18**) or the depraved sexual propensity theory (see **§ 6.21**).

does not invoke the plan theory. In such cases each molestation is simply one in a series of unrelated crimes. Again, the plan theory applies only when the uncharged and charged acts are stages of the same plan. The plan theory would apply, for example, if the defendant was a day care operator who formulated a plan to molest all children attending the center.[287]

The plan theory does not require that the uncharged components of the plan precede the charged component.[288] Depending on the circumstances, the charged and uncharged acts may be separated by a substantial period of time.[289] Uncharged misconduct is admissible despite the fact that the uncharged act could not be prosecuted because of the statute of limitations.[290] The uncharged and charged elements can occur at different locations.[291] Because a plan is a product of the defendant's mind, anonymous acts are inadmissible to establish the plan.[292]

In child abuse litigation, plan is one of the most commonly invoked theories of uncharged misconduct evidence. Unfortunately, the courts sometimes misapply the plan theory, affixing the "plan" label to uncharged misconduct that is actually character evidence barred by Federal Rule of Evidence 404(a).

Hypothetical Nos. 1 and 2 illustrate the plan theory.

Hypothetical No. 1. The defendant was employed as a social worker at a veterans' administration hospital. His assignment was to counsel members of the families of veterans receiving treatment at the hospital. One veteran's 15-year-old daughter received counseling from the defendant three times a week. Almost from the outset, counseling sessions focused on sexual matters. During sessions, the defendant massaged the minor and gave her marijuana, ostensibly to help her relax. The defendant sought to develop a trusting and uninhibited relationship with the minor. Finally, the defendant induced the minor to have sexual relations with him in his office. He urged her not to tell anyone because, in his words, revelation would destroy their relationship. Following the initial molestation,

---

[287] *See* State v. Bennett, 36 Wash. App. 176, 672 P.2d 772 (1983). In *Bennett,* the defendant was charged with sexual abuse of two runaway teenage girls. He invited each victim to his apartment, where he offered to provide food and shelter in exchange for sexual favors. In addition to the testimony of the victims describing the defendant's pattern of conduct with them, the trial court admitted the testimony of two other teenage runaway girls. The defendant was not on trial for his activities with these other girls. The girls described a pattern similar to that described by the victims of the charged crimes. The court approved the uncharged misconduct evidence under a plan theory.

See also Scadden v. State, 732 P.2d 1036 (Wyo. 1987). In *Scadden,* a high school volleyball coach was convicted of molesting several members of the team. The defendant had a plan whereby he ingratiated himself to team members and gradually gained their confidence.

[288] Imwinkelried § 3:21, at 3-53.

[289] *Id.* at 3-53 to -54.

[290] Commonwealth v. Niemetz, 282 Pa. Super. 431, 422 A.2d 1369, 1376 (1980).

[291] *Id.*

[292] Imwinkelried § 3:21, at 3-54.

intercourse occurred at other counseling sessions. Later, the defendant and the minor took a weekend trip to another state. There were frequent acts of intercourse during the trip. The defendant is charged only with acts of intercourse occurring at his office. The government seeks to prove the defendant's plan to gain the child's confidence. The prosecutor offers evidence of the massages, the marijuana, and the weekend trip.[293]

The government's uncharged misconduct evidence is admissible.[294] The evidence establishes that the defendant formulated a step-by-step scheme to seduce the victim. The massages and the marijuana were steps in the plan. Each step was intended to weaken the child's resistance so that the defendant could reach his ultimate goal of sexual intercourse. The uncharged intercourse occurring in another state further evidenced the defendant's unified and continuous plan of molestation. The fact that the out-of-state intercourse occurred after the charged offense does not defeat the logical relevance of the evidence.[295]

Hypothetical No. 2. The defendant is charged with incest with his 13-year-old daughter. When the victim was nine, the defendant initiated a course of sexual touching that began with fondling, progressed to digital penetration and oral copulation, and, when the child was 12, culminated in intercourse. During the past year, the defendant forced the victim to submit to intercourse two or three times a week. He threatened to kill her if she revealed his activities. The defendant is charged only with sexual intercourse. He denies any abuse. The state seeks to prove the uncharged acts of fondling and oral copulation, as well as to establish the defendant's threats. Finally, the state offers testimony from the defendant's two adult daughters, aged 23 and 26, who will testify that when they were the victim's age, the defendant molested them.

The three items of evidence—(1) threats, (2) sibling abuse, and (3) history of abuse of the victim—should be analyzed separately.

1. Threats to maintain silence. The defendant threatened the victim to keep her quiet. The incest and the threats were "connected, mutually dependent, and interlocking"[296] elements of a plan. The defendant threatened the victim for two reasons: to hide the past, and (probably) to secure his opportunity to abuse the victim in the future. The uncharged threats and the charged abuse are part and parcel of one plan, and the prosecutor should be permitted to introduce evidence of the threats to establish the molestation.

---

[293] The facts of this hypothetical are drawn from United States v. Gano, 560 F.2d 990 (10th Cir. 1977).

[294] For a well-reasoned decision applying the plan theory, see Ali v. United States, 520 A.2d 306 (D.C. 1987).

[295] Imwinkelried § 3:21, at 3-53.

[296] *Id.* at 3-54 (footnotes omitted).

2. Abuse of adult daughters. The testimony of the adult daughters should be excluded under the plan theory.[297] The abuse of these women occurred years before the charged incest. It is untenable to suggest that the uncharged abuse of the sisters and the charged abuse were part of a single plan. In all probability, the three incidents are separate and unrelated crimes. It is in this context (when the state offers evidence of similar but unrelated sex crimes), however, that the courts most frequently misapply the plan theory.[298] For example, in *Cox v. State*,[299] the Georgia Court of Appeals affirmed a trial court decision to admit testimony from three adult sisters of the adolescent incest victim. The uncharged acts of abuse occurred from 17 to 22 years prior to the charged offense. Yet the appellate court held that the uncharged incest was properly received "to show defendant's . . . general plan to gratify his lust, passion and sexual desire."[300] Although there is no question that the uncharged misconduct was probative of character, the evidence was not admissible under the plan theory. The *Cox* decision typifies a common problem. In sex offense cases, courts sometimes admit character evidence under the guise of plan.[301] Imwinkelried describes this phenomenon:

---

[297] One could argue for admission of the abuse of the other daughters under the depraved sexual propensity exception discussed in **§ 6.21**. The time lapse may prove difficult to overcome, however.

[298] *See, e.g.,* State v. Friedrich, 135 Wis. 2d 1, 398 N.W.2d 763 (1987). In *Friedrich,* the defendant was charged with sexual abuse of a child. The state, under plan and motive theories, offered uncharged misconduct evidence consisting of alleged incidents of child sexual abuse that occurred five and seven years before trial. The majority of the Wisconsin Supreme Court approved admission of the evidence. In a strident dissent, Chief Justice Heffernan criticized the majority's reasoning:

> The motive, scheme, or plan asserted by the state—to obtain sexual gratification from young females with whom [defendant] had a quasi-familial relationship—is not a motive, scheme, or plan at all. This scheme or plan is simply an assertion that [defendant] had a propensity to commit sexual assaults. The majority allows the state to relabel a "propensity" as a "scheme or plan" and to thus introduce the forbidden propensity or bad character issue.

398 N.W.2d at 779 (Heffernan, C.J., dissenting). *See also* United States v. Munoz, 32 M.J. 359 (C.M.A.), *cert. denied,* 112 S. Ct. 437 (1991) (spurious plan).

[299] 173 Ga. App. 422, 326 S.E.2d 796 (1985).

[300] 326 S.E.2d at 797. In fairness to the *Cox* court, it may have been applying the depraved sexual propensity theory. See **§ 6.21**.

[301] Childs v. State, 177 Ga. App. 257, 339 S.E.2d 311 (1985); Pendleton v. Commonwealth, 685 S.W.2d 549 (Ky. 1985); State v. Matteson, 287 N.W.2d 408 (Minn. 1979); State v. Christeson, 780 S.W.2d 119 (Mo. Ct. App. 1989); State v. Medina, 245 Mont. 25, 798 P.2d 1032 (1990); State v. Just, 184 Mont. 262, 602 P.2d 957 (1979); State v. Plymate, 216 Neb. 722, 345 N.W.2d 327 (1984); State v. DeLeonardo, 315 N.C. 762, 340 S.E.2d 350 (1986); State v. Teeter, 85 N.C. App. 624, 355 S.E.2d 804 (1987); Hancock v. State, 664 P.2d 1039 (Okla. Crim. App. 1983); Driskell v. State, 659 P.2d 343 (Okla. Crim. App. 1983); State v. Catsam, 148 Vt. 366, 534 A.2d 184 (1987); State v. Friedrich, 135 Wis. 2d 1, 398 N.W.2d 763 (1987); Day v. State, 92 Wis. 2d 392, 284 N.W.2d 666 (1979).

Some courts are quite liberal in admitting uncharged misconduct under the rubric of "plan." If the proponent can show a series of similar acts, these courts admit the evidence on the theory that a pattern or systematic course of conduct is sufficient to establish a plan. Similarity or likeness between crimes is a sufficient showing. In effect, these courts convert the doctrine into a plan-to-commit-a-series-of-similar-crimes theory.

This application of the plan theory is troublesome. The commentators often refer to this application as the spurious plan doctrine. The commentators have been almost uniformly critical of the doctrine. Their criticism is well-founded.

In reality, the courts are permitting the proponent to introduce propensity evidence . . . . It is immaterial that there are many instances of similar acts by the defendant; the number of the acts increases the acts' probative value on the issue of defendant's propensity, but standing alone the number of acts cannot change the propensity quality of the theory of relevance. The courts are illicitly allowing the proponent to prove the defendant's character, disposition, or propensity.[302]

The plan theory should be confined to cases in which uncharged and charged acts are part of a single, unified plan. Characterizing a series of unrelated but similar sex offenses as a plan distorts the theory.

3. Uncharged abuse of victim in charged offense. The difficult question raised by Hypothetical No. 2 is the admissibility of the defendant's uncharged sexual abuse of the victim of the charged offense. The defendant's activity extended over five years, beginning with fondling, and progressing to intercourse. Were the uncharged acts of sexual abuse occurring during this period stages of a continuous plan? Arguments are possible both ways.

The defendant will argue that he entertained no plan to have sexual intercourse with his daughter. His situation is not like the counselor in Hypothetical No. 1, who intended all along to seduce the victim. Each of the defendant's uncharged improprieties was a separate and distinct episode. As is typical with

---

[302] Imwinkelried § 3:23, at 3-61 to -62 (footnotes omitted). See also 22 Wright & Graham § 5244, at 499–500, where the authors remark:

> The justification for admitting evidence of other crimes to prove a plan is that this involves no inference as to the defendant's character; instead his conduct is said to be caused by his conscious commitment to a course of conduct of which the charged crime is only a part. The other crime is admitted to show this larger goal rather than to show defendant's propensity to commit crimes. This justification is plausible when there is some other evidence of the plan or when the existence of the plan is the obvious inference from the other crime. However, if not carefully policed, this exception can serve to admit a series of crimes whose most obvious relationship is that they were all committed by the defendant and whose strongest tendency is to prove the defendant's character for crime rather than his planned course of conduct. This expansive use of the plan exception has been criticized by the commentators and condemned by some courts.

(footnotes omitted).

incest, things got progressively out of control, but there was no overriding plan to have intercourse.

The state will counter that there might be merit to the defendant's argument if the 13-year-old were the defendant's only victim. But the defendant did precisely the same thing twice before, with his two adult daughters. He knew exactly what he was doing when he began molesting the present victim, and he knew where it would lead. Each uncharged act with the present victim was a stage in an old and repeated pattern. Thus, the uncharged acts against the 13-year-old should be admissible to prove the defendant's plan.

The defendant's uncharged abuse of the victim of the charged offense should also be admissible under the "entire picture" theory discussed in § **6.20**, or under the depraved sexual propensity theory discussed in § **6.21**.

§ 6.23 Consciousness of Guilt

Uncharged misconduct that reflects consciousness of guilt may be admissible to establish identity, intent, or the criminal act.[303] For further discussion of consciousness of guilt evidence, see **Chapter 3**. Wright and Graham describe the logical relevance of such proof:

> [E]vidence that one of the parties has sought to destroy, conceal, or tamper with witnesses or evidence often involves proof of another crime. Though not listed in rule 404(b), such evidence is admissible. Though it may permit an inference as to the conduct of the party, the basic relevance of spoliation evidence is to show a consciousness of guilt; as such it is not necessary to make any inference as to the character of the spoliator to reach the conclusion that his subjective state of mind is incompatible with the position being asserted in the litigation.[304]

Use of uncharged misconduct to prove consciousness of guilt is illustrated in the following hypothetical:

> The defendant is charged with incest with his seven-year-old daughter. The defendant denies he abused the child. To prove the commission of the offense, and to identify the defendant as the perpetrator, the prosecutor offers the following evidence: The day after the alleged molestation, the defendant took the victim to the hospital because the child was experiencing vaginal bleeding. The emergency room physician will testify that the defendant was very nervous. At

---

[303] *See* United States v. Gonsalves, 668 F.2d 73 (1st Cir.), *cert. denied,* 456 U.S. 909 (1982) (threats to witnesses evidenced consciousness of guilt); United States v. Posey, 611 F.2d 1389 (5th Cir. 1980) (proper to admit evidence that defendant attempted to bribe a police officer into letting defendant escape); Imwinkelried §§ 3:04, 4:09, 5:14.

[304] 22 Wright & Graham § 5240, at 476 (footnotes omitted).

first, the defendant stated that the child injured herself accidentally when she fell on the horizontal bar of a bicycle. Later, he changed his story and asserted that a neighbor molested the girl. The doctor will also testify that the child's vaginal injuries could not have been caused by a fall. A police officer will testify that the officer found the child's blood-stained underpants hidden in a shoe box in the defendant's closet. Finally, the child will testify that the defendant threatened to hurt her if she told what happened, and that he attempted to persuade her to recant.

The government's evidence is admissible to prove consciousness of guilt. In child abuse cases one of the strongest indicators of consciousness of guilt is an implausible or impossible explanation offered to explain a child's injuries.[305] Numerous courts hold that the trier of fact may consider such explanations as circumstantial evidence of guilt.[306] The defendant's inconsistent explanations of the injury and efforts to hide evidence, to cast the blame elsewhere, to silence the victim,[307] and to persuade her to change her story are all admissible to prove consciousness of guilt.

§ 6.24 Modus Operandi to Prove Identity

The state may establish the defendant's identity through evidence of uncharged acts that are strikingly similar to the charged offense.[308] The fact that the same modus operandi (mode of operating) was used in the uncharged and the charged crimes permits an inference that the same person committed them all. When

---

[305] See **Ch. 3**.

[306] *See* Payne v. State, 21 Ark. App. 243, 731 S.W.2d 235 (1987). In *Payne* the court stated:

> A jury may consider and give weight to any false and improbable statements made by an accused in explaining suspicious circumstances . . . . When we consider the defendant's improbable statement in this case together with the nature of the injuries to the child, the medical opinion evidence, and the defendant's opportunity, we are persuaded that, taken together, they are sufficient to constitute substantial evidence of guilt.

731 S.W.2d at 236–37.

[307] *See* United States v. Maddox, 944 F.2d 1223, 1230 (6th Cir. 1991), *cert. denied*, 112 S. Ct. 948 (1992) ("spoliation evidence, including evidence that the defendant threatened a witness, is generally admissible because it is probative of consciousness of guilt").

[308] United States v. Gamble, 27 M.J. 298 (C.M.A. 1988); State v. Phillips, 328 N.C. 1, 399 S.E.2d 293, *cert. denied*, 111 S. Ct. 2804 (1991) (defendant foster parents said child was injured by another child; proper to allow prosecutor to put victim on stand to describe earlier time when defendants injured him; prior act of abuse similar to charged act and supported inference of defendants injuring child); State v. Schultz, 88 N.C. App. 197, 362 S.E.2d 853 (1987), *aff'd*, 322 N.C. 467, 368 S.E.2d 386 (1988); Imwinkelried §§ 3:10 to 3:14, at 3-20 to -35.

the identity of the perpetrator is not in dispute, most courts hold that the modus operandi theory is not applicable.[309]

Evidence of modus operandi to prove identity has two requirements: (1) a very high degree of similarity between the charged and the uncharged acts,[310] and (2) a unique or singular methodology.[311]

On the first requirement—degree of similarity—some portion of the acts constituting the uncharged and charged offenses must be strikingly similar. The similarity required for modus operandi is substantially greater than the similarity required under the doctrine of chances.[312]

In addition to similarity between the charged and uncharged crimes, courts consider the time lapse between the crimes, and whether the crimes occurred in the same general locality.[313] The time and propinquity elements are less important than the degree of similarity, and if the crimes have enough in common, they need not be near in time or place.[314]

On the second requirement—unique methodology—courts use a variety of terms to describe the uniqueness required for the modus operandi theory, including *distinguishing*,[315] *handiwork*,[316] *remarkably similar*,[317] *idiosyncratic*,[318] *signature quality*,[319] and *unique*.[320]

The Florida Supreme Court's decision in *Drake v. State*[321] provides a helpful analysis of the similarity and uniqueness required for the modus operandi theory. Drake was convicted of murdering a woman he met at a bar. After several drinks, the victim left with Drake, never to be seen alive again. Six weeks later, the victim's decomposing body was found in a wooded area. The body had multiple stab wounds. The state contended that the victim had been raped, but the deteriorated condition of the corpse ruled out direct proof of sexual assault. The victim's hands were tied behind her back. The identity of the murderer was

---

[309] Some courts hold that the modus operandi theory is proper when identity is not in dispute. *See, e.g.*, People v. Brown, 214 Ill. App. 3d 836, 574 N.E.2d 190 (1991) (noting split of authority in Illinois).

[310] Imwinkelried § 3:11, at 3-22 to -23.

[311] *Id.* § 3:12, at 3-26.

[312] See § **6.17**.

[313] Imwinkelried § 3:11, at 3-23.

[314] *Id.* at 3-24. *See* State v. Schultz, 362 S.E.2d 853 (N.C. Ct. App. 1987), *aff'd*, 368 S.E.2d 386 (N.C. 1988) (delay of 21 months not too remote).

[315] Cook v. State, 629 S.W.2d 233, 236 (Tex. Ct. App. 1982).

[316] United States v. Morano, 697 F.2d 923, 926 (11th Cir. 1983).

[317] United States v. McCord, 509 F.2d 891, 895 (7th Cir.), *cert. denied*, 423 U.S. 833 (1975).

[318] United States v. Solomon, 490 F. Supp. 373, 375 (S.D. Ga. 1980) (citation omitted).

[319] United States v. Gutierrez, 696 F.2d 753, 755 (10th Cir. 1982), *cert. denied*, 461 U.S. 909 (1983).

[320] Hirst v. Gertzen, 676 F.2d 1252, 1262 (9th Cir. 1982).

[321] 400 So. 2d 1217 (Fla. 1981), *cert. denied*, 466 U.S. 978 (1984).

contested. The trial court permitted the state to establish identity through evidence that on two prior occasions, Drake sexually assaulted women he met in bars. On both occasions Drake bound his victims' hands behind the back. In the uncharged cases the women survived. The Florida Supreme Court reversed the conviction because the requirements of the modus operandi theory were not fulfilled. The court wrote:

> The mode of operating theory of proving identity is based on both the similarity of and the unusual nature of the factual situations being compared. A mere general similarity will not render the similar facts legally relevant to show identity. There must be identifiable points of similarity which pervade the compared factual situations. Given sufficient similarity, in order for the similar facts to be relevant the points of similarity must have some special character or be so unusual as to point to the defendant. The only similarity between the two incidents introduced at trial and [the victim's] murder is the tying of the hands behind the victims' backs and that both had left a bar with the defendant. There are many dissimilarities, not the least of which is that the collateral incidents involved only sexual assaults while the instant case involved murder with little, if any, evidence of sexual abuse. Even assuming some similarity, the similar facts offered would still fail the unusual branch of the test. Binding of the hands occurs in many crimes involving many different criminal defendants. This binding is not sufficiently unusual to point to the defendant in this case, and it is, therefore, irrelevant to prove identity.[322]

Under the modus operandi theory, the state must show substantially more than similarity.[323] "The crimes must be 'nearly identical.'"[324] The exception is not triggered by the fact that the uncharged and charged acts constitute the same crime. Nor is the exception applicable simply because a similar weapon is used in each, or because both occurred at a particular time of day or night. In sex offense cases, similarity of sex act is insufficient unless the act is so out of the ordinary as to be unique.[325] The court evaluates the quantity and quality of characteristics shared by the charged and the uncharged acts to determine whether proof of the uncharged offenses points an accusatory finger at the defendant. In some cases a single shared factor is so unique that it constitutes a signature of guilt. In others, a host of similarities is insufficient.

---

[322] Id. at 1219 (footnote omitted). For another helpful analysis, see Peek v. State, 488 So. 2d 52 (Fla. 1986).

[323] *See* Frisson v. State, 512 So. 2d 1092 (Fla. Dist. Ct. App. 1987) (mere similarity of sexual batteries not sufficient for modus operandi); People v. Esterline, 159 Ill. App. 3d 164, 512 N.E.2d 358, 362 (1987) ("In the present case, we find that any similarities between the crime charged and the other acts were outweighed by the differences so that modus operandi has not been demonstrated").

[324] Imwinkelried § 3:11, at 3-24 (quoting Note, *Admissibility of Evidence under Indiana's "Common Scheme or Plan" Exception,* 53 Ind. L.J. 805, 818 (1978)).

[325] *Id.* § 3:14, at 3-34. Nonunique sex acts include oral copulation, vaginal and anal intercourse, digital penetration, and fondling.

Hypothetical Nos. 1 and 2 illustrate the modus operandi theory.

Hypothetical No. 1. The victim is a 13-year-old minor who was awakened at 2:30 a.m. when the light came on in her bedroom. A man was standing in the doorway. The man motioned with his hand for the victim to come to him. He held a baseball bat in his right hand. As the victim walked toward him, the man grabbed the victim's pajamas and asked her whether any men were in the house. The victim said no. The man then ordered the victim to kiss him, which she did. The man grabbed the victim by the hair, dragged her to her bed, and engaged in anal intercourse with her.

Following the assault, he fled. At trial, the defendant offers an alibi. In rebuttal, the state proposes to call two witnesses. Witness A is a 13-year-old girl who will testify that 10 days after the charged offense, the defendant entered her bedroom at about 9:30 p.m. He grabbed her by the hair after she did not respond to his command to come to him. When A screamed, her mother came into the room. The defendant asked the mother whether any men were in the house. The mother said there were, and the defendant fled. Witness B is a nine-year-old girl who will testify that 10 days before the charged offense, during the early morning hours, the defendant entered her bedroom, picked her up, and took her to an open field across from the house. The defendant removed her clothes and began fondling her genitals. When the victim saw her mother arrive at her house, the defendant allowed the girl to put her nightgown back on, and walked her part way back to her house. The defendant then fled into the night. All three assaults occurred within a four-block radius. The defendant lives in the same area.

The testimony of B should be excluded because the uncharged acts and the charged act are not sufficiently similar and unique to trigger the modus operandi theory. It is true that there are similarities between the assault on B and the charged assault: both victims are minors, the uncharged assault occurred near the time of the charged offense, both acts occurred in the same neighborhood, both assaults occurred at night, the perpetrator entered a bedroom on each occasion, and each case involved a sex offense. There are, however, dissimilarities. No weapon was involved in the assault on B, the sexual acts were different, the defendant took B outside, and the defendant did not ask whether any men were in the house. Furthermore, the modus operandi of the two offenses is not distinguishing, remarkably similar, or unique. Nothing about these crimes ties them together as the work of one person. Rather, they are the work of ordinary, if somewhat daring, criminals.

The testimony of A is a closer case.[326] Note the similarities between the uncharged and the charged acts: both victims are children, the crimes occurred within days of one another, each occurred at night and in the same

---

[326] The fact that the assault on A occurred after the charged assault does not undercut the modus operandi theory. Uncharged acts occurring before or after the charged act can be logically relevant to prove identity if the uncharged acts are sufficiently similar to the charged act.

neighborhood, the assailant entered a bedroom in both cases, the man ordered each victim to come to him, he grabbed each victim, and in each case he asked whether any men were in the house. But note the dissimilarities: no weapon was involved in the offense against A, and no sexual assault occurred.

The shared elements of the assault on A and the charged offense come closer to the similarity required by the modus operandi theory. Yet, the extent of similarity probably falls short of the mark. What is more, there is little that is unique about these crimes. The combination of weak similarity and lack of uniqueness undercuts the argument for admission under the modus operandi theory.

> *Hypothetical No. 2.* The defendant is charged with murdering the infant son of his girlfriend. The infant died from a brain injury caused by a blow to the head. The defendant claims he was out of town when the child was injured. Several adults had custody of the child, and could have inflicted the injuries. There is expert testimony that the injuries were not accidental.[327] To establish identity, the state offers evidence that in the past, the defendant abused two other children. In one case, he severely beat a two-year-old child with a belt, broke the youngster's arm, and inflicted multiple cigarette burns.[328] In the other case, he threw an infant against a wall, inflicting a skull fracture, subdural hematoma, and permanent injury.

The state's identity evidence should be excluded. As to the two-year-old with multiple abusive injuries, the degree of similarity required for the modus operandi theory is lacking. The fact that the uncharged and the charged acts violate the same child abuse statute does not invoke the modus operandi theory.[329]

The same conclusion should be reached concerning the child who suffered head injury at the defendant's hand. It is a tragic fact that head injuries are far from uncommon or unique.[330] Many young children suffer such injuries. Klein states:

> [Forty to seventy percent] of battered children will show some external evidence of trauma to the face and head, with higher incidence noted among those generally more gravely injured. In roentgenograms of 95 consecutive battered children, Kogutt et al. found 22% to show skull fractures and an additional 18% showed suture separation, indicating increased intracranial pressure.[331]

Thus, there is nothing unique about head injury itself. Furthermore, nothing in the evidence indicates that the charged and the uncharged injuries were

---

[327] For discussion of the likelihood that head injuries are accidental, see **Ch. 3**.

[328] For discussion of burns, see **Ch. 3**.

[329] Imwinkelried § 3:14, at 3-34.

[330] See **Ch. 3** for discussion of head injuries.

[331] Klein, *Central Nervous System Injuries, in* Child Abuse and Neglect: A Medical Reference 73 (N. Ellerstein ed. 1981).

inflicted in a novel or idiosyncratic way. The modus operandi theory is not applicable.

§ 6.25 Opportunity or Capacity

The likelihood that a crime was committed by a defendant increases if there is evidence that the defendant had the opportunity or capacity[332] to commit the offense. The facts establishing opportunity or capacity are sometimes uncharged acts.[333] Consider the following hypothetical:

> The defendant is charged with sexual abuse of a child. The child was walking home when she was accosted by a man who stopped his car and offered her candy. When the child approached the car the man pulled her in and committed the charged offense. The child identified the defendant as her attacker. The defense is mistaken identity. The prosecutor seeks to introduce evidence that one hour before the assault, the defendant, who does not live in the neighborhood, purchased marijuana less than a block from the scene of the crime.

The prosecutor's uncharged misconduct evidence should be received because it places the defendant near the scene of the crime and increases the likelihood that the child's identification was correct. The defendant may argue that to avoid unfair prejudice, the court should admit evidence placing the defendant near the scene, but exclude the fact that he purchased drugs. There is merit to this argument. The importance of the uncharged misconduct is not that the defendant bought marijuana, but that he was in the vicinity. Information about drugs has little, if any, evidentiary value, but it has substantial potential for unfair prejudice.

§ 6.26 Proof of Coercion, Force, or Threat

In some child abuse cases the prosecutor must establish that the defendant coerced, forced, or threatened the victim. Evidence of the defendant's uncharged violence and threats against the victim and others may be admissible to establish fear or coercion.[334] In *Calloway v. State,*[335] the defendant was charged with rape and child molestation. The court wrote:

---

[332] State v. Longuskie, 59 Wash. App. 838, 801 P.2d 1004, 1007 (1990) (defendant teacher was charged with sexual abuse of student; defendant claimed he could not achieve an erection; not error to admit testimony from other students of defendant's abuse of them).

[333] Imwinkelried § 3:19, at 3-49 to -50.

[334] Calloway v. State, 199 Ga. App. 272, 404 S.E.2d 811 (1991).

[335] *Id.*

§ 6.26 PROOF OF COERCION

[D]efendant contends that the trial court erroneously allowed the victim to testify over objection that he had a temper and he and her mother fought frequently, as this was brought in only to intimate his violent nature to the jury and impermissibly place his character in evidence. The victim testified that she was afraid of what defendant might have done if she did not do what he told her to do because of the "fights and fusses" he had with her mother. Since force is an essential element of rape, this testimony as to defendant's violence and the victim's fear of him was relevant and admissible. Lack of resistance, induced by fear, is force, and may be shown by "the prosecutrix' state of mind from her prior experience with appellant and subjective apprehension of danger from him . . . ." "It is well-established that if evidence is otherwise relevant and material to the issues being tried, it is not rendered inadmissible merely because it may incidently place the defendant's character in issue."[336]

When rape is charged, the prosecutor must establish force. Force can be overt or constructive.[337] In *United States v. Palmer*,[338] the Court of Military Appeals provides an excellent analysis of constructive force:

> Appellant was convicted of raping and sodomizing his minor stepdaughter. The primary issue on appeal concerns the concept of "constructive force."
>
> To convict an accused of rape, the prosecution must prove, among other things, that the act of sexual intercourse occurred "by force and without [the] consent" of the victim.
>
> * * *
>
> In the law of rape, various types of conduct are universally recognized as sufficient to constitute force. The most obvious type is that brute force which is used to overcome or prevent the victim's active resistance. Physical contact, however, is not the only way force can be established. Where intimidation or threats of death or physical injury make resistance futile, it is said that "constructive force" has been applied, satisfying this element. Closely related to these is the situation in which the victim is incapable of consenting because she is asleep, unconscious, or lacks mental capacity to consent. In such circumstances, the force component is established by the penetration alone.
>
> * * *
>
> The particular bone of contention in this case concerns a species of "constructive force." Many jurisdictions have explicitly recognized that a parent or

---

[336] 404 S.E.2d at 813.

[337] United States v. Hicks, 24 M.J. 3 (C.M.A.), *cert. denied,* 484 U.S. 827 (1987); United States v. Williams, 1992 WL 121410 (A.F.C.M.R. 1992); United States v. Rhea, 1992 WL 110517 (A.F.C.M.R. 1992); United States v. Sargent, 33 M.J. 815 (A.C.M.R. 1991); United States v. Dejonge, 16 M.J. 974 (A.F.C.M.R. 1983); State v. Spaulding, 313 N.W.2d 878 (Iowa 1981); State v. Gillette, 699 P.2d 626 (N.M. Ct. App. 1985); Commonwealth v. Ruppert, 579 A.2d 966, 968–69 (Pa. Super. Ct. 1990); State v. Willis, 370 N.W.2d 193 (S.D. 1985).

[338] 33 M.J. 7 (C.M.A. 1991).

other authority figure can exert a "moral, psychological or intellectual force" over a child which is the compulsory equivalent of a threat or intimidation.

As Justice Martin stated in the oft-quoted opinion of the North Carolina Supreme Court:

> The youth and vulnerability of children, coupled with the power inherent in a parent's position of authority, creates a unique situation of dominance and control in which explicit threats and displays of force are not necessary to effect the abuser's purpose.

State v. Etheridge, 319 N.C. 34, 352 S.E.2d 673, 681 (1987).

To recognize that a parent or authority figure *can* exert a moral, psychological, or intellectual force over a child is merely to recognize the obvious. It is equally obvious, however, that all children do not invariably acquiesce to parental will. The questions thus remain: Was the child forced? and, Did the child consent? "Compulsion of parental command" never becomes an alternative test. If operative, however, it *may* establish that the child was forced and that consent was lacking.[339]

---

[339] *Id.* at 8–11.

CHAPTER 7

HEARSAY

§ 7.1   Introduction

OUT-OF-COURT UTTERANCES

§ 7.2   Hearsay Defined
§ 7.3   —Analyzing Out-of-Court Statements
§ 7.4   Justification for Excluding Hearsay
§ 7.5   Preliminary Rulings on Admissibility
§ 7.6   Verbal Assertions to Prove Other than Matter Asserted
§ 7.7   Written and Drawn Assertions to Prove Other than Matter Asserted
§ 7.8   Nonverbal Assertions to Prove Other than Matter Asserted
§ 7.9   Silence or Inaction as Assertion
§ 7.10   Implied Assertions
§ 7.11   —Verbal and Written Implied Assertions
§ 7.12   —Assertions Implied from Conduct
§ 7.13   Utterances During Sleep
§ 7.14   Verbal Acts and Verbal Parts of Acts
§ 7.15   Assertions to Prove Effect on Listener
§ 7.16   Assertions to Prove Source of Unique Knowledge

EXCEPTIONS TO HEARSAY RULE

§ 7.17   Rationale for Exceptions
§ 7.18   Prior Inconsistent Statements
§ 7.19   —Admissibility Requirements
§ 7.20   —Recurring Issues
§ 7.21   Prior Consistent Statements
§ 7.22   —Admissibility Requirements
§ 7.23   —Fabrication Motivated by Improper Influence, Bias, or Interest
§ 7.24   —Impeachment Through Prior Inconsistent Statements

§ 7.25 —Impeachment Charging Memory Lapse
§ 7.26 Out-of-Court Statements of Identification
§ 7.27 Present Sense Impressions
§ 7.28 Excited Utterances
§ 7.29 —Admissibility Requirements
§ 7.30 —Evaluation Factors
§ 7.31 Fresh Complaint of Rape or Sexual Abuse
§ 7.32 State of Mind
§ 7.33 —Criminal Litigation
§ 7.34 —Civil Litigation
§ 7.35 Diagnosis or Treatment Exception
§ 7.36 —Rationales for Exception
§ 7.37 Past Recollection Recorded
§ 7.38 Business Records
§ 7.39 Public Records
§ 7.40 Learned Treatises
§ 7.41 Proof of Age
§ 7.42 Residual Exception
§ 7.43 —Analysis of Reliability
§ 7.44 —Factors Surrounding Statement
§ 7.45 —Factors Corroborating Statement
§ 7.46 Child Hearsay Exception
§ 7.47 Sufficiency to Support Finding of Fact or Verdict
§ 7.48 Unavailable Hearsay Declarants
§ 7.49 Testimonial Competence of Hearsay Declarants

RIGHT TO CONFRONT ACCUSATORY WITNESSES

§ 7.50 Confrontation Right: Applicability and Elements
§ 7.51 Hearsay and the Confrontation Clause
§ 7.52 —Unavailability Rule
§ 7.53 —Reliability Requirement
§ 7.54 Two-Defendant Trials
§ 7.55 Former Testimony
§ 7.56 Limitations on Cross-Examination
§ 7.57 Applicable Proceedings
§ 7.58 Waiver and Forfeiture of Confrontation Right

§ 7.1 Introduction

Hearsay is immensely important in child abuse litigation.[1] Children's out-of-court statements are critical for three reasons. First, the child's out-of-court statements are sometimes the most compelling evidence of abuse. Second, in many cases the need for the child's out-of-court statements is magnified by a paucity of physical evidence and eyewitnesses.[2] Third, although most children have the cognitive ability to testify,[3] some children are ineffective witnesses, and some cannot take the stand at all. For children who do not testify, out-of-court statements are their only way to communicate with the jury. For children who perform poorly on the witness stand, the willingness of jurors to credit their testimony is enhanced when out-of-court statements are admitted that support in-court testimony.

Out-of-court statements by the alleged perpetrator often constitute powerful evidence of guilt. The defendant's utterances are usually received as party admissions.

This chapter provides an overview of hearsay. The chapter is divided into three parts. The first part discusses out-of-court utterances that fall within and without the definition of hearsay. The second part discusses exceptions to the hearsay rule that play a day-to-day role in child abuse litigation. The final part analyzes the right to confront accusatory witnesses.

OUT-OF-COURT UTTERANCES

§ 7.2 Hearsay Defined

At common law, hearsay was defined as an out-of-court statement offered to prove the truth of the matter asserted. The Federal Rules of Evidence adopt

---

[1] Morgan v. Foretich, 846 F.2d 941, 943 (4th Cir. 1988); People v. McClure, 779 P.2d 864 (Colo. 1989); *In re* E.P., 167 Ill. App. 3d 534, 521 N.E.2d 603, 607 (1988) (hearsay can be probative and valuable evidence); State v. D.R., 109 N.J. 348, 537 A.2d 667 (1988); Note, *A Comprehensive Approach to Child Hearsay in Sex Abuse Cases,* 83 Colum. L. Rev. 1745 (1983).

[2] Pennsylvania v. Ritchie, 480 U.S. 39, 60 (1987) ("Child abuse is one of the most difficult crimes to detect and prosecute, in large part because there often are no witnesses except the victim. A child's feelings of vulnerability and guilt, and his or her unwillingness to come forward are particularly acute when the abuser is a parent"); People v. Bowers, 801 P.2d 511 (Colo. 1990); People v. McClure, 779 P.2d 864, 866 (Colo. 1989); People v. District Ct., 776 P.2d 1083, 1085 n.1 (Colo. 1989); State v. J.C.E., 235 Mont. 264, 767 P.2d 309, 311 (1988); State v. Smith, 16 Utah 2d 374, 401 P.2d 445, 447 (1965); State v. Jones, 112 Wash. 2d 488, 772 P.2d 496 (1989).

[3] See **Ch. 2** for discussion of children's testimonial competence.

this definition. Rule 801(c) defines hearsay as "a statement, other than one made by the declarant while testifying at the trial or hearing, offered in evidence to prove the truth of the matter asserted."[4] Rule 802 provides that hearsay is not admissible unless the requirements of one of the hearsay exceptions are satisfied.[5]

Under the Federal Rules of Evidence, a verbal utterance is hearsay if three requirements are fulfilled: (1) the utterance is a statement, (2) the statement is out-of-court, and (3) the out-of-court statement is offered to prove the truth of the matter asserted. A writing that fulfills these three requirements is hearsay. So too is nonverbal conduct fulfilling the requirements. The three elements of hearsay are examined below.

1. Out-of-Court Utterance Must Be a Statement

The word *statement* is a term of art in hearsay law. Federal Rule of Evidence 801(a) defines a statement as an oral or written assertion or nonverbal conduct that is intended as an assertion.[6] The rules do not define the word *assertion*. McCormick states that "the word [assert] simply means to say that something is so, e.g., that an event happened or that a condition existed."[7] The Advisory Committee note to Rule 801(a) states that "[t]he effect of the definition of 'statement' is to exclude from the operation of the hearsay rule all evidence of conduct, verbal or nonverbal, not intended as an assertion.[8] The key to the definition is that nothing is an assertion unless intended to be one."[9] A child makes an assertion when the child speaks, writes, acts, or fails to act with the *intent* to express some fact or opinion.

---

[4] Fed. R. Evid. 801(c). See Timmons v. State, 584 N.E.2d 1108 (Ind. 1992).

[5] Fed. R. Evid. 802. See Cassidy v. State, 74 Md. App. 1, 536 A.2d 666, 669, *cert. denied*, 312 Md. 602, 541 A.2d 965 (1988) (the hearsay "Rule, in its essence, is a rule of exclusion").

[6] Fed. R. Evid. 801(a). See Cassidy v. State, 74 Md. App. 1, 536 A.2d 666, 668–69, *cert. denied*, 312 Md. 602, 541 A.2d 965 (1988). See also 4 D. Louisell & C. Mueller, Federal Evidence § 415 at 25 (Supp. 1991) [hereinafter Louisell & Mueller] (very helpful discussion of meaning of word *assertion*).

[7] C. McCormick, *McCormick on Evidence* § 246, 729–30 (E. Cleary ed. 1984) (emphasis deleted) [hereinafter McCormick].

[8] Fed. R. Evid. 801(a) advisory committee's note. See In re C.L., 397 N.W.2d 81, 84–85 (S.D. 1986) (parental rights termination case; young sexual abuse victim's play with anatomical dolls was nonassertive and thus not hearsay; child's play admissible as substantive evidence of abuse); State v. Hunt, 48 Wash. App. 840, 741 P.2d 566 (1987) (child engaged in nonassertive nonverbal conduct at preschool that indicated sexual abuse, for example, falling asleep at nap time by bunching blankets under her hips and rocking; she also engaged in overt sex play with another child).

[9] Fed. R. Evid. 801(a) advisory committee's note.

§ 7.2   HEARSAY DEFINED   83

A child's statement may be recorded on audio or videotape.[10] If the statement is admissible, the tape containing the statement is admissible.[11]

Most hearsay statements take the form of declarative sentences. Thus, a child's out-of-court utterance "The man touched me here" is a declarative sentence and hearsay when offered for the truth. Many out-of-court utterances are not formulated as declarative sentences, however. Imwinkelried writes:

> All courts agree that assertive statements fall within the hearsay definition. If the person makes an oral out-of-court statement or reduces the statement to writing out of court, the statement is hearsay. However, it must be remembered that not all statements are assertive. Grammar tells us that there are four types of sentences: declarative, imperative, exclamatory, and interrogatory. As a practical matter, only declarative sentences ordinarily fall within the hearsay definition; they declare or assert facts, including states of mind. Imperative sentences giving orders, exclamatory sentences, and interrogatory sentences posing questions usually fall outside the hearsay definition.[12]

Thus, the grammatical structure of an out-of-court utterance may affect its characterization as a "statement." A child's utterance "Stop it!" gives an order and may not be hearsay. The question "Do I have to do it again?" may be nonassertive.

Although sentence structure is sometimes useful in defining hearsay, commentators warn against placing undue emphasis on grammatical structure.[13] Park writes:

> [H]earsay writers sometimes have placed all utterances that give orders or ask questions in the "nonassertive" category. Under this construction, only declarative sentences are assertions. An imperative ("Put $10 on Native Dancer") or a question ("Is Hector home?") is nonassertive.
>
> This . . . use of the concept [of nonassertive utterances] is highly questionable. When offered to show that the addressee was speeding, the question "Why did you go so fast?" poses the same dangers as a direct declarative sentence. Moreover, questions containing information always can be broken down into interrogative and declaratory components. It would be capricious to treat "You were going so fast. Why?" differently than "Why were you going so fast?" The same can be said of an imperative sentence such as "Throw that thief out of

---

[10] State v. Asfour, 555 So. 2d 1280, 1282 (Fla. Dist. Ct. App. 1990) (videotaped interview is hearsay).

[11] State v. Verley, 106 Or. App. 751, 809 P.2d 723, 724 (1991) (defendant acknowledged that child's statement was admissible, but argued that videotape containing statement was not; rejecting this argument, the court wrote: "The admissibility of the videotape depends on the admissibility of the statements contained in it"). Naturally, the proponent of the videotaped statement must authenticate the tape, and ensure that the tape is the best evidence.

[12] E. Imwinkelried, Evidentiary Foundations 235 (2d ed. 1989).

[13] See 4 Louisell & Mueller § 415, at 24–27 (Supp. 1991) (very useful discussion).

here!" when offered to show that the person referred to was a thief. The [drafters of the hearsay definition] could not have intended such an arbitrary distinction.[14]

Thus, assertions often lurk in imperative and interrogatory sentences, and such sentences should be treated as hearsay despite their grammatical structure.

A reflex response is nonassertive and not hearsay.[15] Thus, if a child screams at the sight of an adult, the child is not consciously asserting a fact or opinion, and if the child's reflexive scream is relevant, a witness may describe the scream. Similarly, if a child begins trembling, or shrinks away when an adult's name is mentioned or when the adult enters the room, such nonassertive conduct is not hearsay.[16]

Suppose a child is alone in a room playing with toys. The child picks up a doll and says, "This is the daddy. Daddy, you are bad 'cause you put your pee-pee in me." The child's statement is hearsay if offered to prove the truth of the assertion. The fact that the child thought no one was listening does not render the utterance nonassertive. Thus, Hamlet's soliloquy from the rampart of Elsinore castle was hearsay even though the ghost had departed and Hamlet was alone.[17]

2. Statement Must Be Out-of-Court

Only out-of-court assertions are hearsay. An assertion is out-of-court if it occurs before the proceeding at which it is offered in evidence. Thus, a child who describes sexual abuse to an interviewer makes an out-of-court statement.[18] A pretrial deposition is an out-of-court statement when the deposition is offered at trial. Finally, testimony offered at trial number 1 is an out-of-court statement when a transcript of the testimony is offered at trial number 2.

In some cases a child testifies at trial by means of closed-circuit television. The child usually testifies from a small room, and the child's testimony is simultaneously conveyed to the courtroom on television monitors. Is such testimony out-of-court? On the one hand, the child is literally outside the courtroom. Yet, contemporaneous video testimony should not be treated as

---

[14] Park, *"I Didn't Tell Them Anything about You": Implied Assertions as Hearsay under the Federal Rules of Evidence,* 74 Minn. L. Rev. 783, 796 (1990) [hereinafter Park] (footnotes omitted).

[15] *See* People v. Clark, 6 Cal. App. 3d 658, 86 Cal. Rptr. 106 (1970).

[16] *See In re* Penelope B., 104 Wash. 2d 643, 709 P.2d 1185, 1192 (1985).

[17] W. Shakespeare, Hamlet, Act I, Scene V, lines 91–112. *See* Wheaton, *What Is Hearsay?,* 46 Iowa L. Rev. 207, 210–11 (1961) ("use of statements overheard from a soliloquy to prove the truth of those statements would involve hearsay").

[18] *See* State v. Asfour, 555 So. 2d 1280, 1282 (Fla. Dist. Ct. App. 1990) ("The child's out-of-court statement given to the police, whether it was videotaped or not, is hearsay. Merely videotaping the out-of-court statement did not transform it into an in-court statement").

out-of-court for hearsay purposes. The testimony is live, the jury sees the child *as the child testifies,* and the child is subject to contemporaneous cross-examination. Unlike the normal hearsay situation, the jury is not listening to a repetition of earlier statements.

Under traditional analysis, an out-of-court statement offered for the truth of the matter asserted is hearsay even though the declarant is present in court and subject to cross-examination after the out-of-court statement is repeated by a witness who overheard the statement. Indeed, the out-of-court statement is hearsay even when the declarant is the one who testifies at trial and repeats the declarant's *own* out-of-court statement. Thus, it is hearsay for the declarant to testify at trial and say, "At the time of the accident I said, 'You should have seen the red car go through the red light.'"

3. Statement Must Be Offered for Truth of Matter Asserted

An out-of-court statement is hearsay only if it is offered to prove the truth of the matter asserted. If the statement is offered for some other purpose, it is not hearsay.[19] The Advisory Committee note to Rule 801(a) explains that assertions "offered as a basis for inferring something other than the matter asserted" are not hearsay.[20] To illustrate this aspect of the hearsay definition, suppose a four-year-old child said, "Daddy's pee-pee was big and hard, and he put it inside me." If the prosecutor offers the child's out-of-court assertion to prove that the child's father penetrated the victim with his penis, the statement is hearsay. There is complete congruence between the out-of-court statement and what it is offered to prove. On the other hand, if the prosecutor offers the child's statement not to prove the truth of the matter asserted, but to prove the child's developmentally unusual knowledge of male sexual arousal, the statement is arguably not hearsay.

In many cases it is a simple matter to analyze an out-of-court statement and to compare it with the purpose for which it is offered. If the statement and the evidentiary purpose are the same, the conclusion is usually easy: the statement is hearsay. By contrast, if the statement and the purpose for which it is offered are not the same, the statement is usually—although not always—not hearsay. Cases in which a statement differs from the purpose for which it is offered raise some of the most interesting hearsay issues.

---

[19] *See* Drumbarger v. State, 716 P.2d 6, 10 (Alaska Ct. App. 1986) (child's out-of-court statement offered to prove that child knew meaning of the word *penis;* defendant had implied that child did not know meaning, thus placing child's knowledge in issue); State v. Emmons, 528 A.2d 1266, 1267 (Me. 1987) (child's statement not offered for truth but to show the timing and circumstances under which the complaint was made); *In re* Jean Marie W., 559 A.2d 625 (R.I. 1989) (four-year-old's verbal and nonverbal conduct admissible to show sexual knowledge far beyond child's years).

[20] Fed. R. Evid. 801(c) advisory committee's note.

When the declarant's words differ from the purpose for which they are offered, it is often necessary to look beyond the words, and to determine what the declarant "really said."[21] Park writes:

> Assertions made metaphorically, sarcastically, or in some other non-literal form, therefore, should be considered hearsay. For example, "Well, *I* never forged a kinsman's will!" would be hearsay when offered to show that the addressee was a forger, if the context indicated that the declarant intended accusation. Similarly, "The sky is on fire" would be hearsay if offered to show that the declarant had seen a sunset, and "Your hands are dirty" would be hearsay when offered as a metaphorical accusation of guilt. When use of the utterance in court requires that the trier assume the declarant intended to assert the proposition that the utterance is being offered to prove, then the utterance must be treated as hearsay, even if its surface form is different because the statement is sarcastic, metaphorical, or veiled. Similarly, "It will stop raining in an hour" is hearsay not only when used for the assertion that it will stop raining, but also when used to show that it is currently raining.[22]

As Park illustrates, hearsay analysis requires more than mechanical comparison of words and evidential purpose. One cannot take literally the proposition that an assertion is not hearsay if it departs in any way from the purpose for which it is offered.

§ 7.3 —Analyzing Out-of-Court Statements

For the proponent, analysis of out-of-court statements includes two steps. First, determine whether the statement is hearsay. Second, if the statement is hearsay, find an exception.

In many cases it is useful to develop a theory under which the statement is *not* hearsay. From the proponent's perspective, there are at least five advantages to characterizing out-of-court statements as nonhearsay:

1. Judges regard hearsay with suspicion. Persuading the court that the statement is not hearsay may reduce the court's suspicion and increase the likelihood the statement is admitted.
2. If the statement is not hearsay, it is not necessary to search for a hearsay exception.[23] By contrast, if the statement is hearsay, the proponent must find an exception, and the opponent can argue that the exception is inapplicable.

---

[21] *See* 4 Louisell & Mueller § 415, at 93–94.

[22] Park at 799, 800.

[23] *See In re* Jean Marie W., 559 A.2d 625, 629 (R.I. 1989) ("Statements not offered to prove the truth of what they assert are not hearsay and as such do not require the assistance of an exception to the hearsay rule in order to be admissible").

3. If the statement is hearsay within an exception, the proper foundation must be laid, and the opponent may find fault with the foundation.[24] If, however, the statement is not hearsay, it is not necessary to lay a hearsay foundation, thus eliminating a potential stumbling block to admissibility.
4. If the statement is not hearsay, it is not necessary to address the question whether hearsay is sufficient to support a finding of fact or verdict.[25]
5. It is useful to adopt the practice of analyzing out-of-court statements for the possibility they are not hearsay. This practice expands the practitioner's options for dealing with out-of-court statements.[26]

Characterizing an out-of-court statement as nonhearsay is not a sufficient reason for admission. The proponent must also establish the relevance of the out-of-court statement. As the California Supreme Court wrote in *People v. Armendariz*,[27] "A hearsay objection to an out-of-court statement may not be overruled simply by identifying a nonhearsay purpose for admitting the statement. The trial court must also find that the nonhearsay purpose is relevant to an issue in dispute."[28]

§ 7.4 Justification for Excluding Hearsay

Witnesses testify before the discerning eye of the jury, under oath, and subject to cross-examination—"the greatest legal engine ever invented for the discovery of truth."[29] The cross-examiner probes the witness's sincerity, memory, and opportunity to perceive and understand crucial events. Cross-examination, oath, and presence of the jury are the law's bulwarks against unreliable testimony.

Hearsay is excluded because the out-of-court statement is not made under oath before the jury, and because the hearsay declarant escapes the crucible of cross-examination.[30] The cross-examiner cannot test the out-of-court declarant's

---

[24] *See* State v. Dollinger, 20 Conn. App. 530, 568 A.2d 1058 (1990) (prosecutor did not lay foundation to admit statements as excited utterances).

[25] See § **7.47** for discussion of the sufficiency of hearsay to support a verdict or finding of fact.

[26] *See* Drumbarger v. State, 716 P.2d 6, 10 (Alaska Ct. App. 1986) (creative theory to admit child's out-of-court description of abuse as nonhearsay).

[27] 37 Cal. 3d 573, 693 P.2d 243, 209 Cal. Rptr. 664 (1984). *See also* People v. Bunyard, 45 Cal. 3d 1189, 1204, 756 P.2d 795, 249 Cal. Rptr. 71, 80 (1988).

[28] 37 Cal. 3d at 585, 693 P.2d at 250, 209 Cal. Rptr. at 671.

[29] 5 J. Wigmore, Evidence in Trials at Common Law § 1367, at 32 (1974) [hereinafter Wigmore].

[30] *See* State v. Allen, 157 Ariz. 165, 755 P.2d 1153, 1160 (1988) ("Obviously, a statement made out-of-court cannot be subjected to rigorous examination the same way that in-court statements can. It is simply not possible to cross-examine hearsay").

Park writes, "[T]he primary reason for excluding hearsay is that the trier of fact has no adequate basis for evaluating the declarant's credibility, because the declarant was not subject to cross-examination under oath in the trier's presence." Park at 785.

Louisell and Mueller write that "[c]ertain it is that [cross-examination] is universally considered the single most important justification for the hearsay doctrine, and the best

sincerity, memory, perception, and narration at the time the out-of-court statement is made.[31]

Although hearsay is sometimes less reliable than in-court testimony,[32] this is not always the case. The Supreme Court stated in *Bourjaily v. United States*[33] that "out-of-court statements are only *presumed* unreliable. The presumption may be rebutted by appropriate proof."[34] Many out-of-court statements have the ring of truth. Hearsay exceptions are created for hearsay statements that are sufficiently reliable to gain admission despite absence of the traditional mechanisms for ensuring the truth.

§ 7.5 Preliminary Rulings on Admissibility

The court decides whether a verbal utterance, a writing, or nonverbal conduct is hearsay.[35] In reaching this decision, the court determines whether the speaker, writer, or actor intended an assertion, that is, intended to make a statement of fact or opinion.[36] When verbal utterances and writings are offered, the court usually assumes that the speaker or writer intended an assertion. As Weinstein and Berger observe, "Most verbal conduct obviously constitutes a statement; *i.e.*, it is intended as a communication about some matter."[37] If the party offering a *verbal* utterance or a *writing* claims it is *not* hearsay because it is not an assertion, the offering party bears the burden of persuading the court that the declarant did not intend an assertion.

In contrast to verbal utterances and writings, when *nonverbal conduct* is offered as *non*hearsay on the theory that the nonverbal conduct is not assertive,

---

  available safeguard against the hearsay risks of ambiguity, lack of memory, and misperception." 4 Louisell & Mueller § 413, at 72. *See also id.* § 413, at 69–70 ("hearsay is excludable because it is generally less reliable than live testimony").

[31] For discussion of the hearsay dangers, see M. Graham, Handbook of Federal Evidence § 801.1, at 704 (3d ed. 1991) [hereinafter Graham]; 4 Louisell & Mueller § 413, at 69–70; McCormick § 245, at 726–27; 4 J. Weinstein & M. Berger, Weinstein's Evidence ¶ 800[01], at 800-11 (1987) [hereinafter Weinstein & Berger] ("The danger against which the hearsay rule is directed is that evidence which is untested by [oath, personal presence at trial, and cross-examination] will be unreliable because faults in the perception, memory and narration of the declarant will not be exposed").

[32] Idaho v. Wright, 110 S. Ct. 3139, 3149 (1990); United States v. Palacios, 32 M.J. 1047, 1050 (A.C.M.R. 1991) ("The purpose of the hearsay rule is to exclude unreliable evidence that cannot be tested in court").

[33] 483 U.S. 171 (1987).

[34] *Id.* at 179.

[35] *See* Fed. R. Evid. 104(a). *See also* 1 Louisell & Mueller § 29, at 196 ("Most preliminary questions which arise when an out-of-court statement is offered in evidence as against a hearsay objection are for the judge to resolve under Rule 104(a)").

[36] See § **7.2** for definition of hearsay.

[37] 4 Weinstein & Berger ¶ 801(a)[01], at 801-57.

who bears the burden of proof on whether the conduct was intended as an assertion? The answer depends on the nonverbal conduct at issue. Some nonverbal conduct is clearly intended as an assertion.[38] Suppose, for example, that a police officer asks a child to point to where she was hurt, and the child points to her genital area. The child's nonverbal conduct seems clearly to be an assertion. If the party offering the child's nonverbal conduct claims the conduct was nonassertive, the offering party bears the burden of persuading the court that the child did not intend an assertion of fact.[39]

Unlike the assertive pointing gesture described above, it is sometimes difficult to tell whether nonverbal conduct was intended as an assertion. Suppose, for example, that a five-year-old is engaged in unsupervised play with anatomical dolls. Without prompting from adults, and without accompanying words, the child places the dolls in sexually explicit positions. Is the child's nonverbal conduct with the dolls assertive, and thus potentially hearsay? If the prosecutor offers the child's conduct with the dolls on the theory that the child was deliberately describing sexual abuse, the prosecutor implicitly argues that the child's conduct was assertive. But what if the prosecutor argues that the child's conduct with the dolls was not intended as an assertion? Does the prosecutor bear the burden of persuading the court that the child did *not* intend an assertion? Or does defense counsel have the burden of persuading the court that the child's conduct *was* assertive and thus hearsay. The Advisory Committee note to Rule 801(a) states:

> When evidence of conduct is offered on the theory that it is not a statement, and hence not hearsay, a preliminary determination will be required to determine whether an assertion is intended. The rule is so worded as to place the burden upon the party claiming that the intention existed; ambiguous and doubtful cases will be resolved against him and in favor of admissibility.[40]

Regarding the child's nonverbal conduct with the dolls, the Advisory Committee note indicates that the burden is on defense counsel to persuade the court that the child intended an assertion. Failure to carry this burden results in a finding that the child's conduct was nonassertive and thus not hearsay.

Weinstein and Berger shed light on the question of which party has the burden of establishing that nonverbal conduct was intended as an assertion:

---

[38] See § 7.2.

[39] *See* 4 Weinstein & Berger ¶ 801(a)[02], at 801-64, where the authors write:

> Although the notes to Rule 801(a) indicate that the burden is ordinarily on the opponent of the evidence to demonstrate that the intention existed, this does not apply where the proffer on its face indicates that the conduct is being used in a way that assumes it was intended by the actor as the equivalent of a statement.

(footnote omitted).

[40] Fed. R. Evid. 801(a) advisory committee's note.

The trial judge will also have to make a preliminary determination on the question of intent. When evidence of conduct is offered, the definition of statement in Rule 801(a) requires that a finding be made whether an assertion was intended. . . . Again, the proponent of the evidence must make a minimum showing to indicate the conduct to be proven and the inference that the trier of fact is intended to draw from the conduct. If at this point the judge is satisfied that the conduct was not intended as an assertion of the matter sought to be proved, the burden of demonstrating the contrary shifts to the opponent of the evidence.[41]

Louisell and Mueller offer this insight on which party bears the burden of proof when nonverbal conduct is offered: "Where conduct is apparently non-assertive in character, the party seeking to exclude evidence of such conduct as hearsay bears the burden of proving to the satisfaction of the trial judge under Rule 104(a) that in fact the actor intended his conduct to be assertive."[42]

Children's nonverbal conduct plays an important role in child abuse litigation. Prosecutors offering such conduct as nonhearsay are sometimes in a position to argue that when the defense objects to such conduct as hearsay, the defense has the burden of persuading the court that the child intended an assertion. The child's conduct is admissible if the defense fails to carry its burden.

Once the court determines that a verbal utterance, a writing, or nonverbal conduct *is* hearsay, the next question is usually whether the hearsay meets the requirements of an exception. The trial court generally determines whether hearsay is within an exception.[43] If a particular exception requires a finding that the declarant is unavailable to testify at trial, the court determines unavailability.[44]

---

[41] 4 Weinstein & Berger ¶ 801(a)[02], at 801-67 (footnotes omitted). *See also id.* at 801-69 ("Rule 801(a), by casting the burden of proving an assertion on the objector, seeks to make relevant evidence, on which people act in their everyday lives, more readily available to the trier of fact").

[42] 4 Louisell & Mueller § 414, at 20 (Pocket Part 1990) (footnote omitted).

[43] *See* 1 Louisell & Mueller § 29, at 197, where the authors write:
 From experience and legal education, the trial judge is best situated to determine whether an out-of-court statement is afflicted with that unreliability or untrustworthiness which forms the basis for the ban of the hearsay rule—in other words, to determine whether the statement is or is not hearsay in the context in which it is offered, or to determine whether the statement (although hearsay) falls within one of the exceptions to the exclusionary policy which are set forth in Rules 803 and 804 . . . .

[44] 1 Louisell & Mueller § 29, at 200 ("When the proponent invokes an exception set forth in Rule 804, the judge must determine whether the declarant is unavailable as a witness").

§ 7.6 Verbal Assertions to Prove Other than Matter Asserted

The most common form of hearsay is a verbal assertion of fact or opinion.[45] "Most verbal conduct obviously constitutes a statement; *i.e.,* it is intended as a communication about some matter."[46] Suppose, for example, that a four-year-old makes the following out-of-court statement, "Daddy's pee-pee was big and hard, like a stick, and it hurt when he pushed it in my mouth, and white glue came out that tasted really yucky." If this powerful statement is offered to prove that the child's father had an erection and ejaculated in the child's mouth, the statement is hearsay. The statement is offered for the truth of the matter asserted.

If the child's statement meets the requirements of an exception to the hearsay rule, the statement may be admitted for the truth of the matter asserted. If the statement does not fall within an exception, it may nevertheless be admissible if the statement is relevant for some purpose *other than* the truth of the matter asserted.[47] The child's statement demonstrates knowledge of sexual matters that one would not expect in a four-year-old. The child's developmentally unusual sexual knowledge is circumstantial evidence of sexual abuse. When the statement is offered to prove sexual knowledge, it is not offered for the truth of the matter asserted, and is not hearsay. The disadvantage of offering the child's statement for this nonhearsay purpose is that the jury is not permitted to consider the statement for its truth, and the court will instruct the jury accordingly. Nevertheless, the prosecutor has a great need for the jury to hear the child's words, and, so long as the jury hears the statement, the prosecutor will settle for limited evidentiary value.

The Rhode Island Supreme Court's decision in *In re Jean Marie W.*[48] provides a good illustration of the nonhearsay use of children's out-of-court statements. In this termination of parental rights case, the four-year-old child was sexually abused while in her mother's custody. After the child was removed from the

---

[45] *See* United States v. Nick, 604 F.2d 1199, 1201–02 (9th Cir. 1979) (three-year-old's statements to physician describing sexual assault were hearsay when doctor repeated statements from the stand, although statements fell within exception for diagnosis or treatment, Fed. R. Evid. 803(4)); Alston v. United States, 462 A.2d 1122 (D.C. 1983) (four-year-old's description of sexual abuse to adults was hearsay not within an exception).

[46] 4 Weinstein & Berger ¶ 801(1)[01], at 801-57. *See* Fed. R. Evid 801(a) advisory committee's note ("It can scarcely be doubted that an assertion made in words is intended by the declarant to be an assertion. Hence verbal assertions readily fall into the category of 'statement'").

[47] *See* Drumbarger v. State, 716 P.2d 6, 10 (Alaska Ct. App. 1986) (child's statement to police officer admissible for nonhearsay purpose of proving that child knew what a penis was; defendant implied child did not know, thus placing her knowledge in issue); State v. Emmons, 528 A.2d 1266 (Me. 1987) (child's statement offered to show timing and circumstances in which complaint was made; not hearsay for this purpose); *In re* Jean Marie W., 559 A.2d 625 (R.I. 1989).

[48] 559 A.2d 625 (R.I. 1989).

mother's home, the child was interviewed with anatomical dolls. During one interview the child engaged the dolls "in various oral, anal, and vaginal sex acts, involving penile and digital penetration . . . ."[49] During a second interview, the child again placed the dolls in sexual positions and used words indicating unusual familiarity with sexual terms and acts.

At the hearing on the petition to terminate the mother's parental rights, the state offered expert testimony from the professionals who observed the child's interaction with the dolls. The mother raised a hearsay objection, which was overruled, and the trial court terminated the mother's parental rights. On appeal, the mother's counsel renewed the hearsay objection. The Rhode Island Supreme Court affirmed the trial court, writing:

> Statements not offered to prove the truth of what they assert are not hearsay and as such do not require the assistance of an exception to the hearsay rule in order to be admissible. Accordingly we find that expert testimony to the verbal and nonverbal conduct of children made during the course of their play with anatomically correct dolls is admissible for nonhearsay purposes if offered to prove something other than the truth of the matter asserted thereby. In this case [the child's] actions were not offered to prove that she was actually molested. Rather her verbal and nonverbal conduct was offered to show that she had explicit sexual knowledge—involving anal, oral, and vaginal sexual intercourse—far in advance of the knowledge of a normal four-year-old. Therefore, we find that the Family Court justice properly admitted the testimony of these experts as nonhearsay.[50]

Other nonhearsay uses of children's out-of-court statements include establishing the timing and circumstances in which a complaint of abuse was made,[51]

---

[49] *Id.* at 628.

[50] *Id.* at 629 (citations omitted).

[51] State v. Emmons, 528 A.2d 1266 (Me. 1987). In *Emmons* the defendant was convicted of child sexual abuse. During cross-examination of the child and the investigating officer, the defendant attempted to "elicit testimony that the charges had been induced by a dream of the child and timed to prevent him from obtaining custody of his own children." *Id.* at 1266. In response to this cross-examination, the state offered the testimony of two of the child's aunts. The court wrote:

> Each aunt testified she had become concerned about the well being of the child because each had witnessed an occasion when the child had awakened from an apparent nightmare, screaming and crying. One aunt testified that the child "kept saying will you get away from me, will you leave me alone." As a result of the aunt's concern, the alleged misconduct was revealed in late 1984. [Defendant] claims the testimony of the child's aunts was inadmissible hearsay within the meaning of M.R.Evid. 801(c). We disagree. The testimony of the aunts did not recite any detail of the child's complaints against [Defendant]. It was offered not as proof of any facts asserted, "but to demonstrate the timing and circumstances under which a complaint was made," and was not hearsay within the meaning of M.R.Evid. 801(c).

Id. at 1267.

§ 7.7 WRITTEN AND DRAWN ASSERTIONS

establishing how social workers became involved in a case and why an investigation was commenced,[52] and for additional purposes.[53]

In some child sexual abuse cases the prosecutor must prove that the defendant acted with the intent to gratify sexual desire. Proof of such intent is discussed in **Chapter 6**. In many cases, the defendant's words at the time of the abuse are probative of intent to arouse or gratify sexual desire.[54] In *Montgomery v. State*,[55] for example, the defendant was charged with sexually abusing his two young daughters "with the intent to arouse and gratify the sexual desire of" the defendant.[56] The defendant said to the victims, "You and I were meant for each other," "Give me your hot love," and "Press my hot lips."[57] Defendant's words are admissible not for the truth of the matter asserted, but as evidence of sexual intent. Even if the words are hearsay, they are admissible under the state of mind exception[58] or as party admissions.[59]

§ 7.7 Written and Drawn Assertions to Prove Other than Matter Asserted

A written statement is hearsay when offered to prove the truth of its contents.[60] Thus, a child's diary in which the child describes abuse is hearsay when offered

---

[52] *See* Altmeyer v. State, 519 N.E.2d 138 (Ind. 1988). In *Altmeyer* "a social worker from the welfare department was permitted to testify about what [two children] had told her concerning the attacks." *Id.* at 142. The defendant raised a hearsay objection. The Indiana Supreme Court rejected the defendant's hearsay argument, writing:

> The State offered the testimony not for truth of the matters asserted, but to show how the social worker became involved in the cases and why the investigation began. . . .
>
> This court has upheld admission of testimony which, although containing out-of-court statements by third parties, was introduced primarily to explain why a particular course of action had been taken. Because the testimony is not offered to prove the truth of the matter stated by the third party, it is admissible.

Id. at 142–43.

[53] See §§ **7.10–7.12** for discussion of implied assertions.

[54] *See* State v. Basker, 468 N.W.2d 413, 416–17 (S.D. 1991) (defendant's specific intent to arouse sexual desire established by defendant's acts and words when fondling children; court did not address hearsay issue).

[55] 810 S.W.2d 372 (Tex. Crim. App. 1990).

[56] *Id.* at 380.

[57] *Id.* at 375.

[58] Fed. R. Evid. 803(3).

[59] Fed. R. Evid. 801(d)(2)(A). When offered as party admissions, defendant's words are technically not hearsay because party admissions are defined as nonhearsay.

[60] Of course, the author of the writing must intend an assertion. Nonassertive writings and artwork are not hearsay.

to prove the truth of the written assertion.[61] Similarly, a picture drawn by a child is hearsay when the picture is drawn with assertive intent and offered for the truth of the matter asserted.[62]

A child's assertive writing or artwork may be admissible as nonhearsay if the writing or artwork is relevant for some purpose other than the truth of the matter asserted.[63] For example, if a preschool-age child draws an erect penis with ejaculate coming out, the picture may be offered to establish the child's developmentally unusual knowledge of sex acts. The drawing is not offered for the truth of the matter asserted, and is not hearsay. A child's diary may contain statements evidencing the child's fear or dislike of an individual. The diary may be admissible on a nonhearsay theory as circumstantial evidence of the child's state of mind regarding the individual. Even if the diary entries are offered for the truth of the matter asserted, they may fall within the state of mind exception.[64]

A picture drawn while the child is testifying at trial is not hearsay. The drawing may be assertive, but it is not out-of-court.

---

[61] *See* United States v. Sheets, 125 F.R.D. 172, 173 (D. Utah 1989) (court pointed out that a diary may not be hearsay if it is offered for something other than the truth, such as evidence of another person's knowledge).

[62] Kenney v. Lewis Revels Rare Coins, Inc., 741 F.2d 378, 383 (11th Cir. 1984) (diagram of accident drawn by police officer was hearsay); State v. Randolph, 190 Conn. 576, 462 A.2d 1011, 1017 (1983) (sketch is hearsay if introduced to establish the truth of what is depicted); Timsah v. General Motors Corp., 225 Kan. 305, 591 P.2d 154, 159–62 (1979); *In re* Alba, 185 Ill. App. 3d 286, 540 N.E.2d 1116 (1989) (child drew picture in response to request that she depict where her father put his "favorite part"; picture was hearsay because it was offered for the truth); Commonwealth v. Rothlisberger, 197 Pa. Super. 451, 178 A.2d 853, 854–55 (1962) (defendants found guilty of fornication and assault and battery after prosecutrix identified defendants at trial; state offered in evidence "pen and ink sketches of two men which had been prepared by a commercial artist upon the request of the prosecutrix four days after the attack; court held sketches were hearsay not within an exception).

[63] *See* 4 Weinstein & Berger ¶ 801(c)[01], at 801-70 to 801-71, where the authors write:

A second major category of statements is excluded from the scope of the hearsay rule by the definition of hearsay in subdivision (c) of Rule 801, which excludes assertive conduct when it is offered as a basis for inferring something other than the matter asserted. . . .

Rule 801 is in accord with the definitions suggested by most scholars in including within the hearsay concept only those statements offered to prove the truth of the matter asserted. It is only in this situation that the trier of fact is faced with the dangers presented by the difficulty of evaluating the credibility an absent declarant.

(footnotes omitted).

See also People v. Arbo, 213 Ill. App. 3d 828, 572 N.E.2d 417 (1991) ("Testimony about an out-of-court writing, which is used for a purpose other than to prove the truth of the matter asserted in the writing, is not hearsay"; not hearsay to state that certain receipts were missing); Crane v. State, 786 S.W.2d 338, 352 (Tex. Crim. App. 1990) ("It is well established that an extra-judicial statement or writing offered for the purpose of showing what was said rather than for the truth of the matter stated therein does not constitute hearsay").

[64] Fed. R. Evid. 803(3). See §§ **7.32–7.34**.

§ 7.8 Nonverbal Assertions to Prove Other than Matter Asserted

Nonverbal conduct intended as an assertion is hearsay when offered to prove the matter asserted.[65] A few examples illustrate the point. A child is asked, "Did the car go through the red light?" The child nods affirmatively. This nonverbal assertion is hearsay when offered to prove that the car passed through the red light. A physician examining a child for possible sexual abuse says, "Did anyone touch you down in the genital area?" The child nods her head up and down. Her nonverbal conduct is the equivalent of words, and is hearsay when offered to prove that she was touched.[66] Finally, a child is being interviewed with the aid of anatomical dolls. The interviewer says, "Can you use the dolls to show what happened?" In response, the child places the dolls in sexually explicit positions. The child's nonverbal conduct with the dolls is assertive, and is hearsay when offered for the truth of the matter asserted.[67] In each of these examples, the child's nonverbal conduct was intended by the child as an assertion.

---

[65] *See* Fed. R. Evid. 801(a)(2), defining an assertion to include "nonverbal conduct of a person, if it is intended by the person as an assertion." *See also* Fed. R. Evid. 801(a) advisory committee's note ("Some nonverbal conduct, such as the act of pointing to identify a suspect in a lineup, is clearly the equivalent of words, assertive in nature, and to be regarded as a statement"); 4 Louisell & Mueller § 414, at 81 ("Often conduct intended as an assertion is easily recognized. A nod or shake of the head, a shrug of the shoulders, a pointing gesture—these are simply word substitutes, entirely assertive in nature, interchangeable with written or spoken verbal expression, part and parcel of the process of communication"); McCormick § 250, at 736 ("nonverbal conduct may unmistakenly be just as assertive in nature as though expressed in words"); 4 Weinstein & Berger ¶ 801(a)[01], at 801-57 ("It has never been doubted that some nonverbal conduct is equivalent to a verbal statement in its intent to communicate information").

See also State v. Wagner, 30 Ohio App. 3d 261, 508 N.E.2d 164, 166 (1986) (three-year-old's play with anatomical dolls was assertive nonverbal conduct).

[66] *See* State v. Maldonado, 13 Conn. App. 368, 536 A.2d 600, 601–02 (1988) (three-year-old shook head in response to questions; the child's nonverbal assertions were hearsay); State v. Bawdon, 386 N.W.2d 484, 487 (S.D. 1986) (six-year-old was examined by a physician who asked, "Did anyone touch you down there in the genital area?" Child nodded affirmatively; trial court ruled child's conduct was not hearsay. Supreme Court held child's nonverbal conduct was assertive and thus hearsay).

[67] United States v. Ellis, 935 F.2d 385 (1st Cir.), *cert. denied,* 112 S. Ct. 201 (1991) (two-year-old half-sister of victim's play with anatomical dolls admissible under residual exception); People v. Bowers, 801 P.2d 511, 523 (Colo. 1990) (child's use of anatomical dolls during interviews was in response to questions and was hearsay); State v. Wagner, 30 Ohio App. 3d 261, 508 N.E.2d 164, 166 (1986) (police officer interviewed three-year-old; officer asked child to use dolls to demonstrate what happened; child's demonstration of what happened was assertive nonverbal conduct); State v. Mayfield, 302 Or. 631, 733 P.2d 438, 446 (1987) (assertive play with anatomical dolls is hearsay).

A child's assertive nonverbal conduct is not hearsay when it is offered to prove something other than the truth of the matter asserted.[68] Thus, in *M.E. v. M.E.E.*,[69] anatomical dolls were used by social workers to help determine whether seven- and three-year-old siblings were sexually abused. The children's conduct with the dolls indicated "sexual knowledge far beyond that of normal seven and three year olds."[70] At the trial of this parental rights termination case, the social workers described what the children did with the dolls. The court of appeals approved, writing:

> From this showing of unusually superior sexual knowledge, the court inferred that some form of sexual abuse had occurred, but did not necessarily determine who had committed such abuse. The testimony was not used to prove the truth of the matters asserted, hence the testimony is not hearsay.[71]

A similar result was achieved in *In re Jean Marie W.*,[72] another termination of parental rights case. The four-year-old child was observed interacting with anatomical dolls.[73] The child "spontaneously positioned the dolls in various sexually explicit positions while making comments such as 'they are humping' and 'most of the time he sticks it in the mouth.'"[74] At trial, the child's mother raised a hearsay objection when the professionals who had observed the child described the child's conduct with the dolls. The trial court overruled the objection and admitted the description to prove the child's explicit sexual knowledge. The Rhode Island Supreme Court affirmed, writing:

> In this case [the child's] actions were not offered to prove that she was actually molested. Rather her verbal and nonverbal conduct was offered to show that she had explicit sexual knowledge—involving anal, oral, and vaginal sexual intercourse—far in advance of the knowledge of a normal four-year-old. Therefore, we find that the Family Court justice properly admitted the testimony of these experts as nonhearsay.[75]

---

[68] In cases involving children's play with dolls and other toys, it is important to begin by asking whether the child's use of the toys is assertive. If the child was not making an assertion, then the child's behavior is not hearsay. Only when the conclusion is reached that the behavior was indeed assertive is it necessary to offer the theory that the assertive behavior is offered to prove something other than the truth of the matter asserted.

[69] 715 S.W.2d 572 (Mo. Ct. App. 1986).

[70] *Id.* at 574.

[71] *Id.* at 575.

[72] 559 A.2d 625 (R.I. 1989).

[73] The case involved two children, one age four and the other age one. The text refers only to the four-year-old.

[74] 559 A.2d at 629.

[75] *Id.* at 629.

§ 7.9 Silence or Inaction as Assertion

Silence or inaction intended as an assertion is hearsay when offered to establish the matter asserted.[76] For example, if X and Y intend to communicate secretly concerning whether an event transpired, they may agree that X will remain silent if the event occurred. When X and Y meet, X's silence is an assertion, and testimony by a third person that X was silent is hearsay when offered to prove the occurrence of the event.

In child abuse litigation, the hearsay implications of silence arise primarily in two situations. First, a person accused of sexual abuse may argue that a child's silence following the alleged event amounts to an assertion that nothing happened. This argument is addressed in **§ 7.12** discussing implied assertions. Second, under proper circumstances, the defendant's silence may constitute an admission.

§ 7.10 Implied Assertions

Few aspects of hearsay cause more confusion than implied assertions.[77] The following two subsections discuss (1) verbal and written implied assertions, and (2) assertions implied from conduct. The overlap is apparent between these sections and **§§ 7.6** through **7.8**. Indeed, the entire discussion of implied assertions could be incorporated into those sections. Although it is tempting to forgo a separate discussion on implied assertions, the temptation is resisted because courts and commentators have traditionally treated implied assertions as a distinct area of law. Moreover, treatment of implied assertions in a single place fosters coherent discussion of this complex subject.

§ 7.11 —Verbal and Written Implied Assertions

The classic implied assertion case is *Wright v. Tatham,*[78] which involved a contest over the will of an English gentleman named John Marsden. In his will, Marsden left his estate to his steward, Wright. Marsden's heir at law, Tatham, brought an action challenging Marsden's testamentary capacity. In an effort to prove that Marsden was competent to make a will, the devisee, Wright,

---

[76] *See* McCormick § 250, at 742–43.

[77] For analysis of the implied assertion doctrine, see Falknor, *The "Hear-Say" Rule as a "See-Do" Rule: Evidence of Conduct,* 33 Rocky Mtn. L. Rev. 133 (1961); Falknor, *Silence as Hearsay,* 89 U. Pa. L. Rev. 194 (1940); Park; Seidelson, *Implied Assertions and Federal Rule of Evidence 801: A Quandary for Federal Courts,* 24 Duq. L. Rev. 741 (1986).

[78] 7 Adolph. & E. 313, 112 Eng. Rep. 488 (Ex. Ch. 1837) (first appeal); 5 Cl. & Fin. 670, 47 Rev. Rep. 136 (H.L. 1838) (second appeal).

introduced letters addressed to Marsden.[79] Two letters were from Marsden's relative in America. The first letter described the voyage to America and the deplorable conditions found upon arrival. The second letter from the relative discussed mutual acquaintances. In addition to the letters from America, Wright offered a letter from a local clergyman requesting Marsden to clear up outstanding business matters with the church. Wright also offered a letter from another cleric, in which the cleric expressed appreciation for favors bestowed by Marsden.

The letters were offered to prove that people who knew Marsden wrote to him as if he were competent. From the letters it was possible to infer the writers' belief that Marsden was competent. Finally, from the writers' belief in Marsden's competence it was possible to infer that Marsden was, in fact, competent.

The letters were objected to as hearsay. The proponent of the letters argued that the missives were not hearsay because they were not offered for the truth of the matters asserted in the letters. Thus, the letters from the relative in America were not offered to prove facts about the voyage or conditions in America. Similarly, the letter from the first cleric was not offered to prove matters of business between Marsden and the church, and the letter from the second cleric was not offered to prove Marsden's kindness. Rather, the letters were offered to prove the writers' belief that Marsden was sane, and for the inference from that belief that Marsden was sane. The opponent argued that the letters were hearsay because they relied for their probative value on the credibility of the writers, all of whom were unavailable at the time of trial, and not subject to cross-examination.[80] The court held the letters were hearsay.

Note that *Wright v. Tatham* did not alter the time-honored rule that verbal and written statements are hearsay when offered to prove the truth of the matter asserted. The significance of *Wright v. Tatham* is that it *expanded* the hearsay doctrine by incorporating within hearsay some verbal or written statements that are *not* offered for the truth of the matter asserted.

An out-of-court verbal or written assertion is an implied assertion when:

1. The assertion is *not* offered to prove the literal truth of the words spoken or written,

2. The assertion *is* offered to prove the declarant's belief, emotion, or knowledge about some matter not expressly articulated in the assertion, and

---

[79] There was considerable conflicting evidence about Marsden's mental state. The letters were but a small part of the evidence.

[80] Park writes that "*Wright v. Tatham* also illustrates how implied assertions derived from *verbal* conduct can involve hearsay dangers. The use of the letters to Marsden requires an inference from the declarant's statement to the declarant's belief to the truth of the belief, so use involves reliance on the declarant's credibility." Park at 791 (footnote omitted).

§ 7.11   IMPLIED VERBAL AND WRITTEN   99

3. The trier of fact is asked to *draw an inference* of relevant fact from the declarant's belief, emotion, or knowledge.[81]

Suppose, for example, that a child is being interviewed about possible sexual abuse at a day care center. When asked a general question about one of the teachers, the child says, "He's really mean." The child's assertion is an implied assertion if: (1) the assertion is *not* offered to prove that the teacher is mean, and (2) the assertion *is* offered to prove the child's fear or dislike of the teacher, and (3) the proponent offers the child's utterance to prove that the teacher did something bad to the child.

Are verbal and written implied assertions hearsay under the Federal Rules of Evidence? Recall that Rule 801(c) defines hearsay as an out-of-court statement "offered in evidence to prove the truth of the matter asserted."[82] Since, by definition, an implied assertion is *not* offered for the literal truth of the matter asserted, an argument can be made that verbal and written implied assertions are not hearsay under the rules. This argument finds support in the Advisory Committee note to Rule 801.[83] The note states that "verbal conduct which is assertive but offered as a basis for inferring something other than the matter asserted [is] excluded from the definition of hearsay by the language of" Rule 801(c).[84] The chief reason for excluding implied assertions from hearsay is that the hearsay

---

[81] Park observes, "An utterance is being used to prove an implied assertion when it depends for value on the credibility of the declarant, but is not being offered to prove the truth of the matter asserted." Park at 783 (footnote omitted). Park goes on:

> To say that an utterance is offered as an "implied assertion" is not to say that the declarant intended to insinuate the fact the proponent is trying to prove. It merely means that the trier is being asked to infer that fact from the declarant's utterance. The utterance containing the implied assertion does not directly assert the proposition it is offered to prove. The trier must infer the proposition by using the utterance as indirect evidence of a belief or state of mind of the declarant. Implied assertions are hearsay under the declarant definition because they depend for value on the declarant's credibility.

Id. at 788 (footnotes omitted).

[82] Fed. R. Evid. 801(c).

[83] *See* Park at 794:

> The Federal rules also deal, perhaps less clearly, with the hearsay status of implied assertions derived from verbal conduct. The Advisory Committee's Note describes two categories of verbal conduct that are excluded from the definition of hearsay by Rule 801(c). These two categories are "nonassertive verbal conduct" and "verbal conduct which is assertive but offered as a basis for inferring something other than the matter asserted."

(footnotes omitted).

[84] Fed. R. Evid. 801(a). *See also* McCormick § 250, at 740; Park at 801 (referring to the Advisory Committee note, Park writes, "Respect for language conventions and for the intent of the Advisory Committee both point toward accepting the proposition that, under the Federal Rules, some verbal conduct will be accepted as nonhearsay even though it depends for value on the credibility of the declarant") (footnote omitted).

risks are often low with implied assertions.[85] The risks of insincerity, misperception, faulty narration, and memory lapse are at their height when assertions are offered for the truth of the matter asserted. By contrast, the hearsay risks—particularly the risk of insincerity—may be lower when an assertion is offered not to prove what the declarant intended to assert, but to prove something else, which the declarant probably was not consciously thinking about at the time.[86] There is authority that verbal and written implied assertions are not hearsay under the Federal Rules of Evidence.[87]

Despite the seemingly clear language of Rule 801(c), several courts hold that assertions implied from verbal and written conduct can be hearsay under the federal rules.[88] These courts emphasize that hearsay risks sometimes accompany implied assertions.[89] With many implied assertions, the trier of fact must rely on the declarant's credibility. Just as assertions offered for the truth are excluded because of the opponent's inability to test credibility through cross-examination, so the argument goes, implied assertions should be excluded because the opponent lacks an opportunity to test the declarant's memory, sincerity, perception, and narration.

The likelihood a court will treat an implied assertion as hearsay turns largely on the extent to which the assertion raises hearsay risks. The more the probative value of the implied assertion depends on the declarant's credibility, the higher the hearsay risks. To determine the extent to which an implied assertion depends on the declarant's credibility, evaluate the degree of similarity between the matter sought to be proved and the declarant's communicative intent.[90] Suppose, for example, that a four-year-old picks up an anatomical doll and says, "He wiggles his pee-pee up and down until white stuff comes out." Obviously, the prosecutor does not offer the child's statement to prove that the *doll* masturbates. Suppose the statement is offered to prove that the child possesses developmentally unusual knowledge of sexual acts, and that from this knowledge it is

---

[85] *See* Fed. R. Evid. 801 advisory committee's note. *See also* McCormick § 250, at 740; Park at 791 ("One can argue that implied assertions derived from verbal conduct should be classified as nonhearsay because dangers of insincerity are reduced by the indirect nature of the inference drawn") (footnote omitted); 4 Weinstein & Berger ¶ 801(a)]01], at 801-61 to 801-62.

[86] For the argument that assertions implied from verbal utterances should be hearsay, see Graham, *"Stickperson Hearsay": A Simplified Approach to Understanding the Rule Against Hearsay*, 1982 U. Ill. L. Rev. 887.

[87] *See* United States v. Groce, 682 F.2d 1359 (11th Cir. 1982); United States v. Zenni, 492 F. Supp. 464 (E.D. Ky. 1980); Park at 810.

[88] *See* Lyle v. Koehler, 720 F.2d 426 (6th Cir. 1983); United States v. Reynolds, 715 F.2d 99 (3d Cir. 1983); Park v. Huff, 493 F.2d 923 (1974), *withdrawn on other grounds,* 506 F.2d 849 (5th Cir.) (en banc), *cert. denied,* 423 U.S. 824 (1975); United States v. Pacelli, 491 F.2d 1108 (2d Cir.), *cert. denied,* 419 U.S. 826 (1974); Park at 803.

[89] The hearsay risks are insincerity, memory lapse, misperception, and ambiguity of narration. See § **7.4** for discussion of the four risks of hearsay.

[90] *See* Park at 801.

possible to infer sexual abuse. Offered for this purpose, the statement could be characterized as an implied assertion. First, the statement is *not* offered for the literal truth of the matter asserted (the doll masturbates). Second, the statement *is* offered to prove the child's sexual knowledge. Third, the trier of fact is asked to infer a relevant fact—sexual abuse—from the child's sexual knowledge.

Should the child's statement about the doll be characterized as hearsay? Compare the degree of similarity between the matter sought to be proved—sexual abuse—and the child's communicative intent. The child may have intended to assert that a *doll* masturbates to ejaculation. The child's statement is offered to prove sexual abuse. There is considerable similarity between the child's communicative intent and the matter sought to be proved. Moreover, the child may actually have intended to assert that the *defendant* masturbates, in which case the child's statement coincides precisely with the matter sought to be proved. Whatever the child intended to assert, the jury is likely to equate the child's communicative intent with the matter sought to be proved. Thus, an argument can be made that the child's statement should be characterized as hearsay.

On the other hand, assuming the child's statement referred to the doll, then the argument is strong that the statement is not offered for the literal truth of the matter asserted, and if the language of Rule 801(c) is to be respected, the child's statement is not hearsay.[91] The proponent of the child's statement can point out that there is a real distinction between the express assertion—a doll masturbated—and the purpose for which the assertion is offered, that is, proof of developmentally inappropriate sexual knowledge. If the jury is properly instructed regarding the limited evidentiary value of the statement, the child's utterance is admissible for a nonhearsay purpose.[92] The proponent may argue that the proper approach to implied assertions is to treat them as nonhearsay and to resort to Rule 403 to determine whether admission will confuse the jury or unfairly prejudice the defendant.

§ 7.12 —Assertions Implied from Conduct

In some cases conduct is the source of an implied assertion. The classic illustration is from *Wright v. Tatham*.[93] A sailing ship was lost at sea. The litigated issue is whether the ship was seaworthy. The party attempting to prove seaworthiness offers a witness who observed the ship's captain inspect the vessel before setting sail with his family and crew. Testimony describing the captain's

---

[91] The Advisory Committee note to Rule 801(a) reinforces the argument that verbal implied assertions are not hearsay.

[92] The principle of multiple admissibility articulated in Rule 105 of the Federal Rules of Evidence clearly contemplates receipt of evidence that is admissible for one purpose but not another.

[93] The famous sea captain example was suggested by the court as a hypothetical case.

inspection is offered to prove the captain's belief that the ship was seaworthy, and from this belief the inference is drawn that the ship was in fact seaworthy. The court in *Wright v. Tatham* suggested the sea captain's conduct would be hearsay when offered to prove seaworthiness because the inference from the captain's conduct to the captain's belief in the ship's seaworthiness raised hearsay risks.[94] Perhaps the captain's perception during the inspection was defective. Perhaps the captain had doubts about the ship's seaworthiness but was willing to take a risk. Perhaps the inspection was inadequate. The point is that it would be useful to cross-examine the captain, who went down with his ship. Since the inference from the captain's conduct to his belief raises hearsay risks, the court concluded the conduct was hearsay.

Another oft-cited example of an assertion implied from conduct is testimony that a pedestrian raised an umbrella, offered to prove it was raining. The chain of inferences is: from the conduct of raising the umbrella one infers that the pedestrian believed it was raining. From this intermediate inference, one infers that it was raining. Arguably, the pedestrian's conduct is hearsay because the inference to the pedestrian's belief that it was raining raises the hearsay dangers of misperception and miscommunication. Perhaps is was not raining. Perhaps the pedestrian raised the umbrella to create shade from the blazing sun. The argument against hearsay is stronger. It seems unlikely the pedestrian was making an assertion of any kind. Even if the pedestrian thought, "Ah, it is raining. I shall raise my umbrella," the hearsay risks are so small that the conduct, which is clearly relevant, should not be lost to the hearsay rule.

A child abuse example is useful. A young child is engaged in unsupervised play with dolls.[95] Without accompanying words, the child picks up an adult doll and uses it to beat a child doll. From this conduct one can infer the child's belief or knowledge that adults beat children. Based on the child's belief or knowledge, a second inference can be drawn to the fact that the child witnessed or experienced abuse. Is the child's nonverbal conduct hearsay? The answer turns on whether the child intended the nonverbal conduct to be an assertion. Certainly, cross-examination is desirable to discover the child's intent regarding the dolls. Cross-examination might elicit relatively benign explanations for the child's behavior. Perhaps the child saw physical violence on

---

[94] Park writes:

> In favor of treating nonverbal conduct offered to show the actor's belief as hearsay, one can argue that the risks are similar to those present when verbal hearsay is received. When using a ship captain's conduct to infer seaworthiness, the trier of fact must rely on the captain's memory and perception to reach the desired inference. Moreover, absent cross-examination, the trier might infer the wrong belief from the conduct. For example, the trier might infer that the captain boarded the ship believing it safe when in fact the captain believed the ship to be dangerous but was willing to take a chance in order to escape.

Park at 790 (footnote omitted).

[95] *See In re* Penelope B., 104 Wash. 2d 643, 709 P.2d 1185 (1985).

television or at a neighbor's house. Thus, offering the child's conduct with the dolls implicates the hearsay risks. Moreover, the child may actually be making an express assertion, which clearly is hearsay if offered for the truth of the matter asserted.

The argument that the child's nonverbal conduct with the dolls is not hearsay rests on the language of Rule 801(a)(2) of the Federal Rules of Evidence, which includes in the definition of a statement "nonverbal conduct of a person, *if it is intended by the person as an assertion.*"[96] The federal rules exclude assertions *implied* from nonverbal conduct from the definition of hearsay. Park writes that "[t]he Advisory Committee drafted Rule 801 to exclude nonassertive nonverbal conduct from the definition of hearsay."[97] The Advisory Committee note states:

> [V]erbal assertions readily fall into the category of "statement." Whether nonverbal conduct should be regarded as a statement for purposes of defining hearsay requires further consideration. Some nonverbal conduct, such as the act of pointing to identify a suspect in a lineup, is clearly the equivalent of words, assertive in nature, and to be regarded as a statement. Other nonverbal conduct, however, may be offered as evidence that the person acted as he did because of his belief in the existence of the condition sought to be proved, from which belief the existence of the condition may be inferred. This sequence is, arguably, in effect an assertion of the existence of the condition and hence properly includable within the hearsay concept. . . . Admittedly evidence of this character is untested with respect to the perception, memory, and narration (or their equivalents) of the actor, but the Advisory Committee is of the view that these dangers are minimal in the absence of an intent to assert and do not justify the loss of the evidence on hearsay grounds. No class of evidence is free of the possibility of fabrication, but the likelihood is less with nonverbal than with assertive verbal conduct. The situations giving rise to the nonverbal conduct are such as virtually to eliminate questions of sincerity. Motivation, the nature of the conduct, and the presence or absence of reliance will bear heavily upon the weight to be given the evidence.[98]

Weinstein and Berger explain the reasons for treating nonassertive conduct as nonhearsay:

> Two principal arguments were usually expressed for removing implied assertions from the scope of the hearsay rule. First, when a person acts in a way consistent with a belief but without intending by his act to communicate that belief, one of the principal reasons for the hearsay rule—to exclude declarations whose veracity cannot be tested by cross-examination—does not apply, because the declarant's sincerity is not then involved. In the second place, the underlying belief is in some cases self-verifying:

---

[96] Fed. R. Evid. 801(a)(2) (emphasis added).
[97] Park at 793 (footnote omitted).
[98] Fed. R. Evid. 801(a) advisory committee's note.

There is frequently a guarantee of the trustworthiness of the inference to be drawn . . . because the actor has based his actions on the correctness of his belief, i.e., his actions speak louder than words.

The Advisory Committee agreed with this analysis. Subdivision (a)(2) of Rule 801 removes implied assertions from the definition of statement and consequently from the operation of the hearsay rule.[99]

Referring again to the child's act of beating one doll with another, if the child's conduct with the dolls was not intended as an assertion, any assertion implied from the conduct is not hearsay. This leaves the opponent with the argument that the child intended an assertion. The problem with this argument is that it is difficult to tell whether the child intended to make an assertion. In such cases, the burden of proof is on the opponent to establish that an assertion was intended. Doubtful and ambiguous cases are resolved against the opponent and in favor of admissibility.[100]

In sexual abuse prosecutions, a defendant who denies that abuse occurred may offer evidence that the child did not report the abuse for a considerable period of time. The defense theory is that if abuse occurred, the child would have told someone quickly. Silence following the alleged abuse undermines the allegation. Could the prosecutor argue that the defense theory involves an implied assertion, and is hearsay? The prosecutor's argument proceeds as follows: From the child's silence one infers the child's belief that sexual abuse did not occur, and from the child's belief one infers the fact that abuse did not occur. The prosecutor's theory should be rejected. The child's silence was not an assertion and therefore not hearsay. Rule 801(a)(2) of the Federal Rules of Evidence states that nonverbal conduct, including silence, is assertive only if the declarant intended an assertion. There is no evidence the child's silence was the equivalent of an assertion that nothing happened.[101] A more productive way to take the sting out of delayed reporting is to have the child explain the reasons for delay,[102] or to offer expert testimony that many sexually abused children delay reporting abuse.[103]

§ 7.13 Utterances During Sleep

Are verbal utterances during sleep hearsay? The small number of decisions addressing this question take three approaches. The first approach treats sleep

---

[99] 4 Weinstein & Berger ¶ 801(a)[01], at 801-61 to 801-62 (footnotes omitted).

[100] See § **7.5**. *See also* Fed. R. Evid. 801(a) advisory committee's note.

[101] *See* 4 Louisell & Mueller § 414, at 89 ("the hearsay objection has been rejected in connection with evidence of noncomplaint, offered to prove the absence of cause for complaint"); McCormick § 250, at 742–43.

[102] See **Ch. 4**.

[103] See **Ch. 4** for discussion of expert testimony on delay in reporting.

utterances as nonhearsay.[104] The Washington Court of Appeals's decision in *State v. Stevens*[105] exemplifies the nonhearsay approach. The court considered the admissibility of utterances by two children, six- and three-year-old siblings. In this sexual abuse case the children "had recurring nightmares during which they would shout words such as "'Arne, don't' and 'Arne, stop, Arne, don't, please don't.'"[106] The court focused its analysis on whether the children's sleep utterances were assertions, that is, *intentional* statements. The court concluded, "The utterances made by [the children] during their sleep are not conscious, intentional assertions of fact or opinion. The nightmare statements are involuntary verbal reactions, and, as such, are nonassertive utterances and not hearsay."[107] Putting the hearsay issue behind it, the court concluded that the children's sleep utterances were admissible as circumstantial evidence "that the children experienced emotional trauma that they associated with [defendant]."[108]

The second approach characterizes sleep utterances as hearsay.[109] The Minnesota Supreme Court's decision in *State v. Posten*[110] typifies the hearsay approach. In this sex offense case the victim was six. While in foster care, the child had frequent nightmares during which she would say such things as, "Ray, stop. Stop it, Ray. Stop it. Stop it." When the child was awakened, she told her foster mother she thought Ray was after her. Unfortunately, the court did not analyze why the child's sleep utterances were hearsay. Instead, the court assumed the utterances were hearsay and admitted them under the residual exception to the hearsay rule. The court observed:

> The real issue is whether this evidence was sufficiently trustworthy. We believe that each case has to be considered on its own. It may be that generally evidence of this sort would be untrustworthy. Here, however, we are not dealing with a conniving person who was out to get someone by faking a bad dream, but with a child who obviously had suffered. The length of time between the last of the defendant's acts and the first of the sleep statements was only a few days.

---

[104] *See* State v. Posten, 302 N.W.2d 638, 642 (Minn. 1981) (Wahl, J., concurring) (Justice Wahl writes that sleep utterances are not hearsay, are unreliable, and should be inadmissible).

[105] 58 Wash. App. 478, 794 P.2d 38 (1990).

[106] 794 P.2d at 40.

[107] *Id.* at 44.

[108] *Id.* at 45.

[109] *See* Godfrey v. State, 258 Ga. 28, 365 S.E.2d 93 (1988). In *Godfrey* the child's sleep utterances were offered under a child hearsay exception. The Georgia Supreme Court did not analyze whether the child's sleep utterances were hearsay. The court concluded that the record before it did not establish that sleep utterances are sufficiently reliable to gain admission under a child hearsay exception. On remand, the Georgia Court of Appeals held that the child's sleep utterances were admissible as part of the res gestae. Godfrey v. State, 187 Ga. App. 319, 370 S.E.2d 183 (1988).

[110] 302 N.W.2d 638 (Minn. 1981).

Finally, and we think importantly, the trial court knew that this was not the only evidence against defendant and that the evidence likely was going to be used primarily for corroborative purposes. If this were the only evidence connecting defendant to the crime, we would say that it was insufficient to support a conviction. But it was just one of a number of items of evidence offered in support of complainant's testimony. Under all these circumstances, the error, if any, was harmless.[111]

An argument can be made that some utterances during sleep are excited utterances.[112] For example, a child's sleep utterance might relate to a startling event and be made while the child continued under the stress of the event. Indeed, one might argue that a nightmare is itself a startling event, and that statements made during the nightmare are excited utterances.[113]

A child's statement upon awakening from a nightmare might qualify as an excited utterance. The startling event could be the original abuse or the nightmare. If the child's statement is made immediately upon awakening, the statement might qualify as a present sense impression.

The third approach concludes that sleep talk is inherently unreliable and, therefore, inadmissible.[114] The concurring opinion of Justice Wahl in *State v. Posten*[115] articulates this position. Justice Wahl wrote:

> I cannot agree that complainant's sleep talk is admissible, as an exception to the hearsay rule or otherwise. . . . Sleep talk falls within neither the language nor the spirit of conduct contemplated as a "statement" by Minn.R.Evid. 801(a). A "statement" is there defined as "(1) an oral or written assertion or (2) nonverbal conduct of a person, if it is intended by him as an assertion."

---

[111] *Id.* at 641–42.

[112] Several courts have rejected the idea that sleep utterances are excited utterances. *See* Godfrey v. State, 258 Ga. 28, 365 S.E.2d 93, 94 (1988) (sleep talk not sufficiently reliable to merit admission in evidence); State v. Posten, 302 N.W.2d 638, 641 (Minn. 1981) ("it is questionable whether the drafters of the rule intended hearsay of this nature to be admissible under this exception").

[113] One might even argue that an utterance during a nightmare is a present sense impression. *See* Fed. R. Evid. 803(1). See also § 7.27 for discussion of the present sense impression exception.

[114] *See* People v. Robinson, 19 Cal. 40 (1861); Gough v. General Box C., 302 S.W.2d 884 (Mo. 1957); State v. Zimmerman, 829 P.2d 861 (Idaho 1992); People v. Smith, 104 A.D.2d 160, 481 N.Y.S.2d 879 (1984) (error to admit defendant's statement made as he slept); Plummer v. Ricker, 71 Vt. 114, 41 A. 1045, 1046 (1898) (dog bite case; child victim described attack while asleep; "Words spoken while in sleep are not evidence of a fact or condition of mind. They proceed from an unconscious and irresponsible condition; they have little or no meaning; they are as likely to refer to unreal facts or conditions as to things real; they are wholly unreliable; and a jury ought not to be allowed to guess that such expressions are produced by a present mental or physical condition").

[115] 302 N.W.2d 638 (Minn. 1981).

> The evidence here was not an assertion. The complainant asserted nothing. She merely called out defendant's name and pleaded that he "stop it." She was clearly involved in the role of a participant in a dream-world fantasy. Even if the dreamer had uttered sleep talk in the form of an assertion about the incident, rather than in the form of an enactment of an incident, such sleep talk could never constitute an assertion in the waking-world sense.
>
> Our knowledge about dreaming indicates that, while dreams are to some degree connected to waking-hours' desires and anxieties, there is no indication that dream sequences accurately mirror actual events. Therefore, sleep talk contains no probative value regarding actual events or the identities of actual participants. Since sleep talk makes the existence of a fact neither more probable nor less probable, it is [not] relevant, as defined by Minn.R.Evid. 401.
>
> Assuming arguendo that such evidence were relevant at all, its inherent unreliability would lead to its exclusion because its probative value is more than substantially outweighed by the dangers of prejudice. Minn.R.Evid. 403. The same concern about the unreliability of the evidence, which led this court to rule inadmissible statements made in a pre-trial hypnotic interview, should be controlling in this case.[116]

A fundamental problem with analyzing sleep utterances as hearsay is that science does not answer the question whether utterances during sleep are assertive. Without an answer to this question, it is impossible to determine with any assurance whether sleep talk is hearsay. A more useful approach is to analyze sleep talk in terms of the four risks of hearsay: inaccurate perception, lapse of memory, inaccurate narration, and insincerity. In view of the scientific uncertainty about the nature of dreams, the risks inherent in admitting sleep talk appear to be high, particularly when the utterances are admitted for the truth. Justice Wahl's concurring opinion in *State v. Posten,* quoted above, presents a strong argument that the risks of admitting sleep utterances usually outweigh the benefits.

In at least two situations, however, a persuasive argument can be made for admitting sleep utterances. First, a sleep utterance may reveal a child's knowledge of facts that are relevant *regardless* of the truth of what the child said, and *regardless* of whether the utterance was assertive. For example, during sleep a child may describe some fact about the defendant or the place where abuse occurred that the child could not know unless the child had contact with the defendant or the place.[117] In such cases the sleep utterance could be admitted not for the truth of the matter asserted, but as circumstantial evidence connecting the child to the defendant or the location. As a second example, suppose a young child utters words that indicate developmentally unusual knowledge of sexual

---

[116] *Id.* at 642–43 (Wahl, J., concurring).

[117] See § **7.16** for discussion of the admissibility of children's statements linking them to the location where abuse occurred.

acts or anatomy. The child's sleep utterance may be circumstantial evidence that the child was exposed to sexual conduct.

The second situation where sleep utterances may be admissible involves child custody litigation in which the child's feelings toward an adult are relevant. The child's sleep talk indicating fear or dislike of the adult is relevant. Admissibility should not turn on whether the child's dream involved a recounting of actual events or was based on fantasy. The child's emotion during the dream provides insight into the child's mind, and may be considered by the court in determining custody.

§ 7.14 Verbal Acts and Verbal Parts of Acts

This section discusses two doctrines: (1) verbal acts, and (2) verbal parts of acts.

Verbal Acts

In certain situations the law attaches legal significance to words themselves.[118] Speaking or writing the words has legal consequences. For example, a contract comes into being when words of offer and acceptance are exchanged. Defamation occurs when damaging untruths are published. Extortion is committed when an illegal threat is made. Words having legal consequence are called verbal acts, and are not hearsay.[119]

The verbal act doctrine is applicable in some child abuse cases. If the crime charged involves an element of threat, coercion, or intimidation, the prohibited conduct usually involves words. The words themselves have legal significance and are not hearsay. In many cases, the perpetrator threatens the victim into silence. If the threat is charged as a separate crime, the threatening words are verbal acts and not hearsay.[120] One of the most destructive forms of

---

[118] *See* 4 Louisell & Mueller § 417, at 103 ("Written or spoken statements often lie at the heart of a litigated dispute, and comprise the operative events at issue"); Park at 794 ("Legally operative language is language that creates or extinguishes legal rights, powers, or duties") (footnote omitted); 4 Weinstein & Berger ¶ 801(c)[01], at 801-86 ("the utterance is an operative fact that gives rise to legal consequences").

[119] Verbal acts are not hearsay because the words are not offered for the truth of the matter asserted. *See* McCormick § 249, at 732.

[120] *See* United States v. Jones, 663 F.2d 567 (5th Cir. 1981) (during sentencing hearing, defendant threatened judge and prosecutor; defendant was charged with threatening federal officer; defendant argued that transcript of sentencing hearing was hearsay; Fifth Circuit stated: "This characterization is patently incorrect. . . . The statement at issue is paradigmatic nonhearsay; it was offered because it contains threats made against officers of the federal courts, i.e., it contains the operative words of this criminal action").

maltreatment is psychological abuse in which the child is belittled, humiliated and/or terrorized. The abusive words are not hearsay when offered to prove psychological abuse. If conspiracy is alleged, the words constituting the conspiracy are verbal acts. Although the common practice in conspiracy cases is to admit the conspirator's statement under the co-conspirator exception, the verbal act doctrine is equally useful in some instances.[121]

Verbal Parts of Acts

Some acts are ambiguous. For example, suppose A hands B a check for $1,000. Is this a gift? A loan? Payment of a debt? The transaction cannot be characterized without further evidence. Suppose that as A put the check in B's hand, A said, "I want you to have this as a token of my appreciation for your kindness." The words accompanying the act help characterize it as a gift. Weinstein and Berger write, "When nonverbal conduct is ambiguous, any accompanying verbal conduct that helps to characterize or define the transaction is not hearsay. The utterance then is merely the verbal part of an act."[122]

The doctrine admitting verbal parts of acts as nonhearsay is applicable in some child abuse cases. Suppose the defendant is charged with maliciously injuring a child. The defendant admits he struck the child but argues he acted without malice and intended only to inflict "reasonable" corporal punishment. Naturally, the nature and extent of the child's injuries may belie this defense.[123] In addition, the defendant's state of mind may be gleaned from the defendant's words as he struck the child. The defendant's inculpatory words are admissible as verbal parts of acts to clarify the defendant's conduct, or as admissions.

As a second example, in a sex offense case the defendant acknowledges touching the child but explains he was administering medicine. If the act was accompanied by sexual words, the ambiguous behavior is explained. The words are admissible as verbal parts of acts, admissions, and perhaps even verbal acts constituting elements of the crime.

---

[121] *See* 4 Louisell & Mueller § 417, at 105–06.

[122] 4 Weinstein & Berger ¶ 801(c)[01], at 801-92 to 801-93 (footnote omitted). Weinstein and Berger go on to add this important observation:

> As in cases falling under the verbal act doctrine, "the words are offered, not for their truth, but merely to show the fact of their expression." This situation must be differentiated from the case where words which clarify an ambiguous situation are relevant only because they are offered for their truth. In such a case, the words constitute hearsay but may be admissible under some exception such as the one for present sense impressions.

Id. at 801-93 to 801-94 (footnotes omitted). *See also* 4 Louisell & Mueller § 417, at 107; McCormick § 249, at 733.

[123] See **Ch. 3** for discussion of proof of intent in physical abuse cases.

§ 7.15 Assertions to Prove Effect on Listener

A person's knowledge or state of mind may be established by out-of-court statements *directed to* the person.[124] Weinstein and Berger write, "An utterance or a writing may be admitted to show the effect on the hearer or reader when this effect is relevant. The policies underlying the hearsay rule do not apply because the utterance is not being offered to prove the truth or falsity of the matter asserted."[125]

In most criminal litigation the victim's state of mind is not relevant. On occasion, however, the victim's state of mind or knowledge is in issue, and out-of-court statements that induced the state of mind or knowledge may be admissible as nonhearsay. For example, many statutes define sexual abuse as a sexual act performed to arouse or gratify the lust of the offender *or* the victim. Under such statutes, the perpetrator's sexualized statements to the victim may be admissible for the nonhearsay purpose of showing the sexual effect of the statements on the victim.[126]

Under some statutes, the victim's fear of the perpetrator is relevant, and under these statutes the defendant's threats to the victim are admissible as nonhearsay to establish the effect of the threats on the victim.[127]

The defendant may inject the child's fear into the case by arguing that the child's long delay in reporting abuse indicates abuse did not occur. Emphasizing delay in reporting invites an explanation from the prosecutor, which may take the form of the defendant's out-of-court threats intended to maintain the victim's silence.

In child custody litigation, the child's feelings toward a caretaker are highly relevant to the child's best interest. The caretaker's statements to the child are admissible nonhearsay to establish the effect of the statements on the child.

In some civil and criminal child sexual abuse litigation, the alleged perpetrator argues that the child was coached into making false allegations.[128] Alternatively, the accused may argue that improper interview techniques led a child to a false belief that abuse occurred.[129] The accused may offer the out-of-court statements of the adults who allegedly coached the child or used improper interview techniques. Are these out-of-court statements hearsay? If the statements are offered to prove their effect on the child, the answer is no. The statements

---

[124] *See* United States v. Payne, 944 F.2d 1458, 1472 (9th Cir. 1991), *cert. denied,* 112 S. Ct. 1598 (1992) (statement to victim of sexual abuse not hearsay because statement not offered for truth, but instead to prove why child remained silent at time of statement). *See also* Graham § 801.5 at 721; 4 Louisell & Mueller § 417, at 110; McCormick § 249, at 733.

[125] 4 Weinstein & Berger ¶ 801(c)[01], at 801-94 to 801-96.

[126] Such statements may constitute part of the crime and be admissible as verbal acts.

[127] *See* 4 Weinstein & Berger ¶ 801(c)[01], at 801-99.

[128] See **Ch. 4**.

[129] See **Ch. 4**.

are not offered for the truth of the matter asserted, but as evidence of the adverse effect of coaching or improper influence.[130]

§ 7.16 Assertions to Prove Source of Unique Knowledge

A child's out-of-court statement may reveal knowledge of a place, person, or thing that the child could not know unless the child had prior contact with the place, person, or thing. Suppose, for example, that a child is abducted and sexually assaulted by a stranger. After the child is released, the child describes the interior and exterior of the van where the molestation occurred. A week later the police spot the defendant driving a van meeting the exterior description provided by the child. The officers discover that the interior of the van is just as the child described it. The defendant does not deny that the child was molested. The defense is mistaken identity. The prosecutor offers the child's out-of-court description of the interior of the van. The defendant objects that the child's description is hearsay. If the prosecutor offers the child's description to establish what the van looked like inside, the out-of-court statement is hearsay. However, the prosecutor may offer the child's description for a nonhearsay purpose: to prove the child's knowledge of the interior of the van. From the child's knowledge it is possible to infer that the child was in the van, thus connecting the defendant to the crime. Offered to prove the child's knowledge, the child's out-of-court statement is not hearsay because it is not offered for the truth of the matter asserted.

---

[130] *See* United States v. Ebens, 800 F.2d 1422 (6th Cir. 1986). In this case the defendant was charged with violating the civil rights of a citizen of Chinese descent by killing him. The defendant was first prosecuted in state court, where he pled guilty to manslaughter and received probation and a small fine. The perceived leniency of the penalty caused public outrage. A private attorney named Lisa Chan formed a group to publicize the killing, to mount criticism of the state prosecutor, and to lobby the Justice Department to bring federal civil rights charges against the killer. At his civil rights trial in federal court, the defendant sought to admit tape recordings of interviews that attorney Chan had conducted with prosecution witnesses. The defendant's theory was that Chan had improperly coached the witnesses to give false testimony against him. The trial court relied on the hearsay rule to exclude the portions of the tapes containing Chan's out-of-court statements to the witnesses. On appeal, the government conceded that it was error to exclude Chan's out-of-court statements. The court wrote:

> Obviously the purpose of introducing the Chan tapes was to show the effect of Chan's statements on the testimony of [the government witnesses]. Plainly, Chan's out of court utterances were admissible to show not the truth of what she said but the effect on [the government witnesses] as bearing on whether the witnesses' subsequent sworn testimony was coached and hence inaccurate. . . . In this light, the tapes were highly relevant and important to the defense.

Id. at 1430.

The foregoing hypothetical is based on *Bridges v. State*.[131] In *Bridges* the seven-year-old victim was accosted by a stranger as she walked home from school. The perpetrator persuaded the child to accompany him to his home, where he molested her. Upon her release, the victim spoke to her mother and police officers, and described the exterior of the house and the interior of the room where she was molested. Among other details, the child mentioned a dresser, chest of drawers, bed, chair with a clock and radio on it, a picture of a woman, two dolls with cloth faces, and three windows. The police drove the victim around hoping she would spot the house where she was molested. Eventually, the child pointed to a house, which turned out to be the defendant's. The police took the child to the bedroom and the child affirmed that this was where she was abused. The room matched the child's previous description in many respects. At trial, the prosecutor offered the child's out-of-court description of the defendant's room. The Supreme Court of Wisconsin ruled the child's description was not hearsay, writing:

> In those [out-of-court] statements she spoke . . . of various matters and features which she remembered and which were descriptive of the exterior and surroundings of the house; and of the room and various articles and the location thereof therein. It is true that testimony as to such statements was hearsay and, as such, inadmissible if the purpose for which it was received had been to establish thereby that there were in fact the stated articles in the room, or that they were located as stated, or that the exterior features or surroundings of the house were as [victim] stated. That, however, was not in this case the purpose for which the evidence as to those statements was admitted. It was admissible in so far as the fact that she had made the statements can be deemed to tend to show that at the time those statements were made—which was a month prior to the subsequent discovery of the room and house . . . —she had knowledge as to articles and descriptive features which, as was proven by other evidence, were in fact in or about that room and house. If in relation thereto [victim] made the statements as to which the officers and her mother testified, then those statements, although they were extra judicial utterances, constituted at least circumstantial evidence that she then had such knowledge; and that such state of mind on her part was acquired by reason of her having been in that room and house prior to making the statements. Under these circumstances there are applicable to the hearsay testimony in question the following propositions stated in Wigmore on Evidence, 3rd Ed., to-wit:
>
> "The condition of a speaker's mind, as to knowledge, belief, rationality, emotion, or the like may be evidenced by his utterances, either used testimonially as assertions to be believed, or used circumstantially as affording indirect inferences. * * * The usual resort is to utterances which circumstantially indicate a specific state of mind causing them. To such a use, then, the hearsay rule makes no opposition, because the utterance is not used for the sake of inducing belief in

---

[131] 247 Wis. 350, 19 N.W.2d 529 (1945). *See also* United States v. Muscato, 534 F. Supp. 969 (E.D.N.Y. 1982).

§ 7.16   PROVING UNIQUE KNOWLEDGE SOURCE

any assertion it may contain. The assertion, if in form there is one, is to be disregarded and the [in]direct inference alone regarded."

* * *

So in this case the proof that [victim] made the statements in question before there was any possibility of having what she stated she remembered about the house, and room, and articles therein, from her first contact therewith, affected or changed by what she learned after the discovery and location thereof . . . is material and significant in so far as it tended to show that she had knowledge of certain things in and about the house and room. The existence of those things in fact could not, however, be established by her hearsay statements, but had to be proven by other evidence which was competent. In other words, although proof of her extra judicial assertions was competent to show such knowledge on her part, it could not be deemed to prove the facts asserted thereby. When for instance, it was proven that [victim] stated during the evening after the alleged assault that there was a picture of a lady in the room, her statement did not constitute competent evidence to prove that there was such a picture in the room. But her statement was competent as evidence to prove that she had knowledge of such an object in the room and for this purpose the utterance is not inadmissible hearsay, but is a circumstantial fact indicating knowledge on the part of [victim] at a particular time.[132]

The *Bridges* case illustrates the principle that out-of-court assertions may be nonhearsay when offered to prove a child's knowledge of facts the child could not know unless the child had certain experience. Louisell and Mueller provide the following insight into *Bridges*:

Critical to *Bridges* were the facts that evidence independent of the girl's statement established the appearance of defendant's quarters, and that the girl would not likely have been able to make her statement unless she had been there on the occasion in question. Any description may be imagined and uttered. But where it fits closely with a detailed reality independently established and unknown to the declarant unless his statement be true, it cannot be explained away as mere coincidence: The utterance is persuasive evidence of memory, and all that memory circumstantially implies. Under such conditions it seems unwise to invoke the hearsay doctrine as a bar to the proof.[133]

The *Bridges* principle is important in child abuse litigation, particularly when the defense is mistaken identity. Thus, a child's description of a tattoo or other unique anatomical feature found on the defendant is admissible not to prove that the defendant had the tattoo or anatomical feature, but to prove that the child knew about it and must, therefore, have had an opportunity to observe it. The child's knowledge connects the child to the defendant and helps establish identity.

---

[132] 19 N.W.2d at 535–36.

[133] 4 Louisell & Mueller § 417, at 119.

EXCEPTIONS TO HEARSAY RULE

§ 7.17 Rationale for Exceptions

Hearsay is excluded because the risks of hearsay make some out-of-court statements less reliable than in-court testimony.[134] Exceptions to the hearsay rule are created for three reasons. First, some hearsay is sufficiently reliable to gain admission in evidence. Thus, excited utterances are reliable because memory loss is unlikely and the exciting event makes lying unlikely. Second, in some cases the need for out-of-court statements supports admission. Thus, dying declarations are admitted in part because of the need for the declarant's final words. Finally, with certain types of out-of-court statements, notably party admissions, the nature of the adversary system justifies receipt of the evidence.

A word about the structure of the Federal Rules of Evidence is appropriate. The rules divide out-of-court statements offered for the truth of the matter asserted into two broad categories. First, Rule 801 defines certain out-of-court statements as not hearsay. Second, Rules 803 and 804(b) catalog exceptions to the hearsay rule.

Rule 801(d)(1) defines certain prior statements of witnesses as not hearsay. Under Rule 801(d)(1) certain prior inconsistent statements, prior consistent statements, and out-of-court statements of identification are not hearsay. Rule 801(d)(2) defines party admissions, including co-conspirator statements, as not hearsay.

Rules 803 and 804(b) contain 28 exceptions to the hearsay rule.[135] It is unnecessary in a book on child abuse to discuss all of the exceptions set forth in Rules 803 and 804(b). The exceptions that play a daily role in child abuse and neglect litigation are discussed in this chapter.

In addition to the hearsay exceptions contained in the Federal Rules of Evidence, **§ 7.46** discusses special exceptions for children's hearsay statements now in force in a majority of jurisdictions. **Section 7.41** discusses a hearsay exception for proof of age of a witness. **Section 7.31** discusses the common law doctrine called *fresh complaint of rape*.

---

[134] The four hearsay risks are misperception, inaccurate narration, lapse of memory, and insincerity. See § **7.4** for discussion of the hearsay dangers.

[135] Rules 803 and 804(b) actually contain 29 exceptions, but since the residual exceptions in Rules 803(24) and 804(b)(5) are identical, they are counted as one exception.

§ 7.18 Prior Inconsistent Statements

A witness's testimony may be impeached with evidence that prior to testifying, the witness told a different story.[136] McCormick describes the theory underlying this mode of impeachment:

> The theory of attack by prior inconsistent statements is not based on the assumption that the present testimony is false and the former statement true but rather upon the notion that talking one way on the stand and another way previously is blowing hot and cold, and raises a doubt as to the truthfulness of both statements.[137]

In child abuse litigation, children are regularly impeached with prior inconsistent statements. Such impeachment is usually proper. Prosecutors should be prepared, however, to respond to such impeachment. In many cases the prosecutor can point to developmental and situational reasons for a child's inconsistency—reasons that explain away the impeaching value of the inconsistency. The reasons children are inconsistent are discussed in **Chapter 4**.

Impeachment with prior inconsistent statements is subject to the collateral fact rule.[138] The witness to be impeached may be asked about prior inconsistent statements on collateral matters. If, however, the witness denies making the statement, the cross-examiner must take the witness's answer, and extrinsic evidence is barred by the collateral fact rule. If the prior inconsistent statement is not collateral, extrinsic evidence is admissible.

Under the doctrine derived from *Queen Caroline's Case*,[139] the cross-examining attorney had to lay a foundation before impeaching with a prior inconsistent statement. If the inconsistent statement was oral, the cross-examiner had to direct the witness's attention to the time, place, and circumstances of the statement before confronting the witness with the statement.[140] If the inconsistent statement was written, the cross-examiner had to give the statement to the witness and afford the witness an opportunity to read it and explain or deny the inconsistency before proceeding with impeachment.[141]

Rule 613 of the Federal Rules of Evidence abolishes much of the traditional foundational requirement for impeachment with prior inconsistent statement. The rule provides:

---

[136] United States v. Hale, 422 U.S. 171, 176 (1975) ("a basic rule of evidence provides that prior inconsistent statements may be used to impeach the credibility of a witness"); 3 Louisell & Mueller § 356, at 545–46.

[137] McCormick § 34, at 74.

[138] See **Ch. 5**.

[139] 2 Brod. & Bing. 284, 129 Eng. Rep. 976, 11 Eng. Ru. Cas. 183 (1820).

[140] *See* Coles v. Harsch, 129 Or. 11, 276 P. 248 (1929); 3 Louisell & Mueller § 357, at 556.

[141] 3 Louisell & Mueller § 357, at 556.

(a) In examining a witness concerning a prior statement made by the witness, whether written or not, the statement need not be shown nor its contents disclosed to the witness at that time, but on request the same shall be shown or disclosed to opposing counsel.

(b) Extrinsic evidence of a prior inconsistent statement by a witness is not admissible unless the witness is afforded an opportunity to explain or deny the same and the opposite party is afforded an opportunity to interrogate the witness thereon, or the interests of justice otherwise require. This provision does not apply to admissions of a party-opponent as defined in rule 801(d)(2).[142]

The trial judge has discretion regarding the adequacy of the foundation for prior inconsistent statements.[143] "This is particularly true when the witness who made the inconsistent statement is a child."[144]

When inconsistent statements are used solely to impeach, the statements are not offered for the truth of the matters asserted, and the hearsay rule is not offended.[145] When prior inconsistent statements are offered for the truth of the matter asserted, however, the common law treated the statements as hearsay.[146] Several states continue to treat prior inconsistent statements as hearsay, but admit such statements under an exception to the hearsay rule.[147] Over the years, judges and scholars argued that some prior statements should be considered nonhearsay.[148] The Federal Rules of Evidence adopt a middle ground between

---

[142] Fed. R. Evid. 613. The Advisory Committee note to Rule 613 states that the rule abolishes the "useless impediment" to cross-examination imposed by *Queen Caroline's Case*.

[143] United States v. Rodko, 34 M.J. 980 (A.C.M.R. 1992) (discussing foundation required to impeach with prior inconsistent statement); Kosbruk v. State, 820 P.2d 1082 (Alaska Ct. App. 1991).

[144] *Id.*

[145] 3 Louisell & Mueller § 356, at 546.

[146] *See* People v. Sambo, 197 Ill. App. 3d 574, 554 N.E.2d 1080, 1086 (1990); State v. Mancine, 124 N.J. 232, 590 A.2d 1107 (1991). *See also* McCormick § 251, at 744, where the author states:

> [T]he traditional view had been that a prior statement of a witness is hearsay if offered to prove the happening of matters asserted therein. This categorization has not, of course, precluded using the prior statement for other purposes, e.g., to impeach the witness by showing a self-contradiction if the statement is inconsistent with his testimony or to support his credibility under certain circumstances when the statement was consistent with his testimony. But the prior statement has been admissible as proof of matter asserted therein, i.e., as "substantive" evidence, only when falling within one of the exceptions to the hearsay rule.

See also Graham § 801.11, at 746; 4 Weinstein & Berger ¶ 801(d)(1)[01], at 801-128 ("the orthodox position that classified all prior statements of a witness as hearsay").

[147] See Cal. Evid. Code § 1235 (West 1992); Ill. Rev. Stat. ch. 38, ¶ 115-10.1; N.J. R. Evid. 63(1)(a).

[148] *See* Fed. R. Evid. 801(d)(1)(A) advisory committee's note. *See also* State v. Mancine, 124 N.J. 232, 590 A.2d 1107, 114 (1991); McCormick § 251 at 744–45; 4 Weinstein & Berger ¶ 801(d)(1)[01], at 801-129 to 801-130.

the view that prior inconsistent statements are hearsay and the position that such statements should be nonhearsay.[149] Rule 801(d)(1)(A) states:

> A statement is not hearsay if the declarant testifies at the trial or hearing and is subject to cross-examination concerning the statement, and the statement is inconsistent with the declarant's testimony, and was given under oath subject to the penalty of perjury at a trial, hearing, or other proceeding, or in a deposition.

§ 7.19 —Admissibility Requirements

Three requirements must be fulfilled to characterize a prior inconsistent statement as nonhearsay under Rule 801(d)(1)(A), and to admit the statement for the truth of the matter asserted:[150] (1) the declarant must be present at trial and subject to cross-examination concerning the prior statement, (2) the prior statement must have been under oath at a prior proceeding, and (3) the prior statement must be inconsistent with the witness's trial testimony.

Before discussing the three requirements of Rule 801(d)(1)(A), it is worth noting that whether or not prior inconsistent statements are excluded from the definition of hearsay, or are admissible as hearsay within an exception, prior inconsistent statements may be used to impeach credibility. When a prior inconsistent statement is limited to impeachment, the statement is not offered for the truth of the matter asserted, and the hearsay rule is not implicated.[151]

1. Testimony and Cross-Examination

The declarant must testify at trial and be subject to cross-examination concerning the prior inconsistent statement. Note that under Rule 801(d)(1)(A) the

---

[149] *See* 4 Weinstein & Berger ¶ 801(d)(1)[01], at 801-133 ("Rule 801(d)(1) thus adopts a compromise position towards classifying the prior statement of a witness as hearsay"). *See also id.* ¶ 801(d)(1)(A)[01], at 801-136.

[150] *See* Fed. R. Evid. 801(d)(1)(A) advisory committee's note ("Prior inconsistent statements traditionally have been admissible to impeach but not as substantive evidence. Under the rule they are substantive evidence"). *See also* Graham § 801.11, at 746–48; 4 Louisell & Mueller § 419, at 167; 4 Weinstein & Berger ¶ 801(d)(1)(A)[01], at 801-134 to 801-135 (two reasons to give substantive effect to prior inconsistent statements: (1) jurors encounter prior inconsistent statements when the statements are used for impeachment, and jurors are likely to use the statements substantively despite limiting instructions, and (2) "statements made closer in time to the event in question and before the exertion of external pressures may be more trustworthy than testimony at trial").

[151] United States v. Hale, 422 U.S. 171, 176(1975) ("A basic rule of evidence provides that prior inconsistent statements may be used to impeach the credibility of a witness"); McCormick § 251, at 744.

declarant must be cross-examinable *concerning the prior statement.*[152] The fact that the declarant cannot be cross-examined regarding the event underlying the prior inconsistent statement does not undermine the substantive admissibility of the statement.[153] Louisell and Mueller observe that "[a] different and harder problem arises where the witness claims a lack of memory or refuses to answer questions concerning *the making* of the prior statement."[154] In this situation it is difficult to see how the declarant can be cross-examined concerning the prior statement. Nevertheless, the United States Supreme Court's decision in *United States v. Owens*[155] indicates that cross-examination is possible when a witness cannot remember the statement. The Court wrote, "Ordinarily a witness is regarded as 'subject to cross-examination' when he is placed on the stand, under oath, and responds willingly to questions."[156] The cross-examiner can focus on the statement despite the fact that the witness cannot remember it. Indeed, the very fact that the witness has forgotten the statement demonstrates the weakness of the witness's testimony.[157]

2. Oath at Prior Proceeding

Not all prior inconsistent statements are defined as nonhearsay under Rule 801(d)(1)(A).[158] The nonhearsay characterization is limited to statements "given under oath subject to the penalty of perjury at a trial, hearing, or other proceeding, or in a deposition."[159] Testimony at a prior trial satisfies the rule, as

---

[152] 4 Louisell & Mueller § 414, at 179–80 ("It should be noted that the Rule does *not* require the witness also to be cross-examinable concerning the underlying event—that is, the matter asserted in the prior statement").

[153] *See* United States v. Owens, 484 U.S. 554, 563 (1988) ("It would seem strange, for example, to assert that a witness can avoid introduction of testimony from a prior proceeding that is inconsistent with his trial testimony, see rule 801(d)(1)(A), by simply asserting lack of memory of the facts to which the prior testimony related"); State v. Bishop, 63 Wash. App. 15, 816 P.2d 738 (1991) (fact that child could not remember one element of the crime did not render child unavailable for cross-examination in the constitutional sense; case discusses child hearsay exception). *See also* 4 Louisell & Mueller § 419, at 179–80; 4 Weinstein & Berger ¶ 801(d)(1)(A)[04].

For lengthy discussion of when cross-examination is sufficient to satisfy Rule 801(d)(1)(A) and the Confrontation Clause, see 4 Weinstein & Berger, ¶¶ 801(d)(1)(A)[02] to 801(d)(1)(A)[08].

[154] 4 Louisell & Mueller § 419, at 180. *See also* 4 Weinstein & Berger ¶ 801(d)(1)(A)[07].

[155] 484 U.S. 554 (1988). *Owens* dealt with out-of-court statements of identification admissible under Rule 801(d)(1)(C). The Court's discussion of when a declarant is subject to cross-examination concerning an out-of-court statement is equally applicable to prior inconsistent statements admissible under Rule 801(d)(1)(A).

[156] 484 U.S. at 561.

[157] *Id.* at 562.

[158] Contrast Rule 801(d)(1)(A) with Cal. Evid. Code § 1235, which allows substantive use of a much broader category of prior inconsistent statements.

[159] Fed. R. Evid. 801(d)(1)(A).

does testimony at a preliminary hearing, deposition, or before the grand jury.[160] "[T]he prior statement need not have been subject to cross-examination at the time made . . . ."[161] The term *other proceeding* does not include statements to law enforcement officials.[162]

A prior inconsistent statement that was not made under oath at a prior proceeding is hearsay if offered for the truth of the matter asserted. The statement may be admissible substantively if it meets the requirements of a hearsay exception. Furthermore, a prior inconsistent statement that does not meet the requirements of Rule 801(d)(1)(A) may be used to impeach.

3. Inconsistency with Trial Testimony

The trial court determines whether inconsistency exists.[163] The Federal Rules of Evidence adopt a liberal approach to the meaning of inconsistency. Clearly, Rule 801(d)(1)(A) is satisfied when the witness's trial testimony diametrically contradicts a prior statement. Rule 801(d)(1)(A) does not insist on such patent inconsistency, however.[164] Weinstein and Berger summarize the majority approach: "The better view, urged by Wigmore, McCormick, and others, and followed by the federal courts, allows the prior statement whenever a reasonable man could infer on comparing the whole effect of the two statements that they had been produced by inconsistent beliefs."[165]

---

[160] *See* Graham § 801.11, at 747 ("Grand jury testimony is included within the concept of 'other proceeding'") (footnote omitted); 4 Louisell & Mueller § 419, at 168–69; 4 Weinstein & Berger ¶ 801(d)(1)(A)[01], at 801-36 to 801-37 ("grand jury testimony is clearly included").

[161] 4 Louisell & Mueller § 419, at 171.

[162] *See* Graham § 801.11, at 747–48; 4 Louisell & Mueller § 419, at 173 ("A stationhouse or streetside declaration made to law enforcement agents, even if in the form of a sworn affidavit, has been quite properly considered to lie outside Rule 801(d)(1)(A)") (footnote omitted).

[163] *See* State v. Murphy, 462 N.W.2d 715, 717 (Iowa Ct. App. 1990) (trial court did not err in refusing to give jury instruction regarding prior inconsistent statements; "the differences were slight and immaterial").

[164] *See* Monn v. State, 811 P.2d 1004, 1006 (Wyo. 1991) ("Inconsistent statements may be found in evasive answers, the inability to recall, silence, or changes of position"). *See also* 3 Louisell & Mueller § 356, at 549–50, where the authors write:

> By better reasoned authority, the requirement of inconsistency may be satisfied by something less than a statement which diametrically opposes or directly contradicts the trial testimony of the witness: So long as the trust of the prior statement differs with the thrust of the testimony, there is inconsistency enough.

(footnote omitted).

[165] 4 Weinstein & Berger ¶ 801(d)(1)(A)[01], at 801-145. *See also* Graham § 613.2, at 569; 4 Louisell & Mueller § 419, at 175–77; McCormick § 34, at 75 ("could the jury reasonably find that a witness who believed the truth of the facts testified to would have been unlikely to make a prior statement of this tenor?"); 3A Wigmore § 1040, at 1048 ("Do the two expressions appear to have been produced by inconsistent beliefs?").

Louisell and Mueller add that "the requirement should be satisfied whenever the thrust of the prior statement differs in any significant way from the thrust of declarant's trial testimony."[166]

Few problems arise when the inconsistency appears on the surface of the statements. Greater difficulty arises in the three recurring situations discussed below.

Specific facts versus general opinion. In the first situation, the witness provides detailed factual testimony conflicting with an out-of-court statement of opinion.[167] Consider, for example, an auto accident involving A and B. A is injured and sues B in negligence. The accident was witnessed by X. At trial, X testifies for B. X gives detailed factual testimony indicating that A probably caused the accident. To impeach X, the attorney for A says, "Isn't it true, X, that not long after the accident you said, and I quote, 'A was not to blame'?" B's attorney objects that there is no inconsistency between the factual trial testimony and the earlier statement in the form of an opinion.

It seems clear in this case that X's out-of-court opinion is inconsistent with X's trial testimony and should be admitted to impeach. Wigmore wrote:

> [T]he only proper inquiry can be, is there within the broad statement of opinion on the general question *some implied assertion of fact* inconsistent with the other assertion made on the stand. If there is, it ought to be received, whether or not it is clothed in or associated with an expression of opinion.[168]

Weinstein and Berger observe that the "liberal approach" is to admit an out-of-court opinion that varies from trial testimony when the opinion "'would be of value to the jury in evaluating [the witness'] testimony.'"[169]

Specific facts versus prior silence. The second troublesome issue is whether an inconsistency exists between trial testimony and earlier silence at a time when it would have been natural to speak. Suppose for example, that A is charged with murdering B during a fight. At trial, A admits he killed B, but testifies he acted in self-defense. To impeach A's credibility, the prosecutor offers the testimony of X, who witnessed the fight. X will testify that as the victim lay dying, X asked A what happened. In response, A did not mention he was acting in self-defense.

Is the defendant's trial testimony describing self-defense inconsistent with his earlier silence on the matter? Louisell and Mueller write:

---

[166] 4 Louisell & Mueller § 419, at 176–77.
[167] See discussion in 3 Louisell & Mueller § 356, at 550–51.
[168] 3 Weinstein & Berger ¶ 607[06], at 607–97, quoting Wigmore.
[169] 3 Weinstein & Berger ¶ 607[06], at 607–96 (quoting Atlantic Greyhound Corp. v. Eddins, 177 F.2d 954, 958 (4th Cir. 1949)).

§ 7.19 ADMISSIBILITY REQUIREMENTS 121

Sometimes mere silence is inconsistent with assertions on other occasions. If a witness says nothing at a time when circumstances make it highly likely that he would assert a fact if the fact were true, his later assertion of the fact in testimony at trial seems inconsistent, and the earlier silence may be shown on cross-examination or by extrinsic evidence.[170]

If X had been a police officer called to the scene of the fight, A's silence may have been reasonable, and thus not inconsistent with his trial testimony describing self-defense.

In some cases, a witness testifies in detail at trial, and the question is whether a prior statement that lacks certain details of the trial testimony is inconsistent. Graham writes that "inconsistency may also consist of the omission from a prior statement of a matter which would reasonably be expected to have been mentioned if true . . . ."[171] Louisell and Mueller observe that "if the prior statement omits a material detail, which under the circumstances would probably have been included in the statement if true, then the prior statement is inconsistent with testimony at trial which includes this detail."[172]

The concept of inconsistency arising from incomplete prior statements is particularly important in child sexual abuse litigation. Suppose, for example, that the child testifies at trial and provides a detailed description of abuse. To impeach the child's credibility, the defendant offers the child's initial disclosure to a social worker followed by a second disclosure to a physician. The disclosures to the social worker and the doctor lack many of the details contained in the child's trial testimony. Moreover, the statement to the doctor was more detailed than the statement to the social worker. Are the child's prior statements inconsistent with the youngster's trial testimony? Defense counsel says yes. When the child talked to the social worker and the doctor, important details were omitted that the child would have included if the allegations were true. Perhaps. But defense counsel's argument ignores the way children disclose sexual abuse. Sorensen and Snow point out that "[d]isclosure of child sexual abuse is best described . . . as a process, not an event. The common presumption that most abused children are capable of immediate active disclosure by providing a coherent, detailed account in an initial investigative interview is not supported" by

---

[170] 3 Louisell & Mueller § 356, at 554. Weinstein and Berger write:

Another perplexing point is whether a failure to assert a fact it would have been natural to affirm amounts to an assertion of the nonexistence of the fact which can be used to impeach testimony in which the witness admitted the fact's existence. According to Wigmore such a failure to make an assertion should be admitted as a prior inconsistent statement, and the federal cases are in accord.

3 Weinstein & Berger ¶ 607[06], at 607-97 to 607-98. *See also* United States v. Langford, 15 M.J. 1090, 1092-93 (A.C.M.R. 1983).

[171] Graham § 613.2, at 570 (footnotes omitted).

[172] 3 Louisell & Mueller § 356, at 550 (footnote omitted).

research or experience.[173] Many sexually abused children disclose a little at a time, testing the water to see how adults respond.[174] Gradual, piecemeal disclosure is the norm, not the exception. Thus, it is not proper to equate partial disclosure with mendacity. The child's progressive disclosure was in keeping with the way children typically disclose sexual abuse.

If the prosecutor is unable to persuade the trial judge that there is no inconsistency between the child's trial testimony and the earlier disclosures, thus blocking impeachment, the prosecutor will use redirect examination to good advantage by affording the child an opportunity to explain away the appearance of inconsistency. Moreover, the prosecutor may give thought to calling an expert witness to explain the dynamics of disclosure and the many reasons children are inconsistent.[175] Whether or not an expert testifies, the prosecutor will use closing argument to help the jury understand the reasons for the child's gradual disclosure.

Specific facts versus inability to remember. Is there inconsistency between a witness's trial testimony and the witness's claimed inability to remember a prior statement? A deliberately false or evasive "I don't remember making that statement" can constitute an implied denial of the facts stated in the prior statement.[176] Weinstein and Berger write:

> The most unsettled aspect of determining what amounts to an inconsistency is presented when a witness denies all recollection of a matter about which he had formerly made a statement. Can this former statement be regarded as inconsistent? The common law practice . . . would not consider such statements inconsistent and would not, therefore, permit their use even for impeachment purposes. Wigmore objected to a rule of blanket exclusion noting that
>
>> the unwilling witness often takes refuge in a failure to remember, and the astute liar is sometimes impregnable unless his flank can be exposed to an attack of this sort. An absolute rule of prohibition would do more harm than good, and the trial Court should have discretion.
>
> . . . . Under the Federal Rules of Evidence, Wigmore's approach would seem most in accord with the broad rule of relevancy stated in rule 401 and the wide discretion granted the trial judge by Rule 403.[177]

---

[173] Sorensen & Snow, *How Children Tell: The Process of Disclosure in Child Sexual Abuse,* 70 Child Welfare 3, 11 (1991). In Sorensen and Snow's study, only 11% of children were in active disclosure at the time of the initial interview.

[174] See **Ch. 4**.

[175] See **Ch. 4**.

[176] People v. O'Quinn, 109 Cal. App. 3d 219, 167 Cal. Rptr. 141 (1980), *cert. denied,* 450 U.S. 928 (1981); Monn v. State, 811 P.2d 1004, 1006 (Wyo. 1991) ("Inconsistent statements may be found in evasive answers, the *inability to recall,* silence, or *changes of position*").

[177] 3 Weinstein & Berger ¶ 607[06], at 607-101 to 607-102 (footnotes omitted).

Louisell and Mueller write:

> Where a witness at one time states that he lacks memory or knowledge about a matter, and at some other time makes a more positive assertion about the same matter, at least theoretically the two statements are entirely consistent, and both might be truthful as well: What is known may be forgotten; what is forgotten may be recalled. But the reality is often very different. On the one hand, claiming a lack of knowledge or memory is a familiar way of keeping distance, of avoiding controversy or strife, and of gaining time in which to think out a position. Consequently, such claims are often untruthful, and may constitute an easy refuge for a witness who is for any reason reluctant to speak. On the other hand, the persuasive force in a positive assertion is diminished where the witness has on an earlier occasion professed a lack of knowledge or memory.
>
> Accordingly, when a witness changes his story in either of the ways suggested above—first making a positive statement and later claiming lack of knowledge or memory, or vice versa—the change often represents a kind of inconsistency, which may reasonably be said to affect credibility in much the same way as outright inconsistencies. It seems that the trial judge should permit impeachment by proof that a witness who makes a positive statement at trial has earlier claimed lack of knowledge or memory, and by proof that a witness who asserts forgetfulness or ignorance at trial has earlier made positive statements, although in the latter situation the judge has a measure of discretion, and should disallow the impeaching effort if he believes that the lapse of memory is real and not feigned.[178]

§ 7.20 —Recurring Issues

In many child abuse cases the defendant's spouse makes statements to police and others implicating the defendant. At trial, however, the spouse exonerates the defendant.[179] The spouse's prior statements inculpating the defendant are admissible to impeach the spouse. In addition, if the requirements of Rule 801(d)(1)(A) are fulfilled, the spouse's prior inconsistent statements are defined as nonhearsay and are admissible for the truth of the matter asserted. In jurisdictions that characterize prior inconsistent statements as hearsay within an exception, the spouse's inculpatory statements may be admissible for the truth.[180]

In two recurring situations, the child is the declarant of the prior inconsistent statement. In the first scenario the child recants before trial. The second scenario involves a child who recants for the first time at trial.

---

[178] 3 Louisell & Mueller § 356, at 551–52 (footnotes omitted).

[179] *See, e.g.,* State v. Hancock, 109 Wash. 2d 760, 748 P.2d 611 (1988); Monn v. State, 811 P.2d 1004 (Wyo. 1991).

[180] *See* Cal. Evid. Code § 1235 (West 1992).

Child Who Recants Before Trial

Most sexually abused children are asked to describe their abuse several times. The child may be interviewed by a police officer, a social worker, a psychologist, and an attorney. The child may testify at a preliminary hearing or before a grand jury. Throughout these interviews and court appearances the child may provide a relatively consistent description of abuse.[181] Some time prior to trial, however, many children recant, denying that abuse occurred.[182]

When a child recants before trial, the prosecutor must decide whether the child is likely to testify favorably at trial. With proper support and preparation, many children recant their recantation and testify for the prosecution. If the child's recantation appears firm, the prosecutor may decline to call the child. If the defense puts the child on the stand, and the child exculpates the defendant, the child's prior descriptions of abuse are inconsistent with the child's trial testimony and may be used for impeachment. Furthermore, if one or more of the child's prior statements meets the requirements of Rule 801(d)(1)(A), or a hearsay exception,[183] the child's prior inconsistent statements are admissible as substantive evidence.

If the prosecutor is relatively sure the child will not testify favorably for the government, may the prosecutor nevertheless call the child as a witness, elicit *unfavorable* testimony, and then offer the child's prior inconsistent statement inculpating the defendant? The answer to this question depends on whether the child's prior inconsistent statement is admissible for the truth of the matter asserted, or is admissible only for the limited purpose of impeachment.

If the child's prior inconsistent statement is admissible substantively under Rule 801(d)(1)(A) or a hearsay exception, the prosecutor may call the child despite the fact that the prosecutor knows the child will provide unfavorable testimony.[184] The prosecutor may offer the child's prior inconsistent statement to

---

[181] Children are seldom entirely consistent over time, particularly regarding peripheral details. There are several reasons for children's inconsistency. See **Ch. 4** for discussion of inconsistency among sexually abused children.

[182] See **Ch. 4** discussing recantation. *See also* Summit, *The Child Abuse Accommodation Syndrome,* 7 Child Abuse & Neglect 177, 188 (1983) (*"Whatever a child says about sexual abuse, she is likely to reverse it"*).

[183] *See* Cal. Evid. Code § 1235 (West 1992).

[184] *See* People v. Freeman, 20 Cal. App. 3d 488, 97 Cal. Rptr. 717 (1971). *Freeman* concerns § 1235 of the California Evidence Code, which creates a hearsay exception for prior inconsistent statements. Unlike Fed. R. Evid. 801(d)(1)(A), the California exception for prior inconsistent statements does not require the statement to be under oath at a legal proceeding. Thus, California allows substantive use of many prior inconsistent statements that would be inadmissible for the truth of the matter asserted under Fed. R. Evid. 801(d)(1)(A). Referring to Cal. Evid. Code § 1235, the *Freeman* court wrote:

> Section 1235 brings California among those jurisdictions which . . . "permit the substantive use of prior inconsistent statements on the theory that the usual dangers of

§ 7.20 RECURRING ISSUES

impeach the child's testimony *and* for the truth of the matter asserted.[185] If, however, the child's prior inconsistent statement will not be admissible for the truth, the prosecutor may not call the child for the sole purpose of impeaching the child with *otherwise inadmissible* hearsay.[186] In *United States v. Gomez-Gallardo*,[187] the Ninth Circuit Court of Appeals wrote: "Federal Rules of Evidence 607 permits the government to impeach its own witness. However, 'the government must not knowingly elicit testimony from a witness in order to impeach him with otherwise inadmissible testimony.'"[188]

Saltzburg, Schinasi, and Schlueter provide a useful summary of the law:

> Rule 607 is intended to permit impeachment, not to permit the introduction of inconsistent statements where there is no reason for impeachment other than to attempt to bring hearsay before [the fact-finder]. If a witness' prior statement satisfies Rule 801(d)(1)(A)'s provisions, it will be admissible as substantive evidence. Any witness can be called and asked about statements that are non-hearsay and admissible under Rule 801(d)(1)(A). However, if a statement does not qualify under Rule 801 as non-hearsay, it is improper for a party to call the witness for the sole purpose of bringing out the prior statements. If the proponent of the witness does elicit some helpful material from the witness but also is damaged by portions of the witness' testimony, impeachment with inconsistent

---

hearsay are largely nonexistent where the witness testifies at trial." The witness' recantation permits the inference that he has something to hide, and this inference provides the earlier version a measure of reliability. The jury may choose which version to believe or reject both versions altogether. When a litigant intentionally brings in the declarant for the purpose of eliciting a predictably false version, he is not misusing section 1235 but utilizing it for the very purpose it is designed to fulfill—that is, to open the door to a second witness with a conceivably reliably indicator of the actual events. The technique conforms to the letter and spirit of section 1235, which supplies fact-finders with a formerly unavailable means for uncovering the truth.

97 Cal Rptr. at 721–22.

[185] People v. Freeman, 20 Cal. App. 3d 488, 97 Cal. Rptr. 717 (1981).

[186] United States v. Kane, 944 F.2d 1406, 1411 (7th Cir. 1991) ("Impeachment of one's own witness cannot be permitted where employed as a mere subterfuge to present to the jury evidence not otherwise admissible"); State v. Tracy, 482 N.W.2d 675 (Iowa 1992); State v. Turecek, 456 N.W.2d 219, 225 (Iowa 1990) ("The State is not entitled under rule 607 to place a witness on the stand who is expected to give unfavorable testimony and then, in the guise of impeachment, offer evidence which is otherwise inadmissible"); People v. Broomfield, 163 A.D.2d 403, 558 N.Y.S.2d 126, 127 (1990) ("there must be no evidence that the prosecutor has called the witness in bad faith, simply hoping to use his or her presence to introduce prior statements which would not otherwise be admissible. In this case, an eight-year-old child witness testified during the People's direct examination that the defendant was not present at the crime scene. This was contrary to her prior testimony and affirmatively damaged the People's case. Therefore, the prior sworn videotaped testimony of the child witness was properly admitted to impeach her trial testimony") (citations omitted); State v. Hancock, 109 Wash. 2d 760, 748 P.2d 611, 612–13 (1988).

[187] 915 F.2d 553 (9th Cir. 1990).

[188] *Id.* at 555, quoting United States v. Whitson, 587 F.2d 948, 952–53 (9th Cir. 1978).

statements directed at the damaging testimony should be allowed. Also, if a party is surprised and hurt by a witness' testimony, impeachment is certainly proper. To be avoided, however, is the calling of a witness who counsel knows has nothing favorable to say in order to bring out inconsistent statements. Since the witness says nothing that helps the calling party, it is clear that this procedure is an attempt to avoid Rule 801 and to smuggle inconsistent statements into a trial in the hope that despite a limiting instruction under Rule 105, [factfinders] will use the statements substantively.[189]

When prior inconsistent statements are not admissible for the truth of the matter asserted, courts consider several factors to determine whether such statements should be admitted for the more limited purpose of impeachment. The court asks whether the prosecutor's primary motive was to offer inadmissible hearsay. The court determines the extent to which the prosecutor had reason to anticipate unfavorable trial testimony from the witness.[190] The court asks whether there was a legitimate need to call the witness,[191] and whether the prosecutor made an effort to elicit relevant and admissible testimony favorable to the government.[192] The court considers the testimony as a whole.[193] In some cases, portions of the witness's testimony are helpful to the government while other portions help the defendant. The more the witness's testimony assists the defense, the more legitimate the prosecutor's claim to impeach with prior inconsistent statements.[194]

Weinstein and Berger argue that the inquiry should not focus primarily on the prosecutor's motivation, writing, "Instead of placing so much emphasis on the motive of the profferer, an approach more consistent with the underlying policy of the federal rules of evidence would be to analyze the problem in terms of Rule 403—is the probative value of the impeaching evidence outweighed by its prejudicial impact?"[195] The approach advocated by Weinstein and Berger is employed in a number of decisions.[196] An important focus of analysis becomes the reliability of the prior inconsistent statement. The following factors assist in

---

[189] S. Saltzburg, L. Schinasi & D. Schlueter, Military Rules of Evidence Manual 640 (3d ed. 1991).

[190] State v. Hancock, 109 Wash. 2d 760, 748 P.2d 611, 613 (1988) (the record did not indicate that there was reason to anticipate that the witness would testify unfavorably).

[191] United States v. Kane, 944 F.2d 1406, 1412 (7th Cir. 1991).

[192] State v. Hancock, 109 Wash. 2d 760, 748 P.2d 611, 613 (1988).

[193] State v. Hancock, 109 Wash. 2d 760, 748 P.2d 611, 614 (1988).

[194] United States v. Kane, 944 F.2d 1406 (7th Cir. 1991); State v. Hancock, 109 Wash. 2d 760, 748 P.2d 611 (1988).

[195] 3 Weinstein & Berger ¶ 607[01], at 607-20. *See also* 3 Louisell & Mueller § 299, 194–99.

[196] *See, e.g.,* State v. Allred, 134 Ariz. 274, 655 P.2d 1326 (1982); State v. Mancine, 124 N.J. 232, 590 A.2d 1107 (1991).

determining the propriety of admitting prior inconsistent statements that may expose the jury to inadmissible hearsay:[197]

1. The reliability of the prior inconsistent statement, which is determined by the totality of the circumstances.[198] (See § **7.44** for discussion of factors affecting reliability.)
2. The degree to which the declarant is interested in the litigation, is biased, or has a motive to fabricate.
3. Assurance the declarant had personal knowledge of the subject matter of the prior statement.
4. The extent to which the declarant can be cross-examined effectively at trial regarding the prior inconsistent statement. The ability to cross-examine is high when the declarant admits making the prior statement and recalls the underlying circumstances.
5. If the declarant is a child, the court asks whether questionable interview techniques were used that may have distorted the child's recollection or coerced the child into inaccurate statements.
6. Whether the prior statement was under oath and subject to the penalty of perjury.
7. Whether the prior statement was against the declarant's interest when made.
8. Whether the declarant was in custody or under investigation at the time of the prior statements, or is beholden to the prosecutor.
9. Whether the prior statement is corroborated.
10. The probative value of the prior inconsistent statement.
11. Whether the prior inconsistent statement is the primary or only evidence on an element of the government's case. If so, is the element essential to a determination of guilt, or is the element merely technical or peripheral?[199]

---

[197] The factors described in the text are drawn from several authorities, including United States v. Leslie, 542 F.2d 285 (5th Cir. 1976); Sheldon v. State, 796 P.2d 831 (Alaska Ct. App. 1990); State v. Allred, 134 Ariz. 274, 655 P.2d 1326 (1982); State v. Mancine, 124 N.J. 232, 590 A.2d 1107 (1991); State v. Gross, 121 N.J. 1, 577 A.2d 806 (1990); 3 Weinstein & Berger ¶ 607[01, at 607-20 to 607-21.

[198] *See* United States v. Leslie, 542 F.2d 285 (5th Cir. 1976).

[199] *See* United States v. Orrico, 599 F.2d 113, 118 (6th Cir. 1979). The court wrote:

> We can conceive of . . . an "unusual case," where, for example, a purely technical element of a crime is established solely through a prior inconsistent statement . . . . But when such evidence is the only source of support for the central allegations of the charge, especially when the statements barely, if at all, meet the minimal requirements of admissibility, we do not believe that a substantial factual basis as to each element of the crime providing support for a conclusion of guilt beyond reasonable doubt has been offered by the Government.

12. The reliability and objectivity of the witness who repeats the prior inconsistent statement at trial.
13. The clarity or ambiguity of the prior statement.
14. Whether the prior statement was recorded or otherwise memorialized.
15. The likelihood of jury confusion or unfair prejudice caused by the statement. The more damaging to the defendant the prior inconsistent statement is, the greater the likelihood the jury will not limit the statement to impeachment but will erroneously use the statement for the truth of the matter asserted.
16. The extent to which the prosecutor is likely to rely on the prior inconsistent statement during trial and/or closing argument.

Child Who Recants for First Time at Trial

In some cases, the child recants for the first time during trial testimony.[200] The prosecutor may impeach the child with prior inconsistent statements.[201] Moreover, if the requirements of Rule 801(d)(1)(A) are fulfilled,[202] or if the state has a hearsay exception for prior inconsistent statements,[203] the child's statements are admissible substantively.

Inconsistency as Sole Evidence

When a prior inconsistent statement is the only evidence supporting an element of a crime, the issue is whether such statement is sufficient to support a finding

---

[200] *See* State v. Moran, 151 Ariz. 378, 728 P.2d 248 (1986).

[201] People v. Broomfield, 163 A.D.2d 403, 558 N.Y.S.2d 126 (1990).

[202] *See* United States v. Button, 31 M.J. 897, 901 (A.F.C.M.R. 1990), *aff'd,* 34 M.J. 139 (1992) (victim recanted at trial; proper to admit verbatim transcript of victim's Article 32 testimony); *see* Sheldon v. State, 796 P.2d 831 (Alaska Ct. App. 1990) (child's grand jury testimony admissible as prior inconsistent statement); State v. Moran, 151 Ariz. 378, 728 P.2d 248, 250 (1986); Commonwealth v. Berrio, 407 Mass. 37, 551 N.E.2d 496 (1990) (child testified at grand jury and implicated defendant; at trial child said nothing happened; child's grand jury testimony properly admitted under Rule 801(d)(1)(A)).

[203] *See* People v. Sambo, 197 Ill. App. 3d 574, 554 N.E.2d 1080 (1990) (physical abuse case; victim told school nurse, counselor, and police officers her parents beat her; at trial child testified her injuries were accidental; court held proper to admit child's prior inconsistent statements substantively); People v. Winfield, 160 Ill. App. 3d 983, 513 N.E.2d 1032 (1987) (six-year-old testified at preliminary hearing that defendant abused her, but at trial child said earlier testimony was "nothing but lies"; court held proper to admit prior inconsistent statement as substantive evidence).

§ 7.20 RECURRING ISSUES

of fact or verdict.[204] Courts are divided on this question.[205] The New Jersey Supreme Court adopted the preferable position with its decision in *State v. Mancine*,[206] writing that "[w]e do not believe it necessary to adopt a *per se* rule barring a conviction based solely on evidence obtained from a prior inconsistent statement."[207] Louisell and Mueller describe the proper analysis:

> That a prior inconsistent statement within Rule 801(d)(1)(A) may be received as substantive evidence does not, of course, mean that it suffices to sustain a criminal conviction, or even a civil judgment. The Senate Report anticipated that such a statement by a government witness might not suffice for conviction,[208] and the Supreme Court has similarly recognized the importance of the question of sufficiency in this context.[209]
>
> In criminal cases, assuming that a statement received under Rule 801(d)(1)(A) is the only evidence for the government on an element in the case against the accused, the following factors should affect the analysis of sufficiency: Whether the statement goes to a central or complex element in the government's case, or only to an element which is technical or simple; whether the matter

---

[204] *See* State v. Moran, 151 Ariz. 378, 728 P.2d 248 (1986) (victim recanted at trial; only evidence of guilt was victim's prior statements to school authorities, detectives, mother, foster mother, friend, and friend's mother; court held child's prior inconsistent statement admissible and sufficient to support verdict).

[205] See § 7.47, discussing the sufficiency of hearsay to support a verdict. *See also* Annotation, *Admissibility of Prior Inconsistent Statements of Witness as Substantive Evidence of Facts to Which They Relate in Criminal Cases—Modern State Cases,* 30 A.L.R.4th 414 (1984). The New Jersey Supreme Court cites most of the cases on both sides in State v. Mancine, 124 N.J. 232, 590 A.2d 1107, 1116 (1991).

[206] 124 N.J. 232, 590 A.2d 1107 (1991).

[207] 590 A.2d at 1117.

[208] Louisell and Mueller's footnote:

> S. Rep. No. 93-1277, 93d Cong., 2d Sess. 16, n. 21 (1974) ("It would appear that some of the opposition to [FRE 801(d)(1)(A)] is based on a concern that a person could be convicted solely upon evidence admissible under this Rule. The Rule, however, is not addressed to the question of the sufficiency of the evidence to send a case to the jury, but merely as [sic] to its admissibility. Factual circumstances could well arise where, if this were the sole evidence, dismissal would be appropriate").

[209] Louisell and Mueller's footnote:

> California v Green (1970) 399 US 149, 170 and 170 n.19, 26 L Ed 2d 489, 503–504 and 504 n.19, 90 S Ct 1930, on remand 3 Cal 3d 981, 92 Cal Rptr 494, 479 P2d 998, cert dismd 404 US 801, 30 L Ed 2d 34, 92 S Ct 20 (after holding that the Confrontation Clause was not offended by the use against the accused of inconsistent statements by a prosecution witness, whether made in proceedings under oath or to a police officer out of court, noting that the California Supreme Court 'may choose to dispose of the case on other grounds,' including 'sufficiency of the evidence to sustain the conviction'; also noting that this issue is 'not insubstantial,' as the conviction 'rests almost entirely on the evidence in Porter's two prior statements which were themselves inconsistent in some respects').

asserted in the prior statement is only formally disputed, or actually contradicted by counterproof adduced by the accused; whether the declarant testifies favorably to the accused at trial, or only asserts a lack of memory; whether, in the latter event, the claimed lack of memory is believable or, on the facts, highly suspect; whether the prior statement is itself direct and certain, or in some way either qualified or equivocal; whether the declarant-witness is impeached in a way which raises doubts concerning his veracity or accuracy in connection with the prior statement.

It must be expected that sometimes a prior inconsistent statement will not satisfy the sufficiency standard. Where, for example, the statement relates to a central element in the government's case, it should not suffice to take the issue to the jury or sustain a conviction if the witness testifies favorably to the accused at trial in a credible manner, or if the prior statement is contradicted by other counterproof or undermined by an attack on the veracity of the witness-declarant: Here a reasonable jury simply could not be convinced of guilt beyond a reasonable doubt. On the other hand, it may be expected that sometimes a prior inconsistent statement can satisfy the sufficiency standard. Where, for example, the witness claims at trial a lack of memory unworthy of belief, while the prior statement is unequivocal and uncontradicted and on the facts entirely believable, the statement may well suffice to establish even an important element in the government's case.[210]

§ 7.21 Prior Consistent Statements

Prior consistent statements play a central role in child abuse litigation. The Alaska Court of Appeals captured the importance of prior consistent statements in *Nitz v. State,*[211] where the court wrote:

Questions concerning the admissibility of prior consistent statements are hardly unique to cases involving the sexual assault of children. Yet, there are perhaps no other cases in which these questions arise so regularly and are imbued with such urgent significance. In cases of sexual assault against children, there are seldom any witnesses to the crime. Often, there is little or no physical evidence capable of lending support to the victim's story. Particularly where a parent or a step-parent is charged, the question of guilt invariably hinges on the

---

[210] 4 Louisell & Mueller § 419, at 183–85 (some footnotes omitted). *See also* 4 Weinstein & Berger ¶ 801(d)(1)(A), where the authors write:

Theoretically, a party may be able to make out a prima facie case even if the only evidence is a previous inconsistent statement of this type. Under the former practice, "if the only evidence of some essential fact is such a previous statement, the party's case falls." In a criminal prosecution, however, it is unlikely that a prior inconsistent statement alone will suffice to support a conviction, since a reasonable juror usually could not be convinced beyond a reasonable doubt by such evidence alone.

801-141 to 801-142 (footnotes omitted).

[211] 720 P.2d 55 (Alaska Ct. App. 1986).

credibility of the victim. The victim is typically an unsophisticated child, inarticulate, and emotionally torn by the experience. Impressionable, readily confused, and incapable of furnishing any detailed verbal account of the offense, the typical victim is hardly an ideal witness.

Thus, in such cases, when the accused attacks the victim's testimony by an express or implied claim of faulty memory or fabrication, the victim's testimony is particularly vulnerable. Jurors are left with virtually no frame of reference for evaluating the credibility of the victim's story, which is bound to seem, at one and the same time, too serious to be accepted uncritically and too shocking to be rejected lightly. Reliance on personal experience and common sense will be of little value to most jurors: because the victim is a child and sexual abuse of children is a subject alien to the experience of most jurors, a realistic context for evaluating truthfulness will be difficult to find. Understandably, then, conscientious jurors may often find themselves in desperate need of reliable information to shed light on the veracity of the victim's testimony.

It is this peculiar context, we believe, that imparts a unique sense of urgency to questions concerning the admissibility of prior consistent statements in cases of sexual assault upon children, for evidence of prior statements by the victim and the circumstances in which those statements were made can be of significant benefit to the jury. When actually relevant to refute a claim of fabrication or false memory, such evidence can, in our view, furnish the jury with a reliable and understandable backdrop against which to judge credibility.[212]

Under the common law, a witness's out-of-court statement that is consistent with trial testimony is admissible to rehabilitate credibility following impeachment charging that the witness's trial testimony is fabricated.[213] A prior consistent statement that is admitted solely to rehabilitate credibility is not offered for the truth of the matter asserted, and therefore, the hearsay rule is not offended.[214]

Rule 801(d)(1)(B) governs admissibility of prior consistent statements under the Federal Rules of Evidence. The rule provides:

> A statement is not hearsay if the declarant testifies at the trial or hearing and is subject to cross-examination concerning the statement, and the statement is consistent with the declarant's testimony and is offered to rebut an express or implied charge against the declarant of recent fabrication or improper influence or motive . . . .[215]

---

[212] *Id.* at 60–61. The court goes on to point out the importance of protecting the defendant from unfair prejudice that may arise from admission of prior consistent statements. *Id.* at 61.

[213] Commonwealth v. Knapp, 374 Pa. Super. 160, 542 A.2d 546, 553 (1988); Graham, *Prior Consistent Statements: Rule 801(d)(1)(B) of the Federal Rules of Evidence, Critique and Proposal,* 30 Hastings L.J. 575 (1979) [hereinafter Graham, Critique].

[214] *See* McCormick § 49, at 118 n. 16.

[215] Fed. R. Evid. 801(d)(1)(B).

Rule 801(d)(1)(B) permits prior consistent statements "to rebut an express or implied charge against the declarant of recent fabrication *or* improper influence or motive . . . ."[216] The language of Rule 801(d)(1)(B) requires explanation. The rule's purpose is to open the way for prior consistent statements when the cross-examiner charges that trial testimony is deliberately untrue or, in the words of the New York Court of Appeals, "fabricated to meet the exigencies of the case."[217] How does the cross-examiner level the charge of fabrication? Often through evidence that improper influence was exerted on the witness or that the witness has a motive to fabricate. Note that under Rule 801(d)(1)(B) improper influence and motive are not ends in themselves, but means to the end of establishing fabrication.[218] The rule would be clarified by deleting the words "improper influence or motive." The rule would then express the intended purpose, which is to allow prior consistent statements "to rebut an express or implied charge of fabrication." Deleting the words "improper influence or motive" would highlight the fact that improper influence and motive are not alternatives to fabrication, but factors which prove fabrication.[219]

Prior consistent statements meeting the requirements under Rule 801(d)(1)(B) are nonhearsay, and are admissible for the truth of the matter asserted.[220] In some states, prior consistent statements are hearsay within an exception.[221] In other states, prior consistent statements are admissible only to rehabilitate credibility, and may not be considered for the truth.[222]

Rule 801(d)(1)(A) states that for prior *in*consistent statements to be defined as nonhearsay, the prior inconsistent statements must be under oath and subject to the penalty of perjury. By contrast, Rule 801(d)(1)(B) "makes no distinctions based upon the setting and nature of the prior statement. Any prior consistent statement, whether sworn or unsworn, oral or written, uttered in or out of court, is potentially within the reach of Rule 801(d)(1)(B)."[223]

---

[216] *Id.* (emphasis added).

[217] People v. Singer, 300 N.Y. 120, 124, 89 N.E.2d 710, 711 (1949).

[218] *See* Graham, Critique, at 583.

[219] *See* Sullivan v. Minneapolis State Ry. Co., 161 Minn. 45, 200 N.W. 922, 924 (1924).

[220] *See* 4 Weinstein & Berger ¶ 801(d)(1)(B) (prior consistent statements should be admissible as nonhearsay because such statements are admissible to rehabilitate, and the jury is unlikely to abide by an instruction against using the statements for the truth).

Some courts interpret Rule 801(d)(1)(B) to allow substantive use of certain prior consistent statements, but to permit other prior consistent statements only to rehabilitate credibility, and not for the truth of the matter asserted. *See* Nitz v. State, 720 P.2d 55 (Alaska Ct. App. 1986) (*Nitz* is discussed infra this section).

[221] *See* Cal. Evid. Code § 1236 (West 1991).

[222] Commonwealth v. Knapp, 374 Pa. Super. 160, 542 A.2d 546, 553 (1988).

[223] 4 Louisell & Mueller § 420, at 187 (footnote omitted). *See also* United States v. Red Feather, 865 F.2d 169 (8th Cir. 1989) (child's diary admissible as prior consistent statement); Smith v. State, 538 So. 2d 66, 68 (Fla. Dist. Ct. App. 1989) (child's notes to friend and mother admissible as prior consistent statements); Cartmill v. State, 748 S.W.2d 581

§ 7.22 —Admissibility Requirements

Three requirements must be fulfilled for a prior consistent statement to be admissible under Rule 801(d)(1)(B).[224] First, the statement must be consistent with trial testimony.[225] The prior statement does not have to be identical to trial testimony. Many sexually abused children disclose progressively more detail. Thus, a child's trial testimony may contain more information than early disclosures. If the child's out-of-court disclosure is consistent with—albeit less detailed than—the child's trial testimony, the prior statement should be admitted.[226]

The second requirement is that the prior consistent statement must rebut a charge of recent fabrication.[227]

The third requirement is that the declarant testify at trial and be subject to cross-examination concerning the statement. A child whose testimony is presented via contemporaneous closed-circuit television testifies "at trial" for purposes of Rule 801(d)(1)(B).[228] In *State v. Lindner*,[229] the Wisconsin Court of Appeals held that a child testified "at trial" when the child's videotaped deposition was played at trial in lieu of the child's testimony. When the deposition was videotaped, the defendant and his attorney were present, as was the judge, and the child was cross-examined.

The court determines pursuant to Rule 104(a) whether the requirements of Rule 801(d)(1)(B) are fulfilled.[230]

A statement admissible under Rule 801(d)(1)(B) may be offered on redirect examination by asking the witness to repeat the witness's own prior consistent statement. Alternatively, the statement may be offered through other witnesses.[231]

(Tex. Ct. App. 1988) (videotape interview admissible as prior consistent statement); 4 Weinstein & Berger ¶ 801(d)(1)(B).

[224] *See* United States v. Red Feather, 865 F.2d 169 (8th Cir. 1989) (describing two requirements); Slater v. Baker, 301 N.W.2d 315, 319 (Minn. 1981); State v. Lucero, 109 N.M. 298, 784 P.2d 1041 (Ct. App. 1989) (describing two requirements); Lacey v. State, 803 P.2d 1364, 1368 (Wyo. 1990) (describing two requirements); 4 Louisell & Mueller § 420, at 186.

[225] Fed. R. Evid. 801(d)(1)(B).

[226] *See* United States v. Red Feather, 865 F.2d 169 (8th Cir. 1989) (child's prior statement was consistent with trial testimony with the exception of one date).

[227] See text accompanying **note 242** for the meaning of "recent fabrication."

[228] See **Ch. 8** for discussion of contemporaneous video testimony as the functional equivalent of testimony from the witness stand.

[229] 142 Wis. 2d 783, 419 N.W.2d 352 (Ct. App. 1987).

[230] *See* 4 Louisell & Mueller § 420, at 76 (Supp. 1990).

[231] *See* United States v. Cherry, 938 F.2d 748 (7th Cir. 1991); 4 Louisell & Mueller § 420, at 188 ("of course such a statement may be proved not merely by redirect examination of the witness, but by extrinsic evidence") (footnote omitted).

Admissibility of prior consistent statements is related to impeachment; thus prior consistent statements must await impeachment.[232] Moreover, only certain types of impeachment trigger admissibility of prior consistent statements.

The theoretical aspects of prior consistent statements are exceedingly complex, and cannot be explored fully in this section. Professor Graham examined the subject at length in a useful article.[233] The goal of the present discussion is to analyze three modes of impeachment that trigger admissibility of prior consistent statements, and that arise in child abuse litigation.

Before turning to impeachment that opens the door to prior consistent statements, it is useful to mention impeachment techniques that usually do not open the door. McCormick writes that "[w]hen the attack takes the form of impeachment of character, by showing misconduct, convictions or bad reputation, it is generally agreed that there is no color for sustaining by consistent statements."[234] Generally, impeachment by contradiction does not trigger admission of prior consistent statements.[235] Suppose, for example, that X testifies a car went through a red light. To impeach this testimony the opponent offers evidence that the light was green. The impeaching effect of the contradiction is not deflected by evidence that before trial X made a statement consistent with his trial testimony. Thus, the prior consistent statement is inadmissible.

Turning now to impeachment that triggers admissibility of prior consistent statements, the charge that trial testimony is fabricated may be express or implied.[236] In most cases the cross-examiner implies fabrication "through insin-

---

[232] United States v. Weil, 561 F.2d 1109, 1111 (4th Cir. 1977) ("Corroborative testimony consisting of prior, consistent statements is ordinarily inadmissible unless the testimony sought to be bolstered has first been impeached"); Wise v. State, 546 So. 2d 1068 (Fla. Dist. Ct. App. 1989); State v. Benton, 759 S.W.2d 427, 433–34 (Tenn. Crim. App. 1988); McCormick § 49, at 115 ("in the absence of an attack upon credibility no sustaining evidence is allowed") (footnote omitted).

[233] See Graham, Critique.

[234] McCormick § 49, at 118. Louisell and Mueller write, "A general imputation of bad character for truth and veracity, such as might result from cross-examination concerning prior bad acts under Rule 608 or prior convictions under Rule 609 or from negative testimony by a character witness, can hardly make prior consistencies relevant . . . ." 4 Louisell & Mueller § 420, at 198.

[235] See 4 Louisell & Mueller § 420, at 198. But see Slater v. Baker, 301 N.W.2d 315 (Minn. 1981) (medical malpractice case; plaintiff's testimony was contradicted by medical records; defense charged that inconsistency between plaintiff's trial testimony and records showed testimony was fabricated; holding that trial court erred in excluding prior consistent statements offered by plaintiff to rebut charge of fabrication).

[236] Fed. R. Evid. 801(d)(1)(B). See Dearing v. State, 100 Nev. 590, 691 P.2d 419, 421 (1984). In *Dearing* it was the intensity of cross-examination that convinced the court to allow prior consistent statements. The court wrote:

We note that appellant's trial counsel cross-examined the child witness at considerable length with the apparent intention of implying that the child's credibility was questionable. Although counsel did not suggest any specific motive for fabrication or indicate

§ 7.22 ADMISSIBILITY REQUIREMENTS

uation, suggestion, inference or imputation . . . ."[237] The charge may come as early as opening statement.[238] For example, the following segment of defense counsel's opening statement contains a rather strong suggestion of fabrication:

> The evidence will show that the child's mother and the child were attempting to get my client to move out of the house at the time these allegations were made. Further, the evidence will show that the child said nothing about the alleged abuse for months. The subject of abuse came up only when marital difficulties erupted between the child's mother and my client. Furthermore, the evidence will show that the child changed her story more than once, and at one point denied that anything happened.

In many cases, the cross-examiner asks the child questions that raise the possibility of bias[239] against the defendant or coaching by interviewers or the

---

where or when such a motive might have arisen, counsel's heavy cross-examination of the victim was directed at impugning her credibility. In light of the heavy cross-examination, the state attempted to rehabilitate the victim's credibility by offering prior consistent statements which the victim had made to her mother just a few days after the attack.

We conclude that the district court did not abuse its discretion by admitting the mother's testimony regarding the prior consistent statements. *See State v. Pitts,* 62 Wash. 2d 294, 382 P.2d 508 (1963). As the court states in *Pitts*: "Repetition adds stature to imputations and insinuations and may well infer recent fabrication. The trial court saw and heard the live performance; it was in a position to weigh any innuendoes and nuances, and it admitted [the prior consistent statement] for the limited purpose stated." 382 P.2d at 510–11.

See also United States v. Cherry, 938 F.2d 748 (7th Cir. 1991) (charge of fabrication inferred from extensive cross-examination); United States v. Farmer, 923 F.2d 1557, 1568 (11th Cir. 1991) ("judge was not required to find an express charge of recent fabrication to admit prior consistent testimony"); United States v. Andrade, 788 F.2d 521, 533 (8th Cir.), *cert. denied,* 479 U.S. 963 (1986) (fabrication may be inferred from extensive cross-examination indicating a well-planned attack on credibility).

[237] Graham, Critique at 585 n.38. *See* State v. King, 115 N.J. Super. 140, 278 A.2d 504 (1971) ("A 'charge' of recent fabrication can be effected through implication by the cross-examiner as well as by direct accusation of the witness. In fact that is the usual way in which the charge is made"); Commonwealth v. Gore, 262 Pa. Super. 540, 396 A.2d 1302, 1307 (1978) ("it is not necessary that the impeachment be explicit, i.e., that an actual allegation of recent fabrication be made, but only that a jury be able to reasonably infer that such is occurring").

[238] United States v. Cherry, 938 F.2d 748 (7th Cir. 1991); State v. Hibbs, 239 Mont. 308, 780 P.2d 182, 185 (1989). *But see* Wise v. State, 546 So. 2d 1068, 1070 (Fla. Dist. Ct. App. 1989) (during opening statement defense counsel indicated general intent to attack child's credibility; this nonspecific intent did not render the child's prior consistent statements to the child's mother admissible).

[239] *See* United States v. Cherry, 938 F.2d 748 (7th Cir. 1991) (defendant extensively cross-examined 13-year-old victim, at one point implying that the victim "felt rejected" because defendant did not consummate the sexual act); Graham, Critique, at 585–86, where the author writes:

> Partiality of a witness may be evidenced either by the circumstances of the witness' situation, or by the conduct of the witness himself. Cross-examination of the witness

136   HEARSAY

prosecutor.[240] In *State v. Bass*,[241] for example, a five-year-old was an eyewitness to his brother's brutal murder by the defendant. At trial, defense counsel

> concerning the existence of facts from which the jury might naturally infer partiality . . . should constitute an implied charge of falsification. However, if the attorney, during cross-examination, inquires beyond the mere existence of either the circumstances of the witness' situation or the conduct of the witness from which partiality may be inferred, and thereby in his questioning directly asserts the existence of the partiality previously left to be inferred by the trier of fact, an express charge of falsification has been levied. In either event, pursuant to Rule 801(d)(1)(B), a prior consistent statement is now admissible if relevant to rebut the implied or express charge.
>
> (footnotes omitted).

[240] *See* Commonwealth v. McEachin, 371 Pa. Super. 188, 537 A.2d 883, 891 (1988). The court wrote:

> An examination of the record indicates that while appellant did not expressly assert fabrication, the following line of questions implies fabrication:
>
> Q: You love your mommy, don't you?
> A: Yes.
> Q: And you love your daddy, don't you?
> A: Yes.
> Q: And, [R.J.], when they tell you to do something you do it.
> A: Yes.
>
> Trial transcript at 178. In addition, appellant's counsel asked questions on cross-examination emphasizing that R.J. and E.J. had gone over their testimony numerous times before trial with the district attorney's office.

See also Smith v. State, 538 So. 2d 66, 68 (Fla. Dist. Ct. App. 1989), in which the court wrote:

> We find on the record an implied charge by Smith that the victim was improperly influenced by her mother and the state to bring charges against her father, and that this influence created in her a motive to lie. For example, in cross-examination of the victim, counsel for Smith asks:
>
> Q. How many times have you talked to your mother about this alleged abuse and the incidents since all of this started when you gave her that note?
> A. I talked to her the same day I gave her the note, before we went to the sheriff's office . . . .
> Q. How many times have you talked to Mr. Moran and the other people in the state attorney's office about this case?
> A. At lease (sic) twice in their office.
> Q. And the people from HRS and Child Protection?
> A. Talked to all them about eleven . . . .
> Q. Did your mother help your memory about what was supposedly said that day four years ago?
> A. A little bit.
> Q. Did you see tell what (sic) was supposedly said back then?
> A. No.

See also United States v. Red Feather, 865 F.2d 169, 171 (8th Cir. 1989) (defense charged child was coached by social workers); United States v. Morgan, 31 M.J. 43, 46 (C.M.A.

asked the child questions such as, "When you forgot, did the detective help you remember that Allen hit him, too?" The clear purpose of the cross-examination was to charge that the detective coached the child, and that the child's trial testimony was fabricated. The court ruled that the child's prior consistent statements were admissible.

Rule 801(d)(1)(B) speaks of "recent fabrication." Graham explains the meaning of the word *recent:*

> "Recent" trial testimony need not have been created just prior to the trial. Rather, a "fabrication" is "recent" if the in-court testimony is expressly or impliedly charged to have been consciously fabricated at any time after the event. Thus, a charge of "recent fabrication" has been made whenever, upon cross-examination of a witness, counsel expressly or impliedly charges that the in-court testimony of the witness, regardless of when the testimony was crystallized, is a result of a *conscious* falsification occurring at any time after the event related.[242]

§ 7.23 —Fabrication Motivated by Improper Influence, Bias, or Interest

The motivation to fabricate testimony springs from several sources.[243] External pressure may be exerted on the witness to fabricate.[244] Alternatively, the

---

1990), *cert. denied,* 111 S. Ct. 959 (1991) (defendant charged recent fabrication by emphasizing child's prior inconsistent statements and "stressing that she had told her story 'over and over again'"); Slater v. Baker, 301 N.W.2d 315, 317, 319 (Minn. 1981) (in medical malpractice case defendant vigorously cross-examined plaintiff about the facts "according to your story"; defendant also challenged plaintiff's truthfulness; this impeachment triggered admission of prior consistent statements); State v. Scheffelman, 820 P.2d 1293 (Mont. 1991) (defendant asserted improper influence by prosecutor); State v. Bass, 221 N.J. Super. 466, 535 A.2d 1, 11 (1987) (cross-examiner asked questions such as "Oh. When you forgot, did the detective help you remember that Allen hit him too?" and "And, Davell, when you forgot things about what happened at the apartment, did they help you remember?"; court wrote, "It is clear that this cross-examination of Davell was an attack on his credibility and was calculated to imply that Davell fabricated his account of the murder of his brother pertaining to defendant at the urging of the prosecutor's investigators"); Lacey v. State, 803 P.2d 1364, 1368 (Wyo. 1990) (adult kidnap victim; defendant "repeatedly asked her if she and the prosecuting attorney had gone over her testimony before trial").

[241] 221 N.J. Super. 466, 535 A.2d 1 (1987).

[242] Graham, Critique, at 582–83.

[243] *See id.* at 585.

[244] United States v. Red Feather, 865 F.2d 169, 171 (8th Cir. 1989) (defense charged coaching by social workers); United States v. Morgan, 31 M.J. 43 (C.M.A. 1990), *cert. denied,* 111 S. Ct. 959 (1991) (defendant charged that child's mother coached child to make allegation); United States v. Jones, 26 M.J. 197 (C.M.A. 1988) (victim was 17 years old and severely retarded; defendant charged she was suggestible); Smith v. State, 538 So. 2d 66, 68 (Fla. Dist. Ct. App. 1989) (defendant implied child was influenced by mother and prosecutor); Commonwealth v. Healey, 27 Mass. App. Ct. 30, 534 N.E.2d 301, 305 (1989) (cross-examiner charged, inter alia,

witness's private allegiances, emotions, or biases may shape testimony.[245] When the cross-examiner expressly or impliedly charges that external pressure or internal motive is responsible for fabricated testimony, prior consistent statements are admissible to rebut the charge.[246] Although Rule 801(d)(1)(B) is silent on the point, courts agree that in most cases, prior consistent

---

that social worker applied improper pressure on child); State v. Bass, 221 N.J. Super. 466, 535 A.2d 1 (1987) (while cross-examining five-year-old eyewitness, defense counsel insinuated that police officers planted the story in the child's mind); State v. Lucero, 109 N.M. 298, 784 P.2d 1041 (Ct. App. 1989) (defendant asserted child's mother influenced child to accuse defendant); Commonwealth v. Knapp, 374 Pa. Super. 160, 542 A.2d 546, 554 (1988) (defense asserted during cross-examination of child that prosecutor told child what to say); Commonwealth v. McEachin, 371 Pa. Super. 188, 537 A.2d 883 (1988); Thomas v. State, 92 Wis. 2d 372, 284 N.W.2d 917, 926 (1979) (defendant charged improper influence by prosecutor and child's mother); State v. Lindner, 142 Wis. 2d 783, 419 N.W.2d 352, 357 (Ct. App. 1987) (defendant charged improper influence by prosecutor).

[245] *See* State v. Littlefield, 540 A.2d 777 (Me. 1988). In *Littlefield* defendant argued that the 16-year-old victim had a crush on him, which he rebuffed. He implied that the victim fabricated the charges of sexual abuse following this rejection. To rebut the charge of fabrication, the prosecutor was allowed to offer the victim's prior consistent statements to her aunt. The prior consistent statements were made shortly following the assault, and the trial court could properly find that the statements were made before the development of the alleged motive to fabricate.

See Nitz v. State, 720 P.2d 55 (Alaska Ct. App. 1986). In *Nitz* the defense theory was that the victim fabricated the allegation because she did not like the defendant, who was her stepfather, and wanted him to leave. To rebut the charge of fabrication, the state offered evidence that the victim was very reluctant to disclose the abuse, and did so only over time. The victim's prior consistent statements supported the state's theory. The court wrote that "[t]o the extent that the evidence of T.K.'s prior statements actually supported this theory, we believe it could properly be deemed relevant to refute Nitz's attack on the credibility of T.K.'s testimony." *Id.* at 68.

See also United States v. Red Feather, 865 F.2d 169, 171 (8th Cir. 1989) (defense charged that victim "was prejudiced against her father because of punishment or discipline by him"); Thompson v. State, 769 P.2d 997 (Alaska Ct. App. 1989) (defense was that child fabricated allegations so her mother would not marry defendant); Nusunginya v. State, 730 P.2d 172 (Alaska Ct. App. 1986) (defendant attempted to show child was lying); Commonwealth v. Healey, 27 Mass. App. Ct. 30, 534 N.E.2d 301, 305 (1989) (defendant charged, inter alia, that child was angry with him for disciplining her and forming a relationship with a woman).

[246] *See* State v. Bass, 221 N.J. Super. 466, 535 A.2d 1 (1987). *See also* 4 Louisell & Mueller § 420, at 188–89, where the authors write:

> Traditionally two kinds of impeaching evidence have been thought to raise [charges of recent fabrication]. One is direct evidence of bias or motive, or evidence (or even mere imputation) that the witness has made it all up, and of course both of these attacks may be mounted by cross-examination of the witness being impeached or through the testimony of others.

(footnotes omitted).

§ 7.23   FABRICATION   139

statements are admissible only when uttered before the motive or pressure to fabricate arose.[247] As Graham writes:

> When partiality is impliedly or expressly charged to have resulted in the witness's falsification of testimony at trial, a consistent statement made prior to the existence of the alleged partiality tends to rebut the suggestion of falsification. On the other hand, a prior consistent statement that occurred after the fabricating influence or motive arose does not rebut the charge that partiality prompted the witness' testimony. Such a statement would show only that the witness made a statement consistent with the testimony at a time when he was under the same pressure to fabricate such testimony as at trial.[248]

In some cases it is difficult to determine when the alleged improper influence or motive to fabricate arose.[249] When the defense concentrates heavily on fabrication, the need for rehabilitation is increased, and courts are likely to admit prior consistent statements despite some uncertainty regarding when the influence or motive arose.[250]

An illustration is useful. Five-year-old Mark's parents are divorced. His mother has custody, and his father exercises visitation. One day, Mark told his mother that sexual abuse occurred during visits with his father. His mother contacted the authorities, and Mark was interviewed by a police officer. During the interview Mark again described the abuse. Two months following the interview, Mark repeated his description to a psychologist. Thus, Mark described abuse consistently to his mother, the police officer, and the psychologist. His

---

[247] United States v. Morgan, 31 M.J. 43, 46 (C.M.A. 1990), *cert. denied,* 111 S. Ct. 959 (1991); United States v. McClaskey, 30 M.J. 188 (C.M.A. 1990); Pennington v. State, 24 Ark. App. 70, 749 S.W.2d 680 (1988) (reversing conviction because of improper admission of prior consistent statements); Wise v. State, 546 So. 2d 1068, 1069 (Fla. Dist. Ct. App. 1989); State v. Littlefield, 540 A.2d 777 (Me. 1988) (proper to conclude that 16-year-old victim's prior consistent statements were made before victim allegedly formed dislike for defendant and fabricated allegations); Commonwealth v. Healey, 27 Mass. App. Ct. 30, 534 N.E.2d 301, 304 (1989); State v. Scheffelman, 820 P.2d 1293, 1297 (Mont. 1991); State v. Harper, 35 Wash. App. 855, 670 P.2d 296 (1983) (improper admission of prior consistent statements was reversible error).

See also McCormick § 49, at 118, where the author writes:

> [I]f the attacker has charged bias, interest, corrupt influence, contrivance to falsify, or want of capacity to observe or remember, the applicable principle is that the prior consistent statement has no relevancy to refute the charge unless the consistent statement was made before the source of the bias, interest, or incapacity originated.

(footnote omitted); 4 Louisell & Mueller § 420, at 193; 4 Weinstein & Berger ¶ 801(d)(1)(B) at 801-188 to 801-189.

[248] Graham, Critique, at 586-87.

[249] United States v. Morgan, 31 M.J. 43 (C.M.A. 1990), *cert. denied,* 111 S. Ct. 959 (1991).

[250] *Id.* Dearing v. State, 100 Nev. 590, 691 P.2d 419 (1984).

father is charged with abuse, which he denies. At trial, Mark testifies for the prosecution and describes the abuse.

At the outset of cross-examination, defense counsel has considerable ability to control the admission of Marks's prior consistent statements.[251] Defense counsel may block prior consistent statements by refraining from cross-examination that renders consistent statements relevant. Suppose, however, that the defendant's theory is that the police officer who interviewed Mark used highly leading questions that effectively coached Mark into fabricated allegations of sexual abuse, and that, following the interview, pressure was maintained on the child to perpetuate the fabrication. Note that a charge of fabrication may take place during cross-examination of Mark or of the police officer.

Once the defense charges fabrication, the door is open for prior consistent statements, and the prosecutor may offer Mark's initial disclosure to his mother. The initial disclosure preceded the interview in which the alleged improper influence occurred. The fact that before the alleged improper influence Mark described the abuse in terms consistent with his trial testimony undermines the claim that Mark's testimony is a product of improper influence. As Weinstein and Berger write, "Evidence that counteracts a suggestion that the witness changed his story in response to some threat or scheme or bribe, by showing that his story was the same prior to the alleged external pressure is highly relevant in shedding light on the witness's credibility."[252]

Mark's statement to the psychologist was made after the police officer's questionable interview. The fact that Mark's description to the psychologist is consistent with his trial testimony may do little to rehabilitate his credibility because the statement to the psychologist could simply be a product of the very improper influence charged by the defense. Weinstein and Berger observe that "[e]vidence that merely shows that the witness said the same thing on other occasions when his motive was the same does not have much probative force, 'for the simple reason that mere repetition does not imply veracity.'"[253]

A change in defense strategy could further restrict admission of Mark's prior consistent statements.[254] If defense counsel argues that Mark's mother was the one who coached Mark into making the initial disclosure to her, then Mark's statements to the police officer and the psychologist occurred after the improper influence arose, and are inadmissible as prior consistent statements.

---

[251] United States v. Morgan, 31 M.J. 43, 46 (C.M.A. 1990), *cert. denied,* 112 S. Ct. 959 (1991) ("admissibility of such declarations is 'a matter of choice by the party opposed by the witness,' who 'may "open the door" to the use of such statements by engaging in a particular kind of impeachment, or leave the door shut by refraining'") (quoting from 4 Louisell & Mueller § 420, at 187).

[252] 4 Weinstein & Berger, ¶ 801(d)(1)(B), at 801-188.

[253] *Id.* at 801-188 to 801-189.

[254] *See* State v. Lucero, 109 N.M. 298, 784 P.2d 1041 (Ct. App. 1989).

§ 7.23 FABRICATION

The ability of the cross-examiner to control admission of prior consistent statements is not unfettered.[255] In Mark's case, for example, defense counsel should not be permitted to charge Mark's mother with improper influence—thereby cutting off *any* prior consistent statements—unless defense counsel shoulders the burden of proving that Mark's mother actually exerted improper influence. The cross-examiner cannot foreclose prior consistent statements with baseless accusations.

As stated above, prior consistent statements usually have greatest probative value when the statements are made before improper influence is exerted.[256] Cases exist, however, where prior consistent statements have rehabilitative value even though uttered following improper influence.[257] *Nitz v. State*[258] is a leading authority approving prior consistent statements uttered following improper influence or motive.[259] The *Nitz* court wrote:

> Under our interpretation of Rule 801(d)(1)(B), the admission of prior consistent statements made after a motive to falsify has arisen should be treated as a question of relevance, for determination on a case-by-case basis. In each instance where admission is sought, the trial court must begin by determining whether the prior statement is actually relevant "to rebut an express or implied charge . . . of recent fabrication or improper influence or motive. . . ." A.R.E.

---

[255] United States v. Cherry, 938 F.2d 748 (7th Cir. 1991) (defendant's argument that victim's motive to fabricate arose before her statements was "highly speculative and is not supported by the evidence"); State v. Lucero, 109 N.M. 298, 784 P.2d 1041 (Ct. App. 1989).

[256] See **note 252**. When impeachment is based on the child's prior inconsistent statements, courts often allow a prior consistent statement that was uttered *after* the utterance of the prior inconsistent statement. *See, e.g.,* State v. Resendez, 82 Or. App. 259, 728 P.2d 562 (1986).

[257] United States v. Payne, 944 F.2d 1458, 1471 (9th Cir. 1991), *cert. denied,* 112 S. Ct. 1598 (1992); United States v. Simmons, 923 F.2d 934 (2d Cir.), *cert. denied,* 111 S. Ct. 2018 (1991); 4 Louisell & Mueller § 420, at 194, 94; 4 Weinstein & Berger ¶ 801(d)(1)(B), at 801-196.

[258] 720 P.2d 55 (Alaska Ct. App. 1986).

[259] *See also* United States v. Farmer, 923 F.2d 1557, 1568 (11th Cir. 1991); United States v. Harris, 761 F.2d 394 (7th Cir. 1985); State v. Lucero, 109 N.M. 298, 784 P.2d 1041, 1042 (Ct. App. 1989), where the court wrote:

> We adopt the position of those circuits which do not make it an absolute condition of admissibility that the declarant's statements have been made prior to the existence of the alleged motive to fabricate. . . . We choose a more flexible position that would permit the trial court to examine the circumstances under which the statement was made and make a determination of the statement's relevancy and probativeness to rebut a charge of recent fabrication or improper influence or motive. While these factors are, of course, more likely to be found where the statement was made prior to the alleged discrediting influence, "temporal priority should not be a condition precedent to admissibility."
>
> We admonish, however, that the approach we take does not allow wide-open admission of just any prior consistent statement.

(references omitted).

801(d)(1)(B). Next, if the court finds the statement to be actually relevant, it must proceed to balance the probative value of the statement against its potential for creating unfair prejudice. A.R.E. 402, 403. Finally, if the court determines the statement to be admissible, it must instruct the jury that the statement should be considered for the limited purpose of determining the credibility of the declarant's trial testimony and that it should not be considered directly as proof that the matters asserted in it are true.[260]

The *Nitz* court wisely focused on the relevance of a particular prior consistent statement, rejecting a rule that prior statements uttered following improper influence are always inadmissible.[261] Under the *Nitz* approach, a prior consistent statement made following undue influence or motive is not admissible for the truth of the matter asserted, and the jury must be instructed that it may consider the statement only insofar as it impacts on the witness's credibility.

It is not difficult to describe child abuse cases in which prior consistent statements should be admitted despite the fact that the statements were uttered following undue influence or motive. The primary rationale for excluding prior consistent statements until the witness has been impeached is that consistent statements are thought to have little value absent a charge of fabrication. As Wigmore put it, "When the witness has merely testified on direct examination, without any impeachment, proof of consistent statement is unnecessary and valueless. The witness is not helped by it; for, even if it is an improbable or untrustworthy story, it is not made more probable or more trustworthy by any number of repetitions of it."[262]

Although Wigmore's observation may be true for adults, the same cannot be said for children. A child's ability to maintain a consistent description of abuse over time is a hallmark of trustworthiness.[263] The cross-examiner has means short of full-scale impeachment to insinuate that a child's trial testimony is unbelievable.[264] The examiner may raise doubts about children's memory or ability to differentiate fact from fantasy. The cross-examiner's efforts may be aided by the disposition of some jurors to doubt children's credibility. However the cross-examiner undermines the child's credibility, the jury's ability to assess

---

[260] State v. Lucero, 720 P.2d at 68.

[261] *Id.* at 66 ("we see little reason to apply a *per se* rule of exclusion, provided that the probative value of the prior statement as rebuttal evidence is determined to outweigh its potential for prejudicial impact").

[262] 4 Wigmore § 1124, at 255 (footnote omitted).

[263] *See* Idaho v. Wright, 110 S. Ct. 3139, 3150 (1990). See also **§ 7.47** for discussion of the role of consistency in evaluating the trustworthiness of hearsay.

See also In re Noel M., 23 Conn. App. 410, 580 A.2d 996 (1990) (juvenile court dependency case does not involve use of prior consistent statements but court emphasized importance of child's consistency in evaluating child's credibility).

[264] Dearing v. State, 100 Nev. 590, 691 P.2d 419 (1984).

credibility is often assisted by admission of the child's prior consistent statements.[265] As the Alaska Court of Appeals observed, prior consistent statements can "furnish the jury with a reliable and understandable backdrop against which to judge credibility."[266] The argument for admission is particularly strong when one or more of the consistent statements preceded the alleged improper influence, motive, fantasy, or memory loss.

Three examples illustrate circumstances in which children's prior consistent statements uttered following alleged improper influence or motive may help assess credibility. Suppose a five-year-old discloses to his mother that he is being sexually abused by his stepfather. The child is interviewed by a social worker. During the social worker's interview, the child again describes the abuse, but adds a unique detail that the child's mother could not know. At trial, the child testifies for the prosecution. Defense counsel charges that the child's mother planted the whole idea in her son's mind. The disclosure to the social worker occurred after the alleged motive to fabricate arose. Nevertheless, the statement to the social worker should be admitted because the statement contains factual data the mother could not have given the child. The fact that the mother cannot be the author of the data supplied to the social worker increases the rehabilitative value of the child's prior consistent statement to the social worker.

A second example involves the common phenomenon of gradual disclosure, in which the child discloses progressively more detail over time.[267] An eight-year-old takes her mother aside and makes her initial, tentative disclosure of sexual abuse by a teacher at school. The child does not tell her mother everything. The case is reported to the police and the child is interviewed. The entire interview is videotaped. During the interview the child discloses a little more. During a second interview a week later the child provides much more detail than was forthcoming during the first interview. At trial, the child testifies consistently with the description she gave during the second interview. Defense counsel charges that the first interview was conducted in a highly suggestive and improper manner that planted the idea of abuse that never occurred. Thus, according to the defense, the child's trial testimony is fabricated. The child's statement to her mother arose before the alleged improper influence and clearly is admissible as a prior consistent statement. The child's fully detailed statement during the second interview should also be admitted as a prior consistent statement provided the prosecutor can establish that the further detail forthcoming during

---

[265] *See* Graham, Critique, at 580 ("The presence of a prior statement made earlier in time does logically tend to support the credibility of the witness").

[266] Nitz v. State, 720 P.2d 55, 61 (Alaska Ct. App. 1986).

[267] For discussion of the disclosure process, see **Ch. 4**. *See also* Nitz v. State, 720 P.2d 55 (Alaska Ct. App. 1986); State v. Resendez, 82 Or. App. 259, 728 P.2d 562 (1986) (child's trial testimony contained greater detail than initial disclosures to baby-sitter and police officer; defense emphasized inconsistency and charged fabrication; prior consistent statements held admissible).

the second interview was not suggested during the first interview. If the prosecutor can carry this burden, then the detail provided during the second interview is not contaminated by the alleged improper influence occurring during the first interview.

As a final example, suppose in an incest case that the victim disclosed to her mother. Her father denies the abuse and asserts that the mother coached the child into false allegations to deprive the father of visitation. Criminal charges are filed against the father, and at the preliminary hearing the child describes the abuse. The child is vigorously cross-examined, but sticks to her story. At trial the child's testimony is consistent with her testimony at the preliminary hearing. During cross-examination, defense counsel expressly asserts coaching. On redirect examination the prosecutor asks the child about her consistent preliminary hearing testimony. The defendant objects that the preliminary hearing occurred long after the alleged improper coaching, and therefore, the child's consistent statement is inadmissible. The objection should be overruled. The child's ability to adhere to her version of events under pressure to recant bolsters her trial testimony.

§ 7.24 —Impeachment Through Prior Inconsistent Statements

One of the most common methods of impeachment is to confront the witness with prior inconsistent statements. McCormick observes that "[t]here is much division of opinion on the question whether impeachment by inconsistent statements opens the door to support by proving consistent statements."[268] When impeachment by prior inconsistent statement does not charge fabrication or lapse of

---

[268] McCormick § 49, at 119-20. McCormick goes on to write:

> A few courts hold generally that the support is permissible. This rule has the merit of easy application in the court room. Some courts, since the inconsistency remains despite all consistent statements, hold generally that it does not. But certain modifications or even a complete departure from these general rules should be recognized. If the attacked witness denies the making of the inconsistent statement then some courts consider that the evidence of consistent statements near the time of the alleged inconsistent one, is relevant to fortify his denial. Again, if in the particular situation, the attack by inconsistent statement is accompanied by, or interpretable as, a charge of a plan or contrivance to give false testimony, then proof of a prior consistent statement *before* the plan or contrivance was formed, tends strongly to disprove that the testimony was the result of contrivance. Here all courts agree. It is for the judge to decide whether the impeachment amounts to a charge of contrivance, and ordinarily this is the most obvious implication. If it does not, then it may often amount to an imputation of inaccurate memory. If so the consistent statement made when the event was recent and memory fresh should be received in support.

(footnotes omitted).

§ 7.24 IMPEACHMENT BY INCONSISTENCIES

memory, prior consistent statements generally are inadmissible.[269] For example, prior consistent statements generally are not allowed when the cross-examiner limits the attack to an assertion that someone whose story changes over time is unbelievable. The theory of such impeachment is not that trial testimony is fabricated, but "that talking one way on the stand and another way previously is blowing hot and cold, and raises a doubt as to the truthfulness of both statements."[270] In some cases, however, the cross-examiner's goal in offering prior inconsistent statements is to assert fabrication.[271] The charge is that the prior statement was true and the inconsistent trial testimony is fabricated. In such cases prior consistent statements are admissible if they are logically relevant to rebut the charge.

The following cases illustrate circumstances in which prior consistent statements may be admitted following impeachment by prior inconsistent statements. The first case illustrates the common scenario in which the witness admits making the prior inconsistent statement and offers an explanation for the inconsistency between the earlier statement and trial testimony. In this

---

[269] United States v. Cherry, 938 F.2d 748, 755 (7th Cir. 1991) ("This court has refused to hold that 'any isolated impeachment on cross-examination gives rise to an implied charge of recent fabrication'"). Evidently, Pennsylvania courts hold that impeachment with prior inconsistent statements does not trigger admission of prior consistent statements. *See* Commonwealth v. Jubilee, 403 Pa. Super. 589, 589 A.2d 1112 (1991). *See also* Graham, Critique, at 592–93, where the author writes:

> To illustrate a situation when the prior consistent statement will be inadmissible, assume that when impeached with a prior inconsistent statement, the witness admits or at least does not deny its making. Assume further that no additional charge is levied by the cross-examiner and that no explanation is offered by the witness. Under such circumstances, the witness has been impeached for unreliability. The jury is being asked to draw the inference that a witness who spoke one way at trial and another way before trial is unworthy of belief. If a prior consistent statement is now offered, the argument against admissibility of the statement to rehabilitate the impeached witness begins with the assertion that the self-contradiction retains its damaging effect; it is not explained away by the presence of a consistent statement.

(footnotes omitted).

[270] McCormick § 34, at 74 (footnote omitted).

[271] Several state evidence codes expressly recognize the fact that charges of fabrication can grow out of impeachment with prior inconsistent statements. See Cal. Evid. Code § 1236 (West 1992); Oregon R. Evid. 801(d)(1)(B) (prior consistent statements allowed "to rebut an inconsistent statement or an express or implied charge against the witness of recent fabrication").

See United States v. Cherry, 938 F.2d 748, 755–56 (7th Cir. 1991) (extensive cross-examination challenged core of victim's testimony); United States v. Morgan, 31 M.J. 43 (C.M.A. 1990), *cert. denied,* 111 S. Ct. 959 (1991) (combination of impeachment with prior inconsistent statement and cross-examiner's stress on fact that child "told her story 'over and over again'" amounted to charge of fabrication); Commonwealth v. Healey, 27 Mass. App. Ct. 30, 534 N.E.2d 301, 305 (1989); Slater v. Baker, 301 N.W.2d 315, 318 (Minn. 1981); Commonwealth v. Knapp, 374 Pa. Super. 160, 542 A.2d 546, 554 (1988); Cartmill v. State, 748 S.W.2d 581, 583 (Tex. Ct. App. 1988); McCormick § 49, at 119.

scenario, courts frequently admit prior consistent statements that help explain the inconsistency.[272]

In an incest case, the victim disclosed to a teacher. Family pressure caused the child to recant. Following the recantation, the child confided to her therapist the reasons for the recantation and reaffirmed the abuse. The child told the therapist she wanted the abuse to stop but felt compelled to comply with her parents' pressure to recant. At trial, the child testified for the government. The defendant impeached the child with the recantation. The cross-examiner implied that the recantation was true and the trial testimony was fabricated. The child acknowledged the recantation. On redirect examination by the prosecutor, the child should be allowed to explain the reasons for the recantation and to repeat her statement to the therapist that is consistent with her trial testimony. Alternatively, the therapist could testify and repeat the child's prior consistent statement. The child's prior consistent statement helps explain the recantation. Graham writes:

> [T]he witness will frequently offer, and, in cases in which the subject matter of the statement is critical, almost invariably will offer, an explanation of why the prior statement, although acknowledged as made, is incorrect or misleading. Along with the proffered explanation, the witness may offer testimony as to a prior consistent statement. In many instances the prior statement will also be related to and thus will support the witness' explanation as a matter of logical relevancy. Since such a prior consistent statement buttresses overall credibility of the witness through its ameliorating effect upon the impeachment, the consistent statement should be admitted as explaining. Statements that support the witness' explanation are properly admitted whether they were made prior or subsequent to the acknowledged inconsistent statement. The prior statement must be significantly related to, and thus sufficiently supportive of the explanation.[273]

The decision in *Hanger v. United States*[274] adds support to admitting the incest victim's statement to her therapist. In *Hanger* the court wrote:

> We think that in the situation where a key witness admittedly changes his story or his recital of important relevant events and admits that his former statements in regard to the proceedings in question were a fabrication, that he should be allowed to not only testify as to what he now swears is a true recital of the events, but to also testify as to the reasons for his fabrication and the reasons why he decided to change his story; and all of the incidents and factors that shed

---

[272] Commonwealth v. Knapp, 374 Pa. Super. 160, 542 A.2d 546, 554 (1988) (cross-examiner emphasized inconsistencies between child's prior statements and trial testimony. "The obvious thrust of the cross examination . . . was to suggest that the victim had recently fabricated his trial testimony").

[273] Graham, Critique, at 595 (footnotes omitted).

[274] 398 F.2d 91 (8th Cir. 1968), *cert. denied,* 393 U.S. 1119 (1969).

§ 7.24 IMPEACHMENT BY INCONSISTENCIES

light upon his credibility, both pro and con, are admitted, subject to the Court's discretion, and left to jury for its evaluation and determination.[275]

Another circumstance in which a child's prior consistent statement helps explain away the impeaching effect of a prior inconsistent statement is illustrated by a case in which the child withheld relevant details at an earlier time because of embarrassment. The child disclosed incest to her best friend. The victim was forced to orally copulate her father. During preliminary hearing testimony, the child described the abuse but omitted a particularly embarrassing detail. Following the preliminary hearing, the child said to her best friend, "I just couldn't tell the judge how stuff comes out of Daddy's pee-pee when he puts it in my mouth. I was too embarrassed." At trial, the child included the embarrassing detail. Defense counsel emphasized the inconsistency between the child's testimony at preliminary hearing and trial and left the impression that the child fabricated the more detailed trial testimony.[276] On redirect the child may explain that she was too embarrassed at the preliminary hearing to provide a full account. The child may also repeat what she said to her friend because the statement to the friend helps explain the victim's behavior at the preliminary hearing.[277]

In the preceding two examples, the child acknowledged the prior inconsistent statement or omission and offered an explanation that was corroborated by a prior consistent statement. In some cases the child denies making the prior inconsistent statement. Courts then often admit prior consistent statements made near in time to the alleged prior inconsistent statement.[278] The fact that at the pertinent time the child made statements consistent with trial testimony lessens the probability the child made the prior inconsistent statement alleged by the cross-examiner.

The impeachment discussed thus far involves confronting the witness with the witness's earlier inconsistent statement. Another form of self-contradiction plays an important role in child abuse litigation. In many cases the victim delays reporting for a substantial period of time. The defense emphasizes the delay and expressly or impliedly charges that if the sexual assault actually occurred, the victim would have spoken sooner.[279] The victim's silence contradicts trial

---

[275] 398 F.2d at 105.

[276] State v. Resendez, 82 Or. App. 259, 728 P.2d 562 (1986).

[277] This hypothetical case is based on People v. Bias, 170 Cal. App. 2d 502, 339 P.2d 204 (1959).

[278] *See* Wise v. State, 546 So. 2d 1068, 1070 (Fla. Dist. Ct. App. 1989) (dicta). *See also* McCormick § 49, at 119, where the author writes; "If the attacked witness denies the making of the inconsistent statement then some courts consider that the evidence of consistent statements near the time of the alleged inconsistent one, is relevant to fortify his denial." (footnote omitted).

[279] United States v. Cherry, 938 F.2d 748, 756 (7th Cir. 1991) (victim's prior consistent statement allowed; defendant extensively cross-examined victim; among other attacks on victim's credibility, defendant "pointed out that she had failed to complain to anyone about the

testimony describing the assault.[280] The inference desired by the defense is that the victim's trial testimony is fabricated. Faced with this form of impeachment, several theories are available to the prosecutor. First, the child's disclosure is admissible as a prior consistent statement. Second, the prosecutor may offer the child's disclosure as a fresh complaint.[281] The advantage in offering the child's disclosure as a prior consistent statement is that under Rule 801(d)(1)(B) the statement is admissible for the truth of the matter asserted. By contrast, in most states, a fresh complaint serves the limited function of corroborating the victim's trial testimony, and is not admissible for the truth. Third, the disclosure may be admissible under a hearsay exception. Finally, impeachment focused on delayed reporting may open the door to expert testimony offered to inform the jury that delay is common among sexually abused children.[282]

When impeachment is by prior inconsistent statement, it is sometimes difficult to determine whether the cross-examiner intends to charge fabrication. The cross-examiner may wait until closing argument to reveal the defense strategy. When the cross-examiner's purpose is not apparent during trial, it is difficult to determine whether rehabilitation with prior consistent statements is permissible. Graham in his 1979 article "Prior Consistent Statements: Rule 801(d)(1)(B) of the Federal Rules of Evidence Critique and Proposal" from volume 30 page 608 of the *Hastings Law Journal* discusses this problem and refers to McCormick for a practical solution:

---

alleged rape in the hours immediately after the incident") (footnote omitted); Redmond v. Baxley, 475 F. Supp. 1111, 1123 (E.D. Mich. 1979) (prison inmate sued prison officials for damages alleging he was raped in prison; the defendants' contention that "rape incident never occurred, as evidenced by the fact that the [victim] did not report the rape to the authorities . . . constituted an implied accusation that the plaintiff fabricated his story of the rape").

[280] See § **7.31** for discussion of the fresh complaint of rape doctrine. *See also* Graham, Critique, at 588:

If counsel, upon cross-examination of a witness, charges that the witness on a previous occasion failed to speak of the matter now being asserted at trial under circumstances in which it would have been natural for the witness to have done so, the witness is being impeached through self-contradiction. The cross-examiner is asserting that the silence of the witness is inconsistent with his in-court testimony. . . .

When a witness is charged with having previously remained silent at a time when it would have been natural for him to speak, evidence of a consistent statement may be relevant to repel the impeaching inference.

See also Redmond v. Baxley, 475 F. Supp. 1111, 1123 (E.D. Mich. 1979) (civil case in which inmate sued prison officials after he was allegedly raped by other inmates; defendants asserted that "rape incident never occurred, as evidenced by the fact that the [victim] did not report the rape to the authorities. This constituted an implied accusation that the [victim] fabricated his story of the rape").

[281] See § **7.31** for discussion of the fresh complaint doctrine.

[282] See **Ch. 4**.

An obvious difficulty is raised when the inference the cross-examiner intends the trier of fact to draw may not be evidenced until closing argument. A charge of either lack of recollection or contrivance would, independent of other possibilities, trigger the admissibility of consistent statements predating the alleged self-contradiction. The charge that the witness is simply not to be believed would not allow the consistent statements to be introduced. The dilemma is of real concern. When the charges are first made during summation, it is obviously too late for a prior consistent statement, not otherwise admissible, to be offered in rebuttal.

Recognizing this dilemma, McCormick in *McCormick on Evidence* § 49 at 119 through 120 offers the following solution:

> [I]f in the particular situation, the attack by inconsistent statement is accompanied by, or interpretable as, a charge of a plan or contrivance to give false testimony, then proof of a prior consistent statement *before* the plan or contrivance was formed, tends strongly to disprove that the testimony was the result of contrivance . . . . It is for the judge to decide whether the impeachment amounts to a charge of contrivance—ordinarily this is the most obvious implication—and it seems he is entitled to have an avowal one way or another from counsel. If it does not, then it may often amount to an imputation of inaccurate memory. If so, the consistent statement made when the event was recent and memory fresh should be received in support.

Thus, when not obviously "interpretable" by the court from the cross-examination itself, McCormick suggests that the cross-examining counsel be required, presumably after completing cross-examination and before redirect, to state to the court what argument he intends to make. He should have to state whether he intends to argue either contrivance, lack of recollection (in which case a predating prior consistent statement will be admissible), or simply that the contradiction shows that the witness is unworthy of belief (in which case a predating prior consistent statement would not be admissible by virtue of the cross-examiner's charge).[283]

§ 7.25 —Impeachment Charging Memory Lapse

The cross-examiner sometimes hopes to undermine a child's trial testimony by asserting or implying that the child's memory is faulty.[284] The impeaching attorney may emphasize inconsistencies between the child's trial testimony and earlier statements on the theory that earlier statements were accurate and the

---

[283] Graham at 608–09 (footnote omitted).

[284] There is some doubt concerning whether Rule 801(d)(1)(B) applies when the cross-examiner charges lapse of memory. *See* 4 Louisell & Mueller § 420, at 196; 4 Weinstein & Berger ¶ 801(d)(1)(B), at 801-192.

child's memory faded in the interim. Impeachment focused on children's memories may be effective because jurors may believe children's memories are weaker than the memories of adults. Although research reveals that this is probably not so,[285] the cross-examiner may nevertheless capitalize on common misconceptions about children's memory. Faced with such impeachment, courts often admit prior consistent statements uttered close in time to the event, when the child's memory was fresh.[286] The fact that the child's trial testimony is consistent with the earlier statement bolsters confidence in the trial testimony.

§ 7.26 Out-of-Court Statements of Identification

In many child abuse cases the identity of the perpetrator is disputed. The child's out-of-court statement identifying the perpetrator may be admissible under the excited utterance exception,[287] the medical diagnosis or treatment exception,[288] or the residual exception.[289] Some states have hearsay exceptions specifically for prior identifications.[290] If the child testifies at trial, the child's prior identification may be admissible as nonhearsay under Federal Rule of Evidence 801(d)(1)(C), which provides that "[a] statement is not hearsay if the declarant testifies at the trial or hearing and is subject to cross-examination concerning the statement, and the statement is one of identification of a person made after perceiving the person."[291]

When trials occur in the movies, the in-court identification is high drama. The prosecutor solemnly addresses the witness and says, "Do you see the person

---

[285] See **Ch. 2** for discussion of children's memory.

[286] *See* Applebaum v. American Export Isbrandsten Lines, 472 F.2d 56, 61–62 (2d Cir. 1972) ("even when the self-contradiction amounts only to an imputation of inaccurate memory a 'consistent statement made when the event was recent and memory fresh should be received'"); United States v. Keller, 145 F. Supp. 692, 697 (D.N.J. 1956); State v. Bruggeman, 161 Ariz. 508, 779 P.2d 823, 825 (Ct. App. 1989) ("During closing argument, appellant's counsel contended that young girls had difficulty remembering what had occurred and that they were confused about what they had seen. When the memory of a witness is attacked, 'a consistent statement made near the time of the event testified to is admissible.'"); State v. Altergott, 57 Haw. 492, 559 P.2d 728 (1977); Slater v. Baker, 301 N.W.2d 315, 319–20 (Minn. 1981); McCormick § 49, at 120.

[287] See **§ 7.28**.

[288] See **§ 7.35**.

[289] See **§ 7.42**. See also 4 Louisell & Mueller § 421, at 212, where the authors write that if a witness is not available to testify at trial, the witness's out-of-court identification may be admissible under the residual exception.

[290] Cal. Evid. Code § 1238 (West 1992); Ill. Ann. Stat. ch. 38, ¶ 115-112. *See* People v. Gould, 54 Cal. 2d 621, 354 P.2d 865, 867, 7 Cal. Rptr. 273 (1960); People v. Hayes, 139 Ill. 2d 89, 564 N.E.2d 803 (1990), *cert. denied,* 111 S. Ct. 1601 (1991); People v. Holveck, 171 Ill. App. 3d 38, 524 N.E.2d 1073, 1083 (1988), *aff'd,* 141 Ill. 2d 84, 565 N.E.2d 919 (1990).

[291] Fed. R. Evid. 801(d)(1)(C).

§ 7.26   STATEMENTS OF IDENTIFICATION   151

in court today?" All eyes rivet on the defendant. "Yes. He's there at counsel table." Case closed! Yet, experienced judges and attorneys know that in-court identifications can be unreliable.[292] The witness's memory may have faded during the delay between the crime and the in-court identification. Furthermore, the witness may have experienced influence or suggestion which casts doubt on the in-court identification. In many cases an out-of-court identification made shortly following the event, when memory was fresh, has more inherent trustworthiness than an in-court identification months or years later.[293] As the Advisory Committee note to Rule 801(d)(1)(C) states, the reason to admit out-of-court identifications "is the generally unsatisfactory and inconclusive nature of courtroom identifications as compared with those made at an earlier time under less suggestive conditions."[294]

A statement of identification meeting the requirements of Rule 801(d)(1)(C) is admissible during the state's case-in-chief.[295] It is not necessary that the child be impeached before admitting the prior identification.[296]

---

[292] 4 Louisell & Mueller § 421, at 204–05; 4 Weinstein & Berger ¶ 801(d)(1)(C), at 801-214 ("identification in the courtroom is a formality that offers little in the way of reliability and much in the way of suggestibility. The experienced trial judge gives much greater credence to the out-of-court identification, especially those made at or near the time of the principal events").

[293] Louisell and Mueller describe the trustworthiness of out-of-court statements of identification with typical insight, and then go on to point out the need in many cases of admitting out-of-court statements of identification. Louisell and Mueller write:

On the matter of necessity, the congressional reports point out the problems to the prosecution caused by delays in arrest, indictment, and trial: The memory of the identifier "will fade" and "his identification will become less reliable." Moreover, with the passage of time, "the defendant or some other party" will have "the opportunity, through bribe or threat, to influence the witness to change his mind." Thus, admitting pretrial identifications helps keep cases from "falling through" because the identifier "can no longer recall the identity" of the culprit, or is no longer willing to testify to it at trial.

4 Louisell & Mueller § 421, at 205 (footnote omitted).

See United States v. Owens, 484 U.S. 554, 562 (1988) ("The premise for Rule 801(d)(1)(C) was that, given adequate safeguards against suggestiveness, out-of-court identifications were generally preferable to courtroom identifications"); People v. Gould, 54 Cal. 2d 621, 354 P.2d 865, 867, 7 Cal. Rptr. 273 (1960); Fells v. State, 345 So. 2d 618, 621 (Miss. 1977) ("it would seem to be a dictate of common sense that the 'best evidence' of identification is normally the first identification because it is nearest in time to the crime"); 4 Wigmore § 1130, at 277-93.

[294] Fed. R. Evid. 801(d)(1)(C) advisory committee's note.

[295] *See* 4 Weinstein & Berger ¶ 801(d)(1)(C), at 801-221, where the authors write, "Rule 801(d)(1)(C) should, therefore, be interpreted as allowing evidence of prior identification by the witness of a photograph or sketch of the person whom he had initially perceived." (footnotes omitted).

[296] 4 Louisell & Mueller § 421, at 208–09 ("the operation of Rule 801(d)(1)(C) in no way depends upon the impeachment process, which makes it unlike subdivisions (b)(1)(A) and

When the child identifies the defendant at trial, the child's out-of-court identification is admissible not just to corroborate the child's in-court identification, but also as substantive evidence of the defendant's identity.[297] But suppose the child will not or cannot identify the defendant in court. The child may not remember who inflicted the abuse. The child may not want to aid the prosecution. Perhaps the defendant's appearance has altered, making identification in court difficult. Some children are so frightened by the proceedings or the defendant's presence that they refuse to make an in-court identification. When the child is present in court but unable or unwilling to identify the defendant, the question is whether a witness to whom the child made an out-of-court identification may repeat the identification in court. The answer under Rule 801(d)(1)(C) is yes, provided the child is subject to cross-examination concerning the prior identification.[298] Thus, if the child told his father that "Bill did it," the child's father could testify, and repeat his son's out-of-court identification.

Rule 801(d)(1)(C) requires the child to testify at trial and be subject to cross-examination concerning the out-of-court identification. Suppose that at trial the child remembers making an out-of-court identification of the defendant, but cannot remember why the defendant was identified, and cannot remember who inflicted the abuse. Can a child who does not remember who inflicted abuse be subjected to cross-examination concerning an out-of-court

---

(b)(1)(B)"); 4 Weinstein & Berger ¶ 801(d)(1)(C), at 801-214 ("Unlike subparagraphs (A) and (B) of Rule 801(d)(1), subparagraph (C) is not related to impeachment of the witness") (footnote omitted).

[297] 4 Louisell & Mueller § 421, at 209. Leading commentators point out that an out-of-court identification, standing alone, may be insufficient to convict. See 4 Louisell & Mueller § 421, at 215; 4 Weinstein & Berger ¶ 801(d)(1)(C)]01[, at 801-223.

[298] State v. Boston, 46 Ohio St. 3d 108, 545 N.E.2d 1220, 1236 (1989); People v. Holveck, 171 Ill. App. 3d 38, 524 N.E.2d 1073, 1083 (1988), aff'd, 141 Ill. 2d 84, 565 N.E.2d 919 (1990). See also 4 Weinstein & Berger ¶ 801(d)(1)(C), at 801-222 where the authors write:

> Under the Rule, however, if at the trial the eyewitness fails to remember or denies that he made the identification, the previous statement of the eyewitness can be proved by the testimony of a person to whom the statement was made, and the statement can be given substantive effect. The legislative history of the provision . . . supports the view that Congress intended that an absence of memory, or even a denial, by the identifying declarant at trial would not bar testimony by a witness to the identification.

(footnote omitted) (reference omitted). See also 4 Louisell & Mueller § 421, at 209, 211 where the authors write:

> [I]f the identifier "waffles" in court, whether from corruption, fear, a desire not to assist in convicting, a lapse of memory, or confusion generated by a change in the appearance of the defendant or by the proceedings themselves, his previous statement of identification can still qualify as "not hearsay" under Rule 801(d)(1)(C).

* * *

Rule 801(d)(1)(C) is broad because it paves the way not only for testimony by the identifier concerning his pretrial identification, but also for testimony to the same end by third persons to whom the identifier was speaking.

(footnote omitted).

identification? The Supreme Court addressed this question in *United States v. Owens.*²⁹⁹ In *Owens,* the defendant was charged with assaulting a correctional counselor at a federal prison. The victim suffered a fractured skull when he was brutally attacked with a metal pipe. The head injury impaired the victim's memory. During the victim's month-long hospitalization, he was visited by several people, including an FBI agent. The FBI agent presented the victim with an array of photographs and the victim identified Owens as his attacker. At trial, the victim testified that he remembered making the out-of-court identification, but on cross-examination the victim acknowledged he could not remember seeing his assailant. Furthermore, the victim acknowledged that he could not remember why he picked Owens's picture from the FBI agent's photo array.³⁰⁰ The trial court admitted the victim's out-of-court identification and the defendant was convicted.³⁰¹

The issue before the Supreme Court was whether admitting the victim's out-of-court identification violated Rule 801(d)(1)(C) or Owens' rights under the Confrontation Clause. As to the Confrontation Clause, the Court ruled that the clause "'guarantees only "an *opportunity* for effective cross-examination, not cross-examination that is effective in whatever way, and to whatever extent, the defense might wish."'"³⁰² The opportunity to cross-examine is not denied when a witness's out-of-court identification is introduced despite the witness's inability to remember the basis for the identification. The Court wrote that the Confrontation Clause is satisfied when "the defendant has the opportunity to bring out such matters as the witness's bias, his lack of care and attentiveness, his poor eyesight, and even (what is often a prime objective of cross-examination) the very fact that he has a bad memory."³⁰³

Turning its attention to Rule 801(d)(1)(C)'s requirement that the witness be subject to cross-examination concerning the out-of-court identification, the Court ruled that the victim in *Owens* was available for cross-examination. The Court wrote that "[o]rdinarily a witness is regarded as 'subject to cross-examination' when he is placed on the stand, under oath, and responds willingly to questions."³⁰⁴ The ability to cross-examine the victim was not undermined by his inability to remember who assaulted him.

Under *Owens,* a child is subject to cross-examination within the meaning of Rule 801(d)(1)(C) if the child remembers making the out-of-court identification but cannot remember why the defendant was identified and cannot recall who committed the abuse. *Owens* did not decide whether a child who cannot

---

[299] 484 U.S. 554 (1988).

[300] *See* United States v. Owens, 789 F.2d 750, 753 (9th Cir. 1986), *rev'd,* 484 U.S. 554 (1988).

[301] The Ninth Circuit reversed the conviction. *See* United States v. Owens, 789 F.2d 750 (9th Cir. 1986). The Supreme Court then granted certiorari in United States v. Owens, 479 U.S. 1084 (1987).

[302] 484 U.S. at 559.

[303] *Id.*

[304] *Id.* at 562.

remember making the out-of-court identification can be cross-examined concerning the identification. If the child remembers the abuse, including the defendant's participation, it may be possible to conduct sufficient cross-examination to permit admission of the out-of-court identification.[305] Furthermore, if the court is persuaded that the child is feigning lack of memory regarding the out-of-court identification, cross-examination may be possible.[306] In *Owens* the Supreme Court hinted that even though the child cannot remember making the out-of-court identification, the child may nevertheless be cross-examinable concerning the statement.[307]

§ 7.27 Present Sense Impressions

Rule 803(1) of the Federal Rules of Evidence excepts from the hearsay rule "[a] statement describing or explaining an event or condition made while the declarant was perceiving the event or condition, or immediately thereafter."[308] Present sense impressions are admissible because they bear special indicia of reliability deriving from the contemporaneousness of the statements.[309]

---

[305] 4 Louisell & Mueller § 486, at 1040; 4 Weinstein & Berger ¶ 801(d)(1)(A)[06], at 801-162.

[306] 4 Weinstein & Berger ¶ 801(d)(1)(A)[07], at 801-163. *See also* 4 Louisell & Mueller § 486, at 1040–41, where the authors discuss unavailability of witnesses under Rule 804(a):

> The key in assessing a claimed lack of memory at trial lies in determining whether the conduct of the witness affords an adequate basis upon which to assess the prior statement. If it does, then the witness should be viewed as cross-examinable, with all that implies for purposes of rule 801(d)(1). . . . Rule 801(d)(1) implies that a claimed lack of memory concerning the matters asserted in the statement is not critical so long as the witness answers questions about the making of the statement. But if a claimed lack of memory at trial leaves the trier with an inadequate basis upon which to assess the prior statement, the witness should be viewed as "unavailable" and not "subject to cross-examination." This may occur where the witness claims a lack of memory as to both the matter asserted or described in the prior statement and the making of the statement. In the unusual case in which a witness recalls the statement and is cross-examinable concerning the making of the statement but has forgotten the underlying matters described or asserted therein, it may be fair to view him as being at once "unavailable" for purposes of Rule 804(a)(3) but "subject to cross-examination" under Rule 801(d)(1).

(footnote omitted).

[307] United States v. Owens, 484 U.S. 554, 562 (1988) (all Rule 801(d)(1)(C) requires is that cross-examination *concern* the statement).

[308] Fed. R. Evid. 803(1).

[309] Fed. R. Evid. 803(1) advisory committee's note ("The underlying theory of Exception (1) is that substantial contemporaneity of event and statement negative the likelihood of deliberate or conscious misrepresentation"). *See also* 4 Louisell & Mueller § 438, at 482 ("It is the idea of contemporaneousness, or immediacy, which lies at the heart of the exception"); 4 Weinstein & Berger ¶ 803(1)[01]; Booth v. State, 306 Md. 313, 508 A.2d 976 (1986) (useful discussion of history of present sense impression exception and reliability of present sense impressions).

§ 7.27 PRESENT SENSE IMPRESSIONS

Contemporaneity reduces two of the risks of hearsay.[310] First, the risk of memory loss is substantially reduced, if not eliminated, by the requirement that the statement be uttered while the declarant is perceiving the event or immediately thereafter. Second, the risk of intentional misstatement is reduced because the immediacy required by the exception reduces the opportunity for conscious fabrication.

In many cases, the person who overheard the present sense impression and repeats it in court also witnessed the event, and serves as a check on the accuracy of the hearsay declarant.[311] The testifying witness can be cross-examined regarding the underlying event as well as the present sense impression.[312]

The exception for present sense impressions has three requirements.[313] First, the declarant must perceive an event or condition.[314] In most cases the declarant sees the event, although perception through other senses is acceptable.[315] The event need not be startling or shocking,[316] and the declarant need not be a participant in the event.[317] Statements by bystanders can qualify as present sense impressions.[318] Second, the statement must be made while the declarant was perceiving the event or condition, or immediately thereafter. The time element is strict.[319] A statement made during the event clearly qualifies.[320] Difficulty arises when the statement is uttered shortly after the event. A few moments

---

[310] See § 7.4 for discussion of the risks of hearsay.

[311] Robinson v. Shapiro, 484 F. Supp. 91, 95 (S.D.N.Y. 1980), *aff'd,* 646 F.2d 734 (2d Cir. 1981).

[312] Rule 803(1) does not require that the individual who repeats a present sense impression in court be a witness to the event. *See* 4 Louisell & Mueller § 438, at 484.

[313] 4 Louisell & Mueller § 438, at 487–91; 4 Weinstein & Berger ¶ 803(1)[01].

[314] The requirement that the declarant perceive the event incorporates the personal knowledge requirement of Rule 602 into the present sense impression exception. *See* 4 Louisell & Mueller § 438, at 490–91.

[315] United States v. Portsmouth Paving Corp., 694 F.2d 312, 323 (4th Cir. 1982) (hearing; "We perceive events with our ears as much as with our eyes"); 4 Louisell & Mueller § 438, at 490–91.

[316] 4 Louisell & Mueller § 437, at 482.

[317] 4 Weinstein & Berger ¶ 803(1)[01].

[318] *Id.* at 803-77 to -78.

[319] 4 Louisell & Mueller § 438, at 487.

[320] State v. Perry, 95 N.M. 179, 619 P.2d 855 (Ct. App. 1980) (rape of adult took place in motel room; declarant in neighboring room heard victim scream and called motel office to complain about noise; declarant's statement to manager was admitted as present sense impression); Walton v. Elftman, 64 Ohio Misc. 45, 410 N.E.2d 1282, 1286 (1980) (auto accident case; child riding in one car involved "exclaimed at about the time of the impact, 'The blue car could not stop'"; properly admitted as present sense impression); Anderson v. State, 454 S.W.2d 740, 741 (Tex. Crim. App. 1970) (statement made while event occurring: "Seems like there is a car being stripped down the street there"); Houston Oxygen Co. v. Davis, 139 Tex. 1, 161 S.W.2d 474, 476 (1942) (passenger in car being passed by another car remarked "they must have been drunk, that we would find them somewhere on the road wrecked if they kept that rate of speed up").

delay between the event and the statement should not disqualify a statement as a present sense impression unless there is evidence of fabrication or other unreliability.[321] When delay extends into minutes or hours, however, the statement is not a present sense impression.[322] Third, the statement must describe or explain the perceived event. This requirement poses few problems, since, in most cases, the statement describes the event.[323] In other cases, the statement interprets or explains the event, and such statements qualify.[324]

In child abuse litigation, the exception for present sense impressions arises infrequently. This is not surprising because abuse almost always occurs in secrecy. There is little likelihood a child's contemporaneous statements will be overheard by anyone but the perpetrator, and if the child later reveals what happened, the time interval is usually too long to satisfy the exception.[325]

---

[321] Michaels v. Michaels, 767 F.2d 1185, 1201 (7th Cir. 1985), *cert. denied,* 474 U.S. 1057 (1986) (telex sent immediately after speaking with defendant was within Rule 803(1)); People v. Burns, 118 Mich. App. 242, 324 N.W.2d 589 (1982); Starr v. Morsette, 236 N.W.2d 183, 186–88 (N.D. 1975) (delay of "a minute or two after the accident occurred" satisfied requirement of Rule 803(1)); 4 Louisell & Mueller § 438, at 488 (the exception "permits enough flexibility to reach statements made a moment after the fact where such small delay . . . appears natural under the circumstances and insufficient to permit reflection, which would raise doubts about trustworthiness") (footnote omitted); 4 Weinstein & Berger ¶ 803(1)[01], at 803-75 ("a slight lapse of time should not result in the loss of valuable evidence") (footnote omitted).

[322] Hilyer v. Howat Concrete Co., 578 F.2d 422, 426 n.7 (D.C. Cir. 1978) (delay of 15 to 45 minutes too long); Tucker v. State, 264 Ark. 890, 575 S.W.2d 684, 685 (1979) (three days too long); Hewitt v. Grand Trunk W.R. Co., 123 Mich. App. 309, 333 N.W.2d 264 (1983) (wrongful death action; eyewitness to accident made statements to police officer within up to 30 minutes of event, but delay too long); State v. Maestas, 92 N.M 135, 584 P.2d 182, 186-66 (Ct. App. 1978) (three hours too long); 4 Louisell & Mueller § 438, at 488 ("More significant delays—those measures in terms of minutes or hours, especially if the declarant has made other statements in the interim—bar resort to rule 803(1)") (footnote omitted).

[323] Walton v. Elftman, 64 Ohio Misc. 45, 410 N.E.2d 1282, 1286 (1980) (auto accident; statement by child riding in car describing accident).

[324] MCA, Inc. v. Wilson, 425 F. Supp. 443, 450–51 (S.D.N.Y. 1976), *aff'd and modified,* 677 F.2d 180 (2d Cir. 1981); 4 Louisell & Mueller § 438, at 491.

[325] State v. Jano, 524 So. 2d 660 (Fla. 1988) (child's statements not present sense impressions; the record did not reflect the time lapsed between the abuse and the child's statements); *In re* C.B., 574 So. 2d 1369, 1372 (Miss. 1990) (statement days or weeks later not present sense impression).

For a case in which the present sense impression exception would apply, see State v. Boodry, 96 Ariz. 259, 394 P.2d 196, *cert. denied,* 379 U.S. 949 (1964) (decided under res gestae rationale). The facts in *Boodry* offer an example of a case in which the present sense impression exception would apply in a sexual abuse case; the victim was rescued from her abuser while the abuse was occurring, and the child immediately began describing what happened).

§ 7.28 Excited Utterances

The excited utterance exception is invoked frequently in child abuse litigation.[326] The exception is codified at Rule 803(2) of the Federal Rules of Evidence, which states that the hearsay rule does not exclude statements "relating to a startling event or condition made while the declarant was under the stress of excitement caused by the event or condition."[327]

The rationale for the excited utterance exception is that statements are trustworthy when made shortly following a startling event, and while the declarant remains affected by the stress of excitement caused by the event.[328] Reliability exists because two of the hearsay risks are reduced.[329] Statements made under the stress of a startling event are not likely to be the product of conscious reflection or fabrication; thus the risk of insincerity is reduced.[330] Furthermore, the risk of memory loss is appreciably reduced because the statement is uttered

---

[326] Note, *A Comprehensive Approach to Child Hearsay in Sex Abuse Cases,* 83 Colum. L. Rev. 1745, 1753 (1983).

[327] Fed. R. Evid. 803(2).

[328] State v. Thomas, 777 P.2d 445 (Utah 1989); Cassidy v. State, 74 Md. App. 1, 536 A.2d 666, 673, *cert. denied,* 312 Md. 602, 541 A.2d 965 (1988); People v. Straight, 430 Mich. 418, 424 N.W.2d 257 (1988); 4 Louisell & Mueller § 439, at 491–92.

[329] The risks of hearsay are misperception, lapse of memory, faulty narration, and lack of sincerity. See **§ 7.4**.

See White v. Illinois, 112 S. Ct. 736, 742 (1992), where the Court wrote; "[T]he evidentiary rationale for permitting hearsay testimony regarding spontaneous declarations . . . is that such out-of-court declarations are made in contexts that provide substantial guarantees of their trustworthiness." (footnote omitted).

[330] See Fed. R. Evid. 803(2) advisory committee's note, where the committee states, "[T]he theory of Exception (2) is simply that circumstances may produce a condition of excitement which temporarily stills the capacity of reflection and produces utterances free of conscious fabrication."

See also Idaho v. Wright, 110 S. Ct. 3139, 3149 (1990) ("The basis for the 'excited utterance' exception . . . is that such statements are given under circumstances that eliminate the possibility of fabrication, coaching, or confabulation"); Lancaster v. People, 200 Colo. 448, 615 P.2d 720, 722 (1980); State v. Messamore, 2 Haw. App. 643, 639 P.2d 413, 418 (1982); State v. Carlson, 311 Or. 201, 808 P.2d 1002, 1010 (1991); 4 Louisell & Mueller § 439, at 491–92; McCormick § 297, at 855.

See also State v. Shaw, 149 Vt. 275, 542 A.2d 1106 (1987). This case involved an adult sexual assault victim. The victim was assaulted in her apartment. She fled the apartment and went to a neighbor's house for help. She did not know the neighbors. She told the neighbors she had been assaulted. Evidently she did not specify that the assault was sexual. The state offered the victim's statements to the neighbors as excited utterances. The defendant objected, arguing that the fact the victim did not specify the type of assault evidenced "conscious reflection on her part." The Vermont Supreme Court rejected this position, holding that the statements were excited utterances.

close in time to the event.[331] In some cases, an excited utterance may be more reliable than trial testimony offered years later.[332]

The excited utterance exception is not without critics.[333] The stress of a startling event may interfere with ability to attend to the event and perceive it accurately, raising the hearsay risk of misperception.[334] Stress may impair narration and memory,[335] although there is evidence that stress may actually improve memory.[336] Stewart writes:

---

[331] State v. Wallace, 37 Ohio St. 3d 87, 524 N.E.2d 466, 468 (1988); 4 Louisell & Mueller § 439, at 492.

[332] White v. Illinois, 112 S. Ct. 736, 742 (1992); State v. D.R., 109 N.J. 348, 537 A.2d 667 (1988); State v. Loughton, 747 P.2d 426, 429 (Utah 1987) (out-of-court statements "made nearer to the time of the incident and removed from the pressure of a courtroom situation, could be the most accurate accounts of the incident available").

[333] McCormick § 297, at 855; 4 Weinstein & Berger ¶ 803(2)[01], at 803-86; Hutchins & Slesinger, *Some Observations on the Law of Evidence: Spontaneous Explanations,* 28 Colum. L. Rev. 432, 437 (1928) ("what the emotion gains by way of overcoming the desire to lie, it loses by impairing the declarant's power of observation") (footnotes omitted).

[334] Peters, *The Influence of Stress and Arousal on the Child Witness, in* The Suggestibility of Children's Recollections: Implications for Eyewitness Testimony 60, 74 (J. Doris ed. 1991). Summarizing his research on the impact of stress on children's memory, Peters writes that "high arousal levels during event witnessing can, at times impair the eyewitness performance of children."

Other researchers have found that stress does not adversely affect children's memory. *See* Goodman, *Commentary: On Stress and Accuracy in Research on Children's Testimony, in* The Suggestibility of Children's Recollections: Implications for Eyewitness Testimony 77 (J. Doris ed. 1991). Goodman discusses her research and that of other psychologists and writes that in some studies "higher stress is associated with increased recall and reduced suggestibility." *Id.* In one study, Goodman "found neither detrimental or beneficial effects of stress on children's memory." *Id.* at 78.

See also Warren-Leubecker, *Commentary: The Influence of Stress and Arousal on the Child Witness, in* The Suggestibility of Children's Recollections: Implications for Eyewitness Testimony 83, 84 (J. Doris ed. 1991) ("Those researching adult eyewitnesses' reports appear to have settled on the conclusion that stress results in a decreased attentional focus and thereby less information encoded or subsequently recalled. Stress may operate similarly on children"); Hutchings & Slesinger, *Some Observations on the Law of Evidence: Spontaneous Exclamations,* 28 Colum. L. Rev. 432 (1928).

[335] See authorities cited in **note 334**. See also **Ch. 2** for discussion of children's memory.

[336] *See* Goodman, Rudy, Bottoms & Aman, *Children's Concerns and Memory: Issues of Ecological Validity in the Study of Children's Eyewitness Testimony, in* Knowing and Remembering in Young Children 249 (R. Fivush & J. Hudson eds. 1990), where the authors discuss research on the impact of stress on memory, particularly their own research on children's memory for the stressful event of receiving an inoculation. The authors write:

[T]here is reason to believe that high levels of stress will have a beneficial effect on memory. As discussed earlier, physiological studies show that high levels of stress are associated with better memory. Psychological studies reveal that events of high

The most unreliable type of evidence admitted under hearsay exceptions is the excited utterance. This exception provides an important source of evidence in cases such as criminal and tort actions which often involve events which produce a high level of emotional stress and its attendant distortions. The events are unexpected and episodic, and a person witnessing them is presented with a vast number of stimuli that far transcend the span of apperception. . . . Excitement is not a guarantee against lying, especially since the courts often hold that excitement may endure many minutes and even hours beyond the event. More important, excitement exaggerates, sometimes grossly, distortion in perception and memory especially when the observer is a witness to a non-routine, episodic event such as occurs in automobile collision cases and crimes. The likelihood of inaccurate perception, drawing of inferences to fill in memory gaps, and the reporting of nonfacts is high. . . . In fact, the theory [behind the excited utterance exception] is merely an artifice for the admission of highly unreliable evidence which is often the only type of evidence available. No justification exists for foregoing cross-examination and admitting such evidence if the declarant is available.[337]

The Advisory Committee on the Federal Rules of Evidence described the rationale for receipt of excited utterances, writing that "circumstances may produce a condition of excitement which temporarily stills the capacity of reflection and produces utterances free of conscious fabrication."[338] There is a dearth of empirical support for the committee's conclusion, although the conclusion has considerable intuitive appeal, which is supported by years of judicial experience. Nevertheless, as Stewart points out, the hearsay risks of misperception, faulty narration, and memory lapse may actually be exacerbated when a statement is made under stress. If a litigant can establish that a particular statement offered as an excited utterance is burdened with too many indicia of unreliability, the evidence may be excluded.[339] Any thought of a frontal attack on the excited utterance exception should be abandoned, however, because the exception "finds support in cases without number."[340]

---

emotionality and personal significance are retained better than events of low emotionality and little personal significance.

* * *

Our general finding was that stress had a facilitative effect on the children's reports. Specifically, planned comparisons revealed that children at the highest stress levels recalled more information than the other children and were less suggestible.

Id. at 272–73.

[337] Stewart, *Perception, Memory, and Hearsay: A Criticism of Present Law and the Proposed Federal Rules of Evidence,* 1970 Utah L. Rev. 1, 28-29 (1970). *See also* Hutchins & Slesinger, *Some Observations on the Law of Evidence: Spontaneous Exclamations,* 28 Colum. L. Rev. 432 (1928).

[338] Fed. R. Evid. 803(2) advisory committee's note.

[339] Exclusion would come under Rule 403.

[340] Fed. R. Evid. 803(2) advisory committee's note.

§ 7.29 —Admissibility Requirements

The excited utterance exception has three requirements. First, there must be an exciting event. Second, the out-of-court statement must relate to the event. Third, the statement must be made while the child is under the excitement induced by the event. The court determines pursuant to Rule 104(a) whether a statement is an excited utterance.[341] An excited utterance may contain conclusions or opinions.[342] Moreover, an excited utterance may contain a direct accusation that the defendant committed the crime.[343] The three requirements of the excited utterance exception are described below.

Startling Event

There must be an event that excites the declarant.[344] The declarant must perceive the event.[345] It is not necessary, however, that the declarant be a participant in the startling event, and the excited utterance of a bystander may be received.[346] It is not enough that the event would excite a reasonable person: the particular declarant must experience excitement.[347] In some situations a child

---

[341] People v. Burton, 433 Mich. 268, 445 N.W.2d 133 (1989); State v. Carlson, 311 Or. 201, 808 P.2d 1002, 1010 (1991).

[342] State v. Carlson, 311 Or. 201, 808 P.2d 1002, 1012 (1991).

[343] Id.

[344] United States v. Pearson, 33 M.J. 913 (A.F.C.M.R. 1991) (startling event established with child's testimony at trial, child's emotional state while in defendant's room and later with his mother, and fact that child's underpants were on backwards); State v. Murphy, 462 N.W.2d 715 (Iowa Ct. App. 1990) (36-year-old defendant was wrestling with 13-year-old victims when he fondled them; this startling event caused a child to shout "pervert"; held admissible as excited utterance); State v. Carlson, 311 Or. 201, 808 P.2d 1002, 1010 (1991); State v. Chapin, 118 Wash. 2d 681, 826 P.2d 194 (1992).

[345] See 4 Weinstein & Berger ¶ 803(2)[01], at 803-89 where the authors remark that "Rule 803(2) does not expressly state that declarant must have perceived the event. Observation is, however, mandated by the requirement that the declarant's excitement be 'caused' by the event or condition."

[346] Fed. R. Evid. 803(2) advisory committee's note ("Participation by the declarant is not required: a non-participant may be moved to describe what he perceives, and one may be startled by an event in which he is not an actor"); 4 Weinstein & Berger ¶ 803(2)[01], at 803-89.

The Advisory Committee note to Rule 803(2) remarks that "when declarant is an unidentified bystander, the cases indicate hesitancy in upholding the statement alone as sufficient, Garrett v. Howden, 73 N.M. 307, 387 P.2d 874 (1963); Beck v. Dye, 200 Wash. 1, 92 P.2d 1113 (1939), a result which would under appropriate circumstances be consistent with the rule."

[347] See State v. Carlson, 311 Or. 201, 808 P.2d 1002, 1011 (1991). In this case the court wrote:

The "startling event or condition" "is the catalyst that shocks the witness' senses, thereby rendering the witness' resulting statement sincere and trustworthy." Rice,

§ 7.29   ADMISSIBILITY REQUIREMENTS   161

may not be excited by an event adults find shocking. For example, a child who has been sexually abused for years may consider the latest incident just another in a long series. If the child discloses the latest incident, it is unlikely the child's statement is an excited utterance.[348] In a similar vein, a child of two or three may not realize that sexual activity is inappropriate, and the child may not find the abuse startling.[349] If the child reveals the event to an adult, the statement does not qualify as an excited utterance. On the other hand, if a child is excited by an event that would not disturb adults, the requisite excitement exists.

Although the subjective excitement of the declarant is decisive, it is difficult to prove the declarant's state of mind, and the usual practice is to establish excitement through objective evidence, including the declarant's verbal and nonverbal reaction.

There are several ways to prove that a startling event occurred. An eyewitness may establish the event and its startling character.[350] The eyewitness may also describe the excited state of the declarant.[351] Alternatively, the proponent may

---

Evidence: Common Law and Federal Rules of Evidence 517 (2d ed. 1990). The "startling-event-or-condition" prerequisite has two components: the occurrence of an event or condition and its startling nature. Whether an event or condition is sufficiently startling cannot be determined from the nature of the event or condition itself. For the purposes of the excited utterance exception, an event or condition is not inherently startling. The startling-nature component is a relational concept, *i.e.,* whether an event is sufficiently startling to qualify cannot be determined without focusing on the event's effect on the declarant.

Often, the very nature of the event or condition (*e.g.,* a violent criminal assault or an automobile accident) will indicate its startling character. The sufficiency of those events or conditions to qualify as startling is, therefore, seldom questioned. . . . An event or condition that does not by its nature indicate a startling quality may, nevertheless, qualify. In determining whether a particular event or condition is startling, the standard is primarily subjective, *i.e.,* the trial judge should "look primarily to the effect [of the event or condition] upon the declarant."

See also United States v. Napier, 518 F.2d 316 (9th Cir.), *cert. denied,* 423 U.S. 895 (1975) (victim was assaulted, requiring seven-week hospitalization; upon returning home the victim was shown a newspaper photograph and said, "He killed me, he killed me"; held that "[t]he display of the photograph . . . qualifie[d] as a sufficiently 'startling' event"); United States v. LeMere, 22 M.J. 61, 68 (C.M.A. 1986).

[348] United States v. Lyons, 33 M.J. 543 (A.C.M.R. 1991) (mentally retarded 18-year-old victim had sexual intercourse with perpetrator on occasions before charged offense, thus rendering it unlikely victim's statement four days following charged offense could be excited utterance); United States v. Fink, 32 M.J. 987 (A.C.M.R. 1991) (record did not contain evidence that child viewed event as startling).

[349] Morgan v. Foretich, 846 F.2d 941, 947 (4th Cir. 1988).

[350] State v. Boodry, 96 Ariz. 259, 394 P.2d 196, *cert. denied,* 397 U.S. 949 (1964); 4 Weinstein & Berger ¶ 803(2)[01], at 803-87 ("In most cases, proof that the event occurred is furnished either by testimony of witnesses other than the declarant, or by circumstantial evidence that something out of the ordinary occurred").

[351] United States v. Iron Shell, 633 F.2d 77 (8th Cir. 1980), *cert. denied,* 450 U.S. 1001 (1981).

offer circumstantial evidence of the event.[352] If the declarant testifies, the declarant may describe the startling event.[353]

Can the out-of-court statement *itself* establish the exciting event?[354] Fortunately, this question does not arise very often because, in the vast majority of cases, there is circumstantial evidence of the event.[355] Courts that have ruled on the question reach differing conclusions.[356] Commentators generally favor allowing the statement to establish the event. McCormick states: "Under generally prevailing practice, the statement itself is taken as sufficient proof of the exciting event and therefore the statement is admissible despite absence of other proof that an exciting event occurred."[357]

Weinstein and Berger advocate a similar approach, writing:

> It would seem, however, that when there is no other evidence to prove the happening, the modern trend is to take "the declaration itself . . . as evidence of the fact of the happening of the startling event." Such an approach though somewhat unsettling theoretically as an example of a statement lifting itself into admissibility by its own bootstraps, is justified by the last sentence of Rule 104(a) which provides that in making preliminary determinations the judge "is not bound by the rules of evidence except those with respect to privileges." A hearsay declaration may be used to establish the foundation for a hearsay

---

[352] United States v. Pearson, 33 M.J. 913 (A.F.C.M.R. 1991); People v. Roy, 201 Ill. App. 3d 166, 558 N.E.2d 1208, 1218 (1990) ("Direct proof of the occurrence is not strictly necessary, as circumstantial evidence corroborating the existence of the shocking event is sufficient"); Commonwealth v. Sanford, 397 Pa. Super. 581, 580 A.2d 784 (1990).

[353] The child's description of the event from the witness stand is sufficient to establish both the event and its startling character.

[354] For discussion of this issue, see 4 Louisell & Mueller § 439, at 509–13; 4 Weinstein & Berger ¶ 803(2)[01], at 803-87 to 803-88. *See also* Travelers' Ins. Co. v. Mosley, 75 U.S. (8 Wall.) 397, 19 L. Ed. 437 (1869); People v. Burton, 433 Mich. 268, 445 N.W.2d 133 (1989) (majority holds statement itself cannot establish event); Commonwealth v. Barnes, 310 Pa. Super. 480, 456 A.2d 1037, 38 A.L.R.4th 1227 (1983) (statement cannot itself establish event).

[355] Fed. R. Evid. 803(2) advisory committee's note ("Whether proof of the startling event may be made by the statement itself is largely an academic question, since in most cases there is present at least circumstantial evidence that something of a startling nature must have occurred"). When deciding admissibility under Rule 104(a), the court uses the civil standard of proof, the preponderance of the evidence. *See* Bourjaily v. United States, 483 U.S. 171 (1987); Graham § 104.1, at 43.

[356] People v. Burton, 433 Mich. 268, 445 N.W.2d 133 (1989). In *Burton* the majority of the Michigan Supreme Court adopted the position that the statement alone is not sufficient to establish the startling event. In a well-reasoned dissent, Justice Boyle took issue with the majority. 445 N.W.2d at 149 (Boyle, J., dissenting). The majority and dissenting opinions in *Burton* offer scholarly and helpful discussion of the competing positions on this issue. *See also* People v. Hughey, 194 Cal. App. 3d 1383, 240 Cal. Rptr. 269, 276 (1987) ("A spontaneous statement can prove that the startling event occurred"); Louisell & Mueller § 439, at 511.

[357] McCormick § 297, at 855 (footnote omitted).

exception. Any other approach would greatly undermine the utility of the exception by causing valuable evidence to be excluded.[358]

As stated above, the out-of-court statement seldom stands in complete isolation. Usually, circumstantial evidence is available to prove the startling event. A hypothetical case is useful. Four-year-old Sally was allegedly abused by a neighbor named Bill. Immediately following the alleged abuse, Sally ran home to her mother and said, "Mommy, Mommy, Bill shook his pee-pee up and down and white stuff came out and got all over my leg!" Bill is charged with sexual abuse. At trial, Bill denies the charge. Sally does not testify, there are no other witnesses, and there is no physical evidence because Bill allegedly washed the semen from Sally's leg before she ran home. Independent evidence establishes that Bill was at home at the time of the alleged abuse.

The prosecutor offers Sally's statement to her mother as an excited utterance. In determining whether a startling event occurred, the court is not bound by the rules of evidence.[359] Thus, the court may consider any evidence that tends to establish the event. Sally's statement itself is strong evidence that the child experienced a startling event. The grammatical structure of the statement—ending as it does with an exclamation point—evidences excitement. When Sally's statement is considered along with the fact that Sally blurted the statement out as she ran to her mother, it is logical to infer a recent startling event as the genesis of the statement. The graphic description of masturbation and ejaculation is further evidence of the event because a four-year-old is unlikely to fabricate such an occurrence. Bill's opportunity to commit the abuse—although not strong evidence—is relevant, and properly considered along with other evidence. Thus, in this case, Sally's statement is the strongest evidence of the event, and the trial court should consider the statement along with other evidence.[360]

The United States Supreme Court's decision in *Bourjaily v. United States*[361] bolsters the argument in favor of considering the child's statement—along with other evidence—to determine whether a startling event occurred. The logic in *Bourjaily*, which considered the admissibility of co-conspirator statements under Rule 801(d)(2)(E), is similar to the logic of using an excited utterance to help determine if a startling event occurred. The co-conspirator exception[362] provides that "[a] statement is not hearsay if the statement is offered against a party and is a statement by a coconspirator of a party during the course and in furtherance

---

[358] 4 Weinstein & Berger ¶ 803(2)[01], at 803-88 (footnotes omitted).

[359] Fed. R. Evid. 104(a). *See* Bourjaily v. United States, 483 U.S. 171 (1987).

[360] Graham § 104.1, at 41 ("an item offered and objected to may itself be considered by the court in ruling on admissibility").

[361] 483 U.S. 171 (1987).

[362] The rule allowing admission of statements of co-conspirators is not actually a hearsay "exception" because co-conspirator statements are defined as nonhearsay. Nevertheless, it is common practice to refer to a co-conspirator "exception," and this admittedly inaccurate practice is continued here.

of the conspiracy."³⁶³ The defendant in *Bourjaily* argued "that in determining whether a conspiracy exists and whether the defendant was a member of it, the court must look only to independent evidence—that is, evidence other than the statements sought to be admitted."³⁶⁴ The Supreme Court rejected the defendant's argument, noting that the trial judge determines pursuant to Rule 104(a) whether the requirements of the co-conspirator exception are fulfilled. Under Rule 104(a), the judge may "consider any evidence whatsoever, bound only by the rules of privilege."³⁶⁵ The Court held that in deciding whether the co-conspirator exception applies, trial judges "may examine the hearsay statements sought to be admitted."³⁶⁶ The Court rejected the argument that considering the statement was improper bootstrapping and noted that when the statement is considered along with other evidence of conspiracy, the statement may have probative value. The Court wrote:

> [I]ndividual pieces of evidence, insufficient in themselves to prove a point, may in cumulation prove it. The sum of an evidentiary presentation may well be greater than its constituent parts. . . . [A] piece of evidence, unreliable in isolation, may become quite probative when corroborated by other evidence. A *per se* rule barring consideration of these hearsay statements during preliminary factfinding is not therefore required. Even if out-of-court declarations by co-conspirators are presumptively unreliable, trial courts must be permitted to evaluate these statements for their evidentiary worth as revealed by the particular circumstances of the case. . . .
>
> We think that there is little doubt that a co-conspirator's statements could themselves be probative of the existence of a conspiracy and the participation of both the defendant and the declarant in the conspiracy.³⁶⁷

As with the co-conspirator exception, statements offered as excited utterances should be considered—along with other evidence—to determine whether the requirements of the excited utterance exception are fulfilled.

Statement Must Relate to Startling Event

The out-of-court statement must "relate" to the startling event. Louisell and Mueller observe that the word *relate* "implies only the loosest sort of relationship."³⁶⁸ A statement may fulfill the relationship requirement without describing

---

³⁶³ Fed. R. Evid. 801(d)(2)(E).

³⁶⁴ 483 U.S. at 176.

³⁶⁵ *Id.* at 178.

³⁶⁶ *Id.* at 181.

³⁶⁷ *Id.* at 179–80.

³⁶⁸ 4 Louisell & Mueller § 439, at 513. *See* People v. Nevitt, 135 Ill. 2d 423, 553 N.E.2d 368, 376–77 (1990).

§ 7.30 EVALUATION FACTORS

or explaining an event, and only statements wholly unrelated to a startling event are excluded.[369]

Statement Must Be Made Under Stress of Event

The statement must be made during the period of excitement caused by the startling event.[370] Courts consider a host of factors to determine whether a statement was made under the stress of a startling event. In most cases, the question boils down to a determination of whether the statement was spontaneous, because spontaneity reduces hearsay risks.[371]

§ 7.30 —Evaluation Factors

In evaluating out-of-court statements by children to determine if they fit the excited utterance exception, courts consider the following factors:

Spontaneity. In evaluating a statement as a possible excited utterance, the most important factor is whether the statement is a product of reflective thought or spontaneous reaction.[372] The more spontaneous the statement, the more likely

---

[369] 4 Louisell & Mueller § 439, at 513. *See also* 4 Weinstein & Berger ¶ 803(2)[01], at 803–95:

Rule 803(2) is in accord with Wigmore in not requiring that the statement elucidate or explain the occurrence . . . . Use of the word "relating" in the federal rule does limit the subject matter of the statement to some degree. The fact that a matter wholly unrelated to the event in question springs to mind through free association does not make a statement about the thought admissible. . . .

If the subject matter of the statement is such as would likely be evoked by the event, the statement should be admitted.

[370] State v. Lafrance, 589 A.2d 43, 45 (Me. 1991) ("'A statement given under the stress of anything other than the *excitement* caused by the startling event is not admissible.' 'The stress of conscience, of guilt, or of fear are [sic] not to be equated with "stress of excitement"'"); State v. Carlson, 311 Or. 201, 808 P.2d 1002, 1012 (1991) ("The spontaneity-of-the-utterance requirement, *i.e.,* the requirement that the statement of the declarant be 'made while the declarant was under the stress caused by the event or condition,' has both a *causal* and a *temporal* dimension. The declarant's excitement must have been caused by the startling event, and the declarant's statement must have been made while the excitement persisted"); 4 Louisell & Mueller § 439, at 495.

[371] Lancaster v. People, 200 Colo. 448, 615 P.2d 720, 723 (1980) ("What is of critical significance to res gestae is the spontaneous character of the statement and its natural effusion from a state of excitement").

[372] Morgan v. Foretich, 846 F.2d 941 (4th Cir. 1988); Haggins v. Warden, 715 F.2d 1050, 1058 (6th Cir. 1983), *cert. denied,* 464 U.S. 1071 (1984); United States v. Fink, 32 M.J. 987, 990 (A.C.M.R. 1991) ("The degree of excitement is not the key to admissibility. Rather it is the spontaneity of the statement"); Lancaster v. People, 200 Colo. 448, 615 P.2d 720, 723 (1980) ("What is of critical significance to res gestae is the spontaneous character of the

it is an excited utterance. If a child had an opportunity to reflect or fabricate, the balance moves away from admissibility.[373]

Lapse of time. The longer the delay between a startling event and an out-of-court statement, the less likely the declarant was excited when the statement was made. Thus, evidence of elapsed time is relevant.[374] Courts agree, however, that lapse of time is not dispositive on the question of excitement.[375]

---

statement and its natural effusion from a state of excitement"); *In re* Doe, 70 Haw. 32, 761 P.2d 299, 303 (1988); *In re* R.A., 225 Neb. 157, 403 N.W.2d 357 (1987) (requirements for excited utterance exception are relaxed with young children); *In re* Deborah M., 544 A.2d 572, 575 (R.I. 1988) (interpreting statute modifying excited utterance exception in child abuse litigation); State v. Shaw, 149 Vt. 275, 542 A.2d 1106 (1987).

See also Commonwealth v. Fuller, 22 Mass. App. Ct. 152, 491 N.E.2d 1083, 1085–86 (1986), *aff'd,* 399 Mass. 678, 506 N.E.2d 852 (1987). In *Fuller* the court wrote:

[I]t is not the quality or degree of the excitement which renders the exclamation admissible. Rather, the "admissibility of the utterance must rest on the fact that it was 'spontaneous to a degree which reasonably negatived premeditation or possible fabrication and tended to qualify, characterize and explain' the [event]." . . . Focusing on the degree of spontaneity (rather than the degree of excitement) is particularly appropriate when the statement is made by a child too young to become excited about the event in issue because he or she cannot appreciate its gravity.

The statement need not be completely spontaneous. *See* State v. Robinson, 44 Wash. App. 611, 722 P.2d 1379, 1383 (1986) ("Nor must an excited utterance be completely spontaneous").

[373] Lyles v. State, 412 So. 2d 458, 460 (Fla. Dist. Ct. App. 1982) (burden was on state to demonstrate spontaneity; state failed to establish that child did not have an opportunity to reflect or deliberate; evidence therefore excluded); People v. Nevitt, 135 Ill. 2d 423, 553 N.E.2d 368, 376 (1990) ("We find no evidence that would explain a motive for the [three-year-old] child to fabricate the statement"); People v. Brown, 170 Ill. App. 3d 273, 524 N.E.2d 742 (1988) (adult's statement not excited utterance because declarant paused to reflect); State v. Stevens, 289 N.W.2d 592, 597 (Iowa 1980) ("Before the statement can be admitted as an exception to the rule excluding hearsay, the court must be persuaded that the utterance was impulsive, not reflective"); State v. Walton, 432 A.2d 1275, 1277 (Me. 1981) ("The trustworthiness of an excited utterance . . . is based upon the theory that the impact of the event produces an utterance that is 'spontaneous and unreflecting.' . . . In this case it is obvious that the victim's stress resulted from reflecting, even brooding, over several past incidents").

[374] Morgan v. Foretich, 846 F.2d 941 (4th Cir. 1988); United States v. Iron Shell, 633 F.2d 77, 85 (8th Cir. 1980), *cert. denied,* 450 U.S. 1001 (1981) ("The lapse of time between the startling event and the out-of-court statement, although relevant, is not dispositive in the application of rule 803(2)"); State v. Jano, 524 So. 2d 660, 662–63 (Fla. 1988); People v. Burton, 433 Mich. 268, 445 N.W.2d 133, 148 (1989); State v. Jones, 362 S.E.2d 330, 333 (W. Va. 1987) ("Usually, the length of time between the occurrence and the victim's statement decides whether the statement is admissible as evidence") (footnote omitted).

[375] Morgan v. Foretich, 846 F.2d 941 (4th Cir. 1988); Gross v. Greer, 773 F.2d 116, 119 (7th Cir. 1985) ("It is well-established that the lapse of time between the startling event and the out-of-court statement, although relevant, is not dispositive in the application of the res gestae exception to the hearsay rule"); United States v. Iron Shell, 633 F.2d 77, 85 (8th Cir. 1980), *cert. denied,* 450 U.S. 1001 (1981) (nine-year-old victim of sexual assault; "The lapse of time between the startling event and the out-of-court statement, although relevant, is not

§ 7.30   EVALUATION FACTORS

Delay is considered in relation to a number of other factors indicating presence or absence of spontaneity and excitement. Furthermore, several decisions state that when the declarant is a child of tender years, the requirements of the excited utterance exception, including lapse of time, are liberally construed in favor of receipt of the evidence.[376] Courts have approved delays ranging from a

---

dispositive in the application of rule 803(2)"); Garcia v. Watkins, 604 F.2d 1297, 1300 (10th Cir. 1979); United States v. Miller, 32 M.J. 843 (N.M.C.M.R. 1991) (lapse of time not dispositive); State v. Allen, 157 Ariz. 165, 755 P.2d 1153, 1161, n. 18 (1988) ("We consider lapse of time as only one factor in determining the admissibility of an excited utterance"; however, court states that time lapse is probably most important factor); State v. Rivera, 139 Ariz. 409, 678 P.2d 1373, 1375 (1984) ("the alleged event occurred from five to ten hours before the statement was made. However, this time lapse is not in itself a bar to admission of the statement"); In re Damon H., 165 Cal. App. 3d 471, 211 Cal Rptr. 623 (1985); In re O.E.P., 654 P.2d 312, 318 (Colo. 1982) ("Although the temporal interval between the 'startling event' and the child's statement is not without significance, it is not conclusive on the question of admissibility"); Alston v. United States, 462 A.2d 1122, 1127 (D.C. 1983) ("while the time element is not controlling, it is of great significance"); People v. Gacho, 122 Ill. 2d 221, 522 N.E.2d 1146, 1155, cert. denied, 488 U.S. 910 (1988) (murder case not involving children; "'The time factor is an elusive element and will vary with the facts of the case'"); People v. Roy, 201 Ill. App. 3d 166, 558 N.E.2d 1208, 1218 (1990), cert. denied, 112 S. Ct. 965 (1992) ("time alone does not control the admissibility of the utterance but rather the critical factor is the lack of opportunity to fabricate"); People v. Cherry, 88 Ill. App. 3d 1048, 411 N.E.2d 61, 66 (1980); State v. Mateer, 383 N.W.2d 533, 535 (Iowa 1986) ("lapse of time is only one of several relevant factors for the trial court to consider in determining the spontaneity of declarant's out-of-court statements"); State v. Daniels, 380 N.W.2d 777, 783 (Minn. 1986) ("Lapse of time between startling event and the excited utterance is not always determinative"); State v. Boston, 46 Ohio St. 3d 108, 545 N.E.2d 1220, 1230–31 (1989); Beavers v. State, 709 P.2d 702, 704 (Okla. Crim. App. 1985) ("There is no fixed rule as to time and distance from the exciting event for statements to be considered excited utterances"); Commonwealth v. McEachin, 371 Pa. Super. 188, 537 A.2d 883, 889 (1988); State v. Bawdon, 386 N.W.2d 484, 486 (S.D. 1986) ("'the time that elapsed between the event and the statement is a factor to be considered, it is not determinative,'" quoting from State v. Percy, 81 S.D. 519, 137 N.W.2d 888 (1965)); State v. Thomas, 777 P.2d 445, 449 (Utah 1989); State v. Shaw, 149 Vt. 275, 542 A.2d 1106, 1109 (1987) ("the key consideration is the condition of the declarant"); State v. Doe, 105 Wash. 2d 889, 719 P.2d 554 (1986); State v. Moats, 156 Wis. 2d 74, 457 N.W.2d 299, 309 (1990).

See Slough, *Spontaneous Statements and State of Mind*, 46 Iowa L. Rev. 224, 243 (1961) ("How long can excitement prevail? Obviously there are no pat answers and the character of the transaction or event will largely determine the significance of the time factor").

[376] United States v. DeNoyer, 811 F.2d 436, 438 (8th Cir. 1987) ("this Circuit follows the modern rule that in cases involving young child witnesses, the administration of justice is served by the admission of statements made in a more relaxed environment without the possible harm of traumatic courtroom encounter"); In re C.A., 201 N.J. Super. 28, 492 A.2d 683, 686 (1985) (court stated that it is proper to make allowances for a child's youth in extending time during which nervous excitement continues); State v. Wagner, 30 Ohio App. 3d 261, 508 N.E.2d 164, 166 (1986) ("Related to the notion of a wide discretion in appellate review is a clear judicial trend to liberalize the requirements for an excited utterance when applied to young children victimized by sexual assaults"); Commonwealth v. Bailey, 353 Pa. Super. 390, 510 A.2d 367, 368 (1986) ("The definition of spontaneity is relaxed when the declarant is the victim of sexual assault"); In re Jean Marie W., 559 A.2d 625, 631 (R.I. 1989); State v.

few minutes to many hours.[377] At the same time, however, courts are careful to reject out-of-court statements in which delay and other factors establish lack of excitement.[378]

Burns, 524 A.2d 564, 567 (R.I. 1987); State v. Bawdon, 386 N.W.2d 484, 486 (S.D. 1986) ("'[W]here the victim is of an age as to render improbable that her utterance was deliberate and its effect premeditated the utterance need not be so nearly contemporaneous with the act as in the case of an older person'"); State v. Logue, 372 N.W.2d 151, 159 (S.D. 1985) ("Thus, particularly where declarant is a child of tender years, a mere lapse of time does not, by itself, disqualify a statement as an excited utterance"); State v. Gollon, 115 Wis. 2d 592, 340 N.W.2d 912, 915 (Ct. App. 1983) (six-year-old victims of sexual abuse; "The exception is liberally applied to statements by a young child involved in a claimed sexual assault"); State v. Doe, 105 Wash. 2d 889, 719 P.2d 554 (1986) ("cases have extended the time limit for young children because the danger of fabrication is more remote"; court rejected a statement offered as an excited utterance when delay was three days); State v. Bouchard, 31 Wash. App. 381, 639 P.2d 761, 763 (1982); State ex rel. Harris v. Schmidt, 69 Wis. 2d 668, 230 N.W.2d 890, 899 (1975) (probation revocation proceeding; court stated that "[a] broad and more liberal interpretation is given to what constitutes an excited utterance when applied to young children especially when the child is alleged to have been the victim of sexual assault").

[377] Morgan v. Foretich, 846 F.2d 941 (4th Cir. 1988) (three hours not too long); United States v. Pearson, 33 M.J. 913 (A.F.C.M.R. 1991) (three hours not too long; child made statement at first safe opportunity); United States v. Miller, 32 M.J. 843, 851 (N.M.C.M.R. 1991) (18 hours not too long); Drumbarger v. State, 716 P.2d 6, 10 (Alaska Ct. App. 1986) (statement made immediately following sexual abuse admissible); Bryan v. State, 288 Ark. 125, 702 S.W.2d 785, 786 (1986) (statement made immediately following event admissible); People v. Trimble, 7 Cal. Rptr. 2d 450 (Ct. App. 1992) (two days not too long); People v. Roark, 643 P.2d 756 (Colo. 1982) (statement by five-year-old eyewitness made 12 hours following a beating held admissible); Ward v. State, 186 Ga. App. 503, 368 S.E.2d 139 (1988) (next day not too long); People v. Nevitt, 135 Ill. 2d 423, 553 N.E.2d 368 (1990) (three-year-old sex abuse victim; five-hour delay not too long in light of circumstances, including first safe opportunity); People v. Fisher, 169 Ill. App. 3d 785, 523 N.E.2d 368 (1988) (four to six hours not too long when child was almost three years old); People v. Robinson, 94 Ill. App. 3d 304, 310, 418 N.E.2d 899, 903-04 (1981) (16-hour delay not too long); People v. Cherry, 88 Ill. App. 3d 1048, 411 N.E.2d 61, 66 (1980) (delay of a few moments acceptable); Goolsby v. State, 517 N.E.2d 54, 60 (Ind. 1987) (five-year-old eyewitness; child witnessed his mother stabbed and beaten; child was also hit by nighttime intruder; 45-minute delay not too long); Hopper v. State, 489 N.E.2d 1209, 1213 (Ind. Ct. App.), cert. denied, 479 U.S. 992 (1986) (delay of a few minutes acceptable); State v. Mateer, 383 N.W.2d 533, 534 (Iowa 1986) (one-hour delay acceptable); State v. Galvan, 297 N.W.2d 344, 346 (Iowa 1980) (delay of two days acceptable); State v. Stevens, 289 N.W.2d 592, 593 (Iowa 1980) (approximately one-hour delay acceptable); State v. Paulsen, 265 N.W.2d 581, 586 (Iowa 1978) (two-hour delay acceptable); State v. Stafford, 237 Iowa 780, 23 N.W.2d 832 (1946) (14-hour delay acceptable); State v. Noble, 342 So. 2d 170 (La. 1977) (statement by four-year-old victim admissible when made two days following event); People v. Hackney, 183 Mich. App. 516, 455 N.W.2d 358, 362 (1990) (three to four hours not too long in case of anal sodomy); State v. Daniels, 380 N.W.2d 777 (Minn. 1986) (delay of one to two hours acceptable); State v. Posten, 302 N.W.2d 638, 641 (Minn. 1981) (delay of a few days between statement and last of defendant's acts acceptable); State v. Plant, 236 Neb. 317, 461 N.W.2d 253, 264 (1990) (two days not too long under circumstances); State v. Gonzales, 219 Neb. 846, 366 N.W.2d 775 (1985) (delay of less than one hour acceptable); Dearing v. State, 100 Nev. 590, 691 P.2d 419, 420 (1984) (delay up to one and one-half hours acceptable); State v. Smith, 315

§ 7.30 EVALUATION FACTORS 169

N.C. 76, 337 S.E.2d 833(1985) (delay of two or three days acceptable); State v. Wallace, 37 Ohio St. 3d 87, 524 N.E.2d 466, 469 (1988) (15 hours not too long; child was brutally assaulted and unconscious during the interval); Beavers v. State, 709 P.2d 702, 704 (Okla. Crim. App. 1985) (delay of two to three hours acceptable); State v. Kendrick, 239 Or. 512, 398 P.2d 471 (1965) (delay of a few moments acceptable); State v. Mace, 67 Or. App. 753, 681 P.2d 140, 143 (1984) (delay of less than two hours acceptable); Commonwealth v. McEachin, 371 Pa. Super. 188, 537 A.2d 883, 890 (1988) ("As long as the statement was clearly a product of overpowering emotion caused by a traumatic and humiliating experience," a lapse in excess of six hours might not be too long); Commonwealth v. Rhoades, 364 Pa. Super. 54, 527 A.2d 148 (1987) (eight-year-old child witnessed her father fatally shoot her mother; child made statements describing the event 30-45 minutes later; these were excited utterances); Commonwealth v. Penn, 497 Pa. 232, 439 A.2d 1154, 1159, *cert. denied,* 456 U.S. 980 (1982) (delay of 15 to 20 minutes not too long); State v. Logue, 372 N.W.2d 151, 159 (S.D. 1985) (two-day delay acceptable); State v. Moats, 156 Wis. 2d 74, 457 N.W.2d 299, 309-10 (1990) (five-year-old's statements within one week after perpetrator left home were excited utterances); Love v. State, 64 Wis. 2d 432, 219 N.W.2d 294 (1974) (statement by three-year-old victim made one day following event admissible); State v. Padilla, 110 Wis. 2d 414, 329 N.W.2d 263, 267 (Ct. App. 1982) ("a three-day time period, as in the case here, is less contemporaneous than the time periods of the other reported cases. This does not matter, however, because spontaneity and stress are the keys").

[378] United States v. LeMere, 22 M.J. 61, 68 (C.M.A. 1986); United States v. Whitney, 18 M.J. 700 (A.F.C.M.R. 1984); Brandon v. State, 778 P.2d 221, 226 (Alaska Ct. App. 1989) (adult victim's statement made at least 45 minutes following severe physical assault could not have been excited utterance; statements by victim's child made at least six hours after child witnessed assault on his mother were also not excited utterances; child was acting normally at time of statement); State v. Allen, 157 Ariz. 165, 755 P.2d 1153, 1161 (1988) (two months too long; child not excited); Pennington v. State, 24 Ark. App. 70, 749 S.W.2d 680, 682 (1988) (six days too long); Alston v. United States, 462 A.2d 1122, 1128 (D.C. 1983) (lapse of more than three hours too long when child was calm during that time); Fitzgerald v. United States, 443 A.2d 1295, 1304 (D.C. 1982) (statement made on day following traumatic event too remote); Lyles v. State, 412 So. 2d 458, 460 (Fla. Dist. Ct. App. 1982) (12-hour delay too long); *In re* Doe, 70 Haw. 32, 761 P.2d 299 (1988) (half a day too long); Mounce v. Commonwealth, 795 S.W.2d 375 (Ky. 1990) (statements 9 to 23 days after abuse too remote); People v. Woith, 126 Ill. App. 3d 817, 467 N.E.2d 614, 617-18 (1984) (statement made on day following event too remote); State v. Lafrance, 589 A.2d 43, 46 (Me. 1991) (statement nearly a day after incident and after period of normal behavior not excited utterance); Cassidy v. State, 74 Md. App. 1, 536 A.2d 666, 675 (1988) (three days too long; "four-and-a-half to five hours seems to represent the extreme outer limit to which the Excited Utterance phenomenon has been pushed"); People v. Straight, 430 Mich. 418, 424 N.W.2d 257 (1988) (one month too long); People v. Pullins, 145 Mich. App. 414, 378 N.W.2d 502, 505 (1985) (seven-hour delay too long); *In re* C.B., 574 So. 2d 1369, 1372 (Miss. 1990) (a week too long); Leatherwood v. State, 548 So. 2d 389, 399 (Miss. 1989) ("Statements made by her some six weeks later simply cannot qualify as having been made 'while the declarant was under the stress of excitement caused by the event'"); Beavers v. State, 709 P.2d 702, 705 (Okla. Crim. App. 1985) (statement made on day following event too remote); State v. Hollywood, 67 Or. App. 546, 680 P.2d 655, 657 (1984) (as much as one month delay too long); State v. Paster, 524 A.2d 587 (R.I. 1987) (nine days too long); State v. Logue, 372 N.W.2d 151, 159 (S.D. 1985) (15 days too long); State v. Williams, 598 S.W.2d 830, 833 (Tenn. Crim. App. 1980) (delay in excess of three hours too long); Vera v. State, 709 S.W.2d 681 (Tex. Ct. App. 1986) (11-year-old sex abuse victim's statement to police officer not an excited utterance; five-hour delay too long when before statement child

First safe opportunity. Most children are abused while under the physical control of the abuser. While a child remains in the custody of the perpetrator, the child is unlikely to risk making a statement that could qualify as an excited utterance. When the child finally leaves the custody of the abuser, however, and feels safe to reveal what happened, a substantial period of time may have elapsed, raising questions about the child's statement as an excited utterance. A growing number of decisions state that when a child makes a statement at the first safe opportunity, the statement is admissible provided there are sufficient indicia of excitement.[379] One indicator of excitement may be that the child's

---

had conversations with her sister and mother and child did not begin to cry until three and one-half hours after event); State v. Roy, 140 Vt. 219, 436 A.2d 1090, 1093 (1981) (delay in excess of an hour too long); State v. Jones, 178 W. Va. 519, 362 S.E.2d 330, 333 (1987) (six months too long).

See also State v. Doe, 105 Wash. 2d 889, 719 P.2d 554, 556 (1986), where the court ruled that a three-day delay was too long. The court wrote:

Normally, in order to fall within the excited utterance exception, a statement must occur immediately after the event in question. Complete spontaneity is not required, however, and we have allowed statements made by declarants a short time after the event in question. . . . The question involved is not how much time has passed, but "whether the statement was made while the declarant was still under the influence of the event to the extent that his statement could not be the result of fabrication, intervening actions, or the exercise of choice or judgment." . . .

Although cases have extended the time limit for young children because the danger of fabrication is more remote, . . . the most amount of time allowed between event and statement was less than 1 day.

[379] Morgan v. Foretich, 846 F.2d 941 (4th Cir. 1988) ("the time lapse to be considered in these cases is not simply the time between the abuse and the declaration. Rather, courts must also be cognizant of the child's first real opportunity to report the incident"); United States v. Nick, 604 F.2d 1199, 1200 (9th Cir. 1979) (statement made by three-year-old child at first safe opportunity to mother admissible); United States v. Arnold, 25 M.J. 129 (C.M.A. 1987), *cert. denied*, 484 U.S. 1060 (1988); United States v. Pearson, 33 M.J. 913 (A.F.C.M.R. 1991); Drumbarger v. State, 716 P.2d 6, 10 (Alaska Ct. App. 1986) (victim's "statement was made immediately after she was discovered by her mother moments after she had been sexually assaulted by her father"; court held that statement was an excited utterance); Weaver v. State, 271 Ark. 853, 612 S.W.2d 324, 327 (Ct. App.), *cert. denied*, 452 U.S. 963 (1981) (after being released from abuser's car, child immediately returned home and told her mother of assault); In re O.E.P., 654 P.2d 312, 318 (Colo. 1982) (child made statement at first safe opportunity); Lancaster v. People, 200 Colo. 448, 615 P.2d 720 (1980) (nearly three-year-old child told her mother about the assault at first safe opportunity, approximately one half hour after assault; held admissible); People v. Sandoval, 709 P.2d 90, 91–92 (Colo. Ct. App. 1985) (victim told her sister about assault at first opportunity she had outside defendant's presence); People v. Bashara, 677 P.2d 1376, 1378 (Colo. Ct. App. 1983) (child "made the statements to her mother after walking directly home from defendant's apartment, upon the first opportunity to do so"); Kilgore v. State, 177 Ga. App. 656, 340 S.E.2d 640 (1986); People v. Nevitt, 135 Ill. 2d 423, 553 N.E.2d 368, 376 (1990) (three-year-old victimized at preschool; court relied on first safe opportunity in conjunction with other factors to hold statement to child's mother some five hours after sexual abuse admissible); People v. Gacho, 122 Ill. 2d 221, 522 N.E. 1146, 1155-56, *cert. denied*, 488

custody by the abuser perpetuated the excitement. The first safe opportunity doctrine helps explain delay, and, as long as there is evidence that the child was excited when the statement was made, the doctrine serves a useful purpose.

Rekindled excitement. An exciting event may be followed by a period of calm during which the child's excitement abates. If the child is subsequently exposed to a stimulus that reminds the child of the startling event, the child's excitement may be rekindled. Consider, for example, a case in which a seven-year-old is kidnapped and assaulted by a stranger. After a day of horror, the child is released. The next day, following a night's sleep in the care of the mother and father, the child is shown a picture of the assailant. The child reacts with fear and blurts out, "That's him, that's the man who took me away and tied me up and hit me with a stick." The excitement of the event is rekindled. Several decisions suggest that rekindled excitement can satisfy the requirement that the declarant speak under the excitement of a startling event.[380]

The rekindled excitement theory raises the question of which event is the exciting event for purposes of the excited utterance exception. Is it the original

---

U.S. 910 (1988) (adult victim was shot and stuffed in trunk; when rescued six hours later, victim made statement; statement held spontaneous declaration because the statement was made at the "first opportunity to speak with anyone after the period of confinement in a seriously wounded condition"); People v. Roy, 201 Ill. App. 3d 166, 558 N.E.2d 1208, 1218–19 (1990), *cert. denied,* 112 S. Ct. 965 (1992); State v. Komurke, 560 So. 2d 986 (La. Ct. App. 1990) (interpreting statutory fresh complaint provision, court recognized first safe opportunity doctrine to explain delay in reporting); People v. Fenner, 136 Mich. App. 45, 356 N.W.2d 1, 2 (1984) (events were disclosed the moment victim was outside presence of defendant); In re Meeboer, 134 Mich. App. 294, 350 N.W.2d 868, 871 (1984) (upon arising around seven o'clock the next morning, victim told first person she talked to, her mother, about incident); State v. Van Orman, 642 S.W.2d 636, 639 (Mo. 1982); State v. Boston, 46 Ohio St. 3d 108, 545 N.E.2d 1220, 1231 (1989); State v. Jensen, 107 Or. App. 35, 810 P.2d 865, 868 (1991) (seriously burned three-year-old made statement to nurse 90 minutes after being immersed in tub of hot water; "he had little opportunity to communicate about the incident to any non-involved person"); State v. Mace, 67 Or. App. 753, 681 P.2d 140, 142 (1984) (excited utterances were made at first safe opportunity for victim to communicate, and were triggered by discomfort and pain related to incident); Commonwealth v. Sanford, 580 A.2d 784, 790 (Pa. Super. Ct. 1990); Commonwealth v. Bailey, 353 Pa. Super. 390, 510 A.2d 367 (1986).

[380] United States v. Napier, 518 F.2d 316, 318 (9th Cir.), *cert. denied,* 423 U.S. 895 (1975) (adult assault victim); *In re* O.E.P., 654 P.2d 312, 319 (Colo. 1982); State v. Shaw, 149 Vt. 275, 542 A.2d 1106, 1109 (1987) (adult rape victim; case does not use term *rekindled excitement,* but may support theory); State v. Lindner, 142 Wis. 2d 783, 419 N.W.2d 352, 356 (Ct. App. 1987) (child made statement shortly after viewing film about good touching and bad touching).

But see Brandon v. State, 778 P.2d 221, 227 (Alaska Ct. App. 1989) (dicta casting doubt on rekindled excitement theory); State v. Jano, 524 So. 2d 660, 663 (Fla. 1988) ("The fact that a declarant long after the occurrence of a startling event once again becomes excited in the course of telling about it would not permit the statement to be introduced as an excited utterance").

event? Or is it the stimulus that reawakens excitement? From an analytical perspective, it is difficult to see how the original occurrence can be the exciting event because a period of calm intervened. Yet, it is plausible in some cases that the original excitement has not dissipated, but is lying somewhere close to the psychological surface. Presentation of a stimulus connected to the original event brings the excitement back to the surface. Thus, the child's statement is made under the stress of excitement caused by the *original* event. In some instances presentation of the reawakening stimulus may be sufficiently startling *in itself* to satisfy the requirement of the exception.[381] In most cases, the statement probably is a product of both sources of excitement. Regardless of the source of excitement, the statement should qualify as an excited utterance if the judge is convinced that genuine excitement is present and that the statement is not contaminated by fabrication.

Emotional condition. A child's emotional condition is obviously important in evaluating whether a statement qualifies as an excited utterance.[382] If the child is upset, the court is more likely to conclude that the statement was made under the stress of excitement caused by the startling event.[383] On the other hand, if

---

[381] United States v. Napier, 518 F.2d 316 (9th Cir.), *cert. denied,* 423 U.S. 895 (1975); *In re* O.E.P.*,* 654 P.2d 312 (Colo. 1982).

[382] Morgan v. Foretich, 846 F.2d 941 (4th Cir. 1988); United States v. Pearson, 33 M.J. 913 (A.F.C.M.R. 1991); People v. Nevitt, 135 Ill. 2d 423, 553 N.E.2d 368 (1990) (three-year-old was sexually abused at day care; child was withdrawn and upset after being picked up by mother); State v. Mateer, 383 N.W.2d 533, 534 (Iowa 1986) (victim was in agitated emotional condition); State v. Daniels, 380 N.W.2d 777, 783 (Minn. 1986) (child was rescued from a burning building and was covered with the blood of another person); Commonwealth v. Sanford, 397 Pa. Super. 581, 580 A.2d 784, 789 (1990) ("there is no requirement that the declarant be emotionally overpowered, but rather must be speaking under the stress of excitement"); State v. Barber, 747 P.2d 436, 438–39 (Utah Ct. App. 1987) (eight-year-old boy's statement when caught red-handed shoplifting was excited utterance).

[383] *See* State v. Ritchey, 107 Ariz. 552, 490 P.2d 558, 561 (1971). The children in *Ritchey* knew and were friendly with the defendant before the assault. The court described the victims' behavior as follows:

> [T]he mother stated that the face of the elder child was streaked as though she might have been crying. She also stated that where the children were usually rowdy and playful when they arrived home, on this evening they were very quiet. The children would always place themselves near the defendant, sometimes sitting on his lap to talk to him, but on this night they stayed to themselves in another room of the house. The mother stated she had never seen the children act in this manner when the defendant was in the house. . . . [T]he children did not seem as happy as usual and were not playing with the defendant or having anything to do with him. When asked to take their toys and play, they stated that they didn't want the toys because the defendant had given the toys to them.

> *See also* Morgan v. Foretich, 846 F.2d 941 (4th Cir. 1988); Brandon v. State, 778 P.2d 221, 226 (Alaska Ct. App. 1989) (adult assault victim "was extremely upset although not

the child is calm when the statement is made, or if there are periods of calm or relaxation before the utterance, the statement is less likely to be an excited utterance.[384] Similarly, if the child was playing contentedly before the statement, a court may decide that the statement falls without the exception.[385]

---

hysterical. She had obviously been severely beaten. Joyce was upset and crying, fearful, and in great pain"); People v. Ortega, 672 P.2d 215, 217 (Colo. Ct. App. 1983) (child was "upset, nervous, shaky, scared"; these factors weighed in favor of admitting child's statements as excited utterances); People v. Nevitt, 135 Ill. 2d 423, 553 N.E.2d 368, 376 (1990) (three-year-old "was visibly upset and withdrawn"); Goolsby v. State, 517 N.E.2d 54, 60 (Ind. 1987) (five-year-old witnessed his mother stabbed and beaten by intruder; child was hit too; when child made hearsay statement he "'was very excitable, he was rambling on about what happened'"); Sanders v. State, 586 So. 2d 792, 795 (Miss. 1991); State v. Coppola, 130 N.H. 148, 536 A.2d 1236 (1987), *cert. denied,* 493 U.S. 969 (1989) (adult rape victim very upset); Dearing v. State, 100 Nev. 590, 691 P.2d 419, 420 (1984) (child made statement minutes following attack, while child was agitated and nervous; court held that child's statements were properly admitted as excited utterances); People v. Knapp, 139 A.D.2d 931, 527 N.Y.S.2d 914, 915 (1988); Commonwealth v. Rhoades, 364 Pa. Super. 54, 527 A.2d 148 (1987) (eight-year-old child witnessed her father fatally shoot her mother 30–45 minutes prior to child's excited utterance; child was very upset); State v. Burns, 524 A.2d 564, 567 (R.I. 1987); State v. Bult, 351 N.W.2d 731, 736 (S.D. 1984) (child was withdrawn, nervous, and still crying; child's statements properly admitted as excited utterances); State v. Shaw, 149 Vt. 275, 542 A.2d 1106, 1109 (1987) (adult sexual assault victim was "crying and trembling"); Martin v. Commonwealth, 4 Va. App. 438, 358 S.E.2d 415 (1987) (statements of two-year-old victim who was upset, crying, and in pain were excited utterances).

But see United States v. Fink, 32 M.J. 987 (A.C.M.R. 1991) (depression does not equate with excitement).

[384] United States v. Fink, 32 M.J. 987 (A.C.M.R. 1991); People v. Jones, 155 Cal. App. 3d 653, 202 Cal. Rptr. 289, 294–95 (1984) (calmness does not defeat spontaneity); State v. Lafrance, 589 A.2d 43, 46 (Me. 1991) (statement nearly one day after incident and after period of normal behavior not excited utterance).

[385] Brandon v. State, 778 P.2d 221, 226–27 (Alaska Ct. App. 1989) (child was playing normally when statement made, at least six hours after child witnessed attack on his mother; held not an excited utterance); State v. Allen, 157 Ariz. 165, 755 P.2d 1153, 1161 (1988); State v. Rivera, 139 Ariz. 409, 678 P.2d 1373 (1984) (three-year-old victim's statements were made following a substantial period of delay and while child was playing; court held statement not spontaneous utterance); Alston v. Untied States, 462 A.2d 1122, 1124 (D.C. 1983) (four-year-old made statements next morning after period of normal play activity; court held that statements did not qualify as excited utterances); Lyles v. State, 412 So. 2d 458, 460 (Fla. Dist. Ct. App. 1982) (four-year-old victim of sexual abuse was "normal and playing in the yard"; child's statements were not excited utterance).

But see People v. Lewis, 147 Ill. App. 3d 249, 498 N.E.2d 1169 (1986), *cert. denied,* 482 U.S. 907 (1987) (fact that child was calm did not mean child's statement not an excited utterance); People v. Hackney, 183 Mich. App. 516, 455 N.W.2d 358, 362 (1990) (fact that child "engaged in normal childhood play with others for some time before finally disclosing incident" did not defeat admission as excited utterance).

Physical condition. A child's physical condition may indicate excitement.[386] For example, if a child is injured[387] or in pain,[388] the child's statements may be excited.

Crying. If a startling event causes a child to cry, and the child is still crying when an out-of-court statement is uttered, the statement is likely to qualify as an excited utterance.[389] The red eyes, streaked face, pouting lip, and sad

---

[386] Goolsby v. State, 517 N.E.2d 54, 60 (Ind. 1987) (five-year-old witnessed his mother stabbed and beaten by intruder; child was hit in face, and urinated in his pants); State v. Mace, 67 Or. App. 753, 681 P.2d 140, 141 (1984) (mother observed blood on child's panties; when child was taken to hospital, staff observed slight tearing of vaginal wall and redness and irritation about vaginal opening; these factors contributed to conclusion that child's statements were excited utterances); State v. Van Orman, 642 S.W.2d 636, 638 (Mo. 1982).

[387] State v. Mace, 67 Or. App. 753, 681 P.2d 140, 141 (1984) (mother observed blood in child's panties; hospital staff observed slight tearing of vaginal wall and redness and irritation of vaginal opening); State v. Van Orman, 642 S.W.2d 636, 638 (Mo. 1982) (victim's vagina was lacerated and irritated at time child made statement); People v. Ortega, 672 P.2d 215 (Colo. Ct. App. 1983) (child's buttocks were injured by sexual abuse); State v. Coppola, 130 N.H. 148, 536 A.2d 1236, 1240 (1987), cert. denied, 493 U.S. 969 (1989) (adult rape victim had been cut attempting to protect herself); Martin v. Commonwealth, 4 Va. App. 438, 358 S.E.2d 415 (1987) (two-year-old's rectum was torn by defendant's penis; victim's statements uttered shortly after the attack were excited utterances).

[388] Brandon v. State, 778 P.2d 221, 225–26 (Alaska Ct. App. 1989) (adult assault victim had been severely beaten and was in great pain); People v. Ortega, 672 P.2d 215, 217 (Colo. Ct. App. 1983) (child was holding his buttock with his hand when he told his mother that "his butt hurt"); State v. Mace, 67 Or. App. 753, 681 P.2d 140, 141 (1984) (child was in pain when she made statement; she started pulling at the crotch of her pants and said "Mommy, it hurts").

[389] Brandon v. State, 778 P.2d 221, 226 (Alaska Ct. App. 1989) (adult assault victim was crying); Weaver v. State, 271 Ark. 853, 612 S.W.2d 324, 327 (Ct. App.), cert. denied, 452 U.S. 963 (1981) ("After Weaver let her out of his car, Donna went home, told her mother the lie that Weaver had told her to tell, and when she did, Donna broke down crying and she then told the truth"; child's statements were properly admitted as excited utterance); In re O.E.P., 654 P.2d 312, 318 (Colo. 1982) (child was crying less than a day following abuse; court stated that "the prolonged crying which occurred after the statement demonstrates that the distressful effects of the mistreatment were still present and quite capable of surfacing on their own power"); State v. Stevens, 289 N.W.2d 592, 594 (Iowa 1980) (victim crying hysterically); State v. Van Orman, 642 S.W.2d 636, 638 (Mo. 1982) ("Before the mother could inquire as to what had happened, the girl commenced crying"); People v. Knapp, 139 A.D.2d 931, 527 N.Y.S.2d 914 (1988); Beavers v. State, 709 P.2d 702, 704 (Okla. Crim. App. 1985) (victim was "tense and crying"); Commonwealth v. Rhoades, 364 Pa. Super. 54, 527 A.2d 148 (1987) (eight-year-old witnessed her father fatally shoot her mother 30–45 minutes before child's excited utterance; child was crying and very upset); State v. Burns, 524 A.2d 564, 567 (R.I. 1987); Vera v. State, 709 S.W.2d 681 (Tex. Ct. App. 1986) (11-year-old victim did not begin to cry until three-and-one-half hours after event; when this fact was combined with a five-hour delay and other factors, court ruled that child's statement to police officer was not excited utterance); State v. Shaw, 149 Vt. 275, 542 A.2d 1106, 1109 (1987) (adult sexual assault victim was crying and trembling).

countenance of a child who was crying a few minutes before making a statement support a finding that the statement was an excited utterance.[390]

Sleep. If a child enjoyed a restful night's sleep between the occurrence of an exciting event and a statement describing the event, the spontaneity required by the excited utterance exception may be lacking. On the other hand, some decisions suggest that when a child makes a statement upon awakening, the statement is unlikely to be fabricated and may qualify as an excited utterance.[391] In a rare case, statements made *during* sleep may be admissible. See § 7.13 for discussion of sleep talk.

Content of statement. The child's words may indicate excitement. Thus, statements such as, "Wow, you should have seen that car smash into the bus!" and "Mommy, Mommy, Bob hurt me right here!" express excitement.[392] As a rough guideline, when the most appropriate punctuation is an exclamation mark, the statement is excited.

Speech pattern. The manner in which a child makes a statement may indicate excitement. For example, pressured or hurried speech indicates excitement.[393] A

---

[390] State v. Ritchey, 107 Ariz. 552, 490 P.2d 558, 561 (1971); Martin v. Commonwealth, 4 Va. App. 438, 358 S.E.2d 415, 418 (1987) (two-year-old victim's "face was red, her eyes watery and tears were running down her cheeks"; her statements shortly after she was sodomized were excited utterances).

[391] George v. State, 306 Ark. 360, 813 S.W.2d 792 (1991) (child's statement upon awakening from nightmare was excited utterance); People v. McNichols, 139 Ill. App. 3d 947, 487 N.E.2d 1252, 1258 (1986); State v. Boston, 46 Ohio St. 3d 108, 545 N.E.2d 1220, 1231 (1989) (two-and-a-half-year-old awoke crying and screaming in middle of night; child's statements were excited utterances); State v. Gollon, 115 Wis. 2d 592, 340 N.W.2d 912, 915 (Ct. App. 1983).

See also State v. Wallace, 37 Ohio St. 3d 87, 524 N.E.2d 466 (1988). In *Wallace,* the child was physically assaulted and strangled by the defendant. The victim was unconscious for approximately 15 hours. As she gradually regained consciousness, she made statements incriminating the defendant. The court held the statements were admissible as excited utterances. The court wrote that "[a] period of unconsciousness, even an extended period, does not necessarily destroy the effect of a startling event upon the mind of the declarant for the purpose of satisfying the excited-utterance exception to the hearsay rule." 524 N.E.2d at 470 (footnote omitted).

[392] Harville v. State, 386 So. 2d 776, 782 (Ala. Crim. App. 1980); In re O.E.P., 654 P.2d 312, 318 (Colo. 1982); People v. Nevitt, 135 Ill. 2d 423, 553 N.E.2d 368, 376 (1990) (three-year-old was sexually abused at day care; child said to her mother, "Teacher Tony bit my ding-dong"; among other factors supporting admission as excited utterance, court stated that "the terminology contained in the child's declaration substantiates its reliability"); In re Meeboer, 134 Mich. App. 294, 350 N.W.2d 868, 871 (1984) (victim used terminology she had never used before).

[393] Goolsby v. State, 517 N.E.2d 54, 60 (Ind. 1987) (five-year-old witnessed his mother stabbed and beaten by intruder; the child was also hit; when child made his hearsay statement he

statement made over cereal at the breakfast table, in the child's normal manner of speaking, lacks excitement.

Lack of recall. Courts occasionally state that inability to recall an event indicates "the declarant was under stress at the time of the statement."[394]

Age. The decisions indicate sensitivity to the age of children who make statements relating to startling events.[395] Younger children may be more excited by certain events than adolescents. At the same time, events of a sexual nature may be more startling to a 13-year-old than a toddler who lacks understanding of societal taboos surrounding sexual activity.

Nature of event. Certain events are more startling than others. Courts consider the nature of the event, and the likely effect such an event would have on a child of similar age and experience.[396]

"'was very excitable, he was rambling on about what happened'"); State v. Mateer, 383 N.W.2d 533, 536 (Iowa 1986) (child was calming down in order to speak intelligibly); Beavers v. State, 709 P.2d 702, 704 (Okla. Crim. App. 1985) (11-year-old was speaking in an excited and fast manner when she made statement regarding incident).

[394] United States v. Iron Shell, 633 F.2d 77, 86 (8th Cir. 1980), *cert. denied,* 450 U.S. 1001 (1981); Hilyer v. Howat Concrete Co., 578 F.2d 422, 426 (D.C. Cir. 1978).

[395] United States v. Renville, 779 F.2d 430, 441 (8th Cir. 1985) (court discusses residual exception, Rule 803(24), and states "we believe that the age of the victim may be a factor guaranteeing the trustworthiness of the declarations. We have held a declarant's young age is a factor that may substantially lessen the degree of skepticism with which we view their motives"); Haggins v. Warden, 715 F.2d 1050, 1058 (6th Cir. 1983), *cert. denied,* 464 U.S. 1071 (1984); United States v. Iron Shell, 633 F.2d 77, 84 (8th Cir. 1980), *cert. denied,* 450 U.S. 1001 (1981) ("the age of the patient also mitigated [sic] against a finding that [the child's] statements are not within the traditional rationale of the rule"); United States v. Pearson, 33 M.J. 913 (A.F.C.M.R. 1991); United States v. LeMere, 22 M.J. 61, 68 (C.M.A. 1986); State v. Ritchey, 107 Ariz. 552, 490 P.2d 558, 561, 562 (1971); People v. Roy, 201 Ill. App. 3d 166, 558 N.E.2d 1208, 1219 (1990), *cert. denied,* 112 S. Ct. 965 (1992) ("it is unlikely a child of tender years would have any reason to fabricate stories of sexual abuse. Their statements may remain void of fabrication for a longer period of time because the child is apt to repress the incident"); Commonwealth v. McEachin, 371 Pa. Super. 188, 537 A.2d 883, 889 (1988); Martin v. Commonwealth, 4 Va. App. 438, 358 S.E.2d 415, 418 (1987) ("reliability of C's declaration is bolstered by her lack of capacity, at age 23 months, to fabricate the statement"); State v. Bryant, 828 P.2d 1121 (Wash. Ct. App. 1992) (three-year-old); State v. Moats, 156 Wis. 2d 74, 457 N.W.2d 299, 309 (1990) ("A broad and liberal interpretation governs the excited utterance exception as applied to young children because such children will tend to repress the stressful incident, will report the incident only to the mother and will be less likely than adults to consciously fabricate the incident over a period of time"); State v. Dwyer, 143 Wis. 2d 448, 422 N.W.2d 121, 124 (Ct. App. 1988), *aff'd,* 149 Wis. 2d 850, 440 N.W.2d 344 (1989) ("We apply a broad and liberal interpretation of what constitutes an excited utterance when young children are involved. . . . Wisconsin cases have consistently held that statements by young children are admissible even though these statements were not made immediately following the incident").

[396] Morgan v. Foretich, 846 F.2d 941, 947 (4th Cir. 1988); Brandon v. State, 778 P.2d 221 (Alaska Ct. App. 1989) (adult victim was severely beaten by her husband); Weaver v. State,

Intelligence. Several decisions indicate that a child's intelligence may influence whether the child's statement is an excited utterance.[397] Certainly, if a child lacks the intelligence to comprehend the exciting nature of an event, a statement describing the event would not qualify. In most cases, however, intelligence has little to do with whether a child's statement is excited.

Questioning. A child may make a statement in response to questions. The way a child is questioned influences whether a statement is an excited utterance.

---

271 Ark. 853, 612 S.W.2d 324, 327 (Ct. App.), *cert. denied,* 452 U.S. 963 (1981) (eight-year-old victim was sexually assaulted by defendant, who also hit her; court wrote that "[w]ithout question, Donna had undergone a startling event and continued in an extremely emotional state of mind when she discussed the event with her mother"); People v. Woith, 126 Ill. App. 3d 817, 467 N.E.2d 614, 618 (1984) (defendant grabbed 14-year-old victim while child's mother was not at home); People v. Cherry, 88 Ill. App. 3d 1048, 411 N.E.2d 61, 67 (1980) (child witnessed shooting of child's mother); Goolsby v. State, 517 N.E.2d 54, 60 (Ind. 1987) (five-year-old witnessed his mother stabbed and beaten by intruder; child was also hit); State v. Bean, 582 So. 2d 947, 951 (La. Ct. App. 1991) (witnessing parent shot was a startling event); State v. Bennett, 549 So. 2d 398 (La. Ct. App. 1989) (witnessing murder of parent certainly a startling event); People v. Hackney, 183 Mich. App. 516, 455 N.W.2d 358, 362 (1990) (child's statements three to four hours following sodomy were excited utterances; "Because the startling event was so traumatic in nature, it is understandable that the effect on the child's emotional state could have persisted up to the time of the statement"); *In re* Meeboer, 134 Mich. App. 294, 350 N.W.2d 868, 871 (1984) (defendant entered child's room and sexually assaulted child); State v. Daniels, 380 N.W.2d 777, 783 (Minn. 1986) (child made statement shortly after being removed from burning building); State v. Coppola, 130 N.H. 148, 536 A.2d 1236 (1987), *cert. denied,* 493 U.S. 969 (1989) (adult rape victim very upset; "The startling character of the experience described by the victim in this case is not open to question"); People v. Knapp, 139 A.D.2d 931, 527 N.Y.S.2d 914, 915 (1988); State v. Bass, 221 N.J. Super. 466, 535 A.2d 1, 10 (1987) (child witnessed his young brother brutally beaten to death by their father); State v. Wallace, 37 Ohio St. 3d 87, 524 N.E.2d 466 (1988) (physical abuse case; child was brutally assaulted); Commonwealth v. Penn, 497 Pa. 232, 439 A.2d 1154, 1159, *cert. denied,* 456 U.S. 980 (1982) (child witnessed stabbing murder of his mother; court wrote that "it is reasonable to conclude that the boy had been continuously upset since witnessing the stabbing of his mother"); Commonwealth v. Rhoades, 364 Pa. Super. 54, 527 A.2d 148 (1987) (eight-year-old girl witnessed her father fatally shoot her mother 30–45 minutes before child's excited utterance); State v. Barber, 747 P.2d 436, 438–39 (Utah Ct. App. 1987) (eight-year-old caught shoplifting; boy's statements when caught were excited utterances); State v. Shaw, 149 Vt. 275, 542 A.2d 1106, 1109 (1987) (adult victim of sexual assault).

[397] People v. Bashara, 677 P.2d 1376, 1377 (Colo. Ct. App. 1983) (mildly mentally retarded child functioning at level of seven-year-old); *In re* Meeboer, 134 Mich. App. 294, 350 N.W.2d 868, 870 (1984) (mentally retarded child).

Courts agree that questioning need not destroy the spontaneity required by this exception.[398] In *State v. Wallace*,[399] the Ohio Supreme Court wrote:

---

[398] Gross v. Greer, 773 F.2d 116, 120 (7th Cir. 1985) ("Her answers to the officer's questions cannot reasonably be deemed insincere or the product of some premeditated deliberation"); United States v. Iron Shell, 633 F.2d 77, 85 (8th Cir. 1980), *cert. denied,* 450 U.S. 1001 (1981); United States v. Pollard, 34 M.J. 1008 (A.C.M.R. 1992); United States v. Pearson, 33 M.J. 913 (A.F.C.M.R. 1991); *In re* O.E.P., 654 P.2d 312, 318 (Colo. 1982) ("Nor does the fact that some general questioning preceded the hearsay declarations destroy their character as excited utterances"); Alston v. United States, 462 A.2d 1122 (D.C. 1983); People v. Nevitt, 135 Ill. 2d 423, 553 N.E.2d 368, 376 (1990) (mother of three-year-old victim asked him, "What's wrong?"; question did not destroy spontaneity required for excited utterance exception); People v. Gacho, 122 Ill. 2d 221, 522 N.E.2d 1146, 1156, *cert. denied,* 488 U.S. 910 (1988) ("That the statement was made in response to a question about 'who did this' does not necessarily destroy its spontaneity"); People v. Roy, 201 Ill. App. 3d 166, 558 N.E.2d 1208, 1219 (1990), *cert. denied,* 112 S. Ct. 965 (1992) ("The fact B.R. made the statement, 'my daddy puts two fingers up my butt,' in response to Caroly's questioning of what was wrong with B.R. or why his butt hurt does not disqualify these statements as spontaneous declarations. Though one of the circumstances to be taken into account is whether the statement was made voluntarily or in response to a question, it is well established asking the declarant what happened is insufficient to destroy the spontaneity of a response"); People v. Watts, 139 Ill. App. 3d 837, 487 N.E.2d 1077, 1086 (1985) ("The key inquiry in deciding whether the statement [responding to questions] should be admitted is whether the statement would have been made if the questions had not been asked"); People v. Cherry, 88 Ill. App. 3d 1048, 411 N.E.2d 61, 67 (1980) (four-year-old's statement to police officer "was made at the first opportunity and not as the result of protracted questioning. It is well established that asking the declarant 'what happened' is insufficient to destroy the spontaneity of the response"); People v. McNichols, 139 Ill. App. 3d 947, 487 N.E.2d 1252, 1258 (1986) ("The fact that Mrs. McNichols asked the boy, 'What happened?' does not destroy the spontaneity of the response"); Hopper v. State, 489 N.E.2d 1209, 1213 (Ind. Ct. App.), *cert. denied,* 479 U.S. 992 (1986) (child made statement to her mother in response to a general question within a few minutes of incident; therefore, statement did not lack requisite spontaneity); People v. Hackney, 183 Mich. App. 516, 455 N.W.2d 358, 362 (1990) (fact that child received "a limited degree of encouragement" by an adult to disclose did not defeat admissibility as excited utterance); State v. Daniels, 380 N.W.2d 777, 783 (Minn. 1986) ("'In summary, an excited utterance is not necessarily rendered inadmissible by the fact the declaration was made in response to a question . . . . The key to admissibility is whether the utterance was spontaneous and excited'" (quoting *In re* Welfare of Chuesberg, 305 Minn. 543, 233 N.W.2d 887 (1975)); Sanders v. State, 586 So. 2d 792, 795 (Miss. 1991); State v. Plant, 236 Neb. 317, 461 N.W.2d 253, 264 (1990); State v. Coppola, 130 N.H. 148, 536 A.2d 1236, 1240 (1987), *cert. denied,* 493 U.S. 969 (1989) (adult rape victim was cut and very upset; "Under such circumstances the fact that the victim gave her statements in answer to questions is in no way inconsistent with the probable spontaneity of her responses"); People v. Knapp, 139 A.D.2d 931, 527 N.Y.S.2d 914, 915 (1988); Commonwealth v. Penn, 497 Pa. 232, 439 A.2d 1154, 1159, *cert. denied,* 456 U.S. 980 (1982) (fact that boy's statement was made in response to question by police officer did not render it inadmissible as an excited utterance); Commonwealth v. Sanford, 397 Pa. Super. 581, 580 A.2d 784, 789 (1990) ("responses to questions are not, per se, excluded from consideration as excited utterances"); *In re* Deborah M., 544 A.2d 572, 575 (R.I. 1988); State v. Burns, 524 A.2d 564, 567 (R.I. 1987) ("The fact that a statement was made in response to an inquiry does not render the spontaneous-utterance doctrine inapplicable. . . . It is merely a factor to be considered in evaluating the statement's spontaneity"); State v. Shaw, 149 Vt. 275,

§ 7.30 EVALUATION FACTORS 179

[T]he admission of a declaration as an excited utterance is not precluded by questioning which: (1) is neither coercive nor leading, (2) facilitates the declarant's expression of what is already the natural focus of the declarant's thoughts, and (3) does not destroy the domination of the nervous excitement over the declarant's reflective faculties.[400]

Some courts wisely acknowledge that with children it is often necessary to draw the child out with questions.[401] As questioning increases, particularly as questions become leading, the spontaneity required by the excited utterance exception may decrease.[402]

Corroboration. In evaluating statements under the excited utterance exception, courts consider whether the statement is corroborated by other evidence. If so, the trustworthiness of the statement is enhanced.[403] Several decisions note

---

542 A.2d 1106, 1109 (1987) (general questions such as "What happened?" do not destroy spontaneity); State v. McKinney, 50 Wash. App. 56, 747 P.2d 1113, 1117 n.4 (1987) (interprets child hearsay exception; "Statements made in response to questions are spontaneous where the child volunteers the information in response to questions that are neither leading nor suggestive"); State v. Robinson, 44 Wash. App. 611, 722 P.2d 1379, 1383 (1986); State v. Bloomstrom, 12 Wash. App. 416, 529 P.2d 1124, 1126 (1974) (spontaneity is not necessarily destroyed by questions asked by child's mother); State v. Lindner, 142 Wis. 2d 783, 419 N.W.2d 352, 356 (1987) (after viewing film about good touching and bad touching, child became upset; teacher asked whether child had any touching problems; question was general and noninflammatory, and did not destroy spontaneity).

But see People v. Pullins, 145 Mich. App. 414, 378 N.W.2d 502, 505 (1985) ("some of the statements were the result of the mother's questioning and thus lack the requisite spontaneity"); State v. Fader, 358 N.W.2d 42, 45 (Minn. 1984) (fact that statement was made in response to question was among reasons to preclude admission as an excited utterance); State v. Roy, 140 Vt. 219, 436 A.2d 1090, 1092 (1981) (child's statement to police officer was not an excited utterance; among other factors, officer elicited information through questions).

[399] 37 Ohio St. 3d 87, 524 N.E.2d 466 (1988).

[400] 524 N.E.2d at 472.

[401] *See, e.g.,* State v. Komurke, 560 So. 2d 986 (La. Ct. App. 1990).

[402] Lyles v. State, 412 So. 2d 458, 460 (Fla. Dist. Ct. App. 1982) (four-year-old's statement to police officer brought out through interrogation); People v. Burton, 433 Mich. 268, 445 N.W.2d 133, 148 (1989) ("The fact that a statement has been made in response to questions is a factor militating against admission"); People v. Straight, 430 Mich. 418, 424 N.W.2d 257, 260 (1988) (statement made after repeated questioning by parents); Sanders v. State, 586 So. 2d 792, 795 (Miss. 1991) ("Certainly police questioning, especially questions that tend to suggest the answers, could raise serious concerns. However, under the excited utterance exception the fact that questions are asked, while relevant to spontaneity, does not *ipso facto* demonstrate a lack of spontaneity in every case"); State v. Griffith, 45 Wash. App. 728, 727 P.2d 247, 253 (1986) (statements made by a child after two hours of leading questioning by parent were not excited utterances).

[403] United Sates v. Renville, 779 F.2d 430, 440 (8th Cir. 1985) ("In assessing the degree of trustworthiness of extra-judicial statements, we must inquire into both the reliability of and necessity for the statement . . . . As with the other enumerated exceptions to the hearsay rule, the reliability of the declaration is assessed in light of the circumstances at the time of

that young children do not fabricate descriptions of explicit sexual acts unless they have been exposed to sexual activity.[404] In evaluating a child's statement as an excited utterance, a court may support other indicia of excitement with the observation that the reliability of the statement is enhanced because it is unlikely the child made it up.[405]

Totality of circumstances. In the final analysis, excited utterances are analyzed on a case-by-case basis. Courts consider the totality of the circumstances to determine whether the statement is uttered under the stress of excitement caused by a startling event.[406]

Trial court discretion. The trial judge has discretion to consider a wide array of factors relating to the spontaneity of a statement, and to determine whether the requirements of the excited utterance exception are satisfied.[407]

---

the declaration and the credibility of the declarant"); United States v. Love, 592 F.2d 1022, 1027 (8th Cir. 1979) ("evidence inadmissible given lack of surrounding circumstances indicative of strong propensity for truthfulness").

[404] Lancaster v. People, 200 Colo. 448, 615 P.2d 720, 723 (1980); *In re* Meeboer, 134 Mich. App. 294, 350 N.W.2d 868 (1984); Martin v. Commonwealth, 4 Va. App. 438, 358 S.E.2d 415 (1987) (two-year-old victim of anal intercourse, which caused physical injury; "particularly in the case of statements made by young children, the element of trustworthiness underscoring the spontaneous and excited utterances exception finds its source in the child's lack of capacity to fabricate rather than the lack of time to fabricate"). *See also In re* Nicole V., 71 N.Y.2d 112, 518 N.E.2d 914, 918, 524 N.Y.S.2d 19 (1987).

[405] *In re* O.E.P., 654 P.2d 312, 318 (Colo. 1982); Lancaster v. People, 200 Colo. 448, 615 P.2d 720, 723 (1980); *In re* Meeboer, 134 Mich. App. 294, 350 N.W.2d 868, 871 (1984); State v. Wagner, 30 Ohio App. 3d 261, 508 N.E.2d 164, 167 (1986) ("As a three-year-old, truly in the age of innocence, he lacked the motive or reflective capacities to prevaricate the circumstances of the attack"); State v. Sorenson, 143 Wis. 2d 226, 421 N.W.2d 77 (1988).

[406] *In re* O.E.P., 654 P.2d 312, 319 (Colo. 1982); People v. Sandoval, 709 P.2d 90, 92 (Colo. Ct. App. 1985); People v. Bashara, 677 P.2d 1376, 1378 (Colo. Ct. App. 1983); Alston v. United States, 462 A.2d 1122, 1128 (D.C. 1983); People v. Nevitt, 135 Ill. 2d 423, 553 N.E.2d 368 (1990) (useful analysis); *In re* Marriage of L.R., 202 Ill. App. 3d 69, 559 N.E.2d 779, 787 (1990); People v. Cherry, 88 Ill. App. 3d 1048, 411 N.E.2d 61, 66 (1980); State v. Mateer, 383 N.W.2d 533, 535 (Iowa 1986); Commonwealth v. Fuller, 22 Mass. App. 152, 491 N.E.2d 1083, 1086 (1986), *aff'd*, 399 Mass. 678, 506 N.E.2d 852 (1987); State v. Posten, 302 N.W.2d 638, 641 (Minn. 1981); State v. Van Orman, 642 S.W.2d 636, 639 (Mo. 1982); State v. Slider, 38 Wash. App. 689, 688 P.2d 538, 541 (1984).

[407] United States v. Renville, 779 F.2d 430, 440 (8th Cir. 1985) (11-year-old victim of sexual abuse; case concerns residual exception and medical diagnosis and treatment exception; "the district court has wide latitude in determining the trustworthiness of an extrajudicial statement"); Commonwealth v. Fuller, 22 Mass. App. Ct. 152, 491 N.E.2d 1083, 1086 (1986), *aff'd*, 399 Mass. 678, 506 N.E.2d 852 (1987) ("In determining whether a spontaneous exclamation meets the test of admissibility, a trial judge is given 'broad discretion,' which should not be 'revised' except in 'clear cases'"); People v. Hackney, 183 Mich. App. 516, 455 N.W.2d 358, 362 (1990).

§ 7.31 Fresh Complaint of Rape or Sexual Abuse

It has long been the law in rape cases that when the adult victim testifies, it is proper to receive evidence that she made complaint shortly following the attack.[408] The complaint of rape doctrine, or, as it is commonly called, the *fresh complaint doctrine,* is not limited to rape cases, however, and numerous decisions approve fresh complaint evidence in other sex offense prosecutions.[409] Moreover, fresh complaint evidence is admissible when consent is not an issue,[410] and, with the exception of Virginia,[411] the fresh complaint doctrine

---

[408] *See* Graham, *The Cry of Rape: The Prompt Complaint Doctrine and the Federal Rules of Evidence,* 19 Willamette L. Rev. 489 (1983); McCormick § 297, at 859 ("In rape cases traditionally, and increasingly in cases of sex offenses generally, evidence has been held admissible that the victim made complaint"); 4 Wigmore § 1134, at 298; 5 Wigmore § 1760, at 240–42.

In Connecticut, fresh complaint evidence is admitted under a theory known as *constancy of accusation. See* State v. Parris, 219 Conn. 283, 592 A.2d 943 (1991). *See also* State v. Saraceno, 15 Conn. App. 222, 545 A.2d 1116, 1129 n.6 (1988), where the court wrote:

> In essence, the constancy of accusation doctrine allows a complainant in a sexual offense case to testify that he or she informed others of the attack. These other individuals are then allowed to testify concerning the complaint made by the victim and are permitted to relate the details of the attack as the victim narrated. . . . This doctrine has been alternatively defined as an exception to the hearsay rule, and the testimony is therefore admissible as substantive evidence of the defendant's guilt, or as evidence simply corroborative of the victim's testimony and therefore relevant only to the credibility of the victim.

See also State v. Dabkowski, 199 Conn. 193, 506 A.2d 118 (1986); C. Tait, Tait and LaPlante's Handbook of Connecticut Evidence § 11.22, at 408 (2d ed. 1988).

[409] Commonwealth v. Brenner, 18 Mass. App. Ct. 930, 465 N.E.2d 1229, 1231 (1984) ("'Fresh complaint' testimony has not been confined to cases of forcible rape, where its rationale is most evidence [sic], . . . but has been received in other cases of sexual assaults, . . . including those where consent is immaterial"); State v. Ramsey, 573 S.W.2d 720 (Mo. Ct. App. 1978) (sodomy); State v. Daniels, 222 Neb. 850, 388 N.W.2d 446 (1986) (child sexual abuse); McCormick § 297, at 859; 4 Wigmore § 1135, at 303.

The Virginia courts appear to limit fresh complaint evidence strictly to rape and attempted rape. *See* Garland v. Commonwealth, 8 Va. App. 189, 379 S.E.2d 146 (1989).

[410] Hollenquest v. State, 394 So. 2d 385 (Ala. Crim. App. 1980), *cert. denied,* 394 So. 2d 389 (1981) (child sex abuse); Commonwealth v. Kirouac, 405 Mass. 557, 542 N.E.2d 270, 274 (1989); Commonwealth v. Brenner, 18 Mass. App. Ct. 930, 465 N.E.2d 1229, 1231 (1984); People v. Taylor, 66 Mich. App. 456, 239 N.W.2d 627 (1976) (statutory rape); State v. Crissman, 31 Ohio App. 2d 170, 287 N.E.2d 642 (1971) (child sex abuse); State v. Hackett, 49 Or. App. 857, 621 P.2d 609 (1980) (fresh complaint doctrine applies where consent not an issue); State v. Murley, 35 Wash. 2d 233, 212 P.2d 801 (1949) (child sex abuse).

But see People v. Hernandez, 88 Ill. App. 3d 698, 412 N.E.2d 572 (1980) (evidence of fresh complaint should not be admissible in child sex abuse case since consent is not an issue).

[411] *See* Leybourne v. Commonwealth, 222 Va. 374, 282 S.E.2d 12 (1981); Kauffmann v. Commonwealth, 8 Va. App. 400, 382 S.E.2d 279, 283 (1989); Garland v. Commonwealth, 8 Va. App. 189, 379 S.E.2d 146 (1989).

applies in sex offense litigation involving children.[412] The fresh complaint doctrine applies to both genders.[413] The doctrine is not articulated in the Federal Rules of Evidence or in most state evidence codes,[414] although several states have statutes codifying the doctrine.[415]

The historical justification supporting admission of the victim's fresh complaint of rape is traced by Wigmore:

> In England, the evidential use of those outcries and explanations came down to us in the 1700s as a traditional relic of the old law of hue and cry. Not only in such cases, but in all charges of violence, the accuser must show, to sustain

---

[412] *In re* Cheryl H., 153 Cal. App. 3d 1098, 200 Cal. Rptr. 789 (1984) (three-year-old victim); State v. True, 438 A.2d 460 (Me. 1981) (teenage victims); Commonwealth v. Kirouac, 405 Mass. 557, 542 N.E.2d 270, 274–75 (1989); Commonwealth v. Lewandowski, 22 Mass. App. 148, 491 N.E.2d 670 (1986) (two-year-old victim); Commonwealth v. Coull, 20 Mass. App. Ct. 955, 480 N.E.2d 323 (1985) (preadolescent victim); Commonwealth v. Brenner, 18 Mass. App. Ct. 930, 465 N.E.2d 1229 (1984) (seven-year-old victim); Commonwealth v. Askins, 18 Mass. App. Ct. 927, 465 N.E.2d 1224 (1984) (seven-year-old-victim); State v. Daniels, 222 Neb. 850, 388 N.W.2d 446 (1986) (nine- and twelve-year-old victims); State v. J.S., 222 N.J. Super. 247, 536 A.2d 769, 771 (1988) ("the rule has been held applicable in child abuse situations"); Commonwealth v. Rodriguez, 343 Pa. Super. 486, 495 A.2d 569 (1985) (14-year-old victim); State v. Sanders, 691 S.W.2d 566 (Tenn. Crim. App. 1984) (five-year-old victim); Heckathorne v. State, 697 S.W.2d 8 (Tex. Ct. App. 1985) (less than five-year-old victim); State v. Ryan, 103 Wash. 2d 165, 691 P.2d 197 (1984) (five-year-old victims); State v. Ferguson, 100 Wash. 2d 131, 667 P.2d 68 (1983) (10-year-old victim).

[413] *See* State v. Cherry, 154 N.J. Super. 157, 381 A.2d 49, 52 (1977), where the court wrote:

> The main thrust of defendant's argument is that the fresh complaint doctrine should be utilized to permit only testimony of complaints of sexual assaults made by female victims. We disagree. While the doctrine has been applied traditionally to complaints by female victims of such assaults, there is no sound reason why it should not be applied to permit testimony about male victims as well. As pointed out above, the doctrine is predicated upon the sense of outrage engendered by the personal indignity forced upon the victim by virtue of the offense. The indignity is the same whether the victim is a male or a female.

[414] It is clear that the doctrine survived adoption of the Federal Rules of Evidence.

[415] *See, e.g.*, Ill. Rev. Stat. ch. 38, ¶ 115-10 (Smith-Hurd 1990); La. Code Evid. 801(D)(1)(d) (when declarant testifies and is subject to cross-examination, statute defines as nonhearsay a statement which is "[c]onsistent with the declarant's testimony and is one of initial complaint of sexually assaultive behavior"); Or. Evid. Code Rule 803(18a) ("The following are not excluded by ORS 40.455, even though the declarant is available as a witness: A complaint of sexual misconduct made by the prosecuting witness after the commission of the alleged offense. Such evidence must be confined to the fact that the complaint was made").

See People v. Branch, 158 Ill. App. 3d 338, 511 N.E.2d 872 (1987) (interpreting statutory fresh complaint provision); State v. Campbell, 299 Or. 633, 705 P.2d 694 (1985); State *ex rel.* Juvenile Dep't v. Karabetsis, 77 Or. App. 583, 713 P.2d 1075 (1986) (holding that fresh complaint evidence is limited by Rule 803 (18a), and that such evidence may not be admitted under the residual exception, Rule 803(24); also holding that a fresh complaint is sufficient evidence to corroborate defendant's confession).

§ 7.31 FRESH COMPLAINTS

his charge, that he made hue and cry, alarming the neighborhood freshly after the occurrence.[416]

The rape victim was required to raise the hue and cry or she could not complain of the offense.[417] Although the original justification for fresh complaint evidence has receded in history, courts continue to receive such evidence on a regular basis.

The theory of fresh complaint evidence is that the victim will naturally speak out shortly after the attack.[418] Absence of prompt complaint "casts doubt on the existence of the rape itself."[419] That is, if the rape occurred, the victim

---

[416] 6 Wigmore § 1760, at 240. *See* H. de Bracton, De Legibus Angliae, f. 147 (ca. 1250), where Bracton wrote:

> When therefore a virgin has been so deflowered and overpowered, against the peace of the lord the king, forthwith and while the act is fresh she ought to repair with hue and cry to the neighboring vills and there display to honest men the injury done to her, the blood and her dress stained with blood, and the tearing of her dress; and so she ought to go to her provost of the hundred and to the sergeant of the lord the king and to the coroners and to the viscount and make her appeal at the first county court.

In today's world, Bracton's requirements seem remarkably insensitive to the emotions of the victim. It seems likely a rape victim may desire to tell as few people as possible, rather than raise the hue and cry throughout the community. *See* United States v. Lips, 22 M.J. 679, 683 (A.F.C.M.R. 1986) (psychological testimony that "between approximately 70–90% [of rapes] go unreported or are delayed in being reported because the victim is ashamed or fearful that no one will believe her").

[417] State v. Murley, 35 Wash. 2d 233, 236–37, 212 P.2d 801, 804 (1949); Graham, *The Cry of Rape: The Prompt Complaint Doctrine and the Federal Rules of Evidence,* 19 Willamette L. Rev. 489, 491 (1983).

[418] The traditional rational is described in an 1877 Virginia case, Haynes v. Commonwealth, 69 Va. (28 Gratt.) 942, 947 (1877), where the Virginia Supreme Court wrote:

> For peculiar reasons, the complaint of the victim of this diabolical outrage and crime . . . must at once make complaint, or she will be suspected of consent. The instincts of human nature, revolting at this unnatural and heinous crime, compels the victim to cry out and denounce its foul perpetrator.

See also Commonwealth v. Snoke, 525 Pa. 295, 580 A.2d 295, 297 (1990) ("The theory is based on the principle that a victim of a violent assault would be expected to complain of the assault at the first safe opportunity"); Graham, *The Cry of Rape: The Prompt Complaint Doctrine and the Federal Rules of Evidence,* 19 Willamette L. Rev. 489 (1983).

Some courts appear to hold that fresh complaint evidence is admissible only if the victim disclosed sexual abuse to a person to whom the child would normally turn to for protection or advice. *See* State v. J.S., 222 N.J. Super. 247, 536 A.2d 769, 774 (1988). This limitation cannot be defended on logical grounds, and should not be imposed.

[419] Commonwealth v. Snoke, 525 Pa. 295, 580 A.2d 295 (1990); Commonwealth v. Powers, 395 Pa. Super. 231, 577 A.2d 194, 197 (1990) (defendant is entitled to present evidence that victim did not make fresh complaint; trial court did not err in refusing to instruct jury that absence of prompt complaint must be considered in determining victim's credibility); Commonwealth v. Rodriguez, 343 Pa. Super. 486, 495 A.2d 569, 572 (1985) (instructive analysis of the justification for complaint of rape evidence).

would have complained. Unexplained silence contradicts the victim's trial testimony alleging rape and amounts to a form of self-contradiction. The fresh complaint is admitted to show that the victim was not silent, thus rebutting the self-contradiction that inheres in silence, and corroborating the victim's testimony. Wigmore explains the justification for fresh complaint evidence:

> [T]he fact of a failure to speak when it would have been natural to do so is in effect an inconsistent statement or self-contradiction. . . .
>
> Now, when a woman charges a man with a rape, and testifies to the details, and the accused denies the act itself, its very commission thus coming into issue, the circumstance that at the time of the alleged rape the woman said nothing about it to anybody constitutes in effect a self-contradiction of the above sort. It was entirely natural, after becoming the victim of an assault against her will, that she should have spoken out. That she did not, that she went about as if nothing had happened, was in effect an assertion that nothing violent had been done.
>
> Thus, the failure of the woman, at the time of an alleged rape, to make any complaint could be offered in evidence (as all concede) as a virtual self-contradiction discrediting her present testimony.
>
> So, where nothing appears on the trial as to the making of such a complaint, the jury might naturally assume that none was made, and counsel for the accused might be entitled to argue upon that assumption. As a peculiarity, therefore, of this kind of evidence, it is only just that the prosecution should be allowed to forestall this natural assumption by showing that the woman was not silent, i.e., that a complaint was in fact made.[420]

The belief that most rape victims speak out shortly following the assault is contradicted by research and experience.[421] Nevertheless, the rationale for the fresh complaint doctrine is viable. Jurors may well entertain the misconception that sexual assault victims disclose immediately. If the victim's fresh complaint is excluded from evidence, the jury may erroneously conclude that no complaint was made, thus undermining the victim's credibility.[422] Therefore, it is appropriate to admit the victim's fresh complaint to ensure that jurors do not

---

[420] 4 Wigmore § 1135, at 298–99 (original emphasis removed).

[421] Many adult victims of sexual assault do not report the offense. The same is true for children. *See* K. Faller, Understanding Child Sexual Maltreatment 31 (1990) ("When the child does tell, there is typically a delay of weeks to years between the onset of the sexual abuse and the child's disclosure"); Russell, *The Incidence and Prevalence of Intrafamilial and Extrafamilial Sexual Abuse of Female Children,* 7 Child Abuse & Neglect 133, 142 (1983) (2% of intrafamilial and 6% of extrafamilial child sexual abuse was reported to authorities). See **Ch. 4** for discussion of the disclosure process.

[422] Such impeachment of the victim is legitimate. It is not improper for defense counsel to argue that delayed reporting undermines the victim's testimony that an assault occurred. *See* Commonwealth v. Snoke, 525 Pa. 295, 580 A.2d 295 (1990) (court discusses the legitimacy of inferring fabrication from delayed reporting; Pennsylvania has a statute that allows the defendant to introduce evidence of delay. Pa. Stat. Ann. tit. 18, § 3105).

§ 7.31   FRESH COMPLAINTS   185

judge the victim's behavior in the false light of misconceptions about the behavior of sexual assault victims.

Although a fresh complaint is an out-of-court statement, it is not hearsay.[423] The complaint is not admitted for the truth, but as corroboration of the victim's testimony.[424] The defendant is entitled to an instruction informing the jury that it may not consider the complaint for the truth.[425] Some decisions[426] and statutes[427] define fresh complaint evidence as hearsay within an exception.

---

[423] People v. Wilmot, 139 Cal. 103, 72 P. 838 (1903); Smith v. Whittier, 95 Cal. 279, 30 P. 529 (1892); People v. Clark, 193 Cal. App. 3d 178, 238 Cal. Rptr. 230, 231 (1987) ("the evidence is not hearsay"); People v. Stewart, 181 Cal. App. 3d 300, 226 Cal. Rptr. 252 (1986); People v. Meacham, 152 Cal. App. 3d 142, 158, 199 Cal. Rptr. 586 (1984) ("In prosecutions for sex offenses, proof of the fact of recent complaints by a minor victim is admissible as original evidence and is not hearsay"); State v. Daniels, 222 Neb. 850, 388 N.W.2d 446, 451 (1986) (child victim's complaint "was relevant, not for the truth of the matter asserted but to confirm Allison's testimony that she made complaint"); State v. Willis, 735 S.W.2d 818, 820 (Tenn. Crim. App. 1987) ("While this Court has spoken of 'fresh complaint' as a 'special exception to the hearsay rule,' it is actually just corroboration of the victim's testimony, not original evidence of the crime charged, unless it qualifies as an 'excited utterance,' in which case it may be received as substantive evidence"); Holland v. State, 802 S.W.2d 696, 699 n. 4 (Tex. Crim. App. 1991) ("properly understood, 'outcry' or 'recent complaint' evidence is not considered hearsay"); Heckathorne v. State, 697 S.W.2d 8, 12 (Tex. Ct. App. 1985); 6 Wigmore § 1761, at 242 ("In the United States, the general consensus has accepted the original and orthodox result, and does not receive the complaints as testimony under a hearsay exception").

[424] Commonwealth v. Gardner, 30 Mass. App. Ct. 515, 570 N.E.2d 1033, 1038 (1991); People v. Zurak, 168 A.D.2d 196, 571 N.Y.S.2d 577 (1991), *cert. denied,* 112 S. Ct. 2276 (1992).

[425] People v. Clark, 193 Cal. App. 3d 178, 238 Cal. Rptr. 230 (1987) (defendant waived right to limiting instruction); People v. Meacham, 152 Cal. App. 3d 142, 199 Cal. Rptr. 586 (1984); Commonwealth v. Amirault, 404 Mass. 221, 535 N.E.2d 193, 199 (1989); Commonwealth v. Bailey, 370 Mass. 388, 348 N.E.2d 746, 751 (1976) ("Our rule does not involve an unfair loading of the case against the defendant. He is entitled to have it impressed on the jury that the testimony may be used for corroborative purposes only; it cannot be used as hearsay to fill gaps in the prosecution's case") (footnote omitted); State v. Daniels, 222 Neb. 850, 388 N.W.2d 446, 451 (1986) ("we believe that the trial court should have given a limiting instruction as to the 'complaint of rape' statement. . . . However, the trial court's failure to give such an instruction was not prejudicial error under the circumstances"); State v. Bethune, 232 N.J. Super. 532, 557 A.2d 1025, 1029 (1989), *aff'd,* 121 N.J. 137, 578 A.2d 364 (1990); State v. J.S., 222 N.J. Super. 247, 536 A.2d 769, 773–74 (1988).

[426] Commonwealth v. Bailey, 370 Mass. 388, 348 N.E.2d 746, 749, 750 n.7 (1976) ("In cases of rape, however, testimony reporting statements made by the victim shortly after the attack are universally admitted to corroborate the victim's testimony. . . . Fresh complaint in cases of sexual crime evolved into a hearsay exception, and was finally rationalized on a basis of corroboration"); State v. Sanders, 691 S.W.2d 566, 568 (Tenn. Crim. App. 1984) (statements by five-year-old victim "were admissible under the fresh complaint exception to the hearsay rule"); State v. DeBolt, 61 Wash. App. 58, 808 P.2d 794, 796 (1991); 6 Wigmore § 1760, at 240 and § 1761, at 242.

[427] *See* Or. Evid. Code 803(18a); State v. Campbell, 299 Or. 633, 705 P.2d 694 (1985) (holding that unexcited utterances of victims must be admitted under Rule 803(18a) rather than the

Fresh complaint evidence is admissible during the state's case-in-chief.[428] As a general rule, the victim must testify before a fresh complaint is admissible.[429] Testimony from the victim is required because the purpose of fresh complaint evidence is to corroborate the victim's trial testimony. However, the fact that the victim does not testify should not lead automatically to exclusion of fresh complaint evidence. In three recurring scenarios fresh complaint evidence may be relevant despite lack of trial testimony from the victim.

First, in some cases where the child does not testify, the child's hearsay statements are admitted at trial. The child's fresh complaint may corroborate the child's hearsay in the same way the complaint would corroborate the child's testimony from the witness stand.[430]

Second, fresh complaint evidence is sometimes relevant when the child does not testify and the child's hearsay statements are not offered. Even though the jury does not hear from the child, the child's fresh complaint may be admissible if the defense concentrates the jury's attention on the fact that the child delayed reporting, and asserts or implies that because there was delay, there was no abuse.[431]

Third, there is authority that when the victim is too young to take the stand, the victim's fresh complaint may be received.[432]

Impeachment of the victim's testimony is not a condition precedent to admission of the victim's fresh complaint.[433] Impeachment is not required because

---

residual exception). *See also* Louisiana Code Evid. 801(D)(1)(d), which defines an initial complaint of sexually assaultive behavior as nonhearsay.

[428] State v. True, 438 A.2d 460, 464 (Me. 1981) ("the bare fact that a complaint has been made is admissible as part of the State's case in chief to forestall the natural assumption that in the absence of a complaint, nothing violent had occurred"); Vera v. State, 709 S.W.2d 681, 685 (Tex. Ct. App. 1986); State v. Alexander, 822 P.2d 1250 (Wash. Ct. App. 1992); State v. Murley, 35 Wash. 2d 233, 212 P.2d 801, 804 (1949); State v. DeBolt, 61 Wash. App. 58, 808 P.2d 794, 796 (1991).

[429] See 4 Wigmore § 1136, at 307, where Wigmore writes that "[s]ince the only object of the evidence is to repel the supposed inconsistency between the woman's present testimony and her former silence, it is obvious that if she has not testified at all, there is no inconsistency to repel, and therefore the evidence is irrelevant." (footnote omitted).

[430] Children's hearsay statements admitted at trial are often made months following the abuse; thus concern about lack of fresh complaint arises with hearsay as well as trial testimony.

[431] The defense often concentrates on delay in reporting. See **Ch. 4** for discussion of reasons for delayed reporting.

[432] People v. Meacham, 152 Cal. App. 3d 142, 199 Cal. Rptr. 586, 597 (1984) ("While it is generally true that evidence that a complaint was made is inadmissible where the prosecutrix does not take the stand, an exception is made where, as in the present case, the child is too young to testify").

[433] State v. Alexander, 822 P.2d 1250 (Wash. Ct. App. 1992). The self-contradiction that exists between trial testimony and silence following the assault exists whether or not the victim is impeached.

§ 7.31 FRESH COMPLAINTS

even without impeachment, the jury may doubt the victim's testimony unless evidence is presented that the victim told someone about the abuse.[434]

Under the traditional view, evidence of fresh complaint is limited to the statement of complaint. Details are not admissible.[435] The justification for limiting fresh complaint evidence to the fact of complaint is that the purpose of the evidence is to establish that the complaint was made so as to "negative the

---

[434] Commonwealth v. Gardner, 30 Mass. App. Ct. 515, 570 N.E.2d 1033, 1038 (1991). *See also* Beck v. State, 544 N.E.2d 204 (Ind. Ct. App. 1989). *Beck* does not deal with fresh complaint evidence. Nevertheless, the court provides the following useful insight into the purpose of fresh complaint evidence:

> The purpose of the fresh complaint rule was to allow the state to meet in advance the negative inference which would be drawn from the absence of evidence that the victim reported the incident to one to whom she would naturally turn for comfort and advice. Thus the credibility of the witness was protected from unfair attack.

Id. at 210.

[435] Hollenquest v. State, 394 So. 2d 385, 387 (Ala. Crim. App. 1980), *cert. denied*, 394 U.S. 389 (1981); Lawson v. State, 377 So. 2d 1115, 1118 (Ala. Crim. App. 1979) ("It is a well established rule in Alabama that testimony concerning the prosecutrix's complaint must be confined to the fact of the complaint. Details of the occurrence such as specifying the identity of the person accused, the injuries claimed to have been sustained, or other minute circumstances of the offense are not admissible"); People v. Baggett, 185 Ill. App. 3d 1007, 541 N.E.2d 1266, 1272 (1989); State v. Naylor, 602 A.2d 187 (Me. 1992); State v. Lafrance, 589 A.2d 43, 45 (Me. 1991); State v. True, 438 A.2d 460, 464 (Me. 1981) ("The *details* of the complaint are not, however, admissible under this rule"); State v. Daniels, 222 Neb. 850, 388 N.W.2d 446, 451 (1986) (although details not admissible, victim could state that "'she submitted to intercourse because of the threat of a knife'"); Vera v. State, 709 S.W.2d 681, 685 (Tex. Ct. App. 1986) ("Outcry is not admissible, however, to 'prove the actual details of the sexual attack or even that the sexual attack actually occurred.' . . . The details of the statement made by the complainant cannot generally be given in evidence; the State is confined to proof of the mere fact that the complaint was made unless the complaint meets the spontaneous utterance exception to the hearsay rule"); State v. Alexander, 64 Wash. App. 147, 822 P.2d 1250 (1992); State v. Ferguson, 100 Wash. 2d 131, 667 P.2d 68, 72 (1983) ("The rule admits only such evidence as will establish that the complaint was timely made. Excluded is evidence of the details of the complaint, including the identity of the offender and the nature of the act"); State v. DeBolt, 61 Wash. App. 58, 808 P.2d 794, 796 (1991) ("Details of the complaint and the identify of the offender are not permitted").

Early California decisions strictly limited fresh complaint evidence to a statement that the victim complained. No details of the offense or the identity of the perpetrator were admissible. *See* People v. Wilmot, 139 Cal. 103, 72 P. 838 (1903); People v. Swist, 136 Cal. 520, 69 P. 223 (1902); People v. Mayes, 66 Cal. 597, 6 P. 691 (1885). In 1961, however, the California Supreme Court expanded the scope of fresh complaint evidence in People v. Burton, 55 Cal. 2d 328, 359 P.2d 433, 11 Cal. Rptr. 65 (1961).

supposed inconsistency of silence by showing that there was not silence."[436] Evidence of details is unnecessary for this limited purpose.[437] Increasingly, however, courts permit such "particulars as are necessary to identify the subject matter,"[438] including the time and place of the complaint,[439] the number of assaults,[440] and "the circumstances under which [the complaint] was made, and the person to whom made, the condition of the victim when making the complaint, the conduct of the prosecutrix at the time she made complaint, and that

---

[436] 4 Wigmore § 1136, at 307.

[437] *Id.*

[438] Elmer v. State, 463 P.2d 14, 19 (Wyo. 1969), *cert. denied,* 400 U.S. 845 (1970). *See also* Kosbruk v. State, 820 P.2d 1082, 1084 (Alaska Ct. App. 1991); People v. Burton, 55 Cal. 2d 328, 359 P.2d 433, 11 Cal. Rptr. 65 (1961); People v. Hudson, 198 Ill. App. 3d 915, 556 N.E.2d 640 (1990) (interpreting Illinois statutory fresh complaint doctrine, court ruled that statute "does not permit testimony which contains a detailed account of the complaint or the identify of the alleged assailant"; court noted, however, that "some detail is necessary to corroborate the fact that the complaint was made and identify the incident as the one before the court"); People v. Baggett, 185 Ill. App. 3d 1007, 541 N.E.2d 1266, 1272 (1989); People v. Robertson, 168 Ill. App. 3d 132, 522 N.E.2d 239, 241 (1988) ("although a corroborative complaint witness cannot testify to all details, the witness must necessarily include some detail to effectively corroborate the fact that the complaint was made and identify the incident as the one before the court"); People v. Branch, 158 Ill. App. 3d 338, 511 N.E.2d 872, 874 (1987) ("Defendant is correct in his assertion that corroborative complaint witnesses cannot testify to all details related to them. . . . What defendant fails to realize, however, is that corroborative complaint testimony must necessarily include some detail to effectively corroborate the fact that a complaint was made and identify the incident as the one before the court"); State v. J.S., 222 N.J. Super. 247, 536 A.2d 769 (1988) (taking the traditional, narrow approach to fresh complaint evidence, court held that admission of too much detail required reversal); State v. Cherry, 154 N.J. Super. 157, 381 A.2d 49, 52 (1977) ("enough of the details must be given to show the nature of the complaint even though it may involve to some extent the particulars").

[439] State v. Grady, 183 N.W.2d 707, 716 (Iowa 1971) (fresh complaint may include "so much of the complaint as identifies 'the time and place with that of the one charged' or in other words, so much as will identify the occurrence complained of with the crime charged"); State v. Bethune, 232 N.J. Super. 532, 557 A.2d 1025, 1028–29 (1989), *aff'd,* 121 N.J. 137, 578 A.2d 364 (1990); State v. Barrett, 299 S.C. 485, 386 S.E.2d 242, 243 (1989); 6 Wigmore § 1136, at 307.

[440] State v. Bethune, 232 N.J. Super. 532, 557 A.2d 1025, 1028–29 (1989), *aff'd,* 121 N.J. 137, 578 A.2d 364 (1990) (child made complaint to social worker, telling worker the abuse happened "a lot of times"; held that social worker could repeat child's fresh complaint that abuse happened "a lot of times" to confirm the child's assertion of multiple attacks; "The recounting of the child's complaint was not required to be limited to a single instance when she complained of multiple attacks").

§ 7.31 FRESH COMPLAINTS 189

she exhibited, if such was the fact, marks of violence and other like indications, as confirmatory of her testimony."[441] Moreover, although most decisions state that the complaint may not identify the perpetrator,[442] some decisions approve fresh complaints identifying the perpetrator.[443] The trend is in the direction of admitting greater detail about the alleged offense,[444] a result which McCormick

---

[441] State v. Bethune, 232 N.J. Super. 532, 557 A.2d 1025 (1989), *aff'd,* 578 A.2d 364 (N.J. 1990) (quoting State v. Saccone, 7 N.J. Super. 263, 266, 72 A.2d 923 (1950)). *See also* Commonwealth v. LeFave, 407 Mass. 927, 556 N.E.2d 83, 92 (1990) (child testified at trial; child's fresh complaint to her mother was more detailed than her trial testimony; nevertheless, the fresh complaint, including details, was properly admitted).

[442] State v. Grady, 183 N.W.2d 707, 718 (Iowa 1971) ("The provision in the rule announced supra permitting 'so much of the complaint as identifies the time and place with the one charged,' is not to be extended to permit testimony on direct examination of the fact the female in making complaint identified the accused"); State v. Hackett, 49 Or. App. 857, 621 P.2d 609 (1980) (error to admit testimony identifying perpetrator); State v. Ferguson, 100 Wash. 2d 131, 667 P.2d 68, 72 (1983); State v. DeBolt, 61 Wash. App. 58, 808 P.2d 794, 796 (1991) (statement of complaint including identification of perpetrator was admitted in error, but error harmless because defendant did not object, identity was not in issue, and the statement of identity was not responsive to the question).

[443] People v. Burton, 55 Cal. 2d 328, 359 P.2d 433, 11 Cal. Rptr. 65 (1961); People v. Meacham, 152 Cal. App. 3d 142, 199 Cal. Rptr. 586, 597 (1984) (victim's statement describing offense and identity of offender, without details, is admissible); People v. Panky, 82 Cal. App. 3d 772, 147 Cal. Rptr. 341 (1978); People v. Alfaro, 61 Cal. App. 3d 414, 132 Cal. Rptr. 356, 364 (1976) ("In a rape prosecution, it is permissible to introduce testimony of a witness as to statements made by the victim shortly after the rape which relate to the nature of the offense and the identity of the person or persons who raped the victim"); State v. Twyford, 85 S.D. 522, 186 N.W.2d 545, 548 (1971) (details not admissible, but "the fact of complaint and the name of complainant and the name of the alleged perpetrator" can be admitted).

[444] *See, e.g.,* Commonwealth v. Bailey, 370 Mass. 388, 348 N.E.2d 746, 749–50 (1976), where the court wrote:

It is said to be the more common view that the prosecution is allowed to introduce only the fact of the complaint . . . , but in the Commonwealth and a few other jurisdictions the rule is settled that "the whole of the statement . . . , including the details, is admissible." . . . [T]he so called "majority" rule permits only the following: "On the direct examination the practice has been merely to ask whether she made complaint that such an outrage had been perpetrated upon her, and to receive in answer only a simple yes or no." . . . It may be doubted whether so perfunctory a reference goes far enough to achieve the intrinsic purpose of the doctrine.

See also People v. Burton, 55 Cal. 2d 328, 359 P.2d 433, 11 Cal. Rptr. 65 (1961), where the California Supreme Court expanded the scope of fresh complaint evidence, writing:

We agree with the reasoning of those cases which point out that testimony to the bare fact that the victim "made a complaint" as to an unspecified subject matter on its face would be meaningless; if the complaint did not relate the alleged offense and

characterizes as "wholly justifiable."[445] In jurisdictions where details of the complaint are admissible, the court has discretion to limit details that could unfairly prejudice the defendant.[446]

A fresh complaint must refer to the charged offense.[447] The decision in *People v. Stewart*[448] raises an interesting issue concerning this requirement. The defendant was charged with oral copulation and attempted incest. The victim was the defendant's 17-year-old daughter. The trial court allowed the prosecutor to introduce evidence of the defendant's long history of molesting the victim leading up to the charged offenses. In addition to this uncharged misconduct evidence, the prosecutor sought to introduce testimony from the victim's mother that the victim complained of the charged assaults. The defendant objected to the fresh complaint evidence, arguing that "the trial court erred in admitting evidence of the prosecutrix's 'fresh complaint' in the absence of a sufficient foundation that the complaint referred to the charged crimes rather than to one

---

(assuming that the victim identified the perpetrator) to the defendant, it would be immaterial to the proof of the People's case; but from the mere receipt of such evidence offered by the prosecution it seems inevitable that the jury would infer that the complaint was that the defendant committed the offense. *We therefore accept the view that although details cannot be recounted, it can be shown by the People "that the complaint related to the matter being inquired into, and not a complaint wholly foreign to the subject; . . . that is, the alleged victim's statement of the nature of the offense and the identity of the asserted offender, without details, is proper."*

See also Inmon v. State, 585 So. 2d 261 (Ala. Crim. App. 1991); Commonwealth v. Gardner, 30 Mass. App. Ct. 515, 570 N.E.2d 1033, 1038 (1991) ("In Massachusetts, the fact that the victim made a complaint is admissible, as well as her entire statement, including the details"); Commonwealth v. Snow, 30 Mass. App. Ct. 443, 569 N.E.2d 838, 840 (1991) ("Fresh complaint witnesses may testify to 'details' where the testimony contains 'no new information' and is 'merely a short summary of the testimony the victim herself gave about the criminal events.' . . . That is, the person to whom the victim complained may testify as to the entire complaint, not merely to the fact that the complaint was made"); Commonwealth v. Adams, 23 Mass. App. Ct. 534, 503 N.E.2d 1315 (1987) (details of the complaint, including a description of ejaculation, admissible); Commonwealth v. Askins, 18 Mass. App. Ct. 927, 465 N.E.2d 1224, 1225–26 (1984) (fresh complaint may contain more detail than trial testimony of victim); State v. Sanders, 691 S.W.2d 566, 568 (Tenn. Crim. App. 1984) ("We note that Tennessee goes farther than most states by allowing proof of the details stated by the victim").

[445] McCormick § 297, at 859 (footnote omitted).

[446] Commonwealth v. Bailey, 370 Mass. 388, 348 N.E.2d 746, 752 (1976) ("We should add that when it appears that admission of details would operate unjustly—as by inciting a jury through a needless rehearsal of the particulars of a gruesome crime—the judge may well limit the testimony in his discretion").

[447] The burden is on the proponent of the fresh complaint to establish the connection between the complaint and the charged offense.

[448] 181 Cal. App. 3d 300, 226 Cal. Rptr. 252 (1986).

§ 7.31 FRESH COMPLAINTS 191

of the uncharged molestations."[449] Indeed, there was some evidence that the victim's complaint referred to an uncharged act of molestation, rather than the charged offense. Nevertheless, the court of appeal upheld the trial judge's decision to admit the fresh complaint. The appellate court wrote:

> The complaint does not have to be detailed. It must, however, relate to the charged crime and to the defendant as the perpetrator.
>
> Defendant maintains that the complaint did not relate to the charged crimes since those crimes allegedly occurred after 11 p.m. and involved oral copulation and attempted incest, while the acts complained of occurred "earlier in the afternoon" and involved "messing . . . on the top and bottom" of Ms. S which her mother understood as meaning "fondling of [her] breasts and vagina."
>
> In cases involving sex crimes against minors, the victim's complaint regarding those crimes as to their nature and time will often be inexact due to the victim's distress, embarrassment or lack of sophistication and knowledge concerning the sexual acts which occurred. As a result, discrepancies may arise between the victim's fresh complaint and testimony at trial. Defendant argues that these discrepancies should preclude the admissibility of the complaint. We disagree. As long as the complaint can be reasonably interpreted as relating to the charged acts any such discrepancies affect the weight and not the admissibility of that complaint.[450]

The *Stewart* court concluded that the trial judge did not err in ruling that the victim's complaint referred to the charged offense. *Stewart* illustrates the fact that when uncharged misconduct evidence and fresh complaint evidence are offered in the same prosecution, it is important to ensure that the fresh complaint relates to the charged offense.

The *Stewart* court wisely acknowledged that discrepancies between a child's fresh complaint and the child's trial testimony go to the weight accorded the complaint, not its admissibility.[451] The court's insight is particularly important with young children, many of whom display inconsistencies between trial testimony and earlier descriptions of abuse. Such inconsistencies are developmentally normal in children, especially regarding peripheral details of events.[452] Thus, discrepancies between a child's fresh complaint and later trial testimony should not cause exclusion of the complaint.

---

[449] *Id.* at 307–08, 226 Cal. Rptr. at 257.

[450] *Id.* at 308, 226 Cal. Rptr. at 257 (citations omitted).

[451] Commonwealth v. LeFave, 407 Mass. 927, 556 N.E.2d 83, 92 (1990) (child testified at trial; child's fresh complaint to mother more detailed than trial testimony, but fresh complaint, including details, was properly admitted; "the trial judge did not err by admitting the 'whole statement including the details' for corroborative purposes only").

[452] See **Ch. 4**.

Most courts hold that a fresh complaint may be repeated at trial by all those who heard it, subject, of course, to the court's authority to limit cumulative evidence.[453] In other words, the testimony is generally not limited to the first witness to hear the complaint. In *Commonwealth v. Crowe*,[454] for example, the trial court permitted fresh complaint testimony from three individuals who heard the complaint at different times on the morning of the rape.

Although fresh complaint evidence is often admitted through the testimony of individuals who overheard the complaint,[455] it is proper to allow the victim to repeat the fresh complaint as a part of the victim's direct testimony.[456]

As the name implies, the fresh complaint doctrine requires a complaint to be made promptly.[457] Modern decisions generally state that a complaint satisfies

---

[453] People v. Belasco, 125 Cal. App. 3d 974, 178 Cal. Rptr. 461 (1981), *cert. denied,* 456 U.S. 979 (1982) (three witnesses were permitted to repeat victim's fresh complaint); People v. Branch, 158 Ill. App. 3d 338, 511 N.E.2d 872, 873 (1987) (more than one adult who overhears child's complaint may testify).

See State v. J.S., 222 N.J. Super. 247, 536 A.2d 769 (1988). The court wrote that a fresh complaint is admissible if "the victim complained of the act within a reasonable time to one to whom she would ordinarily turn for sympathy, protection or advice." 536 A.2d at 771. The court appears to limit the universe of persons to whom a victim may make complaint. This requirement is puzzling. The court is probably correct that most victims disclose to persons they trust, but certainly this is not always the case. It is difficult to discern a logical justification for limiting fresh complaints to those made to persons to whom the victim would ordinarily turn for advice. In child sexual abuse cases, children seek sympathy, protection, or advice from a wide array of individuals, including parents, friends, police officers, medical and mental health professionals, social workers, and teachers.

[454] 21 Mass. App. Ct. 456, 488 N.E.2d 780, 795, *cert. denied,* 479 U.S. 838 (1986).

[455] People v. Wilmot, 139 Cal. 103, 105, 72 P. 838 (1903); People v. Clark, 193 Cal. App. 3d 178, 238 Cal. Rptr. 230 (1987); State v. Daniels, 222 Neb. 850, 388 N.W.2d 446, 449 (1986) ("one to whom the complaining witness has complained may testify to the fact and nature of the complaint"); People v. Gonzalez, 131 A.D.2d 873, 517 N.Y.S.2d 530 (1987) (complaint of rape "can be testified to by either the complainant or by any witnesses who heard her make such complaint"); State v. Willis, 735 S.W.2d 818, 820 (Tenn. Crim. App. 1987) ("such statements may be introduced by the testimony of the person to whom the statements were made").

[456] People v. Wilmot, 139 Cal. 103, 105, 72 P. 838 (1903) (the complaint "may be shown by the prosecutrix and those to whom the complaint is made"); People v. Meacham, 152 Cal. App. 3d 142, 199 Cal. Rptr. 586 (1984); People v. Belasco, 125 Cal. App. 3d 974, 178 Cal. Rptr. 461 (1981), *cert. denied,* 456 U.S. 979 (1982); State v. Hamer, 188 Conn. 562, 452 A.2d 313, 314 (1982) ("it is immaterial that [the statements] are offered through the testimony of the declarant rather than the listener"); People v. Gonzalez, 131 A.D.2d 873, 517 N.Y.S.2d 530 (1987).

[457] People v. Baggett, 185 Ill. App. 3d 1007, 541 N.E.2d 1266, 1273 (1989); Sherrick v. State, 157 Neb. 623, 61 N.W.2d 358 (1953) (child victim's statement one day after sexual assault

§ 7.31   FRESH COMPLAINTS

this requirement if it is made within a reasonable time following the assault.[458] Wigmore points out, however, that since the purpose of the evidence "is merely to negative the supposed silence of the woman, it is perceived that the fact of complaint at any time should be received."[459] Lapse of time between the sexual assault and the complaint should affect weight, not admissibility.[460]

---

too remote); Gibbons v. State, 97 Nev. 299, 629 P.2d 1196 (1981) (delay of several hours too long); People v. Gonzalez, 131 A.D.2d 873, 517 N.Y.S.2d 530 (1987) ("The rule with respect to prompt outcry in cases of forcible rape is that the complaint of injury should be made promptly or at least at the first suitable opportunity"); State v. Willis, 735 S.W.2d 818 (Tenn. Crim. App. 1987) (ruling that fresh complaint should have been excluded because of lack of evidence regarding period of delay between abuse and complaint).

The earlier decisions imposed a rather strict promptness requirement. Graham points out, however, that "[t]he requirement of promptness has . . . been slowly eroding. What was once considered too long a delay is often now considered 'prompt.'" Graham, *The Cry of Rape: The Prompt Complaint Doctrine and the Federal Rules of Evidence,* 19 Willamette L. Rev. 489, 504 (1983).

[458] People v. Clark, 193 Cal. App. 3d 178, 238 Cal. Rptr. 230, 231 (1987) ("It has generally been held that to be admissible on this ground, the complaint must have been volunteered within a reasonable time of the sex offense"); Matter of Cheryl H., 153 Cal. App. 3d 1098, 200 Cal. Rptr. 789, 809 (1984) (statements by three-year-old sexual abuse victim one to two months after alleged abuse too remote to be admitted as fresh complaint; "to be admissible on this ground, the complaint must have been volunteered a short time after the sexual assault. . . . That is, it must truly be 'fresh' and it must truly be in the nature of a 'complaint' and not a response to questions"); Commonwealth v. Dockham, 405 Mass. 618, 542 N.E.2d 591 (1989); Commonwealth v. Amirault, 404 Mass. 221, 535 N.E.2d 193, 198-99 (1989); Commonwealth v. Foskette, 30 Mass. App. Ct. 384, 568 N.E.2d 1167, 1171 (1991) ("Freshness is not, or is not entirely, a matter of counting the hours between the event and first declaration"); Commonwealth v. Gardner, 30 Mass. App. Ct. 515, 570 N.E.2d 1033, 1038 (1991); Gibbons v. State, 97 Nev. 299, 629 P.2d 1196 (1981) (complaint made two to three hours after assault too remote); State v. Bethune, 232 N.J. Super. 532, 557 A.2d 1025 (1989), *aff'd,* 121 N.J. 137, 578 A.2d 364 (1990); State v. True, 438 A.2d 460, 464 (Me. 1981) ("For the fact of a complaint to be admissible . . . , the complaint must have been made within a reasonable time after the alleged rape and the prosecutrix must take the stand at trial"); State v. Baca, 56 N.M. 236, 242 P.2d 1002 (1952) (three-month delay reasonable); State v. Baker, 46 Or. App. 79, 610 P.2d 840, 842 (1980) (delay of 10 to 12 hours reasonable; "Here evidence that defendant was an acquaintance of the 17 year old victim, that the victim had been threatened with a gun and warned to tell no one could be considered by the jury as sufficient circumstances to cause her to delay making her complaint"); State v. Fritz, 44 S.D. 517, 184 N.W. 235 (1921) (complaint one week after event made within reasonable time).

[459] 4 Wigmore § 1135, at 303.

[460] Fitzgerald v. United States, 443 A.2d 1295 (D.C. 1982); State v. Moran, 585 So. 2d 576 (La. Ct. App. 1991) (interpreting fresh complaint statute; complaint does not have to be prompt).

Delay in making complaint may be explained and justified.[461] Thus, delay may be explained by the fact that the child was threatened into silence.[462] If a child makes complaint at the first safe opportunity, the complaint should be received.[463] When a parent abuses a young child, the parent may tell the child

---

[461] People v. Clark, 193 Cal. App. 3d 178, 238 Cal. Rptr. 230 (1987) (five-year-old's complaint made seven to eight months after abuse properly admitted; child complained shortly after attending a class on "good" and "bad" touch; prior to the class, the child's youth prevented the child from realizing the need to report); Fitzgerald v. United States, 443 A.2d 1295, 1305 (D.C. 1982) ("Unless the time lapse on reporting the incident is so long as to deprive the report of reliability, the length of time . . . affects the weight of the evidence in the minds of the jury, but does not diminish the testimony's legal sufficiency as corroboration"; in this case "when there is an explanation for the delay in the child's fear of reprisals, the delay should not render the complaint inadmissible"); People v. Damen, 28 Ill. 2d 464, 193 N.E.2d 25, 30 (1963) ("there is no fixed or definite limit of time within which the complaint must be made, . . . but . . . a complaint made without inconsistent or unexplained delay may properly be shown"); People v. Slavin, 66 Ill. App. 3d 525, 383 N.E.2d 1303 (1978) (seven-hour delay explained); State v. Herrin, 562 So. 2d 1, 10 (La. Ct. App. 1990); Commonwealth v. Dockham, 405 Mass. 618, 542 N.E.2d 591 (1989); Commonwealth v. Titus, 32 Mass. App. Ct. 216, 587 N.E.2d 800 (1992); Commonwealth v. Amirault, 404 Mass. 221, 535 N.E.2d 193, 199 (1989) (defendant threatened four-year-old victim, "telling her that he would kill all of her family if she told anyone"; threat justified 18-month delay in reporting abuse; furthermore, court noted that "[i]t may be that a fresh complaint of child sexual abuse is not possible until the child victim recognizes the nature of the assault and is able to relate the incident"); Commonwealth v. Achorn, 25 Mass. App. Ct. 247, 517 N.E.2d 486, 490 (1988); Commonwealth v. Adams, 23 Mass. App. Ct. 534, 503 N.E.2d 1315 (1987) (victim's mother waited four months after victim's complaint to her before mother told police; delay was mother's, not child's; therefore, complaint was admissible); People v. Gage, 62 Mich. 271, 28 N.W. 835 (1886) (10-year-old victim; delay of three months justified due to fear of defendant); State v. Bethune, 232 N.J. Super. 532, 557 A.2d 1025, 1028 (1989), aff'd, 121 N.J. 137, 578 A.2d 364 (1990); State v. Knapp, 45 N.H. 148, 155 (1863); State v. Baker, 46 Or. App. 79, 610 P.2d 840, 842 (1980) (12- to 13-hour delay explained); Commonwealth v. Snoke, 525 Pa. 295, 580 A.2d 295 (1990) ("consideration should be given to factors inherent in cases involving minor victims which may explain the delay without reflecting on the minor witness' credibility"; useful discussion of why children delay reporting abuse); State v. Twyford, 85 S.D. 522, 186 N.W.2d 545, 548 (1971) (fresh complaint made "in the neighborhood of some 67 to 82 days after the alleged incident" was not too late); McCormick § 297, at 859; 4 Wigmore § 1135, at 301 ("the silence may nevertheless be *explained away* as due to fear, shame, or the like, so that it loses its significance as a suspicious inconsistency") (footnote omitted).

[462] People v. Clark, 193 Cal. App. 3d 178, 238 Cal. Rptr. 230 (1987); Commonwealth v. Amirault, 404 Mass. 221, 535 N.E.2d 193, 199 (1989); Commonwealth v. Gardner, 30 Mass. App. Ct. 515, 570 N.E.2d 1033, 1039 (1991).

[463] State v. Komurke, 560 So. 2d 986, 988 (La. Ct. App. 1990) ("A very young child raped by an adult standing in the position of parent, caretaker or friend cannot be expected to immediately come forward with a complete and exact report of the event. The courts have recognized that the child may be unable to speak about the incident until she considers herself safely in the presence of a compassionate adult whom she can trust"); State v. Burt, 546 So. 2d 931 (La. Ct. App. 1989); Commonwealth v. Souther, 31 Mass. App. Ct. 219, 575 N.E.2d 1150 (1991); Commonwealth v. Gardner, 30 Mass. App. Ct. 515, 570 N.E.2d 1033 (1991)

§ 7.31   FRESH COMPLAINTS

the behavior is normal, or their "little secret."[464] The child is likely to accept the parent's explanation, with the result that disclosure is delayed.[465] The adult's misuse of parental authority explains delayed reporting.[466] Whether abuse occurs inside the home or out, some young children do not realize the inappropriateness of sexual behavior, and do not complain until they learn that what happened was wrong.[467] In several cases, children disclosed abuse after viewing a film or demonstration about "good" and "bad" touch.[468] In sex offense cases

---

(court should consider how long the child is away from the abusive setting); People v. Gonzalez, 131 A.D.2d 873, 517 N.Y.S.2d 530 (1987) ("The rule with respect to prompt outcry in cases of forcible rape is that the complaint of injury should be made promptly or at the first suitable opportunity"); Commonwealth v. Snoke, 525 Pa. 295, 580 A.2d 295, 297 (1990) ("The theory is based on the principle that a victim of a violent assault would be expected to complain of the assault at the first safe opportunity").

[464] Commonwealth v. Snoke, 525 Pa. 295, 580 A.2d 295 (1990).

[465] Commonwealth v. Snoke, 525 Pa. 295, 580 A.2d 295, 299 (1990) ("Where no physical force is used to accomplish the reprehensible assault, a child victim would have no reason to promptly complain of the wrong-doing, particularly where the person involved is in a position of confidence. Where such an encounter is of a nature that a minor victim may not appreciate the offensive nature of the conduct, the lack of a complaint would not necessarily justify an inference of a fabrication").

[466] *Id.*

[467] Commonwealth v. Lane, 521 Pa. 390, 555 A.2d 1246 (1989) ("It is also possible that the immaturity of the victim would cause the child not to appreciate the offensiveness of the encounter and the need for its prompt disclosure").

[468] *See* People v. Clark, 193 Cal. App. 3d 178, 238 Cal. Rptr. 230 (1987). In *Clark* the court of appeal ruled that a trial judge did not err in admitting a five-year-old's complaint made seven to eight months after the sex offense. The child complained shortly after she attended a class on "good" and "bad" touch. The court wrote:

It has generally been held that to be admissible on this ground, the complaint must have been volunteered within a reasonable time of the sex offense. . . .

Appellant contends that the testimony regarding [the victim's] complaint should not have been admitted on the ground that the complaint was not "fresh" due to the seven- to eight-month delay between the incident and the complaint.

An unexplained delay of seven months would undoubtedly cause a complaint to fall outside the fresh complaint doctrine. The longest delay permitted by a court thus far has been approximately one month. However, the complaint here was made shortly after [the victim] attended the class on molestation and learned of the importance of reporting such incidents.

Most children do not view a sexual episode as shocking or particularly unusual and may not know that what happened to them is wrong. . . . When discussing a delay of approximately one month between a five-year-old child's complaint and the incident, the court in *People v. Bianchino* (1907) 5 Cal. App. 633, 637, 91 P. 112, noted that "[t]he child was too young to be fully conscious of anything wrong in the act, or to experience any sense of shame, and, considering the relations of defendant to the family and his familiarity with the child, she may not have comprehended the nature of the act or thought of complaining earlier than she did. When the disease [vaginitis]

involving children, courts have not insisted on great promptness in making the complaint.[469]

The lapse of time that satisfies the fresh complaint doctrine is often too long for the excited utterance exception. Thus, a statement that fails as an excited utterance may be admissible as a fresh complaint.[470]

---

developed and she found herself suffering additional pain the complaint was naturally renewed."

Before the offense, [the victim] had neither demonstrated any knowledge of sexual matters nor witnessed any sexual conduct. Further, she was told to keep the incident a secret. Thus, [the victim] did not have the impetus to make the complaint until she attended the molestation class. Nevertheless, once [the victim] became aware of what had happened to her, she promptly made the complaint. Therefore, the complaint was "fresh" in the sense of [the victim's] cognizance and, in light of the rationale behind this doctrine, was properly admitted.

238 Cal. Rptr. at 231-32 (citations omitted). *See also* Commonwealth v. Amirault, 404 Mass. 221, 535 N.E.2d 193, 199 (1989); Commonwealth v. Snoke, 525 Pa. 295, 580 A.2d 295 (1990).

[469] Commonwealth v. Dockham, 405 Mass. 618, 542 N.E.2d 591 (1989) (in evaluating reasonableness of delay, court considers child's age, amount of time child has been away from the scene of the abuse, whether the abuser used threats or coercion, and the relationship between the child and the abuser); Commonwealth v. Brenner, 18 Mass. App. Ct. 930, 465 N.E.2d 1229, 1231 (1984); State v. Duncan, 53 Ohio St. 2d 215, 373 N.E.2d 1234 (1978); State v. Baker, 46 Or. App. 79, 610 P.2d 840, 842 (1980) ("Such delay may be excused by sufficient explanation 'found in the particular circumstances of the case, including the age of the prosecutrix, her degree of intelligence, and threats by the perpetrator of the wrong'"); State v. Twyford, 85 S.D. 522, 186 N.W.2d 545 (1971) (12-year-old victim's complaint made between 67 and 82 days after event admissible due to age of child); State v. Bouchard, 31 Wash. App. 381, 639 P.2d 761 (1982); McCormick § 297, at 859 n.49 ("A tendency is apparent in cases of sex offenses against children of tender years to be less strict with regard to permissible time lapse").

See Commonwealth v. Amirault, 404 Mass. 221, 535 N.E.2d 193, 198-99 (1989), where the court wrote:

There is no absolute rule of law as to the time within which a sexual assault victim must make her first complaint for that complaint to be admissible in evidence as a fresh complaint. . . . The determination whether statements are sufficiently prompt to constitute fresh complaint rests within the sound discretion of the trial judge. . . . The test is whether the victim's actions were reasonable in the particular circumstances of the case. . . .

Courts have not insisted on great promptness for fresh complaints in prosecutions involving child sexual abuse. . . . Because child sexual abusers are often related to or friends of the child victim, and because the victim's silence has been induced by threats or coercion, courts are flexible in applying the usual fresh complaint strictures. . . . The cases involving child sexual abuse constitute a factually distinct branch of the fresh complaint doctrine that gives special consideration to the natural fear, ignorance, and susceptibility to intimidation that is unique to a young child's make-up.

[470] Fitzgerald v. United States, 443 A.2d 1295 (D.C. 1982) (child's statement not excited utterance because not made under stress of excitement caused by a startling event, but statement

§ 7.31 FRESH COMPLAINTS

A fresh complaint is generally thought to be a type of spontaneous exclamation.[471] If the statement is elicited through questioning, the necessary spontaneity may be lost,[472] although this is not always so.[473] Because it is often necessary

---

admissible as fresh complaint); McCormick § 297, at 859 ("The only time requirement is that the complaint have been made without a delay which is unexplained or is inconsistent with the occurrence of the offense, in general a less demanding time aspect than with the typical excited utterance situation") (footnote omitted).

[471] People v. Hubbell, 54 Cal. App. 2d 49, 128 P.2d 579 (1942) ("the fact of complaint expresses a spontaneous reaction to an unusual and disturbing experience"); Commonwealth v. Snoke, 525 Pa. 295, 580 A.2d 295, 297 (1990).

[472] Matter of Cheryl H., 153 Cal. App. 3d 1098, 1129, 200 Cal. Rptr. 789, 809 (1984) (three-year-old victim made statement "while she was being questioned at length by Dr. Powell. These 'complaints' were neither fresh nor volunteered and thus are inadmissible under the 'fresh complaint' theory"); People v. Orduno, 80 Cal. App. 3d 738, 145 Cal. Rptr. 806 (1978), *cert. denied,* 439 U.S. 1074 (1979); State v. Bethune, 232 N.J. Super. 532, 557 A.2d 1025, 1027 (1989), *aff'd,* 121 N.J. 137, 578 A.2d 364 (1990); State v. J.S., 222 N.J. Super. 247, 536 A.2d 769, 772 (1988) ("In our view, to qualify as a complaint the victim's statement must at least be self-motivated and not extracted by interrogation").

[473] People v. Hudson, 198 Ill. App. 3d 915, 556 N.E.2d 640, 646 (1990); People v. Morton, 188 Ill. App. 3d 95, 543 N.E.2d 1366, 1372 (1989); People v. Branch, 158 Ill. App. 3d 338, 511 N.E.2d 872, 874 (1987) ("The fact that a complaint is made in response to questioning, however, does not necessarily destroy the admissibility"); State v. Herrin, 562 So. 2d 1, 9 (La. Ct. App. 1990) (foster parent reassured child that no harm would come to child if he spoke; such questioning did not render child's statement inadmissible; it is often necessary to draw the child out with questions); Commonwealth v. Amirault, 404 Mass. 221, 535 N.E.2d 193, 199 (1989); Commonwealth v. Brenner, 18 Mass. App. Ct. 930, 465 N.E.2d 1229, 1231 (1984) ("moreover, the 'complaint' itself has been held admissible despite the fact that it was elicited by questioning"); 4 Wigmore § 1135, at 305-06 n.10 ("The fact that the complaint was *elicited by questions* should not of itself exclude the fact of complaint—certainly in the case of young children").

See State v. Bethune, 232 N.J. Super. 532, 557 A.2d 1025, 1027–28 (1989), *aff'd,* 121 N.J. 137, 578 A.2d 364 (1990), where the court wrote:

> [I]n order for a statement by a victim of a sexual assault to be admitted under the "fresh complaint" rule, it must have been self-motivated and not extracted by interrogation.
>
> * * *
>
> [This victim's] complaint was not spontaneous, but flowed from questioning by Ms. Foster.
>
> * * *
>
> At least with regard to children of tender years, the fact that the complaint was made in response to questioning need not be fatal to admissibility. It must be considered that there may be a reluctance on the part of an abused, and consequently confused and troubled young child, to discuss a traumatic sexual incident. . . . It is only natural and realistic not to require that the complaint be entirely volunteered and spontaneous. Having established that a jury may weigh the value of the complaint where freshness is in issue, we see no reason why that same consideration should not extend

to question children to help them disclose sexual abuse, use of questions normally should go to the weight accorded a fresh complaint, not its admissibility.[474]

In the usual case, out-of-court statements are admissible only if the witness possessed testimonial competence *at the time* the out-of-court statement was made.[475] Fresh complaint evidence is an exception to this rule. A fresh complaint is admissible even though the declarant was not testimonially competent when the complaint was made.[476]

Depending on the circumstances in which a child discloses sexual abuse, the disclosure may be admissible under several theories, the most common of which are: (1) fresh complaint of sexual assault, (2) excited utterance, (3) statement for purposes of medical diagnosis or treatment, (4) hearsay admissible under a residual or child hearsay exception, (5) prior consistent statement, or (6) prior inconsistent statement. In most states a child's fresh complaint of sexual assault is not admissible as substantive evidence[477] and is limited in the amount of permissible detail. Because of the limits inherent in fresh complaint evidence, it is usually advantageous to offer the child's disclosure as hearsay

---

to the circumstances under which the complaint was made, i.e., whether in response to questioning or volunteered. . . .

A proper instruction will focus the jury's attention on the issue of whether the "complaint" is truly from the child in all of the circumstances, including whether it was volunteered or the result of interrogation. . . . In many cases the child's first opportunity for complaint may be coincidental with interrogation. We except that the scenario often follows a pattern where the child is upset, crying and otherwise disturbed and is then questioned by a parent or other authority figure, and for the first time discloses what has taken place.

[474] State v. Komurke, 560 So. 2d 986, 988 (La. Ct. App. 1990) ("Because the child has no clear understanding of what has been done to her, her 'original complaint' often consists of responses to the questioning of a patient, persistent adult who draws the child's story from her").

[475] See § **7.49**.

[476] People v. Figueroa, 134 Cal. 159, 66 P. 202 (1901); People v. Meacham, 152 Cal. App. 3d 142, 199 Cal. Rptr. 586 (1984); People v. Orduno, 80 Cal. App. 3d 738, 145 Cal. Rptr. 806 (1978), *cert. denied,* 439 U.S. 1074 (1979); People v. Guldbrandsen, 35 Cal. 2d 514, 218 P.2d 977 (1950); State v. Ryan, 103 Wash. 2d 165, 691 P.2d 197, 203–4 (1984) ("If the declarant was not competent at the time of making the statements, the statements may not be introduced through hearsay repetition. . . . The exceptions to this general rule are res gestae utterances of fresh complaints") (footnote omitted).

See also 6 Wigmore § 1761, at 246:

Where the prosecutrix is a child *too young to be a witness,* the statements should nevertheless be receivable; because although in general a hearsay declarant must not lack the qualifications of an ordinary witness . . . , yet the peculiar nature of the present exception . . . renders this principle substantially inapplicable to children; furthermore, the orthodox common-law limitations as to children's testimonial capacity are inherently unsound and impractical . . . and should not be extended by analogy.

[477] State v. Willis, 735 S.W.2d 818, 820 (Tenn. Crim. App. 1987).

§ 7.32 STATE OF MIND

within an exception or as nonhearsay admissible substantively. For example, if the child's statement qualifies as an excited utterance, the statement is substantive evidence of the abuse, and all details are admissible, including the identity of the perpetrator.

§ 7.32 State of Mind

The state of mind exception allows out-of-court statements describing a person's physical or emotional condition at the time the statement is made.[478] The exception is contained in Rule 803(3) of the Federal Rules of Evidence, which states that the following is not excluded by the hearsay rule:

> A statement of the declarant's then existing state of mind, emotion, sensation, or physical condition (such as intent, plan, motive, design, mental feeling, pain, and bodily health), but not including a statement of memory or belief to prove the fact remembered or believed . . . .[479]

Admission of state of mind evidence is justified by the need for the evidence and by its trustworthiness. Statements of existing state of mind are considered trustworthy because two of the risks of hearsay are lowered.[480] First, the risk of memory loss is reduced, if not eliminated, because the statement must be made while the declarant is experiencing a physical or emotional condition.[481] There is no time to forget. In many cases, a statement describing contemporaneous physical or mental feeling is more reliable than trial testimony months later, when the person attempts to reconstruct from memory how they felt earlier.[482] Second, the risk of misperception is low because one knows one's own mind.[483] Statements of

---

[478] The state of mind exception is a special application of the present sense impression exception. Both exceptions allow admission of statements made contemporaneously with an event including, in the case of the state of mind exception, feelings and emotions. *See* Rule 803(3) advisory committee's note (the state of mind exception "is essentially a specialized application of Exception (1) presented separately to enhance its usefulness and accessibility").

[479] Fed. R. Evid. 803(3). The state of mind exception does allow statements of memory or belief to prove facts remembered or believed relating to wills. This aspect of the exception is not relevant to child abuse litigation and is not discussed.

[480] The hearsay risks are insincerity, misperception, memory loss, and inaccurate narration. See § **7.4** for discussion of the hearsay risks.

[481] *See* 4 Louisell & Mueller § 440, at 519 ("the risk of flawed memory is virtually nonexistent. The state-of-mind exception reaches only utterances offered to prove declarant's *then-existing* mental or physical condition, and not past conditions").

[482] *See* Mutual Life Ins. Co. v. Hillmon, 145 U.S. 285, 295 (1892) ("his own memory of his state of mind at a former time is no more likely to be clear and true than a bystander's recollection of what he then said").

[483] 4 Louisell & Mueller § 440, at 518 ("The risk of misperception is usually negligible").

existing state of mind are also reliable because often they are spontaneous.[484] Of course, the risks of insincerity and miscommunication exist, but these risks are not thought to justify exclusion of the evidence. Added to the trustworthiness of state of mind evidence is the need for its admission. Sometimes the only insight into a person's mind is the person's out-of-court statements.[485]

Statements of Physical Condition

The state of mind exception includes statements of physical condition, including pain and other physical sensation.[486] The exception admits a child's statement of pain or discomfort experienced at the time of the statement. Thus, the statements "My leg really hurts" and "My private parts feel funny" are admissible under this exception. The state of mind exception does not include statements describing physical conditions experienced earlier.[487] Thus, the statement "My leg really hurt yesterday" is not within the exception.[488]

---

[484] See McCormick § 291, at 839, where the author writes:

> Judicial opinions have frequently said that, in order to qualify under this hearsay exception, the statement must be a "natural and spontaneous" expression of present bodily condition. . . .
>
> While [Rule 803(3)] in terms contains no requirement that the statement be spontaneous, it is clear from the Advisory Committee's Note to the Federal Rule that the rule is a specialized application of the broader rule recognizing a hearsay exception for statements describing a present sense impression, the cornerstone of which is spontaneity.

(footnotes omitted).

[485] 4 Louisell & Mueller § 440, at 520.

[486] McCormick § 291, at 838 ("Statements of the declarant's present bodily condition and symptoms, including pain and other feelings, to prove the truth of the statements have been generally recognized as an exception to the hearsay rule").

[487] McCormick § 291, at 838 ("The exception is, however, limited to descriptions of present condition, and therefore excludes description of past pain or symptoms as well as accounts of the events furnishing the cause of the condition") (footnotes omitted).

But see Cal. Evid. Code § 1251 (West 1992), which provides:

> [E]vidence of a statement of the declarant's state of mind, emotion, or physical sensation (including a statement of intent, plan, motive, design, mental feeling, pain, or bodily health) at a time prior to the statement is not made inadmissible by the hearsay rule if:
>
> (a) The declarant is unavailable as a witness; and
>
> (b) The evidence is offered to prove such prior state of mind, emotion, or physical sensation when it is itself an issue in the action and the evidence is not offered to prove any fact other than such state of mind, emotion, or physical condition.

[488] The statement in the text may be admissible under some other hearsay exception. For example, if the statement was made to a physician, the statement may constitute part of the child's medical history and be admissible under Rule 803(4), the medical diagnosis or treatment exception.

A child's out-of-court statement of *present* pain or physical sensation is admissible under the state of mind exception even though the event causing the pain or sensation occurred earlier.[489] Furthermore, it is reasonable to infer from a statement of present physical condition that the condition has existed for some time. However, the child's statement of *present* pain cannot be used to prove the cause of the pain.[490]

A child's statement describing an existing physical sensation is admissible even though self-serving. Moreover, the statement does not have to be made to a doctor or other professional.[491]

In a physical abuse case it may be critical to prove when abuse was inflicted. For example, an accused parent may blame the baby-sitter and assert that the child was injured on Saturday, while in the sitter's care. If, however, the child made statements of pain on Friday, before the baby-sitter came into the picture, the child's statements are admissible under the state of mind exception, and go far toward undermining the parent's explanation.

Statements of Emotion, Intent, and Other Mental States

The state of mind exception is a theoretical labyrinth with evidentiary minotaurs lurking around every corner. Although the exception—in all its complexity—arises in child abuse litigation, it is unnecessary in these pages to assume the role of Theseus. The reader is referred to the authorities for analysis of the more esoteric aspects of the state of mind exception.[492] It will do for now to catalog the more common situations in which state of mind issues arise in child abuse litigation.

The state of mind exception is used relatively infrequently in criminal child abuse litigation.[493] In civil litigation, by contrast, the state of mind exception plays an important role.

---

[489] 4 Louisell & Mueller § 440, at 522–23 ("an utterance may be within Rule 803(3) even though the present pain described in the statement was caused by a blow or an accident many days earlier, for the instant exception contains no requirement that the statement be contemporaneous with the precipitating event") (footnote omitted).

[490] *Id.* at 523 ("the instant exception does not embrace statements offered to show the cause of a physical ailment") (footnote omitted); McCormick § 291, at 838–39.

[491] 4 Louisell & Mueller § 440, at 524; McCormick § 291, at 838 ("declarations of present bodily condition generally have not been required to be made to a physician in order to qualify for the present exception").

[492] There is no better discussion than that found in 4 Louisell & Mueller §§ 441, 442.

[493] It is not that the defendant's state of mind is not important in criminal child abuse litigation. Rather, most of the time, the defendant's out-of-court statements are admitted as party admissions rather than under the state of mind exception.

§ 7.33 —Criminal Litigation

In criminal litigation, the victim's state of mind is seldom relevant.[494] In some cases, however, a particular state of mind—fear—is in issue. California, for example, provides that a person who sexually abuses a child "by use of force, violence, duress, menace, or fear of immediate and unlawful bodily injury" is guilty of a felony.[495] Federal law is similar.[496] Such statutes require the prosecutor to prove the defendant threatened the child. The child's out-of-court statements expressing fear of the defendant are probative of the defendant's threats.

When the defendant is charged under a statute that does not require proof of threats, the defendant's trial strategy sometimes makes threats relevant. For example, the defense often attacks the child's credibility on the theory that delayed disclosure of abuse undermines the child's testimony. When the defense emphasizes delayed disclosure, the prosecutor may respond with evidence that threats induced the delay.

A child's statement of existing fear is admissible under the state of mind exception to prove the child's fear. Louisell and Mueller write that "it is settled that statements by the alleged victim indicating his fear of the accused are admissible to prove his fear."[497] Although a child's statement is admissible to prove fear of the defendant, the statement is *not* admissible to prove that the defendant actually threatened the child.[498] The statement may, however, connect the defendant's threats to the child if there is independent evidence of the threats. When the threats are established by other evidence, the child's statement is admissible to connect the child's fear to the defendant's acts, and to eliminate other explanations for the child's fear.[499]

---

[494] Kauffmann v. Commonwealth, 8 Va. App. 400, 382 S.E.2d 279 (1989) (victim's state of mind not relevant in prosecution of father for sexual abuse).

[495] Cal. Penal Code § 288(b) (West 1992).

[496] 18 U.S.C. § 2242 (aggravated sexual abuse; "Whoever . . . knowingly causes another person to engage in a sexual act (1) by using force against that other person; or (2) by threatening or placing that other person in fear that any person will be subjected to death, serious bodily injury, or kidnapping" shall be punished).

[497] 4 Louisell & Mueller § 441, at 527 (footnote omitted). Although in the quote, Louisell and Mueller are discussing extortion cases, their observation is equally relevant in child abuse litigation where the prosecutor must prove threats against the child. *See also* McCormick § 294, at 844 ("Common examples of statements used to prove mental state at the time of the statement include . . . statements of ill will to show malice or the required state of mind in criminal cases, and statements showing fear").

[498] *See* 4 Louisell & Mueller § 441, at 534 n.75. *Id.* § 441, at 535 n.75 ("evidence of out-of court statements of fear by alleged victims is not merely insufficient as proof of defendant's conduct—it is incompetent as proof of such conduct").

[499] Referring to threats in extortion cases, Louisell and Mueller write:

[S]tatements of fear by the victim in extortion cases are especially useful because they are competent to prove the *source* or *direction* of the fear. The fact that they cannot prove *that the defendant acted in a certain way* should not be allowed to obscure the

Statements evidencing fear and other states of mind sometimes take the form of direct references to state of mind, such as "I'm afraid of him." Equally often, however, the statement is not a direct reference to state of mind, but a factual assertion from which state of mind is inferred.[500] Thus, it is possible to infer fear from the statement "Daddy said he'd whip me if I told anyone that he put his finger in me." The state of mind exception admits the inference of fear from the child's statement. However, the state of mind exception does not authorize admission of the child's statement to prove that the father digitally penetrated the child.[501] Needless to say, jurors will have difficulty ignoring the portion of the statement directly implicating the father.[502] In this case, the permissible use of the child's statement pales in comparison to the impermissible use, and the judge may exclude the statement as unfairly prejudicial to the defendant.[503]

---

fact . . . that if other evidence indicates defendant's conduct, the victim's statements are competent under FRE 803(3) to prove that it was that conduct, rather than something else, which caused declarant's fear.

4 Louisell & Mueller § 441, at 535 n.75.

[500] See 4 Louisell & Mueller § 441, at 532-33, where the authors write:

Statements shedding light upon declarant's mental condition usually include assertions of fact, and often consist entirely of such assertions. Even so, when offered as proof of declarant's mental condition, any such statement should be viewed as hearsay, but within the state-of-mind exception, rather than as a "verbal act" or anything else which might be taken as "circumstantial evidence" of declarant's state of mind. . . . [T]he dependability of a statement as evidence of declarant's state of mind is the same, whether the statement is partly or entirely factual in nature or purely descriptive of declarant's thoughts or intention.

(footnotes omitted).

[501] Of course, the child's statement might be admissible in its entirety under some other hearsay exception.

[502] See McCormick § 294, at 845, where the author writes:

Declarations such as those involved here frequently include assertions other than as to state of mind, as, for example, assertions that the defendant's acts caused the state of mind. The truth of those assertions may coincide with other issues in the case, such as whether the defendant's acts did in fact cause the state of mind. When this is so, the normal practice is to admit the statement and direct the jury to consider it only in proof of the state of mind and to disregard it as evidence of the other issues. Compliance with these instructions is probably beyond the jury's ability and almost certainly beyond their willingness. Where there is adequate evidence on the other issues, this probably does little harm. But in a case where the mental state is provable by other available evidence and the danger of harm from improper use by the jury of the offered declarations is substantial, the judge's discretion to exclude the statements has been recognized.

(footnotes omitted).

[503] Louisell and Mueller address the problem of statements offered under the state of mind exception that contain inadmissible factual assertions. Louisell and Mueller write:

Where an external fact asserted in a statement has no logical bearing upon the case, and tends in no way to prejudice the cause of any party objecting to the evidence, there is no reason for concern. Unfortunately matters are seldom so simple, for it is perhaps

In some cases the prosecutor must prove that the defendant committed acts to arouse or gratify the defendant's sexual desire.[504] If the defendant made statements of sexual pleasure at the time of the offense, such statements are admissible under the state of mind exception. Alternatively, the defendant's statements may be admissible as verbal acts or admissions.[505]

If the substantive law requires proof that the defendant committed acts to arouse the sexual interest *of the victim*,[506] the victim's statements of interest or arousal are admissible under the state of mind exception. Note that when it is the child's state of mind that is relevant, resort cannot be had to the admissions doctrine because the child is not a party to the litigation.

Intent is a state of mind, and it is well established that statements of intent are admissible under the state of mind exception to prove that the declarant acted in conformity with intent.[507] Thus, the statement "I'm going to the store" is admissible to prove that the declarant went to the store.[508] A criminal

---

in the nature of things that relevant conditions are affected by relevant facts, or by facts which are for some reason either irrelevant or inadmissible for reasons of prejudice. In any such case the question whether the statement should be received depends upon weighing probative worth against the danger of jury misuse of the statement as proof of the fact asserted, and against the risks of confusing the issues or misleading the jury—in short, upon the factors set forth in Rule 403.

4 Louisell & Mueller § 441, at 533 (footnote omitted). *See also id.* § 441, at 538, 551.

[504] See **Ch. 6** for discussion of methods to prove that defendant acted with the intent to arouse or gratify sexual desire.

[505] 4 Louisell & Mueller § 441, at 525 ("where a party seeks to prove the state of mind of his adversary by means of the latter's out-of-court statements, resort to the admissions doctrine is likely to be the basis upon which the evidence is received") (footnote omitted).

[506] *See, e.g.*, Cal. Penal Code § 288(a) (West 1992).

[507] 4 Louisell & Mueller § 442, at 540 ("It has long been settled that the state-of-mind exception may be used as the basis for introducing statements showing the forward-looking intent of the declarant for the purpose of proving that he thereafter acted in accordance with that intent"); McCormick § 295, at 847 ("it is now clear that out-of-court statements which tend to prove a plan, design, or intention of the declarant are admissible, subject to the usual limitations as to remoteness in time and perhaps apparent sincerity common to all statements of mental state, to prove that the plan, design, or intention of the declarant was carried out by the declarant") (footnotes omitted); 4 Weinstein & Berger ¶ 803(3)[04], at 803-122 ("statements of intention to prove a subsequent act had been previously admitted in a variety of contexts, and continue to be admitted pursuant to Rule 803(3)") (footnote omitted).

The declarant need not be unavailable for evidence of intent to be admitted to prove conduct in conformity with intent. *See* 4 Louisell & Mueller § 442, at 547. The subject of when, if ever, one person's statement of intent or plan is admissible to prove the conduct of another person is a complex topic taken up in detail in 4 Louisell & Mueller § 442. *See also* McCormick § 295, at 848-51.

[508] The admissibility of statements of intent to prove subsequent conduct is clear. McCormick points out, however, that the admissibility of such statements does not mean statements of intent are necessarily sufficient evidence to prove subsequent conduct. McCormick § 295, at 850–51.

defendant's statement "I'm going to get you, kid" is admissible to prove the defendant's assault on the child.[509]

Intent is not the only state of mind that actuates conduct. Louisell and Mueller write:

> But of course it is not intent alone which bears a causal connection to declarant's subsequent conduct. Statements indicating various emotional conditions, such as affection, jealousy, anger, hate, fear, prejudice, and so forth may bear upon declarant's probable subsequent conduct, and may sometimes be proved by statements offered under the instant exception.[510]

In sexual abuse prosecutions involving adolescent victims, the defense sometimes asserts that the child fabricated the allegations to get even with the defendant for imposing discipline. The victim's pre-accusation statements evidencing love of the defendant should be admissible under the state of mind exception to help establish that the child probably did not invent a vindictive lie designed to hurt the defendant.

Sometimes a person's description of a past event sheds light on the person's intent *at the time* the event is described. Suppose, for example, that the defendant is charged with incest. The victim is the defendant's 12-year-old daughter. At trial, the child's mother testifies for her husband, stating that her daughter fabricated the allegations. The prosecutor must undermine the mother's testimony. Suppose that shortly following the victim's disclosure, the victim's mother told her, "No one must ever know your father had sex with you." From the mother's statement describing a prior event—sexual abuse—it is possible to infer her intent to protect her husband. From the mother's intent, it is possible to infer that the mother's trial testimony is fabricated. The mother's statement to the victim is admissible for this purpose under the state of mind exception.

§ 7.34 —Civil Litigation

In child custody and visitation litigation incident to divorce, the child's feelings, fears, likes, and dislikes are central to the child's best interest. The child's state of mind is in issue in such litigation,[511] and the child's hearsay statements

---

[509] For discussion of statements of intent to prove subsequent conduct, see 4 Louisell & Mueller § 441, at 540–43. *See id.* § 442, at 544–45 ("statements indicating an intent to inflict harm upon oneself or upon another may be received under Rule 803(3) to prove subsequent conduct in conformity therewith"). A defendant could not object that evidence of the threat constitutes inadmissible character evidence. *See* Fed. R. Evid. 404(a). It is clear that uncharged misconduct evidencing intent is admissible under Rule 404(b).

[510] 4 Louisell & Mueller § 442, at 554.

[511] See McCormick § 294, at 843, where the author writes, "The substantive law often makes legal rights and liabilities hinge upon the existence of a particular state of mind or feeling in a person involved in the transaction at issue. . . . When this is so the mental or

revealing state of mind are admissible. Thus, it is proper to admit the child's out-of-court statement describing the child's "intimidation by the father and desire to live with the mother."[512] Similarly, a child's hearsay statements describing parental misconduct are admissible insofar as the statements reveal the child's fear of a parent.[513]

In custody and visitation litigation involving allegations of sexual abuse, the state of mind exception is particularly important.[514] For example, in some cases there is considerable evidence of sexual abuse, but it is impossible to determine who molested the child. In other cases, the evidence creates a strong suspicion of sexual abuse by a parent but falls short of a preponderance of the evidence. In both scenarios, the child is at risk of further abuse, yet, under traditional notions of burden of proof, there is not enough evidence to justify an order to protect the child from the likely perpetrator. The court may fear that doing nothing consigns the child to further abuse, yet feels powerless to take action. In a proper case, statements admissible under the state of mind exception may be used to protect a child despite the fact that sexual abuse or the identify of the perpetrator cannot be substantiated. For instance, the child's out-of-court statements expressing fear or dislike of the parent accused of sexual abuse constitute sufficient evidence to support a custody or visitation order.[515] Similarly, if the child believes abuse occurred, placing limits on interaction with the parent may be in the child's best interest whether or not the child's belief is accurate. Such use of state of mind evidence does not wink at the requirement that allegations of sexual abuse must be established. Rather, evidence of a child's feelings, beliefs, and fears constitute an independent and sufficient source of proof regarding the child's best interests.

---

emotional state of the person becomes an ultimate object of search." McCormick points out that when a declarant's out-of-court statement offered to prove state of mind is not offered to prove the literal truth of the words spoken, the statement may not be hearsay at all, thus making resort to the state of mind exception unnecessary. *See* McCormick § 294, at 843. *See also* 4 Weinstein & Berger ¶ 803(3)[03], at 803-112.

[512] Griffin v. Griffin, 81 N.C. App. 665, 344 S.E.2d 828, 830 (1986).

[513] Crabtree v. Crabtree, 716 S.W.2d 923 (Tenn. Ct. App. 1986). In *Crabtree* the court wrote:

> The statements of the child to third persons, offered to prove the misconduct of one of the parents, are generally excluded as hearsay. But, as they relate to the child's state of mind, statements that would ordinarily be excluded may be introduced. . . . And where the child's state of mind shows that he or she has a real fear of one parent based on the real or imagined mistreatment by that parent, that is sufficient to persuade this court to exclude the child from the company of that parent except under proper supervision.

716 S.W.2d at 927. The fact that the child's out-of-court statements from which state of mind is inferred contain allegations of wrongdoing by a parent should not lead to exclusion of the evidence under Rule 403. At least in most states, there is no jury in custody litigation, and the court can be trusted to consider the child's hearsay statement for the limited purpose of establishing state of mind.

[514] *See* Crabtree v. Crabtree, 716 S.W.2d 923 (Tenn. Ct. App. 1986).

[515] See *id.*

§ 7.34 CIVIL LITIGATION

The admissibility of state of mind evidence in juvenile court dependency proceedings turns in the first instance on statutes governing adjudication of child abuse. A statute that requires proof that a particular caretaker inflicted specified abuse has much in common with criminal child abuse statutes. As in criminal litigation, where the victim's state of mind is not in issue, under juvenile court statutes that parallel the proof required in criminal cases, the child's state of mind probably also is not in issue. Thus, under such statutes a child's out-of-court statements evidencing state of mind would not be admissible to prove the facts described in the statements.[516]

Under some juvenile court statutes, however, the child's state of mind is in issue,[517] and evidence of the child's fear or emotions may constitute a sufficient basis to adjudicate the child dependent regardless of whether abuse can be established.

Regardless of the statutory scheme governing juvenile court adjudication, intervention should be allowed when evidence establishes that a child is suffering serious fear, anxiety, or depression, and parents fail or refuse to seek appropriate professional help. The child's mental suffering can be established in whole or part through the child's hearsay statements admissible under the state of mind exception. It is reasonable to infer that the mental anguish disclosed in the child's out-of-court statements continues to the present, necessitating juvenile court intervention when parents refuse to act.[518]

Memory and belief are states of mind that are not admissible to prove facts remembered or believed under Federal Rule of Evidence 803(3).[519] However, when a child's welfare is at stake in civil litigation, a persuasive argument can

---

[516] *See In re* Custody of Jennifer, 25 Mass. App. Ct. 241, 517 N.E.2d 187 (1988) (care and protection proceeding; trial judge erroneously relied on state of mind exception to admit child's statements as proof of facts remembered).

[517] *See Id.* at 189 ("We have no question that a child's state of mind may be a material issue in a care and protection proceeding").

[518] See 4 Louisell & Mueller § 441, at 529–31, where the authors write:

> [T]he statement must indicate declarant's then-existing state of mind. It is not within Rule 803(3) if it describes only a previous mental condition. But Monday's statement describing declarant's then-existing state of mind often sheds light upon his mental condition on the previous Sunday and the following Tuesday. Where it is reasonable to assume a kind of continuity, either backward or forward from the moment of a present-tense statement which is otherwise admissible under Rule 803(3) as proof of declarant's state of mind, the evidentiary effect of such a statement may be expanded accordingly, and need not be confined to the moment it was uttered.

(footnotes omitted). *See also* McCormick § 294, at 844 ("Although it is required that the statement describe a state of mind or feeling existing at the time of the statement, the evidentiary effect of the statement is broadened by the notion of the continuity in time of states of mind").

[519] The classic case taking the position that statements of memory are inadmissible to prove facts remembered is Shepard v. United States, 290 U.S. 96 (1933) (opinion by Cardozo, J.). *See also* McCormick § 296.

be made that in selected cases the child's statements of memory or belief should be admissible to prove facts remembered or believed, that is, to prove abuse or neglect.[520] Scholars support selective admissibility of memory or belief to prove facts remembered or believed if the declarant is not available to testify at trial.[521] In an oft-cited article, Payne wrote:

> Suppose a material fact in a given case is whether or not A went to the movies on Sunday. A is not available at the trial. Under the doctrine of [*Mutual Life Insurance Co. v. Hillmon*[522]], W would be permitted to testify that on Saturday he was witness to A's declarations of intention to attend the movies on the following day. The reasoning involved in the offer of proof has been explored. However, Seligman argues that logically W should be permitted to testify that on Monday he was witness to A's declarations that A had been to the movies on the previous day.
>
> What is the sense in permitting W to testify in the first instance and refusing to permit him to testify in the second instance? If logical relevance be taken to exclude considerations of the possibility of intentional misstatement and faulty memory, it is submitted that A's declarations in the second case are more cogent than his declarations in the first case. In other words, as a matter of common sense and logic in evaluating its effectiveness as proof, A's mental state on Monday has a greater tendency to prove the doing of the act on Sunday than A's mental state on Saturday has to prove the doing of the act on Sunday. With regard to the perception of the mental state itself, there is virtually no problem in either case. There is, however, a problem of perception and memory with reference to the doing of the act in the second case which was not involved in the first case. If the act perceived is a simple one, the problem of perception would not seem to be large. With regard to the problem of memory, in which perception

---

[520] The proposed Federal Rules of Evidence adopted by the Supreme Court contained a rule allowing limited admissibility of statements of memory to prove facts remembered. Proposed Rule 804(b)(2) stated:

> The following are not excluded by the hearsay rule if the declarant is unavailable as a witness: (2) A statement, not in response to the instigation of a person engaged in investigating, litigating, or settling a claim, which narrates, describes, or explains an event or condition recently perceived by the declarant, made in good faith, not in contemplation of pending or anticipated litigation in which he was interested, and while his recollection was clear.

51 F.R.D. 315, 438 (1971). The proposed rule was not approved by Congress and is not part of the Federal Rules of Evidence.

[521] *See* 4 Louisell & Mueller § 442, at 568-84; McCormick § 296; Seligman, *An Exception to the Hearsay Rule,* 26 Harv. L. Rev. 146 (1912); 4 Weinstein & Berger ¶ 803(3)[05], at 803-129 to 803-130.

[522] 145 U.S. 285 (1892). The *Hillmon* case is most well known for the proposition that statements of intent are admissible to prove conduct in conformity with intent. On a more subtle level, the Supreme Court's decision in *Hillmon* arguably paves the way for certain statements of memory to prove facts remembered. For thorough analysis of the *Hillmon* case, see 4 Louisell & Mueller § 442.

plays a part, if the time lapse between the act and declared memory is not too great—a question of degree—and the declarant himself is possessed of ordinary mental powers, in many conceivable cases, including the illustration used here, the probability of default in memory is no greater than, and perhaps not so great as, the probability of frustration or alteration of intention presented on the facts of the *Hillmon* case itself.[523]

When a child is unavailable to testify at trial, or appears at trial but cannot communicate effectively, a strong argument can be made in civil proceedings to admit the child's statement of memory to prove facts remembered. Consider a case in which a nine-year-old told her friend, "I'm going to run away because my dad molests me every day and I know he won't stop." A dependency trial is underway in juvenile court. The child is unavailable because she is unwilling to testify. If it is relevant to prove that the child ran away from home, the state of mind exception allows admission of the child's statement to prove her intent to run away and her subsequent conduct in conformity with that intent. However, when attention shifts from intent (which looks to the future) to memory (which looks to the past) Rule 803(3) seems to preclude admission of the child's statement. The rule states that an out-of-court statement of memory—in this case memory of molestation—is not admissible to prove the fact remembered. Yet, the child's statement may be reliable.[524] The statement indicates that the abuse occurs every day. Thus, the child's memory of the abuse is recent. The matter was not in litigation when the victim spoke to her friend, and there is no indication of motive to fabricate. The hearsay risks of misperception, miscommunication, and insincerity seem low. If the state of mind exception is flexible enough to accommodate statements of intent looking to the future, the exception should also accommodate certain statements of memory looking to the past. If the court refuses to expand the state of mind exception to receive the child's statement, however, the statement should be admissible under a residual or child hearsay exception.[525]

§ 7.35 Diagnosis or Treatment Exception

Certain hearsay statements made for purposes of obtaining treatment or a diagnosis are sufficiently reliable to be admitted in evidence. Statements to

---

[523] Payne, *The Hillmon Case—An Old Problem Revisited*, 41 Va. L. Rev. 1011, 1023–24 (1955).

[524] See 4 Louisell & Mueller § 422 for detailed analysis of the potential reliability of state of mind evidence to prove facts remembered.

[525] 4 Louisell & Mueller § 442, at 581 ("Hearsay objections to statements of intent, offered for purposes of proving previous facts motivating or explaining declarant's contemplated conduct, might of course be overcome by resort to the catchall exceptions of Rule 803(24) or Rule 804(b)(5)").

physicians providing treatment have long been received.[526] Under the influence of the Federal Rules of Evidence, a growing number of states also admit statements for purposes of diagnosis, whether or not the patient seeks treatment from the diagnostician.[527] Rule 803(4) of the Federal Rules of Evidence codifies the diagnosis or treatment exception as follows:

> The following are not excluded by the hearsay rule, even though the declarant is available as a witness: Statements made for purposes of medical diagnosis or treatment and describing medical history, or past or present symptoms, pain, or sensations, or the inception or general character of the cause or external source thereof insofar as reasonably pertinent to diagnosis or treatment.[528]

The proponent of hearsay offered under the diagnosis or treatment exception has the burden of establishing that the exception applies.[529] The trial court determines admissibility pursuant to Rule 104(a).

---

[526] State v. Aguallo, 318 N.C. 590, 350 S.E.2d 76 (1986) (helpful discussion of when statements are for purposes of diagnosis or treatment and when they are for purposes of litigation only); State v. Nelson, 138 Wis. 2d 418, 406 N.W.2d 385, 390 (1987) (helpful discussion of rationale of diagnosis or treatment exception); Cassidy v. State, 74 Md. App. 1, 536 A.2d 666, *cert. denied,* 312 Md. 602, 541 A.2d 965 (1988) (extended discussion of treatment exception).

See also McCormick § 292, at 839 ("Statements of presently existing bodily condition made by a patient to a doctor consulted for treatment have almost universally been admitted as evidence of the facts stated"); Mosteller, *Child Sexual Abuse and Statements for the Purpose of Medical Diagnosis or Treatment,* 67 N.C. L. Rev. 257 (1989); 4 Weinstein & Berger ¶ 803(4)[01], at 803-143 ("All jurisdictions admit some statements made with a view to treatment as an exception to the hearsay rule, but considerable dissension exists about the scope of the exception").

[527] *See* McCormick § 293, at 841–42. Some statements purely for purposes of diagnosis probably are unreliable. For example, a personal injury plaintiff may retain a physician to testify as an expert witness on the plaintiff's behalf. The plaintiff's statements to the doctor may lack indicia of reliability. Indeed, the patient may have a litigation-induced incentive to be less than candid with the doctor.

Other statements for purposes of diagnosis bear the hallmarks of reliability that underlie the present exception. For example, a patient may consult a specialist not for treatment, but simply for a diagnosis. The specialist's diagnosis may be passed along to a treating physician or used in some other way by the patient. The patient has every incentive to be accurate and candid with the specialist. McCormick writes that "[t]he fact that no treatment was actually given is not controlling, but subsequent reliance upon advice of a treatment nature given by the physician is strong evidence of a treatment motive for the initial consultation." McCormick § 293, at 842 (footnote omitted).

The Federal Rules of Evidence reject a distinction between statements for purposes of diagnosis or treatment, expressly authorizing admission of both types of statements.

[528] Fed. R. Evid. 803(4).

[529] Oldsen v. People, 732 P.2d 1132, 1135 n.7 (Colo. 1986).

§ 7.35 DIAGNOSIS OF TREATMENT EXCEPTION

Rule 803(4) includes statements describing past[530] as well as present symptoms.[531] Thus, the patient's medical history is admissible.[532] The exception also embraces the patient's description of the cause of illness or injury, provided the cause is pertinent to diagnosis or treatment.[533] Although Rule 803(4) allows statements describing the cause of illness or injury, traditional practice under this exception excludes statements attributing fault. To use the Advisory Committee's example, "a patient's statement that he was struck by an automobile would qualify but not his statement that the car was driven through a red light."[534]

In child abuse litigation, courts have carved out an exception to the rule against statements attributing fault. The majority of courts hold that children's statements identifying the perpetrator of abuse are sometimes pertinent to

---

[530] See McCormick § 292, at 839-40, where the author writes:

> Because of this strong assurance of reliability courts tend to expand the exception to include statements made by a patient to a physician concerning *past* symptoms. This seems appropriate, as patients are likely to recognize the importance to their treatment of accurate statements as to past as well as present symptoms.

(footnotes omitted). *See also* Federal Rule of Evidence 803(4) advisory committee's note ("The same guarantee of trustworthiness extends to statements of past conditions and medical history, made for purposes of diagnosis or treatment"); 4 Louisell & Mueller § 444, at 605 ("statements may satisfy the pertinency requirement even though they describe (and are offered to prove) previous physical sensations, symptoms, or events").

[531] Statements of present bodily sensation are also admissible under the state of mind exception. See § **7.32**.

[532] *See* Fed. R. Evid. 803(4) advisory committee's note ("The same guarantee of trustworthiness extends to statements of past conditions and medical history, made for purposes of diagnosis or treatment"). *See also* United States v. Balfany, 1992 W.L. 97006 (8th Cir. 1992); Lewis v. State, 161 Ga. App. 209, 288 S.E.2d 278, 279 (1982); State v. Bellotti, 383 N.W.2d 308, 312 (Minn. Ct. App. 1986); In re James A., 505 A.2d 1386, 1388 (R.I. 1986); State v. Bawdon, 386 N.W.2d 484, 487 (S.D. 1986) (six-year-old child was taken to hospital after it was learned she may have been abused; examining doctor asked if anyone touched her in the genital area; child nodded in the affirmative; court stated, "This is the type of hearsay contemplated as admissible by the medical diagnosis exception").

[533] See McCormick § 292, at 840, where the author writes:

> In some cases the special assurance of reliability—the patient's belief that accuracy is essential to effective treatment—also applies to statements concerning the cause, and a physician who views this as related to diagnosis and treatment might reasonably be expected to communicate this to the patient and perhaps take other steps to assure a reliable response.

(footnote omitted). *See also* People v. Hudson, 198 Ill. App. 3d 915, 556 N.E.2d 640, 645 (1990) ("Generally, statements concerning a cause of injury made to a treating physician are admissible under the physician-patient exception to the hearsay rule"); Mosteller, *Child Sexual Abuse and Statements for the Purpose of Medical Diagnosis or Treatment*, 67 N.C. L. Rev. 257, 260 (1989).

[534] Fed. R. Evid. 803(4) advisory committee's note.

diagnosis or treatment.[535] A minority of courts reject statements of identification.[536] The majority has the better argument. Treatment of child abuse includes removing the child from the abusive setting, and to this end the doctor often needs to know the identity of the perpetrator.[537] If the physician has reason to

---

[535] United States v. Balfany, 1992 W.L. 97006 (8th Cir. 1992); United States v. George, 960 F.2d 97 (9th Cir. 1992); Morgan v. Foretich, 846 F.2d 941, 949 (4th Cir. 1988); United States v. Shaw, 824 F.2d 601, 608 (8th Cir. 1987), *cert. denied,* 484 U.S. 1068 (1988); United States v. Renville, 779 F.2d 430 (8th Cir. 1985); United States v. Deland, 22 M.J. 70 (C.M.A.), *cert. denied,* 479 U.S. 856 (1986); United States v. Lingle, 27 M.J. 704 (A.F.C.M.R. 1988); United States v. Brown, 25 M.J. 867 (A.C.M.R. 1988); State v. Robinson, 153 Ariz. 191, 735 P.2d 801, 810 (1987) ("in many child sexual abuse cases . . . the abuser's identity *is* critical to effective diagnosis and treatment"); State v. Thompson, 146 Ariz. 552, 707 P.2d 956, 962 (Ct. App. 1985); Stallnacker v. State, 19 Ark. App. 9, 715 S.W.2d 883 (1986); People v. Oldsen, 697 P.2d 787 (Colo. Ct. App. 1984), *aff'd,* 732 P.2d 1132 (Colo. 1986); State v. Dollinger, 20 Conn. App. 530, 568 A.2d 1058, 1060 (1990) ("If the sexual abuser is a member of the child victim's immediate household, it is reasonable for a physician to ascertain the identity of the abuser to prevent recurrences and to facilitate the treatment of psychological and physical injuries"); State v. Maldonado, 13 Conn. App. 368, 536 A.2d 600, 604-04 (1988); Flanagan v. State, 586 So. 2d 1085 (Fla. Dist. Ct. App. 1991); State v. Tracy, 482 N.W.2d 675 (Iowa 1992); State v. Hebert, 480 A.2d 742, 748 (Me. 1984); People v. Meeboer, 484 N.W.2d 621 (Mich. 1992); *In re* Rinesmith, 144 Mich. App. 475, 376 N.W.2d 139, 141 (1985); People v. Wilkins, 134 Mich. App. 39, 349 N.W.2d 815, 817 (1984); State v. Red Feather, 205 Neb. 734, 289 N.W.2d 768, 771 (1980); State v. Bullock, 320 N.C. 780, 360 S.E.2d 689 (1987); State v. Aguallo, 318 N.C. 590, 350 S.E.2d 76 (1986); State v. Smith, 315 N.C. 76, 337 S.E.2d 833 (1985); State v. Gregory, 78 N.C. App. 565, 338 S.E.2d 110, 112 (1985); State v. Moen, 309 Or. 45, 786 P.2d 111, 120 (1990) (not child abuse case); State v. Logan, 105 Or. App. 556, 806 P.2d 137, 139-40 (1991) (identity of perpetrator pertinent even though perpetrator had already been removed from home; identity pertinent to visitation and appropriate treatment); State v. Vosika, 83 Or. App. 298, 731 P.2d 449, *on reconsideration,* 85 Or. App. 148, 735 P.2d 1273 (1987); State v. Garza, 337 N.W.2d 823, 825 (S.D. 1983); Fleming v. State, 819 S.W.2d 237 (Tex. Ct. App. 1991); Tissier v. State, 792 S.W.2d 120, 125 (Tex. Ct. App. 1990) (in physical abuse case, trial court did not err in allowing physician to repeat child's statement that defendant hit him in the stomach and later told him not to tell anyone); State v. Butler, 53 Wash. App. 214, 766 P.2d 505 (1989); State v. Fitzgerald, 39 Wash. App. 652, 694 P.2d 1117, 1122 (1985); State v. Sorenson, 143 Wis. 2d 226, 421 N.W.2d 77, 87 (1988); State v. Nelson, 138 Wis. 2d 418, 406 N.W.2d 385 (1987); Goldade v. State, 674 P.2d 721 (Wyo. 1983), *cert. denied,* 467 U.S. 1253 (1984).

[536] People v. LaLone, 432 Mich. 103, 437 N.W.2d 611 (1989); People v. Hudson, 198 Ill. App. 3d 915, 556 N.E.2d 640 (1990); People v. Pluskis, 162 Ill. App. 3d 449, 515 N.E.2d 480 (1987); People v. Sexton, 162 Ill. App. 3d 607, 515 N.E.2d 1359, 1364 (1987); Cassidy v. State, 74 Md. App. 1, 536 A.2d 666, 682-90, *cert. denied,* 312 Md. 602, 541 A.2d 965 (1988).

In a jurisdiction where statements of identification are inadmissible under the diagnosis or treatment exception, such statements may be admissible under other exceptions. For example, the statement may be admissible as a statement of identification under Rule 801(d)(1)(C). *See* State v. Boston, 46 Ohio St. 3d 108, 545 N.E.2d 1220, 1236 (1989).

[537] See State v. Robinson, 153 Ariz. 191, 735 P.2d 801, 810 (1987), where the court wrote:

> [I]n many child sexual abuse cases . . . the abuser's identity *is* critical to effective diagnosis and treatment. . . .[I]t matters who abused Nicole. Dr. Davis's testimony in

§ 7.35 DIAGNOSIS OF TREATMENT EXCEPTION 213

suspect that a child has a sexually transmitted disease, it is pertinent to know who had sexual contact with the child.[538] If the child was threatened into silence, the source of the threats may be pertinent to psychological treatment.[539]

Rule 803(4) is premised on the theory that the four hearsay risks are low with statements for diagnosis or treatment.[540] The risk of insincerity is low because the patient has a strong incentive to be truthful with the doctor.[541] After

---

this case echoed the conclusion reached by numerous courts: "The exact nature and extent of the psychological problems which ensue from child [sexual] abuse often depend on the identity of the abuser." . . . The psychological sequelae of sexual molestation by a father, other relative, or family friend may be different and require different treatment than those resulting from abuse by a stranger. . . . Furthermore, effective treatment may require that the victim avoid contact with the abuser, not just to prevent further abuse, but also to facilitate recovery from past abuse.

At least in child sexual abuse cases, we therefore join the growing number of jurisdictions which recognize that statements regarding the abuser's identity fall within Rule 803(4) whenever, as here, identity is relevant to proper diagnosis and treatment. . . . When the abuser's identity is elicited and given to further treatment, the doctor's and the declarant's "selfish interest[s]" in giving and obtaining proper treatment are sufficient guarantees of trustworthiness to at least allow the jury to evaluate the statements.

[538] *See* People v. Meeboer, 181 Mich. App. 365, 449 N.W.2d 124, 127 (1989), *aff'd*, 484 N.W.2d 621 (Mich. 1992). In this case the court wrote:

[W]e have no doubt in the instant case that the identity of the perpetrator was reasonably necessary for Amy's [six-year-old victim] medical care and treatment. We note that following a rape the identity of the perpetrator as the 'inception or general character of the cause or external source thereof' (MRE 803[4]) is medically necessary to treat or rule out the transmission of venereal diseases or Acquired Immune Deficiency Syndrome. With venereal diseases at epidemic levels and with the rapid spread of AIDS, the perpetrator of every rape needs to be identified and evaluated as part of the victim's care and treatment. Accordingly, we hold that in cases of rape the identity of the attacker is reasonably necessary for the victim's medical care and treatment.

[539] *See* United States v. Cherry, 938 F.2d 748, 757 (7th Cir. 1991).

[540] White v. Illinois, 112 S. Ct. 736, 743 (1992); 4 Louisell & Mueller § 444, at 593–94. In addition to the trustworthy nature of statements within this exception, there is often a need to admit statements describing the patient's symptoms. As Weinstein and Berger write, "[T]here is often a real need for the statement since no other evidence will be available concerning subjective symptoms." 4 Weinstein & Berger ¶ 803(4)[01], at 803-144 (footnote omitted). *See also* 4 Louisell & Mueller § 444, at 594.

[541] Morgan v. Foretich, 846 F.2d 941, 951 (4th Cir. 1988) (Powell, J. concurring and dissenting) ("the declarant's purpose in making the statement normally assures its trustworthiness because diagnosis and treatment may depend on what the patient tells the physician"); United States v. Edens, 31 M.J. 267, 269 (C.M.A. 1990); State v. Robinson, 153 Ariz. 191, 735 P.2d 801, 809 (1987); Oldsen v. People, 732 P.2d 1132, 1135 (Colo. 1986); State v. Moen, 309 Or. 45, 786 P.2d 111, 118–19 (1990); Fleming v. State, 819 S.W.2d 237 (Tex. Ct. App. 1991); McCormick § 292, at 839 ("reliability is assured by the likelihood that the patient believes that the effectiveness of the treatment he receives may depend largely upon the

all, the patient's health—even life—may depend on the accuracy of information supplied the doctor. The risk of miscommunication is low because the patient is motivated to be clear and unambiguous. The likelihood of memory loss is reduced because, in most cases, the patient reports on recent events. Finally, the risk of misperception is low because the patient reports on the patient's own symptoms.

Statements to nonphysicians are admissible under the diagnosis or treatment exception.[542] The Advisory Committee note to Rule 803(4) states, "Under the exception the statement need not have been made to a physician. Statements to hospital attendants, ambulance drivers, or even members of the family might be included."[543] Although most of the reported decisions involve patient-physician communication,[544] a child's statement to an ambulance driver,[545] nurse,[546]

---

accuracy of the information he provides the physician"); 4 Weinstein & Berger ¶ 803(4)[01], at 803-144.

See also Mosteller, *Child Sexual Abuse and Statements for the Purpose of Medical Diagnosis or Treatment,* 67 N.C. L. Rev. 257, 257 (1989):

> Statements made to a physician for the purpose of receiving medical treatment have long been received under an exception to the rule that excludes hearsay. The theory of the exception in its archetypal form is straightforward: a patient's selfish interest in receiving appropriate treatment guarantees the trustworthiness of the statement. In this archetypal form, the exception is among the most solidly founded within the hearsay rules.

If there is no indication the professional was performing diagnostic or treatment-related services, the exception does not apply. In Begley v. State, 483 So. 2d 70, 73-74 (Fla. Dist. Ct. App. 1986), the court held that statements to a counselor at a sexual assault center were not within the exception. The counselor stated she interviewed the victim "just to see how she was doing and what was troubling her at the time." The court wrote that "at a minimum, there must be a showing (a) that the statements were made for the purposes of diagnosis or treatment, and (b) that the individual making the statement knew the statements were being made for this purpose. The record is devoid of any such showing."

[542] 4 Louisell & Mueller § 444, at 608; McCormick § 292, at 840; 4 Weinstein & Berger ¶ 803(4)[01], at 803-144 to 803-145. A few decisions decline to extend the diagnosis or treatment exception beyond physicians. See State v. J.C.E., 235 Mont. 264, 767 P.2d 309 (1988) (court declined to extend exception beyond medical doctors).

[543] Fed. R. Evid. 803(4) advisory committee's note.

[544] United States v. Renville, 779 F.2d 430, 438 (8th Cir. 1985); W.C.L. v. People, 685 P.2d 176 (Colo. 1984); State v. Hebert, 480 A.2d 742 (Me. 1984); In re Rinesmith, 144 Mich. App. 475, 376 N.W.2d 139 (1985); People v. Wilkins, 134 Mich. App. 39, 349 N.W.2d 815 (1984); State v. Red Feather, 205 Neb. 734, 289 N.W.2d 768 (1980); State v. Gregory, 78 N.C. App. 565, 338 S.E.2d 110 (1985); State v. Fearing, 315 N.C. 167, 337 S.E.2d 551 (1985); State v. Garza, 337 N.W.2d 823 (S.D. 1983); State v. Fitzgerald, 39 Wash. App. 652, 694 P.2d 1117 (1985); Goldade v. State, 674 P.2d 721 (Wyo. 1983), *cert. denied,* 467 U.S. 1253 (1984).

[545] State v. Smith, 315 N.C. 76, 337 S.E.2d 833, 839 (1985).

[546] United States v. Fink, 32 M.J. 987 (A.C.M.R. 1991); Goldade v. State, 674 P.2d 721 (Wyo. 1983), *cert. denied,* 467 U.S. 1253 (1984).

§ 7.35 DIAGNOSIS OF TREATMENT EXCEPTION

psychologist,[547] social worker,[548] psychiatrist,[549] hospital receptionist,[550] relative,[551] or other individual[552] will be admitted if the rationale supporting the exception is present.

The person making the out-of-court statement need not be the patient.[553] With ill children, for example, a parent may communicate with the professional. The parent's incentive to be accurate often justifies receipt of the parent's statements under this exception.[554]

---

[547] Morgan v. Foretich, 846 F.2d 941, 949 n.17 (4th Cir. 1988) ("Statements to psychiatrists or psychologists are admissible under 803(4) the same as statements to physicians"); United States v. Nelson, 25 M.J. 110 (C.M.A. 1987), *cert. denied,* 484 U.S. 1061 (1988); United States v. Welch, 25 M.J. 23 (C.M.A. 1987); United States v. Deland, 22 M.J. 70 (C.M.A.), *cert. denied,* 479 U.S. 856 (1986); United States v. Armstrong, 33 M.J. 1011, 1013 (A.C.M.R. 1991); United States v. Miller, 32 M.J. 843 (N.M.C.M.R. 1991); United States v. Fink, 32 M.J. 987 (A.C.M.R. 1991); State v. Nelson, 138 Wis. 2d 418, 406 N.W.2d 385, 390 (1987) ("we recognize that statements made to a psychologist, if made for the purposes of diagnosis or treatment, are also admissible").

[548] United States v. Fink, 32 M.J. 987 (A.C.M.R. 1991); United States v. Balfany, 1992 WL 97006 (8th Cir. 1992); United States v. Miller, 32 M.J. 843 (N.M.C.M.R. 1991); United States v. Cottriel, 21 M.J. 535 (N.M.C.M.R. 1985); State v. Jones, 89 N.C. App. 584, 367 S.E.2d 139, 144 (1988) (child interviewed by social worker at child protection center; "Statements made to a medical worker, if pertinent to diagnosis or treatment, are admissible under Rule 803(4)"); *In re* Jean Marie W., 559 A.2d 625, 630 (R.I. 1989) (statements to social worker within exception; "Statements do not have to be made to a physician").

[549] Of course, psychiatrists are physicians. Nevertheless, the work of psychiatrists often has more in common with that of psychologists and social workers than with physicians in nonpsychiatric practice. *See* Morgan v. Foretich, 846 F.2d 941, 949 n.17 (4th Cir. 1988) ("Statements to psychiatrists and psychologists are admissible under 803(4) the same as statements to physicians").

[550] Fed. R. Evid. 803(4) advisory committee's note.

[551] State v. Smith, 315 N.C. 76, 337 S.E.2d 833 (1985) (grandmother); State v. Jones, 89 N.C. App. 584, 367 S.E.2d 139, 143–44 (1988) (mother).

[552] The identity of the person to whom the child speaks is not the important factor. What is important is that the child make the statement for the purpose of obtaining diagnosis or treatment. Thus, a statement to the child's school bus driver, teacher, baby-sitter, or parent would be admissible if the child's motivation were to receive treatment.

See State v. Maldonado, 13 Conn. App. 368, 536 A.2d 600 (1988). In this case a three-and-a-half-year-old victim of sexual abuse was taken to the hospital for treatment of a vaginal discharge. The child spoke only Spanish. In order to obtain the child's medical history, the doctor enlisted the assistance of a Spanish-speaking security guard. The guard informed the child that he was questioning the child to assist the doctor. Outside the doctor's presence, the child revealed her sexual abuse to the guard. The court held that the child's statements to the security guard fell within the medical treatment exception.

[553] *See* 4 Louisell & Mueller § 444, at 606.

[554] *See* State v. Bauman, 98 Or. App. 316, 779 P.2d 185 (1989). In this case the child's mother described to a physician what happened to the child. The court wrote that under the diagnosis or treatment exception, "statements made for medical diagnosis and treatment by a family member other than the person who is the subject of the diagnosis or treatment are admissible." 779 P.2d at 186. *See also* State v. Dollinger, 20 Conn. App. 530, 568 A.2d 1058

Increasingly, children who may be sexually abused are referred to centers specializing in interviewing children and conducting thorough medical evaluations. Such centers have a multidisciplinary staff, often composed of physicians, nurses, and nonmedical professionals with expertise on child sexual abuse. The child is interviewed and receives a medical examination. Part of the examination consists of taking the medical history, including a description of abuse. If evidence of sexual abuse is discovered, the professional documents the evidence for purposes of treatment and use in possible legal proceedings. The professional may prescribe appropriate medical or psychological treatment.

The argument is sometimes made that children's statements to physicians and other employees of specialized centers are made for purposes of diagnosis only, and not for purposes of treatment. Moreover, critics argue that professionals in specialized centers are as interested in prosecution as in treatment. The perceived alignment with law enforcement, emphasis on diagnosis, and deemphasis of treatment prompts critics to conclude that children's statements to professionals at specialized centers should not be admitted under the diagnosis or treatment exception. This argument besmirches the integrity of professionals working in specialized centers and finds virtually no support in the literature or experience.[555] Admittedly, a few medical or mental health workers may lose

---

(1990) (rejecting defendant's argument that child's mother took child to professional not to seek treatment but to gain advantage in custody battle); 4 Weinstein & Berger ¶ 803(4)[01], at 803-145, where the authors write:

> Nor need the statements refer to the *declarant's* physical condition. Statements relating to someone else's symptoms, pains, or sensations would be admissible, provided again, that they were made for purposes of diagnosis or treatment. The relationship between declarant and patient will usually determine admissibility. In the case of a child, a court would undoubtedly assume the absence of any motive to mislead on the part of his parents.

Naturally, Weinstein and Berger's observation holds true only in cases where the parents are not suspected of inflicting abuse on their child.

[555] *See* State v. Jones, 89 N.C. App. 584, 367 S.E.2d 139 (1988). In *Jones,* the four-year-old victim was taken by her mother to a child protection center for evaluation of suspected sexual abuse. The child was interviewed by a social worker. During the interview the child described abuse by the defendant. Following the social worker's interview and a physical examination, professionals at the center concluded the child had been sexually abused. The child received psychotherapy. At trial, the social worker repeated the child's statements during the interview. The court of appeals upheld admission of the statements under the diagnosis or treatment exception. In arguing against admission, the defendant pointed out that the child's mother was referred to the center by the prosecutor as well as by a psychologist. Defense counsel asserted that the victim's statements to the interviewer "were not for the purpose of treatment or diagnosis, but were instead for the purpose of gathering evidence for the State." 367 S.E.2d at 144. The court remarked that one factor considered "[i]n determining the purpose of a medical examination [is] whether the examination was requested by persons involved in the prosecution of the case." *Id.* However, the fact that the

their professional bearings and become "cops in white coats." However, the overwhelming majority of professionals working in specialized centers concentrate their efforts on providing high-quality medical and mental health services for children. These professionals are aware of the forensic implications of their work, but the primary emphasis remains diagnosis and treatment. If anything, the expertise of these professionals enhances the trustworthiness of children's statements. As with all statements offered under the diagnosis or treatment exception, the inquiry should be whether the rationale supporting the exception is present. The argument that medical and mental health professionals who devote their professional energies to assisting abused children are not to be trusted is as cynical as it is meritless.

§ 7.36 —Rationales for Exception

The primary rationale supporting admission of statements for purposes of diagnosis or treatment is the patient's self-interest in accuracy.[556] In addition to the patient's self-interest, a second rationale supports the exception. The second rationale is described in an opinion by Justice Powell following his retirement from the Supreme Court. Justice Powell sat by designation on *Morgan v. Foretich*.[557] In a concurring and dissenting opinion, Justice Powell wrote that at common law "a fact reliable enough to serve as a basis for a physician's diagnosis or treatment generally is considered sufficiently reliable to escape hearsay proscription."[558] Along similar lines, Weinstein and Berger write that "the integrity and specialized skill of the expert will keep him from basing his opinion on questionable matter. . . . [A]s a matter of policy, a fact reliable enough to serve as the basis for a diagnosis is also reliable enough to escape hearsay proscription."[559] McCormick adds that "[t]he general reliance upon 'subjective' facts by the medical profession and the ability of its members to evaluate the accuracy of statements made to them is considered sufficient protection against

---

child was referred by the prosecutor did not mean the child's statements were inadmissible. Other factors supported admission of the child's statements.

See also United States v. Iron Shell, 633 F.2d 77, 83 (8th Cir. 1980), *cert. denied,* 450 U.S. 1001 (1981) (rejecting defendant's argument that physician who examined child on night of assault was really an investigator "seeking to solve a crime, rather than a doctor treating or diagnosing a patient"); United States v. Cottriel, 21 M.J. 535 (N.M.C.M.R. 1985); Flanagan v. State, 586 So. 2d 1085 (Fla. Dist. Ct. App. 1991) (doctor who was part of child protection team not arm of law enforcement); State v. Aguallo, 318 N.C. 590, 350 S.E.2d 76, 79-80 (1986) (rejecting defense claim that doctor was simply gathering evidence for the state).

[556] R.S. v. Knighton, 125 N.J. 79, 592 A.2d 1157 (1991).

[557] 846 F.2d 941 (4th Cir. 1988) (Powell, J., concurring and dissenting).

[558] *Id.* at 951 (Powell, J., concurring and dissenting).

[559] 4 Weinstein & Berger ¶ 803(4)[01], at 803-146.

contrived symptoms."[560] Thus, the second rationale for the diagnosis or treatment exception is the doctor's special skill.

In sum, the diagnosis or treatment exception finds support in two rationales. The first is the patient's self-interest, which lowers the hearsay risks to acceptable levels. The second is the unique skill of physicians, which allows them to differentiate accurate from inaccurate information. Each rationale, standing alone, provides sufficient justification for admitting hearsay under the diagnosis or treatment exception. In an increasing number of decisions, however, courts combine the two rationales into one, two-part test, in which both rationales must be present before a statement is admissible under the exception. The trend toward combining the two rationales into a single test began with the Eighth Circuit Court of Appeals's decision in *United States v. Iron Shell*,[561] a child abuse case. The Eighth Circuit recognized that the two rationales are independent. For reasons that do not appear in the opinion, however, the court combined the two rationales into one test. In a later decision, *United States v. Renville*,[562] the Eighth Circuit described its two-part test as follows: "first, the declarant's motive in making the statement must be consistent with the purposes of promoting treatment; *and* second, the content of the statement must be such as is reasonably relied on by a physician in treatment or diagnosis."[563] Several courts have adopted the Eighth Circuit's two-part test.[564]

Combining the two rationales is analytically questionable and potentially counterproductive. Cases arise in which one of the rationales is absent, yet the hearsay is reliable. For example, suppose a young child makes a statement to a doctor without understanding the need to be truthful with the doctor. The first rationale is absent. Yet, the child's statement may supply the type of information physicians reasonably rely on in diagnosing or treating patients, and, for this reason, the statement may be sufficiently reliable to be admitted. Under the Eighth Circuit's two-part test, the statement may be inadmissible because only one of the rationales is present. If the Eighth Circuit recognized that each rationale stands on its own, the child's statement might be admissible.

Alternatively, suppose a child makes a statement to a doctor with the actual, subjective belief that the doctor needs the information to treat the child. However, the child is mistaken. The information is irrelevant to diagnosis or treatment. The first rationale for the exception is present, but the second is not. Under the Eighth Circuit's test, the child's statement may have to fulfill both rationales, and, since it does not, the statement may be inadmissible despite fulfilling the traditional rationale supporting the exception.

---

[560] McCormick § 293, at 842 (footnote omitted).

[561] 633 F.2d 77 (8th Cir. 1980), *cert. denied*, 450 U.S. 1001 (1981).

[562] 779 F.2d 430 (8th Cir. 1985).

[563] *Id.* at 436 (emphasis added).

[564] *See* Morgan v. Foretich, 846 F.2d 941 (4th Cir. 1988); State v. Robinson, 153 Ariz. 191, 735 P.2d 801, 809 (1987).

§ 7.36 RATIONALES FOR EXCEPTION

A more useful approach to the diagnosis or treatment exception is to recognize the independent validity of both rationales. Although it may be true that in most cases hearsay offered under this exception achieves greatest trustworthiness when both rationales are present, some reliable hearsay finds support in only one of the rationales. The fact that only one of the rationales is present should not lead automatically to exclusion.

When considering the applicability of the diagnosis or treatment exception to children, it is useful to focus on each rationale supporting the exception. Concentrating first on the self-interest rationale, a number of courts question whether young children understand the importance of being truthful with health care providers.[565] Mosteller urges that admission of statements under the self-interest rationale should turn on the patient's understanding that personal well-being is likely to be affected by the statement to the doctor.[566]

Children's comprehension of the need for accuracy with doctors is a question of developmental psychology, not law. The medical and psychological literature contain information on children's understanding of illness and the roles of medical professionals. As one would expect, children's understanding follows a developmental progression.[567] One author concludes, "Logical concepts such as

---

[565] Ring v. Erickson, 1992 WL 155797 (8th Cir. 1992); Morgan v. Foretich, 846 F.2d 941, 951-53 (4th Cir. 1988) (Powell, J., concurring and dissenting); State v. Robinson, 153 Ariz. 191, 735 P.2d 801, 809 (1987) ("Because of their young age, sexually abused children may not always grasp the relation between their statements and receiving medical treatment. It is particularly important, therefore, to ask whether the information sought by the treating doctor was reasonably pertinent to effective treatment"); Oldsen v. People, 732 P.2d 1132, 1135-36 (Colo. 1986) (child was incompetent to testify and there was no evidence she was capable of understanding "the need to provide accurate information for purposes of medical diagnosis or treatment"); W.C.L. v. People, 685 P.2d 176, 181 (Colo. 1984); Cassidy v. State, 74 Md. App. 1, 536 A.2d 666, 680, *cert. denied,* 312 Md. 602, 541 A.2d 965 (1988) ("the two-year-old declarant in this case lacked the motive or purpose which is the heart of the trustworthiness guarantee"); People v. Meeboer, 484 N.W.2d 621 (Mich. 1992); State v. Harris, 247 Mont. 405, 808 P.2d 453 (1991); State v. Boston, 46 Ohio St. 3d 108, 545 N.E.2d 1220, 1234 (1989); Fleming v. State, 819 S.W.2d 237 (Tex. Ct. App. 1991).

[566] Mosteller, *Child Sexual Abuse and Statements for the Purpose of Medical Diagnosis or Treatment,* 67 N.C. L. Rev. 257, 268 (1989).

[567] Bibace & Walsh, *Children's Conceptions of Illness, in* New Directions for Child Development: Children's Conceptions of Health, Illness, and Bodily Functions 31, 33 (R. Bibace & M. Walsh eds., No. 16, 1981) ("the child's concept of illness changes in certain specifiable directions with age and/or development. . . . [It] is clearly related to the child's developmental status"); Bibace & Walsh, *Development of Children's Concepts of Illness,* 66 Pediatrics 912 (1980); Brewster, *Chronically Ill Hospitalized Children's Concepts of Their Illness,* 69 Pediatrics 355 (1982); Burbach & Peterson, *Children's Concepts of Physical Illness: A Review and Critique of the Cognitive-Development Literature,* 5 Health Psychol. 307, 315 (1986) ("Children's overall understanding of illness concepts increases with age"); Eiser, Patterson & Tripp, *Illness Experience and Children's Concepts of Health and Illness,* 10 Child Care Health & Development 157 (1984); Neuhauser, Amsterdam, Hines & Steward, *Children's Concepts of Healing: Cognitive Development and Locus of Control Factors,* 48 Am. J. Orthopsychiatry 335 (1978); Perrin, Sayer & Willett, *Sticks and Stones May Break*

cause of illness, necessity of treatment, and role of medical personnel are often beyond the inherent developmental ability of the young patient."[568]

Two examples from the writing of child psychologist Margaret Steward provide insight into children's knowledge. Steward describes three-year-old Sammy, who was knocked off his tricycle by a passing car, causing a concussion and fractured skull. When Steward interviewed Sammy in the pediatric ward, he was a solemn little boy. Steward talked with Sammy about being in the hospital, and asked, "Are the doctors helping you get well?" Sammy replied, "No, the doctors are berry mean." Little Sammy did not understand that the unfamiliar and sometimes painful things the doctors did to him were designed to help him. To Sammy, the doctors were "berry mean."[569]

Steward offers another illustration of the limits of young children's understanding. In a study involving kindergartners and third-graders, the kindergartners knew that a hypodermic syringe was used to give shots, but many of the young children did not understand why shots were given. By contrast, most third-graders, that is, eight- and nine-year-olds, knew shots were given to prevent or cure illness.[570]

The literature indicates that some three- to six-year-olds believe medical procedures are administered as punishment because they have been bad.[571] Children

---

My Bones . . . Reasoning about Illness Causality and Body Functioning in Children Who Have a Chronic Illness, 88 Pediatrics 608 (1991); Perrin & Gerrity, *There's a Demon in Your Belly: Children's Understanding of Illness,* 67 Pediatrics 841 (1981); Potter & Roberts, *Children's Perceptions of Chronic Illness: The Roles of Disease Symptoms, Cognitive Development, and Information,* 9 J. Pediatric Psychol. 13 (1984); Steward, *Illness: A Crisis for Children, in* Crisis Counseling, Intervention, and Prevention in the Schools 109, 123 (J. Sandoval ed. 1988) ("Children's understanding of medical procedures done for diagnostic and therapeutic purposes also seems to follow a developmental progression").

[568] Brewster, *Chronically Ill Hospitalized Children's Concepts of Their Illness,* 69 Pediatrics 355, 361 (1982).

[569] Steward & Steward, *Children's Conceptions of Medical Procedures, in* New Directions for Child Development: Children's Conceptions of Health, Illness, and Bodily Functions 67 (R. Bibace & M. Walsh eds., No. 16, 1981). A young child might mistakenly conclude that the doctor actually caused the illness. *See* Redpath & Rogers, *Healthy Young Children's Concepts of Hospitals, Medical Personnel, Operations, and Illness,* 9 J. Pediatric Psychol. 29, 37-38 (1984) ("Because of the tendency of preschoolers to confuse cause and effect, clinicians or teachers working with them should be prepared to help these youngsters understand that body state, germs, and/or accidents, not the doctor, may be the cause of illness").

[570] Steward & Regalbuto, *Do Doctors Know What Children Know?,* 45 Am. J. Orthopsychiatry 146 (1975).

[571] Bibace & Walsh, *Children's Conceptions of Illness, in* New Directions for Child Development: Children's Conceptions of Health, Illness, and Bodily Functions 31 (R. Bibace & M. Walsh eds., No. 16, 1981); Brewster, *Chronically Ill Hospitalized Children's Concepts of Their Illness,* 69 Pediatrics, 355 (1982); Perrin & Gerrity, *There's a Demon in Your Belly: Children's Understanding of Illness,* 67 Pediatrics 841, 846 (1981) ("Children's ideas regarding illness frequently involve punishment, guilt, and self-blame. . . . Hospitalized children often ascribe the cause of their illness to disobedience of parental commands and

of this tender age may not associate doctors with health or illness.[572] By the time children reach age five or six, most understand that the purpose of medical procedures is to help them get well.

The diagnosis or treatment exception was designed with adults in mind. When the exception is applied to young children, the developmental fit may not be very good, raising legitimate questions about young children's understanding of the need for truthfulness with the doctor, and casting doubt on the reliability of certain statements by young children. It is important to add, however, that children of a particular age are far from uniform.[573] One four-year-old may understand quite clearly the need for accuracy with the doctor, while another may not.[574] Assessment of children's understanding should proceed on a case-by-case basis.[575]

Children's understanding of the relationship between what they say and their well-being may be particularly tenuous when the professional is not a physician or nurse providing traditional medical care, but a psychiatrist, psychologist, or

---

interpret their hospitalization as rejection or punishment"); Burbach & Peterson, *Children's Concepts of Physical Illness: A Review and Critique of the Cognitive-Developmental Literature,* 5 Health Psychol. 307, 318 (1986) ("Older, less anxious, and cognitively mature children seemed to reject the notion that illness and misbehavior are related. Younger, highly anxious, and less cognitively mature children did perceive of illness in a moralistic way and, furthermore, exhibited more self-blame for the etiology of illness").

[572] Steward & Regalbuto, *Do Doctors Know What Children Know?,* 45 Am. J. Orthopsychiatry 146, 149 (1975) ("kindergartners did not associate doctors with health or illness").

[573] *See* Burbach & Peterson, *Children's Concepts of Physical Illness: A Review and Critique of the Cognitive-Developmental Literature,* 5 Health Psychol. 307, 308 (1986) ("age simply is not an accurate predictor of cognitive maturity").

[574] United States v. Edens, 31 M.J. 267 (C.M.A. 1990) (statements by three- and five-year-olds admissible); State v. Dollinger, 20 Conn. App. 530, 568 A.2d 1058, 1061 (1990) (statements by two-and-one-half-year-old admissible); State v. Maldonado, 13 Conn. App. 368, 536 A.2d 600 (1988) (three-and-one-half-year-old understood need to be truthful); Commonwealth v. Sanford, 397 Pa. Super. 581, 580 A.2d 784, 791-92 (1990) (statements by three-year-old admissible); State v. Sorenson, 143 Wis. 2d 226, 421 N.W.2d 77, 87 (1988) (children as young as three can understand the need to be truthful with doctor); State v. Nelson, 138 Wis. 2d 418, 406 N.W.2d 385 (1987) (court held that a three-year-old was capable of understanding need to tell the truth to doctor; "We do not believe that, because a child is only three or four years of age at the time he or she goes to a doctor, the child is unable to comprehend that the child is involved in the process of receiving diagnosis or treatment").

[575] United States v. Cherry, 938 F.2d 748, 757 (7th Cir. 1991); United States v. Edens, 31 M.J. 267, 269 (C.M.A. 1990); Cook v. Hoppin, 783 F.2d 684, 690 (7th Cir. 1986); People v. Meeboer, 484 N.W.2d 621 (Mich. 1992); State v. Moen, 309 Or. 45, 786 P.2d 111, 119 (1990) (declarant's "motive in making the statements at issue must necessarily be determined by reference to the circumstances in which they were made"); State v. Logan, 105 Or. App. 556, 806 P.2d 137, 139 (1991) ("We cannot say as a matter of law that a four-year old child is too young to understand the nature of a medical examination. The decision must be based on the facts in each case").

social worker providing psychological treatment.[576] There are several reasons why a child may not understand the special need to be accurate with the psychotherapist. The child may not understand that sessions with the professional are therapeutic. Psychotherapy usually occurs in surroundings that would not remind a child of a "doctor's office." Psychotherapy is likely to occur in a comfortable room with soft furniture. The room may be filled with toys, and the child may be encouraged to play.[577] Some courts limit the medical diagnosis or treatment exception to statements to physicians providing traditional medical care. Other courts admit statements to mental health professionals.[578] A categorical rule against admitting statements to mental health professionals should be rejected in favor of individualized analysis. If one or both of the rationales supporting the exception is present, the statement may be admitted.[579]

---

[576] *See* People v. LaLone, 432 Mich. 103, 437 N.W.2d 611, 613 (1989) ("statements made in the course of the treatment of psychological disorders may not always be as reliable as those made in the course of the treatment of physical disorders"); 4 Louisell & Mueller § 444, at 610–12; Mosteller, *Child Sexual Abuse and Statements for the Purpose of Medical Diagnosis or Treatment,* 67 N.C. L. Rev. 257, 268 (1989).

[577] In State v. Nelson, 138 Wis. 2d 418, 406 N.W.2d 385 (1987), the Supreme Court of Wisconsin ruled that a child's statements to a psychologist during psychotherapy were sufficiently reliable to be admitted under the diagnosis or treatment exception. The court wrote:

> In the present case a number of factors support a finding that T.N. was aware that her statements were being used as a basis for medical diagnosis or treatment. T.N.'s sessions with Dr. McClean, although mainly conducted in a play therapy room, were scheduled and conducted in a manner consistent with the provision of diagnosis and treatment. Dr. McClean had a waiting room in which T.N. and her mother would await their regularly scheduled appointments. T.N. was aware that she saw Dr. McClean on an appointment basis and that he was not her peer. Very early in the treatment, Dr. McClean made it clear to T.N. that he was an authority figure, not a playmate. T.N. began her treatment with Dr. McClean by undergoing a series of tests and evaluations. Although most of the sessions were conducted in a play therapy room, T.N. would occasionally sit and speak with Dr. McClean in his formal office. T.N. was described as a very intelligent child. We conclude that T.N. was aware that she was being observed, with a goal towards treatment.
>
> Furthermore, there is nothing in the record to indicate that T.N.'s motive in making the statements to Dr. McClean and Dr. Silberglitt was other than as a patient seeking treatment. It is always difficult for a court to determine whether a very young child completely understands the context in which information is sought from the child. However, we do not believe that, because a child is only three or four years of age at the time he or she goes to a doctor, the child is unable to comprehend that the child is involved in the process of receiving diagnosis or treatment. A child is no less aware of the existence of emotional or mental pain than physical pain and, thus, is equally aware of the necessity and beneficial nature of therapy.

406 N.W.2d at 390–91.

[578] *See* State v. Robinson, 153 Ariz. 191, 735 P.2d 801 (1987); State v. Nelson, 138 Wis. 2d 418, 406 N.W.2d 385, 390 (1987) ("we recognize that statements made to a psychologist, if made for the purposes of diagnosis or treatment, are also admissible").

[579] *See* 4 Weinstein & Berger ¶ 803(4)[01], at 803-150.

Turning to the second rationale supporting the diagnosis or treatment exception, statements to physicians are considered reliable because of the special skill of the doctor. When it comes to child sexual abuse, however, this rationale is lacking in some cases. The psychological and developmental aspects of child sexual abuse are more complex than the typical broken bone or sore throat. Moreover, most physicians lack expertise regarding child sexual abuse. Finally, many of the professionals making diagnostic and treatment decisions about child sexual abuse are not physicians, and some of these nonmedical professionals are not highly trained.[580] Thus, in some cases, with some professionals, the second rationale for this exception is lacking.

Several factors may increase confidence that a child's statement meets the requirements of the diagnosis or treatment exception.[581] In some cases there is concrete evidence that the child understood the purpose of treatment and understood the need to be truthful and accurate.[582] For example, a child's medical record may reveal that the professional informed the child of the purpose of the examination or interview.[583] Some children have a history of involvement with medical professionals.[584] The experience of such children may increase their understanding of the purpose of medical treatment and the importance of candor.

In *State v. Ochoa*,[585] the Florida Court of Appeal rejected the argument that the child must be available at trial to determine whether the requirements of the medical diagnosis or treatment exception are satisfied. The court wrote that "[w]here, as here, the declarant is unavailable, the necessary predicate can be established through other evidence. In the present case, that was done by the testimony of the examining physician."[586]

---

[580] *See* Mosteller, *Child Sexual Abuse and Statements for the Purpose of Medical Diagnosis or Treatment,* 67 N.C. L. Rev. 257 (1989).

[581] *See* State v. Larson, 472 N.W.2d 120, 126 (Minn. 1991), *cert. denied,* 112 S. Ct. 965 (1992) (discussing seven factors that indicated reliability).

[582] State v. Larson, 472 N.W.2d 120, 126 (Minn. 1991), *cert. denied,* 112 S. Ct. 965 (1992) (child knew she was being examined in doctor's office); Fleming v. State, 819 S.W.2d 237 (Tex. Ct. App. 1991).

[583] *See* Morgan v. Foretich, 846 F.2d 941, 949 (4th Cir. 1988) (Powell, J., concurring and dissenting) (Justice Powell was concerned that psychologist did not explain to child "that his questions and relationship with her arise, at least in part, from a desire to treat her"); United States v. Dean, 31 M.J. 196 (C.M.A. 1990), *cert. denied,* 111 S. Ct. 1106 (1991); United States v. Armstrong, 33 M.J. 1011, 1013 (A.C.M.R. 1991); United States v. Miller, 32 M.J. 843 (N.M.C.M.R. 1991); United States v. Tornowski, 29 M.J. 578 (A.F.C.M.R. 1989); State v. Ochoa, 576 So. 2d 854, 856 (Fla. Dist. Ct. App. 1991) ("The doctor introduced himself as such"); State v. Logan, 105 Or. App. 556, 806 P.2d 137 (1991) (physician informed child she was a doctor and was going to do a checkup).

[584] State v. Logan, 105 Or. App. 556, 806 P.2d 137, 139 (1991) (child had been to doctor before).

[585] 576 So. 2d 854 (Fla. Dist. Ct. App. 1991).

[586] *Id.* at 856.

In *Oldsen v. People*,[587] the Colorado Supreme Court discussed the impact of testimonial incompetence on admissibility of children's statements under the diagnosis or treatment exception.[588] In *Oldsen* the five-year-old victim made statements to a physician and a mental health professional. The record was devoid of evidence that at the time of the child's statements she understood "the need to provide accurate information for purposes of medical diagnosis or treatment within the meaning of [Colorado Rules of Evidence] 803(4)."[589] At trial, the child was testimonially incompetent.[590] The Supreme Court wrote:

> [A] finding that a child is incompetent to testify . . . does not automatically render inadmissible all hearsay statements of the child . . . . However, where the asserted exception depends on the declarant's ability to understand the purpose of questioning and to relate accurate information, it is significant that the declarant has been disqualified . . . .[591]

Of course, as the *Oldsen* court recognized, a child who cannot testify competently at trial may nevertheless have understood the necessity, at an earlier time, of truthfulness with a health care provider. In *Morgan v. Foretich*,[592] the party accused of abuse argued that the child's testimonial incompetence at trial rendered her statements to a psychologist inadmissible. The court rejected the argument, writing that "[a]n individual's statements made for purposes of medical diagnosis or treatment have frequently been admitted into evidence regardless of whether that individual was competent to testify at trial."[593]

In the final analysis, many statements by children—even preschool children—meet the requirements of the diagnosis or treatment exception. In other cases, doubts arise about the applicability of the exception; yet, the statement seems trustworthy. In such cases, the best course is sometimes to depart the diagnosis or treatment exception and to resort to a residual or child hearsay exception.[594]

§ 7.37 Past Recollection Recorded

Memory being what it is, people forget. If the forgetful witness made a record of the now-forgotten event when the event was fresh in memory, the record

---

[587] 732 P.2d 1132 (Colo. 1986).

[588] *See also* W.C.L. v. People, 685 P.2d 176 (Colo. 1984).

[589] 732 P.2d at 1135 (footnote omitted).

[590] It appeared the child was psychologically conflicted about testifying.

[591] 732 P.2d at 1135.

[592] 846 F.2d 941 (4th Cir. 1988).

[593] *Id.* at 949.

[594] *See* United States v. Dean, 31 M.J. 196 (C.M.A. 1990), *cert. denied*, 111 S. Ct. 1106 (1991); Oldsen v. People, 732 P.2d 1132 (Colo. 1986) (ruling that lower court erred in admitting five-year-old's statement under diagnosis or treatment exception; however, child's statements were admissible under residual exception).

§ 7.37 PAST RECOLLECTION RECORDED

may be admissible under the hearsay exception for past recollection recorded. Rule 803(5) states:

> The following are not excluded by the hearsay rule, even though the declarant is available as a witness: A memorandum or record concerning a matter about which a witness once had knowledge but now has insufficient recollection to enable the witness to testify fully and accurately, shown to have been made or adopted by the witness when the matter was fresh in the witness' memory and to reflect that knowledge correctly. If admitted, the memorandum or record may be read into evidence but may not itself be received as an exhibit unless offered by an adverse party.

Documents containing past recollections are reliable for several reasons.[595] First, since the document is made while memory is fresh, the risk of memory loss is low. Second, in some cases the document is made under circumstances likely to impress the declarant with the importance of accuracy. Third, Rule 803(5) requires that the document accurately reflect the declarant's knowledge. Fourth, although the declarant cannot be cross-examined about the now-forgotten event, the declarant can be cross-examined about the document containing the recorded recollection as well as other matters. Indeed, the fact that the witness has forgotten the event may help the cross-examiner, who can urge the jury to give the document little weight because its author is forgetful and thus a doubtful witness.[596] Added to these markers of reliability is the need to admit past recollection recorded. Because the declarant has forgotten the underlying event, the record may be the only available evidence.

The proponent of a writing as past recollection recorded must fulfill four requirements. The trial judge determines pursuant to Rule 104(a) whether the requirements are satisfied.[597] The court usually conducts an admissibility hearing outside the presence of the jury.

The first requirement is that the declarant have insufficient recollection to testify fully and accurately about the event.[598] Feigned memory loss is probably sufficient.[599] Complete lapse of memory is unnecessary.[600] The normal practice is to use the document in an effort to refresh the witness's recollection.[601] When refreshment fails, memory lapse is demonstrated. Weinstein and Berger write:

---

[595] *See* 4 Louisell & Mueller § 445, at 618.

[596] *See* United States v. Owens, 484 U.S. 554 (1988) (pointing out memory problems may be the very purpose of cross-examination).

[597] 4 Louisell & Mueller § 445, at 642-43.

[598] United States v. Gans, 32 M.J. 412 (C.M.A. 1991) (very instructive analysis of past recollection recorded exception).

[599] 4 Louisell & Mueller § 445, at 623 ("Probably use of Rule 803(5) is proper even in cases in which it is suspected that the claimed lack of memory is phony") (footnote omitted).

[600] United States v. Gans, 32 M.J. 412 (C.M.A. 1991); 4 Weinstein & Berger ¶ 803(5)[01], at 803-159 ("memory need not be wholly exhausted before the memorandum can be used").

[601] 4 Louisell & Mueller § 445, at 619.

If the witness answers some questions without hesitation, but then becomes vague or evasive or claims he cannot remember a particular aspect of the event in question, even after he has been shown the memorandum to refresh his recollection, the trial judge should admit at least those portions of the memorandum which failed to restore his memory. Admissibility should be determined on a question by question basis rather than by viewing the witness' testimony as a whole.[602]

The exception for past recollection recorded is useful when a witness remembers the general contours of an event but has forgotten relevant details.[603] For example, a child may remember an abusive episode, but forget penetration. If the requirements of the exception are fulfilled, a document containing the child's description of penetration is admissible under the exception.

It is worth recalling the difference between refreshing recollection and past recollection recorded.[604] A witness's memory may be refreshed with anything that revives memory.[605] Once the witness's memory is refreshed, the witness testifies from present recollection. The document or other item used to refresh recollection is not admitted in evidence. By contrast, with past recollection recorded, the witness is unable to remember the event despite efforts to refresh recollection, and the document is offered for the truth of the matter asserted. Thus, a document used to refresh recollection is not evidence, whereas a document offered as past recollection recorded is substantive evidence.

The second requirement for past recollection recorded is that the document correctly reflect the declarant's knowledge of the now-forgotten event.[606] The dilemma, of course, is proving that a document accurately reflects an event that the author cannot remember. Declarants sometimes remember making an accurate record of an event even though the event has faded. In many cases, however, the declarant remembers neither the event nor the document. On this score Louisell and Mueller write:

> When [the declarant] cannot recall preparing the record despite the fact that the occasion was unique or non-routine in his life, perhaps simply because of the passage of time, or for indeterminable reasons which may spring from psychology or interest, the question arises whether it suffices to satisfy the second

---

[602] 4 Weinstein & Berger ¶ 803(5)[01], at 803-159 to 803-160 (footnotes omitted).

[603] See 4 Louisell & Mueller § 445, at 622, where the authors write:

> [I]t is proper to use past recollection recorded to establish specific points which the witness recalls on the stand only generally (that the accident occurred at 9:30 AM, for example, where the witness only remembers that it was "in the morning"), and to bring out details which the witness has forgotten altogether (the license number of the getaway car, for example, where the witness remembers only the make and color).

See also 4 Weinstein & Berger ¶ 803(5)[01], at 803-160.

[604] 4 Weinstein & Berger ¶ 803(5)[01], at 803-157.

[605] See **Ch. 5** for discussion of refreshing recollection.

[606] The declarant must have had personal knowledge of the event. 4 Weinstein & Berger ¶ 803(5), at 803-162.

requirement if he testifies simply that he would not have signed or prepared the record if it were not true. Commentators have suggested, albeit reluctantly, that such a response suffices if none better may be had, and some cases go along. A statement of this sort is nothing more than an assertion of general honesty and integrity which sheds only a very faint circumstantial light upon the making of the statement in question, and represents the kind of thing that nearly anyone would be willing to say under pressure by questioning counsel nearly always. Accepting such a statement as enough tends to make the accuracy requirement a sham, which suggests at least that trial judges should have discretion to exclude statements offered on this basis where accuracy is suspect. And some decisions in fact require exclusion where the witness can be led only to such a minimal endorsement.[607]

Suppose a child not only claims to forget the underlying event, but repudiates as false the document offered as past recollection recorded? Rule 803(5) requires the child to affirm the document as an accurate reflection of the child's knowledge. It seems under these circumstances that the requirements of the exception cannot be satisfied.[608] In such cases the document may be inconsistent with the child's trial testimony, in which case the document may be used to impeach the child or, if the requirements of Rule 801(d)(1)(A) are fulfilled, as substantive evidence.[609]

The third requirement for past recollection recorded is that the record be made or adopted by the declarant. The declarant's own writing will do. The rule does not require formalities such as signature, attestation, acknowledgement, or oath.[610] Thus, a child's diary may qualify. Audio and videotaped statements also qualify. A document prepared by someone else may be adopted by the child.[611]

In child abuse cases, the child may be interviewed by an adult who takes notes of the child's statements. The interviewer's notes may be admissible under this exception if the child adopted the notes. In such cases, however, two witnesses are required to lay the foundation.[612] The child establishes that an event

---

[607] 4 Louisell & Mueller § 445, at 625-27 (footnotes omitted). *See also* McCormick § 303, at 868; 4 Weinstein & Berger ¶ 803(5)[01], at 803-166 (the witness "can testify that he recognizes his handwriting and would not have written, signed, initialed or marked the memorandum, as the case may be, unless he had been convinced it was correct").

[608] 4 Louisell & Mueller § 445, at 629 ("Where the person who made or adopted a statement either repudiates it at trial, or fails completely to endorse the statement as accurate, it should not be received under Rule 803(5)").

[609] 4 Weinstein & Berger ¶ 803(5)[01], at 803-160.

[610] 4 Louisell & Mueller § 445, at 633.

[611] 4 Weinstein & Berger ¶ 803(5)[01], at 803-166 ("The witness need not himself have been the person who actually wrote the memorandum. It is admissible if the witness can testify that he saw the memorandum when the matter it concerned was fresh in his memory, and that he then knew it to be correct. Only the witness who adopted the memorandum need be called").

[612] 4 Louisell & Mueller § 445, at 634; 4 Weinstein & Berger ¶ 803(5)[01], at 803-166.

occurred that cannot be remembered. The child also testifies that during the interview the child accurately described the event to the interviewer. The interviewer testifies that the notes accurately reflect what the child said.

The fourth requirement for past recollection recorded is that the document be made when the event is fresh in the declarant's memory. The time requirement is flexible.[613] Weinstein and Berger write:

> In determining whether the matter was sufficiently fresh to guarantee the memory's trustworthiness, the trial judge will probably wish to take into account such factors as the time when the memorandum was made, the quality of the memory embodied in the memorandum, whether it was made before the litigation commenced, whether it was made spontaneously or in answer to a request by an interested party and other pertinent circumstances.[614]

An out-of-court statement that would not qualify as an excited utterance may be admissible as past recollection recorded. It is worth noting that unlike the excited utterance exception, the exception for past recollection recorded does not require that the event be startling.

A child's statement offered as past recollection recorded is admissible against the defendant in a criminal case despite the fact that the defendant cannot cross-examine the child about the underlying event.[615] "[C]ourts have consistently rejected defense challenges under the Confrontation Clause to the use against the accused of past recollection recorded."[616]

Rule 803(5) provides that the document may be read to the jury, but may not be received as an exhibit.[617] The jury may not take the document to the jury room during deliberations. If the document is an audio or videotape of the child, the tape is played for the jury. The opponent may make the document or tape an exhibit.[618]

§ 7.38 Business Records

The business records exception is found in Rule 803(6) of the Federal Rules of Evidence. Rule 803(6) is very broad, covering records "in any form." The exception provides:

---

[613] 4 Louisell & Mueller § 445, at 638.

[614] 4 Weinstein & Berger ¶ 803(5)[01], at 803-164 to 803-165.

[615] *Id.* at 803-161 to 803-162.

[616] 4 Louisell & Mueller § 445, at 641 (footnote omitted).

[617] *See* 4 Weinstein & Berger ¶ 803(5)[01], at 803-168 ("Upon stipulation the document may be sent into the jury. If there is no such stipulation the jury can be called back and the document read to it").

[618] 4 Louisell & Mueller § 445, at 645 ("if the opponent of the offering party offers the memorandum or record, clearly it may be received as an exhibit for all purposes, and may properly be given to the jury during deliberations").

§ 7.38 BUSINESS RECORDS

The following are not excluded by the hearsay rule, even though the declarant is available as a witness: A memorandum, report, record, or data compilation, in any form, of acts, events, conditions, opinions, or diagnoses, made at or near the time by, or from information transmitted by, a person with knowledge, if kept in the course of a regularly conducted business activity, and if it was the regular practice of that business activity to make the memorandum, report, record, or data compilation, all as shown by the testimony of the custodian or other qualified witness, unless the source of information or the method or circumstances of preparation indicate lack of trustworthiness. The term "business" as used in this paragraph includes business, institution, association, profession, occupation, and calling of every kind, whether or not conducted for profit.[619]

The business records exception is based on trustworthiness and necessity.[620] Business records are reliable because the individuals who produce them are charged with accuracy of record keeping. Trustworthiness is bolstered by the procedures established to produce and maintain records generated in the regular course of business. Moreover, the requirement that business records be prepared close in time to the event, and from information gleaned through personal knowledge, increases accuracy. In addition to trustworthiness, the need to admit records of regularly conducted activities justifies the business records exception. In many cases, the individual preparing business records observes hundreds of similar events and makes an equal number of records. The individual's memory for individual occurrences blurs with repetition; consequently the record of a particular episode becomes not only the best, but, in many cases, the only source of information.

The business records exception reaches much further than IBM and General Motors. The term *business* includes hospitals, clinics, nonprofit as well as for-profit organizations, and businesses large and small.[621] Thus, the records of a pediatrician or psychotherapist in private practice are potentially admissible under this exception. In addition to records of businesses and professionals in private practice, courts employ the business records exception to admit records of public entities.[622] Thus, the records of a public hospital or child protective service agency may be admitted as business records. It should be noted, however, that public records are not invariably admissible under the business records exception. The Federal Rules of Evidence provide a specific exception for public records.[623] The public records exception contains limitations on admission of public records against defendants in criminal litigation. To the extent the public

---

[619] Fed. R. Evid. 803(6).

[620] 4 Louisell & Mueller § 446, at 646–47.

[621] *See* State v. Brunette, 501 A.2d 419 (Me. 1985) (motel registration documents admissible under 803(6)).

[622] *See In re* J.L.G., 762 P.2d 42, 45 (Wyo. 1988) (termination of parental rights case; social services file admissible under 803(6)).

[623] Fed. R. Evid. 803(8), discussed in **§ 7.39**. See 4 Weinstein & Berger ¶ 803(6)[03], at 803-185.

records exception bars admission of public agency records against a defendant, a prosecutor may not circumvent the prohibitions established in the public records exception by resort to the business records exception.[624]

The business records exception has four requirements. The court determines pursuant to Rule 104(a) whether the requirements are fulfilled.

The first requirement is that the business have a practice of producing records, and that the proferred record be produced in the regular course of business.[625] Thus, medical records of hospital patients are within this exception. Weinstein and Berger urge that "Rule 803(6) should be interpreted so that the absence of routineness without more is not sufficiently significant to require exclusion of the record. Nonroutine records made in the course of a regularly conducted 'business' should be admissible if they meet the other requirements of Rule 803(6) . . . ."[626]

The second requirement of the business records exception is that the record be made at or near the time of the event memorialized in the record. The purpose here is to enhance accuracy by ensuring that the record is made when memory is fresh.[627] The time requirement is flexible, and the business records exception tolerates delays considerably longer than delays that satisfy the excited utterance exception.

The third requirement is that the record be made by, or from information transmitted by, a person with personal knowledge of the event. The original source of information must have personal knowledge.[628] A physician who examines a child and personally writes a medical record fulfills this requirement. It is not necessary, however, that the individual with personal knowledge actually create the record. For example, the physician who examined the child might dictate a medical record. The actual record is created by a typist in the hospital records department. The fact that the typist lacks personal knowledge of the child is immaterial because the source of the information in the report had personal knowledge.

---

[624] See 4 Louisell & Mueller § 452, at 711, where the authors write:

> Congress carefully amended Rule 803(8) so as to avoid qualifying certain kinds of public records when offered against the accused in a criminal case, and it would frustrate a clear congressional purpose to admit under Rule 803(6) records which could not be received under Rule 803(8) on account of these restrictions.

(footnote omitted). *See also* 4 Weinstein & Berger ¶ 803(8)[04].

[625] 4 Louisell & Mueller § 446, at 654.

[626] 4 Weinstein & Berger ¶ 803(6)[03], at 803-182.

[627] 4 Louisell & Mueller § 446, at 662.

[628] See *id.* at 659-60, where the authors write, "[T]he source of the information must be a person with knowledge. . . . The source must have personal knowledge, but others involved in the chain of transmission of the information ultimately recorded, including the person who physically causes the record to be made, need not have such knowledge." (footnote omitted).

§ 7.38 BUSINESS RECORDS

The fourth requirement of the business records exception is that the first three requirements be established through the testimony of the custodian of records or some other qualified witness.[629] The custodian need not have personal knowledge of the event described in the record. Nor is it required that the custodian have prepared the record. Thus, the custodian of medical records at a hospital can lay the foundation required by this exception. In addition to laying the foundation, the custodian authenticates the records.

Medical Records; Opinions and Diagnoses

Rule 803(6) authorizes admission of records containing a patient's medical history.[630] The exception also admits records documenting the patient's condition while in the hospital,[631] results of laboratory tests,[632] administration of treatments and medications, and autopsy reports.[633]

Rule 803(6) expressly allows records containing opinions and diagnoses. Before a diagnosis or professional opinion is admitted, however, the proponent should establish the expertise of the professional.[634] Battered child syndrome is a well-accepted medical diagnosis, and records containing this diagnosis should

---

[629] See 4 Weinstein & Berger ¶ 803(6)[02], at 803-177 to 803-178, where the authors write, "Records of regularly conducted activity are not normally self proving as public records may be. . . . The testimony of the custodian or other qualified witness who can explain the record-keeping of his organization is ordinarily essential. The phrase 'other qualified witness' should be given the broadest interpretation . . . ." (footnotes omitted). *See also* 4 Louisell & Mueller § 446, at 662.

[630] See 4 Louisell & Mueller § 451, at 695–97, where the authors write:

A patient's medical history is clearly provable by means of hospital records, including statements by the patient describing his symptoms and the cause of his injuries, insofar as such history and statements are germane to diagnosis or treatment . . . . Such records are also routinely received, and properly so, to prove the physical condition of the patient upon arrival at the hospital, and to prove relatively routine measurements taken during hospitalization (pulse, temperature, etc.), as well as treatment and medication administered.

(footnotes omitted). *See also* Ziegler v. Tarrant County Child Welfare Unit, 680 S.W.2d 674 (Tex. Ct. App. 1984) (medical records admissible under 803(6)).

[631] State v. Morrison, 437 N.W.2d 422 (Minn. Ct. App.), *cert. denied*, 493 U.S. 858 (1989) (autopsy report admissible under Rule 803(6)).

[632] Department of Social Welfare v. Miller, 595 A.2d 288 (Vt. 1991) (documents from private laboratory admissible to prove chain of custody of blood for paternity tests); State v. Thompson, 503 A.2d 689 (Me. 1986) (chain of custody of blood samples for paternity testing was properly established with documents admitted under business records exception); 4 Weinstein & Berger ¶ 803(6)[06], at 803-199. *But see* Grantham v. State, 580 So. 2d 53 (Ala. Crim. App. 1991) (Confrontation Clause barred admission of toxicologist's report when toxicologist was not available).

[633] State v. Morrison, 437 N.W.2d 422, 427 (Minn. Ct. App.), *cert. denied*, 493 U.S. 858 (1989); Vasquez v. State, 814 S.W.2d 773 (Tex. Ct. App. 1991).

[634] 4 Louisell & Mueller § 446, at 660.

be admitted.[635] It is less clear whether a diagnosis of child sexual abuse is admissible under the business records exception. Some professionals assert that diagnostic terminology is inapplicable to sexual abuse. Opponents of diagnostic terminology argue that sexual abuse is an event, not a diagnosable disease. The majority of professionals disagree with this reasoning, however, and assert that the word *diagnosis* is sufficiently flexible to cover sexual abuse.[636] Proponents of diagnostic terminology agree that sexual abuse is an event, but point out that physical abuse is an event, too. Like physical abuse, sexual abuse sometimes has diagnosable physical and psychological effects.[637] The American Academy of Child and Adolescent Psychiatry states that "[t]he effects of child sexual abuse are diagnosable in the same sense that other medical conditions are diagnosable . . . ."[638] In some cases, medical evidence points strongly to sexual abuse, and in such cases the diagnosis should be admissible under the business records exception. In other cases, the evidence is less clear, and the diagnosis depends largely on the child's statement and the professional's assessment of psychological factors. Some courts demonstrate reluctance to admit diagnoses in complex cases, particularly when the diagnosis turns on psychological symptoms.[639] In

---

[635] See **Ch. 3** for discussion of battered child syndrome. Other diagnoses are equally well accepted, including shaken baby syndrome.

[636] State v. Verley, 106 Or. App. 751, 809 P.2d 723, 724, n.1 (1991) (physician testified that child sexual abuse is an accepted medical diagnosis); State v. Logan, 105 Or. App. 556, 806 P.2d 137, 139 (1991) (physician characterized child sexual abuse as legitimate medical diagnosis).

[637] See **Ch. 4**.

[638] *Guidelines for the Clinical Evaluation of Child and Adolescent Sexual Abuse,* 27 J. Am. Acad. Child & Adolescent Psychiatry 655, 657 (1988).

[639] See 4 Weinstein & Berger ¶ 803(6)[06], at 803-199 to 803-201, where the authors discuss admissibility of psychiatric diagnoses. The authors describe the disinclination of some courts to admit psychiatric diagnoses, writing:

> In practice most federal courts reached an accommodation between the need for relevant information and the fear of uncross-examined opinion. They drew a distinction between diagnoses involving "conjecture and opinion" and diagnoses upon which "competent physicians would not differ." As applied, this distinction usually resulted in the admission of entries relating to a physical condition, (including the results of tests administered by hospital personnel), and the rejection of psychiatric diagnoses which "must perforce be based upon many subjective factors requiring judgment evaluation" and upon which psychiatrists often disagree.
>
> Rule 803(6) in accord with the trend of state decisions and the conclusion of leading legal authorities rejects any attempt to exclude a particular class of hospital records. Diagnoses and opinions, without restriction to routine vis-a-vis conjectural, or physical as against psychiatric, are included as proper subjects of admissible entries in addition to acts, events and conditions. As in the case of any other record, however, the last phrase of Rule 803(6) authorizes the trial judge to exclude a particular record where indications of trustworthiness are shown to be lacking, either by the record itself, or by other evidence indicating that the opinion lacks factual basis or expert qualification. . . . If the expert is available and the diagnostic opinion is of a kind

§ 7.38   BUSINESS RECORDS   233

appropriate cases, however, a diagnosis of sexual abuse should be admissible under the business records exception.

Even if a medical record containing a diagnosis of child abuse is admissible, it is difficult to imagine a prosecutor who would rely solely on such a record—which is hearsay—to establish the ultimate issue of abuse.[640] In nearly all cases, the diagnosing professional is called as a witness.

Reports Under Child Abuse Reporting Laws

Every state has a statute requiring professionals to report suspected abuse and neglect. A record containing such a report may be a business record under Rule 803(6). A report filed by a government employee may be a public record under Rule 803(8).[641] Reports filed under reporting statutes are in some respects similar to accident reports maintained by businesses. Courts are inclined to admit accident reports as business records when the reports are required by statute, and are prepared by individuals who are neither involved in the accident nor likely to become parties to litigation arising out of the accident.[642]

Multiple Hearsay

The business records exception often involves multiple layers of hearsay.[643] For example, a child taken to a hospital describes abuse to a nurse, who relays the child's disclosure to a physician who, in turn, dictates a medical record that is typed by an employee of the medical records department. This example involves four layers of hearsay.

For the proponent, solving multiple hearsay problems involves three steps. First, identify each declarant. Second, determine whether each declarant's utterance is hearsay. Third, for each hearsay statement, locate an exception. Returning to the example in the preceding paragraph, the four declarants are the child, the nurse, the doctor, and the typist. The child's disclosure is hearsay when

---

    competent physicians may disagree upon, the judge has discretion to require the expert to testify to ensure trustworthiness through cross-examination, particularly if the medical issue is crucial, and the patient's liberty is at stake.

    (footnotes omitted). *See also* 4 Louisell & Mueller § 451, at 701-07.

[640] See § **7.47** for discussion of the sufficiency of hearsay to support a finding of fact or verdict.

[641] A professional in private practice might be acting as a delegate of government authority in filing a child abuse report. If so, the report may be admissible under Rule 803(8) as a public record. *See* 4 Weinstein & Berger ¶ 803(8)[02], at 803-240 to 803-244.

[642] 4 Louisell & Mueller § 450, at 692-94.

[643] Rule 805 of the Federal Rules of Evidence provides that "[h]earsay included within hearsay is not excluded under the hearsay rule if each part of the combined statements conforms with an exception to the hearsay rule provided in these rules." *See* 4 Louisell & Mueller § 448; 4 Weinstein & Berger ¶ 803(6)[04].

offered for the truth of the matter asserted. The nurse's statement to the doctor is hearsay because it is offered to prove what the nurse told the doctor. Similarly, the doctor's dictation is hearsay because it is offered to prove the doctor's statement. Finally, the typist made an assertion for hearsay purposes by creating the medical record.

The nurse, doctor, and typist were acting within the scope of their employment when they made their out-of-court statements; therefore, all of their hearsay statements are admissible under the business records exception. As Louisell and Mueller write:

> So long as both the source and the recorder of information embodied in a business record are acting in the regular course of business, and so long as every person in the chain of transmission between source and recorder is doing likewise, the clear message of Rule 803(6) is that the fact of multiple hearsay does not matter. To put it another way, rule 803(6) creates a hearsay exception for the message conveyed by each such person in the chain.[644]

The child's disclosure to the nurse is not within the business records exception, however, because the child is an outsider to the business. Thus, it is necessary to find another exception for the child's statement. If the child's disclosure to the nurse was pertinent to diagnosis or treatment, the child's statement may be admitted under the diagnosis or treatment exception.[645] Alternatively, the child's statement may be admissible under the excited utterance exception,[646] or under a residual[647] or child hearsay exception.[648] Portions of the child's statement describing existing physical or emotional states may be admissible under the state of mind exception.[649] If no hearsay exception applies to the child's statement, the medical record must be excluded despite the fact that the statements of the nurse, doctor, and typist fall within the business records exception.

A business record offered in evidence may incorporate a business record prepared by another organization.[650] For example, a physician's medical record on a patient may include laboratory reports from independent laboratories. If each record qualifies under Rule 803(6), the entire medical record, including the lab reports, is admissible.

---

[644] 4 Louisell & Mueller § 446, at 681.

[645] Fed. R. Evid. 803(4). See §§ **7.35** and **7.36** for discussion of the diagnosis or treatment exception.

[646] Fed. R. Evid. 803(2). See §§ **7.28–7.30** for discussion of the excited utterance exception.

[647] Fed. R. Evid. 803(24), 804(b)(5). See §§ **7.42–7.45** for discussion of the residual exception.

[648] See § **7.46** for discussion of child hearsay exceptions.

[649] Fed. R. Evid. 803(3). See §§ **7.32–7.34** for discussion of the state of mind exception.

[650] 4 Louisell & Mueller § 446, at 658.

§ 7.39 Public Records

Rule 803(8) creates a broad exception for public records. The rule states:

> The following are not excluded by the hearsay rule, even though the declarant is available as a witness: Records, reports, statements, or data compilations, in any form, of public offices or agencies, setting forth (A) the activities of the office or agency, or (B) matters observed pursuant to duty imposed by law as to which matters there was a duty to report, excluding, however, in criminal cases matters observed by police officers and other law enforcement personnel, or (C) in civil actions and proceedings and against the Government in criminal cases, factual findings resulting from an investigation made pursuant to authority granted by law, unless the sources of information or other circumstances indicate lack of trustworthiness.[651]

Public records are "considered trustworthy because of the great public duty which attends the discharge of official functions."[652] Because public records are presumed to be reliable, "the opponent to admissibility has the burden of showing that a public record is untrustworthy."[653] The exception is also predicated on the need for public documents.[654] The officials generating the reams of public documents seldom remember the underlying events. Thus, the document often constitutes the only evidence of the event.

Unlike the business records exception, which requires the proponent to lay a foundation through the custodian of records or some other witness, the proponent of public records usually does not have to call a witness to lay a foundation.[655] Public documents are often self-authenticating.[656]

Rule 803(8) is applicable to agencies of federal, state, and local government. The rule creates three categories of public records. The lines separating the categories are sometimes fuzzy, allowing overlap. The court determines pursuant to Rule 104(a) whether records are admissible under this exception.

(A) Agency Activities

Subpart (A) allows admission of factual documents evidencing routine internal operations of public agencies. For example, a sheriff's return of service is

---

[651] Fed. R. Evid. 803(8).

[652] 4 Louisell & Mueller § 454, at 720.

[653] *In re* Air Crash Disaster at Stapleton Int'l Airport, 720 F. Supp. 1493, 1497 (D. Colo. 1989). *See also* Moss v. Ole South Real Estate, Inc., 933 F.2d 1300, 1305 (5th Cir. 1991) ("In light of the presumption of admissibility, the party opposing the admission of the report must prove the report's untrustworthiness").

[654] 4 Louisell & Mueller § 454, at 720.

[655] 4 Louisell & Mueller § 454, at 721.

[656] *See* Fed. R. Evid. 902.

admissible under subpart (A) to prove personal service. Reports that focus primarily on individuals or events outside the agency generally do not fall within subpart (A).[657] Thus, a report filed under a child abuse reporting statute probably does not fall within subpart (A).

(B) Matters Observed Pursuant to Legal Duty

Unlike subpart (A), which focuses primarily on the internal operations of an agency, subpart (B) allows records describing people and events outside the agency. Records admissible under subpart (B) set forth matters observed and recorded pursuant to legal duty. There must be a legal duty to report the observation.[658] Subpart (B) is concerned primarily with factual observations. A child's school attendance record should be admissible under subpart (B) to establish days the child attended school. (If the goal is to establish nonattendance, admissibility is through Rule 803(10)). A government employee's report under a child abuse reporting statute should be admissible under subpart (B) insofar as the report contains factual data.[659] Moreover, reports filed by mandated reporters in the private sector may be admissible under subpart (B) if the reporter is viewed as a delegate of government authority for purposes of reporting. If the private sector reporter is not a government agent for this limited purpose, subpart (B) does not apply. Of course, if an exception can be found for the private sector reporter (for example, a business record exception), then the agency document incorporating the report is admissible under subpart (B), and the multiple hearsay problem is solved. Thus, when the report filed by a private practitioner is a business record under Rule 803(6), and this business record is incorporated into a public record admissible under Rule 803(8), the entire document is admissible.

Subpart (B) of Rule 803(8) contains an important limitation. Matters observed by police officers and other law enforcement personnel are not admissible in criminal cases. On its face, this language appears to prohibit both the prosecution and the defense from offering reports generated by the police. The legislative history of subpart (B) reveals, however, that Congress was concerned with protecting criminal defendants, and several decisions allow the defendant to employ subpart (B) to admit public records containing matters observed by the police.[660]

In child abuse litigation it is important to determine whether the professionals directly and indirectly involved in investigation of the case are "other law enforcement personnel" for purposes of Rule 803(8)(B). Courts generally hold

---

[657] 4 Louisell & Mueller § 455, at 724–27.

[658] *Id.* at 727.

[659] *See id.* at 728.

[660] *See id.* at 744.

§ 7.39 PUBLIC RECORDS

that medical examiners conducting autopsies are not law enforcement personnel.[661] Whether laboratory technicians performing tests are "law enforcement personnel" depends on the facts of the case, particularly the degree of alignment between the technician and police or prosecutorial authorities.[662] In *State v. Tavares*,[663] the Rhode Island Supreme Court held that a health department toxicologist who analyzed a rape kit was not operating as law enforcement. The court wrote:

> [T]he toxicologist, a health department employee . . . does not become a law-enforcement person by virtue of the fact that he or she has a statutory obligation to cooperate with the police and to perform scientific crime-detection tests.
>
> In practice the toxicologist's cooperation consists of receiving the rape kit from the hospital, analyzing the specimens, and forwarding the laboratory results to the authorities. There appears to be no close contact between the toxicologist and the police. It does not appear that the toxicologist has seen the police report or has been informed of any details relating to the alleged crime. Accordingly we rule that health department toxicologists are not law-enforcement personnel for purposes of Rule 803(8)(B).[664]

Are professionals employed in the increasing number of multidisciplinary centers for interviewing and examining children "other law enforcement personnel"? Most of these centers are government agencies. Many centers are in university hospitals. There is no pat answer to whether professionals in these centers are "other law enforcement personnel." A center could be so closely aligned with law enforcement that everyone in the center, including medical and mental health professionals, is properly viewed as "law enforcement." On the other hand, centers generally are not an arm of the law despite the fact that police and prosecutors refer children to the centers and experts from the centers testify for the government.[665] In some centers, certain employees may be law

---

[661] *See* Manocchio v. Moran, 919 F.2d 770, 777 (1st Cir. 1990), *cert. denied*, 111 S. Ct. 1695 (1991) (medical examiner not law enforcement personnel); Vasquez v. State, 814 S.W.2d 773 (Tex. Ct. App. 1991) (not error to permit assistant medical examiner to testify regarding autopsy report prepared by another doctor; assistant medical examiner not law enforcement personnel; autopsy report admissible as business record).

[662] *See* United States v. Oates, 560 F.2d 45 (2d Cir. 1977) (U.S. Customs Service chemist who analyzed heroin was "other law enforcement personnel" because of chemist's important role in law enforcement effort).

[663] 590 A.2d 867 (R.I. 1991).

[664] *Id.* at 872.

[665] *See* Flanagan v. State, 586 So. 2d 1085 (Fla. Dist. Ct. App. 1991) (rejecting defense claim that physician serving as member of child protection team was serving primarily a law enforcement function); State v. Aguallo, 318 N.C. 590, 350 S.E.2d 76, 79 (1986) (rejecting defense claim that statements to physician were inadmissible under diagnosis or treatment exception because doctor was allegedly concerned with gathering evidence for the state; record reflected that doctor was concerned with diagnosis and treatment).

enforcement personnel while other employees are not.[666] The key factors are usually whether the employee in question has law enforcement responsibilities, and, if so, whether those responsibilities supplied the primary motivation for creating the record.

(C) Factual Findings from Investigation

Subpart (C) of the public records exception allows admission in civil proceedings, and in criminal cases against the prosecution, of factual findings resulting from official investigations.[667] In *Beech Aircraft Corp. v. Rainey*,[668] the Supreme Court defined the term *factual findings* to include conclusions and opinions based on factual investigation.[669]

§ 7.40 Learned Treatises

Courts allow expert witnesses to be impeached with books and articles from the professional literature.[670] Such publications are referred to as *learned treatises*. Although impeachment is permitted, learned treatises are hearsay, and

---

[666] In some centers, for example, a prosecutor has an office in the center.

[667] See 4 Louisell & Mueller § 455, at 734-35, where the authors write:

> Records within clause (C), like those in clause (B), have essentially no subject limitations, provided only that they relate to matters which the agency is authorized to investigate. . . .
>
> A great advantage of clause (C) is that it embraces records based upon statements or testimony by outsiders to government, so there is no need to show that the source was an official with personal knowledge. . . . Like records within clause (A), those within clause (C) should be considered to satisfy foundation requirements if properly authenticated as public records . . . .
>
> The idea behind clause (C) is to pave the way to receive reports by public officials, even when evaluation and interpretation of outside data (including statements by outsiders) are required.

(footnotes omitted).

[668] 488 U.S. 153 (1988).

[669] *Id.* at 170. The Court wrote:

> We hold, therefore, that portions of investigatory reports otherwise admissible under Rule 803(8)(C) are not inadmissible merely because they state a conclusion or opinion. As long as the conclusion is based on a factual investigation and satisfies the Rule's trustworthiness requirement, it should be admissible along with other portions of the report.

Id. (footnote omitted). *See also* Moss v. Ole South Real Estate, Inc., 933 F.2d 1300, 1305 (5th Cir. 1991) ("Opinions and conclusions, as well as facts, are covered by Rule 803(8)(C)").

[670] States impose various restrictions on such impeachment. *See* 4 Louisell & Mueller § 466, at 841; McCormick § 321, at 900 ("Virtually all courts have, to some extent, permitted the use of learned materials in the cross-examination of an expert witness"); 4 Weinstein & Berger at ¶ 803(18)[02].

§ 7.40   LEARNED TREATISES   239

cannot be offered for the truth of matters contained therein unless an exception applies.[671] Rule 803(18) creates an exception, and allows limited substantive use of learned treatises.[672] The rule states:

> The following are not excluded by the hearsay rule, even though the declarant is available as a witness: To the extent called to the attention of an expert witness upon cross-examination or relied upon by the expert witness in direct examination, statements contained in published treatises, periodicals, or pamphlets on a subject of history, medicine, or other science or art, established as a reliable authority by the testimony or admission of the witness or by other expert testimony or by judicial notice. If admitted, the statements may be read into evidence but may not be received as exhibits.[673]

Learned treatises are reliable because the author has a strong incentive to be accurate.[674] The author realizes the treatise will be scrutinized by peers and relied on by practitioners in the field.

The proponent of a learned treatise must establish that the treatise is reliable. Reliability can be established in three ways. First, the expert testifying at trial can establish that the treatise is reliable.[675] Second, reliability can be established by testimony from other expert witnesses. The second method may be used when the expert on the stand refuses to concede the reliability of the treatise. Third, the court may take judicial notice of the reliability of certain well-known treatises.

Much of the literature on child abuse is contained in journals. It is useful to distinguish juried from nonjuried journals.[676] Unlike law reviews, most of which

---

[671] Fed. R. Evid. 803(18) advisory committee's note ("The writers have generally favored the admissibility of learned treatises . . . , but the great weight of authority has been that learned treatises are not admissible as substantive evidence though usable in the cross-examination of experts"); McCormick § 321, at 900 ("Traditionally, however, the material may be considered only as going to the witness' competency or the accuracy of his conclusions; most courts have been unwilling to adopt a broad exception to the hearsay rule for treatises and other professional literature").

[672] 4 Weinstein & Berger ¶ 803(18)[01], at 803-324 ("Rule 803(18), in allowing learned treatises to be admitted as substantive evidence provided certain conditions are met, adopts a view long advocated by legal writers, but contrary to the great weight of authority").

[673] Fed. R. Evid. 803(18).

[674] 4 Louisell & Mueller § 446, at 846.

[675] See 4 Louisell & Mueller § 446, at 848–49, where the authors write:

> Perhaps the most certain and thorough way to satisfy the first requirement is to obtain expert testimony that the book or article is in fact reliable authority. This requirement should be considered satisfied by testimony from the expert (i) that he knows professionally and respects the author of the work in question and considers that work reliable, or (ii) that experts in the field generally accept the author and the work in question as authoritative, even if the witness himself might differ with this assessment.

[676] For additional discussion of juried journals, see **Ch. 4**.

are edited by students, the psychological and medical literature is edited by professionals. The better journals are juried. Each manuscript submitted for possible publication is sent to two or three experts in the field. The author's name is removed from the manuscript so that the reviewer does not know who wrote the manuscript. The reviewer critically reviews the manuscript and makes recommendations for or against publication. In most cases, it is appropriate to place greater confidence in juried than nonjuried journals.

It is useful to differentiate clinical reports from empirical research. Empirical research relies to a greater or lesser extent on the experimental method to increase the reliability of findings. Clinical literature, by contrast, does not employ the experimental method. It is often appropriate to place greater confidence in conclusions drawn from rigorously controlled empirical studies than from clinical research. This is not to say, however, that clinical research is unreliable. The reliability of particular articles is analyzed on a case-by-case basis.

Rule 803(18) does not allow unfettered substantive use of treatises. A treatise is admissible only if an expert testifies at trial who can chaperon the treatise by explaining it to the jury.[677] Furthermore, a treatise is admissible on direct examination only if the expert relied on the treatise during direct. To be admissible during cross-examination, the examiner must bring the treatise to the expert's attention.

The court determines pursuant to Rule 104(a) whether the requirements of Rule 803(18) have been fulfilled.[678]

§ 7.41 Proof of Age

In many child abuse cases the prosecutor must prove the child's age. Testimony from the child concerning the child's own age or date of birth can be characterized as hearsay because the testimony necessarily relies on what others told the child.[679] The hearsay objection is seldom raised, however, and when it is,

---

[677] McCormick's treatise states that "[a] significant limitation is that the publication must be called to the attention of an expert on cross-examination or relied upon by him in direct examination, a provision designed to ensure that the materials are used only under the chaperonage of an expert to assist and explain in applying them." McCormick § 321, at 901.

[678] 4 Louisell & Mueller § 466, at 861.

[679] See 2 Wigmore § 667, at 926–28, where Wigmore wrote:

> Strictly speaking, one cannot exactly know his *own age* except upon hearsay information; for he is not capable of knowing this, or anything, until an appreciable time after birth. But practically a person's belief on this point has a satisfactory basis. Courts have commonly preferred to accept this practical certainty rather than to insist on academic nicety.
>
> But in any case one may know whether at a *particular time* he was of one age or another, if the difference is as much as the time that must have brought him to the age of observation. Moreover, a person who does not know the date of another's birth or of

§ 7.41 PROOF OF AGE

courts reject it.[680] Wigmore wrote that a person's knowledge of their own age is a "satisfactory basis" for admitting such testimony.[681] In *Antelope v. United States*,[682] the court stated:

> Testimony by one as to his age and date of his birth is in a sense hearsay, but is an exception to the rule that hearsay testimony may not be received in evidence. Courts generally recognize that one is competent to testify as to his age and the date of his birth although of necessity such facts are based upon hearsay and family history.[683]

Testimony regarding one's own age should be admissible under a residual or child hearsay exception. Rule 804(b)(4) allows statements regarding a person's own birth provided the person is unavailable at trial. Louisiana has a specific hearsay exception for "[a] witness' testimony as to his own age."[684]

A persuasive argument can be made that testimony regarding one's own age should be characterized as nonhearsay because the hearsay risks are extremely low. The risk a child will lie about age is remote. The risk of memory loss is low. With so concrete and simple a fact as age, the risks of misperception and ambiguity are virtually eliminated. For children, age is an important marker of

---

> his own may know, by the association of events, whether he or the other was over or under a certain age at a certain time.
>
> Even if testimony to one's own age is not to be received from the present point of view, yet it may be regarded as asserting the family reputation on the subject, and the latter may thus be received under the exception to the hearsay rule.
>
> The parents of an *adoptive child,* not having been present at its birth, have not personal knowledge, in the strictest sense, of the child's age. But their belief, based on the statements of the natural parents or of the original custodians of the child, together with their observation of the child's behavior during its growth, has for practical purposes a sufficient probability of correctness—the probative value varying with the age at which the child was adopted and with the other circumstances of their acquisition of the child. To reject their testimony would be pedantic.
>
> For similar reasons a member of a family is qualified to testify to *place of birth* or of *death, place* and *time of residence,* and similar facts of family history or of the life of a *member of a family.*

(footnotes omitted). *See* United States v. Brown, 548 F.2d 1194 (5th Cir. 1977).

[680] People v. Williams, 477 N.W.2d 877 (Mich. Ct. App. 1991) (defendant objected on hearsay grounds to victim's testimony regarding her age; rejecting defendant's argument the court wrote, "It has long been established in this state that a person is competent to testify regarding his own age").

[681] 2 Wigmore § 667, at 926, quoted in **note 679**.

[682] 185 F.2d 174 (10th Cir. 1950).

[683] *Id.* at 175 (footnote omitted). *See also* United States v. Estrella, 21 M.J. 782 (A.C.M.R. 1986); Slater v. State, 575 So. 2d 1208, 1209 (Ala. Crim. App. 1990) (victim testified to his own age); People v. Bessette 564 N.Y.S.2d 605, 606 (A.D. 1991) ("A person is competent to testify as to his own age").

[684] La. R. Evid. 803(24).

accomplishment and social status, thus children are interested in their age, and are likely to possess accurate information.

Any argument that testimony regarding one's age is an inadmissible lay opinion should be rejected. The rules of evidence permit lay witnesses to opine on matters such as age.

Parents may testify regarding their child's age, and such testimony is not hearsay. Parents have personal knowledge of the child's birth.

If the defendant's age must be established, the defendant's in-court or out-of-court statement regarding age may be received as a party admission. Statements by one spouse may suffice to establish the other spouse's age.[685]

Age can be established with a person's birth certificate.[686] Rule 803(9) paves the way for admission of birth certificates.[687] The rule states that "[t]he following are not excluded by the hearsay rule, even though the declarant is available as a witness: Records or data compilations, in any form, of births, fetal deaths, deaths, or marriages, if the report thereof was made to a public office pursuant to requirements of law."[688] Age can also be established by resort to records of religious organizations (Rules 803(11) and 803(12)) and family records (Rule 803(13)).

§ 7.42 Residual Exception

The Federal Rules of Evidence contain an exception admitting reliable hearsay that does not fall within one of the traditional exceptions. This so-called residual or catchall exception is found in two rules: 803(24) and 804(b)(5). The language of the two rules is identical. The only difference is that under Rule 804(b)(5) the declarant must be unavailable.[689] Rule 803(24) states:

> The following are not excluded by the hearsay rule, even though the declarant is available as a witness: A statement not specifically covered by any of the

---

[685] *See* People v. Buhrle, 744 P.2d 747 (Colo. 1987) (defendant's age could be established, at least at preliminary hearing, by out-of-court statements of defendant's spouse relating defendant's age to third parties).

[686] United States v. Austrew, 202 F. Supp. 816, 822 (D. Md. 1962), *aff'd per curiam,* 317 F.2d 926 (4th Cir. 1963) (child's age established with birth certificate); 4 Weinstein & Berger ¶ 803(9).

[687] 4 Louisell & Mueller § 457, at 778 ("Under the instant exception, birth certificates are admissible over a hearsay objection when offered to prove the date, time, and place of birth") (footnote omitted).

[688] Fed. R. Evid. 803(9).

[689] 4 Louisell & Mueller § 472, at 922 ("Rule 803(24) is but one of two identically-worded catchall exceptions, the other being found in Rule 804(b)(5). There is no real difference between them") (footnotes omitted).

§ 7.42   RESIDUAL EXCEPTION   243

foregoing exceptions but having equivalent circumstantial guarantees of trustworthiness, if the court determines that (A) the statement is offered as evidence of a material fact;[690] (B) the statement is more probative on the point for which it is offered than any other evidence which the proponent can procure through reasonable efforts;[691] and (C) the general purposes of these rules and the interests of justice will best be served by admission of the statement into evidence.[692] However, a statement may not be admitted under this exception unless the proponent of it makes known to the adverse party sufficiently in advance of the trial or hearing to provide the adverse party with a fair opportunity to prepare to meet it,[693] the proponent's intention to offer the statement and the particulars of it, including the name and address of the declarant.[694]

The residual exception is included in the rules of evidence to leave the door ajar for reliable hearsay that does not fit within one of the traditional exceptions. The Advisory Committee note to Rule 803(24) states, "It would . . . be presumptuous to assume that all possible desirable exceptions to the hearsay rule have been catalogued and to pass the hearsay rule to oncoming generations as a closed system. Exception (24) and its companion provision in Rule 804(b)(5) are accordingly included."[695] Congress intended the residual exception to be used

---

[690] 4 Weinstein & Berger ¶ 803(24)[01], at 803-378 (referring to the requirement that the statement be offered to prove a material fact, the authors write, "This would, in any event, be required by Rules 401 and 402").

[691] *In re* C.B., 574 So. 2d 1369, 1373 (Miss. 1990) (residual exception "would not be available to admit the disputed hearsay unless the hearsay statement offered is more probative on point for which it is offered than any other evidence which the proponent can procure through reasonable efforts. Hence, if the child were available to testify, then this catch-all exception would not be available").

[692] 4 Weinstein & Berger ¶ 803(24)[01], at 803-379 (referring to the requirement that admission must comport with the purposes of the rules and the interests of justice, the authors write, "This is a restatement of Rule 102").

[693] See *Id.* at 803-380, where the authors discuss the notice requirement of the residual exception. The authors recognize that on occasion the proponent of hearsay will not be able to provide notice before trial. They write, "[I]f the question arises during trial through no fault of the proponent—something bound to occur from time to time, no matter how careful is discovery—the court can comply with the rule by granting a continuance."

[694] Fed. R. Evid. 803(24). *See* United States v. Renville, 779 F.2d 430, 439 (8th Cir. 1985) (discussing requirements of residual exception).

[695] Fed. R. Evid. 803(24) advisory committee's note.

sparingly, and in criminal cases courts are particularly cautious.[696] Nevertheless, courts regularly employ the residual exception in child abuse litigation.[697]

The requirement that hearsay offered under the residual exception must be more probative than other evidence arises as an issue in some child abuse cases.[698] Children's hearsay plays a critical role in abuse litigation, and in some instances the child's out-of-court statements are the most powerful evidence of abuse. The need for children's out-of-court statements is particularly high when the child is "too frightened and uncommunicative to testify meaningfully, or the child ha[s] recanted her earlier accusations . . . ."[699] In *State v. McCafferty*,[700] the South Dakota Supreme Court considered hearsay statements of a seven-year-old child. The court wrote that "[i]t is . . . obvious that the statement is more probative than any other evidence the State could produce through reasonable efforts. In this type of loco-parentis and child situation, it is difficult to envision any evidence more probative than the statements and action of the victim."[701] In *United States v. Shaw*,[702] the 11-year-old victim testified at trial and described her sexual abuse. In addition to the child's testimony, the trial judge

---

[696] United States v. Ellis, 935 F.2d 385, 394 (1st Cir.), *cert. denied,* 112 S. Ct. 201 (1991) ("Congress, however, intended the residual hearsay exception to 'be used very rarely, and only in exceptional circumstances'"; two-year-old's play with anatomical dolls admissible under residual exception); United States v. Renville, 779 F.2d 430, 439 (8th Cir. 1985) ("Congress intended that the residual exception 'be used very rarely, and only in exceptional circumstances'"); Brandon v. State, 778 P.2d 221, 227 (Alaska Ct. App. 1989); In re C.B., 574 So. 2d 1369, 1373 (Miss. 1990) (juvenile court dependency case; "This catch-all exception should be carefully considered and applied rarely, so as not to devour the hearsay rule"); State v. Nelson, 777 P.2d 479, 482 (Utah 1989).

[697] Idaho v. Wright, 110 S. Ct. 3139 (1990); United States v. Ellis, 935 F.2d 385, 393–94 (1st Cir.), *cert. denied,* 112 S. Ct. 201 (1991); United States v. Shaw, 824 F.2d 601, 609 (8th Cir. 1987), *cert. denied,* 484 U.S. 1068 (1988) ("We have recognized that while Congress intended the residual exception to be 'used very rarely' and only in exceptional circumstances, . . . one such exceptional circumstance generally exists when a child abuse victim relates to an adult the details of the abusive events"); United States v. Renville, 779 F.2d 430 (8th Cir. 1985); United States v. Cree, 778 F.2d 474 (8th Cir. 1985); United States v. Frazier, 678 F. Supp. 499 (E.D. Pa.), *aff'd,* 806 F.2d 255 (3d Cir. 1986); United States v. Giambra, 33 M.J. 331 (C.M.A. 1991); United States v. Williamson, 26 M.J. 115 (C.M.A. 1988); United States v. Barror, 23 M.J. 370 (C.M.A. 1987); United States v. Pollard, 34 M.J. 1008 (A.C.M.R. 1992); State v. Allen, 157 Ariz. 165, 755 P.2d 1153 (1988); State v. J.C.E., 235 Mont. 264, 767 P.2d 309, 315 (1988); State v. Taylor, 103 N.M. 189, 704 P.2d 443 (Ct. App. 1985); State v. Hollywood, 67 Or. App. 546, 680 P.2d 655 (1984); State v. Sorenson, 143 Wis. 2d 226, 421 N.W.2d 77 (1988).

[698] State v. Nelson, 777 P.2d 479, 482 (Utah 1989) (victim's hearsay not admissible under residual exception because hearsay was not more reliable than other available evidence).

[699] United States v. Shaw, 824 F.2d 601, 609–10 (8th Cir. 1987), *cert. denied,* 484 U.S. 1068 (1988).

[700] 356 N.W.2d 159 (S.D. 1984), *cert. denied,* 476 U.S. 1172 (1986).

[701] *Id.* at 162.

[702] 824 F.2d 601 (8th Cir. 1987), *cert. denied,* 484 U.S. 1068 (1988).

§ 7.43 ANALYSIS OF RELIABILITY 245

approved use of the residual exception to admit the child's out-of-court statements given during interviews. The interview statements covered much the same ground as the victim's trial testimony. On appeal, the defendant argued that because the victim "testified to essentially the same matters addressed in the hearsay statements, the 'more probative' requirement of Rule 803(24) was not met."[703] The Eighth Circuit Court of Appeals rejected this argument, writing:

> [The victim's] hearsay testimony undoubtedly retraced some of [the victim's trial] testimony. But this alone does not render erroneous the district court's ruling. As Judge Weinstein emphasized, "[e]ven though the evidence may be somewhat cumulative, it may be important in evaluating other evidence and arriving at the truth so that the 'more probative' requirement can not be interpreted with cast iron rigidity."[704] The district court reasoned that [the victim's hearsay] was "more probative" than [the victim's trial testimony] for several reasons. [The victim's hearsay] reflected the first known statements of [the victim] made to anyone about the sexual incidents. The hearsay statements were made just days after the last sexual incidents. And most importantly, they contained specific details as to the dates of the incidents—details that [the victim] could not provide at trial. The record supports these conclusions. We hold that the trial court did not abuse its discretion in allowing [the victim's hearsay].[705]

§ 7.43 —Analysis of Reliability

When hearsay is offered under a residual exception, the primary issue usually is whether the hearsay is sufficiently reliable. That is, does the hearsay possess indicia of reliability "equivalent" to the reliability supporting other exceptions.[706] The starting place for analysis of reliability is the United States Supreme Court's decision in *Idaho v. Wright*.[707] In *Wright* the Court endorsed the universal judicial practice of assessing reliability in light of "the totality of the circumstances."[708] Insofar as the Court reaffirmed the totality of the circumstances approach to reliability, the Court's analysis is unremarkable. However, the majority in *Wright* broke new and troubling ground. The majority

---

[703] 824 F.2d at 609.

[704] 4 Weinstein & Berger ¶ 803(24)[01], at 803-379.

[705] 824 F.2d at 610 (citation omitted).

[706] For discussion of the meaning of the word *equivalent,* see Huff v. White Motor Corp., 609 F.2d 286, 293 (7th Cir. 1979) ("the circumstantial guarantees of trustworthiness necessary under the residual exception are to be 'equivalent' to guarantees that justify the specific exceptions"); United States v. Pollard, 34 M.J. 1008 (A.C.M.R. 1992); United States v. Quick, 22 M.J. 722, 723 (A.C.M.R. 1986), *aff'd,* 26 M.J. 460 (C.M.A. 1988) (evidence "must possess certain guarantees of trustworthiness. These guarantees are generally similar to those associated with the specific exceptions under Rule 803").

[707] 110 S. Ct. 3139 (1990).

[708] *Id.* at 3148.

held that in criminal cases, the Confrontation Clause requires that when evaluating the totality of the circumstances, "the relevant circumstances include only those that surround the making of the statement and that render the declarant particularly worthy of belief."[709] The trial judge may not consider evidence that does not surround the statement, even though such evidence corroborates the statement. Thus, according to the *Wright* majority, the Sixth Amendment prohibits a court from considering corroborating evidence such as medical or physical evidence of abuse, the defendant's opportunity to commit the offense, or the testimony of another witness identifying the defendant as the perpetrator.[710]

Why did the *Wright* majority hold that assessment of reliability must focus only on circumstances surrounding the making of the out-of-court statement? The majority's reasoning appears to proceed as follows: Only hearsay that has circumstantial guarantees of reliability equivalent to those found in specific hearsay exceptions is admissible under the residual exception. Examination of other hearsay exceptions, such as excited utterances, dying declarations, and statements for purposes of diagnosis or treatment, reveals that the indicia of reliability for these exceptions derive from the circumstances in which they are made. That is, excited utterances are reliable because they are made shortly following a startling event and before the declarant has time to fabricate. A dying declaration is reliable because those who know they are about to die will not want to meet their maker with a lie upon their lips. And statements for diagnosis or treatment are reliable because of the patient's incentive to be truthful with the doctor. Because the reliability of such statements derives from the circumstances in which they are made, and because the residual exception requires that hearsay proffered under that exception possess guarantees of trustworthiness that are "equivalent" to the reliability of the other exceptions, it follows that, like the other exceptions, the reliability of hearsay offered under the residual exception must be gauged by the circumstances in which the statement is made.

With great respect for the majority, this reasoning seems flawed.[711] It is true that under the residual exception, hearsay must possess circumstantial guarantees of trustworthiness equivalent to those justifying other exceptions. But equivalence is an elastic concept. Louisell and Mueller write that "[i]f a statement appears under the circumstances to be trustworthy, it should make no difference for purposes of the instant exception that the factors leading to this conclusion differ markedly from those underlying any or all of the specific exceptions."[712] The majority slips into logical error when it concludes that corroborating

---

[709] *Id.*

[710] *Id.* at 3152.

[711] *See* George v. State, 306 Ark. 360, 813 S.W.2d 792 (1991) (Glaze, J. concurring) (criticizing the *Wright* majority opinion).

[712] 4 Louisell & Mueller § 472, at 925.

§ 7.43 ANALYSIS OF RELIABILITY

evidence is completely irrelevant in assessing reliability.[713] As Louisell and Mueller remark, corroborative evidence "tends obviously to confirm the trustworthiness of the statement."[714] Prior to *Idaho v. Wright,* the great majority of courts factored corroborative evidence into the reliability assessment.[715]

To illustrate the error in prohibiting consideration of corroborating evidence, imagine a case in which a four-year-old's hearsay statement describes an act of anal intercourse. Six items of evidence are available regarding the statement. Three of these items surround the making of the statement:

1. The statement was spontaneous
2. The child had no motive to fabricate
3. The child's statement demonstrated developmentally unusual knowledge of anal intercourse.

Three of the items of evidence do not immediately surround the making of the statement, but tend to corroborate the child's description:

4. Medical evidence of anal intercourse
5. The defendant's inculpatory statement
6. The day after the assault, the defendant attempted to dispose of the victim's bloody underwear.

When is a trial judge justified in placing the greatest confidence in the child's statement? When all six items of evidence are considered? Would a judge place as much confidence in the statement when the three items of corroborative evidence are eliminated altogether from consideration? It seems that the more evidence there is for a proposition—in this case reliability—the more likely the proposition is to be true,[716] and evidence is probative whether it accompanies the statement or corroborates it. The majority's decision that corroborative evidence must be ignored when evaluating the reliability of hearsay offered under a residual exception is logically unsound.

In a persuasive dissent, Justice Kennedy took issue with the majority's rejection of corroborative evidence as an aid in assessing reliability. Justice Kennedy wrote:

> The majority errs, in my view, by adopting a rule that corroboration of the statement by other evidence is an impermissible part of the trustworthiness inquiry.

---

[713] *See* Chambers v. Mississippi, 410 U.S. 284, 300–01 (1973).

[714] 4 Louisell & Mueller § 472, at 929 (footnote omitted).

[715] *See* State v. Robinson, 153 Ariz. 191, 735 P.2d 801, 812 (1987) ("Although Rules 803(24) and 804(b)(5) do not require corroboration, corroborating evidence obviously bolsters the reliability of Nicole's statements").

[716] *See* E. Morgan, Basic Problems of Evidence 185–88 (1961).

The Court's apparent ruling is that corroborating evidence may not be considered in whole or in part for this purpose. . . .

I see no constitutional justification for this decision to prescind corroborating evidence from consideration of the question whether a child's statements are reliable. It is a matter of common sense for most people that one of the best ways to determine whether what someone says is trustworthy is to see if it is corroborated by other evidence. . . . [M]ost federal courts have looked to the existence of corroborating evidence or the lack thereof to determine the reliability of hearsay statements not coming within one of the traditional hearsay exceptions. . . .

[C]orroboration has been an essential element in our past hearsay cases, and there is no justification for a categorical refusal to consider it here. . . .

The short of the matter is that both the circumstances existing at the time the child makes the statements and the existence of corroborating evidence indicate, to a greater or lesser degree, whether the statements are reliable.[717]

Justice Kennedy has the better argument. Although it may be true in many cases that the best way to assess reliability is through circumstances immediately surrounding the statement,[718] cases exist in which corroborative evidence supports reliability. Wholesale disregard of corroborating evidence is unwarranted.

In certain cases it may be possible to escape *Wright*'s prohibition of corroborative evidence to assess reliability. It is clear that *Wright* is based squarely on the Sixth Amendment. The Court wrote that "[t]o be admissible under the Confrontation Clause, hearsay evidence used to convict a defendant must possess indicia of reliability by virtue of its inherent trustworthiness, not by reference to other evidence at trial."[719] If, however, the declarant is available at trial and subject to cross-examination, the Court's decision in *California v. Green*[720] indicates that the Confrontation Clause is satisfied, and hearsay is admissible without affront to the Sixth Amendment. The argument can be made that in criminal cases where the child testifies at trial, *Idaho v. Wright*'s limits on assessing reliability are not applicable because the Sixth Amendment is fulfilled.[721] If the

---

[717] 110 S. Ct. at 3153–56 (Kennedy, J., dissenting).

[718] On this point Justice Kennedy wrote:

If the Court means to suggest that the circumstances surrounding the making of a statement are the best indicators of reliability, I doubt this is so in every instance. And, if it were true in a particular case, that does not warrant ignoring other indicators of reliability such as corroborating evidence . . . .

110 S. Ct. at 3156 (Kennedy, J., dissenting).

[719] *Id.* at 3150.

[720] 399 U.S. 149 (1970).

[721] *See* United States v. Spotted War Bonnet, 933 F.2d 1471 (8th Cir. 1991), *cert. denied,* 112 S. Ct. 1187 (1992).

Sixth Amendment is satisfied, it is permissible to turn to nonconstitutional principles of evidence to determine reliability, and under evidentiary principles, corroborative evidence is relevant.

Another potential escape from the limitations imposed by *Idaho v. Wright* exists in civil litigation. In most jurisdictions, the residual exception applies in civil cases. For example, the residual exception plays an important role in juvenile court proceedings to protect abused and neglected children. A question that did not arise in *Idaho v. Wright* is whether corroborative evidence may be considered to evaluate reliability when hearsay is offered in civil litigation. Again, *Wright* is based squarely on the Sixth Amendment's Confrontation Clause. The Sixth Amendment does not apply in juvenile court dependency proceedings. In juvenile court, the Due Process Clause of the Fourteenth Amendment affords parents accused of maltreatment a right to confront accusatory witnesses.[722] However, confrontation rights under the Due Process Clause are not as extensive as rights guaranteed by the Sixth Amendment. In juvenile court proceedings it can be argued persuasively that corroborative evidence that could not be considered in criminal litigation may be considered to assess the reliability of children's hearsay statements offered under residual exceptions.[723]

Idaho v. Wright's restriction on corroborative evidence in assessing reliability under residual exceptions is equally applicable to child hearsay exceptions. As discussed in **§ 7.46**, child hearsay exceptions are "first cousins" of the residual exception. In reality, child hearsay exceptions are simply residual exceptions for children's out-of-court statements.

The following two sections discuss factors that bear on the reliability of hearsay offered under residual and child hearsay exceptions. **Section 7.44** discusses factors that surround the making of the out-of-court statement, and that meet the requirement set forth in *Idaho v. Wright* for assessing reliability. **Section 7.45** discusses corroborative factors that probably cannot be considered under *Wright*, but that nevertheless relate to reliability, and that are important when *Wright* does not control. Often, there is no clear line separating "surrounding factors" from "corroborating factors." Factors that surround in one case corroborate in another.

The reliability of hearsay offered under the residual exception is a preliminary matter decided by the court pursuant to Rule 104(a). The rules of evidence do not govern the factors the court may consider in evaluating reliability.[724]

---

[722] See § **7.57**.

[723] *See In re* Linda S., 148 Misc. 2d 169, 560 N.Y.S.2d 181 (Fam. Ct. 1990).

[724] State v. Jones, 112 Wash. 2d 488, 772 P.2d 496, 498–99 (1989) (decision concerns child hearsay exception; holding that rules of evidence do not govern what trial court may consider when evaluating whether child's statement is corroborated).

§ 7.44 —Factors Surrounding Statement

Prior testimony. If the child's out-of-court statement was under oath at a prior hearing at which the adversary had the opportunity to cross-examine the child, the statement assumes added reliability.[725]

Testimonial competence when statement was made. The fact that a child possessed or lacked the competence to testify as a witness *at the time* of an out-of-court statement may impact reliability. The fact that a child was testimonially competent when a statement was made means the child possessed the ability to observe, remember, and relate events, as well as an understanding of the difference between truth and falsehood *at that time*.[726] A child's out-of-court statement may be reliable despite the fact that the child lacked an element of testimonial competence when the child spoke.[727]

Testimonial competence at time of trial. The fact that a child lacks testimonial competence at trial does not necessarily mean the child's out-of-court statements are unreliable.[728] In *Idaho v. Wright*,[729] the defendant argued that the child's out-of-court statements were unreliable because the trial judge found that the child could not communicate at trial. The Supreme Court rejected the defendant's argument, writing:

> [W]e have in any event held that the Confrontation Clause does not erect a *per se* rule barring the admission of prior statements of a declarant who is unable to communicate to the jury at the time of trial. . . . Although such inability might be relevant to whether the earlier hearsay statement possessed particularized guarantees of trustworthiness, a *per se* rule of exclusion would not only frustrate the truth-seeking purpose of the Confrontation Clause, but would also hinder States in their own "enlightened development in the law of evidence . . . ."[730]

---

[725] State v. Bellotti, 383 N.W.2d 308, 315 (Minn. Ct. App. 1986).

[726] Huff v. White Motor Corp., 609 F.2d 286, 293–94 (7th Cir. 1979); M.N.D. v. B.M.D., 356 N.W.2d 813 (Minn. Ct. App. 1984); Buckley v. State, 758 S.W.2d 339, 343 (Tex. Ct. App. 1988), *aff'd*, 786 S.W.2d 357 (Tex. Crim. App. 1990).

[727] *See* State v. Gribble, 60 Wash. App. 374, 804 P.2d 634 (1991) (holding that if trial judge finds child's statement reliable, judge need not make separate finding that child was testimonially competent when statement was made).

[728] State v. Doe, 105 Wash. 2d 889, 719 P.2d 554 (1986).

[729] 110 S. Ct. 3139 (1990).

[730] *Id.* at 3151–52.

§ 7.44   FACTORS SURROUNDING STATEMENT   251

Other courts agree.[731] In *State v. Bellotti*,[732] the Minnesota Court of Appeals wrote:

> Appellant claims that there were insufficient indicia of reliability because the trial court found [the child] incompetent to testify at trial. We disagree. Incompetency to testify at trial does not alone render a statement inadmissible. Competency to testify concerns, in part, the child's present ability to remember. If a child cannot remember at trial an incident occurring months previously, she may nevertheless have remembered the incident and truthfully related it at the time she made the out-of-court statement.[733]

Spontaneity. Spontaneity is an important indicator of reliability. The more spontaneous a statement, the less likely the statement is a product of fabrication.[734] Of course, spontaneity is not always indicative of reliability. As the

---

[731] People v. Bowers, 801 P.2d 511, 519 (Colo. 1990) ("A finding, for example, that a very young child is incompetent to testify because of the child's reluctance to answer questions in a formal courtroom environment does not necessarily impair any particularized guarantees of reliability that otherwise inhere in a child's hearsay statement"); State v. Doe, 105 Wash. 2d 889, 719 P.2d 554 (1986); State v. Robinson, 44 Wash. App. 611, 722 P.2d 1379, 1385 (1986) ("That the victim was incompetent to testify does not necessarily render her hearsay statements unreliable"); State v. Oliver, 161 Wis. 2d 140, 467 N.W.2d 211, 214 (Ct. App. 1991) (four-year-old victim could not communicate at trial; victim's out-of-court statement to his father was nevertheless reliable; "There is no suggestion that he did not know the difference between a truthful statement and a lie").

[732] 383 N.W.2d 308 (Minn. Ct. App. 1986).

[733] *Id.* at 314. *See also* State v. Lanam, 459 N.W.2d 656 (Minn. 1990), *cert. denied,* 111 S. Ct. 693 (1991).

[734] Idaho v. Wright, 110 S. Ct. 3139, 3150 (1990); United States v. Ellis, 935 F.2d 385, 393–94 (1st Cir.), *cert. denied,* 112 S. Ct. 201 (1991) (two-year-old's play with anatomical dolls was spontaneous); Morgan v. Foretich, 846 F.2d 941 (4th Cir. 1988); State v. Allen, 157 Ariz. 165, 755 P.2d 1153, 1162 (1988) (child's statements were not spontaneous; for this and other reasons, hearsay should not have been admitted); State v. Robinson, 153 Ariz. 191, 735 P.2d 801, 811 (1987) (five-year-old child; "Nicole's statements were spontaneous; she explained what had occurred with little prompting. If there is evidence of prior interrogation, prompting, or manipulation by adults, spontaneity may be an inaccurate indicator of trustworthiness. But under the facts of this case, Nicole's spontaneity indicates truthfulness"); People v. Bowers, 801 P.2d 511, 521 (Colo. 1990); People v. District Ct., 776 P.2d 1083, 1089 (Colo. 1989); Rayburn v. State, 194 Ga. App. 676, 391 S.E.2d 780, 782, *cert. denied,* 111 S. Ct. 434 (1990); State v. Bratt, 250 Kan. 264, 824 P.2d 983 (1992); State v. Conklin, 444 N.W.2d 268, 276 (Minn. 1989) (discussing child hearsay exception); State v. Oslund, 469 N.W.2d 489, 494 (Minn. Ct. App. 1991); State v. Smith, 384 N.W.2d 546, 549 (Minn. Ct. App. 1986); State v. Bellotti, 383 N.W.2d 308, 313 (Minn. Ct. App. 1986) (child hearsay exception); D.A.H. v. G.A.H., 371 N.W.2d 1 (Minn. Ct. App. 1985) (residual exception; child's statements to psychologist admitted in part because they were spontaneous); State v. Boyer, 803 S.W.2d 132 (Mo. Ct. App. 1991) (three-year-old spontaneously disclosed to her mother); State v. J.C.E., 235 Mont. 264, 767 P.2d 309, 315 (1988); State v. Floody, 481 N.W.2d 242 (S.D. 1992); Buckley v. State, 758 S.W.2d 339, 343 (Tex. Ct. App. 1988), *aff'd,* 786 S.W.2d 357 (Tex. Crim. App. 1990); State v. Cooley, 48 Wash. App. 286, 738

Court noted in *Wright*, "[I]t is possible that '[i]f there is evidence of prior interrogation, prompting, or manipulation by adults, spontaneity may be an inaccurate indicator of trustworthiness.'"[735] Nevertheless, courts put considerable stock in the spontaneity of children's statements.

Statement overheard by more than one person. The fact that a child's out-of-court statement was overheard by more than one person may enhance confidence in the statement.[736]

Statement elicited by questioning. The reliability of a child's out-of-court statement may be influenced by the type of questions used to elicit the statement.[737] When questioning is leading, the possibility exists that the questioner influenced the child's statement, raising questions about reliability.[738] As the

---

P.2d 705 (1987); State v. Robinson, 44 Wash. App. 611, 722 P.2d 1379, 1385 (1986); State v. Sorenson, 143 Wis. 2d 226, 421 N.W.2d 77, 86 (1988) ("Contemporaneity and spontaneity of statements are not as crucial in admitting hearsay statements of young sexual assault victims under the residual exception"); *In re* Dependency of S.S., 61 Wash. App. 488, 814 P.2d 204, 210 (1991) ("any statements made that are not the result of leading or suggestive questions are spontaneous"); State v. Lindner, 142 Wis. 2d 783, 419 N.W.2d 352, 356 (Ct. App. 1987).

See State v. Carlson, 61 Wash. App. 865, 812 P.2d 536 (1991). In *Carlson,* the court wrote:

For purposes of a child hearsay analysis, spontaneous statements are statements the child volunteered in response to questions that were not leading and did not in any way suggest an answer. Unlike an excited utterance, the statements need not be contemporaneous with the event in question.

812 P.2d at 540.

[735] 110 S. Ct. at 3152.

[736] People v. District Ct., 776 P.2d 1083, 1090 (Colo. 1989); State v. Ryan, 103 Wash. 2d 165, 691 P.2d 197, 205 (1984); *In re* Dependency of S.S., 61 Wash. App. 488, 814 P.2d 204, 210 (1991); State v. Cooley, 48 Wash. App. 286, 738 P.2d 705 (1987).

[737] United States v. Ellis, 935 F.2d 385, 394 (1st Cir.), *cert. denied,* 112 S. Ct. 201 (1991) (social worker asked no leading questions; "The child was never asked to reenact the situation, but was simply given the [anatomical] dolls to play with"); United States v. Giambra, 33 M.J. 331, 334 (C.M.A. 1991); United States v. Barror, 23 M.J. 370 (C.M.A. 1987); United States v. King, 16 M.J. 990 (A.C.M.R. 1983); State v. Boyer, 803 S.W.2d 132 (Mo. Ct. App. 1991) (child was interviewed; court ruled that fact that victim's mother was in room just before interview had no bearing on reliability of child's statements).

[738] Idaho v. Wright, 110 S. Ct. 3139 (1990); United States v. Stivers, 33 M.J. 715 (A.C.M.R. 1991); United States v. Quick, 22 M.J. 722, 724 (A.C.M.R. 1986), *aff'd,* 26 M.J. 460 (C.M.A. 1988); People v. District Ct., 776 P.2d 1083, 1089 (Colo. 1989); State v. Bellotti, 383 N.W.2d 308, 313 (Minn. Ct. App. 1986) (child hearsay exception); State v. Carver, 380 N.W.2d 821, 826 (Minn Ct. App. 1986) (in applying child hearsay exception, court held that hearsay

Supreme Court pointed out in *Idaho v. Wright,* however, use of leading questions does not necessarily render children's statements untrustworthy.[739] Use of leading questions during interviews is discussed in **Chapter 4**.

Mental health counseling before statement. Following abuse, the victim may receive mental health services. During counseling sessions, the child may be asked about abuse. In *State v. Carlson,*[740] the Washington Court of Appeals considered whether a child's participation in counseling undermined the reliability of statements the child made following counseling. The court wrote:

> We recognize that a lapse of time and intervening counseling could affect the reliability of a child's statements regarding abuse. . . . "[I]t is *possible* that '[i]f there is evidence of prior interrogation, prompting, or manipulation by adults, spontaneity may be an inaccurate indicator of trustworthiness.'" (Emphasis added.) *Idaho v. Wright,* 110 S. Ct. 3139 (1990). However, as the *Wright* court's careful language makes clear, these factors will not affect reliability in all cases.

---

statements by young children were not sufficiently reliable when statements were elicited by questions from physician); State v. Robinson, 153 Ariz. 191, 735 P.2d 801, 811 (1987).
See also State v. Allen, 157 Ariz. 165, 755 P.2d 1153, 1162 (1988), where the court wrote:

> The statements of the child Cara were not spontaneous. They were the result of a conversation initiated by Cara's mother after a therapy session. The facts indicate that the child was being encouraged to reflect and report any previous molestation. "If there is evidence of prior interrogation, prompting, or manipulation by adults, spontaneity may be an inaccurate indicator of trustworthiness." . . . The circumstances of the conversation with her mother negate any idea of spontaneity.

See State v. Carlson, 61 Wash. App. 865, 812 P.2d 536 (1991). In *Carlson,* the court analyzed whether a delay between abuse and a child's description of the abuse, combined with intervening mental health counseling, undermined reliability. The court wrote, "We hold, therefore, that a trial judge may find child hearsay statements unreliable on the ground that there has been a lapse of time and intervening counseling between the abuse and the statements at issue only when the evidence demonstrates that the lapse or counseling somehow affected the child's statements." 812 P.2d at 540.

[739] 110 S. Ct. at 3148. Dana v. Department of Corrections, 958 F.2d 237 (8th Cir. 1992), *cert. denied,* 112 S. Ct. 3043 (1992); People v. Edwards, 224 Ill. App. 3d 1017, 586 N.E. 2d 1326 (1992); State v. Oslund, 469 N.W.2d 489, 494 (Minn. Ct. App. 1991) (three-year-old's statements "were reasonably spontaneous, and leading questions, when used, were not overly suggestive"); State v. McKinney, 50 Wash. App. 56, 747 P.2d 1113, 1117 n.4 (1987) (case interpreting child hearsay exception; "Statements made in response to questions are spontaneous where the child volunteers the information in response to questions that are neither leading nor suggestive"); State v. Robinson, 44 Wash. App. 611, 722 P.2d 1379, 1385 (1986) ("Although some of the statements were in response to questions, the record reveals the questions were not leading"); State v. Sorenson, 143 Wis. 2d 226, 421 N.W.2d 77, 86 (1988); State v. Lindner, 142 Wis. 2d 783, 419 N.W.2d 352 (Ct. App. 1987).

[740] 61 Wash. App. 865, 812 P.2d 536 (1991).

[Court's footnote: Such a rule would be unworkable in any event. Were the courts to hold as a matter of law that counseling affects a child's reliability, an abused child would be prevented from receiving much needed help until after trial. . . .]

We hold, therefore, that a trial judge may find child hearsay statements unreliable on the ground that there has been a lapse of time and intervening counseling between the abuse and the statements at issue only when the evidence demonstrates that the lapse or counseling somehow affected the child's statements.[741]

The Montana Supreme Court has expressed doubt about the reliability of children's statements made to therapists.[742]

Taped interviews. If a child discloses abuse during an interview that is video or audiotaped, the court can evaluate firsthand whether improper questions were asked. Recording is not the sine qua non of reliability, however.[743] As the Court observed in *Idaho v. Wright,* "Out-of-court statements made by children regarding sexual abuse arise in a wide variety of circumstances,"[744] many of which do not lend themselves to video or audiotaping. The Court declined "to read into the Confrontation Clause a preconceived and artificial litmus test for the procedural propriety of professional interviews in which children make hearsay statements against a defendant."[745] Although the fact that an interview is recorded may bolster confidence in a child's statement,[746] recording is not synonymous with trustworthiness.[747]

Consistent statements. Reliability may be enhanced when a child repeats an out-of-court statement more than once, and when each version is consistent.[748] If

---

[741] 812 P.2d at 540.

[742] State v. Mayes, 825 P.2d 1196 (Mont. 1992); State v. Harris, 247 Mont. 405, 808 P.2d 453 (1991).

[743] United States v. Palacios, 32 M.J. 1047 (A.C.M.R. 1991) (court was not convinced that videotaped interview was reliable).

[744] 110 S. Ct. at 3148.

[745] *Id.*

[746] *Id.* ("Although the procedural guidelines propounded by the court below may well enhance the reliability of out-of-court statements of children regarding sexual abuse"); McCafferty v. Leapley, 944 F.2d 445 (8th Cir. 1991), *cert. denied,* 112 S. Ct. 1277 (1992); United States v. Ellis, 935 F.2d 385, 394 n.8 (1st Cir.), *cert. denied,* 112 S. Ct. 201 (1991) ("It might have been desirable had LM's play in front of the social worker been videotaped, but we do not think this was essential to a finding of trustworthiness," citing *Idaho v. Wright*); United States v. Harjak, 33 M.J. 577, 582-83 (N.M.C.M.R. 1991).

[747] United States v. Ellis, 935 F.2d 385, 394 n.8 (1st Cir.), *cert. denied,* 112 S. Ct. 201 (1991).

[748] Idaho v. Wright, 110 S. Ct. 3139, 3150 (1990); United States v. Cree, 778 F.2d 474 n.5 (8th Cir. 1985) (physical abuse case; "the fact that [the victim] made such a statement separately to the two school officials and later made similar statements to Chaussee and Agent Hellekson in our view enhances [the victim's] credibility"); United States v. Stivers, 33 M.J. 715 (A.C.M.R. 1991); R.O. v. Pike County Dep't Human Resources, 578 So. 2d 1312, 1313

§ 7.44 FACTORS SURROUNDING STATEMENT

the description varies each time abuse is described, reliability may be questioned.[749] Consistency is a complex issue, however, and complete consistency is not necessary for reliability. Indeed, a degree of inconsistency is the norm rather than the exception. When a child's description of abuse never varies, suspicion arises that the child is repeating a memorized script.

Children disclose sexual abuse in many ways. Sorensen and Snow observe that disclosure is a process, not an event.[750] Many children disclose a little at a time. Thus, children's descriptions of abuse may change over time. The psychological reasons for children's inconsistency are explored in **Chapter 4**. The Eighth Circuit Court of Appeals took the correct approach to inconsistencies in children's statements in *United States v. Dorian.*[751] In *Dorian* the five-year-old victim made several inconsistent statements regarding her abuse. The court held that such inconsistency did not render the child's out-of-court statements unreliable under Rule 803(24). The court wrote:

> Nor do the conflicts in Roxanne's statement necessarily render her July 10 statement untrustworthy. As a clinical psychologist testifying as an expert witness explained, the contradictions may well have been a function of Roxanne's concern

---

(Ala. Civ. App. 1990); State v. Oslund, 469 N.W.2d 489, 494 (Minn. Ct. App. 1991); State v. Smith, 384 N.W.2d 546, 549 (Minn. Ct. App. 1986); D.A.H. v. G.A.H., 371 N.W.2d 1 (Minn. Ct. App. 1985) (child's statements to psychologist admitted); M.N.D. v. B.M.D., 356 N.W.2d 813 (Minn. Ct. App. 1984); State v. Allen, 157 Ariz. 165, 755 P.2d 1153, 1162 (1988); State v. Kuone, 243 Kan. 218, 757 P.2d 289, 292 (1988); State v. Conklin, 444 N.W.2d 268, 276 (Minn. 1989) (discussing child hearsay exception); State v. Gill, 806 S.W.2d 48, 54 (Mo. Ct. App. 1991); State v. Boyer, 803 S.W.2d 132 (Mo. Ct. App. 1991); State v. J.C.E., 235 Mont. 264, 767 P.2d 309, 316 (1988); State v. Buller, 484 N.W.2d 883 (S.D. 1992); State v. Floody, 481 N.W.2d 242 (S.D. 1992); State v. Gallagher, 150 Vt. 341, 554 A.2d 221, 225, *cert. denied,* 488 U.S. 995 (1988) (discussing child hearsay exception, court mentioned child's description of abuse and internal consistency and detail); State v. Robinson, 153 Ariz. 191, 735 P.2d 801, 811 (1987) (five-year-old victim; "Consistency does not always guarantee trustworthiness; it could be evidence that the statements were rehearsed. In this case, however, Nicole's [consistent] statements were made in stressful situations or were directly responsive to normal, nonleading questions. In these circumstances, a five-year old's consistency, like her spontaneity, indicates truthfulness"); People v. Kulakowski, 135 A.D.2d 1119, 523 N.Y.S.2d 288 (1987); Buckley v. State, 758 S.W.2d 339, 343 (Tex. Ct. App. 1988), *aff'd,* 786 S.W.2d 357 (Tex. Crim. App. 1990); State v. Robinson, 44 Wash. App. 611, 722 P.2d 1379, 1385 (1986).

[749] United States v. Lockwood, 23 M.J. 770, 771 (A.F.C.M.R. 1987); United States v. Crayton, 17 M.J. 932 (A.F.C.M.R. 1984); State v. Taylor, 103 N.M. 189, 704 P.2d 443 (Ct. App. 1985) (holding that three-year-old's hearsay statement identifying defendant was unreliable because child named no less than five perpetrators, parents suggested identity of defendant, and there was no corroboration of child's identification); State v. Smith, 384 N.W.2d 546, 549 (Minn. Ct. App. 1986) (case involved child hearsay exception; court held that child's statements were not sufficiently reliable, in part because statements lacked consistency).

[750] Sorensen & Snow, *How Children Tell: The Process of Disclosure in Child Sexual Abuse,* 70 Child Welfare 3 (1991).

[751] 803 F.2d 1439 (8th Cir. 1986).

about how the information would be received, and whether she would be punished for what she said. According to the psychologist, it frequently takes a long time for children to share what is really going on and they may then do so in stages, telling a little more each time.[752]

It is important to determine whether inconsistencies relate to core aspects of the abuse or peripheral details. Inconsistency regarding peripheral detail is inevitable with children and adults alike. Moreover, inconsistency regarding core events, although pertinent to reliability, need not brand a statement unreliable.

State of mind and emotion when statement was made. A child may display feeling or emotion that supports the reliability of an out-of-court statement.[753] For example, a child may demonstrate embarrassment or shame one would expect when a child discloses sexual abuse. It is important to note, however, that many abused children are not emotional when they describe abuse. Many victims are severely traumatized. Others are depressed. Still others have told their story over and over again. These and other factors cause many abused children to describe their abuse in flat, matter-of-fact terms.

Play and gestures coinciding with description of abuse. A young child's play or gestures while describing abuse may enhance the reliability of the child's statement. For example, if a child spontaneously places the penis of an anatomical doll in the mouth of another doll or in the child's mouth while describing sexual abuse, the child's verbal statement may gain trustworthiness.[754]

Developmentally unusual sexual knowledge.[755] Young children lack the experience required to fabricate or fantasize detailed accounts of sexual acts.[756] It is difficult to imagine a four-year-old sexually naive child capable of inventing a detailed and anatomically accurate account of fellatio, including ejaculation, unless the child has either experienced fellatio or been exposed to it.[757] Naturally,

---

[752] *Id.* at 1444.

[753] Idaho v. Wright, 110 S. Ct. 3139, 3150 (1990); Morgan v. Foretich, 846 F.2d 941, 948 (4th Cir. 1988); United States v. Quick, 22 M.J. 722, 724 (A.C.M.R. 1986), *aff'd,* 26 M.J. 460 (C.M.A. 1988); People v. District Ct., 776 P.2d 1083, 1089–90 (Colo. 1989).

[754] United States v. Pollard, 34 M.J. 1008 (A.C.M.R. 1992); People v. Bowers, 801 P.2d 511, 521 (Colo. 1990). See **Ch. 4** for discussion of use of anatomical dolls during interviews.

[755] In some cases developmentally unusual sexual knowledge may be corroborative in nature. *See* State v. Jones, 112 Wash. 2d 488, 772 P.2d 496, 500 (1989).

[756] E. Matthews & K. Saywitz, California Ctr. for Judicial Educ. & Research, Vol. 12, Child Victim Witness Manual (1992). Matthews and Saywitz write, "Even though young children are capable of intentionally lying and misstating reality, studies show that they have limited knowledge of adult sexual behavior from which to invent detailed descriptions." *Id.* at 24.

[757] Dana v. Department of Corrections, 958 F.2d 237 (8th Cir. 1992), *cert. denied,* 1992 WL 103799 (1992); McCafferty v. Leapley, 944 F.2d 445 (8th Cir. 1991), *cert. denied,* 112 S. Ct. 1277 (1992); Nelson v. Farrey, 874 F.2d 1222 (7th Cir. 1989), *cert. denied,* 493 U.S.

1042 (1990) (case deals with medical diagnosis or treatment exception; child described "white mud" coming from penis); Morgan v. Foretich, 846 F.2d 941 (4th Cir. 1988); United States v. Dorian, 803 F.2d 1439, 1445 (8th Cir. 1986) (five-year-old sex abuse victim described an erection and sexually explicit behavior by defendant and demonstrated what happened with anatomical dolls; "It is unlikely that Roxanne could have fabricated the story she told . . . and repeated . . . , and ordinary experience suggests that Roxanne would not have engaged in the behavior with the anatomically correct dolls that Monica Whiting observed absent some prior similar experience"); United States v. Cree, 778 F.2d 474, 477–78 (8th Cir. 1985) (physical abuse case; "It is highly unlikely that a four-year-old child would fabricate such accusations of abuse"); United States v. Pollard, 34 M.J. 1008; People v. Bowers, 801 P.2d 511, 521 (Colo. 1990) ("In some circumstances the sexual terminology employed by a young child in describing a sexual offense can lend some measure of reliability to the child's statement"); Lancaster v. People, 200 Colo. 448, 615 P.2d 720, 723 (1980) ("children of tender years are generally not adept at reasoned reflection and at concoction of false stories under such circumstances"); People v. Anita B., 592 N.E.2d 274 (Ill. Ct. App. 1992); State v. Myatt, 237 Kan. 17, 697 P.2d 836, 841 (1985) ("children do not have enough knowledge about sexual matters to lie about them"); In re Meeboer, 134 Mich. App. 294, 350 N.W.2d 868 (1984); State v. Taylor, 103 N.M. 189, 704 P.2d 443 (Ct. App. 1985); State v. Oslund, 469 N.W.2d 489, 494 (Minn. Ct. App. 1991); State v. Allen, 157 Ariz. 165, 755 P.2d 1153, 1163 (1988) (court recognized that age-inappropriate sexual knowledge may support reliability of child's hearsay statement; however, in this case, there were explanations for child's sexual knowledge; thus child's knowledge did not support reliability of child's hearsay); People v. Diefenderfer, 784 P.2d 741 (Colo. 1989); People v. District Ct., 776 P.2d 1083, 1089 (Colo. 1989); Oldsen v. People, 732 P.2d 1132. 1136 (Colo. 1986); State v. D.R., 109 N.J. 348, 537 A.2d 667, 673 (1988); Buckley v. State, 758 S.W.2d 339, 343 (Tex. Ct. App. 1988), aff'd, 786 S.W.2d 357 (Tex. Crim. App. 1990); State v. Edwards, 1992 WL 118977 (Minn. 1992); State v. Lanam, 444 N.W.2d 882, 885 (Minn. Ct. App. 1989), aff'd, 459 N.W.2d 656 (Minn. 1990), cert. denied, 111 S. Ct. (1991); State v. Herrin, 562 So. 2d 1, 9 (La. Ct. App. 1990); State v. J.C.E., 235 Mont. 264, 767 P.2d 309, 315 (1988); State v. Robinson, 44 Wash. App. 611, 722 P.2d 1379, 1382 (1986) (three-year-old described "soap" coming out of defendant's "tail"); State v. Jagielski, 161 Wis. 2d 67, 467 N.W.2d 196, 199 (Ct. App. 1991).

See also State v. Sorenson, 143 Wis. 2d 226, 421 N.W.2d 77 (1988), where the court wrote that "a child at such a young age is unlikely to review an incident of sexual assault and calculate the effect of a statement about it. . . . Additional support for the trustworthiness of the hearsay is [her] knowledge well beyond the ordinary familiarity of a child her age. A young child is unlikely to fabricate a graphic account of sexual activity because it is beyond the realm of his or her experience." 421 N.W.2d at 85, 87; *see also* K. MacFarlane & J. Waterman, Sexual Abuse of Young Children 27 (1986), where the authors write:

> [I]ssues of truth versus lying are complex in the preschool years. Children in this age group may tell lies under two circumstances: in order to avoid a problem or punishment (e.g., "Susie was the one who did it, not me") and in order to impress adults or get attention (e.g., telling tall tales, such as that there was a hippopotamus in the back yard last night). However, children cannot manufacture stories based on information that they have not learned or experienced. For example, children will not make up a story about the comings and goings of Eskimos if they have never been exposed to any learning about Eskimos, and will not say someone attempted oral copulation with them if they have not had either direct or vicarious experience with that act.

United States v. Quarles, 25 M.J. 761 (N.M.C.M.R. 1987) (reliability is undermined if there is an alternative explanation for a child's developmentally unusual knowledge of sexual acts).

care must be taken to rule out innocent explanations for a child's developmentally unusual knowledge of sexual acts, anatomy, or vocabulary.

Idiosyncratic detail. Presence in a child's statement of idiosyncratic detail of sexual abuse may point toward reliability.[758] Jones and McQuiston write that "[i]diosyncracy in the sexual abuse account is exemplified by children who describe smells and tastes associated with rectal, vaginal or oral sex."[759] Lack of idiosyncratic detail does not render a child's statement unreliable. Many forms of sexual abuse lack unique detail. Fondling through clothing is an example. In some cases, paucity of detail is a product of the child's psychological defenses. In young children, difficulty with free recall memory may limit the amount of detail in the child's description.[760]

Age and maturity. A child's youth may render the child's statement more reliable.[761]

---

[758] Nelson v. Farrey, 874 F.2d 1222 (7th Cir. 1989), *cert. denied,* 493 U.S. 1042 (1990) (child described white mud coming from perpetrator's penis); State v. Robinson, 44 Wash. App. 611, 722 P.2d 1379, 1382 (1986) (three-year-old said "he had touched her with his tail and that soap had come out of his tail"). *See also* E. Matthews & K. Saywitz, California Ctr. for Judicial Educ. & Research, Vol. 12, Child Victim Witness Manual 24 (1992), where the authors write:

> Even though young children are capable of intentionally lying and misstating reality, studies show that they have limited knowledge of adult sexual behavior from which to invent detailed descriptions. While a minority of preschoolers may be familiar with the idea of genital penetration for the purpose of reproduction, knowledge of oral and anal sex as well as details related to orgasm (pace of breathing) and ejaculation (taste of semen) are entirely unfamiliar. Unless young children have been personally or vicariously exposed to adult sexual activity, they do not possess the knowledge to fabricate detailed and believable descriptions of such activity.

[759] D. Jones & M. McQuiston, Interviewing the Sexually Abused Child 30 (1985).

[760] For discussion of free recall memory in children, see **Ch. 2**.

[761] Dana v. Department of Corrections, 958 F.2d 237 (8th Cir. 1992), *cert. denied,* 112 S. Ct. 3043 (1992); Morgan v. Foretich, 846 F.2d 941 (4th Cir. 1988); United States v. Dorian, 803 F.2d 1439, 1445 (8th Cir. 1986); United States v. Cree, 778 F.2d 474, 477 (8th Cir. 1985) (physical abuse of four-year-old victim; "Maurcie's age is a significant factor supporting the finding that the challenged statements are trustworthy"); United States v. Renville, 779 F.2d 430, 441 (8th Cir. 1985) ("a declarant's young age is a factor that may substantially lessen the degree of skepticism with which we view their motives"); Roberts v. Hollocher, 664 F.2d 200, 205 (8th Cir. 1981); United States v. Iron Shell, 633 F.2d 77 (8th Cir. 1980), *cert. denied,* 450 U.S. 1001 (1981); United States v. Quick, 22 M.J. 722, 724 (A.C.M.R. 1986), *aff'd,* 26 M.J. 460 (C.M.A. 1988); State v. Robinson, 153 Ariz. 191, 735 P.2d 801, 811 (1987); People v. Diefenderfer, 784 P.2d 741 (Colo. 1989); State v. McCafferty, 356 N.W.2d 159, 164 (S.D. 1984), *cert. denied,* 476 U.S. 1172 (1986); State v. Slider, 38 Wash. App. 689, 688 P.2d 538, 543 (1984); State v. J.C.E., 235 Mont. 264, 767 P.2d 309, 315 (1988); State v. Sorenson, 143 Wis. 2d 226, 421 N.W.2d 77, 84 (1988) (excellent discussion

Developmentally appropriate terminology. When a young child's initial disclosure of abuse is made in terminology one would expect from a child of that age, the reliability of the statement may be enhanced.[762] By contrast, if a child's initial disclosure employs adult terminology, the possibility arises that an adult coached the child. The words used by the child are not a litmus test for reliability, however. Many abused children are subjected to multiple interviews, and it is not uncommon for abused children to pick up adult terms like *molest* and *penetration* during interviews, and to incorporate such terms into their descriptions of abuse. Similarly, an abused child who would not spontaneously use adult terminology may first reveal abuse to a parent who, while questioning the child, introduces a term that seems unusual coming from a child. An abused child with a sophisticated vocabulary might use adult-like terms during initial disclosure. Thus, when considering the child's terminology, it is important to assess the child's developmental and linguistic level, along with the number of times the child has been interviewed and by whom.

Statement against interest. Individuals are generally not disposed to make statements against their penal, economic, or other interests.[763] When they do, the statements may be more reliable.[764] A statement that a child knew could result in punishment or loss of privilege may have enhanced reliability.

---

of factors affecting reliability); State v. Robinson, 44 Wash. App. 611, 722 P.2d 1379, 1383 (1986).

The diagnosis or treatment exception is addressed in State v. Nelson, 138 Wis. 2d 418, 406 N.W.2d 385 (1987). In its discussion of the reliability of a three-year-old declarant's statements to her psychologist, the court remarked:

[W]e find that the age of the declarant and the nature of the allegations manifest indicia of trustworthiness. Although there exists considerable debate as to whether out-of-court statements by children which allege sexual abuse are intrinsically reliable, there is significant support for the proposition that such statements are reliable.

[762] United States v. Quick, 22 M.J. 722, 724 (A.C.M.R. 1986), *aff'd*, 26 M.J. 460 (C.M.A. 1988); People v. Bowers, 801 P.2d 511, 521 (Colo. 1990) ("In some circumstances the sexual terminology employed by a young child in describing a sexual offense can lend some measure of reliability to the child's statement"); State v. Robinson, 44 Wash. App. 611, 722 P.2d 1379, 1382 (1986) (three-year-old described "soap" coming out of defendant's "tail").

[763] *See* Fed. R. Evid. 804(b)(3).

[764] Huff v. White Motor Corp., 609 F.2d 286, 292 (7th Cir. 1979); United States v. Pollard, 34 M.J. 1008 (A.C.M.R. 1992); State v. Ortlepp, 363 N.W.2d 39, 44 (Minn. 1985); Buckley v. State, 758 S.W.2d 339, 343 (Tex. Ct. App. 1988), *aff'd*, 786 S.W.2d 357 (Tex. Crim. App. 1990).

Motive to fabricate. Evidence that a child had or did not have a motive to fabricate impacts reliability.[765] Similarly, the motivation of adults is considered.[766]

Personal knowledge. Proof that the child had personal knowledge of the event and ample opportunity to observe enhances reliability.[767]

Level of certainty regarding event. If a child's answers to questions indicate that the child lacks understanding of basic factual matters described in the child's statement, reliability may be called into question.[768] Reliability may be enhanced when a child does not agree with everything a questioner asks, or when a child corrects a questioner. Disagreement and correction demonstrate

---

[765] United States v. Stivers, 33 M.J. 715 (A.C.M.R. 1991); United States v. Miller, 32 M.J. 843 (N.M.C.M.R. 1991) (child had no motive to fabricate); State v. Edwards, 1992 WL 118977 (Minn. 1992); *In re* Dependency of S.S., 61 Wash. App. 488, 814 P.2d 204 (1991); State v. Robinson, 44 Wash. App. 611, 722 P.2d 1379, 1385 (1986) (three-year-old "had no apparent motive to lie").

[766] Children are sometimes convinced by parents or other adults to make untrue statements. It is unfortunately true that in a small percentage of contested child custody disputes unscrupulous parents fabricate allegations of sexual abuse and persuade or coach children to make false allegations. The issue of fabricated allegations in custody disputes is extremely complex, and snap judgments are dangerous and unwarranted. See **Ch. 4**. *See also* Myers, *Allegations of Child Sexual Abuse in Custody and Visitation Litigation: Recommendations for Improved Fact Finding and Child Protection*, 28 J. Fam. L.1 (1989–90); *In re* Marriage of L.R., 202 Ill. App. 3d 69, 559 N.E.2d 779 (1990) (cautioning courts to consider motivation of parents involved in custody or visitation dispute when considering children's hearsay statements related by contesting parent).

See also Idaho v. Wright, 110 S. Ct. 3139, 3150 (1990); Huff v. White Motor Corp., 609 F.2d 286, 292 (7th Cir. 1979); United States v. Williamson, 26 M.J. 115 (C.M.A. 1988); United States v. Palacios, 32 M.J. 1047 (A.C.M.R. 1991) (mother had custody of child; mother was antagonistic to defendant); R.O. v. Pike County Dep't Human Resources, 578 So. 2d 1312, 1313 (Ala. Civ. App. 1991) (adults repeating child's statements had high credibility); State v. Allen, 157 Ariz. 165, 755 P.2d 1153, 1164 (1988) (child disliked defendant; "Cara was not without improper motivation in her accusations against the defendant"); People v. Bowers, 801 P.2d 511, 521 (Colo. 1990); People v. District Court, 776 P.2d 1083, 1089 (Colo. 1989); State v. Kuone, 243 Kan. 218, 757 P.2d 289, 292–93 (1988) ("There appears to have been no ill feeling between the families of the victim and the defendant, and no reason for her to concoct an untrue story"); State v. Bellotti, 383 N.W.2d 308, 313 (Minn. Ct. App. 1986) (child hearsay exception); D.A.H. v. G.A.H., 371 N.W.2d 1 (Minn. Ct. App. 1985); State v. Gill, 806 S.W.2d 48, 53 (Mo. Ct. App. 1991) (child's mother was not present during interview, thus eliminating source of possible parental pressure to make statement); State v. J.C.E., 235 Mont. 264, 767 P.2d 309, 315 (1988); Buckley v. State, 758 S.W.2d 339, 343 (Tex. Ct. App. 1988), *aff'd*, 786 S.W.2d 357 (Tex. Crim. App. 1990); State v. Slider, 38 Wash. App. 689, 688 P.2d 538, 543 (1984); State v. Sorenson, 143 Wis. 2d 226, 421 N.W.2d 77, 85 (1988).

[767] United States v. Carlson, 547 F.2d 1346 (8th Cir. 1976), *cert. denied*, 431 U.S. 914 (1977); R.O. v. Pike County Dep't Human Resources, 578 So. 2d 1312, 1313 (Ala. Civ. App. 1990).

[768] State v. Smith, 384 N.W.2d 546, 549 (Minn. Ct. App. 1986). Young children are not adept at interpreting ambiguous events, nor are they good at understanding the motivation or thinking of other people.

§ 7.44 FACTORS SURROUNDING STATEMENT

that the child has a firm mental picture of the matter described. Furthermore, disagreement and correction indicate the child is not simply responding unthinkingly, or answering questions to please the questioner.[769]

Possibility of memory loss. A statement about an act that occurred in the past raises the possibility of memory loss.[770] Memory issues are of little concern when statements describe then-existing events or feelings.[771] When statements describe past events, reliability may be influenced by the amount of time between the event and the child's description of the event.[772] In *State v. Carlson*,[773] the Washington Court of Appeals held that lapse of time does not undermine reliability unless there is evidence that the lapse actually affected the child's out-of-court statement.[774] The court observed that "[t]o treat a lapse of time between abuse and accusatory statements as necessarily indicative of unreliability would also overlook the tendency of abuse victims to delay reporting that abuse occurred."[775] When evaluating lapse of time, the court considers the strength of the child's memory and intervening factors that may have interfered with memory.[776]

Expert testimony regarding reliability. American courts agree that expert witnesses may not offer expert testimony that comments *directly* on the credibility of individual children or sexually abused children as a group before the trier of fact.[777] However, the psychological literature reveals that properly qualified professionals possess information that, in some instances, can assist judges to evaluate the truthfulness of children's out-of-court statements. Under Rule 104(a) of the Federal Rules of Evidence, the decision to admit hearsay is a preliminary matter for the trial judge, and the rules of evidence do not apply.

---

[769] State v. Bellotti, 383 N.W.2d 308, 313 (Minn. Ct. App. 1986).

[770] Dutton v. Evans, 400 U.S. 74 (1970).

[771] State v. Robinson, 44 Wash. App. 611, 722 P.2d 1379, 1385 (1986) (the three-year-olds's "statements were assertions of either present facts of the victim's discomfort or of facts which had occurred immediately prior to her making the statements").

[772] State v. Carlson, 61 Wash. App. 865, 812 P.2d 536, 540 (1991); State v. Stange, 53 Wash. App. 638, 769 P.2d 823 (1989) (fact that child's statement describes past event not very helpful in determining reliability); State v. Robinson, 44 Wash. App. 611, 722 P.2d 1379, 1385 (1986) (child's statement described abuse that occurred immediately before statement).

[773] 61 Wash. App. 865, 812 P.2d 536 (1991).

[774] 812 P.2d at 540.

[775] *Id.* at 540, n.3.

[776] Dutton v. Evans, 400 U.S. 74, 88–89 (1970); State v. Ryan, 103 Wash. 2d 165, 691 P.2d 197, 205 (1984); State v. Carlson, 61 Wash. App. 865, 812 P.2d 536 (1991); State v. Robinson, 44 Wash. App. 611, 722 P.2d 1379, 1383 (1986) ("no intervening influences militate against the reliability of the statements").

[777] See **Ch. 4**.

Thus, in deciding reliability, a judge theoretically could consider expert testimony on the reliability of a child's hearsay statement.

Four hearsay risks. In all cases it is useful to analyze statements in terms of the hearsay risks of insincerity, memory loss, ambiguity, and misperception.[778] When the risks are low, admission is appropriate.

§ 7.45 —Factors Corroborating Statement

Many factors that do not surround the making of an out-of-court statement may nevertheless bolster confidence in the reliability of the statement.

Medical or physical evidence of abuse. A child's statement may be corroborated by medical, laboratory, scientific, or physical evidence.[779]

---

[778] See 4 Weinstein & Berger ¶ 803(24)[01], at 803-375, where the authors write:

Cases decided pursuant to Rule 803(24) indicate that the courts have been willing to admit hearsay evidence when the declarant is available and subject to cross-examination, and the hearsay statement in question was not the product of faulty perception, memory or meaning, the dangers against which the hearsay rule seeks to guard.

(footnote omitted).

[779] Morgan v. Foretich, 846 F.2d 941 (4th Cir. 1988); United States v. Dorian, 803 F.2d 1439, 1445 (8th Cir. 1986); United States v. Cree, 778 F.2d 474, 477 (8th Cir. 1985); United States v. Quick, 22 M.J. 722, 724 (A.C.M.R. 1986), aff'd, 26 M.J. 460 (C.M.A. 1988) (sexual abuse case; "we note that the child's statements were corroborated by the physical evidence of inflammation of her vagina"); Thompson v. State, 769 P.2d 997, 1000 (Alaska Ct. App. 1989) (case does not interpret child hearsay exception, but does contain helpful discussion of medical evidence as corroboration of child's out-of-court statements); People v. Bowers, 801 P.2d 511, 525 (Colo. 1990); People v. District Court, 776 P.2d 1083, 1090 (Colo. 1989); State v. Kuone, 243 Kan. 218, 757 P.2d 289, 292 (1988) (blood in victim's underwear); People v. Landis, 593 N.E.2d 893 (Ill. Ct. App. 1992); People v. Ward, 207 Ill. App. 3d 365, 565 N.E.2d 740 (1991); State v. Soukup, 376 N.W.2d 498, 501 (Minn. Ct. App. 1985) (hearsay corroborated by medical evidence); State v. Taylor, 103 N.M. 189, 704 P.2d 443, 452 (Ct. App. 1985) (young victim stated that defendant "stuck finger" in child's "butt"; child's statement was corroborated by medical evidence that child's rectum was irritated; examining physician may corroborate child's statement by describing physical examination); State v. Swan, 114 Wash. 2d 613, 790 P.2d 610, 615, 622–23 (1990), cert. denied, 111 S. Ct. 752 (1991) (child's statement was corroborated somewhat by child's statements of physical pain); State v. Bishop, 63 Wash. App. 15, 816 P.2d 738, 746 (1991) (child's hearsay statement describing painful urination corroborated her statement to professional describing penetration); State v. Gribble, 60 Wash. App. 374, 804 P.2d 634 (1991); State v. Robinson, 44 Wash. App. 611, 722 P.2d 1379 (1986) (semen stain on child's blanket); State v. Gitchel, 41 Wash. App. 820, 706 P.2d 1091 (1985).

§ 7.45   FACTORS CORROBORATING STATEMENT   263

Changes in behavior. When a child's behavior alters in a way that corroborates the child's description of abuse, it may be appropriate to place increased confidence in the child's statement.[780]

Developmentally unusual sexual knowledge. In many cases, a young child's developmentally unusual knowledge of sexual acts, anatomy, or terminology surrounds the child's out-of-court statement and may be considered in assessing the reliability of the child's statement.[781] In other cases, the child's developmentally unusual knowledge corroborates the child's statement.[782]

Play and gestures indicative of abuse. In some cases a child's play or gestures may corroborate the child's statement describing sexual abuse.[783]

Corroborative hearsay statements. A child's hearsay statement offered under a residual or child hearsay exception may be corroborated by another hearsay statement admissible under a different exception.[784]

---

[780] State v. Robinson, 153 Ariz. 191, 735 P.2d 801, 812 (1987); State v. Ritchey, 107 Ariz. 552, 490 P.2d 558, 561 (1971) (excited utterance exception; court's discussion of children's altered behavior useful in analysis of residual exception); People v. Bowers, 801 P.2d 511, 522, 525 (Colo. 1990); People v. Diefenderfer, 784 P.2d 741 (Colo. 1989) (child demonstrated extreme anxiety and masturbated on being questioned regarding sexual abuse by stepfather); State v. Kuone, 243 Kan. 218, 757 P.2d 289, 292 (1988); People v. Ridgeway, 194 Ill. App. 3d 881, 551 N.E.2d 790 (1990); State v. Carver, 380 N.W.2d 821, 826 (Minn. Ct. App. 1986); M.N.D. v. B.M.D., 356 N.W.2d 813 (Minn. Ct. App. 1984) (abnormal behavior following visits with alleged abuser); Leatherwood v. State, 548 So. 2d 389, 402 (Miss. 1989) (victim of rape experienced severe emotional reaction); State v. Taylor, 103 N.M. 189, 704 P.2d 443, 452 (Ct. App. 1985) ("He had nightmares, was sick, and refused to allow himself to be touched"); Buckley v. State, 758 S.W.2d 339, 343 (Tex. Ct. App. 1988), *aff'd,* 786 S.W.2d 357 (Tex. Crim. App. 1990); State v. Gribble, 60 Wash. App. 374, 804 P.2d 634 (1991); State v. Gitchel, 41 Wash. App. 820, 706 P.2d 1091 (1985) (nightmares).

[781] *See* People v. Bowers, 801 P.2d 511 (Colo. 1990), in which a majority of the Colorado Supreme Court ruled that the trial judge may not consider the child's statement itself as corroborative evidence. In a persuasive dissent, Chief Justice Rovira argued that in some cases the content of the child's statement may have corroborative value. 801 P.2d at 527, 532 (Rovira, C.J., dissenting).

[782] *In re* Nicole V., 71 N.Y.2d 112, 518 N.E.2d 914, 524 N.Y.S.2d 19 (1987); State v. Swan, 114 Wash. 2d 613, 790 P.2d 610, 615, 620–21 (1990), *cert. denied,* 111 S. Ct. 752 (1991); State v. Jones, 112 Wash. 2d 488, 772 P.2d 496, 500 (1989) (child's precocious knowledge of urolagina corroborated her hearsay statement); State v. Bishop, 63 Wash. App. 15, 816 P.2d 738, 746 (1991) (nine-year-old child's complaint of painful urination constituted precocious sexual knowledge).

[783] State v. Swan, 114 Wash. 2d 613, 790 P.2d 610, 622 (1990), *cert. denied,* 111 S. Ct. 752 (1991) (child's play with anatomical dolls provided some corroboration).

[784] State v. Bishop, 63 Wash. App. 15, 816 P.2d 738 (1991).

Reliability of person who overheard statement. The court may consider the reliability of the individual who overheard the child's out-of-court statement and proposes to repeat it at trial.[785]

Writing. The fact that a child took time to reduce a statement to writing may indicate reliability.[786]

More than one child with same story. Two or more children may be exposed to the same event. If the children are interviewed separately, and each tells a similar story, their statements are mutually corroborative, enhancing the reliability of each.[787] If, on the other hand, the children are interviewed together, the fact that they tell the same story does little to bolster the reliability of their statements, since one child may have been influenced by the other.[788]

Eyewitness. The testimony at trial of an eyewitness may strengthen the reliability of a child's hearsay statement describing the event.[789]

---

[785] *See* State v. McKinney, 50 Wash. App. 56, 747 P.2d 1113 (1987). The *McKinney* case concerned a child hearsay exception. The defendant argued that the four-year-old's statements were unreliable not because the child was unreliable, but because the witness who repeated the child's hearsay statements at trial was unreliable. The witness proposed to testify to additional statements made by the child that the witness had not previously remembered. The court of appeals rejected the defendant's argument, writing:

> The constitutional requirement that there be adequate indicia of reliability surrounding a child's hearsay statements refers to the circumstances that "'existed *at the time that statement was made* . . . .'" [State v. Ryan, 103 Wash. 2d 165, 691 P.2d 197 (1984)] does not require the trial court to determine if the *witness's* memory or articulation of the child's statement is reliable. Indeed, any deficiencies in the witness's memory or perception may be explored on cross examination. . . . We reject [defendant's] attempt to alter the focus of the *Ryan* analysis from the reliability of the victim's statement to the reliability of the witness's recollection.

747 P.2d at 1116.

[786] 4 Weinstein & Berger ¶ 803(24)9010, at 803-376.

[787] Murray v. State, 770 P.2d 1131 (Alaska Ct. App. 1989); Clifton v. State, 758 P.2d 1279 (Alaska Ct. App. 1988); *In re* Nicole V., 71 N.Y.2d 112, 518 N.E.2d 914, 524 N.Y.S.2d 19 (1987); Commonwealth v. Haber, 351 Pa. Super 79, 505 A.2d 273, 285 (1986); State v. Swan, 114 Wash. 2d 613, 790 P.2d 610, 618 (1990), *cert. denied,* 111 S. Ct. 752 (1991).

[788] State v. Carver, 380 N.W.2d 821, 826 (Minn. Ct. App. 1986) (interpreting child hearsay exception; holding that hearsay statements by young children were not sufficiently reliable, in part because children were interviewed together).

[789] State v. Robinson, 153 Ariz. 191, 735 P.2d 801, 812 (1987) (five-year-old victim; "Nicole's statements were corroborated by Carla's testimony, by physical evidence, and by Nicole's behavioral changes. . . . Although Rules 803(24) and 804(b)(5) do not require corroboration, corroborating evidence obviously bolsters the reliability of Nicole's statements"); State v. Boodry, 96 Ariz. 259, 394 P.2d 196, *cert. denied,* 379 U.S. 949 (1964) (case arose before adoption of residual exception; adult witnessed five-year-old child being sexually abused by her father); People v. Bowers, 801 P.2d 511, 525 (Colo. 1990); State v. Petry, 524 N.E.2d 1293 (Ind. Ct. App. 1988); State v. Swan, 114 Wash. 2d 613, 790 P.2d 610, 615 (1990), *cert.*

§ 7.45 FACTORS CORROBORATING STATEMENT

Defendant's opportunity to commit act. The fact that the defendant had the opportunity to commit the act described in a child's statement may increase the reliability of the statement.[790]

Admission by defendant. An admission or confession by the defendant corroborates the child's statement.[791]

Evidence of defendant's prior uncharged misconduct. Evidence that a defendant has a history of activity similar to that complained of by a child may support the child's assertion.[792]

Character evidence. Although the rules of evidence bar the prosecutor from offering evidence of the defendant's character to prove that the defendant acted in conformity with character on a particular occasion,[793] the rules do not govern the preliminary question of corroboration. An argument can be made that if a pertinent trait of the defendant's character tends to corroborate a child's hearsay statement, the character trait should be admissible on the issue of corroboration.[794]

Expert testimony that child was abused. Expert testimony that the child was abused may corroborate the child's statement.[795]

---

denied, 111 S. Ct. 752 (1991); State v. Jones, 112 Wash. 2d 488, 772 P.2d 496, 500 (1989); State v. Justiniano, 48 Wash. App. 572, 740 P.2d 872, 875 (1987) (corroboration supplied by eyewitness testimony from another child).

[790] State v. Bellotti, 383 N.W.2d 308, 313 (Minn. Ct. App. 1986) (child hearsay exception); Buckley v. State, 758 S.W.2d 339, 343–44 (Tex. Ct. App. 1988), *aff'd*, 786 S.W.2d 357 (Tex. Crim. App. 1990); State v. Sorenson, 143 Wis. 2d 226, 421 N.W.2d 77, 85 (1988); State v. Oliver, 161 Wis. 2d 140, 467 N.W.2d 211, 214 (Ct. App. 1991).

[791] State v. Allen, 157 Ariz. 165, 755 P.2d 1153, 1166 (1988) (child's hearsay was not corroborated by defendant's statement that was too ambiguous to constitute consciousness of guilt); People v. Bowers, 801 P.2d 511, 525 (Colo. 1990); People v. Diefenderfer, 784 P.2d 741 (Colo. 1989) (defendant made inculpatory statements to investigator); Perez v. State, 536 So. 2d 206 (Fla. 1988), *cert. denied*, 492 U.S. 923 (1989) (defendant's admission to police officer constituted corroboration); D.A.H. v. G.A.H., 371 N.W.2d 1 (Minn. Ct. App. 1985) (residual exception; child's statements to psychologist admitted; trustworthiness bolstered by admissions of abuser); State v. Swan, 114 Wash. 2d 613, 790 P.2d 610, 615 (1990), *cert. denied*, 111 S. Ct. 752 (1991); State v. Frey, 43 Wash. App. 605, 718 P.2d 846 (1986).

[792] People v. Bowers, 801 P.2d 511, 525 (Colo. 1990); State v. Jones, 112 Wash. 2d 488, 772 P.2d 496, 500–01 (1989) (defendant's prior acts of urolagina with other persons corroborated child's statement that defendant asked victim to urinate in his mouth). See **Ch. 6** for analysis of uncharged misconduct evidence in child abuse litigation.

[793] Fed. R. Evid. 404(a).

[794] State v. Jones, 112 Wash. 2d 488, 772 P.2d 496, 501 (1989).

[795] People v. Bowers, 801 P.2d 511, 525 (Colo. 1990); *In re* Donna K., 132 A.D.2d 1004, 518 N.Y.S.2d 289 (1987) (expert testimony on sexual abuse sufficient to corroborate child's hearsay statement); Dutchess County Dep't of Social Servs. v. Bertha C., 130 Misc. 2d 1043, 498 N.Y.S.2d 960 (Fam. Ct. 1986).

§ 7.46 Child Hearsay Exception

Beginning in 1982 in the state of Washington, an increasing number of states enacted hearsay exceptions for children's statements describing sexual abuse.[796] The Washington statute states:

> A statement made by a child when under the age of ten describing any act of sexual contact performed with or on the child by another, or describing any attempted act of sexual contact with or on the child by another, not otherwise admissible by statute or court rule, is admissible in evidence in dependency proceedings . . . and criminal proceedings, including juvenile offense adjudications, in the courts of the state of Washington if:
>
> (1) The court finds, in a hearing conducted outside the presence of the jury, that the time, content, and circumstances of the statement provide sufficient indicia of reliability; and
>
> (2) The child either:
>
> (a) Testifies at the proceedings; or
>
> (b) Is unavailable as a witness: Provided, That when the child is unavailable as a witness, such statement may be admitted only if there is corroborative evidence of the act.
>
> A statement may not be admitted under this section unless the proponent of the statement makes known to the adverse party his intention to offer the statement and the particulars of the statement sufficiently in advance of the proceedings to provide the adverse party with a fair opportunity to prepare to meet the statement.[797]

---

[796] See Ala. Code §§ 15-25-31, 15-25-32 (Cum. Supp. 1990); Alaska Stat. § 12.40.110 (1990) (applies only in grand jury proceedings); Colo. Rev. Stat. § 13-25-129 (1986 Replacement); Fla. Stat. Ann. § 90.802(23) (West Cum. Supp. 1991); Ga. Code Ann. § 24-3-16 (Michie Cum. Supp. 1991); Idaho Code § 19-3024 (1987); Ill. Ann. Stat. ch. 38, ¶ 115-10 (Smith-Hurd 1990); Ind. Code Ann. § 35-37-4-6 (West Cum. Supp. 1991); Kan. Stat. Ann. § 60-460(dd) (Cum. Supp. 1989); Me. Rev. Stat. Ann. tit. 14, § 1205 (West Cum. Supp. 1990); Md. Cts. & Jud. Proc. Code Ann. § 9-103.1 (1989); Mass. Gen. Laws Ann. ch. 233, §§ 81-83 (West Cum. Supp. 1990); Minn. Stat. Ann. § 595.02 (West 1988); Miss. Code Ann § 13-1-403 (Cum. Supp. 1990); Mo. Ann. Stat. § 491.075 (Vernon Cum. Supp. 1991); Nev. Rev. Stat. Ann. § 51.385 (Michie 1986); N.J. R. Evid. 63(33); Okla. Stat. Ann. tit 12, § 2803.1 (West Cum. Supp. 1991); Or. Rev. Stat. § 40.460(18a) (1987); Pa. Stat. Ann. tit. 42, § 5985.1 (Cum. Supp. 1991); S.D. Codified Laws Ann. § 19-16-38 (1987); Tex. Crim. Proc. Code Ann. § 38.072 (West Cum. Supp. 1991); Utah Code Ann. § 76-5-411 (1990); Vt. R. Evid. 804a; Wash. Rev. Code Ann. § 9A.44.110 (West 1988).

Prior to the current generation of child hearsay exceptions, a few states had so-called tender years hearsay exceptions. See J. Myers, Child Witness Law and Practice § 5.38, at 373 (John Wiley & Sons 1987).

[797] Wash. Rev. Code Ann. § 9A.44.120.

§ 7.46 CHILD HEARSAY EXCEPTION

Most child hearsay exceptions follow the Washington model. Several require the child to be unavailable before hearsay is admissible.[798] Others require the child to be available to testify at trial before hearsay is admissible.[799]

Many states have both a residual exception and a child hearsay exception. In *People v. Bowers*,[800] the Colorado Supreme Court stated that the Colorado child hearsay exception, "rather than the residual hearsay exception of CRE 803(24), provides 'the sole basis upon which hearsay evidence, which otherwise comes within the terms of that statute, may be admitted.'"[801]

Several issues arise in litigation under child hearsay exceptions.[802] The issues most often before the courts concern: (1) the hearing to determine reliability, (2) assessment of reliability, (3) the finding of unavailability, (4) corroborative evidence when the child is unavailable, and (5) admissibility of repetitive hearsay.

Hearing to Determine Reliability

Most child hearsay exceptions require the trial judge to hold a hearing to determine the reliability of hearsay offered under the exception.[803] Some courts hold

---

[798] See Ind. Code. Ann § 35-37-4-6 (Cum. Supp. 1991); Kan. Stat. Ann. § 60-460(dd) (Cum. Supp. 1989); Mass. Gen. Laws Ann. ch. 233, § 81 (West Cum. Supp. 1991); Vt. R. Evid. 804a.

[799] See Ga. Code Ann. § 24-3-16 (Cum. Supp. 1991); Tex. Crim. Proc. Code Ann. § 38.072 (West Cum. Supp. 1991). For discussion of the Texas exception, see Holland v. State, 802 S.W.2d 696 (Tex. Crim. App. 1991); Garza v. State, 828 S.W.2d 432 (Tex. Ct. App. 1992).

[800] 801 P.2d 511 (1990). The court's first decision holding that the child hearsay exception must be used rather than the residual exception was People v. Diefenderfer, 784 P.2d 741 (Colo. 1989).

[801] 801 P.2d at 517, *quoting* People v. Diefenderfer, 784 P.2d 741, 752 (Colo. 1989).

[802] See Sosebee v. State, 257 Ga. 298, 357 S.E.2d 562 (1987). In *Sosebee* the issue on appeal was whether the Georgia child hearsay exception permitted the state to use the five-year-old's hearsay statements without calling the child to testify. The defendant argued that such a procedure would require him to call the child himself or forgo cross-examination, and that such a procedure would violate his right to confront accusatory witness. The Georgia Supreme Court held:

> [I]f the prosecution invokes the Child Hearsay Statute to introduce out-of-court declarations by the alleged victim, the court shall do as follows: Before the state rests, the court shall, at the request of either party, cause the alleged victim to take the stand. The court shall then inform the jury that it is the court who has called the child as a witness, and that both parties have the opportunity to examine the child.

357 S.E.2d at 563.

Most child hearsay exceptions require the prosecutor to give advance notice to the defendant of the state's intention to offer hearsay under the exception. *See* People v. Wood, 743 P.2d 422, 427 (Colo. 1987) (although prosecutor did not comply with notice requirement, hearsay properly admitted; defendant knew substance of hearsay statement).

[803] In People v. Bowers, 801 P.2d 511, 518 (Colo. 1990), the Colorado Supreme Court held that when the propriety of admitting a child's hearsay is considered on appeal, the appellate court generally considers only the evidence presented at the hearing required by the child

that the reliability hearing must be fully adversarial.[804] Failure to hold a hearing is error,[805] although the error may be harmless.[806] The right to a hearing can be waived.[807] The court should make specific findings on the record regarding the reliability of hearsay offered under a child hearsay exception.[808] In some cases, the witness who will repeat the child's out-of-court statement at trial testifies at the hearing, although the Minnesota Supreme Court ruled in *State v. Dana*[809]

---

hearsay exception. The appellate court considers the evidence admitted at trial only insofar as the entire record helps the court determine whether erroneous admission of hearsay was harmless or plain error. *Bowers* should be compared with the Washington Supreme Court's instructive decision in State v. Swan, 114 Wash. 2d 613, 790 P.2d 610 (1990), *cert. denied*, 111 S. Ct. 752 (1991), where the court stated that it was proper on appeal to "consider all evidence in the record in assessing corroboration of claimed abuse." 790 P.2d at 616 n.16.

[804] Miller v. State, 531 N.E.2d 466 (Ind. 1988).

[805] State v. Lanter, 237 Kan. 309, 699 P.2d 503, 505 (1985); State v. Smith, 384 N.W.2d 546, 549 (Minn. Ct. App. 1986); Lytle v. State, 816 P.2d 1082 (Nev. 1991); State v. Foell, 416 N.W.2d 45 (S.D. 1987) (court erred when it failed to determine child's availability); State v. Sammons, 47 Wash. App. 762, 737 P.2d 684 (1987).

[806] State v. Burns, 394 N.W.2d 495, 497–98 (Minn. 1986) (failure to hold separate hearing did not prejudice defendant because record made it clear hearsay was properly admitted); State v. Leavitt, 49 Wash. App. 348, 743 P.2d 270, 274–75 (1987), *aff'd*, 111 Wash. 2d 66, 758 P.2d 982 (1988) (defendant waived objection to lack of hearing; even if issue of failure to hold hearing had been preserved for appeal, failure to hold hearing under facts of this case would have been harmless).

[807] State v. Warren, 55 Wash. App. 645, 779 P.2d 1159, 1162 (1989) (it is usually error not to hold required hearing; however, defendant failed to object to absence of hearing, precluding appellate review); Martinez v. State, 732 S.W.2d 401, 403 (Tex. Ct. App. 1987) (defendant waived right to hearing); State v. Leavitt, 49 Wash. App. 348, 743 P.2d 270, 274–75 (1987), *aff'd*, 111 Wash. 2d 66, 758 P.2d 982 (1988).

[808] People v. Bowers, 801 P.2d 511, 519 (Colo. 1990) (requiring trial court to make findings regarding reliability, unavailability, and corroboration); Weatherford v. State, 561 So. 2d 629, 633 (Fla. Dist. Ct. App. 1990) (child hearsay exception required court to make specific findings regarding reliability; trial court's failure to make such findings was reversible error); Fricke v. State, 561 So. 2d 597 (Fla. Dist. Ct. App. 1990) (trial court must make specific findings).

[809] 422 N.W.2d 246 (Minn. 1988), *cert. denied*, 112 S. Ct. 3043 (1992). In this case the Minnesota Supreme Court discussed the type of hearing required under the Minnesota child hearsay exception. At trial, the court held a hearing out of the presence of the jury to determine the competence of the two victims. The court determined that only one of the victims was competent. The hearing then turned to whether the victims' hearsay statements were admissible. The defense argued that a proper reliability hearing required the court to listen to the testimony of the witnesses who would repeat the children's statements. The defense asserted that only by listening to the various witnesses prior to their trial testimony could the court properly evaluate the reliability of the children's statements. The trial court refused to call the witnesses, and based its reliability determination on the following: (1) the relevant papers in the file, (2) the circumstances under which the statements were made, (3) a finding that the witnesses who would relate the children's statements were reliable, (4) a determination that no purpose would be served by having witnesses testify at the hearing prior to their trial testimony, and (5) the arguments of counsel. The Minnesota Supreme Court ruled that the trial judge did not err "in deciding the admissibility issue on the record

that this is not always necessary. Based on the facts in *Dana,* the court stated, "There were no significant factual issues underlying the admissibility decision, only the basically legal issue of the reliability of the statements."[810] When substantial factual issues exist, it may be appropriate for the trial court to hear from the witnesses who will repeat the child's out-of-court statements.

Assessment of Reliability

Child hearsay exceptions admit reliable hearsay that is not admissible under other exceptions. In terms of the reliability requirement, there is no difference between child hearsay exceptions and the residual exceptions contained in Rules 803(24) and 804(b)(5).[811] Thus, factors considered in assessing reliability are identical under child hearsay and residual exceptions. Moreover, the Supreme Court's decision in *Idaho v. Wright,*[812] which places limits on assessing reliability under residual exceptions, applies with equal vigor in criminal litigation where hearsay is offered under child hearsay exceptions.[813] Factors pertinent to reliability are outlined in **§ 7.44**, and the reader is referred to that section.

The admissibility of hearsay under a child hearsay exception is determined by the trial court pursuant to Rule 104(a). The court determines by a preponderance of the evidence whether the conditions of admissibility are satisfied.[814]

Unavailability

Most child hearsay exceptions provide that a child's out-of-court statement is admissible regardless of whether the child testifies at trial or is unavailable.[815]

---

he had, without requiring those who would be summarizing the statements of the children to testify separately and out of the presence of the jury in advance of their trial testimony." 422 N.W.2d at 249. The court emphasized that "[t]here were no significant factual issues underlying the admissibility decision, only the basically legal issue of the reliability of the statements." *Id.* If substantial factual issues exist, it may be appropriate for the court to hear from witnesses. *Id.*

[810] 422 N.W.2d at 249.

[811] The residual exception is discussed in **§§ 7.42–7.45**.

[812] 110 S. Ct. 3139 (1990).

[813] The restrictions of *Idaho v. Wright* may not apply in civil litigation. See **§ 7.43**.

[814] Bourjaily v. United States, 483 U.S. 171 (1987); People v. Bowers, 801 P.2d 511, 518 (Colo. 1990) ("The preponderance of the evidence standard, therefore, applies to a trial court's ruling on whether the statutory conditions for admitting a child's hearsay statements under section 13-25-129 have been satisfied").

[815] *See* State v. Bishop, 63 Wash. App. 15, 816 P.2d 738 (1991) (child testified at trial; court considered whether the child was available in the constitutional sense of the word; ruling that the fact that child could not remember one element of crime [penetration] did not render child unavailable). A few child hearsay exceptions apply only when the child is unavailable to testify (see **note 789**). A few exceptions apply only when the child is available (see **note 799**).

Several child hearsay exceptions expressly provide that psychological trauma may render children unavailable.[816] For example, the Florida child hearsay exception states, "[U]navailability shall include a finding by the court that the child's participation in the trial or proceeding would result in a substantial likelihood of severe emotional or mental harm . . . ."[817] Factors rendering children unavailable are discussed in § 7.48.

Corroborative Evidence When Child Is Unavailable

The majority of child hearsay exceptions state that when the child is unavailable to testify at trial, the child's out-of-court statement is admissible only if there is corroborative evidence of the abuse.[818] That is, there must be evidence of abuse *in addition to* the child's statement. Each act of abuse described by the child must be corroborated.[819]

Wigmore stated that "'[c]orroboration' means literally 'strengthening.'"[820] Evidence corroborates if it has any tendency to make a proposition more likely.[821] To put it another way, evidence corroborates if it is relevant as that term

---

[816] *See, e.g.,* Ala. Code § 15-25-32(2)(a)(6) (Cum. Supp. 1990) ("Substantial likelihood that the child would suffer severe emotional trauma from testifying at the proceeding or by means of closed circuit television"); Ind. Code Ann. § 35-37-4-6 (d)(3)(A) (Cum. Supp. 1991) ("a psychiatrist, physician, or psychologist has certified that the participation of the protected person in the trial creates a substantial likelihood of emotional or mental harm to the protected person").

[817] Fla. Stat. Ann. § 90.803(23)(a)(2)(b) (West Cum. Supp. 1991).

[818] State v. Jones, 112 Wash. 2d 488, 772 P.2d 496, 499 (1989) (helpful discussion of basis for corroboration requirement). In People v. Bowers, 801 P.2d 511 (Colo. 1990), the Colorado Supreme Court stated that the corroboration requirement is "directed at the sexual act described in the child's statement and not at the identity of the perpetrator." 801 P.2d at 522.

[819] State v. Jones, 112 Wash. 2d 488, 722 P.2d 496, 500 (1989); State v. Bishop, 63 Wash. App. 15, 816 P.2d 738, 745 (1991).

[820] J. Wigmore, The Science of Judicial Proof as Given by Logic, Psychology, and General Experience and Illustrated in Judicial Trials § 23 (1937).

[821] *See* T. Anderson & W. Twining, Analysis of Evidence 445 (1991). Anderson and Twining define corroboration as follows:

Literally, strengthening, as when two witnesses independently testify to the truth of the same proposition (cf. convergence). The term is used in at least two senses: (1) to signify the production of an additional witness or two, duplicating the assertion of a prior witness; or (2) to signify the auxiliary evidential facts offered by a proponent to *negative the explanations* by which the opponent seeks to weaken the inference from some original evidentiary fact of the proponent. In the latter aspect, "corroboration" involves not a new logical process, but a new stage in the presentation of evidence.

See also L. Cohen, The Probable and the Provable 94 (1977) ("At its simplest testimonial corroboration occurs when two witnesses both testify, independently of one another, to the truth of the same proposition"); People v. Bowers, 801 P.2d 511, 524 (Colo. 1990):

To "corroborate" means "to make strong or strengthen," "to provide evidence of the truth of," or to "make more certain," and the word "corroborative" means "serving or

§ 7.46   CHILD HEARSAY EXCEPTION

is defined in Rule 401.[822] "Corroborative evidence need not be conclusive—it need only support a reasonable inference that the acts alleged in the hearsay statements occurred."[823] Corroborative evidence may be direct, as in eyewitness testimony.[824] More commonly, however, corroborative evidence is circumstantial.[825] The types of evidence that may corroborate abuse are potentially limitless, and case-by-case analysis is required.[826] The corroboration requirement should be applied flexibly so that reliable hearsay is not excluded "by a stubborn insistence on corroboration that is impossible to obtain."[827] Factors that corroborate children's hearsay statements are discussed in § **7.48**.

---

tending to corroborate." Webster's Third International Dictionary 512 (1986). In the context of evidence, corroborative or corroborating evidence means evidence "supplementary to that already given and tending to strengthen or confirm it" or, stated somewhat differently, "[a]dditional evidence of a different character to the same point." Black's Law Dictionary 311 (5th ed. 1979). The term "corroborative evidence," in its commonly accepted meaning, therefore, connotes evidence independent of and supplementary to a fact and tending to strengthen or confirm that fact.

See also Stevens v. People, 796 P.2d 946, 951 (Colo. 1990) (corroborative evidence "comprises evidence, direct or by proof of surrounding circumstances, that tends to establish the fact sought to be proved"); State v. Swan, 114 Wash. 2d 613, 790 P.2d 610 (1990), *cert. denied,* 111 S. Ct. 752 (1991).

[822] Rule 401 states, "'Relevant evidence' means evidence having any tendency to make the existence of any fact that is of consequence to the determination of the action more probable or less probable than it would be without the evidence."

[823] State v. Bishop, 63 Wash. App. 15, 816 P.2d 738, 746 (1991).

[824] State v. Jones, 112 Wash. 2d 488, 772 P.2d 496, 500 (1989) ("Certainly the best sort of corroborative evidence would be direct physical or testimonial evidence of the abuse"); State v. Justiniano, 48 Wash. App. 572, 740 P.2d 872 (1987) (eyewitness testimony).

[825] See State v. Jones, 112 Wash. 2d 488, 772 P.2d 496 (1989), where the court wrote, "Fairly commonly, however, such direct evidence is not available. Thus, evidence that is only indirectly corroborative must be deemed sufficient in many cases." 772 P.2d at 500. In a footnote the court added, "The nonviolent nature of the acts in which Jones allegedly involved Sonja, and Sonja's apparent compliance with her father's directions, are characteristic of cases of child abuse and help explain the lack of direct corroborative evidence in such cases." 772 P.2d at 500 n.5. See also People v. Bowers, 801 P.2d 511, 522 (Colo. 1990), where the Colorado Supreme Court wrote:

[T]he term "corroborative evidence" means evidence, whether direct or circumstantial, that tends to establish the fact sought to be proved—namely, the sexual offense described in the child's statement—and that the quantum of corroborative evidence needed to support the admission of a child's hearsay statement "must be enough to induce a person of ordinary prudence and caution conscientiously to entertain a reasonable belief that the sexual abuse that is the subject of the child's hearsay statement occurred."

See also State v. Bishop, 63 Wash. App. 15, 816 P.2d 738, 745 (1991).

[826] State v. Swan, 114 Wash. 2d 613, 790 P.2d 610, 615 (1990), *cert. denied,* 111 S. Ct. 752 (1991); State v. Jones, 112 Wash. 2d 488, 772 P.2d 496, 500 (1989) ("The determination must proceed case by case"); State v. Bishop, 63 Wash. App. 15, 816 P.2d 738 (1991).

[827] State v. Jones, 112 Wash. 2d 488, 772 P.2d 496, 500 (1989). *See also* Stevens v. People, 796 P.2d 946, 952 (Colo. 1990).

The corroboration requirement is separate from, and in addition to, the requirement that hearsay be sufficiently reliable.[828] The proponent of a child's hearsay statement should distinguish the two requirements.

The court determines the existence of corroborative evidence pursuant to Rule 104(a), and the formal rules of evidence do not apply.[829]

Constitutional Challenges

Child hearsay exceptions have been subjected to constitutional attack. Attacks on the facial constitutionality of the exceptions have been largely unsuccessful,[830] and for good reason. Statutes based on the Washington model are designed to protect defendants' rights to confrontation and due process. Naturally, statutes that are constitutional on their face can be applied in an unconstitutional fashion.

Admission of Repetitive Hearsay

In some cases the jury hears the child's description of abuse more than once. For example, the child may testify and relate what happened. The prosecutor

---

[828] Stevens v. People, 796 P.2d 946, 952 (Colo. 1990); Beck v. State, 544 N.E.2d 204, 208 (Ind. Ct. App. 1989) ("the corroboration requirement is separate from the reliability requirement and evidence going to support the reliability of the statement does not necessarily provide corroborative evidence of the act alleged in the statement"); State v. Swan, 114 Wash. 2d 613, 790 P.2d 610, 615 (1990), *cert denied,* 111 S. Ct. 752 (1991).

[829] State v. Jones, 112 Wash. 2d 488, 772 P.2d 496, 499 (1989) ("The determination . . . that 'there is corroborative evidence of the act' of sexual contact alleged by a child against a criminal defendant similarly may be made free from evidentiary constraints"). *But see* People v. Bowers, 801 P.2d 511 (Colo. 1990).

[830] Glendening v. State, 536 So. 2d 212 (Fla. 1988), *cert. denied,* 492 U.S. 907 (1989) (rejecting argument that child hearsay statute constituted an ex post facto law); Perez v. State, 536 So. 2d 206 (Fla. 1988), *cert. denied,* 492 U.S. 923 (1989); State v. Myatt, 237 Kan. 17, 697 P.2d 836 (1985); State v. Bellotti, 383 N.W.2d 308, 314–16 (Minn. Ct. App. 1986); State v. Wright, 751 S.W.2d 48 (Mo. 1988); State v. Renly, 111 Or. App. 453, 827 P.2d 1345 (1992); State v. Loughton, 747 P.2d 426 (Utah 1987) (upholding child hearsay exception against challenge that limitation of hearsay exception to children under age of 10 violated equal protection); Buckley v. State, 786 S.W.2d 357 (Tex. Crim. App. 1990) (rejecting facial challenge to Texas child hearsay exception); State v. Ryan, 103 Wash. 2d 165, 691 P.2d 197 (1984).

But see George v. State, 306 Ark. 360, 813 S.W.2d 792 (1991) (Arkansas statute unconstitutional in light of *Idaho v. Wright*); State v. Robinson, 153 Ariz. 191, 735 P.2d 801 (1987) (court struck down Arizona child hearsay exception because: (1) statute creating the exception "impermissibly infring[ed] on this court's constitutional authority to make procedural rules for the judiciary," and (2) statute created situations where unreliable hearsay could be admitted); Hall v. State, 539 So. 2d 1338 (Miss. 1989) (child hearsay exception unconstitutional because judiciary, not legislature, has authority to adopt rules of evidence).

then uses the child hearsay exception to offer the child's out-of-court statements describing the abuse.[831] It seems clear that out-of-court statements qualifying for admission under a child hearsay exception can be used to fill in gaps in a child's trial testimony. To the extent out-of-court statements become cumulative or unfairly prejudicial to the defendant, the trial court has discretion to reject them. Failure to object to repetitive hearsay waives objection.[832]

Miscellaneous Issues

In *Russell v. State*,[833] the Florida Court of Appeal ruled that the Florida child hearsay statute allows admission of out-of-court statements of child witnesses other than the victim.

In *People v. McClure*,[834] the Colorado Supreme Court held that the child hearsay exception "is in derogation of common law, and must be strictly construed. . . . Further, the statute must be strictly construed in favor of the accused."[835]

In *People v. Serna*,[836] the nine-year-old victim made out-of-court statements describing how the defendant abused him. The court wrote:

> Defendant next argues that certain portions of the hearsay statements were not admissible under the statute because they contained information other than a description of the specific sexual conduct alleged. Specifically, defendant contends that the trial court improperly allowed those parts of the statements that included the setting in which the act occurred, the names of others present, what was going on in the room where the act occurred, whether defendant was drinking, looking at sexual materials, breathing hard, or doing something with his free hand, the frequency with which this occurred, how the victim reacted to defendant's actions, how it made him feel about defendant, and the reasons why the victim delayed telling anyone about his father's conduct.
>
> Clearly, the attendant circumstances are often necessary to provide an adequate description of the alleged sexual conduct. Hence, with the exception of the statements regarding the victim's reaction to his father's actions, how it made him feel about his father, and the reason why he delayed in telling anyone about his father's conduct, the statements allowed by the trial court where within the scope of [the Colorado child hearsay exception] in that they provided descriptive information about the sexual conduct alleged.[837]

---

[831] *See* Cogburn v. State, 292 Ark. 564, 732 S.W.2d 807 (1987); Pardo v. State, 596 So. 2d 665 (Fla. 1992).

[832] Goodwin v. State, 573 N.E.2d 895, 896 (Ind. Ct. App. 1991).

[833] 572 So. 2d 940 (Fla. Dist. Ct. App. 1990).

[834] 779 P.2d 864 (Colo. 1989).

[835] *Id.* at 866.

[836] 738 P.2d 802 (Colo. Ct. App. 1987).

[837] *Id.* at 804.

§ 7.47 Sufficiency to Support Finding of Fact or Verdict

Hearsay plays a central role in child abuse litigation. The out-of-court statements of the victim and others may be the strongest, and, in some cases, the only evidence of abuse or the identity of the abuser. In light of the importance of hearsay, it is necessary to ask whether a finding of fact or verdict may be based on hearsay.

It is clear that hearsay properly admitted under an exception is substantive evidence that may be considered along with nonhearsay evidence.[838] The same is generally true for inadmissible hearsay admitted without objection.[839] Difficulty arises, however, when the *only* evidence supporting an element of a cause of action or a crime is hearsay. The sufficiency of hearsay *alone* to support a verdict turns primarily on the type of case—civil or criminal—and the reliability of the hearsay.

---

[838] Haggins v. Warden, 715 F.2d 1050 (6th Cir. 1983), *cert. denied,* 464 U.S. 1071 (1984); United States v. Iron Shell, 633 F.2d 77 (8th Cir. 1980), *cert. denied,* 450 U.S. 1001 (1981).

[839] United States v. Alvarez, 584 F.2d 694, 697 (5th Cir. 1978); Carpenter Steel Co. v. Pellegrin, 237 Cal. App. 2d 35, 46 Cal. Rptr. 502 (1965) (hearsay constitutes substantive evidence, but such evidence must be considered with caution); Estate of Ballard, 210 Cal. App. 2d 799, 26 Cal. Rptr. 832, 834 (1962) (probate proceeding); State v. Cuvelier, 175 Conn. 100, 394 A.2d 185, 189 (1978) (defendant was committed for mental health treatment following judgment of acquittal on grounds of mental disease or defect; in discussing certain evidence, court remarked that "even if this testimony were deemed to be inadmissible hearsay . . . where such evidence is admitted without objection, it may properly be considered for whatever it is worth on its face in determining the facts in issue"); Kern v. State, 237 Ind. 144, 144 N.E.2d 705 (1957); Barlow v. Verrill, 88 N.H. 25, 183 A. 857, 858–59 (1936); State v. White, 215 S.C. 450, 55 S.E.2d 785, 787 (1949); Menges v. Board of County Comm'rs, 290 Or. 251, 621 P.2d 562, 571 (1980) (zoning case; "It is well established that at least when hearsay evidence is not objected to, . . . such evidence is 'competent evidence sufficient to support a verdict' in an action at law"); Laubach v. Industrial Indem. Co., 286 Or. 217, 593 P.2d 1146, 1150 (1979) (personal injury action; "when such testimony is received without objection it is competent evidence sufficient to support a verdict"); Smith v. J.C. Penney Co., 269 Or. 643, 525 P.2d 1299, 1302 (1974) (products liability action; "Hearsay evidence admitted without objection is substantial evidence sufficient to support a verdict"); Shepard v. Purvine, 196 Or. 348, 248 P.2d 352, 363–64 (1952); Chambers v. State, 711 S.W.2d 240, 247 (Tex. Crim. App. 1986) (en banc); Stevens v. Mirakian, 177 Va. 123, 12 S.E.2d 780, 783 (1941) (personal injury action; "The general rule is that hearsay testimony admitted without objection may properly be considered and given its natural effect. It may be the only relevant and material evidence obtainable. . . . It is our view that the hearsay statement was evidence to go to the jury. Its weight was also for the jury, and upon this testimony the jury could have found that the defendant knew of the defective condition of the chair"); W.W. Conner Co. v. McCollister & Campbell, Inc., 9 Wash. 2d 407, 115 P.2d 370, 372 (1941) (action for brokerage commission); 30 Am. Jur. 2d *Evidence* §§ 1089, 1103 (1967).

But see Germany v. State, 235 Ga. 836, 221 S.E.2d 817 (1976) (hearsay has no probative value); Shaver v. State, 199 Ga. App. 428, 405 S.E.2d 281, 282 (1991).

§ 7.47 FINDING OF FACT OR VERDICT

In the context of civil litigation, including juvenile court dependency proceedings,[840] many courts hold that hearsay is sufficient to support a finding of fact or judgment.[841] In *W.W. Conner Co. v. McCollister & Campbell, Inc.*,[842] for example, the Washington Supreme Court stated that "hearsay evidence, admitted without objection, has the force and effect of proper evidence and is to be accorded its natural probative value; and that such evidence alone is sufficient to sustain a verdict or a finding of fact."[843] The California Court of Appeal wrote in a similar vein in *In re Ballard's Estate*,[844] observing that "it is well established that hearsay admitted without objection is evidence sufficient to sustain a verdict or findings."[845] Although the majority of courts agree that in civil litigation, hearsay alone is sufficient to sustain a finding of fact or judgment, many decisions state that such evidence must be considered with caution,[846] and if hearsay is unreliable, it will not support a finding or verdict.

In criminal litigation, where the right to confront accusatory witnesses looms large, courts are understandably hesitant to rest a verdict on out-of-court statements.[847] Even here, however, the majority rule is that hearsay is sometimes sufficient to support a finding of fact or verdict.[848]

---

[840] Matter of Jaclyn P., 578 N.Y.S. 2d 252 (App. Div. 1992); *See* Matter of Christina F., 74 N.Y.2d 532, 548 N.E.2d 1294, 549 N.Y.S.2d 643 (1989); Nassau County Dep't of Social Servs. v. Steven K., 574 N.Y.S.2d 767 (A.D. 1991).

[841] See authorities cited in **note 839**. *But see* Gallagher v. Pequot Spring Water Co., 2 Conn. Cir. Ct. 354, 199 A.2d 172, 175 (1963) (hearsay has no probative value); Warren v. Waterville Urban Renewal Auth., 235 A.2d 295, 300 (Me. 1967), *cert. denied*, 390 U.S. 1006 (1968) ("hearsay evidence may properly be considered and given its natural and logical probative effect. The fact finder must always, however, weigh such evidence with caution, mindful of its inherent weakness, the same weakness which leads to exclusion upon objection. . . . Such evidence may [be corroborative], but will not alone support a verdict or finding"); Goldhwaite v. Sheraton Restaurant, 154 Me. 214, 145 A.2d 362, 367–68 (1958); 30 Am. Jur. 2d *Evidence* § 1103, at 271–72 (1967) ("In a few jurisdictions the rule is that hearsay is without any probative value at all and may not be considered even where admitted without objection").

[842] 9 Wash. 2d 407, 115 P.2d 370 (1941).

[843] 115 P.2d at 372.

[844] 210 Cal. App. 2d 799, 26 Cal. Rptr. 832 (1962).

[845] 26 Cal. Rptr. at 834.

[846] Carpenter Steel Co. v. Pellegrin, 237 Cal. App. 2d 35, 46 Cal. Rptr. 502 (1965); W.W. Conner Co. v. McCollister & Campbell, Inc., 9 Wash. 2d 407, 115 P.2d 370 (1941).

[847] Cote v. State, 711 S.W.2d 240, 245–47 (Tex. Crim. App. 1985) (en banc) (thorough analysis of probative value of hearsay); Annotation, *Consideration, in Determining Facts, of Inadmissible Hearsay Evidence Introduced Without Objection*, 79 A.L.R.2d 890 (1961).

[848] United States v. Bey, 526 F.2d 851, 855 (5th Cir.), *cert. denied*, 426 U.S. 937 (1976) ("the jury may consider [hearsay] for whatever value it may have; such evidence is to be given its natural probative value as if it were in law admissible"); United States v. Alvarez, 584 F.2d 694, 697 (5th Cir. 1978) ("Absent plain error, hearsay that is not subjected to proper objection is ordinarily admissible at trial for any relevant purpose"); State v. Allen, 157 Ariz. 165, 755 P.2d 1153, 1159 (1988); State v. Hernandez, 167 Ariz. 236, 805 P.2d 1057, 1061

In many of the criminal cases concerning the sufficiency of hearsay to support a finding or verdict, the out-of-court statement is a prior inconsistent statement.[849] Under Rule 801(d)(1)(A) of the Federal Rules of Evidence, certain prior inconsistent statements are nonhearsay.[850] Whether or not a prior inconsistent statement is defined as hearsay, the question remains whether a prior inconsistent statement alone is sufficient to support a verdict in a criminal case. Weinstein and Berger write:

> Theoretically, a party may be able to make out a prima facie case even if the only evidence is a previous inconsistent statement of this type. Under the former practice, "if the only evidence of some essential fact is such a previous statement, the party's case falls." In a criminal prosecution, however, it is unlikely that a prior inconsistent statement alone will suffice to support a conviction, since a reasonable juror usually could not be convinced beyond a reasonable doubt by such evidence alone.[851]

Despite Weinstein and Berger's observation, a number of well-reasoned decisions uphold verdicts based largely on prior inconsistent statements.[852]

In delinquency litigation in juvenile court, the principles outlined in this section govern use of hearsay to support an adjudication.[853] In dependency proceedings, by contrast, reliable hearsay should be regarded as sufficient to support an

---

(Ct. App. 1990) ("In a criminal case, hearsay evidence admitted without objection is competent evidence admissible for all purposes unless its admission amounts to fundamental error"); Chambers v. State, 711 S.W.2d 240, 245–47 (Tex. Crim. App. 1986) ("we will follow the majority rule now embraced by Tex. R. Ev. 802 and treat inadmissible hearsay admitted without objection the same as all other evidence in the sufficiency context, i.e., it is capable of sustaining a verdict").

Commentators raise the question whether a pretrial identification is alone sufficient to support the conclusion that the defendant is the perpetrator of crime. *See* 4 Louisell & Mueller § 421, at 215; 4 Weinstein & Berger ¶ 801(d)(1)(C)[01], at 801-223.

[849] *See* United States v. Orrico, 599 F.2d 113, 118 (6th Cir. 1979) (helpful discussion). The *Orrico* court concluded that out-of-court statements in the form of prior inconsistent statements and past recollection recorded were not sufficient to support a verdict, stating:

> [W]hen such evidence is the only source of support for the central allegations of the charge, especially when the statements barely, if at all, meet the minimal requirements of admissibility, we do not believe that a substantial factual basis as to each element of the crime providing support for a conclusion of guilt beyond reasonable doubt has been offered by the Government.

See also State v. Moran, 151 Ariz. 378, 728 P.2d 248 (1986) (child's prior inconsistent statements sufficient to support verdict); State v. Allred, 134 Ariz. 274, 655 P.2d 1326 (1982).

[850] See § **7.18**.

[851] 4 Weinstein & Berger ¶ 801(d)(1)(A)[01], at 801-141 to 801-142 (footnotes omitted).

[852] See § **7.20**.

[853] *In re* Miguel L., 32 Cal. 3d 100, 649 P.2d 703, 185 Cal. Rptr. 120 (1982) (juvenile court delinquency case; accomplice's out-of-court statements identifying juvenile as participant, which were repudiated at trial, were insufficient to sustain adjudication of delinquency).

adjudication of abuse or neglect. The California Supreme Court ruled in *In re Malinda S.*[854] that "social studies" prepared for the juvenile court by social workers are admissible and competent to support dependency adjudication despite the fact that such studies are hearsay.[855]

The rule excluding hearsay applies in child custody and visitation litigation incident to divorce.[856] In such litigation reliable hearsay should be sufficient to support a custody determination.[857]

§ 7.48 Unavailable Hearsay Declarants

When a hearsay declarant is unavailable to testify at trial, issues arise under the rules of evidence and the Confrontation Clause of the Sixth Amendment. Under Rule 804(b) of the Federal Rules of Evidence, unavailability is required for admission of former testimony, dying declarations, statements against interest, and statements of personal or family history. Under Rule 803, the availability of the declarant is immaterial for admission of present sense impressions, excited utterances, declarations of state of mind, statements for medical diagnosis or treatment, recorded recollections, business records, public records, and statements admissible under the residual exception. Turning to the Sixth Amendment, the Confrontation Clause requires the prosecutor to establish the declarant's unavailability as a precondition to offering out-of-court statements made during prior judicial proceedings.[858]

---

[854] 51 Cal. 3d 368, 795 P.2d 1244, 272 Cal. Rptr. 787 (1990).

[855] The court ruled that certain California statutes created a hearsay exception for social reports.

[856] Hearsay issues do not arise very often in appellate decisions concerning child custody and visitation. There is no doubt, however, that the hearsay rule applies in such proceedings. *See In re* Marriage of Williams, 303 N.W.2d 160 (Iowa 1981) (report of court-appointed custody evaluator was hearsay and should have been excluded); Shunk v. Walker, 87 Md. App. 389, 589 A.2d 1303 (1991) (evidence of mother's conversations with child's school principal and National Center for Missing and Exploited Children not hearsay because not admitted for the truth; conversations were admitted to show why mother commenced custody modification proceeding); *In re* Marriage of Cavitt, 564 S.W.2d 53 (Mo. Ct. App. 1978) (social agency report was inadmissible hearsay, but admission was harmless error in bench trial); Murdoch v. Murdoch, 200 Neb. 429, 264 N.W.2d 183 (1978) (statement of child to father expressing affection was not hearsay because it was not offered for the truth; the child's statement was relevant because it was made); Griffin v. Griffin, 81 N.C. App. 665, 344 S.E.2d 828 (1986); Fuhrman v. Fuhrman, 254 N.W.2d 97 (N.D. 1977) (error requiring reversal to admit and consider hearsay report of social worker regarding custody); Crabtree v. Crabtree, 716 S.W.2d 923 (Tenn. Ct. App. 1986).

[857] Crabtree v. Crabtree, 716 S.W.2d 923 (Tenn. Ct. App. 1986); Bingham v. Bingham, 811 S.W.2d 678, 684 (Tex. Ct. App. 1991) (social worker's report in custody case was public record within Rule 803(8)).

[858] White v. Illinois, 112 S. Ct. 736 (1992).

A witness on the stand may be unavailable.[859] Weinstein and Berger write that "the crucial factor is not the unavailability of the witness but rather the unavailability of his testimony."[860] The Mississippi Supreme Court adds that "[t]he availability of the child to testify is not measured solely in terms of physical presence but refers as well to the child's ability to communicate in a trial setting."[861]

Although unavailability under the Confrontation Clause may not be identical to unavailability under evidence law,[862] the overlap is considerable, and for most purposes a witness who is unavailable under the rules of evidence is unavailable for constitutional purposes.

The court determines unavailability pursuant to Rule 104(a).[863] The burden of establishing unavailability is on the party asserting it.[864]

Nine types of unavailability are discussed below.

Claim of privilege.[865] A witness who claims a privilege such as the psychotherapist-patient privilege or the privilege against self-incrimination is unavailable regarding matters within the privilege.[866] Rule 804(a)(1) contemplates putting the witness on the stand, where the witness claims the privilege and the court rules that the privilege applies.[867]

---

[859] State v. Foell, 416 N.W.2d 45, 46 n.3 (S.D. 1987) ("the terms 'available' and 'present' are clearly not synonymous").

[860] 4 Weinstein & Berger ¶ 804(a)[01], at 804-36 (footnote omitted).

[861] Griffith v. State, 584 So. 2d 383 (Miss. 1991).

[862] See United States v. Inadi, 475 U.S. 387, 393 n.5 (1986), where the Supreme Court wrote:

> Federal Rule of Evidence 804 also imposes an unavailability requirement before allowing the admission of prior testimony. The Rule 804 requirement is part of the law of evidence regarding hearsay. While it "may readily be conceded that hearsay rules and the Confrontation Clause are generally designed to protect similar values," . . . the overlap is not complete.

See also State v. Lindner, 142 Wis. 2d 783, 419 N.W.2d 352, 355 (1987) ("unavailability in the constitutional sense is not the equivalent of unavailability as a state law prerequisite to claiming an exception to the hearsay rule").

[863] 4 Louisell & Mueller § 486, at 1026.

[864] State v. Allen, 157 Ariz. 165, 755 P.2d 1153, 1158 (1988) ("The burden is on the state to prove unavailability when it offers a declarant's out-of-court statements"); People v. Stritzinger, 34 Cal. 3d 505, 668 P.2d 738, 746, 194 Cal. Rptr. 431 (1983).

[865] Fed. R. Evid. 804(a)(1). See United States v. Chapman, 866 F.2d 1326 (11th Cir.), cert. denied, 493 U.S. 932 (1989) (witness who claimed marital privilege was unavailable).

[866] United States v. Inadi, 475 U.S. 387 (1986) (claim of privilege against self-incrimination rendered witness unavailable); McCormick § 253, at 754; 4 Weinstein & Berger ¶ 804(a)[01].

[867] 4 Weinstein & Berger ¶ 804(a)[01], at 804-39 ("Rule 804(a)(1) requires a ruling by the judge, thereby implying that an actual claim of privilege must be made") (footnote omitted); 4 Louisell & Mueller § 486, at 1028 ("Since there must be a 'ruling of the court' which exempts the witness from testifying (or excludes his testimony), a party relying upon this kind of unavailability should be required to produce the witness so that a claim of privilege may be made and ruled upon").

§ 7.48   UNAVAILABLE HEARSAY DECLARANTS

Refusal to testify.[868]   A witness is unavailable who refuses to testify despite a court order to do so.[869] Children sometimes refuse to testify despite the best efforts of the judge and counsel. For example, some children are too frightened of the defendant to testify.[870] Such children are unavailable. Mere reluctance to testify does not render a witness unavailable.[871]

Lack of memory.[872]   Genuine lack of memory about the subject matter of an out-of-court statement renders the witness unavailable regarding the matter.[873] The proponent should call the witness to the stand and establish actual memory

---

[868] Fed. R. Evid. 804(a)(2).

[869] The witness must take the stand and refuse to testify. Louisell and Mueller write:

> A refusal to answer as contemplated by Rule 804(a)(2) clearly involves calling the declarant to the witness stand and obtaining a court order requiring him to testify: A mere representation that the declarant will not testify does not suffice to establish his unavailability, nor does a mere claim of privilege amount to such refusal. Clearly the wording of Rule 804(a)(2) contemplates a refusal "despite judicial pressures" to testify . . . .

4 Louisell & Mueller § 486, at 1032–33 (footnotes omitted). *See also* McCormick § 253, at 754; 4 Weinstein & Berger ¶ 804(a)[01], at 804-40.

See also United States v. Ruffin, 12 M.J. 952 (A.F.C.M.R. 1982); Tucker v. State, 564 A.2d 1110 (Del. 1989) (defendant's Confrontation Clause rights not violated by admission of child's out-of-court statements; child appeared at trial, but was unable or unwilling to respond to defendant's questions); People v. Johnson, 118 Ill. 2d 501, 517 N.E.2d 1070 (1987) (reluctance to testify not sufficient for unavailability); State v. R.C., 494 So. 2d 1350 (La. Ct. App. 1986) (five-year-old who refused to answer questions on cross-examination was unavailable within meaning of Louisiana statute permitting admission of videotaped interviews only if child was present at trial and subject to cross-examination); Commonwealth v. Kirouac, 405 Mass. 557, 542 N.E.2d 270 (1989) (defendant's right to cross-examine victim was violated when six-year-old refused to answer nearly all questions during cross-examination; court stated that such refusal is similar to case in which witness is unavailable); State v. Boston, 46 Ohio St. 3d 108, 545 N.E.2d 1220 (1989) (three-year-old who refused to answer questions about abuse was unavailable); State v. Justiniano, 48 Wash. App. 572, 740 P.2d 872, 876 (1987) (four-year-old victim was unable to answer questions; child was properly declared unavailable).

[870] 4 Louisell & Mueller § 486, at 1031 ("unavailability is also established where the witness simply refuses to testify out of fear of the party against whom his prior statement is then offered, or refuses for other reasons or for no stated reason to answer proper questions").

[871] State v. Hester, 801 S.W.2d 695, 697 (Mo. 1991).

[872] Fed. R. Evid. 804(a)(3).

[873] State v. Marcum, 750 P.2d 599 (Utah 1988) (child's inability to answer one question due to lack of memory does not render child unavailable); McCormick § 253, at 754-55 ("A claim of lack of memory made by the witness on the stand should satisfy the requirement of unavailability. If the claim is genuine, the testimony is simply unavailable by any realistic standard"); 4 Weinstein & Berger ¶ 804(a)[01].

loss.[874] If a witness has partial recollection, the witness may be partially unavailable.[875] Louisell and Mueller write:

> [W]here a witness recalls part of a transaction but not other parts, or one of a series of related events but not others, so that his memory is fragmented and his present account confused, the proponent should be permitted to introduce a prior statement describing coherently the whole transaction or series of related events, assuming that the statement otherwise qualifies within Rule 804(b). And the important point is the state of the declarant's recollection about the underlying realities described or asserted in his prior statement: The fact that the declarant either does or does not remember making the statement itself does not bear upon the question at hand.[876]

McCormick indicates that even though a claimed lack of memory is insincere, the witness should probably be considered unavailable if the witness adheres to the claim.[877] Children, like adults, sometimes falsely claim lack of memory, and if a child remains adamant in such a claim, the child may be unavailable.

Death.[878] Death obviously renders a witness unavailable.[879]

Physical illness or incapacity.[880] A witness may be unavailable due to physical illness or incapacity.[881] When the illness or incapacity is temporary, the proper course may be to continue the trial rather than declare the witness unavailable.[882] The decision to postpone the witness's testimony or declare the witness unavailable lies within the discretion of the trial court, guided by

---

[874] 4 Louisell & Mueller § 486, at 1036. Louisell & Mueller add that "[i]t would be reasonable for the trial judge to require the proponent to attempt to refresh the memory of the witness as to his prior statement . . . ." *Id.* at 1037 n.54.

[875] McCormick § 253, at 755 ("If the forgetfulness is only partial, the appropriate solution would appear to be resort to present testimony to the extent of recollection, implementing with the hearsay testimony to the extent required") (footnote omitted).

[876] 4 Louisell & Mueller § 486, at 1038 (footnotes omitted).

[877] McCormick § 253, at 755; 4 Weinstein & Berger ¶ 804(a)[01].

[878] Fed. R. Evid. 804(a)(4).

[879] 4 Louisell & Mueller § 486, at 1041-42; McCormick § 253, at 755; 4 Weinstein & Berger ¶ 804(3)[01].

[880] Fed. R. Evid. 804(a)(4).

[881] 4 Louisell & Mueller § 486, at 1041-44; McCormick § 253, at 755–56; 4 Weinstein & Berger ¶ 804(a)[01].

[882] McCormick § 253, at 755 ("The relative scarcity of decisions passing upon the degree of permanency required supports the conclusion that most of the cases are handled by continuance"); 4 Louisell & Mueller § 486, at 1042–43; 4 Weinstein & Berger ¶ 804(a)[01], at 804-44 ("Certainly in a case where the hearsay statement is being offered against an accused, some delay to permit the witness to attend seems imperative under the confrontation clause where the nature of the disability is such that its alleviation or disappearance can be expected") (footnote omitted).

several factors, including the importance of the out-of-court statement, the likelihood and timing of recovery, and the inconvenience or prejudice caused by delay.[883]

Psychological factors.[884] It is useful to consider three categories of unavailability caused by psychological factors: (1) the effects of mental illness or retardation, (2) children who are so shy or timid they cannot testify, (3) children who would be so psychologically traumatized by testifying that they should be considered unavailable. These categories are not watertight, and considerable overlap is possible.

1. Mental illness, retardation, or brain damage. The effects of mental illness, mental retardation,[885] or brain damage may rob the witness of the capacity to testify, rendering the person unavailable.[886] As is true with physical impairments, the court should ascertain whether a continuance will afford the witness time to overcome mental impairment.[887] If the condition is permanent or longstanding, the witness is unavailable.[888]

2. Unavailability caused by shyness or timidity. The unavailability discussed in this subsection differs from unavailability due to mental illness or retardation. Some children who are mentally and emotionally healthy, and fully capable of effective communication under normal circumstances, find testifying

---

[883] 4 Louisell & Mueller § 486, at 1043; McCormick § 253, at 755; 4 Weinstein & Berger ¶ 804(a)[01]; 5 Wigmore § 1406(a), at 158.

[884] Fed. R. Evid. 804(a)(4).

[885] State v. Kuone, 243 Kan. 218, 757 P.2d 289 (1988) (child was mentally retarded); Griffith v. State, 584 So. 2d 383 (Miss. 1991) (10-year-old mentally retarded victim; "We note that Sally's ability to communicate in court may be jeopardized by her retarded condition").

[886] McCormick § 253, at 755-56 ("Mental incapacity, including failure of faculties due to disease, senility, or accident, is also a good ground of unavailability").

[887] See 4 Weinstein & Berger ¶ 804(a)[01], at 804–46, where the authors write:

In the case of a mental rather than a physical disability, the trial judge's task is harder because there is often greater uncertainty as to the patient's prognosis. Opposing medical experts may disagree about the efficacy of treatment. In the case of a hearsay statement against the accused, particularly if it is indispensable to the prosecution's case, the court should order a continuance if there is any medical testimony suggesting that an improvement in the declarant's condition is to be expected within a reasonable time.

(footnote omitted). State v. Drusch, 139 Wis. 2d 312, 407 N.W.2d 328 (1987) (child broke down on the stand; continuance not practical).

[888] Burns v. Clusen, 798 F.2d 931 (7th Cir. 1986) (mental illness need not be permanent to declare person unavailable); Walden v. Sears, Roebuck & Co., 654 F.2d 443 (5th Cir. 1981) (products liability case in which six-year-old suffered head injury when he fell off bicycle; 19 months later he gave deposition describing accident; at trial, nine years after accident, memory loss induced by accident caused him to forget details of the event; trial court excluded boy's deposition; Fifth Circuit reversed, holding that boy's lack of memory caused by injury rendered him unavailable).

exceedingly difficult or impossible.[889] The prospect of facing the defendant renders some children mute. Before such children are declared unavailable, steps may be taken to eliminate the source of the child's discomfort. For example, if the child is frightened by the courtroom full of strangers, the courtroom can be cleared.[890] If presence of the defendant is too much for the child, a support person may stand by the child[891] or, if necessary, consideration may be given to abridging the defendant's right to face-to-face confrontation.[892] In civil litigation, the court has considerable discretion to make testifying less difficult for children.[893] In the end, the shyness and timidity of some children makes it impossible for them to testify despite the best efforts of court and counsel. The out-of-court statements of such children should not be lost, and such children should be considered unavailable.

3. Unavailability caused by psychological trauma of testifying. For some children, testifying poses a risk of psychological trauma. The law does not close its eyes to the trauma of testifying, and, in exceptional cases, the threat of psychological harm renders children unavailable.[894] It is clear that the harm

---

[889] Government of Virgin Islands v. Riley, 754 F. Supp. 61 (D.V.I. 1991); People v. Johnson, 118 Ill. 2d 501, 517 N.E.2d 1070, 1074 (1987) ("we feel compelled to acknowledge the special difficulties presented by cases such as these, where the witness in question is a young child whose fear and reticence is probably non-volitional and hence understandable"); State v. Chandler, 324 N.C. 172, 376 S.E.2d 728 (1989) (child was in court and trial judge had ample opportunity to observe that child could not testify); State v. Lindner, 142 Wis. 2d 783, 419 N.W.2d 352, 355 (Ct. App. 1987) (child was not unavailable; trial court's concern that child was not a good witness at preliminary hearing did not suffice to declare her unavailable at trial); State v. Drusch, 139 Wis. 2d 312, 407 N.W.2d 328 (Ct. App. 1987) (child was called to stand and began to cry; soon she could not respond to questions; she told victim-witness coordinator she could not testify; child had reacted similarly whenever she talked about the trial; held that child was unavailable).

[890] See **Ch. 8** for discussion of constitutional restraints on clearing the courtroom.

[891] For discussion of support persons for children, see **Ch. 8**.

[892] For discussion of abridging face-to-face confrontation, see **Ch. 8**.

[893] See **Ch. 8**.

[894] People v. Diefenderfer, 784 P.2d 741 (Colo. 1989); State v. Yednock, 14 Conn. App. 333, 541 A.2d 887 (1988) (child had great difficulty on stand and could not describe details of abuse; court admitted child's hearsay statement to supply missing details; child was fully cross-examined); Warren v. United States, 436 A.2d 821 (D.C. 1981); Perez v. State, 536 So. 2d 206, 210 (Fla. 1988), *cert. denied,* 492 U.S. 923 (1989); State v. Kuone, 243 Kan. 218, 757 P.2d 289 (1988) (it was likely the child would suffer severe psychological injury; child was mentally retarded; child suffered serious psychological symptoms following a preliminary examination); State v. Eaton, 244 Kan. 370, 769 P.2d 1157, 1167–68 (1989); State v. Twist, 528 A.2d 1250, 1257 (Me. 1987); Wildermuth v. State, 310 Md. 496, 530 A.2d 275, 296-87 (1987); State v. Sheppard, 197 N.J. Super. 411, 484 A.2d 1330 (1984); State v. Gilbert, 109 Wis. 2d 501, 326 N.W.2d 744 (1982) (trial court erred in quashing subpoena for child's testimony, but court and counsel were to make an effort to reduce possible trauma); 4 Louisell &

§ 7.48 UNAVAILABLE HEARSAY DECLARANTS

must be "more than *de minimis, i.e.,* more than 'mere nervousness or excitement or some reluctance to testify. . . .'"[895] In *People v. Stritzinger,*[896] the California Supreme Court stated that psychological trauma must render testifying relatively impossible.[897]

In reaching a decision on unavailability due to psychological trauma, the court considers the psychological condition of the child,[898] the nature of the crime, the degree of violence or threat involved, the probability of psychological injury if testimony is required, the seriousness of probable injury,[899] the anticipated duration of injury,[900] the importance of the testimony to the prosecution, the trustworthiness of the child's out-of-court statements,[901] and the feasibility of taking the child's testimony under circumstances that would not induce trauma.[902] The court should make particularized findings on the record of the likely trauma.[903]

Mueller § 486, at 1044 ("But a witness who is competent enough to testify but suffers from mental affliction such that exposure to formal questioning and cross-examination in court is likely to cause further damage should be viewed as unavailable").

[895] Maryland v. Craig, 110 S. Ct. 3157, 3169 (1990) (discussing trauma needed to dispense with face-to-face confrontation and permit child to testify via closed circuit television); People v. Diefenderfer, 784 P.2d 741, 751 (Colo. 1989) ("We emphasize that mere inconvenience or discomfort at the prospect of testifying does not meet the statutory standard of unavailability"); People v. Johnson, 118 Ill. 2d 501, 517 N.E.2d 1070, 1074 (1987) ("the mere *unwillingness* of an otherwise available witness to testify simply does not rise to the high level of the Federal Rule 804 standards").

[896] 34 Cal. 3d 505, 668 P.2d 738, 194 Cal. Rptr. 431 (1983).

[897] 668 P.2d at 747.

[898] 4 Louisell & Mueller § 486, at 1044 (quoted at **note 894**).

[899] People v. Diefenderfer, 784 P.2d 741, 750 (Colo. 1989) (requiring substantial impairment).

[900] *Id.* (psychological impairment must be "long standing rather than transitory in nature"); State v. Drusch, 139 Wis. 2d 312, 407 N.W.2d 328, 331 (Ct. App. 1987) (Wisconsin law "does not require permanent testimonial incapacity in order for prior testimony to be admitted into evidence").

[901] *See* State v. Robinson, 153 Ariz. 191, 735 P.2d 801 (1987). In *Robinson* the court considered several factors to conclude that the defendant's Sixth Amendment rights were not violated when the child was declared unavailable. The court wrote:

[I]t is difficult to find a clear violation of the confrontation clause when, as here, the state has facially valid reasons for not calling the declarant, the state's hearsay evidence is supported by particularized guarantees of trustworthiness, the record supports the trial court's finding that the witness is incapable of testifying, and the defendant makes no attempt to call the witness even though she was physically present.

735 P.2d at 813 n.15.

[902] Warren v. United States, 436 A.2d 821, 830 n.18 (D.C. 1981).

[903] People v. Diefenderfer, 784 P.2d 741, 750 (Colo. 1989).

Expert testimony is often helpful,[904] although it is not always necessary for a finding of unavailability.[905] Lay testimony from adults, particularly parents or other caretakers, often provides insight into the probability of harm.[906] If a child can do so without serious trauma, it is often useful for the child to appear before the court, perhaps in chambers, so the judge has an opportunity to evaluate the likelihood of psychological harm.[907]

Several states have statutes authorizing courts to declare witnesses psychologically unavailable.[908] For example, California Evidence Code § 240(c) states that a witness may be declared unavailable on the basis of "[e]xpert testimony which establishes that physical or mental trauma resulting from an alleged crime has caused harm to a witness of sufficient severity that the witness is physically unable to testify or is unable to testify without suffering substantial trauma . . . ." The Indiana child hearsay exception provides that a child is unavailable if "a psychiatrist, physician, or psychologist has certified that the

---

[904] People v. Stritzinger, 34 Cal. 3d 505, 668 P.2d 738, 746, 194 Cal. Rptr. 431 (1983). In *Stritzinger* the California Supreme Court appears to require expert testimony. The court wrote that "[r]eviewing courts have typically and properly required either expert testimony on the witness's present condition, or the witness's own express refusal to testify at trial." 668 P.2d at 746.

[905] Expert testimony may add little in cases where the child appears in court and the judge has a firsthand opportunity to determine that the child cannot testify. *See* State v. Chandler, 324 N.C. 172, 376 S.E.2d 728 (1989); State v. Drusch, 139 Wis. 2d 312, 407 N.W.2d 328, 331 (Ct. App. 1987) ("Nor do we believe expert medical testimony is essential to the determination").

[906] There is authority that lay testimony alone may not suffice to determine psychological unavailability. *See* People v. Stritzinger, 34 Cal. 3d 505, 668 P.2d 738, 194 Cal. Rptr. 431 (1983); State v. Gollon 115 Wis. 2d 592, 340 N.W.2d 912, 916 (Ct. App. 1983). Although it probably is true in the run of cases that expert testimony is helpful to determine psychological unavailability, exceptions certainly exist to this generalization. In some cases the probability of psychological damage can be ascertained without resort to experts. This is particularly so when the trial judge has an opportunity to meet the child and determine firsthand the probable impact of testifying.

[907] State v. Robinson, 153 Ariz. 191, 735 P.2d 801, 813 (1987) ("Although it is generally preferable for the trial judge to personally examine the declarant, the court of appeals correctly determined that there was sufficient evidence in this case for the judge, in his discretion, to find that Nicole's in-court testimony was 'unavailable'"); State v. Gollon, 115 Wis. 2d 592, 340 N.W.2d 912, 916 (Ct. App. 1983).

[908] *See, e.g.,* Ala Code § 15-25-32(2)(6) (Supp. 1990) (child hearsay exception; unavailability includes "[s]ubstantial likelihood that the child would suffer severe emotional trauma from testifying at the proceeding or by means of closed circuit television"); Cal. Evid. Code § 240(c) (West 1992); Fla. Stat. Ann. § 90.803(23)(a)(2)(b) (West Cum. Supp. 1991) (child hearsay exception; "Unavailability shall include a finding by the court that the child's participation in the trial or proceeding would result in a substantial likelihood of severe emotional or mental harm"); Miss. R. Evid 804(a)(6); Utah Code Ann. § 77-35-15.5(l)(h).

§ 7.48 UNAVAILABLE HEARSAY DECLARANTS   285

participation of the protected person in the trial creates a substantial likelihood of emotional or mental harm . . . ."[909]

Absence.[910] If a witness's presence in court cannot be secured because the witness is beyond the jurisdictional reach of the court or because the witness cannot be located, the witness is unavailable.[911] When the prosecutor has an obligation to produce a witness, the prosecutor must make a good faith effort to secure the witness's attendance at trial.[912]

Lack of testimonial competence. If a child is incompetent to testify as a witness, the child is effectively unavailable because the child cannot be subjected to cross-examination.[913] If the state argues that a child is unavailable because the

---

[909] Ind. Code Ann. § 35-37-4-6(d)(3)(A) (Cum. Supp. 1991).

[910] Fed. R. Evid. 804(a)(5). *See* 4 Louisell & Mueller § 486, at 1045-68; McCormick § 253, at 756-58; 4 Weinstein & Berger ¶ 804(a)[01], at 804-47 to 804-56.

[911] *See* United States v. Crockett, 21 M.J. 423 (C.M.A. 1986); United States v. Palacios, 32 M.J. 1047 (A.C.M.R. 1991) (child was sexually abused in Germany; child was unavailable for trial in Germany because she had been taken back to United States by her mother, who refused to return her to Germany for trial; prosecution did not have power to subpoena child); Rouse v. State, 548 So. 2d 643 (Ala. Crim. App. 1989) (murder case involving admissibility of former testimony of prosecution witness; state failed to show that witness, who was out of state on vacation, was unavailable); People v. Arguello, 737 P.2d 436 (Colo. Ct. App. 1987) (child had already testified twice; she was out of state at time of third trial, and her parents refused to bring her back for trial; trial court did not err in holding her unavailable).

[912] Ohio v. Roberts, 448 U.S. 56 (1980) (young adult witness was away from home; parents did not know where to find her, and prosecution sought unsuccessfully to subpoena her; witness was unavailable "in the constitutional sense"); Mancusi v. Stubbs, 408 U.S. 204 (1972) (declarant was unavailable when living in another country and prosecution had no way to secure his attendance); Barber v. Page, 390 U.S. 719 (1968) (declarant was in prison in another state; prosecutor made no effort to secure declarant's attendance even though procedures existed to make attendance possible; holding that defendant's confrontation rights violated when absent declarant's preliminary hearing testimony was admitted); United States v. Ferdinand, 29 M.J. 164 (C.M.A. 1989), *cert. denied,* 493 U.S. 1044 (1990); United States v. Cokeley, 22 M.J. 225 (C.M.A. 1986); State v. Roman, 248 N.J. Super. 144, 590 A.2d 686 (1991) (prosecutor failed to exercise due diligence in obtaining child's presence; fact that child's mother refused to honor subpoena was not sufficient; prosecutor could have resorted to Uniform Act to Secure Attendance of Witnesses); State v. Chandler, 324 N.C. 172, 376 S.E.2d 728, 733 (1989).

[913] People v. Orduno, 80 Cal. App. 3d 738, 145 Cal. Rptr. 806 (1978), *cert. denied,* 439 U.S. 1074 (1979); People v. Diefenderfer, 784 P.2d 741 (Colo. 1989); Lancaster v. People, 200 Colo. 448, 615 P.2d 720, 723 (1980) (three-year-old "declarant in this case was unavailable as a witness due to her age"); People v. District Court, 776 P.2d 1083, 1086-88 (Colo. 1989); State v. Lanam, 459 N.W.2d 656 (Minn. 1990), *cert. denied,* 111 S. Ct. 693 (1991); State v. Bellotti, 383 N.W.2d 308, 313, 315 (Minn. Ct. App. 1986); State v. Bounds, 71 Or. App. 744, 694 P.2d 566 (1985); Lancaster v. People, 200 Colo. 448, 615 P.2d 720 (1980);

child is incompetent, must the state produce the child for a competency examination? In *State v. Campbell*,[914] the Oregon Supreme Court appears to answer in the affirmative. *Campbell* involved a three-year-old sexual abuse victim. The prosecutor and defense counsel stipulated that the child was incompetent. The court disapproved the stipulation and wrote that "before any out-of-court declaration of any available living witness may be offered against a defendant in a criminal trial, the witness must be produced and declared incompetent by the court."[915]

The *Campbell* decision may be contrasted with the Washington Court of Appeals' decision in *State v. Robinson*.[916] In *Robinson* the prosecutor and defense attorney interviewed the three-year-old victim and agreed that she was testimonially incompetent. Defense counsel did not object to the trial judge's ruling that the child was incompetent. The court of appeals held that, on these facts, the trial court did not err in accepting the stipulation of the parties that the child was incompetent.

State v. Oslund, 469 N.W.2d 489, 493 (Minn. Ct. App. 1991); State v. Doe, 105 Wash. 2d 889, 719 P.2d 554 (1986); State v. Hunt, 48 Wash. App. 840, 741 P.2d 566, 568 (1987) ("A child found incompetent to testify is 'unavailable' as a witness within the meaning of" the state's child hearsay exception); State v. Robinson, 44 Wash. App. 611, 722 P.2d 1379 (1986); State v. Gitchel, 41 Wash. App. 820, 706 P.2d 1091, 1095 (1985); State v. Gove, 148 Wis. 2d 936, 437 N.W.2d 218, 219 (1989); State v. Dwyer, 143 Wis. 2d 448, 422 N.W.2d 121 (Ct. App. 1988), *aff'd,* 149 Wis. 2d 850, 440 N.W.2d 344 (1989).

In its 1984 decision in State v. Ryan, 103 Wash. 2d 165, 691 P.2d 197, 202–03 (1984), a majority of the Washington Supreme Court stated that an incompetent child is not necessarily unavailable. Although the *Ryan* majority was undoubtedly correct in concluding that incompetence and unavailability are different legal concepts, it seems that in nearly all cases where a trial judge finds it necessary to declare a child incompetent, the child will also be unavailable. Justice Dolliver expressed this view in his concurring opinion in *Ryan* where he remarked that "if . . . a finding of incompetency is made by the trial court, this then may be considered the legal equivalent of unavailability." 691 P.2d at 207 (Dolliver, J., concurring).

In its 1986 decision in State v. Doe, 105 Wash. 2d 889, 719 P.2d 554 (1986), the Washington Supreme Court appears to back away from its statement in *Ryan*. In *Doe,* the court wrote, "While the concepts of availability and competency do not overlap entirely, it is quite clear that an incompetent child is not available. The term 'available' denotes a witness who can be confronted and cross-examined. . . . A child unable to take the stand obviously cannot respond to opposing counsel's questions." 719 P.2d at 557.

[914] 299 Or. 633, 705 P.2d 694 (1985).

[915] 705 P.2d at 706. The court's decision was based on both the Oregon and United States constitutions. *See also* State v. Doe, 105 Wash. 2d 889, 719 P.2d 554 (1986); State v. Ryan, 103 Wash. 2d 165, 691 P.2d 197, 203 (1984); State v. Gollon, 115 Wis. 2d 592, 340 N.W.2d 912, 916 (Ct. App. 1983) (if child physically available, child should appear in court to determine psychological unavailability).

[916] 44 Wash. App. 611, 722 P.2d 1379 (1986).

Unavailability in fact. It is not possible to enumerate all the circumstances in which witnesses are unavailable. Courts evaluate the circumstances of each case. McCormick put his finger on it when he wrote, "In principle probably anything which constitutes unavailability in fact ought to be considered adequate."[917]

§ 7.49 Testimonial Competence of Hearsay Declarants

A hearsay declarant is a witness,[918] and, like witnesses who testify at trial, hearsay declarants ordinarily must posses testimonial capacity. Wigmore described the requirement:

> The hearsay rule is merely an additional test or safeguard to be applied to testimonial evidence otherwise admissible. The admission of hearsay statements, by way of exception to the rule, therefore presupposes that the assertor possessed the *qualifications of a witness* in regard to knowledge and the like. These qualifications are fundamental as rules of relevancy. Thus these extrajudicial statements may be inadmissible because of their failure to fulfil the ordinary rules about qualifications, even though they meet the requirements of a hearsay exception.[919]

Under some hearsay exceptions, out-of-court statements are admissible only if the declarant was testimonially competent *at the time* the statement was made. If the declarant was testimonially competent when the statement was made, incompetence at trial normally does not bar receipt of the statement.[920]

In child abuse litigation, there are important exceptions to the rule that hearsay declarants must be testimonially competent when out-of-court statements are made. Courts generally hold that excited utterances are admissible despite the fact that the declarant was testimonially incompetent when the

---

[917] McCormick § 253, at 754. *See* United States v. Arruza, 26 M.J. 234 (C.M.A. 1988), *cert. denied*, 489 U.S. 1011 (1989) (child's testimony at Article 32 investigation admissible at trial; child was unavailable at trial due to intimidation by defense counsel).

[918] Maryland v. Craig, 110 S. Ct. 3157, 3165 (1990) (referring to the Confrontation Clause, the Court stated that "a declarant [is] undoubtedly as much a 'witness against' a defendant as one who actually testifies at trial").

[919] 5 Wigmore § 1424, at 255 (footnote omitted).

[920] Idaho v. Wright, 110 S. Ct. 3139 (1990). See also **§ 7.29**.

excited utterance was made.[921] Trial courts retain discretion to exclude excited utterances that appear particularly unreliable.[922]

---

[921] Morgan v. Foretich, 846 F.2d 941, 946 (4th Cir. 1988) ("We agree with the majority of courts that have studied this issue and have reached the conclusion that 'although a child is incompetent to testify, testimony as to his spontaneous declarations or *res gestae* statements is nevertheless admissible'"); State v. Bauer, 146 Ariz. 134, 704 P.2d 264, 267 (Ct. App. 1985) ("In Arizona excited utterances of children who are incompetent to testify because of their age are admissible in evidence"); Bryan v. State, 288 Ark. 125, 702 S.W.2d 785 (1986); *In re* Basilio T., 4 Cal. App. 4th 155, 5 Cal. Rptr. 2d 450 (1992); People v. Orduno, 80 Cal. App. 3d 738, 145 Cal. Rptr. 806, 808 (1978), *cert. denied*, 439 U.S. 1074 (1979) ("we note that while there is a split in authority in other jurisdictions, the majority admit evidence of spontaneous declarations by children too young to testify"); Lancaster v. People, 200 Colo. 448, 615 P.2d 720, 722, (1980); People v. Cherry, 88 Ill. App. 3d 1048, 411 N.E.2d 61, 65 (1980); People v. Miller, 58 Ill. App. 3d 156, 373 N.E.2d 1077 (1978); Henry Vogt Mach. Co. v. Chamberlain, 279 S.W.2d 224 (Ky. 1955) (res gestae statements of a testimonially incompetent insane person properly admitted); Johnson v. State, 63 Md. App. 485, 492 A.2d 1343, 1346–47 (1985); Moore v. State, 26 Md. App. 556, 338 A.2d 344 (1975) (testimonial incompetence does not bar admission of spontaneous declaration of a young child); State v. Gorman, 229 Minn. 524, 40 N.W.2d 347 (1949) (res gestae utterance of incompetent child admissible); State v. Simmons, 52 N.J. 538, 247 A.2d 313 (1968), *cert. denied*, 395 U.S. 924 (1969); People v. Knapp, 139 A.D.2d 931, 527 N.Y.S.2d 914, 915 (1988); State v. Boston, 46 Ohio St. 3d 108, 545 N.E.2d 1220 (1989); State v. Wallace, 37 Ohio St. 3d 87, 524 N.E.2d 466, 472–73 (1988).

See also Bishop v. State, 581 P.2d 45, 48 (Okla. Crim. App. 1978), where the court wrote:

The defendant contends that since the [six-year-old] victim was deemed incompetent to testify because of her age, any rationale for admitting excited utterances as an exception to the hearsay rule is thereby negated and that, therefore, the excited utterances should have been excluded. . . . Hearsay evidence is excluded because there is no way to test the credibility of the declarant; an excited utterance is admissible though hearsay, because it is thought to have independent indicia of reliability. That is, an excited utterance made contemporaneous with a specific event, which relates to or describes the event, is held to be reliable because its nearness to the stimulating event excludes the possibility of premeditation and fabrication. . . . We are of the opinion that the fact a witness is ruled incompetent to testify because of age does not by itself negate the independent indicia of reliability which excited utterances possess, and which are the key to their admissibility.

See also State v. Galvan, 297 N.W.2d 344, 346–47 (Iowa 1980). In this case the child witnessed a brutal murder. The court wrote:

Over defense counsel's objections, Mrs. Perez testified that two days after these events she observed her two year old daughter . . . behaving in a way that was, for the child, unique. The child had taken a belt from her mother's robe and bound her own hands with it. Then she made several gestures as if beating her own chest. . . . [T]he witness's daughter was undoubtedly not competent to take an oath as a witness. The authorities make it clear that admissibility in such cases does not turn on the competence of the child to take the oath, but on the spontaneity of the utterance or act described.

[922] Oldham v. State, 167 Tex. Crim. 644, 322 S.W.2d 616 (1959).

The authorities agree that a statement of fresh complaint of sexual offense is admissible despite the testimonial incompetence of the declarant at the time of the complaint.[923]

An important question under residual and child hearsay exceptions is whether the child must be testimonially competent when the out-of-court statement is made.[924] The Washington Court of Appeal addressed this issue in *State v. Hunt*.[925] In *Hunt* the victim was between two-and-a-half and three-and-a-half when she made out-of-court statements that were admitted at trial. The defendant argued on appeal that a child's out-of-court statements should be inadmissible under the child hearsay exception unless "the child was testimonially competent at the time the statements were made."[926] The appellate court rejected the defendant's argument and held that the trial court is not required to "make a separate finding regarding testimonial competency of the child declarant at the time the statements were made."[927] The court noted that "reliability is the touchstone of admissibility under the child abuse hearsay exception."[928] A child's out-of-court statement may be reliable despite the fact that the child is testimonially incompetent when the statement is made.[929] Thus, testimonial competence is one factor among many in the reliability calculation.

Testimonial competence at the time an out-of-court statement is made is sometimes relevant when a child's statement is offered under the medical diagnosis or treatment exception.[930] The primary rationale for admitting statements under this exception is that the child understands the need to be accurate with

---

[923] *In re* Basilio T., 4 Cal. App. 4th 155, 5 Cal. Rptr. 2d 450 (1992); State v. Ryan, 103 Wash. 2d 165, 691 P.2d 197, 203–04 (1984); State v. Lounsbery, 74 Wash. 2d 659, 445 P.2d 1017, 1019 (1968) ("we have held that it is proper to permit a witness to testify that a child made complaint, even though the child is too young to be a competent witness").

[924] Perez v. State, 536 So. 2d 206 (Fla. 1988), *cert. denied*, 492 U.S. 923 (1989) (fact that young child is not testimonially competent does not mean child's statement is not sufficiently reliable to gain admission under child hearsay exception).

[925] 48 Wash. App. 840, 741 P.2d 566 (1987).

[926] 741 P.2d at 568.

[927] *Id.* at 570.

[928] *Id.* at 569.

[929] *In re* Dependency of S.S., 61 Wash. App. 488, 814 P.2d 204 (1991); State v. Gribble, 60 Wash. App. 374, 804 P.2d 634, 639 (1991) ("We hold that once the trial court has found sufficient indicia of reliability to make the hearsay statements admissible, it is not necessary to also make a finding of testimonial competence at the time the statements are made").

[930] Morgan v. Foretich, 846 F.2d 941, 949–50 (4th Cir. 1988) (four-year-old's statements to therapist admissible under medical diagnosis or treatment exception whether or not child competent to testify); Oldsen v. People, 732 P.2d 1132, 1135 n.6 (Colo. 1986) ("A finding that a child is incompetent to testify . . . does not automatically render inadmissible all hearsay statements of the child . . . . However, where the asserted exception depends on the declarant's ability to understand the purpose of questioning and to relate accurate information, it is significant that the declarant has been disqualified").

the doctor.[931] If, at the time the child talks to a doctor, the child does not understand the difference between truth and falsehood, or does not understand the importance of telling the truth, the child may be equally oblivious of the need to be truthful with the doctor.[932] Thus, the child's testimonial incompetence at the time of the out-of-court statement may assist in determining admissibility under the medical diagnosis or treatment exception.

There is a second rationale for the medical diagnosis or treatment exception.[933] Under the second rationale, statements that physicians rely on to make treatment decisions are considered sufficiently reliable to be admitted. With this rationale, the primary question is whether the information supplied by the child is the type of information relied on by physicians. Under this rationale the testimonial competence of the child is of minor importance.

RIGHT TO CONFRONT ACCUSATORY WITNESSES

§ 7.50 Confrontation Right: Applicability and Elements

The Confrontation Clause of the Sixth Amendment states that "in all criminal prosecutions, the accused shall enjoy the right . . . to be confronted with the witnesses against him."[934] In *Pointer v. Texas*,[935] the Supreme Court ruled "that the Sixth Amendment's right of an accused to confront the witnesses against him is . . . a fundamental right and is made obligatory on the States by the Fourteenth Amendment."[936] In *Lee v. Illinois*,[937] the Court observed that "the right to confront and cross-examine adverse witnesses contributes to the

---

[931] See §§ **7.35** and **7.36** for analysis of the diagnosis or treatment exception.

[932] Some elements of testimonial competence are more pertinent to admissibility than others. For example, the fact that a child has difficulty communicating with the doctor or has poor memory for the event is of less importance than the child's difficulty differentiating fact from fantasy.

[933] See § **7.36**.

[934] U.S. Const. amend. VI.

[935] 380 U.S. 400 (1965).

[936] *Id.* at 403. In *Pointer* the Court wrote:

There are few subjects, perhaps, upon which this Court and other courts have been more nearly unanimous than in their expressions of belief that the right of confrontation and cross-examination is an essential and fundamental requirement for the kind of fair trial which is this country's constitutional goal.

Id. at 405.

[937] 476 U.S. 530 (1986).

establishment of a system of criminal justice in which the perception as well as the reality of fairness prevails."[938]

State constitutions contain confrontation clauses, many of which employ the same language as the Sixth Amendment of the United States Constitution. Other state constitutions guarantee defendants a right to confront witnesses face to face.[939] Regardless of the language, state courts generally hold that state confrontation clauses provide the same rights as the Confrontation Clause of the federal Constitution.[940]

The fundamental purpose of the Confrontation Clause is to increase the accuracy of the fact-finding process.[941] The clause strives for accuracy through four requirements. When one or more of the requirements is absent, Confrontation Clause issues arise.

First, "the Confrontation Clause reflects a preference for face-to-face confrontation at trial."[942] The defendant normally has the right to a face-to-face meeting with accusatory witnesses.[943] Although the Confrontation Clause does not require accusatory witnesses to look at the defendant,[944] the witnesses normally must testify in the defendant's physical presence.

---

[938] *Id.* at 540.

[939] *See, e.g.,* N.H. Const. part I, art. 15.

[940] State v. Schaal, 806 S.W.2d 659, 662 (Mo. 1991), *cert. denied,* 112 S. Ct. 976 (1992); State v. Hester, 801 S.W.2d 695, 697 (Mo. 1991) (Missouri Constitution guarantees face-to-face confrontation; court holds that Missouri and United States confrontation clauses protect the same rights). *But see* Commonwealth v. Ludwig, 594 A.2d 281 (Pa. 1991).

[941] Maryland v. Craig, 110 S. Ct. 3157, 3163 (1990) ("The central concern of the Confrontation Clause is to ensure the reliability of the evidence against a criminal defendant"); Lee v. Illinois, 476 U.S. 530, 540 (1986) ("The right to confront and cross-examine witnesses is primarily a functional right that promotes reliability in criminal trials"); Dutton v. Evans, 400 U.S. 74, 89 (1970) ("the mission of the Confrontation Clause is to advance a practical concern for the accuracy of the truth-determining process in criminal trials").

[942] Ohio v. Roberts, 448 U.S. 56, 63 (1980). *See also* Maryland v. Craig, 110 S. Ct. 3157, 3165 (1990) ("our precedents establish that 'the Confrontation Clause reflects a *preference* for face-to-face confrontation at trial'").

[943] *See* Maryland v. Craig, 110 S. Ct. 3157, 3163 (1990); Coy v. Iowa, 487 U.S. 1012, 1016 (1988) ("We have never doubted, therefore, that the Confrontation Clause guarantees the defendant a face-to-face meeting with the witnesses appearing before the trier of fact"); California v. Green, 399 U.S. 149, 157 (1970) ("it is this literal right to 'confront' the witness at the time of trial that forms the core of the values furthered by the Confrontation Clause").

[944] Coy v. Iowa, 487 U.S. 1012, 1019 (1988) ("The Confrontation Clause does not, of course, compel the witness to fix his eyes upon the defendant; he may studiously look elsewhere, but the trier of fact will draw its own conclusions"); Stanger v. State, 545 N.E.2d 1105 (Ind. Ct. App. 1989) (turning witness chair away from defendant did not violate Sixth Amendment; jury, witness, and defendant could all see and hear one another); Commonwealth v. Groff, 378 Pa. Super. 353, 548 A.2d 1237 (1988) (not error to tell child she did not have to look at defendant).

Second, accusatory witnesses generally must testify under oath or affirmation, thus impressing them with "the seriousness of the matter and guarding against the lie by the possibility of a penalty for perjury."[945]

Third, the defendant has a right to have the jury evaluate the demeanor of accusatory witnesses.[946] Confrontation "permits the jury that is to decide the defendant's fate to observe the demeanor of the witness in making his statement, thus aiding the jury in assessing his credibility."[947] In many cases, witnesses testifying at trial repeat their own out-of-court statements. The Confrontation Clause is not violated by the fact that the jury cannot view the witness's demeanor *at the time* the out-of-court statement was made.[948]

Fourth, the Confrontation Clause includes the right to cross-examine accusatory witnesses.[949] Although the term *cross-examination* does not appear in the

---

[945] California v. Green, 399 U.S. 149, 158 (1970). *See also* Maryland v. Craig, 110 S. Ct. 3157, 3163 (1990); Ohio v. Roberts, 448 U.S. 56, 64 n.6 (1980).

[946] Maryland v. Craig, 110 S. Ct. 3157, 3163 (1990); California v. Green, 399 U.S. 149, 158 (1970); Barber v. Page, 390 U.S. 719, 725 (1968) (confrontation "includes both the opportunity to cross-examine and the occasion for the jury to weigh the demeanor of the witness"). In Mattox v. United States, 156 U.S. 237, 242–43 (1895), the Supreme Court wrote:

> The primary object of the constitutional provision in question was to prevent depositions or *ex parte* affidavits, such as were sometimes admitted in civil cases, being used against the prisoner in lieu of a personal examination and cross-examination of the witness in which the accused has an opportunity, not only of testing the recollection and sifting the conscience of the witness, but of compelling him to stand face to face with the jury in order that they may look at him, and judge by his demeanor upon the stand and the manner in which he gives his testimony whether he is worthy of belief.

[947] Maryland v. Craig, 110 S. Ct. 3157, 3163 (1990).

[948] California v. Green, 399 U.S. 149, 160 (1970) (the Court discounted "as a constitutional matter the fact that the jury at trial is foreclosed from viewing the declarant's demeanor when he first made his out-of-court statement").

[949] See Pointer v. Texas, 380 U.S. 400, 404 (1965), where the Court wrote:

> It cannot seriously be doubted at this late date that the right of cross-examination is included in the right of an accused in a criminal case to confront the witnesses against him. . . . [T]he decisions of this Court throughout the years have constantly emphasized the necessity for cross-examination as a protection for defendants in criminal cases.

(footnote omitted).

See also Kentucky v. Stincer, 482 U.S. 730 (1987); Richardson v. Marsh, 481 U.S. 200, 206 (1987); Cruz v. New York, 481 U.S. 186, 189 (1987); Ohio v. Roberts, 448 U.S. 56, 63 (1980); Davis v. Alaska, 415 U.S. 308, 315 (1974) ("Confrontation means more than being allowed to confront the witness physically. 'Our cases construing the [confrontation] clause hold that a primary interest secured by it is the right of cross-examination'"); Douglas v. Alabama, 380 U.S. 415, 418 (1965); Mattox v. United States, 156 U.S. 237, 242 (1895); Brady v. State, 575 N.E.2d 981, 985 (Ind. 1991) ("the defendant's opportunity for cross-examination has been interpreted as being the essential purpose of the federal confrontation right"); Hodges v. State, 524 N.E.2d 774, 781 (Ind. 1988) (defendant's right to confront and cross-examine was not infringed when child "could not specify the time, order, or location

Sixth Amendment, it is clear that the right to cross-examine is of constitutional stature.[950]

Although the right to confront accusatory witnesses is fundamental,[951] it is not absolute.[952] The defendant's confrontation right may be balanced against competing interests. In *Mattox v. United States*,[953] the Supreme Court wrote of the Confrontation Clause that "general rules of law of this kind, however beneficent in their operation and valuable to the accused, must occasionally give way to considerations of public policy and the necessities of the case."[954] In *Ohio v. Roberts*,[955] the Court "recognized that competing interests, if 'closely examined,' may warrant dispensing with confrontation at trial."[956]

Interests that may be balanced against the defendant's confrontation right include the state's "strong interest in effective law enforcement,"[957] the state's compelling "interest in the physical and psychological well-being of child abuse victims,"[958] the state's interest "in the development and precise formulation of the rules of evidence applicable in criminal proceedings,"[959] and the "societal interest in accurate factfinding."[960]

---

of the offenses"); Hosford v. State, 525 So. 2d 789, 790 (Miss. 1988) (discussing importance of cross-examination); Commonwealth v. Kirouac, 405 Mass. 557, 542 N.E.2d 270 (1989); State v. Cooper, 291 S.C. 351, 353 S.E.2d 451 (1987).

The right to cross-examine applies to each witness against the defendant. *See* Delaware v. Van Arsdall, 475 U.S. 673, 680 (1986). *See also* 1 Wigmore § 8, at 608 (referring to cross-examination as "the most efficacious expedient ever invented for the extraction of truth").

[950] United States v. Owens, 484 U.S. 554, 557 (1988) ("The Confrontation Clause . . . has long been read as securing an adequate opportunity to cross-examine adverse witnesses"); Barber v. Page, 390 U.S. 719, 725 (1968) (confrontation "includes both the opportunity to cross-examine and the occasion for the jury to weigh the demeanor of the witness"). *See also* 4 Louisell & Mueller § 418, at 126 ("right to confront includes a right 'to cross-examine'").

[951] Brady v. State, 575 N.E.2d 981, 985 (Ind. 1991) ("The right of confrontation is a fundamental right").

[952] Maryland v. Craig, 110 S. Ct. 3157, 3163 (1990); Chambers v. Mississippi, 410 U.S. 284, 295 (1973) ("Of course, the right to confront and cross-examine is not absolute and may, in appropriate cases, bow to accommodate other legitimate interests in the criminal trial process"); Brady v. State, 575 N.E.2d 981, 987 (Ind. 1991); Wildermuth v. State, 310 Md. 496, 530 A.2d 275, 284 (1987) ("the right to confrontation, fundamental as it is, is not absolute. It 'must occasionally give way to considerations of public policy and the necessities of the case'").

[953] 156 U.S. 237 (1895).

[954] *Id.* at 243.

[955] 448 U.S. 56 (1980).

[956] *Id.* at 64 (citation omitted).

[957] Ohio v. Roberts, 448 U.S. 56, 64 (1980).

[958] Maryland v. Craig, 110 S. Ct. 3157, 3167 (1990).

[959] Ohio v. Roberts, 448 U.S. 56, 64 (1980).

[960] Bourjaily v. United States, 483 U.S. 171, 182 (1987).

The Confrontation Clause impacts four aspects of criminal litigation:[961] (1) admissibility of hearsay (see §§ 7.51 to 7.55), (2) limitations on cross-examination (see § 7.56), (3) pretrial discovery (see **Chapter 1**), and (4) limitations on face-to-face confrontation at trial (see **Chapter 8**).

§ 7.51 Hearsay and the Confrontation Clause

The hearsay rule and the Confrontation Clause share the goal of excluding unreliable evidence.[962] Under the Confrontation Clause, hearsay is assumed to be unreliable until proven otherwise,[963] and the clause undoubtedly excludes some hearsay.[964] Indeed, the Confrontation Clause could be interpreted to exclude any

---

[961] When the Supreme Court refers to its Confrontation Clause cases, the Court usually mentions two categories: admissibility of out-of-court statements, and court imposed limitations on cross-examination. *See* Kentucky v. Stincer, 482 U.S. 730, 737 (1987); Delaware v. Fensterer, 474 U.S. 15, 18 (1985) ("This Court's Confrontation Clause cases fall into two broad categories: cases involving the admission of out-of-court statements and cases involving restrictions imposed by law or by the trial court on the scope of cross-examination").

[962] Idaho v. Wright, 110 S. Ct. 3139, 3146 (1990); Dutton v. Evans, 400 U.S. 74, 86 (1970) (the Confrontation Clause and the hearsay rule "stem from the same roots"); California v. Green, 399 U.S. 149, 155 (1970) ("hearsay rules and the Confrontation Clause are generally designed to protect similar values").

Although the Confrontation Clause and the hearsay rule serve similar values, the overlap between the clause and the rule is not complete. Idaho v. Wright, 110 S. Ct. 3139, 3146 (1990); United States v. Owens, 484 U.S. 554, 560 (1988); People v. Bastien, 129 Ill. 2d 64, 541 N.E.2d 670, 675 (1989) ("The Supreme Court has made clear that the scope of the confrontation clause is not coextensive with the rules of hearsay and their exceptions").

In some cases hearsay admissible under evidence law violates the Confrontation Clause. *See* Idaho v. Wright, 110 S. Ct. 3139, 3146 (1990) (Confrontation Clause "bars the admission of some evidence that would otherwise be admissible under an exception to the hearsay rule"); Barber v. Page, 390 U.S. 719 (1968); Grantham v. State, 580 So. 2d 53, 55 (Ala. Crim. App. 1991); State v. Robinson, 44 Wash. App. 611, 722 P.2d 1379, 1383 (1986). In other cases out-of-court statements barred by the hearsay rule are admissible under the Confrontation Clause. *See* Chambers v. Mississippi, 410 U.S. 284 (1973) (decided on due process grounds); Dutton v. Evans, 400 U.S. 74 (1970).

In the main, hearsay admissible under evidence law is equally admissible under the Confrontation Clause. *See* Bourjaily v. United States, 483 U.S. 171, 182 (1987) (the requirements for admission of co-conspirator statements under Rule 801(d)(2)(E) are identical to the requirements of the Confrontation Clause).

[963] Bourjaily v. United States, 483 U.S. 171, 179 (1987) ("out-of-court statements are only *presumed* unreliable. The presumption may be rebutted by appropriate proof").

[964] Idaho v. Wright, 110 S. Ct. 3139, 3146 (1990) ("The Confrontation Clause . . . bars the admission of some evidence that would otherwise be admissible under an exception to the hearsay rule"; holding that hearsay admissible under Idaho residual exception not sufficiently reliable to withstand challenge based on Confrontation Clause); Ohio v. Roberts, 448 U.S. 56, 63 (1980) ("The historical evidence leaves no doubt, however, that the Clause was intended to exclude some hearsay"). *See also* 4 Louisell & Mueller § 418, at 127.

out-of-court statement by a declarant who is unavailable to testify at trial.[965] The Supreme Court has never construed the clause as a complete bar to hearsay, however, and it is settled that the Confrontation Clause tolerates admission of reliable hearsay.[966] In *Idaho v. Wright*[967] the Court wrote:

> From the earliest days of our Confrontation Clause jurisprudence, we have consistently held that the Clause does not necessarily prohibit the admission of hearsay statements against a criminal defendant, even though the admission of such statements might be thought to violate the literal terms of the Clause. We reaffirmed only recently that "[w]hile a literal interpretation of the Confrontation Clause could bar the use of any out-of-court statements when the declarant is unavailable, this Court has rejected that view as 'unintended and too extreme.'"[968]

The Confrontation Clause is not offended by admission of hearsay when the declarant testifies at trial and is available for cross-examination.[969] In *California v. Green*,[970] the Court wrote "that the Confrontation Clause is not violated by admitting a declarant's out-of-court statements, as long as the declarant is testifying as a witness and subject to full and effective cross-examination."[971] The fact that the defendant cannot cross-examine the declarant *at the time* the out-of-court statement is made is not material. Cross-examination at trial is

---

[965] *See* Idaho v. Wright, 110 S. Ct. 3139, 3145 (1990); Maryland v. Craig, 110 S. Ct. 3157, 3165 (1990); Bourjaily v. United States, 483 U.S. 171, 182 (1987); Ohio v. Roberts, 448 U.S. 56, 64 (1980) ("If one were to read this language literally, it would require, on objection, the exclusion of any statement made by a declarant not present at trial. . . . But, if thus applied, the Clause would abrogate virtually every hearsay exception, a result long rejected as unintended and too extreme"); State v. Nelson, 138 Wis. 2d 418, 406 N.W.2d 385, 392 (1987).

[966] Ohio v. Roberts, 448 U.S. 56, 63 (1980); Dutton v. Evans, 400 U.S. 74, 80 (1970) ("It is not argued, nor could it be, that the constitutional right to confrontation requires that no hearsay evidence can ever be introduced"); California v. Green, 399 U.S. 149 (1970); Mattox v. United States, 156 U.S. 237 (1895) (former testimony admissible when declarant had died prior to trial).

[967] 110 S. Ct. 3139 (1990).

[968] *Id.* at 3145 (citations omitted).

[969] United States v. Gibson, 29 M.J. 379 (C.M.A. 1990), *cert. denied*, 497 U.S. 907 (1990); United States v. Hines, 23 M.J. 125, 132 (C.M.A. 1986); United States v. Fink, 32 M.J. 987, 990 (A.C.M.R. 1991); State v. Boyer, 803 S.W.2d 132, 136 (Mo. Ct. App. 1991); State v. Loughton, 747 P.2d 426 (Utah 1987); State v. Bishop, 63 Wash. App. 15, 816 P.2d 738 (1991) (child was available even though she could not remember one element of the crime).

[970] 399 U.S. 149 (1970).

[971] *Id.* at 158. The Court went on to write, "Where the declarant is not absent, but is present to testify and to submit to cross-examination, our cases, if anything, support the conclusion that the admission of his out-of-court statements does not create a confrontation problem." *Id.* at 162.

sufficient under the Confrontation Clause.[972] Cross-examination can certainly be effective when the declarant acknowledges making the prior statement and remembers the events underlying the statement.[973] The declarant need not acknowledge the statement or recall the underlying events for cross-examination to be effective, however.[974] Cross-examination is possible when the declarant is placed under oath and responds willingly to questions.[975] Cross-examination generally is possible despite the fact that the witness is unable to remember one element of the crime.[976] Cross-examination is particularly effective when normal avenues of impeachment are available to the cross-examiner.[977] Moreover, the important factor is the *opportunity* for cross-examination, not the degree to which cross-examination is effective.[978]

With its 1980 decision in *Ohio v. Roberts*,[979] the Court established a two-part framework for admissibility of hearsay under the Confrontation Clause.[980] First, "[i]n the usual case . . . the prosecution must either produce, or demonstrate the unavailability of, the declarant whose statement it wishes to use against the defendant."[981] Second, if the declarant is unavailable, the out-of-court statement "is admissible only if it bears adequate 'indicia of reliability.' Reliability can be

---

[972] Ohio v. Roberts, 448 U.S. 56 (1980); Mancusi v. Stubbs, 408 U.S. 204 (1972); Nelson v. O'Neil, 402 U.S. 622 (1971); California v. Green, 399 U.S. 149 (1970). See 4 Louisell & Mueller § 418, at 141, where the authors write of *California v. Green* that "[t]he Court emphatically established . . . that deferred cross-examination—that is, cross-examination at trial of a witness whose pretrial statement has been introduced—satisfies the Confrontation Clause, *at least* where the cross-examination is 'full and effective' . . . ."

[973] California v. Green, 399 U.S. 149, 158 (1970) (referring to out-of-court statement inconsistent with trial testimony, Court wrote that "[i]f the witness admits the prior statement is his, or if there is other evidence to show the statement is his, the danger of faulty reproduction is negligible and the jury can be confident that it has before it two conflicting statements by the same witness").

[974] Nelson v. O'Neil, 402 U.S. 622 (1971) (rejecting idea that cross-examination can only be effective when declarant admits making out-of-court statement). *See also* United States v. Owens, 484 U.S. 554 (1988); Delaware v. Fensterer, 474 U.S. 15 (1985).

[975] *See* United States v. Owens, 484 U.S. 554 (1988).

[976] State v. Bishop, 63 Wash. App. 15, 816 P.2d 738, 743 (1991). In *Bishop* the court held that a child victim was available for cross-examination even though the child could not describe an element of the crime, in this case penetration.

[977] United States v. Owens, 484 U.S. 554, 559 (1988).

[978] United States v. Owens, 484 U.S. 554 (1988); State v. Bishop, 63 Wash. App. 15, 816 P.2d 738, 743 (1991) ("This confers only an *opportunity* for effective cross-examination, however, not the right to an effective cross-examination").

[979] 448 U.S. 56 (1980).

[980] The Court has applied the Roberts framework in subsequent cases. *See* Idaho v. Wright, 110 S. Ct. 3139 (1990); United States v. Inadi, 475 U.S. 387 (1986). In White v. Illinois, 112 S. Ct. 736 (1992), however, the Court may have limited *Roberts* to former testimony cases.

[981] 448 U.S. at 65. The framers of the Sixth Amendment preferred face-to-face confrontation at trial. It is this preference that requires the prosecutor to produce or establish the unavailability of hearsay declarants. *Id.*

inferred without more in a case where the evidence falls within a firmly rooted hearsay exception. In other cases, the evidence must be excluded, at least absent a showing of particularized guarantees of trustworthiness."[982] The Court's two-part framework is discussed below.

§ 7.52 —Unavailability Rule

The first component of the *Roberts* framework states that "[i]n the usual case" the prosecutor must produce the out-of-court declarant at trial or establish the declarant's unavailability.[983] For convenience, this component will be referred to as the *unavailability rule*.[984] The *Roberts* Court held that the unavailability rule applies to former testimony. Thus, a prosecutor seeking to offer former testimony must produce the declarant at trial or establish the declarant's unavailability.[985] The unavailability rule does not apply to all hearsay, however, and in *Roberts* the Court stated that "[a] demonstration of unavailability . . . is not always required."[986] In *United States v. Inadi*,[987] the Court ruled that the unavailability rule does not apply when the prosecutor offers out-of-court statements under the co-conspirator exception of Rule 801(d)(2)(E). In *White v. Illinois*,[988] the Court further narrowed the unavailability rule. The Court stated that "*Roberts* stands for the proposition that unavailability analysis is a necessary part of the Confrontation Clause inquiry *only* when the challenged out-of-court statements were made in the course of a prior judicial proceeding."[989] The Court's use of the word *only* may mean that the prosecutor has a duty to produce the declarant or establish unavailability only when former testimony is offered. The *White* Court held that the unavailability rule does not apply to hearsay offered under the excited utterance or medical diagnosis or treatment exceptions.[990]

---

[982] *Id.* at 66 (footnote omitted).

[983] *Id.* at 65. *See* Grantham v. State, 580 So. 2d 53 (Ala. Crim. App. 1991) (emphasizing importance of producing declarant at trial; Confrontation Clause violated by admission of toxicologist's report when toxicologist did not testify at trial and prosecutor made no effort to produce toxicologist).

[984] This is the term used by the Court to describe this component of the *Roberts* framework. *See* White v. Illinois, 112 S. Ct. 736, 742 n.6 (1992).

[985] It makes no difference whether the former testimony was given at a preliminary hearing or a prior trial. The unavailability rule applies to both types of former testimony.

[986] 448 U.S. at 65 n.7.

[987] 475 U.S. 387 (1986).

[988] 112 S. Ct. 736 (1992).

[989] *Id.* at 741 (emphasis added).

[990] In *White,* the Court had little good to say about the unavailability rule, stating that "while an unavailability rule would therefore do little to improve the accuracy of factfinding, it is likely to impose substantial additional burdens on the factfinding process." 112 S. Ct. at 742.

If the unavailability rule applies, the prosecutor's duty is to make a good faith effort to obtain the witness's presence at trial.[991] In *Ohio v. Roberts,* the Court described the prosecutor's responsibility:

> The basic litmus of Sixth Amendment unavailability is established: "[A] witness is not 'unavailable' . . . "unless the prosecutorial authorities have made a *good-faith effort* to obtain his presence at trial."
>
> Although it might be said that the Court's prior cases provide no further refinement of this statement of the rule, certain general propositions safely emerge. The law does not require the doing of a futile act. Thus, if no possibility of procuring the witness exists (as, for example, the witness' intervening death), "good faith" demands nothing of the prosecution. But if there is a possibility, albeit remote, that affirmative measures might produce the declarant, the obligation of good faith *may* demand their effectuation. "The lengths to which the prosecution must go to produce a witness . . . is a question of reasonableness."[992]

The demands of good faith turn on the circumstances of the case. If the prosecutor's efforts to secure the declarant's presence are reasonable under the circumstances, the purpose of the constitutional requirement is fulfilled.[993]

If the prosecutor asserts that a declarant is unavailable, the prosecutor must establish unavailability by a preponderance of the evidence.[994]

---

[991] *See* Barber v. Page, 390 U.S. 719 (1968). *Barber v. Page* concerned admission of former testimony. The Court wrote that "a witness is not 'unavailable' for purposes of foregoing exception to the confrontation requirement unless the prosecutorial authorities have made a good-faith effort to obtain his presence at trial." *Id.* at 724–25. The declarant was incarcerated in another state. The prosecutor made no effort to obtain the declarant's presence at the trial where the prosecutor offered the declarant's former testimony. The Court held that the defendant's rights under the Confrontation Clause were violated because means were available to secure the declarant's presence, yet the prosecutor did nothing.

In Mancusi v. Stubbs, 408 U.S. 204 (1972), another former testimony case, the prosecutor offered the former trial testimony of a declarant. Following the former trial, the declarant moved permanently to Sweden. The prosecutor had no ability to secure the declarant's presence at the trial where the prior testimony was offered. The defendant's rights under the Confrontation Clause were not violated by admission of the unavailable declarant's former testimony.

[992] Ohio v. Roberts, 448 U.S. 56, 74 (1980).

[993] Ohio v. Roberts, 448 U.S. 56, 69 (1980) (what is required is substantial compliance with the purposes of the Confrontation Clause); United States v. Casamento, 887 F.2d 1141 (2d Cir. 1989), *cert. denied,* 493 U.S. 1081 (1990).

[994] Ohio v. Roberts, 448 U.S. 56, 74 (1980) ("The ultimate question is whether the witness is unavailable despite good-faith efforts undertaken prior to trial to locate and present that witness. As with other evidentiary proponents, the prosecution bears the burden of establishing this predicate"). In Bourjaily v. United States, 483 U.S. 171 (1987), the Court ruled that the preponderance of the evidence standard applies to questions of admissibility of evidence under Rule 104(a).

§ 7.53 —Reliability Requirement

The second component of the *Roberts* framework provides that hearsay "is admissible only if it bears adequate 'indicia of reliability.'"[995] Hearsay within a firmly rooted exception bears sufficient indicia of reliability to be admitted.[996] Hearsay not within a firmly rooted exception is "'presumptively unreliable and inadmissible for Confrontation Clause purposes,' and 'must be excluded, at least absent a showing of particularized guarantees of trustworthiness.'"[997]

In *Bourjaily v. United States*,[998] the Court indicated that a hearsay exception is firmly rooted when lengthy judicial experience with the exception leads to the conclusion that hearsay within the exception is generally reliable.[999] The *Bourjaily* Court held that statements admissible under the co-conspirator exception are firmly rooted for Confrontation Clause purposes.[1000]

---

[995] Ohio v. Roberts, 448 U.S. 56, 66 (1980).

[996] *Id.* ("Reliability can be inferred without more in a case where the evidence falls within a firmly rooted hearsay exception"). In *Roberts* the Court applied this "indicia of reliability" requirement principally by concluding that certain hearsay exceptions rest upon such solid foundations that admission of virtually any evidence within them comports with the "substance of the constitutional protection. *Id.* at 66.

See also White v. Illinois, 112 S. Ct. 736, 743 (1992) ("where proffered hearsay has sufficient guarantees of reliability to come within a firmly rooted exception to the hearsay rule, the Confrontation Clause is satisfied").

[997] Idaho v. Wright, 110 S. Ct. 3139, 3148 (1990). *See* Ohio v. Roberts, 448 U.S. 56, 66 (1980) (when hearsay is not within a firmly rooted exception, "the evidence must be excluded absent a showing of particularized guarantees of trustworthiness") (footnote omitted); Manocchio v. Moran, 919 F.2d 770 (1st Cir. 1990), *cert. denied,* 111 S. Ct. 1695 (1991) (autopsy report bore sufficient indicia of reliability to be admitted despite absence of doctor who prepared report).

[998] 483 U.S. 171 (1987).

[999] *Id.* at 183. In holding that the co-conspirator exception is firmly rooted, the Court wrote:

We think that the co-conspirator exception to the hearsay rule is firmly enough rooted in our jurisprudence that, under this Court's holding in *Roberts,* a court need not independently inquire into the reliability of such statements. . . . [T]he co-conspirator exception to the hearsay rule is steeped in our jurisprudence. . . . [C]o-conspirators' statements, when made in the course and in furtherance of the conspiracy, have a long tradition of being outside the compass of the general hearsay exclusion. Accordingly, we hold that the Confrontation Clause does not require a court to embark on an independent inquiry into the reliability of statements that satisfy the requirements of Rule 801(d)(2)(E).

Id. at 183–84 (footnote omitted).

See also Nelson v. Farrey, 874 F.2d 1222, 1233 (7th Cir. 1989), *cert. denied,* 493 U.S. 1042 (1990) (Flaum, J., concurring) (in *Bourjaily* "the Court held that a firmly-rooted hearsay exception has 'a long tradition of being outside the compass of the general hearsay exclusion.' Thus, the test of 'firmly-rooted' is simply the longevity of the exception's existence").

[1000] 483 U.S. at 183–84.

Under the *Bourjaily* approach, exceptions that should qualify as firmly rooted include: prior inconsistent statements,[1001] prior consistent statements,[1002] statements of identification,[1003] party admissions,[1004] statements of co-conspirators,[1005] present sense impressions,[1006] excited utterances,[1007] the state of mind exception,[1008] past recollection recorded,[1009] the business records exception,[1010] the public records exception,[1011] records of vital statistics,[1012] the learned treatise exception,[1013] former testimony,[1014] dying declarations,[1015]

[1001] Fed. R. Evid. 801(d)(1)(A).

[1002] Fed. R. Evid. 801(d)(1)(B).

[1003] Fed. R. Evid. 801(d)(1)(C). *See* United States v. Owens, 484 U.S. 554, 560 (1988). In *Owens* the Court declined to adopt a rule that out-of-court statements of identification are inherently less reliable than other out-of-court statements simply because of the possibility of suggestive identification procedures.

[1004] Fed. R. Evid. 801(d)(2).

[1005] Fed. R. Evid. 801(d)(2)(E). *See* Bourjaily v. United States, 483 U.S. 171, 183–84 (1987) (holding that the co-conspirator exception is firmly rooted).

[1006] Fed. R. Evid. 803(1).

[1007] Fed. R. Evid. 803(2). White v. Illinois, 112 S. Ct. 736, 742 n.8 (1992) ("there can be no doubt" that the excited utterance exception is firmly rooted); United States v. Vazquez, 857 F.2d 857 (1st Cir. 1988); Vann v. State, 1992 WL 105295 (Ark. 1992); State v. Plant, 236 Neb. 317, 461 N.W.2d 253 (1990); State v. Jensen, 107 Or. App. 35, 810 P.2d 865 (1991); State v. Robinson, 44 Wash. App. 611, 722 P.2d 1379, 1383, 1385 (1986) ("these statements fall within the 'firmly rooted' excited utterance hearsay exception").

[1008] Fed. R. Evid. 803(3). *See* State v. Stager, 329 N.C. 278, 406 S.E.2d 876 (1991); State v. Faucette, 326 N.C. 676, 392 S.E.2d 71 (1990).

[1009] Fed. R. Evid. 803(5).

[1010] Fed. R. Evid. 803(6). *See* Ohio v. Roberts, 448 U.S. 56, 66 n.8 (1980) (dicta indicating that business records exception is firmly rooted); United States v. Franks, 939 F.2d 600 (8th Cir. 1991) (business records exception is firmly rooted); United States v. Ray, 920 F.2d 562 (9th Cir. 1990), *cert. denied*, 111 S. Ct. 1084 (1991) (business records exception is firmly rooted); People v. Lendabarker, 215 Ill. App. 3d 540, 575 N.E.2d 568, 580 (1991), *cert. denied*, 112 S. Ct. 1561 (1992) ("As for the second prong of the *Roberts* test, it is clear that the business-records exception to the rule against hearsay is firmly rooted in the law").

In Manocchio v. Moran, 919 F.2d 770 (1st Cir. 1990), *cert. denied*, 111 S. Ct. 1695 (1991), the court indicated that autopsy reports sometimes contain information going beyond routine medical records. Thus, autopsy reports may not be firmly rooted. The court provides a useful approach to analyzing the reliability of autopsy reports.

[1011] Fed. R. Evid. 803(8). *See* United States v. McKenney, 846 F.2d 528 (9th Cir. 1988); Goldsberry v. United States, 598 A.2d 376 (D.C. 1991).

[1012] Fed. R. Evid. 803(9).

[1013] Fed. R. Evid. 803(18).

[1014] Fed. R. Evid. 804(b)(1). *See* Ohio v. Roberts, 448 U.S. 56, 66 n.8 (1980); United States v. Salim, 664 F. Supp. 682 (E.D. N.Y. 1987), *aff'd*, 855 F.2d 944 (2d Cir. 1988).

[1015] Fed. R. Evid. 804(b)(2). *See* Ohio v. Roberts, 448 U.S. 56, 66 n.8 (1980); Ellis v. State, 558 So. 2d 826 (Miss. 1990).

§ 7.53 RELIABILITY REQUIREMENT   301

statements against interest,[1016] statements of personal or family history,[1017] and fresh complaint of rape.[1018]

The hearsay exception admitting statements for purposes of diagnosis or treatment requires particular attention.[1019] In *White v. Illinois*,[1020] the Supreme Court stated that "[t]here can be no doubt" that the medical diagnosis or treatment exception is firmly rooted.[1021] With great respect, the Court's assertion is only half correct. Statements to professionals providing *treatment* have long been admitted in evidence, and this aspect of the diagnosis or treatment exception clearly is firmly rooted.[1022] Statements to professionals providing diagnostic services alone, *without treatment,* are another matter. If the patient seeks diagnostic services with an *eye toward treatment,* the patient's statements should be considered within a firmly rooted exception because the patient has a motive to be truthful with the diagnostician. The patient's motive is identical to the motive of patients talking to treating professionals. For example, a general practitioner may refer a patient to a specialist for diagnostic workup. The patient has a strong incentive to be accurate with the specialist because the general practitioner will rely on the specialist's diagnosis in prescribing treatment. In the child abuse context, children are often taken to physicians for examination. Whether or not the physician treats the child, the child's statements to the physician should be considered firmly rooted if the child's motive in talking to the doctor was consistent with receiving treatment.

[1016] Fed. R. Evid. 804(b)(3).

[1017] Fed. R. Evid. 804(b)(4).

[1018] Although fresh complaint evidence is not technically speaking hearsay, some courts consider fresh complaint evidence hearsay, and some states have statutes rendering fresh complaint evidence hearsay within an exception. See § **7.31**. In Inmon v. State, 585 So. 2d 261 (Ala. Crim. App. 1991), the court stated that "a victim's complaint that she has been sexually abused is a 'firmly rooted' exception to the hearsay rule."

[1019] Fed. R. Evid. 803(4). *See* United States v. George, 960 F.2d 97 (9th Cir. 1992); Dana v. Department of Corrections, 958 F.2d 237 (8th Cir. 1992), *cert. denied,* 112 S. Ct. 3043 (1992) (medical diagnosis or treatment exception is firmly rooted); State v. Ochoa, 576 So. 2d 854, 858 (Fla. Dist. Ct. App. 1991) (medical diagnosis or treatment exception is firmly rooted); State v. Larson, 472 N.W.2d 120, 126 (Minn. 1991) (dicta), *cert. denied,* 112 S. Ct. 965 (1992); State v. Moen, 309 Or. 45, 786 P.2d 111 (1990) (medical diagnosis or treatment exception is firmly rooted); Mosteller, *Child Sexual Abuse and Statements for the Purpose of Medical Diagnosis or Treatment,* 67 N.C. L. Rev. 257 (1989).

[1020] 112 S. Ct. 736 (1992).

[1021] *Id.* at 742 n.8.

[1022] See § **7.35**. *See also* Nelson v. Farrey, 874 F.2d 1222, 1234 (7th Cir. 1989), *cert. denied,* 493 U.S. 1042 (1990) (Flaum, J. concurring). The clearest case for considering statements for purposes of treatment firmly rooted is when the patient talks to a physician about a physical ailment. When the professional is a psychiatrist, psychologist, or social worker providing psychotherapy, it is more difficult to argue that statements to such professionals are within a firmly rooted exception.

Statements to diagnosticians retained for the limited purpose of testifying as expert witnesses are admissible as a matter of evidence law under the medical diagnosis or treatment exception.[1023] Admissibility of statements to testifying experts does not have "a long tradition of being outside the compass of the general hearsay exclusion,"[1024] however, and such statements probably should not be considered firmly rooted.

An increasing number of courts hold that children's statements identifying the perpetrator of abuse are sometimes admissible under the diagnosis or treatment exception.[1025] Traditionally, statements attributing fault were not admissible under this exception.[1026] The trend toward admitting identifying statements is a recent phenomenon, beginning in 1983.[1027] It seems safe to conclude—despite the broad language of *White v. Illinois*—that statements identifying the perpetrator are not firmly rooted.[1028]

The disadvantage of dissecting the diagnosis or treatment exception into firmly rooted and not firmly rooted components is that the exception becomes difficult to administer in the heat of trial, potentially frustrating one of the objectives of the Confrontation Clause, which is to "increas[e] certainty and consistency in the application of the Confrontation Clause."[1029]

In *Idaho v. Wright*,[1030] the Supreme Court held that the residual exception is not firmly rooted for Confrontation Clause purposes.[1031] The child hearsay

---

[1023] Fed. R. Evid. 803(4).

[1024] Bourjaily v. United States, 483 U.S. 171, 183 (1987).

[1025] See § **7.35**.

[1026] *Id.*

[1027] *See* Goldade v. State, 674 P.2d 721 (Wyo. 1983), *cert. denied,* 467 U.S. 1253 (1984).

[1028] *See* Nelson v. Farrey, 874 F.2d 1222, 1233 (7th Cir. 1989), *cert. denied,* 493 U.S. 1042 (1990) (Flaum, J., concurring), where Judge Flaum, in a concurring opinion, wrote:

> The Wisconsin Supreme Court held that T's statements identifying the defendant as the abuser fit within the medical diagnosis or treatment exception to the hearsay rule and the validity of this interpretation is not an issue in this habeas corpus case. At common law, the admission into evidence of statements made to others for purposes of treatment was a well-established practice. The common law version of this exception, however, did not embrace statements of fault; the admission of these types of statements under this particular exception is the product of the Federal Rules of Evidence (enacted in 1974) and recent court decisions. Since this development represents a marked deviation from and expansion of the common law approach, *Bourjaily* dictates that an individualized examination into the reliability of T's statements is required.

(citations omitted).

[1029] Ohio v. Roberts, 448 U.S. 56, 73 n.12 (1980).

[1030] 110 S. Ct. 3139 (1990).

[1031] *Id.* at 3147. The Court's holding refers to the Idaho residual exception. There is no doubt, however, that the holding applies with equal force to Rule 803(24) of the Federal Rules of Evidence and state residual exceptions. *See also* United States v. Stivers, 33 M.J. 715 (A.C.M.R. 1991).

exceptions in force in a majority of states are residual exceptions, and are not firmly rooted.[1032]

When a court has doubts concerning the reliability of hearsay, the following factors may influence admissibility:[1033] (1) extent to which the hearsay risks of insincerity, misperception, memory loss, and ambiguity are present,[1034] (2) extent to which the evidence is peripheral or crucial to the prosecution and devastating to the defendant,[1035] (3) motive of the declarant to be accurate or to lie,[1036] (4) spontaneity of the out-of-court statement,[1037] (5) possibility the statement was coerced,[1038] (6) extent to which the statement was against the declarant's interest,[1039] (7) assurance that the declarant possessed personal knowledge,[1040] (8) extent to which the out-of-court statement describes then-existing events rather than past facts,[1041] (9) prosecutorial misconduct,[1042] (10) use of the statement at a joint trial,[1043] (11) extent to which the evidence was prepared under procedures indicating reliability,[1044] and (11) extent to which the defendant's right to cross-examination was impaired or denied.[1045]

§ 7.54 Two-Defendant Trials

Confrontation Clause issues arise when two people commit a crime, and the hearsay statement of one participant is admitted at a joint trial.[1046] Thus, the

---

[1032] State v. Renly, 111 Or. App. 453, 827 P.2d 1345 (1992); State v. Robinson, 44 Wash. App. 611, 722 P.2d 1379, 1385 (1986) (Washington child hearsay exception "is not a firmly rooted hearsay exception").

[1033] In Dutton v. Evans, 400 U.S. 74 (1970), the Court determined that the reliability of an out-of-court statement may impact the admissibility of the statement under the Confrontation Clause. *See* 4 Louisell & Mueller § 418, at 142.

[1034] See § **7.4** for discussion of the four hearsay risks. *See also* Dutton v. Evans, 400 U.S. 74, 89 (1970).

[1035] Dutton v. Evans, 400 U.S. 74, 87 (1970); Pointer v. Texas, 380 U.S. 400 (1965) (unavailable declarant was principal witness against the defendant); Douglas v. Alabama, 380 U.S. 415 (1965).

[1036] Dutton v. Evans, 400 U.S. 74, 89 (1970); Manocchio v. Moran, 919 F.2d 770, 777 (1st Cir. 1990), *cert. denied*, 111 S. Ct. 1695 (1991).

[1037] Dutton v. Evans, 400 U.S. 74, 89 (1970).

[1038] *Id.* at 87.

[1039] *Id.* at 89.

[1040] *Id.* at 88.

[1041] *Id.*

[1042] *Id.* at 87.

[1043] *Id.*

[1044] Manocchio v. Moran, 919 F.2d 770, 777 (1st Cir. 1990), *cert. denied*, 111 S. Ct. 1695 (1991).

[1045] Mancusi v. Stubbs, 408 U.S. 204, 213 (1972); Dutton v. Evans, 400 U.S. 74, 87 (1970).

[1046] The same issues arise when there are three or more codefendants.

right to cross-examination, guaranteed by the Confrontation Clause, can be infringed at a joint trial when hearsay statements that implicate one codefendant, the declarant, (and are *admissible* under the hearsay rule against the declarant), also implicate another codefendant (but are *inadmissible* under the hearsay rule against the nondeclarant codefendant). The Confrontation Clause is not offended if the declarant codefendant (against whom the statement *is* admissible) testifies at trial and is subject to cross-examination by the nondeclarant codefendant (against whom the statement is *not* admissible).[1047] However, when the declarant codefendant cannot be cross-examined, admission of the hearsay statement implicating the nondeclarant codefendant may violate the nondeclarant codefendant's confrontation rights.[1048]

The foregoing scenario is illustrated by the leading case of *Bruton v. United States*,[1049] which involved a joint trial of two defendants for armed postal robbery. One of the defendants confessed to a postal inspector. The confession directly inculpated both defendants. The confession was admitted at trial against the confessing defendant. The jury was instructed that it could consider the confession against the confessing defendant, but not against the other defendant. The confessing defendant did not testify. The Court ruled that "because of the substantial risk that the jury, despite instructions to the contrary, looked to the incriminating extrajudicial statements in determining [the nonconfessing defendant's] guilt, admission of [the] confession in this joint trial violated [the nonconfessing defendant's] right of cross-examination secured by the Confrontation Clause . . . ."[1050]

[1047] Nelson v. O'Neil, 402 U.S. 622 (1971); California v. Green, 399 U.S. 149, 163 (1970) (referring to *Bruton* the Court wrote "no confrontation problem would have existed if Bruton had been able to cross-examine his co-defendant") (footnote omitted).

[1048] Bruton v. United States, 391 U.S. 123 (1968). In Cruz v. New York, 481 U.S. 186 (1987), the Court wrote, "Where two or more defendants are tried jointly, therefore, the pretrial confession of one of them that implicates the others is not admissible against the others unless the confessing defendant waives his Fifth Amendment rights so as to permit cross-examination." 481 U.S. at 189–90.

[1049] 391 U.S. 123 (1968). For discussion of *Bruton,* see 4 Louisell & Mueller § 418, at 137; 1 Weinstein & Berger ¶ 105[05]. *Bruton* errors are subject to harmless error analysis. *See* Harrington v. California, 395 U.S. 250 (1969).

[1050] 391 U.S. at 126. Judges periodically acknowledge the difficulty jurors have following instructions. In a concurring opinion in Krulewitch v. United States, 336 U.S. 440, 453 (1949), Justice Jackson wrote, "The naive assumption that prejudicial effects can be overcome by instructions to the jury . . . all practicing lawyers know to be unmitigated fiction."
In a footnote in *Bruton,* the Court wrote:
Judge Hand addressed the subject several times. The limiting instruction, he said, is a "recommendation to the jury of a mental gymnastic which is beyond, not only their powers, but anybody's [sic] else," *Nash v. United States,* 54 F. 2d 1006, 1007; "nobody can indeed fail to doubt whether the caution is effective, or whether usually the practical result is not to let in hearsay," *United States v. Gottfried,* 165 F. 2d 360, 367; "it is indeed very hard to believe that a jury will, or for that matter can, in practice observe the admonition," *United States v. Delli Paoli,* 229 F. 2d 319, 321. Judge Hand

§ 7.54 TWO-DEFENDANT TRIALS

In *Lee v. Illinois*,[1051] the Court stated that confessions of codefendants are particularly unreliable.[1052] In *Lee* the confession of one defendant in a joint trial was admitted for the truth of the matter asserted against the other defendant. Neither defendant testified, and thus the defendant against whom the confession was admitted had no opportunity to cross-examine the confessing defendant. Introduction of the confession violated the confrontation rights of the nonconfessing defendant.

In *Cruz v. New York*,[1053] the Court considered the joint murder trial of Benjamin Cruz and his brother Eulogio. Both defendants confessed, and their confessions interlocked. Neither defendant testified at trial. The trial judge instructed the jury not to consider Benjamin's confession against Eulogio. The Court held that despite the jury instruction, introduction of Benjamin's confession violated Eulogio's confrontation rights. The Court wrote:

> Where two or more defendants are tried jointly, therefore, the pretrial confession of one of them that implicates the others is not admissible against the others unless the confessing defendant waives his Fifth Amendment rights so as to permit cross-examination.
>
> Ordinarily, a witness is considered to be a witness "against" a defendant for purposes of the Confrontation Clause only if his testimony is part of the body of evidence that the jury may consider in assessing his guilt. Therefore, a witness whose testimony is introduced in a joint trial with the limiting instruction that it be used only to assess the guilt of one of the defendants will not be considered

---

referred to the instruction as a "placebo," medically defined as "a medicinal lie." Judge Jerome Frank suggested that its legal equivalent "is a kind of 'judicial lie': It undermines a moral relationship between the courts, the jurors, and the public; like any other judicial deception, it damages the decent judicial administration of justice." *United States v. Gruenwald*, 233 F. 2d 556, 574.

391 U.S. at 132 n.8.

Despite concerns about jurors' ability or willingness to follow instructions in joint trials, the Court stated in Tennessee v. Street, 471 U.S. 409, 415 n.6 (1985), that "[t]he assumption that jurors are able to follow the court's instructions fully applies when rights guaranteed by the Confrontation Clause are at issue."

[1051] 476 U.S. 530 (1986).

[1052] The Court wrote:

> Our cases recognize that this truth-finding function of the Confrontation Clause is uniquely threatened when an accomplice's confession is sought to be introduced against a criminal defendant without the benefit of cross-examination. As has been noted, such a confession "is hearsay, subject to all the dangers of inaccuracy which characterize hearsay generally . . . . More than this, however, the arrest statements of a codefendant have traditionally been viewed with special suspicion. Due to his strong motivation to implicate the defendant and to exonerate himself, a codefendant's statements about what the defendant said or did are less credible than ordinary hearsay evidence."

476 U.S. at 541.

[1053] 481 U.S. 186 (1987).

to be a witness "against" the other defendants. In *Bruton,* however, we held that this principle will not be applied to validate, under the Confrontation Clause, introduction of a nontestifying codefendant's confession implicating the defendant, with instructions that the jury should disregard the confession insofar as its consideration of the defendant's guilt is concerned.

* * *

This case is indistinguishable from *Bruton* with respect to those factors the Court has deemed relevant in this area: the likelihood that the instruction will be disregarded, the probability that such disregard will have a devastating effect, and the determinability of these facts in advance of trial.

We hold that, where a nontestifying codefendant's confession incriminating the defendant is not directly admissible against the defendant, . . . the Confrontation Clause bars its admission at their joint trial, even if the jury is instructed not to consider it against the defendant, and even if the defendant's own confession is admitted against him.[1054]

Confrontation issues in joint trials usually arise when the out-of-court statement of defendant X is properly admitted against X, and the jury is instructed that the statement may not be considered against defendant Y. In most cases the reason X's statement may not be considered against Y is that, as to Y, the statement violates the hearsay rule. If, however, the hearsay rule allows admission of X's out-of-court statement against both X *and* Y, then Y's confrontation rights usually are not violated by admission of the statement, despite Y's inability to cross-examine X. LaFave and Israel write:

> In *Bruton,* the Court emphasized that it was dealing with a case in which "the hearsay statement inculpating petitioner was clearly inadmissible against him under traditional rules of evidence." Lower courts have thus concluded that *Bruton* has no application when a statement by defendant's partner in crime is received under some exception to the hearsay rule. Illustrative are cases where the evidence was admissible because the statement was made by a co-conspirator during the course of and in furtherance of the conspiracy or fell within the spontaneous exclamation or business record exception to the hearsay rule. These decisions seem correct in light of *Dutton v. Evans,* where the Supreme Court upheld the use of hearsay evidence in the form of a statement by a co-conspirator not on trial made during the concealment phase of the conspiracy. Distinguishing *Bruton* because the instant case did not involve evidence which was "devastating" or "a confession made in the coercive atmosphere of official interrogation," the Court in *Dutton* held the admitted statement was "sufficiently clothed with 'indicia' of reliability," that it, was properly "placed before the jury though there is no confrontation with the declarant." In short, the "right of confrontation . . . is not absolute."[1055]

[1054] *Id.* at 189–90, 193 (citations omitted).

[1055] 2 W. LaFave & J. Israel, Criminal Procedure § 17.2(b), at 364 (1984).

Not every out-of-court statement that implicates a codefendant raises *Bruton* problems.[1056] In *Richardson v. Marsh*,[1057] the Court contrasted confessions that directly implicate a codefendant with confessions that are not incriminating on their face, and that become incriminating "only when linked with evidence introduced later at trial . . . ."[1058] The Court concluded that in such "linkage" cases, jurors are capable of obeying the judge's instruction to disregard the statement insofar as it relates to one codefendant.[1059]

Bruton issues usually are resolved before trial. In some instances, the appropriate solution is severance and separate trials.[1060] In some cases it is possible to redact offending language from a confession.[1061]

In addition to joint trials, Confrontation Clause issues arise when participants in the same crime are tried separately. *Douglas v. Alabama*,[1062] for example, was not a joint trial. The defendant and an accomplice were tried separately for assault with intent to commit murder. At the defendant's trial, the prosecutor called the accomplice as an adverse witness. The accomplice refused on Fifth

---

[1056] See *id.* at 366, where the authors write:

> Because the *Bruton* rule was stated in terms of "a codefendant's confession inculpating the defendant," sometimes the question is whether that has occurred. The courts are generally rather demanding in that regard, insisting that "the challenged statements must be clearly inculpatory." This means that *Bruton* will likely be deemed inapplicable if the confession contains only "linkage evidence," that is, information which by itself does not incriminate the other defendant but which does have some tendency to link him to the crime when it is considered together with other evidence admitted at the trial.

(footnotes omitted). See also 1 Weinstein & Berger ¶ 105[04], at 105-29.

[1057] 481 U.S. 200 (1987).

[1058] *Id.* at 208. The Court remarked that "the calculus changes when confessions that do not name the defendant are at issue." *Id.* at 211.

[1059] 481 U.S. at 208 ("while it may not always be simple for the members of a jury to obey the instruction that they disregard an incriminating inference, there does not exist the overwhelming probability of their inability to do so that is the foundation of *Bruton*'s exception to the general rule" that jurors do obey instructions).

[1060] Severance is not always appropriate. In *Richardson v. Marsh*, 481 U.S. 200, 209–10 (1987), the Court wrote:

> One might say, of course, that a certain way of assuring compliance would be to try defendants separately whenever an incriminating statement of one of them is sought to be used. That is not as facile or as just a remedy as might seem. Joint trials play a vital role in the criminal justice system, accounting for almost one-third of federal criminal trials in the past five years. . . . It would impair both the efficiency and the fairness of the criminal justice system to require, in all these cases of joint crimes where incriminating statements exist, that prosecutor bring separate proceedings . . . .

[1061] See Richardon v. Marsh, 481 U.S. 200, 211 (1987) ("We hold that the Confrontation Clause is not violated by the admission of a nontestifying codenfendant's confession with a proper limiting instruction when, as here, the confession is redacted to eliminate not only the defendant's name, but any reference to his existence") (footnote omitted).

[1062] 380 U.S. 415 (1965).

Amendment grounds to answer questions. The accomplice's confession directly implicating the defendant was then read to the jury by the prosecutor under the rather transparent guise of refreshing the accomplice's recollection. Arguably, the accomplice's confession was not substantive evidence because it was nominally used for the nonsubstantive purpose of refreshing recollection. The defendant was unable to cross-examine the accomplice. The Court ruled that the jury may well have considered the confession for the truth of the matter asserted, and that the defendant's inability to cross-examine the accomplice violated the defendant's rights under the Confrontation Clause.

Tennessee v. Street[1063] teaches that in some circumstances limiting instructions are effective to overcome potential Confrontation Clause problems. In *Street* the defendant confessed to a murder. At trial he claimed that his confession was coerced by the sheriff. The defendant asserted that during police interrogation, the sheriff read the confession of another participant in the crime and instructed the defendant to give a similar confession. The other participant's confession inculpated the defendant. To rebut the defendant's theory, the prosecutor called the sheriff to the stand, and the sheriff denied coercing the defendant. To corroborate the sheriff's testimony, the prosecutor sought to point out the differences between the two confessions. To this end, the sheriff read the other participant's confession. Before the other participant's confession was read, "the trial judge twice informed the jury that it was admitted 'not for the purpose of proving the truthfulness of his statement, but for the purpose of rebuttal only.'"[1064] The Supreme Court found no violation of the Confrontation Clause. Jurors are assumed to follow the court's instructions,[1065] and in this case the trial judge was careful to instruct the jury on the limited purpose for which the confession could be used.

§ 7.55 Former Testimony

Many of the Supreme Court's Confrontation Clause cases involve former testimony. The former testimony exception is found at Rule 804(b)(1), and reads:

> The following are not excluded by the hearsay rule if the declarant is unavailable as a witness: Testimony given as a witness at another hearing of the same or a different proceeding, or in a deposition taken in compliance with law in the course of the same or another proceeding, if the party against whom the testimony is now offered . . . had an opportunity and similar motive to develop the testimony by direct, cross, or redirect examination.[1066]

[1063] 471 U.S. 409 (1985).

[1064] *Id.* at 412.

[1065] *Id.* at 415.

[1066] Fed. R. Evid. 804(b)(1). For discussion of the former testimony exception, see 4 Louisell & Mueller § 497; 4 Weinstein & Berger ¶ 804(b)(1).

§ 7.55   FORMER TESTIMONY

The present section outlines highlights from the Supreme Court's former testimony cases. In *Pointer v. Texas*,[1067] the defendant was not represented by counsel at his preliminary hearing. A witness who testified against the defendant at the preliminary hearing was unavailable at trial, and the unavailable witness's preliminary hearing testimony was admitted against the defendant. The Court held that because the defendant was not represented by counsel at the preliminary hearing, admission of the preliminary hearing testimony violated the Confrontation Clause.

In *California v. Green*,[1068] the Court ruled that a defendant's Confrontation Clause rights were not violated by admission at trial of the preliminary hearing testimony of a witness who was available for cross-examination at trial. The Court ruled that on the facts before it, preliminary hearing testimony could be equated with testimony given at a former trial.[1069] The Court also stated that if the prosecutor is responsible for the declarant's unavailability at trial, the opportunity to cross-examine at an earlier time may not suffice for purposes of the Confrontation Clause.[1070]

In *Ohio v. Roberts*,[1071] the Court considered the admissibility of preliminary hearing testimony. The defendant in *Roberts* was represented by different attorneys at the preliminary hearing and trial. The Court stated that different lawyers at the two proceedings did not violate the Confrontation Clause.

The *Roberts* Court ruled that when former testimony is offered at trial, the trial judge ordinarily does not inquire into the effectiveness of cross-examination at the earlier proceeding. In *Mancusi v. Stubbs*,[1072] the Court had inquired into the effectiveness of cross-examination at an earlier trial. But *Mancusi* was unique because a lower court had already ruled that defense counsel at the earlier trial had been ineffective. In *Roberts* the Court referred to *Mancusi* and wrote:

> Under those unusual circumstances, it was necessary to explore the character of the actual cross-examination to ensure that an adequate opportunity for full cross-examination had been afforded to the defendant. . . . We hold that in all but such extraordinary cases, no inquiry into "effectiveness" is required. A holding that every case involving prior testimony requires such an inquiry would frustrate the principal objective of generally validating the prior-testimony exception in the first place—increasing certainty and consistency in the application of the Confrontation Clause.[1073]

[1067] 380 U.S. 400 (1965).

[1068] 399 U.S. 149 (1970).

[1069] *Id.* at 175.

[1070] *Id.* at 166.

[1071] 448 U.S. 56 (1980).

[1072] 408 U.S. 204 (1972).

[1073] 448 U.S. at 73 n.12.

The Supreme Court's former testimony cases indicate that "an adequate opportunity for cross-examination may satisfy the [confrontation] clause even in the absence of physical confrontation."[1074] The Court's decisions suggest that what is important under the Confrontation Clause is the opportunity for cross-examination.[1075] If the opportunity for effective cross-examination exists, the defendant's rights usually are protected.

In *Barber v. Page*,[1076] the Court ruled that a defendant does not waive the right to cross-examine witnesses at trial by declining to cross-examine at a preliminary hearing. The Court also stated that one justification for admitting former testimony is the need for such evidence.[1077]

§ 7.56 Limitations on Cross-Examination

The right to cross-examine accusatory witnesses is an integral part of the Sixth Amendment confrontation right.[1078] Confrontation issues arise when restrictions are "imposed by law or by the trial court on the scope of cross-examination."[1079]

[1074] Douglas v. Alabama, 380 U.S. 415, 418 (1965).

[1075] *See* Delaware v. Fensterer, 474 U.S. 15, 20 (1985) ("Generally speaking, the Confrontation Clause guarantees an *opportunity* for effective cross-examination"); Ohio v. Roberts, 448 U.S. 56, 70 (1980) (Court did not decide whether mere opportunity would suffice); Douglas v. Alabama, 380 U.S. 415, 418 (1965).

[1076] 390 U.S. 719 (1968).

[1077] *Id.* at 722.

[1078] Delaware v. Van Arsdall, 475 U.S. 673, 678 (1986); Davis v. Alaska, 415 U.S. 308, 316–17 (1974). The Supreme Court's opinions frequently refer to the confrontation right as a trial right. In *Barber v. Page,* 390 U.S. 719, 725 (1968) the Court wrote, "The right to confrontation is basically a trial right. It includes both the opportunity to cross-examine and the occasion for the jury to weigh the demeanor of the witness."

The right to cross-examine applies to each accusatory witness. Delaware v. Van Arsdall, 475 U.S. 673, 680 (1986). Spencer and Flin comment on the reverance in which common law lawyers hold cross-examination, "Among English-speaking lawyers no belief is more deeply held than the value of cross-examination. It has been the subject of fervent professions of faith in so many speeches and writings that a collection of them would fill a sizeable book." J. Spencer & R. Flin, The Evidence of Children: The Law and the Psychology 222 (1990). Lawyers in Europe are not so impressed by cross-examination. A French judge and legal writer had this to say:

> The Anglo-American system has grave faults which cry out for it to be abolished. In the first place, it over-uses the right of questioning, to which it attributes an exaggerated efficency in the case of suspect witnesses, whilst paying insufficient respect to witnesses who are sincere. Even more deplorably, it takes absolutely no precautions against the witness being influenced, or even badgered, and it takes no account of the distorting effect of suggestive questions, which get worse as the case is more bitterly contested.

F. Gorphe, La Critique du Temoignage 90 (2d ed. 1927).

[1079] Delaware v. Fensterer, 474 U.S. 15, 18 (1985).

§ 7.56 LIMITATIONS ON CROSS-EXAMINATION

Sixth Amendment issues also arise when interference with cross-examination is due not to the court, but to the unwillingness or inability of the witness to answer questions.[1080] These two sources of interference with cross-examination are discussed in this section.

Limitations Imposed by Trial Court

Supreme Court decisions make clear the importance of cross-examination. "[T]he Court has recognized that cross-examination is the "'greatest legal engine ever invented for the discovery of the truth.'"[1081] Restrictions on cross-examination can "effectively . . . emasculate the right of cross-xamination."[1082] In *Davis v. Alaska*,[1083] the Court wrote that "[c]onfrontation means more than being allowed to confront the witness physically. 'Our cases construing the [confrontation] clause hold that a primary interest secured by it is the right of cross-examination.'"[1084] Defense counsel must be afforded fairly wide latitude to cross-examine accusatory witnesses.[1085] The *Davis* Court wrote:

> [T]he cross-examiner is not only permitted to delve into the witness' story to test the witness' perceptions and memory, but the cross-examiner has traditionally been allowed to impeach, *i.e.*, discredit, the witness. . . . We have recognized that the exposure of a witness' motivation in testifying is a proper and important function of the constitutionally protected right of cross-examination.[1086]

In *Ohio v. Roberts*,[1087] the Court added that "one critical goal of cross-examination is to draw out discrediting demeanor to be viewed by the fact-finder."[1088]

[1080] United States v. Berrio-Londono, 946 F.2d 158 (1st Cir. 1991), *cert. denied*, 112 S. Ct. 1223 (1992) (witness's refusal to answer questions during cross-examination did not violate defendant's Sixth Amendment rights).

[1081] California v. Green, 399 U.S. 149, 158 (1970) (quoting 5 Wigmore § 1367).

[1082] Smith v. Illinois, 390 U.S. 129, 131 (1968). *See also* Delaware v. Fensterer, 474 U.S. 15, 19 (1985).

[1083] 415 U.S. 308 (1974). In *Davis* the Court ruled that the defendant's right to confront accusatory witnesses outweighed the state's interest in protecting the confidentiality of juvenile court records. *See* Stamps v. State, 107 Nev. 372, 812 P.2d 351 (1991) (defendant had right to cross-examine witness on statements contained in confidential juvenile court file).

[1084] *Id.* at 315. *See also* Douglas v. Alabama, 380 U.S. 415, 418 (1965).

[1085] State v. Allison, 595 A.2d 1089, 1094 (N.H. 1991) ("cross-examination is subject to limitation at the discretion of the trial judge. However, the defendant may not be denied the opportunity to make at least a threshold level of inquiry"); State v. Ramos, 553 A.2d 1059 (R.I. 1989) (defendant should have been permitted to cross-examine child about delay in reporting sexual abuse).

[1086] Davis v. Alaska, 415 U.S. 308, 316–17 (1974).

[1087] 448 U.S. 56 (1980).

[1088] *Id.* at 63 n.6.

In *Delaware v. Van Arsdall,*[1089] the Court ruled that the Confrontation Clause was violated when the trial judge precluded the defendant from all cross-examination of a prosecution witness regarding dismissal of charges pending against the witness. The charges were dropped when the witness agreed to speak to the prosecutor about the crime allegedly committed by the defendant. The Court wrote:

> We think that a criminal defendant states a violation of the Confrontation Clause by showing that he was prohibited from engaging in otherwise appropriate cross-examination designed to show a prototypical form of bias on the part of the witness, and thereby "to expose to the jury the facts from which jurors . . . could appropriately draw inferences relating to the reliability of the witness."[1090]

Restrictions on cross-examination that violate a defendant's right to confront accusatory witnesses are subject to harmless error analysis.[1091] In *Delaware v. Van Arsdall,*[1092] the Court held:

> [C]onstitutionally improper denial of a defendant's opportunity to impeach a witness for bias, like other Confrontation Clause errors, is subject to *Chapman* harmless-error analysis. The correct inquiry is whether, assuming that the damaging potential of the cross-examination were fully realized, a reviewing court might nonetheless say that the error was harmless beyond a reasonable doubt. Whether such an error is harmless in a particular case depends upon a host of factors, all readily accessible to reviewing courts. These factors include the importance of the witness' testimony in the prosecution's case, whether the testimony was cumulative, the presence or absence of evidence corroborating or contradicting the testimony of the witness on material points, the extent of cross-examination otherwise permitted, and, of course, the overall strength of the prosecution's case.[1093]

The right to cross-examine accusatory witnesses is not absolute.[1094] In *Van Arsdall* the Court wrote:

> [T]rial judges retain wide latitude insofar as the Confrontation Clause is concerned to impose reasonable limits on such cross-examination based on concerns

---

[1089] 475 U.S. 673 (1986).

[1090] *Id.* at 680.

[1091] United States v. Vargas, 933 F.2d 701 (9th Cir. 1991).

[1092] 475 U.S. 673 (1986).

[1093] *Id.* at 684.

[1094] Davis v. Alaska, 415 U.S. 308, 316 (1974) ("the broad discretion of a trial judge to preclude repetitive and unduly harassing interrogation"); United States v. Berrio-Londono, 946 F.2d 158 (1st Cir. 1991), *cert. denied,* 112 S. Ct. 1223 (1992); United States v. Torres, 937 F.2d 1469, 1473 (9th Cir. 1991), *cert. denied,* 112 S. Ct. 886 (1992). *See also* Kentucky v. Stincer, 482 U.S. 730 (1987) (exclusion of defendant from preliminary competency examination of child witness did not violate defendant's right to cross-examine child; *Stincer* is discussed in **Ch. 2**).

§ 7.56 LIMITATIONS ON CROSS-EXAMINATION 313

about, among other things, harassment, prejudice, confusion of the issues, the witness' safety, or interrogation that is repetitive or only marginally relevant. . . . "[T]he Confrontation Clause guarantees an *opportunity* for effective cross-examination, not cross-examination that is effective in whatever way, and to whatever extent, the defense might wish."[1095]

In *United States v. Garcia-Rosa,*[1096] the First Circuit remarked:

Once the defendant has been afforded a reasonable opportunity to question a witness' veracity and motivation, the trial judge enjoys broad discretion in determining the scope and extent of cross-examination. . . . "The court need not permit unending excursions into each and every matter touching upon veracity if a reasonably complete picture has already been developed." . . . The trial judge must balance the probative value of the proposed inquiry against the twin dangers of unfair prejudice and unnecessary delay in the proceedings.[1097]

Rule 611(a) of the Federal Rules of Evidence codifies the trial court's authority to "exercise reasonable control over the mode . . . of interrogating witnesses . . . so as to . . . protect witnesses from harassment or undue embarrassment."[1098]

The trial judge has authority[1099] to limit or forbid cross-examination in the following areas:

Embarrassing questions. The court may limit unduly embarrassing questions.[1100] In the context of child sexual abuse, the nature of the crime often makes it necessary for the cross-examiner to delve into embarrassing matters.

[1095] 475 U.S. at 679.

[1096] 876 F.2d 209 (1st Cir. 1989).

[1097] *Id.* at 237 (citations omitted).

[1098] Fed. R. Evid. 611(a).

[1099] *In re* Martha, 407 Mass. 319, 553 N.E.2d 902 (1990) (trial court did not err in denying mother right to cross-examine child she and her husband abused; juvenile court judge had ample evidence to support finding of abuse); State v. Anthony, 89 N.C. App. 93, 365 S.E.2d 195, 196 (1988).

See also Garcia v. State, 629 S.W.2d 196 (Tex. Ct. App. 1982). In *Garcia,* the defendant raped the 13-year-old victim. The child testified for the state and was cross-examined at length. After the state rested, the defendant sought to recall the victim for further cross-examination. The court held a conference in chambers with counsel during which the defendant's lawyer was invited to articulate the need for further cross-examination. No showing was made. The court permitted the defendant to recall the victim, but did not allow leading questions or impeachment. The defendant argued on appeal that this limitation on cross-examination was error. The court of appeal affirmed the defendant's conviction, holding that the trial court did not abuse its discretion in limiting cross-examination.

[1100] *See* People v. District Court, 719 P.2d 722, 726 (Colo. 1986); State v. John C., 503 A.2d 1296 (Me. 1986) (proper to exclude embarrassing questions under Rules 403 and 611).

Marginally relevant or collateral matters. The court may disallow cross-examination on marginally relevant and collateral matters.[1101]

Developmentally inappropriate questions. The court should prohibit questions that employ language or concepts the child cannot understand.[1102] Such questions are developmentally inappropriate. California Evidence Code § 765(b) is a good model. Section 765(b) states:

> With a witness under the age of 14, the court shall take special care to protect him or her from undue harassment or embarrassment, and to restrict the unnecessary repetition of questions. The court shall also take special care to insure that questions are stated in a form which is appropriate to the age of the witness. The court may in the interests of justice, on objection by a party, forbid the asking of a question which is in a form that is not reasonably likely to be understood by a person of the age of the witness.[1103]

Confusing questions. The court may instruct counsel to refrain from questions that are confusing, misleading, ambiguous, or unintelligible.[1104]

Harassment. The court may curtail questions designed to harass or annoy the witness.[1105] Psychological literature reveals that intimidating cross-examination may make children more suggestible and less accurate. Spencer and Flin write that "[t]he characteristics of a typical . . . cross-examination appear to violate all the principles of best practice, with the predicted outcome of maximising the risk of contaminating the evidence."[1106]

[1101] Delaware v. Van Arsdall, 475 U.S. 673, 679 (1986); United States v. Berrio-Londono, 946 F.2d 158 (1st Cir. 1991), *cert. denied,* 112 S. Ct. 1223 (1992); United States v. Torres, 937 F.2d 1469, 1473 (9th Cir. 1991), *cert. denied,* 112 S. Ct. 886 (1992); People v. District Court, 719 P.2d 722, 726 (Colo. 1986); Chastain v. State, 257 Ga. 54, 354 S.E.2d 421 (1987) (not error for trial court to refuse to permit cross-examination of 11-year-old sex abuse victim regarding fact that she once slept with an uncle); Jennette v. State, 197 Ga. App. 580, 398 S.E.2d 734 (1990) (questions regarding prior sexual experience of child irrelevant to molestation charge); Johns v. State, 181 Ga. App. 510, 352 S.E.2d 826, 827 (1987) (not error to prohibit defendant from cross-examining victim about victim's juvenile court record; "Such matters were not relevant to the issue before the court"); State v. Hyde, 735 S.W.2d 746, 747–48 (Mo. Ct. App. 1987); State v. Moton, 749 P.2d 639 (Utah 1988).

[1102] State v. Dwyer, 149 Wis. 2d 850, 440 N.W.2d 344 (1989) (discusses need to question children in language they understand).

[1103] Cal. Evid. Code § 765(b) (West 1991).

[1104] *See* Delaware v. Van Arsdall, 475 U.S. 673 (1986).

[1105] *Id.*; Davis v. Alaska, 415 U.S. 308, 316 (1974); People v. District Court, 719 P.2d 722, 726 (Colo. 1986); *In re* C.B., 574 So. 2d 1369, 1374 (Miss. 1990) ("The youth court must, also, have some control over the manner in which questions are put to a child witness so as to protect the witness from improper or excessive intimidation").

[1106] J. Spencer & R. Flin, The Evidence of Children: The Law and the Psychology 257 (1990).

§ 7.56 LIMITATIONS ON CROSS-EXAMINATION

Undue consumption of time. The court may limit examination that constitutes an undue consumption of time,[1107] or that is unduly repetitive.[1108]

Questions designed to elicit inadmissible evidence. The court has discretion to forbid questions that are designed to, or that are likely to, elicit inadmissible evidence.[1109]

Limitations Caused by Unwillingness or Inability to Answer Questions

A witness's refusal to answer questions on cross-examination may violate the defendant's right to confrontation.[1110] In *Commonwealth v. Kirouac*,[1111] the six-year-old victim testified, but "resisted answering nearly all questions put to her on cross-examination."[1112] The Massachusetts Supreme Judicial Court ruled that the defendant's inability to cross-examine the child violated the Confrontation Clause. The court wrote:

> In deciding whether a defendant's constitutional right to cross-examine and thus confront a witness against him has been denied because of an unreasonable limitation of cross-examination, a court must weigh the materiality of the witness's direct testimony and the degree of the restriction on cross-examination. The determination can only be made on a case-by-case basis. Cross-examination that is somewhat impeded, but not totally foreclosed, presents a weaker case for finding a denial of rights than a complete absence of cross-examination. . . .
>
> Valerie's testimony was crucial to the prosecution's case, and her total refusal to cooperate on cross-examination was so prejudicial as to deny the defendant his constitutional right to cross-examine her. . . . This case more closely parallels a case in which a witness declines to answer all questions on cross-examination or, because of illness or otherwise, is unavailable for cross-examination.[1113]

In some cases a witness's memory loss interferes with effective cross-examination. Decisions indicate, however, that memory loss seldom interferes so

---

[1107] Fed. R. Evid. 611(a)(2).

[1108] Davis v. Alaska, 415 U.S. 308, 316 (1974).

[1109] People v. District Court, 719 P.2d 722, 726 (Colo. 1986).

[1110] *In re* J.D.S., 436 N.W.2d 342 (Iowa 1989) (defendant juvenile was not denied effective cross-examination when victim refused to respond to a few questions).

[1111] 405 Mass. 557, 542 N.E.2d 270 (1989).

[1112] 542 N.E.2d at 272.

[1113] *Id.* at 273 (footnote omitted).

completely with cross-examination as to violate the Sixth Amendment.[1114] In *Delaware v. Fensterer*,[1115] the Supreme Court wrote:

> [T]he Confrontation Clause guarantees an *opportunity* for effective cross-examination, not cross-examination that is effective in whatever way, and to whatever extent, the defense might wish. . . . The Confrontation Clause includes no guarantee that every witness called by the prosecution will refrain from giving testimony that is marred by forgetfulness, confusion, or evasion.[1116]

So long as forgetful witnesses testify under oath in the presence of the accused, where the jury can observe their demeanor, cross-examination can be effective in most instances.[1117] Cross-examination is particularly effective when the cross-examiner is allowed free rein to impeach credibility.[1118] Indeed, in many instances a witness's memory problems actually help the cross-examiner persuade the jury to disbelieve the witness.[1119] Courts analyze the facts of each case to determine whether an opportunity exists for effective cross-examination.[1120]

[1114] Delaware v. Fensterer, 474 U.S. 15, 19 (1985) ("it does not follow that the right to cross-examination is denied by the State whenever the witness' lapse of memory impedes one method of discrediting him"); United States v. Spotted War Bonnet, 933 F.2d 1471 (8th Cir. 1991), *cert. denied*, 112 S. Ct. 1187 (1992) ("a perfectly satisfactory cross-examination is not required by the Clause, and a witness who cannot remember the details of statements she has made in the past can still be sufficiently available for cross-examination to satisfy the constitutional requirement"); Commonwealth v. Amirault, 404 Mass. 221, 535 N.E.2d 193, 202 (1989) (in response to questions during cross-examination, child sometimes responded that she could not remember; defendant's right to cross-examination was not violated; "not comparable to a refusal to answer questions. . . . Nor is this case equivalent to a denial of the right to examine a witness. . . . because [defendant] had ample *opportunity* to cross-examine the child. . . . The defendant could have used, and did use, the child's memory lapse and unresponsiveness to impeach her credibility") (footnotes omitted); State v. Bishop, 63 Wash. App. 15, 816 P.2d 738 (1991).

[1115] 474 U.S. 15 (1985).

[1116] *Id.* at 20, 21–22.

[1117] Delaware v. Fensterer, 474 U.S. 15, 20 (1985).

[1118] United States v. Owens, 484 U.S. 554, 559 (1988) ("It is sufficient that the defendant has the opportunity to bring out such matters as the witness' bias, his lack of care and attentiveness, his poor eyesight, and even (what is often a prime objective of cross-examination . . .) the very fact that he has a bad memory"); Delaware v. Fensterer, 474 U.S. 15, 22 (1985) ("the Confrontation Clause is generally satisfied when the defense is given a full and fair opportunity to prove and expose these infirmities through cross-examination, thereby calling to the attention of the factfinder the reasons for giving scant weight to the witness' testimony").

[1119] United States v. Owens, 484 U.S. 554 (1988).

[1120] United States v. Spotted War Bonnet, 933 F.2d 1471 (8th Cir. 1991), *cert. denied*, 112 S. Ct. 1187 (1992) (analyzes cross-examination of the six- and seven-year-old children and concludes that cross-examination was adequate to satisfy the Confrontation Clause; defendant was able to imply that children had been coached by interviewers).

In some cases, an intellectually disabled witness has difficulty responding to questions during cross-examination. In most cases, however, mental illness or retardation does not undermine the ability to cross-examine.[1121]

§ 7.57 Applicable Proceedings

The Confrontation Clause applies in "criminal prosecutions." Clearly, this language embraces the trial of a criminal case. The confrontation right also is applicable during preliminary hearings and hearings on motions to suppress evidence, although in such settings the right may be more limited than the trial right.[1122] In *Kentucky v. Stincer*,[1123] the Supreme Court ruled that a defendant's Sixth Amendment right to cross-examine accusatory witnesses was not violated when he was excluded from the competency examination of a child witness.[1124]

The right to confront accusatory witnesses applies at the adjudicatory stage of delinquency proceedings in juvenile court.[1125] The right probably also applies in

---

[1121] *See* United States v. Lyons, 33 M.J. 543 (A.C.M.R. 1991).

[1122] United States v. Gunter, 631 F.2d 583, 589 (8th Cir. 1980) (defendant has right to be present at evidentiary hearing); Wilcox v. United States, 425 F. Supp. 895 (D. Conn. 1975) (right to be present at suppression hearing can be waived); United States v. Lopez, 328 F. Supp. 1077, 1088 (E.D.N.Y. 1971) (same); Singletary v. United States, 383 A.2d 1064, 1070 (D.C. 1978) (same); Poteat v. United States, 330 A.2d 229, 231 (D.C. 1974) (suppression hearing); State v. Grey, 256 N.W.2d 74, 76 (Minn. 1977) (suppression hearing).

See also 1 W. LaFave & J. Israel, Criminal Procedure § 10.5(e), at 805 (1984):

As indicated in McCray v. Illinois, [386 U.S. 300 (1967)] defendant's right of cross-examination at the suppression hearing may be substantially narrower than that available at trial. McCray held that neither due process nor the confrontation cause was violated when the suppression hearing judge refused to allow defense counsel to force the arresting officer, on cross-examination, to reveal the name and address of the informant alleged to have provided probable cause for defendant's arrest. . . . Courts have stressed, however, that limitations on the opportunity for confrontation must be carefully circumscribed to fit the state's justification for restricted disclosure.

See also Annotation, *Right of Accused to Be Present at Suppression Hearing or at Other Hearing or Conference Between Court and Attorneys Concerning Evidentiary Questions*, 23 A.L.R.4th 955 (1983).

[1123] 482 U.S. 730 (1987).

[1124] See **Ch. 2** for discussion of *Stincer*.

[1125] *In re* Gault, 387 U.S. 1, 56 (1967) ("confrontation and sworn testimony by witnesses available for cross-examination were essential for a finding of 'delinquency' and an order committing Gerald to a state institution"); R.L.R. v. State, 487 P.2d 27, 31 (Alaska 1971); *In re* Malinda S., 51 Cal. 3d 368, 795 P.2d 1244, 272 Cal. Rptr. 787, 795 n.16 (1990) ("parties in civil proceedings also have a due process right to cross-examine and confront witnesses"); *In re* Dennis H., 19 Cal. App. 3d 350, 96 Cal. Rptr. 791 (1971); *In re* J.D.S., 436 N.W.2d 342, 344 (Iowa 1989); *In re* M.O., 13 Kan. App. 2d 381, 770 P.2d 856, 857 (1989) ("Confrontational rights, of course, apply to juvenile proceedings"); *In re* B., 43 A.D.2d 688, 350 N.Y.S.2d 426 (1973); *In re* Dwayne M., 287 S.C. 413, 339 S.E.2d 130 (1986)

juvenile court proceedings to transfer or certify a case from juvenile to adult court.[1126]

There is a dearth of authority regarding applicability of the confrontation right in status offense cases in juvenile court. Such litigation involves noncriminal misconduct such as truancy, curfew violation, and running away from home. In view of the fact that in most jurisdictions a child who is adjudicated a status offender may be institutionalized, the child should be afforded the right to confront and cross-examine accusatory witnesses.[1127]

Child abuse and neglect proceedings in juvenile court are civil rather than criminal. As such, the Sixth Amendment does not apply.[1128] This is not to say, however, that persons accused of neglect or abuse in dependency proceedings do

---

(appellant was adjudged a juvenile delinquent for committing a "lewd act on a minor and indecent exposure"; during adjudicatory hearing, judge ordered appellant to leave room while six-year-old victim testified; South Carolina Supreme Court held that it was error to exclude appellant from the courtroom, and stated that "[t]he right to be present and to confront witnesses applies in juvenile court proceedings in the same manner as in criminal court proceedings"); *In re* Dino, 359 So. 2d 586, 589 (La.), *cert. denied,* 439 U.S. 1047 (1978) ("The constitutional privilege against self-incrimination and the rights to counsel and to confront and cross-examine witnesses are applicable in the case of juveniles as they are with respect to adult accused"). *See also* S. Davis, Rights of Juveniles § 5.6, at 5-22 (1986).

The confrontation right in juvenile delinquency proceedings, which are nominally civil, is based on principles of due process rather than the Sixth Amendment, which by its terms is limited to criminal prosecutions. Several states have statutes conferring a right to confrontation in delinquency proceedings. *See, e.g.,* Conn. Gen. Stat. Ann. § 46b-135(a) (West 1986); Wyo. Stat. Ann. § 14-6-223(b)(ii) (1986).

[1126] P.H. v. State, 504 P.2d 837, 843 (Alaska 1972). *But see In re* Ralph M., 211 Conn. 289, 559 A.2d 179 (1989) (rules of evidence do not apply during transfer hearing; court may consider hearsay despite fact that such hearsay might not be admissible at trial; consideration of hearsay does not deprive minor of due process or confrontation).

[1127] The potential loss of liberty and stigma attached to an adjudication as a status offender dictate that minors accused of status offenses have the same confrontation rights as minors accused of delinquency.

[1128] R.O. v. Pike County Dep't Human Resources, 578 So. 2d 1312, 1313 (Ala. Civ. App. 1990); *In re* Kerry O., 210 Cal. App. 3d 326, 258 Cal. Rptr. 448 (1989); *In re* Long, 313 N.W.2d 473, 478–79 (Iowa 1981) (court stated that Sixth Amendment does not apply in neglect proceedings; court assumed without expressly deciding that persons accused of neglect have a right to confront accusatory witnesses); *In re* L.K.S. 451 N.W.2d 819, 822 (Iowa 1990) ("there is no sixth amendment right to confrontation in CHINA proceedings"); *In re* Michael C., 557 A.2d 1219 (R.I. 1989) (not error for trial judge to question adolescent sex abuse victim in camera; parents did not have right to face-to-face confrontation); *In re* M.W., 374 N.W.2d 889, 893 (S.D. 1985) ("The constitutional implications of the confrontation clause . . . are not present in a civil action. . . . We recently held that dependency and neglect proceedings are civil in nature. . . . Therefore, in determining whether the statement bears sufficient indicia of reliability, the trial court is not faced with the highly onerous burden placed upon it in criminal cases"); *In re* James A., 505 A.2d 1386 (R.I. 1986).

not possess a right to confront accusatory witnesses.[1129] In dependency litigation the confrontation right springs from principles of due process rather than from the Sixth Amendment. In dependency cases the trial judge has considerable discretion regarding the manner in which cross-examination and confrontation occur. For example, in *In re Noel M.*,[1130] the judge questioned the child in chambers. The parent was not present. The parent's attorney was present, although all questioning was done by the court. Counsel was afforded the opportunity to submit questions in advance. Furthermore, during the judge's examination of the child, counsel was permitted to suggest further questions. On appeal, the parent did not dispute her exclusion from the in-chambers examination of the child, but argued that her rights to confrontation and cross-examination were violated when her attorney was not allowed to cross-examine the child directly. The court of appeal disagreed, holding that "the procedure employed did not deprive the respondent of her rights to confrontation and cross-examination."[1131]

Proceedings to terminate parental rights are commenced either in juvenile court or in a civil court of general jurisdiction. Because such litigation is not criminal, the Sixth Amendment does not apply. No one denies, however, that the most fundamental rights are at stake;[1132] thus, the Due Process Clause of the Fourteenth Amendment and state due process clauses apply in such proceedings to afford parents a right to confront and cross-examine the witnesses for the state.

Although the Sixth Amendment right of confrontation does not apply in administrative proceedings that are not criminal or quasi-criminal in nature, principles of due process may impose a right of confrontation and cross-examination.[1133] Davis writes:

[1129] *See ex parte* McAllister, 541 So. 2d 1104, 1106–07 (Ala. 1989) (trial court did not err in juvenile court dependency case when it took child's testimony in camera; parent's attorney was present while child testified); *In re* Kerry O., 210 Cal. App. 3d 326, 258 Cal. Rptr. 448 (1989); *In re* Mary S., 186 Cal. App. 3d 414, 230 Cal. Rptr. 726 (1986) (persons accused of child abuse in juvenile court have right to confront witnesses; right not without exception, however; primary goal of juvenile court proceedings is to protect child; proper for trial court in juvenile court proceeding to permit children to testify outside physical presence of their parents when children testified that they were afraid of their parents); *In re* Tanya P., 120 Cal. App. 3d 66, 174 Cal. Rptr. 533 (1981); *In re* Long, 313 N.W.2d 473, 478–79 (Iowa 1981); Diggs v. Tyler, 525 So. 2d 1263, 1266 (La. Ct. App. 1988) (in child custody litigation incident to divorce, court may interview child in camera without parents present); *In re* C.B., 574 So. 2d 1369, 1374 (Miss. 1990) ("This is not a criminal case, but we are of the opinion that the right of confrontation should be accorded to an accused parent in such cases as this").

[1130] 23 Conn. App. 410, 580 A.2d 996 (1990).

[1131] 580 A.2d at 1002.

[1132] Santosky v. Kramer, 455 U.S. 745 (1982).

[1133] Seering v. Department of Social Servs., 194 Cal. App. 3d 298, 239 Cal. Rptr. 422 (1987) (administrative proceeding to revoke license of day care center where child was sexually abused by operator; during victim's testimony, ALJ excluded alleged perpetrator from room; appellate court upheld this procedure, finding a right to confront witnesses at an

One element in a full trial-type hearing is opportunity to be confronted by the adverse witnesses. When adjudicative facts are in dispute, our legal tradition is that the party affected is entitled not only to rebut or explain but also to "confront his accusers" and to cross-examine them. . . . For a full hearing, the accused must have a chance to know the identity of the accuser, to see and hear him testify, and he must have a chance to explain, to submit rebuttal evidence and argument, and to cross-examine.

The Supreme Court held in Goldberg v. Kelly, 397 U.S. 254, 268 (1970), that welfare could not be terminated, even temporarily, without a full trial-type hearing, including "an effective opportunity to defend by confronting any adverse witnesses." . . .

One who has a sufficient interest at stake is entitled to confront the witnesses against him on a question of adjudicative fact.[1134]

The goal of enhancing the truth-finding process, which lies at the heart of the Sixth Amendment right to confront accusatory witnesses, finds expression in civil and administrative proceedings through the principles of fundamental fairness and due process of law.

§ 7.58 Waiver and Forfeiture of Confrontation Right

A defendant may waive the Sixth Amendment right to confront accusatory witnesses.[1135] Like the waiver of constitutional rights generally, waiver must

---

administrative proceeding, but right not absolute); *In re* E.P. 167 Ill. App. 3d 534, 521 N.E.2d 603 (1988); *In re* Wolf, 231 N.J. Super. 365, 555 A.2d 722 (1989) (tenured teacher had right to face students accusing him of sexual impropriety).

[1134] 2 K. Davis, Administrative Law Treatise § 12:9, at 444–47 (2d ed. 1979). *See also* Willner v. Committee on Character & Fitness, 373 U.S. 96, 103–04 (1963) ("procedural due process often requires confrontation and cross-examination of those whose word deprives a person of his livelihood").

[1135] Barber v. Page, 390 U.S. 719, 725 (1968); Brookhart v. Janis, 384 U.S. 1, 3 (1966); Thomas v. Gunter, 962 F.2d 1477 (10th Cir. 1992); United States v. Barror, 23 M.J. 370 (C.M.A. 1987) (defendant did not waive confrontation right in this case); State v. Davis, 830 P.2d 1309 (Mont. 1992); *In re* Kerry O., 210 Cal. App. 3d 326, 258 Cal. Rptr. 448 (1989); State v. Gove, 148 Wis. 2d 936, 437 N.W.2d 218 (1989) (defendant waived objection to court's decision that child was unavailable by failing to object at trial). See also United States v. Carlson, 547 F.2d 1346, 1357–58 (8th Cir. 1976), *cert. denied,* 431 U.S. 914 (1977), where the court wrote:

> The Sixth Amendment right of confrontation is, by its language and historical underpinnings, a personal right of the accused and is intended for his benefit. As such, this right, like other federally guaranteed constitutional rights, can be waived by the accused. To constitute a valid waiver there must be "an intentional relinquishment or abandonment of a known right or privilege" by the accused.

See also 4 Louisell & Mueller § 418, at 166.

§ 7.58 WAIVER AND FORFEITURE

be voluntary, knowing, and intelligent. Thus, a defendant may stipulate to receipt of unconfronted hearsay evidence,[1136] and may forgo the right to cross-examine witnesses.[1137]

In most cases, failure to make timely objection based on the Confrontation Clause constitutes a waiver of the right to object on appeal.[1138] If, however, unconfronted hearsay is admitted because the defendant fails to object, an appellate court may nevertheless consider the evidence under the plain error rule.[1139]

A defendant may forfeit the right to confrontation through misconduct.[1140] In *United States v. Carlson*,[1141] the Eighth Circuit Court of Appeals explained:

> The Sixth Amendment does not stand as a shield to protect the accused from his own misconduct or chicanery. "A defendant who murders a witness ought not to be permitted to invoke the right of confrontation to prohibit the use of his accusation." Similarly, a defendant should not be afforded the protection of the confrontation clause if he achieves his objective of silencing a witness by less drastic, but equally effective means. [The defendant] cannot be heard to complain that he was denied the right of cross-examination and confrontation when he himself was the instrument of the denial.[1142]

The defendant may lose the right of confrontation if a child is rendered unavailable through the misconduct of the defendant or someone acting on the defendant's behalf. For example, if the defendant intimidates or coerces the child into silence, the defendant's misconduct constitutes a forfeiture of the confrontation right.[1143]

[1136] *See* United States v. Carlson, 547 F.2d 1346 (8th Cir. 1976), *cert. denied,* 431 U.S. 914 (1977); 4 Louisell & Mueller § 418, at 166. *But see* State v. Campbell, 299 Or. 633, 705 P.2d 694 (1985) (prosecutor and defense counsel may not stipulate as to incompetence of three-year-old sexual abuse victim so as to render child unavailable as a witness; such a practice may violate right to confrontation).

[1137] *See* 4 Louisell & Mueller § 418, at 166.

[1138] United States v. Szabo, 789 F.2d 1484, 1486–87 (10th Cir. 1986) ("'Ordinarily, a confrontation clause objection cannot be raised on appeal unless it was also raised sometime during the trial court proceedings'"; court recognized, however, that confrontation right is "an important constitutional right," and that appellate court sometimes will consider confrontation issue even though it is not raised below); State v. Gove, 148 Wis. 2d 936, 437 N.W.2d 218 (1989); 4 Louisell & Mueller § 418, at 166.

[1139] United States v. Szabo, 789 F.2d 1484, 1486–87 (10th Cir. 1986).

[1140] Brandon v. State, 778 P.2d 221, 227–28 (Alaska Ct. App. 1989). A defendant who persists in disruptive and contumacious behavior may be excluded from the courtroom and thus be denied the constitutional right to be present at trial. *See* Illinois v. Allen, 397 U.S. 337 (1970).

[1141] 547 F.2d 1346 (8th Cir. 1976), *cert. denied,* 431 U.S. 914 (1977).

[1142] *Id.* at 1359.

[1143] State v. Black, 291 N.W.2d 208, 214 (Minn. 1980) (adult witness intimidated into silence by defendant; right to confront forfeited).

CHAPTER 8

ALTERING THE COURTROOM TO ACCOMMODATE CHILDREN

§ 8.1   Support Persons
§ 8.2   Sequestering Witnesses
§ 8.3   Altering Courtroom Practices and Configurations
§ 8.4   Defendant's Right to Public Trial
§ 8.5   Right to Attend Criminal Trials
§ 8.6   Right of Access to Court Records
§ 8.7   Video Testimony
§ 8.8   —Confrontation Clause
§ 8.9   —Assistance of Counsel
§ 8.10 —Impartial Jury
§ 8.11 —Compulsory Process Clause
§ 8.12 —Due Process Clause
§ 8.13 —Right to Be Present
§ 8.14 Jury's Perception of Children's Credibility

§ 8.1   Support Persons

Testifying is difficult for most children, and it is not surprising when young witnesses respond in childlike ways. Some have great difficulty speaking above a whisper.[1] Others break into tears. Some simply refuse to speak. Consider the six-year-old who "refused to listen to questions and placed her fingers in her ears."[2]

---

[1] United States v. Romey, 32 M.J. 180 (C.M.A.), *cert. denied*, 112 S. Ct. 337 (1991) (defendant's confrontation rights not violated when child whispered to her mother who repeated what child said).

[2] Pendleton v. Commonwealth, 685 S.W.2d 549, 551 (Ky. 1985).

To reduce the anxiety caused by testifying, it is often useful to allow an adult to serve as a support person for a child.[3] If the child has difficulty, the support person may sit at counsel table or stand beside or behind the child. With young children, the child may sit in the adult's lap. Such practices are not objectionable unless the support person coaches or prompts the child. There should be no hard and fast rules in this area. Each child is unique. The jury may be instructed to infer nothing from the presence of the support person.

Although reducing children's stress is a sufficient reason to allow support persons, empirical research discloses an additional justification for their use: For some children, presence of a supportive adult actually increases the ability to testify. Research by Goodman and her colleagues reveals that the presence of a supportive adult increases children's ability to answer the prosecutor's questions.[4] Of equal importance, the reassurance afforded by a supportive adult helps children cope with cross-examination. Thus, when a support person is present, children are less likely during cross-examination to recant the identity of the perpetrator, recant central details of the abuse, or provide inconsistent answers regarding peripheral details. The truth-finding function of the trial is measurably enhanced by the simple expedient of allowing a supportive adult to remain in the courtroom while the child testifies.

---

[3] United States v. Johnson, 15 M.J. 518 (A.C.M.R. 1982); State v. Menzies, 603 A.2d 419 (Conn. App. Ct. 1992); Baxter v. State, 522 N.E.2d 362 (Ind. 1988); Stanger v. State, 545 N.E.2d 1105 (Ind. Ct. App. 1989) (permitting support person to sit near child not improper); Commonwealth v. Amirault, 404 Mass. 221, 535 N.E.2d 193, 207 (1989) (court permitted parent to attend children); State v. Pollard, 719 S.W.2d 38, 42 (Mo. Ct. App. 1986) (not error to allow six-year-old's mother to sit near counsel table); Commonwealth v. Pankraz, 382 Pa. Super. 116, 554 A.2d 974 (1989) (not abuse of discretion to permit young child to sit in grandmother's lap while testifying); Commonwealth v. Meadows, 381 Pa. Super. 354, 553 A.2d 1006, 1011–12 (1989) (trial court did not err in refusing to grant mistrial when rape counselor who was familiar with child comforted child while judge and attorneys adjourned to adjacent room for legal argument; child, deaf and mute, was confused about why judge and attorneys left); State v. Jones, 178 W. Va. 519, 362 S.E.2d 330, 332 (1987) (defendant not prejudiced by trial court's decision permitting seven-year-old witness to sit in foster mother's lap while testifying; child was extremely anxious; no evidence that foster mother prompted child; "The court may have allowed Rachel to sit on her foster mother's lap to keep the child from being distracted"). *See* Cal. Penal Code § 868.5 (West); Wis. Stat. Ann. § 950.005 (West).

[4] G. Goodman, E. Taub, D. Jones, P. England, L. Port, L. Ruby & L. Prado-Estrada, The Emotional Effects of Criminal Court Testimony on Child Sexual Assault Victims (Monographs of the Soc'y for Research in Child Dev., in press).

§ 8.2 Sequestering Witnesses

Witnesses may be excluded from the courtroom while they are not testifying. The purpose of exclusion is to prevent witnesses from shaping their testimony in light of what others say.[5] Louisell and Mueller write:

> Excluding witnesses serves two main purposes. The first is to prevent the testimony of one witness from being tailored by what he hears in the testimony of another. Where one of two witnesses, both called by the same party and generally in sympathy with that party's cause, hears the testimony of the other, the one may consciously or semi-consciously try to mold his testimony into greater consistency with that of the other, or his memory may be shaped, without conscious effort at all, by what he has heard. Where the sympathies of the witnesses are aligned with opposing sides, similar distortions may occur, but to the end of artificially increasing conflicts and inconsistencies between their stories. The second reason is to assist the parties in detecting error or falsehood by the witnesses.[6]

Rule 615 of the Federal Rules of Evidence articulates the exclusion rule:

> At the request of a party the court shall order witnesses excluded so that they cannot hear the testimony of other witnesses and it may make the order of its own motion. This rule does not authorize exclusion of (1) a party who is a natural person, or (2) an officer or employee of a party which is not a natural person designated as its representative by its attorney, or (3) a person whose presence is shown by a party to be essential to the presentation of the party's cause.[7]

Under Rule 615 the court must exclude witnesses on request of a party. Some states permit the court to exercise discretion in deciding whether to exclude witnesses.[8]

---

[5] Fed. R. Evid. 615 advisory committee's note ("The efficacy of excluding or sequestering witnesses has long been recognized as a means of discouraging and exposing fabrication, inaccuracy, and collusion"); 6 J. Wigmore, Evidence in Trials at Common Law § 1837, at 455–60 (1976) [hereinafter Wigmore].

See also United States v. Leggett, 326 F.2d 613 (4th Cir.), *cert. denied,* 377 U.S. 955 (1964) (exclusion prevents "the possibility of one witness shaping his testimony to match that given by other witnesses at the trial"); Commonwealth v. Knapp, 374 Pa. Super. 160, 542 A.2d 546, 555 (1988); State v. Barker, 178 W. Va. 736, 364 S.E.2d 264 (1987).

[6] 3 D. Louisell & C. Mueller, Federal Evidence § 370, at 595–96 (1979) [hereinafter Louisell & Mueller]. *See also* 3 J. Weinstein & M. Berger, Weinstein's Evidence ¶ 615[01] (1987) [hereinafter Weinstein & Berger]; 6 Wigmore § 1838, at 461–67.

[7] Fed. R. Evid. 615.

[8] *See* Minn. R. Evid. 615 ("At the request of a party the court may order witnesses excluded so that they cannot hear the testimony of other witnesses"); State v. Posten, 302 N.W.2d 638, 640 (Minn. 1981) (not error to refuse to exclude six-year-old victim's father and foster mother; "In Minnesota sequestration is not a matter of right but a matter left to the trial court's discretion").

In child abuse litigation, the exclusion rule becomes important when a child witness needs the supportive presence of a person who is also a witness, and who normally would be subject to exclusion. In states where the trial judge has discretion regarding exclusion, the court may allow a support person to remain.[9] If the prosecutor knows the child will need support, the prosecutor can arrange for a support person who is not a witness. If the only appropriate support person is a witness, the support person may testify before the child.[10]

Rule 615 exempts from exclusion persons who are essential to the presentation of the party's case. In some cases, a child's need for a support person who is also a witness makes the presence of the support person essential to the prosecution's case.[11] This argument is particularly persuasive when the support person has already testified and the child is unable to testify without support. The Third Circuit embraced this approach in *Government of Virgin Islands v. Edinborough*.[12] Edinborough was convicted of raping a 13-year-old minor. At trial, the prosecution's only witnesses were the victim and her mother. When the child was called as the government's first witness, defense counsel asked that the mother be excluded. The trial judge refused to sequester the mother, and the Third Circuit affirmed, writing:

> It is also possible to view the circumstances of this case as falling within an explicit exception to Rule 615. Subsection (3) of the Rule permits an exception for "a person whose presence is shown by a party to be essential to the presentation of his cause." This indicates that Rule 615 has not entirely eliminated all judicial discretion, . . . but rather has changed the burden of proof . . . . While the party desiring sequestration previously had to convince the court to grant it, under Rule 615 sequestration must be given unless the party opposing the exclusion has convinced the court to exercise its discretion to except a particular witness from the sequestration order on the basis of his or her necessity to the presentation of a party's cause. . . .
>
> At oral argument, defense counsel suggested that so long as the child is a competent witness, the presence of one acting *in loco parentis* cannot be viewed as essential for purposes of subsection (3). We disagree. Persons unfamiliar with judicial proceedings often find that the necessity of testifying produces anxiety.

---

[9] State v. Posten, 302 N.W.2d 638, 640 (Minn. 1981); Commonwealth v. Berry, 355 Pa. Super. 243, 513 A.2d 410, 415 (1986) (trial court did not err in allowing 15-year-old rape victim's mother to remain; "where . . . there is minimal risk that subsequent witnesses will merely echo preceding witnesses, the court may allow those witnesses to remain, with good cause, despite a sequestration order"); State v. Barker, 178 W. Va. 736, 364 S.E.2d 264 (1987) (10-year-old victim; trial court did not err in allowing state's expert witness, a psychologist who had discussed abuse with child on several occasions, to remain in courtroom throughout trial to provide support for child).

[10] The defendant may object on the ground that it may be necessary to recall the support person later. Wigmore supports this argument. *See* 3 Wigmore § 1840, at 470.

[11] *See* State v. Barker, 178 W. Va. 736, 364 S.E.2d 264 (1987).

[12] 625 F.2d 472 (3d Cir. 1980).

It follows that children, particularly those who must testify about sexual molestation, will find the judicial experience even more frightening if they are required to testify in the unfamiliar surroundings of a sterile courtroom without the sight of a familiar and protective individual. Defendant's interpretation of Rule 615 would require the automatic exclusion of even the parents of a seven-year-old child. We conclude that subsection (3) authorizes the court to exercise its discretion to permit the presence of a parent of a young witness.[13]

§ 8.3 Altering Courtroom Practices and Configurations

Most criminal courtrooms are similarly configured and furnished. May these solemn halls of justice be modified to make children more comfortable? If modification decreases children's stress and increases their ability to provide accurate and complete testimony, the answer should be yes.

The origins of the contemporary American courtroom are found in England. Historical research discloses that the physical layout of today's courtroom is more the product of practical necessity and convenience than law or principle. Birks writes that "[d]uring the Middle Ages, and even later, courts were rough and noisy places."[14] The bar that separates the judge and attorneys from the spectators was initially installed to protect the former from the latter. In early times, the judge sat on a wooden bench and had no writing desk. "When law reports began to be printed in the sixteenth century and the practice of examining witnesses in open court was generally adopted, a desk for the judges obviously became desirable."[15] Today, of course, the judge's desk is the most prominent feature in the courtroom.

The point of this historical sojourn is that the modern courtroom is not sacrosanct. Nothing in law or the Constitution forbids circumspect modification of the courtroom to facilitate children's testimony.

The courtroom is a forbidding place for many children. Increasing attention is directed to making the courtroom less intimidating. A California statute provides that "[i]n the court's discretion the judge, parties, witnesses, support persons, and court personnel, may be relocated within the courtroom to facilitate a more comfortable and personal environment for the child witness."[16] Flexibility is particularly appropriate in juvenile court dependency proceedings.[17] In *In re C.B.*,[18] the Mississippi Supreme Court wrote that in dependency cases "[t]he

---

[13] *Id.* at 474–75.

[14] Birks, *Court Architecture, in* Selected Readings: Courthouses and Courtrooms 2 (G. Winters ed. 1972).

[15] *Id.* at 3.

[16] Cal. Penal Code § 868.8(c) (West).

[17] *In re* C.M., 595 A.2d 293 (Vt. 1991).

[18] 574 So. 2d 1369 (Miss. 1990).

courtroom need not be made to appear a place of horrors and is not required, by law, to have any particular configuration. It may look like a playroom, a school room, a family room or living room, so long as the necessary persons are present."[19]

In an enlightened decision, *Commonwealth v. Amirault*,[20] the Massachusetts Supreme Judicial Court considered a trial judge's decision to alter the courtroom for young witnesses in a day care sexual abuse case. The Supreme Judicial Court wrote:

> At trial, the judge allowed the child witnesses to testify from a child-sized table and chair placed in front of the jury box. The judge and questioning attorneys sat around the table. The defendant sat at counsel table. The child was allowed to bring a toy into the courtroom and had a parent sit behind him or her. The judge instructed the attorneys to make objections quietly into a microphone during a child's testimony. The judge ruled on the objections immediately and heard arguments based on the objections after the testimony.
>
> On appeal, the defendant makes a broad objection to the inability of counsel effectively to register valid objections and the prejudicial nature of the courtroom set-up, and argues that he was thereby deprived of his rights to effective assistance of counsel and to a fair trial. . . . We find no error.
>
> A judge is afforded wide discretion in fashioning procedures and modifying standard trial practices to accommodate the special needs of child witnesses. . . . We have recognized the plight of child sexual abuse victims, and the difficulties a particular child may face in trying to testify in a traditional courtroom setting. . . . "[A] judge may require that the environment in which a witness is to give testimony may be made less formal and intimidating." . . .
>
> The judge here protected the child witnesses to the extent possible while also safeguarding the defendant's rights. The judge permitted defense counsel to confer with each other and with the defendant and then to return to the witness with additional questions following the conferences. Furthermore, the judge explained the special practices to the jury to avoid any possible prejudice to the defendant. The defendant's right to a fair trial and assistance of counsel were not compromised.[21]

So long as the seriousness of the proceeding is not compromised, there is no objection to alterations which accommodate children.[22] Thus, the witness chair

---

[19] *Id.* at 1374. The court went on to state, "Trial courts have substantial control over such matters and can, with sufficient prior planning, preliminary consultation and experimentation, eliminate most of the features of a court appearance that disturbs children." *Id.*

[20] 404 Mass. 221, 535 N.E.2d 193 (1989).

[21] 535 N.E.2d at 207.

[22] Hunter v. State, 194 Ga. App. 711, 391 S.E.2d 695, 697 (1990) (during preliminary competency examination of four-year-old, judge sat on floor with child, played with her, and gave her a soft drink; defendant failed to object at the time, and could not complain on appeal); State v. Dunbar, 152 Vt. 399, 566 A.2d 970, 973 (1989); *In re* C.M., 595 A.2d 293, 295 (Vt.

may be turned slightly away from the defendant, provided the child and defendant can see and hear each other, and the jury can see the child.[23] Reducing the child's anxiety in this way may lead to more accurate testimony. Some children cannot speak above a whisper. In *United States v. Romey,*[24] the Court of Military Appeals held that a defendant's Sixth Amendment right to confront accusatory witnesses was not violated when the victim whispered her testimony to her mother, who repeated it for the record.[25]

Although there are limits to the accommodations that may be made for children,[26] defendants will be hard-pressed to argue that minor tinkering with time-honored courtroom traditions runs afoul of the Constitution. The matter is eminently one for trial court discretion.[27] Accommodations for child witnesses can be explained to jurors to prevent them from drawing improper inferences.[28]

Trial judges have discretion to recess the proceedings to allow children to rest and regain their composure.[29] See **Chapter 5** for discussion of recesses.

In *People v. Puhl,*[30] the Illinois Appellate Court urged attorneys not to use children's names in court briefs.[31]

The court may appoint a guardian ad litem for a child in criminal or civil litigation.[32]

1991) ("even in criminal cases some accommodation may be made to protect juvenile witnesses from the stress and fright that may surround their testimony in court").

[23] United States v. Thompson, 31 M.J. 168 (C.M.A. 1990), *cert. denied,* 111 S. Ct. 956 (1991); United States v. Williams, 33 M.J. 754 (A.C.M.R. 1991); State v. Davis, 830 P.2d 1309 (Mont. 1992) (screen between child and defendant); Ortiz v. State, 188 Ga. App. 532, 374 S.E.2d 92 (1988) (not error to turn young witness's chair away from defendant; child could still see defendant by turning her head); Stanger v. State, 545 N.E.2d 1105 (Ind. Ct. App. 1989) (turning witness chair away from defendant did not violate Sixth Amendment; jury, witness, and defendant could all see and hear one another); Commonwealth v. Groff, 378 Pa. Super. 353, 548 A.2d 1237 (1988) (Sixth Amendment not violated by telling child she did not have to look at defendant).

[24] 32 M.J. 180 (C.M.A.), *cert. denied,* 112 S. Ct. 337 (1991).

[25] A record was made at trial to justify this procedure. Although the Court of Military Appeals was not persuaded that sufficient effort was made to find a party more neutral than the child's mother to repeat the child's testimony, any error was harmless. *Id.* at 183 n.2.

[26] Duffitt v. State, 525 N.E.2d 607, 608 (Ind. 1988) (court disapproved trial judge's decision to decorate the courtroom with posters; "the practice of decorating in deference to [a] certain witness is altogether inappropriate"); State v. Mannion, 19 Utah 505, 57 P. 542 (1899) (six-year-old victim was afraid of defendant, who was her father; error to turn witness chair toward jury and require defendant to sit in corner of courtroom where he could not hear child or confer with counsel).

[27] Commonwealth v. Amirault, 404 Mass. 221, 535 N.E.2d 193, 207 (1989).

[28] *Id.*

[29] Commonwealth v. Brusgulis, 398 Mass. 325, 496 N.E.2d 652, 656 (1986).

[30] 211 Ill. App. 3d 457, 570 N.E.2d 447 (1991).

[31] 570 N.E.2d at 458.

[32] People v. Pitts, 223 Cal. App. 3d 606, 273 Cal. Rptr. 757, 906 (1990) ("appointment of counsel for minor victims is constitutionally and statutorily permissible, but . . . proper

§ 8.4 Defendant's Right to Public Trial

The Sixth Amendment states, "In all criminal prosecutions, the accused shall enjoy the right to a . . . public trial." The right to a public trial is personal to the defendant.[33] Neither the press nor the public shares the Sixth Amendment right.[34] Although the defendant has a right to a public trial, the opposite is not true. The defendant cannot insist on a private trial.[35]

The right to a public trial is not absolute.[36] Competing interests may be balanced against the defendant's right, and in compelling cases, the right yields. Denial of a public trial must be the exception, however, not the rule. In *Waller v. Georgia*,[37] the Supreme Court established guidelines to ensure protection of the right to a public trial, writing:

> [T]he party seeking to close the hearing must advance an overriding interest that is likely to be prejudiced, the closure must be no broader than necessary to protect that interest, the trial court must consider reasonable alternatives to closing the proceeding, and it must make findings adequate to support the closure.[38]

When children are involved, the balance sometimes tips in favor of closing the proceeding or excluding selected persons during a child's testimony. Closure is particularly appropriate in sex offense litigation where the child must describe

---

procedures were not followed in the instant case"); People v. Sambo, 197 Ill. App. 3d 574, 554 N.E.2d 1080 (1990).

See D. Whitcomb, U.S. Dep't of Justice, Guardians ad Litem in the Criminal Courts (1988); D. Duquette, Advocating for the Child in Protective Proceedings: A Guide for Child Advocates (1990); Bischoff, *The Voice of a Child: Independent Legal Representation of Children in Private Custody Disputes When Sexual Abuse Is Alleged*, 138 U. Pa. L. Rev. 1383 (1990).

[33] United States v. Hershey, 20 M.J. 433 (C.M.A. 1985), *cert. denied*, 474 U.S. 1062 (1986) (right to public trial applies at courts-martial); State v. Webb, 467 N.W.2d 108 (Wis.), *cert. denied*, 112 S. Ct. 249 (1991) (ruling that conviction following fair and errorless trial cures any error in closing preliminary hearing); Commonwealth v. Jubilee, 403 Pa. Super. 589, 589 A.2d 1112 (1991) (defendant not denied public trial when trial judge ordered that courtroom doors be locked to prevent children who attended the trial from running in and out; court did not want jury distracted during court's charge to jury).

[34] Gannett Co. v. DePasquale, 443 U.S. 368 (1979).

[35] *Id.*

[36] People v. Holveck, 141 Ill. 2d 84, 565 N.E.2d 919 (1990) (trial court did not err in excluding spectators during children's testimony; press was allowed to remain; Supreme Court upholds Illinois statute allowing trial court to exercise discretion to exclude spectators during children's testimony); State v. Guajardo, 605 A.2d 217 (N.H. 1992).

[37] 467 U.S. 39 (1984).

[38] *Id.* at 48. *See* United States v. Galloway, 963 F.2d 1388 (10th Cir. 1992).

§ 8.4 RIGHT TO PUBLIC TRIAL 331

degrading and embarrassing acts.[39] The need for closed proceedings is described by the Seventh Circuit Court of Appeals in *United States ex rel. Latimore v. Sielaff.*[40] In this federal habeas corpus case, the state trial judge excluded the public during the testimony of the 21-year-old rape victim. The Seventh Circuit upheld the lower court's decision, writing:

> [E]xclusion of spectators during the testimony of an alleged rape victim "is a frequent and accepted practice when the lurid details of such a crime must be related by a young lady." . . . Primary justification for this practice lies in protection of the personal dignity of the complaining witness. The Supreme Court has recognized that, short of homicide, rape is the "ultimate violation of self." . . . Rape constitutes an intrusion upon areas of the victim's life, both physical and psychological, to which our society attaches the deepest sense of privacy. Shame and loss of dignity, however unjustified from a moral standpoint, are natural byproducts of an attempt to recount details of a rape before a curious and disinterested audience. The ordeal of describing an unwanted sexual encounter before persons with no more than a prurient interest in it aggravates the original injury. Mitigation of the ordeal is a justifiable concern of the public and of the trial court.[41]

Several considerations may be added to those outlined in *Sielaff*. The state has a compelling interest in "the protection of minor victims of sex crimes from further trauma and embarrassment."[42] Exclusion of the public is sometimes necessary to effectuate this interest. Moreover, the courtroom may be more terrifying for children than adults. A room full of adults may immobilize a child, making accurate testimony impossible. Finally, there is reason to shield young children from press coverage that may result from their testimony.

The need to protect children from trauma and embarrassment does not justify exclusion of the public in every case.[43] Trial judges "determine on a case-by-case basis whether closure is necessary to protect the welfare of a minor victim."[44] In doing so, courts consider such factors as the child's age, the nature of

---

[39] Press-Enterprise Co. v. Superior Court, 478 U.S. 1 (1986) (holding that limited First Amendment right of press to attend criminal proceedings applies to preliminary hearing stage; interests of sex crimes victims sometimes justify exclusion of press and public); United States v. Galloway, 963 F.2d 1388 (10th Cir. 1992); State v. Guajardo, 605 A.2d 217 (N.H. 1992).

[40] 561 F.2d 691 (7th Cir. 1977), *cert. denied,* 434 U.S. 1076 (1978).

[41] 561 F.2d at 694–95. *See also* Press-Enterprise Co. v. Superior Court, 478 U.S. 1 (1986).

[42] Globe Newspaper Co. v. Superior Court, 457 U.S. 596, 607 (1982) (addressing First Amendment right of press and public to attend criminal trials, not defendant's Sixth Amendment right to public trial).

[43] State v. Hightower, 376 N.W.2d 648 (Iowa Ct. App. 1985) (prosecutor failed to articulate overriding reason to clear courtroom).

[44] Globe Newspaper Co. v. Superior Court, 457 U.S. 596, 608 (1982).

the crime, the psychological fragility of the child, the preference of the parents, and the desires of the child.[45] In every case, the party seeking closure must persuade the court that closure is necessary to protect "an overriding interest that is likely to be prejudiced."[46]

In states where criminal trials are televised, the trial court may exempt the victim from the camera. Such a decision does not violate the defendant's right to a public trial.[47]

§ 8.5 Right to Attend Criminal Trials

The public and the press have a limited First Amendment right to attend criminal trials.[48] The Supreme Court has remarked that this right finds support in two aspects of the criminal justice system. First, there is a long tradition of open criminal trials,[49] and second:

> [T]he right of access to criminal trials plays a particularly significant role in the functioning of the judicial process and the government as a whole. Public scrutiny of a criminal trial enhances the quality and safeguards the integrity of the factfinding process, with benefits to both the defendant and to society as a whole. Moreover, public access to the criminal trial fosters an appearance of fairness, thereby heightening public respect for the judicial process. And in the broadest terms, public access to criminal trials permits the public to participate in and serve as a check upon the judicial process—an essential component in our structure of self-government. In sum, the institutional value of the open criminal trial is recognized in both logic and experience.[50]

---

[45] *Id.*

[46] Waller v. Georgia, 467 U.S. 39, 48 (1984).

[47] Commonwealth v. Cordeiro, 401 Mass. 843, 519 N.E.2d 1328 (1988) (in rape case involving adult victim, trial court did not err in exempting victim from camera coverage during her testimony and while she was in courtroom; limits on camera coverage did not implicate defendant's right to public trial).

[48] Richmond Newspapers, Inc. v. Virginia, 448 U.S. 555 (1980); Press-Enterprise Co. v. Superior Court, 478 U.S. 1 (1986) ("the First Amendment right of access . . . applies to preliminary hearings conducted in California"); Press-Enterprise Co. v. Superior Court, 464 U.S. 501 (1984) (right of access to criminal trials extends to voir dire of jury); Globe Newspaper Co. v. Superior Court, 457 U.S. 596, 603 (1982) ("This Court's recent decision in *Richmond Newspapers* firmly established for the first time that the press and general public have a constitutional right of access to criminal trials"); United States v. Raffoul, 826 F.2d 218, 222 (3d Cir. 1987) ("The First Amendment guarantees the right of the press and the public to attend a criminal trial"); United States v. Jacobson, 785 F. Supp. 563, 567 (E.D. Va. 1992).

[49] Press-Enterprise Co. v. Superior Court, 464 U.S. 501, 505 (1984) ("The roots of open trials reach back to the days before the Norman Conquest when cases in England were brought before 'moots,' a town meeting kind of body such as the local court of the hundred or the county court") (footnote omitted); Globe Newspaper Co. v. Superior Court, 457 U.S. 596, 606 (1982).

[50] Globe Newspaper Co. v. Superior Court, 457 U.S. 596, 606–07 (1982).

§ 8.5 RIGHT TO ATTEND TRIALS

The public's right of access to criminal trials is not absolute, and in some instances involving children, the public and press may be excluded.[51] The Supreme Court's 1982 decision in *Globe Newspaper Co. v. Superior Court*[52] is directly on point. In *Globe Newspaper*, the Court struck down a Massachusetts statute requiring trial judges to exclude the press and public whenever a young sex offense victim testified. The Court began its analysis by reiterating the importance of public access to criminal proceedings. From there the Court wrote:

> Although the right of access to criminal trials is of constitutional stature, it is not absolute. . . . But the circumstances under which the press and public can be barred from a criminal trial are limited; the State's justification in denying access must be a weighty one. Where, as in the present case, the State attempts to deny the right of access in order to inhibit the disclosure of sensitive information, it must be shown that the denial is necessitated by a compelling governmental interest, and is narrowly tailored to serve that interest.[53]

In *Globe Newspaper*, the state argued that its interest in protecting young sex offense victims from further trauma justified exclusion of the press and public from the courtroom during the victim's testimony. The Supreme Court agreed that "safeguarding the physical and psychological well-being of a minor"[54] is a compelling governmental interest that occasionally overrides the public's right of access, but went on to hold that mandatory exclusion in every case is unconstitutional. The Court wrote that, despite the compelling nature of the state's interest, the need to protect sex offense victims

> does not justify a *mandatory* closure rule, for it is clear that the circumstances of the particular case may affect the significance of the interest. A trial court can determine on a case-by-case basis whether closure is necessary to protect the welfare of a minor victim. Among the factors to be weighed are the minor victim's age, psychological maturity and understanding, the nature of the crime, the desires of the victim, and the interests of parents and relatives.[55]

Under the authority of *Globe Newspaper*, trial judges have limited discretion to override the First Amendment right of the press and public to attend criminal

---

[51] Wildermuth v. State, 310 Md. 496, 530 A.2d 275, 286 n.12 (1987) ("If a child witness's psychological problem has to do with testifying before a large number of strangers (courtroom spectators), the courtroom could be closed, if the facts were sufficiently strong to warrant that drastic action"); Commonwealth v. Cordeiro, 401 Mass. 843, 519 N.E.2d 1328, 1331 (1988) (trial court's order limiting television coverage of adult rape victim during her testimony did not implicate "public or press rights of access to trial"); People v. Mateo, 73 N.Y.2d 928, 536 N.E.2d 1146, 1147, 539 N.Y.S.2d 727 (1989) ("A witness' embarrassment or anxiety might in appropriate circumstances warrant closure").

[52] 457 U.S. 596 (1982).

[53] *Id.* at 606–07.

[54] *Id.* at 607.

[55] *Id.* at 608–09.

trials. Before an exclusion order may be entered, however, evidence must be adduced from which the judge concludes that "closure is essential to preserve higher values."[56] Any exclusion must be narrowly tailored to serve those values. The court must make specific findings in support of its order so that its decision can be scrutinized on appeal.[57] Finally, the press is entitled to "an opportunity to be heard on the question of their exclusion."[58]

The foregoing discussion pertains to the First Amendment right of the press and public to attend criminal trials. Courts traditionally hold that there is no corresponding right to attend adjudicatory hearings in juvenile court.[59]

§ 8.6 Right of Access to Court Records

The public and press have a common law right to inspect and copy court records.[60] In addition to the common law right, the First Amendment protects access to court documents.[61]

The constitutional and common law rights to inspect and copy court documents are not absolute.[62] In *Nixon v. Warner Communications*,[63] the Supreme

---

[56] Press-Enterprise Co. v. Superior Court, 464 U.S. 501, 510 (1984).

[57] *Id.* at 510.

[58] Globe Newspaper Co. v. Superior Court, 457 U.S. 596, 609 n.25 (1982).

[59] San Bernardino County Dep't of Pub. Social Servs. v. Superior Court, 232 Cal. App. 3d 188, 283 Cal. Rptr. 332 (1991) (constitutional right to attend criminal trials does not extend to juvenile court dependency proceedings); *In re* T.R., 52 Ohio St. 3d 6, 556 N.E.2d 439, *cert. denied*, 111 S. Ct. 386 (1990) (excellent discussion of public access to juvenile court dependency proceedings; holding such proceedings presumptively closed to public; useful guidelines on when to open dependency proceedings); Division of Youth & Family Servs. v. J.B., 120 N.J. 112, 576 A.2d 261 (1990) (very useful discussion of public access to dependency proceedings; holding such proceedings presumptively closed); *In re* J.S., 140 Vt. 458, 438 A.2d 1125 (1981).

[60] Nixon v. Warner Communications, 435 U.S. 589 (1978); *In re* Application of National Broadcasting Co., 828 F.2d 340 (6th Cir. 1987); United States v. Raffoul, 826 F.2d 218, 222 (3d Cir. 1987) (common law right of public to inspect and copy judicial records is older than Constitution); United States v. Beckham, 789 F.2d 401, 409–10 (6th Cir. 1986).

[61] *In re* Washington Post Co., 807 F.2d 383, 390 (4th Cir. 1986) ("First Amendment right of access applies to documents filed in connection with plea hearings and sentencing hearings in criminal cases, as well as to the hearings themselves"); United States v. Smith, 776 F.2d 1104 (3d Cir. 1985); United States v. Peters, 754 F.2d 753, 763 (7th Cir. 1985) (right of press and public access to court records "is of constitutional magnitude through the First Amendment"); *In re* Globe Newspaper Co., 729 F.2d 47, 51 (1st Cir. 1984) (constitutional right of access "has also been extended to documents filed in pretrial proceedings"); Associated Press v. United States District Court, 705 F.2d 1143, 1145 (9th Cir. 1983) ("the public and press have a first amendment right of access to pretrial documents in general").

[62] United States v. Jacobson, 785 F. Supp. 563, 569 (E.D. Va. 1992).

[63] 435 U.S. 589 (1978).

Court considered the common law right. The Court decided that the press had properly been denied the right to copy audiotapes of White House telephone conversations that were admitted in evidence at the criminal trials of individuals charged with conspiring to obstruct justice in the Watergate investigation. The Court wrote:

> It is clear that the courts of this country recognize a general right to inspect and copy public records and documents, including judicial records and documents. In contrast to the English practice, . . . American decisions generally do not condition enforcement of this right on a proprietary interest in the document or upon a need for it as evidence in a lawsuit. The interest necessary to support the issuance of a writ compelling access has been found, for example, in the citizen's desire to keep a watchful eye on the workings of public agencies, . . . and in a newspaper publisher's intention to publish information concerning the operation of government . . . .
>
> It is uncontested, however, that the right to inspect and copy judicial records is not absolute. Every court has supervisory power over its own records and files, and access has been denied where court files might have become a vehicle for improper purposes. For example, the common-law right of inspection has bowed before the power of a court to insure that its records are not "used to gratify private spite or promote public scandal" through the publication of "the painful and sometimes disgusting details of a divorce case." . . . Similarly, courts have refused to permit their files to serve as reservoirs of libelous statements for press consumption, . . .
>
> It is difficult to distill from the relatively few judicial decisions a comprehensive definition of what is referred to as the common-law right of access or to identify all the factors to be weighed in determining whether access is appropriate. The few cases that have recognized such a right do agree that the decision as to access is one best left to the sound discretion of the trial court, a discretion to be exercised in light of the relevant facts and circumstances of the particular case.[64]

In child abuse litigation, the exquisite sensitivity of many documents—particularly videotapes of children—justify limits on the right of the press and public to inspect or copy records. In many cases, complete closure of records is appropriate.

§ 8.7 Video Testimony

During the 1980s, a majority of states enacted statutes authorizing video testimony by children in child abuse litigation. Video testimony statutes fall into four

---

[64] *Id.* at 598–99. *See also* Matter of Estate of Hearst, 67 Cal. App. 3d 777, 136 Cal. Rptr. 821 (1977); Copley Press, Inc. v. Superior Court, 7 Cal. Rptr. 2d 841 (Cal. Ct. App. 1992).

categories: (1) videotaped depositions,[65] (2) videotaped interviews,[66] (3) videotaped preliminary hearing testimony,[67] and (4) contemporaneous video testimony at trial.

Video testimony raises several constitutional issues, which are discussed in §§ **8.8** through **8.13**. In addition to constitutional issues, use of video technology raises procedural and evidentiary issues. For example, when a child testifies via video technology, a recurring issue is whether the jury should be permitted to view the tape again during deliberations. Courts are concerned that allowing the jury to replay the tape places undue emphasis on the child's testimony.[68]

Most video cameras have a zoom lens. In *Strickland v. State*,[69] a child's deposition was videotaped for use at trial. During the deposition, the technician operating the camera zoomed in on the child's face when the child was asked the critical question about what the defendant did to her. The appellate court remarked that such theatrics are highly improper. Although the court did not reverse, it stated that it would reverse in future cases if such "highly improper" techniques were used.

During videotaping, who should be on camera? Naturally, the child must always be in view.[70] In *Commonwealth v. Tufts*,[71] the court stated that normally the camera should show everyone in the room.[72] Attorneys may appear in profile. Defendants should be on camera so that their reactions can be observed.

---

[65] People v. Bastien, 129 Ill. 2d 64, 541 N.E.2d 670 (1989) (Illinois video deposition statute required that defendant and defense counsel be permitted to attend, but did not allow defense counsel to cross-examine child at deposition; cross-examination was postponed until trial; holding that statute unconstitutional; defendant had right to contemporaneous cross-examination); State v. Conklin, 444 N.W.2d 268 (Minn. 1989) (court upheld facial constitutionality of statute permitting removal of defendant from room where child gives deposition provided proper showing of trauma is made).

[66] Burke v. State, 820 P.2d 1344 (Okla. Crim. App. 1991), *cert. denied,* 112 S. Ct. 2940 (1992) (video interview statute unconstitutional); State v. Pilkey, 776 S.W.2d 943 (Tenn. 1989), *cert. denied,* 494 U.S. 1032 (1990) (video interview statute unconstitutional).

[67] *See* Cal. Penal Code § 1346 (West 1992).

[68] Chambers v. State, 504 So. 2d 476 (Fla. Dist. Ct. App. 1987) (not per se reversible error to permit jury to view videotaped deposition again during deliberation; defendant failed to object); Pfaff v. State, 830 P.2d 193 (Okla. Crim. App. 1992); Martin v. State, 747 P.2d 316, 319 (Okla. Crim. App. 1987); Chambers v. State, 726 P.2d 1269, 1277 (Wyo. 1986) (conviction reversed because trial judge twice permitted jury to replay videotaped interview of child); Taylor v. State, 727 P.2d 274 (Wyo. 1986) (error to allow unsupervised viewing of videotape by jurors during deliberation).

[69] 550 So. 2d 1042 (Ala. Crim. App. 1988), *aff'd,* 550 So. 2d 1054 (Ala. 1989).

[70] Commonwealth v. Tufts, 405 Mass. 610, 542 N.E.2d 586 (1989).

[71] *Id.*

[72] Commonwealth v. Amirault, 404 Mass. 221, 535 N.E.2d 193, 206–07 (1989) ("Ideally, all persons present in the room during the taping would be visible in the videotape. It is not, however, a fatal flaw to an otherwise satisfactory videotape" if one or more persons are not visible); State v. Warford, 223 Neb. 368, 389 N.W.2d 575, 582 (1986) ("The camera should

§ 8.8 —Confrontation Clause

The Sixth Amendment to the United States Constitution provides that "[i]n all criminal prosecutions, the accused shall . . . be confronted with the witnesses against him." The most serious constitutional issue raised by video testimony is the extent to which the technology infringes the right to confront accusatory child witnesses. There are four elements of effective confrontation: cross-examination, oath, the jury's opportunity to view the witness's demeanor,[73] and face-to-face confrontation between the witness and the accused.[74]

Some forms of video testimony are the functional equivalent of live, in-court testimony.[75] Such testimony raises few, if any, confrontation problems. Consider,

---

be so situated that persons viewing the examination in the courtroom will be able to see the witness, the examiner, and any other person (other than the cameraman) present in the room where the examination is being conducted").

[73] In State v. Crandall, 120 N.J. 649, 577 A.2d 483 (1990), the New Jersey Supreme Court upheld the New Jersey video testimony statute. The defendant argued that the trial judge must make a case-specific finding that the child cannot testify in the presence of the jury. The New Jersey Supreme Court wrote that "the ultimate purpose of the confrontation clause is not to protect eye-to-eye contact between the jury and witness. . . . Rather, the ultimate purpose of that clause is to further the truth-seeking process of the trial by ensuring that the jury can observe the demeanor of the witness." 577 A.2d at 487. The court held that if the child fears only the defendant, and not the jury, the trial judge should authorize video testimony in which the child testifies outside the courtroom "unless defendant requests that the child testify before the jury." *Id.* If the defendant makes such a request, the defendant

> should be informed of the possible adverse consequences of such a procedure, namely, that he or she could not be present in the courtroom during the child's testimony and that he or she would be required to waive the right of presence. In essence, to insist that the child testify before the jury, a defendant must execute a knowing and intelligent waiver of the right to be present.

Id.

[74] See **Ch. 7** for discussion of the elements of confrontation.

[75] Maryland v. Craig, 110 S. Ct. 3157, 3166 (1990); Coy v. Iowa, 487 U.S. 1012 (1988) (O'Connor, J., concurring) ("many such procedures may raise no substantial Confrontation Clause problem since they involve testimony in the presence of the defendant"); United States v. Binder, 769 F.2d 595 (9th Cir. 1985), *cert. denied,* 484 U.S. 1073 (1988) ("Videotape testimony is unique. It enables the jury to observe the demeanor and to hear the testimony of the witness. It serves as the functional equivalent of a live witness." 769 F.2d at 600. "Often, videotapes are substitutes for live testimony and therefore distinct from audiotapes. We remain convinced that in this case the videotape was the functional equivalent of live testimony and not analogous to an audiotape." *Id.* at 601 n.1); People v. Schmitt, 204 Ill. App. 3d 820, 562 N.E.2d 377 (1990); Commonwealth v. Willis, 716 S.W.2d 224, 228 (Ky. 1986) (video testimony is "the functional equivalent of testimony in court"); State v. Thomas, 150 Wis. 2d 374, 442 N.W.2d 10, *cert. denied,* 110 S. Ct. 188 (1989) ("The videotaped deposition is, therefore, the functional equivalent of in-court testimony and . . . the defendant is confronting the opposing witness prior to trial rather than at trial, and

for example, contemporaneous video testimony in which a child testifies at trial from a special room outside the courtroom. The child's image and voice are transmitted to the courtroom, where the jury views the child as the child testifies. The child can see the judge and jury on a video screen. The attorneys and the defendant are seated in the special room. The child can see the defendant, and the defendant can see and hear the child. Direct and cross-examination proceed as usual. In this video testimony configuration the elements of effective confrontation are satisfied. The child is under oath. Cross-examination is unimpaired. In fact, the less forbidding atmosphere of a small, comfortable room may help the child to testify more accurately.[76] As long as proper video equipment is used and operated by competent technicians, the image viewed by the factfinder is accurate and sufficiently detailed to permit meaningful evaluation of demeanor.[77] Finally, the requirement of face-to-face confrontation between accuser and accused is satisfied.

Although some forms of video testimony are the functional equivalent of traditional courtroom testimony, most are not. A substantial number of permutations are possible on the video testimony theme, some of which are closely analogous to traditional in-court testimony, and some of which stray quite far from the conventional mold.[78]

For Confrontation Clause purposes, it is useful to array the various video testimony alternatives along a continuum. At one end of the continuum are alternatives that satisfy completely the elements of effective confrontation. At the

---

before the jury"); Note, *The Testimony of Child Victims in Sex Abuse Prosecutions: Two Legislative Innovations,* 98 Harv. L. Rev. 806, 814 (1985).

But see State v. Vess, 157 Ariz. 236, 756 P.2d 333, 335 (Ct. App. 1988) (questioning whether video testimony is functional equivalent of in-court testimony; court stated that although "the jury did not wholly lose its capacity to judge demeanor . . . [,] there is a difference between live testimony and that seen by television. . . . In circumstances where the jury may be disadvantaged in making credibility determinations, any deviation from standard procedures must be justified by necessity"); Commonwealth v. Bergstrom, 402 Mass. 534, 524 N.E.2d 366, 375–76 (1988) (powerful argument that video technology interferes with jury's ability to evaluate child's demeanor).

[76] Maryland v. Craig, 110 S. Ct. 3157, 3169 (1990) (Court acknowledged that in some cases use of video technology may help frightened children testify more accurately); Hill & Hill, *Videotaping Children's Testimony: An Empirical View,* 85 Mich. L. Rev. 809 (1987); Saywitz & Nathanson, *Children's Testimony and Perceived Stress in and out of the Courtroom,* Child Abuse & Neglect (to be published in 1993).

[77] People v. Schmitt, 204 Ill. App. 3d 820, 562 N.E.2d 377 (1990). *But see* Commonwealth v. Bergstrom, 402 Mass. 534, 524 N.E.2d 366, 375–76 (1988) (powerful argument that video technology interferes with jury's ability to evaluate child's demeanor).

[78] In some cases, for example, the child does not see the defendant, and thus there is no face-to-face confrontation. In other cases, the defendant's attorney is not in the same room with the child during the child's testimony. In still others, the attorney is in the room with the child, but not in the same room with the client. Finally, in some instances, the child's testimony is recorded on videotape before trial. When a pretrial videotape is admitted at trial, the jury arguably does not observe the child at the moment the child testifies.

other end are alternatives that satisfy none of the elements. Most video testimony configurations lie somewhere between these extremes. In other words, most applications of video testimony infringe to some extent one or more elements of traditional in-court, face-to-face confrontation. The greater the infringement, the greater the likelihood the video technique oversteps constitutional limits.

Coy v. Iowa and *Maryland v. Craig*

The element of confrontation affected most seriously by video testimony is usually face-to-face confrontation between the witness and the defendant. The United States Supreme Court's decisions in *Coy v. Iowa*[79] and *Maryland v. Craig*[80] are the starting point for analysis of the face-to-face confrontation right. In *Coy,* the Court made clear that face-to-face confrontation is of co-equal importance with the other elements of confrontation.[81]

Although *Coy* leaves no doubt about the importance of face-to-face confrontation, the Supreme Court noted that the Confrontation Clause does not require a witness to look at the defendant. Thus, literal eye-to-eye confrontation is not required by the Sixth Amendment. The Court wrote that "[t]he Confrontation Clause does not, of course, compel the witness to fix his eyes upon the defendant; he may studiously look elsewhere, but the trier of fact will draw its own conclusions."[82]

In *Coy,* the Supreme Court reserved decision on whether a defendant's Sixth Amendment right to face-to-face confrontation may be curtailed to protect child witnesses. The Court clearly held, however, that any exceptions to face-to-face confrontation must be based on an individualized showing of necessity.[83] With its 1990 decision in *Maryland v. Craig,*[84] the Supreme Court answered the

---

[79] 487 U.S. 1012 (1988).

[80] 110 S. Ct. 3157 (1990).

[81] *See also* State v. Jarzbek, 204 Conn. 683, 529 A.2d 1245, 1249 (1987), *cert. denied,* 484 U.S. 1061 (1988) (right to face-to-face confrontation is fundamental component of confrontation).

[82] 487 U.S. at 1019. *See* Ortiz v. State, 188 Ga. App. 532, 374 S.E.2d 92 (1988); Stanger v. State, 545 N.E.2d 1105 (Ind. Ct. App. 1989); *In re* J.D.S., 436 N.W.2d 342, 345 (Iowa 1989); Commonwealth v. Melchionno, 29 Mass. App. Ct. 939, 558 N.E.2d 18, 20 (1990) (during prosecutor's questioning of five-year-old victim, child denied abuse; prosecutor pressed for answer he expected, and told victim to look at him, not defendant; "It was not unreasonable of the prosecutor to ask that when he put a question that she look at him so that he might have her attention and so that she would not be subject to signals, whether intended or unintended, from the defendant"); Commonwealth v. Groff, 378 Pa. Super. 353, 548 A.2d 1237, 1248–50 (1988) (not error to inform seven-year-old victim that it was not necessary to look at anyone other than attorney asking questions).

[83] *See* State v. Benny E., 110 N.M. 237, 794 P.2d 380 (Ct. App. 1990) (failure of trial judge to make required finding of harm necessitated remand).

[84] 110 S. Ct. 3157 (1990).

question reserved in *Coy,* and held that, in appropriate cases, the Sixth Amendment right to face-to-face confrontation gives way to the state's compelling interest in protecting children from trauma.[85]

Before face-to-face confrontation may be curtailed, the state must make a sufficient case-specific showing of necessity.[86] The Court did not determine "the minimum showing of emotional trauma required" to curtail face-to-face confrontation,[87] although it provided some guidance on the necessity issue. The Court wrote that "the trial court must find that the emotional distress suffered by the child witness in the presence of the defendant is more than de minimis, i.e., more than 'mere nervousness or excitement or some reluctance to testify.'"[88] The Court stated that a showing a child will suffer serious emotional distress that interferes with the child's ability to communicate suffices for constitutional purposes.

The Court further stated that the trial judge must "find that the child witness would be traumatized, not by the courtroom generally, but by the presence of the defendant."[89] If the child's trauma is a product of testifying in open court, the judge may close the courtroom or take other steps to make testifying easier for the child without sacrificing the defendant's right to confront the child.[90]

The Court held that the Constitution does not require that a child be forced to endure actual face-to-face confrontation before video technology may be used.[91] An unsuccessful attempt at face-to-face confrontation might strengthen the justification to dispense with a face-to-face encounter, but the Court ruled that it

---

[85] The Court held that "a State's interest in the physical and psychological well-being of child abuse victims may be sufficiently important to outweigh, at least in some cases, a defendant's right to face his or her accusers in court." 110 S. Ct. at 3167. The Court has spoken several times of the importance of the state interest in children. *See* New York v. Ferber, 458 U.S. 747, 757 (1982) ("The prevention of sexual exploitation and abuse of children constitutes a government objective of surpassing importance"); Globe Newspaper Co. v. Superior Court, 457 U.S. 596 (1982) (state has compelling interest in protecting children); Prince v. Massachusetts, 321 U.S. 158 (1944).

See also State v. Jarzbek, 204 Conn. 683, 529 A.2d 1245, 1253–54 (1987), cert. denied, 108 S. Ct. 1017 (1988); People v. Kahan, 15 N.Y.2d 311, 312, 206 N.E.2d 333, 334, 258 N.Y.S.2d 391, 392 (1965) (Fuld, J., concurring) (characterizing society's interest in welfare of children as "transcendent").

[86] Maryland v. Craig, 110 S. Ct. 3157, 3169 (1990). The Court wrote that "[t]he requisite finding of necessity must of course be a case-specific one: the trial court must hear evidence and determine whether use of the one-way closed circuit television procedure is necessary to protect the welfare of the particular child witness who seeks to testify." *Id. See* State v. Chisholm, 825 P.2d 147 (Kan. 1992).

[87] *Id.*

[88] *Id.*

[89] *Id. See* Thomas v. People, 803 P.2d 144, 148 (Colo. 1990); State v. Conklin, 444 N.W.2d 268, 274 (Minn. 1989).

[90] For discussion of closing the courtroom, see §§ **8.4** and **8.5**.

[91] 110 S. Ct. at 3171.

is not necessary to traumatize a child as a predicate for protection.[92] The Court also held that it is not necessary to attempt two-way closed-circuit television before resorting to one-way television.[93]

Following the Supreme Court's 1988 decision in *Coy v. Iowa,* a substantial number of courts addressed the complex issues raised by video testimony. Most of this post-*Coy* law remains viable following the Supreme Court's 1990 decision in *Maryland v. Craig*. With rare exception,[94] the post-*Coy* courts agree that the right to face-to-face confrontation is not absolute, and that the confrontation right sometimes yields to competing interests.[95] Courts also agree that face-to-face confrontation "can be abridged only where there is 'a case-specific finding of necessity.'"[96]

A defendant may forfeit the right to face-to-face confrontation. Many children are threatened by their abusers. When a child must sit a few feet from an adult who has promised severe retribution for answering questions, it can be argued that the defendant has forfeited the right to confrontation.[97]

Showing of Necessity Required to Curtail Face-to-Face Confrontation

Courts follow three approaches to the showing that must be made to curtail face-to-face confrontation:[98]

---

[92] *Id.*

[93] *Id.*

[94] Commonwealth v. Ludwig, 594 A.2d 281 (Pa. 1991).

[95] *See, e.g.,* State v. Bonello, 210 Conn. 51, 554 A.2d 277, 281, *cert. denied,* 490 U.S. 1082 (1989) ("Coy does not establish an absolute right to face-to-face confrontation"); State v. Chisholm, 245 Kan. 145, 777 P.2d 753 (1989) (Kansas video testimony statute can be interpreted as constitutional "by reading into the statute the individualized determination required by Coy"); State v. Conklin, 444 N.W.2d 268, 272 (Minn. 1989) ("Protecting child witnesses under 10 years of age from trauma is certainly an important public policy").

[96] State v. Crandall, 120 N.J. 649, 577 A.2d 483 (1990) (in an instructive post-*Craig* case, the New Jersey Supreme Court upheld the constitutionality of closed-circuit video testimony); People v. Cintron, 75 N.Y.2d 249, 551 N.E.2d 561, 552 N.Y.S.2d 68 (1990) (upholding constitutionality of video testimony statute against facial challenge); State v. Davis, 229 N.J. Super. 66, 550 A.2d 1241 (1988); State v. Eastham, 39 Ohio St. 3d 307, 530 N.E.2d 409 (1988); State v. Rogers, 293 S.C. 505, 362 S.E.2d 7 (1987); State v. Pilkey, 776 S.W.2d 943, 949 (Tenn. 1989), *cert. denied,* 494 U.S. 1032 (1990).

[97] See **Ch. 7**. *See also* United States v. Carlson, 547 F.2d 1346 (8th Cir. 1976), *cert. denied,* 431 U.S. 914 (1977); United States v. Balano, 618 F.2d 624 (10th Cir. 1979), *cert. denied,* 449 U.S. 840 (1980); Black v. Woods, 651 F.2d 528 (8th Cir.), *cert. denied,* 454 U.S. 847 (1981); State v. Jarzbek, 204 Conn. 683, 529 A.2d 1245, 1252–53 (1987), *cert. denied,* 484 U.S. 1061 (1988); State v. Sheppard, 197 N.J. Super. 411, 484 A.2d 1330 (1984).

[98] All cases agree that confrontation can be curtailed only after "an individualized finding that the witness is in need of such protection." People v. Bastien, 129 Ill. 2d 64, 541 N.E.2d 670, 674 (1989); State v. Albert, 13 Kan. App. 2d 671, 778 P.2d 386 (1989).

1. Trauma rendering child unavailable. Several courts hold that confrontation may be curtailed only when a face-to-face encounter would be so difficult for the child that the child would be unavailable as a witness.[99]

2. Undermining trustworthiness of child's testimony. The Connecticut Supreme Court holds that before face-to-face confrontation may be dispensed with, the trial court must be convinced that testifying in the defendant's presence would undermine the trustworthiness of the child's testimony.[100] Under the Connecticut approach, the most important consideration is the accuracy of the child's testimony. The state must establish that "the minor victim would be so intimidated, or otherwise inhibited, by the physical presence of the defendant that the trustworthiness of the victim's testimony would be seriously called into question."[101] Although the trial judge may consider trauma to the child, trauma is not the focal point of analysis.

3. Trauma short of rendering child unavailable. The third approach focuses on trauma to the child caused by face-to-face confrontation. The prosecutor need not establish that trauma will render the child unavailable.[102] In *Thomas v. People*,[103] the Colorado Supreme Court stated that the child's emotional or psychological health must be substantially impaired, and impairment must be long-standing rather than transitory.

Establishing Trauma to Child

Several decisions require clear and convincing evidence to curtail face-to-face confrontation.[104] A number of courts state that the trial judge normally should

---

[99] State v. Vincent, 159 Ariz. 418, 768 P.2d 150 (1989); Thomas v. People, 803 P.2d 144 (Colo. 1990) (interpreting statute requiring unavailability at trial to admit videotaped deposition); State v. Black, 537 A.2d 1154 (Me. 1988); State v. Twist, 528 A.2d 1250 (Me. 1987); State v. Conklin, 444 N.W.2d 268 (Minn. 1989); State v. Davidson, 764 S.W.2d 731 (Mo. Ct. App. 1989); State v. Taylor, 562 A.2d 445 (R.I. 1989).

[100] State v. Bonello, 210 Conn. 51, 554 A.2d 277 *cert. denied*, 490 U.S. 1082 (1989); State v. Jarzbek, 204 Conn. 683, 529 A.2d 1245 (1987), *cert. denied*, 108 S. Ct. 1017 (1988); State v. Darby, 19 Conn. App. 445, 563 A.2d 710 (1989).

[101] State v. Jarzbek, 204 Conn. 683, 529 A.2d 1245, 1255 (1987), *cert. denied*, 484 U.S. 1061 (1988).

[102] Glendening v. State, 536 So. 2d 212 (Fla. 1988); State v. Hoversten, 437 N.W.2d 240 (Iowa), *cert. denied*, 493 U.S. 875 (1989); In re J.D.S., 436 N.W.2d 342 (Iowa), *cert. denied*, 492 U.S. 907 (1989); State v. Chisholm, 250 Kan. 153, 825 P.2d 147 (1992); State v. Albert, 13 Kan. App. 2d 671, 778 P.2d 386 (1989); State v. Crandall, 120 N.J. 649, 577 A.2d 483, 486 (1990) (post-*Craig* case holding that finding of severe emotional or mental distress is sufficient for constitutional purposes); State v. Thomas, 150 Wis. 2d 374, 442 N.W.2d 10, *cert. denied*, 493 U.S. 867 (1989).

[103] 803 P.2d 144 (Colo. 1990).

[104] State v. Bonello, 210 Conn. 51, 554 A.2d 277, *cert. denied*, 490 U.S. 1082 (1989); State v. Jarzbek, 204 Conn. 683, 529 A.2d 1245 (1987), *cert. denied*, 484 U.S. 1061 (1988); State v.

§ 8.8 CONFRONTATION CLAUSE

examine the child personally.[105] Although expert testimony is often helpful, it should not invariably be required.[106] In *State v. Spigarolo*,[107] the Connecticut Supreme Court held that expert testimony is not always necessary. Lay testimony suffices in some cases. The court noted, for example, that parents have ample opportunity to observe their child before trial, and can testify about the child's behavior as the time to testify approaches. In *State v. Jarzbek*,[108] the Connecticut court approved a combination of lay and expert testimony.[109]

Albert, 13 Kan. App. 2d 671, 778 P.2d 386 (1989); *In re* B.F., 230 N.J. Super. 153, 553 A.2d 40 (1989); State v. Taylor, 562 A.2d 445 (R.I. 1989).

[105] State v. Vincent, 159 Ariz. 418, 768 P.2d 150 (1989); State v. Conklin, 444 N.W.2d 268, 274 (Minn. 1989) (encouraging trial judge to talk to child in chambers); State v. Crandall, 120 N.J. 649, 577 A.2d 483, 490 (1990) ("Trial courts should conduct a thorough face-to-face interview with the child and make detailed findings concerning the child's objective manifestations of fear"); State v. Chisholm, 245 Kan. 145, 777 P.2d 753 (1989) (trial judge was able to compare child's ability to testify effectively outside defendant's presence with her relative inability to testify in defendant's presence); State v. Presley, 542 So. 2d 1171 (La. Ct. App. 1989) (trial judge interviewed child to determine her availability to testify; child "was very ashamed of what had happened to her and extremely frightened to testify in front of her father and a jury"; *Id.* at 1174; holding that individualized showing of necessity was made to dispense with face-to-face confrontation); Commonwealth v. Dockham, 405 Mass. 618, 542 N.E.2d 591, 595 (1989) (four-year-old victim able to describe sexual abuse without much prompting in judge's chambers; however, in open court before defendants, child was able to answer only general background questions; when questioning turned to sexual abuse, he "kicked, turned around in his chair, bit his shirt, could not speak, put his head on the railing, had difficulty sitting up in his chair, and was unresponsive to questions[,] saying that he 'didn't know it anymore,' that he 'didn't remember any of it,' that 'enough's enough,' and that he had 'already said it.'" Held that trial judge had ample information to determine need for video testimony; expert testimony not needed).

[106] Thomas v. Gunter, 962 F.2d 1477 (10th Cir. 1992) (expert testimony regarding trauma was sufficient to dispense with face-to-face confrontation); Gonzales v. State, 818 S.W. 756 (Tex. Crim. App. 1991) (lay testimony illustrated need to dispense with face-to-face confrontation); State v. Crandall, 120 N.J. 649, 577 A.2d 483, 490 (1990) ("We decline to hold that expert testimony is required to show that a child will suffer severe emotional or mental distress from testifying in open court. If . . . a court is unable to make a determination on its own, it may then appoint an expert to evaluate the child"). *But see* State v. Taylor, 562 A.2d 445 (R.I. 1989) (court appears to require expert testimony).

Although expert testimony is not always required, the Minnesota Supreme Court noted in State v. Conklin, 444 N.W.2d 268 (1989) that expert testimony may be necessary if the child has difficulty testifying, and "where the cause of the child's testimonial difficulties and trauma is not clear." *Id.* at 274.

[107] 210 Conn. 359, 556 A.2d 112, *cert. denied,* 493 U.S. 933 (1989).

[108] 204 Conn. 683, 529 A.2d 1245 (1987), *cert. denied,* 484 U.S. 1061 (1988).

[109] *See* Commonwealth v. Dockham, 405 Mass. 618, 542 N.E.2d 591 (1989) (expert testimony not always needed; trial judge had ample opportunity to observe child); State v. Conklin, 444 N.W.2d 268, 274 (Minn. 1989) ("The finding may be based on the trial court's personal observation of the witness").

What factors should courts examine to determine whether to curtail face-to-face confrontation?[110] It is clear that mere unwillingness to testify is not sufficient.[111] In *State v. Crandall*,[112] the New Jersey Supreme Court provides a useful list of factors:

> Apart from expert testimony, other factors may enable a court to determine the likelihood that a child will suffer severe emotional or mental distress from testifying in open court. Those include: the commission of the offense was especially heinous; the child is particularly susceptible to harm because of a preexisting mental condition; the defendant occupied a position of authority with respect to the child witness; the offense or offenses charged were part of an ongoing course of conduct committed by the defendant against the child over an extended period of time; a deadly weapon or dangerous instrument was allegedly used during the commission of the crime; the defendant had inflicted serious physical injury upon the child; the defendant expressly or impliedly threatened harm to the child or a third person if the child were to report the incident; the defendant was living in the same household with, has ready access to, or was providing substantial financial support for, the child; or the child has previously been the victim of abuse or incest.[113]

The following sources of information provide concrete data on which judges can base findings of trauma:

Reaction to prior encounters with defendant. One way to predict how a child will react to face-to-face confrontation is to determine whether the child has had other face-to-face encounters with the defendant. If so, and the child fared poorly, then the court has data to predict the impact of face-to-face confrontation at trial. For example, if the child was abducted by a stranger, the child may have attended a police lineup. In an incest case, the child's reaction to visits with the defendant may provide insight.

Reaction when testifying is discussed. If testifying is mentioned at home, during therapy, or in other situations, the child's reaction is important.

Symptoms of stress as trial approaches. Some children demonstrate increasing stress as the day for testifying approaches. Often, the most compelling evidence of trauma comes not from mental health professionals but from caretakers who watch the child fall apart before their eyes as the day for testifying draws nigh.

---

[110] In State v. Eaton, 244 Kan. 370, 769 P.2d 1157 (1989), the Kansas Supreme Court lists four factors: (1) probability of psychological injury from testifying, (2) degree of anticipated injury, (3) expected duration of injury, and (4) whether the expected injury is substantially greater than the reaction of the average victim of rape, kidnapping, or other violent acts.

[111] People v. Thomas, 770 P.2d 1324 (Colo. Ct. App. 1989), *aff'd in part and rev'd in part*, 803 P.2d 144 (Colo. 1990) (mere unwillingness to testify is not sufficient).

[112] 120 N.J. 649, 577 A.2d 483 (1990).

[113] 577 A.2d at 490.

Psychiatric diagnosis. The child may have a psychiatric condition that renders the child psychologically fragile.

Threats. The court should know of threats against the child, including the severity of the child's fear. Threats an adult would not take seriously may paralyze a child.

Impact on ability to communicate. Any concrete data suggesting that face-to-face confrontation will likely impair a child's ability to communicate effectively is critical.

Psychological Research

It is undoubtedly true that many children are traumatized by face-to-face confrontation.[114] Although testifying is difficult, there is little support for the position that a substantial number of children are seriously harmed.[115] Berliner and Barbieri suggest that some children benefit from testifying.[116]

Empirical research is beginning on the extent to which involvement in legal proceedings traumatizes children.[117] Runyan found that children who testified in juvenile court appeared to resolve their psychological distress more rapidly than

---

[114] Commonwealth v. Amirault, 404 Mass. 221, 535 N.E.2d 193, 206 (1989) (child's therapist "testified that the child became more anxious, concerned, and aggressive as he prepared to testify in court"; child was reluctant to talk about his abuse at day care, and "reacted to the topic by holding his knees up, covering his eyes, clenching his fists, and grinding his teeth"); State v. Albert, 13 Kan. App. 2d 671, 778 P.2d 386 (1989) (child's therapist opined that testifying would be very difficult for child, who had serious ulcer and who cried every time subject of testifying was mentioned).

[115] *See* State v. Conklin, 444 N.W.2d 268, 273 (Minn. 1989) ("not all children experience trauma when testifying"). *See also* G. Goodman, E. Taub, D. Jones, P. England, L. Port, L. Rudy & L. Prado-Estrada, The Emotional Effects of Criminal Court Testimony on Child Sexual Assault Victims (Monographs of the Soc'y for Research in Child Dev. to be published in 1993).

[116] Berliner & Barbieri, *The Testimony of Child Victims of Sexual Assault,* 40 J. Soc. Issues, 125, 135 (1984) ("the experience of testifying in court can have a therapeutic effect for the child victim. The child can learn that social institutions take children seriously. Some children report feeling empowered by their participation in the process").

[117] G. Goodman, E. Taub, D. Jones, P. England, L. Port, L. Rudy & L. Prado-Estrada, The Emotional Effects of Criminal Court Testimony on Child Sexual Assault Victims (Monographs of the Soc'y for Research in Child Dev. to be published in 1993); R. Flin, R. Bull, J. Boon & A. Knox, Child Witnesses in Scottish Criminal Trials (manuscript submitted for publication in 1992. Available from Dr. Rhona Flin, The Robert Gordon Institute of Technology, Kepplestone House, Viewfield Road, Aberdeen AB9 2 PW United Kingdom); Tedesco & Schnell, *Children's Reactions to Sex Abuse Investigation and Litigation,* 11 Child Abuse & Neglect 267 (1987) (litigation not necessarily harmful to children); D. Whitcomb, D. Runyan, E. De Vos, W. Hunter, T. Cross, M. Everson, N. Peeler, C. Porter, P. Toth & C. Cropper, Child Victim as Witness Research and Development Program (1992).

children who did not testify.[118] Runyan cautions against extrapolating findings in juvenile court to testimony in criminal court.

Goodman studied 218 children involved as witnesses in the criminal justice system.[119] Most children's psychological adjustment improved over time whether or not they testified. Thus, time plays a healing role. Of the children who testified, certain factors were related to improved psychological functioning. Children with maternal support improved more rapidly than children without such support. Children whose testimony was corroborated by other evidence fared better. On the negative side, the more often a child testified, the slower the psychological improvement.

Most children in Goodman's study had negative feelings about testifying face-to-face with the defendant. Children who were most upset about testifying in front of the defendant experienced greater difficulty answering the prosecutor's questions. This finding provides significant support for the position that face-to-face confrontation interferes with accurate testimony for some children.

§ 8.9 —Assistance of Counsel

The Sixth Amendment provides that "[i]n all criminal prosecutions, the accused shall enjoy the right . . . to have the assistance of counsel for his defense."[120] When video testimony is used, the child usually testifies in one room while the defendant listens from another. In most cases, defense counsel is in the room with the child. Thus, the defendant is physically separated from counsel. If a means of contemporaneous communication is provided, the right to counsel is not infringed. However, if the defendant cannot communicate effectively with defense counsel during the child's testimony, the right to counsel may be violated.[121]

---

[118] Runyan, Everson, Edelsohn, Hunter & Coulter, *Impact of Legal Intervention on Sexually Abused Children,* 113 J. Pediatrics 647 (1988). Runyan and his colleagues write:

> We hypothesized that a child's testimony would result in greater harm to the mental health status of the child. This hypothesis was refuted in the context of juvenile court testimony. Our findings lend support to the assertion that the opportunity to testify in juvenile court may expert a protective effect on the child victim.

Id. at 652.

[119] G. Goodman, E. Taub, D. Jones, P. England, L. Port, L. Rudy & L. Prado-Estrada, The Emotional Effects of Criminal Court Testimony on Child Sexual Assault Victims (Monographs of the Soc'y for Research in Child Dev. to be published in 1993).

[120] U.S. Const. amend. VI.

[121] People v. Kasben, 158 Mich. App. 252, 404 N.W.2d 723 (1987) (at preliminary hearing, four-year-old testified from another room, and defendant viewed child on TV monitor; defendant could not communicate with counsel during cross-examination; right to counsel not violated); State v. Warford, 223 Neb. 368, 389 N.W.2d 575 (1986) (conviction reversed on due process and confrontation grounds; defendant could not communicate with counsel).

The defendant in a criminal trial has a right to self-representation.[122] A defendant may argue that the right to self-representation is denied by allowing a child to testify outside the defendant's physical presence.[123]

§ 8.10 —Impartial Jury

The Sixth Amendment provides that "[i]n all criminal prosecutions, the accused shall enjoy the right to . . . an impartial jury."[124] Defendants occasionally argue that video testimony deprives them of an impartial jury. The defendant may argue that use of video equipment interferes with the jury's capacity to evaluate the child's demeanor.[125] The Arkansas Supreme Court rejected this argument in *McGuire v. State*,[126] writing that when video testimony is properly presented, it "is useful and does not deprive the jury of the opportunity of determining the victim's credibility."[127]

When a child's trial testimony is taken in a separate room and transmitted to the courtroom, the defendant usually remains in the courtroom, seated at counsel table. Under these conditions, the defendant can argue that the jury is certain to wonder why the child is not testifying in the courtroom. Jurors are likely to conclude—correctly—that the child is testifying elsewhere to avoid facing the defendant. From here it is a short hop to the conclusion that there must be a good reason to protect the child, namely, the defendant is guilty. The defendant argues that the potential prejudice inherent in contemporaneous video testimony denies the defendant an impartial jury. There is strength to this argument. In response, it may be argued that under proper instructions the jury will carry out its responsibility.[128]

§ 8.11 —Compulsory Process Clause

Statutes in a few states permit pretrial depositions or interviews to be videotaped and admitted at trial in lieu of the child's testimony. If the defendant is denied an opportunity to subpoena the child for trial, an argument can be made that the defendant's Sixth Amendment right to compel the attendance of

---

[122] Faretta v. California, 422 U.S. 806 (1975).

[123] *See* Wildermuth v. State, 310 Md. 496, 530 A.2d 275 (1987).

[124] U.S. Const. amend. VI.

[125] Commonwealth v. Bergstrom, 402 Mass. 534, 524 N.E.2d 366, 375–76 (1988) (powerful argument that video technology interferes with jury's ability to evaluate child's demeanor).

[126] 288 Ark. 388, 706 S.W.2d 360 (1986).

[127] 706 S.W.2d at 362.

[128] For jury instructions, see Cal. Penal Code § 1347 (West 1992); N.Y. Crim. Proc. Law § 65.30(6) (McKinney 1992).

witnesses is infringed.[129] This argument is particularly strong when the child is the most important witness against the defendant. The argument also has merit when defense counsel acquires information about the child that could be used during cross-examination, but that was not available at the time of the deposition or interview.

A satisfactory solution to the compulsory process issue is found in the Alabama video deposition statute, which provides that a videotaped deposition may be admitted in lieu of the child's trial testimony unless the trial judge finds that the absence of live trial testimony will unduly prejudice the defendant.[130] If prejudice is established, the defendant may call the child at trial.

§ 8.12 —Due Process Clause

The Due Process Clause of the Fourteenth Amendment is offended if video testimony deprives the defendant of a fair trial.[131] In *State v. Daniels*,[132] the defendant was charged with physical abuse of her school-age son. The trial judge granted the prosecutor's motion to use live, contemporaneous video testimony in which the child testified from another room, where he could not see his mother. The attorneys were in the room with the child, and the defendant

---

[129] The Sixth Amendment provides in part that "[i]n all criminal prosecutions, the accused shall enjoy the right to . . . have compulsory process for obtaining witnesses in his favor." For discussion of the right to compel attendance of witnesses, see Weston, *Confrontation and Compulsory Process: A Unified Theory of Evidence for Criminal Cases,* 91 Harv. L. Rev. 567 (1978). *See also* McGuire v. State, 288 Ark. 388, 706 S.W.2d 360, 363 (1986) (court gave short shrift to argument that use of video deposition at trial violated defendant's right to compel attendance of witnesses).

[130] *See* Ala. Code § 15-25-2(a) (Supp. 1991).

[131] In Spoerri v. State, 561 So. 2d 604 (Fla. Dist. Ct. App. 1990), the trial court granted the prosecution's pretrial motion to allow the child to testify via two-way closed-circuit television. At trial, the prosecutor elected to have the child testify in open court. Part way through the child's courtroom testimony, the prosecutor asked the judge to allow the child to continue her testimony from the judge's chambers via the two-way television procedure. The defendant objected, but the court granted the prosecutor's request. The court of appeal reversed, writing:

> This procedure, in starting K.G.'s testimony in the courtroom and then removing the child to complete her testimony from the judge's chambers, thereby highlighting K.G.'s fear of the defendant, prejudiced the defendant. In effect, the clear impression conveyed to the jury was that the *judge* felt that this particular witness, K.G., needed to be protected from testifying in the presence of this particular defendant. The inference that K.G. needed to be shielded from the sight of the defendant cast a negative aspersion upon the defendant's credibility and created the appearance that the judge felt that the child was afraid of the defendant, thus prejudicing the defendant's right to a fair trial.

Id. at 605-06.

[132] 484 So. 2d 941 (La. Ct. App. 1986).

§ 8.12   DUE PROCESS CLAUSE   349

could communicate with her attorney throughout the child's testimony. Full cross-examination was permitted. On appeal, the defendant argued that the video procedure "resulted in a denial of due process."[133] The Louisiana Court of Appeals disagreed, writing:

> [T]his trial technique serve[d] as the functional equivalent of in-court testimony. The process employed did not significantly affect the flow of information to the jury. It did not confer any advantage on the state which would affect fundamental fairness. Scrutiny under the due process clause of the Fourteenth Amendment is not warranted.[134]

Contrast the facts of *Daniels* with those in *State v. Warford*.[135] *Warford* involved a four-year-old victim of sexual abuse. The child appeared at trial, but was unable or unwilling to testify. When it became apparent that the child would proceed no further, the state requested that her testimony be taken in another room and relayed to the courtroom with video equipment. There was no showing that the child would be traumatized by testifying in court. The trial judge granted the request for video testimony over the defendant's objection. The judge and the attorneys accompanied the child to a separate room. The defendant and the jury remained in the courtroom, and viewed the testimony on a monitor. "The defendant did not have any means of communication with his attorney during this part of the proceedings, nor could the judge monitor what was happening in the courtroom."[136] Once in the separate room, the child persisted in her refusal to testify. At that point, the prosecutor requested that the child's therapist be permitted to conduct the direct examination with no one else in the room. The judge approved this procedure. The child was able to testify when questioned by her therapist.

The Nebraska Supreme Court reversed the ensuing conviction, holding that the video testimony approved by the trial judge violated the defendant's right to due process and confrontation. The court wrote:

> The record before us does not show a compelling need to protect the child witness from further injury. The record does show that the attempt to examine the child in open court was frustrated by the child's failure to cooperate. There should also be a particularized showing on the record that the child would be further traumatized or was intimidated by testifying in the courtroom in front of the defendant. Without such a showing the use of closed-circuit television will not withstand constitutional scrutiny.
>
> Once the State has made an adequate showing on the record, the use of a new evidentiary tool such as closed-circuit television must be as minimally intrusive

---

[133] *Id.* at 945.
[134] *Id.*
[135] 223 Neb. 368, 389 N.W.2d 575 (1986).
[136] 389 N.W.2d at 578.

as possible. . . . At the very least, the defendant must at all times have a means of communicating with his attorney, and the court must be able to control the examination by interrupting the questioning to rule on objections. . . .

Initially, and again during cross-examination, the defendant in this case was in the courtroom while his attorney was in chambers where the witness was testifying. The defendant could not physically confront his accuser, nor could he confront the witness through counsel because he had no means of communicating with his attorney. Even when the attorneys and the judge returned to the courtroom, the defendant did not have a meaningful opportunity to confront the witness because the court had no control over the examination process. This lack of communication between the courtroom and the room in which the witness was testifying unduly inhibited the defendant's confrontation right and was therefore constitutionally objectionable.[137]

The impact of video testimony on fairness is assessed on a case-by-case basis. In *Daniels* the video procedure did not undermine basic fairness, whereas in *Warford* the cumulative intrusions on the defendant's rights went too far.

§ 8.13 —Right to Be Present

The defendant in a criminal trial has a right to be present during "every stage of his trial."[138] In *United States v. Gagnon,*[139] the Supreme Court wrote:

The constitutional right to presence is rooted to a large extent in the Confrontation Clause of the Sixth Amendment, but we have recognized that this right is

---

[137] *Id.* at 581–82.

[138] Illinois v. Allen, 397 U.S. 337, 338 (1970); Valenzuela-Gonzalez v. United States District Court, 915 F.2d 1276, 1279 (9th Cir. 1990) ("The Supreme Court has long recognized that the accused has a right to be present at all critical stages of the proceeding against him"). *See also* Fed. R. Crim. P. 43; 3 W. LaFave & J. Israel, Criminal Procedure § 23.2(c) (1991 pocketpart) (right to be present "is not restricted to situations where the defendant is 'actually confronting witnesses or evidence against him,' but encompasses all trial-related proceedings at which defendant's presence '"has a relation, reasonably substantial, to the fullness of his opportunity to defend against the charge"'").

See also State v. Thompson, 430 N.W.2d 151 (Minn. 1988) (defendant had no constitutional right to be present at child's in-chambers examination regarding testimonial competence; however, Rule 26.03 of Minnesota Rules of Criminal Procedure is broader than constitutional right to be present, and affords defendant right to be present at competency examination); State v. Crandall, 120 N.J. 649, 577 A.2d 483 (1990) (defendant who insists that traumatized child testify before jury must waive right to be present in court while child testifies); State v. Ogburne, 235 N.J. Super. 113, 561 A.2d 667, 669 (1989) ("A criminal defendant has a fundamental right to be present at every critical stage of a trial"; ruling defendant could not be excluded from in-camera hearing conducted pursuant to rape shield statute to determine admissibility of evidence of victim's previous sexual activity).

[139] 470 U.S. 522 (1985).

§ 8.13   RIGHT TO BE PRESENT

protected by the Due Process Clause in some situations where the defendant is not actually confronting witnesses or evidence against him. In *Snyder v. Massachusetts,* 291 U.S. 97 (1934), the Court explained that a defendant has a due process right to be present at a proceeding "whenever his presence has a relation, reasonably substantial, to the fulness of his opportunity to defend against the charge. . . ."[140]

In a number of cases, defendants argued that video testimony deprived them of the right to be present at trial.[141] In *Wildermuth v. State,*[142] for example, the defendant objected to a procedure that allowed the child to testify from another room. The Maryland Court of Appeals rejected this argument, writing:

> In Maryland, "a criminal defendant's right to be present at every stage of his trial is a common law right, is to some extent protected by the Fourteenth Amendment to the United States Constitution, and is guaranteed by Maryland Rule 724". . . . To some degree the right of confrontation and the right to be present may overlap, but the latter extends beyond the former in certain respects. For example, examination of jurors on voir dire does not involve a confrontation between accused and accusers. Nevertheless, it is a critical stage of the trial, and absent waiver, the defendant is entitled to be present at it. . . .
>
> In [defendant's] case there is no question of waiver of the right to be present, nor is there any doubt that the child witness's testimony was a critical stage of his trial. The only issue is whether use of closed-circuit television, as described previously, deprived [defendant] of the right. We hold that it did not.
>
> With respect to the Fourteenth Amendment, the right to be present that we now consider applies only when the defendant's presence has a reasonably substantial relationship to the fullness of the opportunity to defend; that is, the defendant's presence must in some way contribute to the fairness of the hearing. . . . As Justice Cardozo once explained: "So far as the Fourteenth Amendment is concerned, the presence of a defendant is a condition of due process to the extent that a fair and just hearing would be thwarted by his absence, and to that extent only." . . .
>
> [Defendant] notes cases . . . in which the accused's right to be present was held to have been denied even when he was in the courtroom where certain proceedings took place. From this premise he argues that his right to be present was denied because the witness testified in a separate room, in which he was not permitted. But [such cases] involved bench conferences, from which defendants were excluded. They could not hear what was taking place at the bench conferences and had no effective way of participating in them. That is not the situation here. [Defendant] could see the witness as she testified, could hear the questions asked of her and her responses, and could communicate with his lawyer in order to convey information or suggest questions to ask. The statutory procedure did

---

[140] *Id.* at 526.

[141] Wildermuth v. State, 310 Md. 496, 530 A.2d 275 (1987).

[142] *Id.*

not thwart a fair and just hearing in terms of due process. Thus, there was no violation of [defendant's] due process right to be present.

As to the Maryland common law right to be present, the legislature can change the common law.... If [the video testimony statute] narrows the common law right to be present, this was an alteration the General Assembly was entitled to make.[143]

The right to be present is not absolute, and a defendant may waive or forfeit the right.[144] In *Illinois v. Allen*,[145] the Court wrote:

[A] defendant can lose his right to be present at trial if, after he has been warned by the judge that he will be removed if he continues his disruptive behavior, he nevertheless insists on conducting himself in a manner so disorderly, disruptive, and disrespectful of the court that his trial cannot be carried on with him in the courtroom. Once lost, the right to be present can, of course, be reclaimed as soon as the defendant is willing to conduct himself consistently with the decorum and respect inherent in the concept of courts and judicial proceedings.[146]

§ 8.14 Jury's Perception of Children's Credibility

Eyewitness testimony is not always accurate, and a number of courts permit expert testimony regarding the weaknesses of eyewitness testimony.[147] With children, psychological research indicates that many jurors "enter the courtroom with doubts about the credibility of child witnesses."[148] The psychological

---

[143] 530 A.2d at 291–92.

[144] Illinois v. Allen, 397 U.S. 337 (1970).

[145] *Id.*

[146] *Id.* at 343 (footnote omitted).

[147] For a thorough review of case law, see Campbell v. People, 814 P.2d 1, 7 (Colo. 1991) ("in some cases the admission of expert testimony on the reliability of eyewitness identification may be proper, but we decline to adopt a *per se* rule of admissibility.... [T]his matter is best left to the trial court's discretion"). *See* Annotation, *Admissibility, at Criminal Prosecution, of Expert Testimony on Reliability of Eyewitness Testimony,* 46 A.L.R.4th 1047 (1986).

[148] Goodman, Golding & Haith, *Jurors' Reactions to Child Witnesses,* 40 J. Soc. Issues 139 (1984). *See also* Goodman, Bottoms, Herscovici & Shaver, *Determinants of the Child Victim's Perceived Credibility, in* Perspectives on Children's Testimony 1 (S. Ceci, D. Ross & M. Toglia eds. 1989); Ross, Dunning, Toglia & Ceci, *Age Stereotypes, Communication Modality, and Mock Jurors' Perceptions of the Child Witness, in* Perspectives on Children's Testimony 37 (S. Ceci, D. Ross & M. Toglia eds. 1989).

Although jurors may entertain doubts about the credibility of young witnesses, when jurors hear the evidence, children are believed. See Wells, Turtle & Luus, *The Perceived Credibility of Child Eyewitnesses: What Happens When They Use Their Own Words?, in*

§ 8.14   CHILDREN'S CREDIBILITY 353

literature also reveals, however, that children are more capable witnesses than some adults believe.[149]

It was once common to instruct jurors to consider children's testimony with care. Such instructions are unwarranted, however, and should not be given.[150] Children should not be singled out as more or less credible than adult witnesses.[151]

Perspectives on Children's Testimony 23, 33 (S. Ceci, D. Ross & M. Toglia eds. 1989), where the authors write:

> We propose that eight-year-old, twelve-year-old, and adult eyewitnesses are nearly equivalent in the perceived accuracy and believability of their testimony. Although a negative stereotype of the young eyewitness probably exists, we propose that this stereotype is mitigated when triers-of-fact observe actual testimony delivered by young eyewitnesses.

[149] See Goodman, Bottoms, Herscovici & Shaver, *Determinants of the Child Victim's Perceived Credibility, in* Perspectives on Children's Testimony 1, 5 (S. Ceci, D. Ross & M. Toglia eds. 1989), where the authors write:

> Recent research indicates that children, by at least the age of four years, can be quite accurate in reporting the main actions witnessed or experienced in real-life events. Young children are also surprisingly resistant to suggestive questions concerning actions associated with abuse, such as being hit or having one's clothes removed.

[150] The trial court does not err in refusing a special instruction regarding the credibility of a child witness. *See* United States v. Bear Ribs, 562 F.2d 563, 565 (8th Cir.), *cert. denied,* 434 U.S. 974 (1977); People v. Boyette, 201 Cal. App. 3d 1527, 247 Cal. Rptr. 795 (1988) (not error to refuse special instruction regarding child witnesses); People v. Estorga, 200 Colo. 78, 612 P.2d 520, 524 (1980); State v. James, 211 Conn. 555, 560 A.2d 426 (1989); Ivy v. State, 522 So. 2d 740 (Miss. 1988); State v. Hewett, 93 N.C. App. 1, 376 S.E.2d 467, 478 (1989) ("A trial judge is not required to give a special instruction on the credibility of child witnesses").

[151] See Cal. Penal Code § 1127f (West Cum. Pocket Part 1991), which states:

> In any criminal trial or proceeding in which a child 10 years of age or younger testifies as a witness, upon the request of a party, the court shall instruct the jury, as follows:
>
> In evaluating the testimony of a child, you should consider all of the factors surrounding the child's testimony, including the age of the child and any evidence regarding the child's level of cognitive development. Although, because of age and level of cognitive development, a child may perform differently as a witness from an adult, that does not mean that a child is any more or less credible a witness than an adult. You should not discount or distrust the testimony of a child solely because he or she is a child.

TABLE OF CASES

Case	Book §
A.C., *In re,* 573 A.2d 1235 (D.C. 1990)	§ 3.17
Adoption of Abigail, *In re,* 23 Mass. App. Ct. 191, 499 N.E.2d 1234 (1986)	§ 3.20
Adoption of R.I., *In re,* 468 Pa. 287, 361 A.2d 294 (1976)	§ 3.24
Adoption of T.M., *In re,* 389 Pa. Super. 303, 566 A.2d 1256 (1989)	§ 3.25
Agent Orange Prod. Liab. Litig., *In re,* 611 F. Supp. 1223 (E.D.N.Y. 1985), *aff'd,* 818 F.2d 187 (2d Cir. 1987)	§ 4.11
Agosto, *In re,* 553 F. Supp. 1298 (D. Nev. 1983)	§ 1.12
A.H.B., *In re,* 491 A.2d 490 (D.C. 1985)	§§ 2.1, 2.11, 2.12, 2.14, 2.15, 2.18
Air Crash Disaster at Stapleton Int'l Airport, *In re,* 720 F. Supp. 1493 (D. Colo. 1989)	§ 7.39
A.J.H., *In re,* 210 Ill. App. 3d 65, 568 N.E.2d 964 (1991)	§ 6.18
Alba, *In re,* 185 Ill. App. 3d 286, 540 N.E.2d 1116 (1989)	§ 7.7
Aldridge v. State, 175 Ga. App. 837, 334 S.E.2d 881 (1985)	§ 2.1
Ali v. United States, 520 A.2d 306 (D.C. 1987)	§ 6.22
Allan v. State, 92 Nev. 318, 549 P.2d 1402 (1976)	§ 6.20
Allen v. Department of Human Resources, 540 S.W.2d 597 (Ky. 1976)	§ 1.17
Allgire v. State, 575 N.E.2d 600 (Ind. 1991)	§§ 4.45, 6.21
Allison v. State, 256 Ga. 851, 353 S.E.2d 805 (1987)	§ 4.37
Alston v. United States, 462 A.2d 1122 (D.C. 1983)	§§ 7.6, 7.30
Altmeyer v. State, 519 N.E.2d 138 (Ind. 1988)	§§ 5.7, 7.6
Alvin v. State, 253 Ga. 740, 325 S.E.2d 143 (1985)	§§ 2.1, 2.18
A&M, *In re,* 61 A.D.2d 426, 403 N.Y.S.2d 375 (1978)	§ 1.12
Amber B., *In re,* 191 Cal. App. 3d 682, 236 Cal. Rptr. 623 (1987)	§§ 4.16, 4.18, 4.35, 4.37
A.M.C., *In re,* 148 Ill. App. 3d 775, 500 N.E.2d 104 (1986)	§ 2.12
Amin v. State, 686 P.2d 593 (Wyo. 1984)	§ 5.25
A.M.S., *In re,* 419 N.W.2d 723 (Iowa 1988)	§ 3.19
Amy M., *In re,* 232 Cal. App. 3d 849, 283 Cal. Rptr. 788 (1991)	§§ 2.1, 2.14
Anderson v. State, 749 P.2d 369 (Alaska Ct. App. 1988)	§ 2.22, 5.16
Anderson v. State, 454 S.W.2d 740 (Tex. Crim. App. 1970)	§ 7.27
Andrea G., *In re,* 221 Cal. App. 3d 547, 270 Cal. Rptr. 534 (1990)	§ 3.21
Antelope v. United States, 185 F.2d 174 (10th Cir. 1950)	§§ 5.7, 7.41
Appeal in Cochise County, *In re,* 133 Ariz. 157, 650 P.2d 459 (1982)	§§ 3.16, 3.17

Case	Book §
Appeal of E.S., 82 Pa. Commw. 168, 474 A.2d 432 (1984)	§ 3.2
Applebaum v. American Export Isbrandsten Lines, 472 F.2d 56 (2d Cir. 1972)	§ 7.25
Application of Nat'l Broadcasting Co., *In re*, 828 F.2d 340 (6th Cir. 1987)	§ 8.6
Archie v. Commonwealth, 1992 WL 131928 (Va. Ct. App. 1992)	§ 3.29
Arnett v. State, 551 So. 2d 1158 (Ala. Crim. App. 1989)	§ 2.22
Asendorf v. M.S.S., 342 N.W.2d 203 (N.D. 1983)	§§ 3.19, 6.6
Associated Press v. United States Dist. Court, 705 F.2d 1143 (9th Cir. 1983)	§ 8.6
Athey v. State, 106 Nev. 520, 797 P.2d 956 (1990)	§§ 3.9, 3.11, 3.28, 3.32
Atlantic Greyhound Corp. v. Eddins, 177 F.2d 954 (4th Cir. 1949)	§ 7.19
B., *In re*, 43 A.D.2d 688, 350 N.Y.S.2d 426 (1973)	§ 7.57
Baby X., *In re*, 97 Mich. App. 111, 293 N.W.2d 736 (1980)	§ 3.23
Bachman v. Leapley, 953 F.2d 440 (8th Cir. 1992)	§ 4.45
Badr v. Hogan, 75 N.Y.2d 629, 554 N.E.2d 890, 555 N.Y.S.2d 249 (1990)	§ 5.20
Baggett v. State, 514 N.E.2d 1244 (Ind. 1987)	§ 5.37
Bailey v. Bailey, 184 Mont. 418, 603 P.2d 259 (1979)	§ 5.7
Ballard v. Superior Court, 64 Cal. 2d 159, 410 P.2d 838, 49 Cal. Rptr. 302 (1966)	§ 5.16
Ballou v. Henri Studios, Inc., 656 F.2d 1147 (5th Cir. 1981)	§ 6.13
B.A.M., *In re*, 290 N.W.2d 498 (S.D. 1980)	§ 3.18
Barber v. Page, 390 U.S. 719 (1968)	§§ 7.48, 7.50, 7.51, 7.52, 7.55, 7.58
Barcus v. State, 92 Nev. 289, 550 P.2d 411 (1976)	§ 5.7
Barger v. State, 562 So. 2d 650 (Ala. Crim. App. 1989)	§ 5.16
Barlow v. Verrill, 88 N.H. 25, 183 A. 857 (1936)	§ 7.47
Barnes v. State, 173 Ga. App. 907, 328 S.E.2d 583 (1985)	§§ 2.12, 2.18
Barnes v. United States, 600 A.2d 821 (D.C. 1991)	§ 2.18
Barrera v. United States, 599 A.2d 1119 (D.C. 1991)	§ 2.22
Barrett v. State, 23 Ark. App. 144, 744 S.W.2d 741 (1988)	§ 2.18
Bartlett v. State, 196 Ga. App. 174, 396 S.E.2d 31 (1990)	§ 1.14
Basilio T., *In re*, 4 Cal. App. 4th 155, 5 Cal. Rptr. 2d 450 (1992)	§ 7.49
Baxter v. State, 522 N.E.2d 362 (Ind. 1988)	§ 8.1
B.B., *In re*, 440 N.W.2d 594 (Iowa 1989)	§ 3.26
B.E. v. State, 564 So. 2d 566 (Fla. Dist. Ct. App. 1990)	§ 1.13
Beavers v. State, 709 P.2d 702 (Okla. Crim. App. 1985)	§ 7.30
Beck v. Dye, 200 Wash. 1, 92 P.2d 1113 (1939)	§ 7.29
Beck v. State, 544 N.E.2d 204 (Ind. Ct. App. 1989)	§§ 7.31, 7.46
Beech Aircraft Corp. v. Rainey, 488 U.S. 153 (1988)	§ 7.39
Begley v. State, 483 So. 2d 70 (Fla. Dist. Ct. App. 1986)	§§ 5.7, 7.35
Bell v. Commonwealth, 684 S.W.2d 282 (Ky. Ct. App. 1984)	§ 3.5
Benjamin D., *In re*, 227 Cal. App. 3d 1464, 278 Cal. Rptr. 468 (1991)	§ 6.5

CASES

Case	Book §
Bently v. Bently, 86 A.D.2d 926, 448 N.Y.S.2d 559 (1982)	§ 1.12
Berger v. United States, 295 U.S. 78 (1935)	§ 1.1
Berkey Photo, Inc. v. Eastman Kodak Co., 74 F.R.D. 613 (S.D.N.Y. 1977)	§ 5.12
Betty J.B. v. Department of Social Servs., 460 A.2d 528 (Del. 1983)	§ 1.17
B.F., In re, 230 N.J. Super. 153, 553 A.2d 40 (1989)	§ 8.8
Bingham v. Bingham, 811 S.W.2d 678 (Tex. Ct. App. 1991)	§ 7.47
Bishop v. Goins, 586 N.E.2d 905 (Ind. Ct. App. 1992)	§ 1.18
Bishop v. State, 581 P.2d 45 (Okla. Crim. App. 1978)	§ 7.49
Black v. Gray, 540 A.2d 431 (Del. 1988)	§ 3.25
Black v. Woods, 651 F.2d 528 (8th Cir.), cert. denied, 454 U.S. 847 (1981)	§ 8.8
Blackwelder, In re, 139 Misc. 2d 776, 528 N.Y.S.2d 759 (Sup. Ct. 1988)	§ 3.26
Bludsworth v. State, 98 Nev. 289, 646 P.2d 558 (1982)	§ 6.17
Blume v. State, 797 P.2d 664 (Alaska Ct. App. 1990)	§§ 2.1, 2.18
Bobby M., In re, 103 A.D.2d 777, 477 N.Y.S.2d 589 (1984)	§ 3.19
Bodnar v. Bodnar, 441 F.2d 1103 (5th Cir.), cert. denied, 404 U.S. 413 (1971)	§ 2.22
Boland v. Leska, 308 Pa. Super. 169, 454 A.2d 75 (1982)	§ 3.2
Bolden v. State, 720 P.2d 957 (Alaska Ct. App. 1986)	§ 6.21
Bond v. District Court, 682 P.2d 33 (Colo. 1984)	§ 1.12
Booth v. State, 306 Md. 313, 508 A.2d 976 (1986)	§ 7.27
Bourjaily v. United States, 483 U.S. 171 (1987)	§§ 7.4, 7.29, 7.46, 7.50, 7.51, 7.52, 7.53
Boutwell v. State, 719 S.W.2d 164 (Tex. Crim. App. 1985)	§§ 6.15, 6.20, 6.21
Bowling v. State, 560 N.E.2d 658 (Ind. 1990)	§ 6.21
Bradburn v. Peacock, 135 Cal. App. 2d 161, 286 P.2d 972 (1955)	§ 2.1
Brady v. Maryland, 373 U.S. 83 (1963)	§§ 1.13, 5.11
Brady v. State, 575 N.E.2d 981 (Ind. 1991)	§ 7.50
Brady v. State, 540 N.E.2d 59 (Ind. Ct. App. 1989)	§ 5.8
Brandon v. State, 778 P.2d 221 (Alaska Ct. App. 1989)	§§ 7.30, 7.42, 7.58
Brenda H., In re, 119 N.H. 382, 402 A.2d 169 (1979)	§ 1.17
Brewer v. State, 562 N.E.2d 22 (Ind. 1990)	§§ 1.1, 2.1, 4.40, 6.21
Brewington v. State, 802 S.W.2d 691 (Tex. Crim. App. 1991)	§ 4.50
Bridges v. State, 247 Wis. 350, 19 N.W.2d 529 (1945)	§ 7.16
Broderick v. King's Way Assembly of God Church, 808 P.2d 1211 (Alaska 1991)	§§ 4.11, 4.18, 4.37
Brookhart v. Janis, 384 U.S. 1 (1966)	§ 7.58
Brown v. State, 512 N.E.2d 173 (Ind. 1987)	§ 3.11
Brown v. State, 736 P.2d 1110 (Wyo. 1987)	§ 6.14
Bruce L., Jr., In re, 140 Misc. 2d 757, 531 N.Y.S.2d 438 (Fam. Ct. 1988)	§ 3.17
Bruton v. United States, 391 U.S. 123 (1968)	§ 7.54
Bryan v. State, 288 Ark. 125, 702 S.W.2d 785 (1986)	§§ 7.30, 7.49
Bryant v. State, 685 S.W.2d 472 (Tex. Ct. App. 1985)	§ 5.8

Case	Book §
Buchanan v. State, 554 P.2d 1153 (Alaska 1976)	§ 5.15
Buck v. Board of Educ., 17 Fed. R. Serv. 2d (Callaghan) 165 (E.D.N.Y. 1973)	§ 2.22
Buckley v. State, 758 S.W.2d 339 (Tex. Ct. App. 1988), aff'd, 786 S.W.2d 357 (Tex. Crim. App. 1990)	§§ 7.44, 7.46
Burdette v. Lobban, 174 W. Va. 120, 323 S.E.2d 601 (1984)	§ 2.22
Burke v. State, 624 P.2d 1240 (Alaska 1980)	§§ 6.20, 6.21
Burke v. State, 820 P.2d 1344 (Okla. Crim. App. 1991), cert. denied, 112 S. Ct. 2940 (1992)	§ 8.7
Burkett v. State, 439 So. 2d 737 (Ala. Crim. App. 1983)	§§ 2.1, 2.16, 2.18
Burns v. Clusen, 798 F.2d 931 (7th Cir. 1986)	§ 7.48
Burr v. Sullivan, 618 F.2d 583 (9th Cir. 1980)	§ 5.21
Burroughs v. State, 186 Ga. App. 40, 366 S.E.2d 378 (1988)	§ 5.3
Busby v. State, 174 Ga. App. 536, 330 S.E.2d 765 (1985)	§§ 2.1, 2.12, 2.14
Bussey v. State, 536 N.E.2d 1027 (Ind. 1989)	§ 5.7
Buttram v. State, 269 Ind. 598, 382 N.E.2d 166 (1978)	§ 2.1
C. Children, In re, 169 A.D.2d 481, 564 N.Y.S.2d 354 (1991)	§ 3.2
C.A., In re, 201 N.J. Super. 28, 492 A.2d 683 (1985)	§ 7.30
Cabello v. State, 471 So. 2d 332 (Miss. 1985), cert. denied, 476 U.S. 1164 (1986)	§§ 1.12, 5.7
Cabrera, In re, 381 Pa. Super. 100, 552 A.2d 1114 (1989)	§ 3.17
Caldwell v. State, 260 Ga. 278, 393 S.E.2d 436 (1990)	§§ 4.18, 4.19
California v. Green, 399 U.S. 149 (1970)	§§ 7.20, 7.43, 7.50, 7.51, 7.54, 7.55, 7.56
Calloway v. State, 199 Ga. App. 272, 404 S.E.2d 811 (1991)	§§ 5.9, 5.34, 6.26
Calloway v. State, 520 So. 2d 665 (Fla. Dist. Ct. App. 1988)	§ 4.45
Campbell v. Commonwealth, 405 S.E.2d 1 (Va. Ct. App. 1991)	§§ 3.2, 3.10, 3.28, 3.29, 3.32
Campbell v. People, 814 P.2d 1 (Colo. 1991)	§§ 3.30, 8.14
Carlita B., In re, 185 W. Va. 163, 408 S.E.2d 365 (1991)	§§ 3.21, 6.5
Carney v. Carney, 525 So. 2d 357 (La. Ct. App. 1988)	§§ 1.12, 1.17, 1.18
Carpenter v. Commonwealth, 186 Va. 851, 44 S.E.2d 419 (1947)	§ 3.2
Carpenter Steel Co. v. Pellegrin, 237 Cal. App. 2d 35, 46 Cal. Rptr. 502 (1965)	§ 7.47
Carsey v. United States, 392 F.2d 810 (D.C. Cir. 1967)	§ 5.15
Cartmill v. State, 748 S.W.2d 581 (Tex. Ct. App. 1988)	§§ 7.21, 7.24
Cason v. Jackson, 466 So. 2d 1188 (Fla. Dist. Ct. App. 1985)	§ 1.16
Cassidy v. State, 74 Md. App. 1, 536 A.2d 666, cert. denied, 312 Md. 602, 541 A.2d 965 (1988)	§§ 7.2, 7.28, 7.30, 7.35, 7.36

CASES

Case	Book §
C.B., *In re,* 574 So. 2d 1369 (Miss. 1990)	§§ 7.27, 7.30, 7.42, 7.56, 7.57, 8.3
Celeste v. State, 805 S.W.2d 579 (Tex. Ct. App. 1991)	§§ 5.20, 6.21
CFB, *In re,* 497 S.W.2d 831 (Mo. Ct. App. 1973)	§ 3.17
Chadwick v. State, 176 Ga. App. 296, 335 S.E.2d 674 (1985), *aff'd,* 255 Ga. 376, 339 S.E.2d 717 (1986)	§§ 2.1, 2.12, 2.14, 2.18
Chambers v. Mississippi, 410 U.S. 284 (1973)	§§ 5.19, 7.43, 7.50, 7.51
Chambers v. State, 504 So. 2d 476 (Fla. Dist. Ct. App. 1987)	§ 8.7
Chambers v. State, 711 S.W.2d 240 (Tex. Crim. App. 1986)	§ 7.47
Chambers v. State, 726 P.2d 1269 (Wyo. 1986)	§ 8.7
Chastain v. State, 257 Ga. 54, 354 S.E.2d 421 (1987)	§ 7.56
Cheryl H., *In re,* 153 Cal. App. 3d 1098, 200 Cal. Rptr. 789 (1984)	§ 7.31
Chuesberg, *In re,* 305 Minn. 543, 233 N.W.2d 887 (1975)	§ 7.30
Chicago & Alton R.R. v. Springfield & Northwestern R.R., 67 Ill. 142 (1873)	§ 4.13
Childs v. State, 177 Ga. App. 257, 339 S.E.2d 311 (1985)	§ 6.22
Childs v. State, 744 P.2d 567 (Okla. Crim. App. 1987)	§ 3.9
Christina F., *In re,* 74 N.Y.2d 532, 548 N.E.2d 1294, 549 N.Y.S.2d 643 (1989)	§ 7.47
Christina H., *In re,* 127 A.D.2d 997, 513 N.Y.S.2d 65 (1987)	§ 3.26
Christine C., *In re,* 191 Cal. App. 3d 676, 236 Cal. Rptr. 630 (1987)	§ 4.18
Cicero, *In re,* 101 Misc. 2d 699, 421 N.Y.S.2d 965 (Sup. Ct. 1979)	§ 3.17
Cissna v. State, 170 Ind. App. 437, 352 N.E.2d 793 (1976)	§ 1.12
C.L., *In re,* 397 N.W.2d 81 (S.D. 1986)	§§ 4.35, 7.2
Clark v. Clark, 220 Neb. 771, 371 N.W.2d 749 (1985)	§ 1.18
Clark, *In re,* 185 N.E.2d 128 (Ohio Ct. C.P. 1962)	§ 3.17
Cleaveland v. State, 490 N.E.2d 1140 (Ind. Ct. App. 1986)	§ 5.8
Cleopatra D., *In re,* 193 Cal. App. 3d 694, 238 Cal. Rptr. 426 (1987)	§ 6.6
Clifton v. State, 758 P.2d 1279 (Alaska Ct. App. 1988)	§§ 3.29, 7.45
Clinebell v. Commonwealth, 235 Va. 319, 368 S.E.2d 263 (1988)	§ 5.34
C.M., *In re,* 595 A.2d 293 (Vt. 1991)	§§ 5.7, 8.3
C.N.G., *In re,* 531 So. 2d 345 (Fla. Dist. Ct. App. 1988)	§ 3.20
C.O., *In re,* 36 Colo. App. 298, 541 P.2d 330 (1975)	§ 3.19
Coachman v. State, 692 S.W.2d 940 (Tex. Ct. App. 1985)	§§ 2.1, 2.12, 2.18
Cogburn v. State, 292 Ark. 564, 732 S.W.2d 807 (1987)	§ 7.46
Cohoon v. United States, 387 A.2d 1098 (D.C. 1978)	§§ 3.9, 3.11
Cole v. Detroit Auto. Inter-Ins. Exch., 137 Mich. App. 603, 357 N.W.2d 898 (1984)	§ 5.9
Coles v. Harsch, 129 Or. 11, 276 P. 248 (1929)	§ 7.18
Collin R., *In re,* 63 Md. App. 684, 493 A.2d 1083 (1985)	§ 3.15
Collins v. United States, 491 A.2d 480 (D.C. 1985), *cert. denied,* 475 U.S. 1124 (1986)	§§ 2.22, 5.16

Case	Book §
Commonwealth v. Achorn, 25 Mass. App. Ct. 247, 517 N.E.2d 486 (1988)	§ 7.31
Commonwealth v. Adams, 23 Mass. App. Ct. 534, 503 N.E.2d 1315 (1987)	§ 7.31
Commonwealth v. Amirault, 404 Mass. 221, 535 N.E.2d 193 (1989)	§§ 5.27, 7.31, 7.56, 8.1, 8.3, 8.7, 8.8
Commonwealth v. Anderson, 381 Pa. Super. 1, 552 A.2d 1064 (1988)	§§ 2.1, 2.8, 2.18
Commonwealth v. Appenzeller, 565 A.2d 170 (Pa. Super. Ct. 1989)	§ 5.35
Commonwealth v. Arthur, 31 Mass. App. Ct. 178, 575 N.E.2d 1147 (1991)	§ 5.24
Commonwealth v. Askins, 18 Mass. App. Ct. 927, 465 N.E.2d 1224 (1984)	§ 7.31
Commonwealth v. Azar, 32 mass. App. Ct. 290, 588 N.E.2d 1352 (1992)	§ 3.5
Commonwealth v. Bailey, 370 Mass. 388, 348 N.E.2d 746 (1976)	§ 7.31
Commonwealth v. Bailey, 353 Pa. Super. 390, 510 A.2d 367 (1986)	§ 7.30
Commonwealth v. Bailey, 322 Pa. Super. 249, 469 A.2d 604 (1983)	§ 2.8
Commonwealth v. Baran, 21 Mass. App. Ct. 989, 490 N.E.2d 479 (1986)	§§ 2.1, 5.7
Commonwealth v. Barnes, 310 Pa. Super. 480, 456 A.2d 1037 (1983)	§ 7.29
Commonwealth v. Barnhart, 345 Pa. Super. 10, 479 A.2d 616 (1985), *cert. denied,* 488 U.S. 817 (1988)	§ 3.17
Commonwealth v. Bergstrom, 402 Mass. 534, 524 N.E.2d 366 (1988)	§§ 8.8, 8.10
Commonwealth v. Berrio, 407 Mass. 37, 551 N.E.2d 496 (1990)	§ 7.20
Commonwealth v. Berry, 355 Pa. Super. 243, 513 A.2d 410 (1986)	§ 8.2
Commonwealth v. Black, 337 Pa. Super. 548, 487 A.2d 396 (1985)	§ 5.36
Commonwealth v. Brenner, 18 Mass. App. Ct. 930, 465 N.E.2d 1229 (1984)	§ 7.31
Commonwealth v. Bristow, 372 Pa. Super. 48, 538 A.2d 1343 (1988)	§ 2.1
Commonwealth v. Brusgulis, 398 Mass. 325, 496 N.E.2d 652 (1986)	§ 8.3
Commonwealth v. Byuss, 372 Pa. Super. 395, 539 A.2d 852 (1988)	§ 1.14
Commonwealth v. Calcagno, 31 Mass. App. Ct. 25, 574 N.E.2d 420 (1991)	§§ 6.20, 6.21
Commonwealth v. Cauto, 369 Pa. Super. 381, 535 A.2d 602 (1987)	§ 5.21
Commonwealth v. Clancy, 402 Mass. 664, 524 N.E.2d 395 (1988)	§ 1.14

Case	Book §
Commonwealth v. Collett, 387 Mass. 424, 439 N.E.2d 1223 (1982)	§ 1.16
Commonwealth v. Corbett, 26 Mass. App. Ct. 773, 533 N.E.2d 207 (1989)	§§ 2.1, 2.12, 2.14
Commonwealth v. Cordeiro, 401 Mass. 843, 519 N.E.2d 1328 (1988)	§§ 8.4, 8.5
Commonwealth v. Coull, 20 Mass. App. Ct. 955, 480 N.E.2d 323 (1985)	§ 7.31
Commonwealth v. Crowe, 21 Mass. App. Ct. 456, 488 N.E.2d 780, *cert. denied,* 479 U.S. 838 (1986)	§ 7.31
Commonwealth v. Davis, 518 Pa. 77, 541 A.2d 315 (1988)	§ 4.45
Commonwealth v. Day, 409 Mass. 719, 569 N.E.2d 397 (1991)	§§ 3.5, 3.31
Commonwealth v. Devlin, 460 Pa. 598, 333 A.2d 888 (1975)	§§ 1.1, 1.3, 1.4
Commonwealth v. Dockham, 405 Mass. 618, 542 N.E.2d 591 (1989)	§§ 7.31, 8.8
Commonwealth v. Donahue, 519 Pa. 532, 549 A.2d 121 (1988)	§ 6.17
Commonwealth v. Douglass, 403 Pa. Super. 105, 588 A.2d 53 (1991)	§ 5.16
Commonwealth v. Dunkle, 385 Pa. Super. 317, 561 A.2d 5 (1989) *aff'd in part, rev'd in part,* 602 A.2d 830 (Pa. 1992)	§§ 1.14, 4.37, 4.44
Commonwealth v. Eck, 605 A.2d 1248 (Pa. Super Ct. 1992)	§ 1.15
Commonwealth v. Elder, 389 Mass. 743, 452 N.E.2d 1104 (1983)	§ 5.36
Commonwealth v. Fanelli, 377 Pa. Super. 555, 547 A.2d 1201 (1988)	§§ 1.3, 1.4
Commonwealth v. Foskette, 30 Mass. App. Ct. 384, 568 N.E.2d 1167 (1991)	§ 7.31
Commonwealth v. Fuller, 22 Mass. App. Ct. 152, 491 N.E.2d 1083 (1986), *aff'd,* 399 Mass. 678, 506 N.E.2d 852 (1987)	§ 7.30
Commonwealth v. Gallagher, 519 Pa. 291, 547 A.2d 355 (1988)	§ 4.34
Commonwealth v. Garcia, 403 Pa. Super. 280, 588 A.2d 951 (1991)	§§ 4.44, 4.50
Commonwealth v. Gardner, 30 Mass. App. Ct. 515, 570 N.E.2d 1033 (1991)	§ 7.31
Commonwealth v. Gibbons, 383 Pa. Super. 297, 556 A.2d 915 (1989)	§ 4.44
Commonwealth v. Gomes, 11 Mass. App. Ct. 933, 416 N.E.2d 551 (1981)	§ 5.24
Commonwealth v. Gore, 262 Pa. Super. 540, 396 A.2d 1302 (1978)	§ 7.22
Commonwealth v. Groff, 378 Pa. Super. 353, 548 A.2d 1237 (1988)	§§ 1.3, 1.4, 7.50, 8.3, 8.8
Commonwealth v. Haber, 351 Pa. Super. 79, 505 A.2d 273 (1986)	§§ 2.18, 7.45

Case	*Book §*
Commonwealth v. Hart, 501 Pa. 174, 460 A.2d 745 (1983)	§ 2.18
Commonwealth v. Healey, 27 Mass. App. Ct. 30, 534 N.E.2d 301 (1989)	§§ 7.23, 7.24
Commonwealth v. Ianello, 401 Mass. 197, 515 N.E.2d 1181 (1987)	§ 4.45
Commonwealth v. Jones, 404 Mass. 339, 535 N.E.2d 221 (1989)	§§ 1.14, 1.15
Commonwealth v. Joyce, 382 Mass. 222, 415 N.E.2d 181 (1981)	§ 5.28
Commonwealth v. Jubilee, 403 Pa. Super. 589, 589 A.2d 1112 (1991)	§§ 7.24, 8.4
Commonwealth v. Kennedy, 604 A.2d 1036 (Pa. Super. Ct. 1992)	§ 1.15
Commonwealth v. King, 387 Mass. 464, 441 N.E.2d 248 (1982)	§§ 1.1, 6.18, 6.21
Commonwealth v. Kirouac, 405 Mass. 557, 542 N.E.2d 270 (1989)	§§ 7.31, 7.48, 7.50, 7.56
Commonwealth v. Knapp, 374 Pa. Super. 160, 542 A.2d 546 (1988)	§§ 2.14, 7.21, 7.23, 7.24, 8.2
Commonwealth v. Kyle, 367 Pa. Super. 484, 533 A.2d 120 (1987)	§§ 1.14, 1.15
Commonwealth v. Lane, 521 Pa. 390, 555 A.2d 1246 (1989)	§ 7.31
Commonwealth v. LaPierre, 10 Mass. App. Ct. 871, 408 N.E.2d 883 (1980)	§ 5.24
Commonwealth v. Lazarovich, 28 Mass. App. Ct. 147, 547 N.E.2d 940 (1989)	§§ 3.5, 3.9, 3.10, 3.11, 3.29, 3.30
Commonwealth v. LeFave, 407 Mass. 927, 556 N.E.2d 83 (1990)	§§ 2.15, 2.18, 4.5, 7.31
Commonwealth v. Lewandowski, 22 Mass. App. 148, 491 N.E.2d 670 (1986)	§ 7.31
Commonwealth v. Lloyd, 523 Pa. 427, 567 A.2d 1357 (1989)	§ 1.14
Commonwealth v. Ludwig, 594 A.2d 281 (Pa. 1991)	§§ 7.50, 8.8
Commonwealth v. Mamay, 407 Mass. 412, 553 N.E.2d 945 (1990)	§ 4.34
Commonwealth v. McEachin, 371 Pa. Super. 188, 537 A.2d 883 (1988)	§§ 5.3, 5.9, 7.22, 7.23, 7.30
Commonwealth v. Meadows, 381 Pa. Super. 354, 553 A.2d 1006 (1989)	§ 8.1
Commonwealth v. Melchionno, 29 Mass. App. Ct. 939, 558 N.E.2d 18 (1990)	§§ 4.28, 8.8
Commonwealth v. Merola, 405 Mass. 529, 542 N.E.2d 249 (1989)	§§ 3.5, 3.8, 3.9, 3.11, 3.29, 3.30, 3.32
Commonwealth v. Moore, 261 Pa. Super. 92, 395 A.2d 1328 (1978)	§ 3.28

CASES

Case	Book §
Commonwealth v. Niemetz, 282 Pa. Super. 431, 422 A.2d 1369 (1980)	§§ 1.1, 1.3, 6.22
Commonwealth v. O'Brien, 27 Mass. App. Ct. 184, 536 N.E.2d 361 (1989)	§ 1.15
Commonwealth v. Ogin, 373 Pa. Super. 116, 540 A.2d 549 (1988)	§§ 3.2, 3.13
Commonwealth v. Pankraz, 382 Pa. Super. 116, 554 A.2d 974 (1989)	§ 8.1
Commonwealth v. Payton, 258 Pa. Super. 140, 392 A.2d 723 (1978)	§ 2.14
Commonwealth v. Penn, 497 Pa. 232, 439 A.2d 1154, *cert. denied*, 456 U.S. 980 (1982)	§ 7.30
Commonwealth v. Perry, 588 A.2d 917 (Pa. Super. Ct. 1991)	§§ 4.21, 4.28
Commonwealth v. Powers, 395 Pa. Super. 231, 577 A.2d 194 (1990)	§ 7.31
Commonwealth v. Purcell, 589 A.2d 217 (Pa. Super. Ct. 1991)	§§ 5.9, 5.36
Commonwealth v. Rathburn, 26 Mass. App. Ct. 699, 532 N.E.2d 691 (1988)	§ 1.14
Commonwealth v. Reid, 400 Mass. 534, 511 N.E.2d 331 (1987)	§ 2.14
Commonwealth v. Repoza, 382 Mass. 119, 414 N.E.2d 591 (1980)	§ 3.32
Commonwealth v. Rhoades, 364 Pa. Super. 54, 527 A.2d 148 (1987)	§ 7.30
Commonwealth v. Ritchie, 509 Pa. 357, 502 A.2d 148 (1985) *aff'd in part, rev'd in part,* 480 U.S. 39 (1987)	§ 1.14
Commonwealth v. Robinson, 30 Mass. App. Ct. 62, 565 N.E.2d 1229 (1991)	§§ 3.27, 3.28, 3.30
Commonwealth v. Rochon, 398 Pa. Super. 494, 581 A.2d 239 (1990)	§§ 3.2, 3.13
Commonwealth v. Rodgers, 364 Pa. Super. 477, 528 A.2d 610 (1987)	§§ 3.5, 3.6, 3.30
Commonwealth v. Rodriguez, 343 Pa. Super. 486, 495 A.2d 569 (1985)	§ 7.31
Commonwealth v. Roldan, 524 Pa. 366, 572 A.2d 1214 (1990)	§ 5.9
Commonwealth v. Rothlisberger, 197 Pa. Super. 451, 178 A.2d 853 (1962)	§ 7.7
Commonwealth v. Ruffen, 399 Mass. 811, 507 N.E.2d 684 (1987)	§ 5.35
Commonwealth v. Ruppert, 579 A.2d 966 (Pa. Super Ct. 1990)	§ 6.26
Commonwealth v. Sanford, 397 Pa. Super. 581, 580 A.2d 784 (1990)	§§ 7.29, 7.30, 7.35
Commonwealth v. Scott, 408 Mass. 811, 564 N.E.2d 370 (1990)	§§ 6.14, 6.18
Commonwealth v. Sees, 605 A.2d 307 (Pa. 1992)	§ 4.44
Commonwealth v. Seese, 512 Pa. 439, 517 A.2d 920 (1986)	§ 4.45

Case	Book §
Commonwealth v. Short, 278 Pa. Super. 581, 420 A.2d 694 (1980)	§§ 2.8, 2.18
Commonwealth v. Snoke, 525 Pa. 295, 580 A.2d 295 (1990)	§ 7.31
Commonwealth v. Snow, 30 Mass. App. Ct. 443, 569 N.E.2d 838 (1991)	§ 7.31
Commonwealth v. Souther, 31 Mass. App. Ct. 219, 575 N.E.2d 1150 (1991)	§ 7.31
Commonwealth v. Stockhammer, 409 Mass. 867, 570 N.E.2d 992 (1991)	§§ 1.15, 5.36
Commonwealth v. Stohr, 361 Pa. Super. 293, 522 A.2d 589 (1987)	§ 2.1
Commonwealth v. Thek, 376 Pa. Super. 390, 546 A.2d 83 (1988)	§ 1.4
Commonwealth v. Titus, 32 Mass. Ct. App. 216, 587 N.E.2d 800 (1992)	§ 7.31
Commonwealth v. Trenholm, 14 Mass. App. 1038, 442 N.E.2d 745 (1982)	§ 5.8
Commonwealth v. Tufts, 405 Mass. 610, 542 N.E.2d 586 (1989)	§ 8.7
Commonwealth v. Vidmosko, 393 Pa. Super. 236, 574 A.2d 96 (1990)	§§ 1.1, 1.3, 5.9
Commonwealth v. Wall, 606 A.2d 449 (Pa. Super. Ct. 1992)	§ 5.35
Commonwealth v. Welansky, 316 Mass. 383, 55 N.E.2d 902 (1944)	§ 3.28
Commonwealth v. Willis, 716 S.W.2d 224 (Ky. 1986)	§ 8.8
Commonwealth v. Wilson, 602 A.2d 1290 (Pa. 1992)	§ 1.15
Commonwealth *ex rel.* Ruczynski v. Powers, 421 Pa. 2, 219 A.2d 460 (1966)	§ 3.25
Conley v. State, 20 Ark. App. 56, 723 S.W.2d 841 (1987)	§ 2.12
Cook v. Hoppin, 783 F.2d 684 (7th Cir. 1986)	§ 7.36
Cook v. State, 629 S.W.2d 233 (Tex. Ct. App. 1982)	§ 6.24
Cooney v. State, 803 S.W.2d 422 (Tex. Ct. App. 1991)	§ 2.18
Copley Press, Inc. v. Superior Court, 7 Cal. Rptr. 2d 841 (Cal. Ct. App. 1992)	§ 8.6
Cote v. State, 711 S.W.2d 240 (Tex. Crim. App. 1985)	§ 7.47
Covenant House/Under 21, *In re,* 169 A.D.2d 723, 564 N.Y.S.2d 473 (A.D. 1991)	§ 1.14
Covington v. State, 703 P.2d 436 (Alaska Ct. App.), *different results reached on other grounds,* 711 P.2d 1183 (Alaska 1985)	§§ 1.6, 5.34
Cox v. Court C.P., 42 Ohio App. 3d 171, 537 N.E.2d 721 (1988)	§ 3.17
Cox v. State, 173 Ga. App. 422, 326 S.E.2d 796 (1985)	§§ 6.21, 6.22
Cox v. State, 51 Md. App. 271, 443 A.2d 607 (1982), *aff'd,* 298 Md. 173, 468 A.2d 319 (1983)	§ 5.34
Coy v. Iowa, 487 U.S. 1012 (1988)	§§ 1.14, 5.3, 7.50, 8.8
Cozad v. State, 303 Ark. 137, 792 S.W.2d 606 (1990)	§ 1.16
Crabtree v. Crabtree, 716 S.W.2d 923 (Tenn. Ct. App. 1986)	§§ 7.34, 7.47

Case	Book §
Crane v. State, 786 S.W.2d 338 (Tex. Crim. App. 1990)	§ 7.7
Crisp v. State, 667 P.2d 472 (Okla. Crim. App. 1983)	§ 6.20
Critchlow v. Critchlow, 347 So. 2d 453 (Fla. Dist. Ct. App. 1977)	§ 1.18
Crossman v. State, 797 S.W.2d 321 (Tex. Ct. App. 1990)	§ 6.21
Crozier v. State, 723 P.2d 42 (Wyo. 1986)	§ 6.20
Cruz v. New York, 481 U.S. 186 (1987)	§§ 7.50, 7.54
Cruz v. State, 737 S.W.2d 74 (Tex. Ct. App. 1987)	§ 1.13
Custody of a Minor, In re, 375 Mass. 733, 379 N.E.2d 1053 (1978)	§ 3.17
Custody of a Minor, In re, 16 Mass. App. Ct. 998, 454 N.E.2d 924 (1983)	§ 1.18
Custody of Jennifer, In re, 25 Mass. App. Ct. 241, 517 N.E.2d 187 (1988)	§ 7.34
Czajka v. Hickman, 703 F.2d 317 (8th Cir. 1983)	§ 5.25
D. v. D., 108 N.J. Super. 149, 260 A.2d 255 (1969)	§ 1.18
D.A.H. v. G.A.H., 371 N.W.2d 1 (Minn. Ct. App. 1985)	§§ 7.44, 7.45
Damon H., In re, 165 Cal. App. 3d 471, 211 Cal. Rptr. 623 (1985)	§ 7.30
Dana v. Department of Corrections, 958 F.2d 237 (8th Cir. cert. denied, 112 S. Ct. 3043 (1992)	§§ 7.44, 7.46, 7.53
Daniel C.H., In re, 220 Cal. App. 3d 814, 269 Cal. Rptr. 624 (1990)	§ 1.12
Danielle M., In re, 151 A.D.2d 240, 542 N.Y.S.2d 525 (1989)	§ 3.18
Daniels v. Department of Human Resources, 530 So. 2d 841 (Ala. Civ. App. 1988)	§ 3.19
Daniels v. State, 767 P.2d 1163 (Alaska Ct. App. 1989)	§ 5.36
Darby v. State, 538 So. 2d 1168 (Miss. 1989)	§ 6.20
Davis v. Alaska, 415 U.S. 308 (1974)	§§ 1.14, 4.45, 5.21, 5.25, 5.36, 7.50, 7.56
Davis v. State, 569 So. 2d 1317 (Fla. Dist. Ct. App. 1990)	§ 4.28
Day v. State, 92 Wis. 2d 392, 284 N.W.2d 666 (1979)	§ 6.22
De Groot v. Winter, 261 Mich. 660, 247 N.W. 69 (1933)	§ 4.13
De Los Santos v. Superior Court, 27 Cal. 3d 677, 613 P.2d 233, 166 Cal. Rptr. 172 (1980)	§ 1.12
Dearing v. State, 100 Nev. 590, 691 P.2d 419 (1984)	§§ 7.22, 7.23, 7.30
Deborah M., In re, 544 A.2d 572 (R.I. 1988)	§ 7.30
DeBruhl v. State, 544 N.E.2d 542 (Ind. Ct. App. 1989)	§ 5.32
Decker, In re, 20 Ohio App. 3d 203, 485 N.E.2d 751 (1984)	§ 1.17
Dehring v. Northern Mich. Exploration Co., 104 Mich. App. 300, 304 N.W.2d 560 (1981)	§ 5.7
Delaware v. Fensterer, 474 U.S. 15 (1985)	§§ 7.50, 7.51, 7.55, 7.56
Delaware v. Van Arsdall, 475 U.S. 673 (1986)	§§ 5.21, 5.23, 5.36, 7.50, 7.56
DeMotte v. State, 555 N.E.2d 1336 (Ind. Ct. App. 1990)	§§ 2.14, 4.45, 5.27
Dennis H., In re, 19 Cal. App. 3d 350, 97 Cal. Rptr. 791 (1971)	§ 7.57
Department of Human Resources v. Smith, 494 U.S. 872 (1990)	§ 3.17

Case	Book §
Department of Human Servs. v. Smith, 785 S.W.2d 336 (Tenn. 1990)	§ 3.21
Department of Social Welfare v. Miller, 595 A.2d 288 (Vt. 1991)	§ 7.38
Dependency of S.S., *In re,* 61 Wash. App. 488, 814 P.2d 204 (1991)	§§ 7.44, 7.49
Devone, *In re,* 86 N.C. App. 57, 356 S.E.2d 389 (1987)	§ 3.26
Diehl v. Commonwealth, 9 Va. App. 191, 385 S.E.2d 228 (1989)	§ 3.32
Diggs v. Tyler, 525 So. 2d 1263 (La. Ct. App. 1988)	§ 7.57
Dino, *In re,* 359 So. 2d 586 (La.), *cert. denied,* 439 U.S. 1047 (1978)	§ 7.57
Ditchley v. State, 542 N.E.2d 996 (Ind. 1989)	§ 5.29
Dittrick Infant, *In re,* 80 Mich. App. 219, 263 N.W.2d 37 (1977)	§ 3.17
Division of Youth & Family Servs. v. J.B., 120 N.J. 112, 576 A.2d 261 (1990)	§ 8.5
D.K., *In re,* 245 N.W.2d 644 (S.D. 1976)	§§ 1.12, 1.17
D.M. v. State, 515 P.2d 1234 (Alaska 1973)	§ 3.25
D.N. v. Commonwealth Dep't Pub. Welfare, 127 Pa. Commw. 580, 562 A.2d 433 (1989)	§ 3.2
Dockery v. State, 504 N.E.2d 291 (Ind. Ct. App. 1987)	§ 1.15
Dodge, *In re,* 29 Wash. App. 486, 628 P.2d 1343 (1981)	§ 1.17
Doe v. United States, 666 F.2d 43 (4th Cir. 1981)	§§ 5.28, 5.31
Doe, *In re,* 70 Haw. 32, 761 P.2d 299 (1988)	§ 7.30
Doe, *In re,* 97 N.M. 69, 636 P.2d 888 (Ct. App. 1981)	§ 3.19
Doe Children, *In re,* 93 Misc. 2d 479, 402 N.Y.S.2d 958 (1978)	§ 1.17
Donna K., *In re,* 132 A.D.2d 1004, 518 N.Y.S.2d 289 (1987)	§ 7.45
Dorothy I., *In re,* 162 Cal. App. 3d 1154, 209 Cal. Rptr. 5 (1984)	§ 6.3
Dorsett v. State, 761 S.W.2d 432 (Tex. Ct. App. 1988)	§ 4.50
Douglas v. Alabama, 380 U.S. 415 (1965)	§§ 7.50, 7.53, 7.54, 7.55, 7.56
Dovidio, *In re,* 56 Misc. 2d 79, 288 N.Y.S.2d 21 (Fam. Ct. 1968)	§ 1.18
Drake v. State, 400 So. 2d 1217 (Fla. 1981), *cert. denied,* 466 U.S. 978 (1984)	§ 6.24
Driskell v. State, 659 P.2d 343 (Okla. Crim. App. 1983)	§ 6.22
Drumbarger v. State, 716 P.2d 6 (Alaska Ct. App. 1986)	§§ 7.2, 7.3, 7.6, 7.30
D.T., *In re,* 229 N.J. Super. 509, 552 A.2d 189 (1988)	§ 3.30
Duckett v. State, 797 S.W.2d 906 (Tex. Crim. App. 1990)	§§ 4.9, 4.10, 4.42
Duffitt v. State, 519 N.E.2d 216 (Ind. Ct. App.), *aff'd,* 525 N.E.2d 607 (Ind. 1988)	§§ 2.22, 5.9, 8.3
Duley v. State, 56 Md. App. 275, 467 A.2d 776 (1983)	§ 3.31
Dull, *In re,* 521 N.E.2d 972 (Ind. Ct. App. 1988)	§ 3.20
Dunham v. State, 762 P.2d 969 (Okla. Crim. App. 1988)	§§ 2.14, 2.16, 2.17, 2.18
Dunnington v. State, 740 S.W.2d 896 (Tex. Ct. App. 1987)	§§ 4.44, 4.45

CASES

Case	*Book §*
Dutchess County Dep't of Social Servs. v. Bertha C., 130 Misc. 2d 1043, 498 N.Y.S.2d 960 (Fam. Ct. 1986)	§ 7.45
Dutton v. Evans, 400 U.S. 74 (1970)	§§ 7.44, 7.50, 7.51, 7.53
Dwayne M., *In re,* 287 S.C. 413, 339 S.E.2d 130 (1986)	§ 7.57
Edmonds v. State, 380 So. 2d 396 (Ala. Crim. App. 1980)	§ 4.28
Edwards v. State, 500 N.E.2d 1209 (Ind. 1986)	§ 5.37
E.G., *In re,* 133 Ill. 2d 98, 549 N.E.2d 322 (1989)	§ 3.17
E.H. v. Department of Health & Rehabilitation Servs., 443 So. 2d 1083 (Fla. Dist. Ct. App. 1984)	§ 1.17
Ellis v. State, 558 So. 2d 826 (Miss. 1990)	§ 7.53
Elmer v. State, 463 P.2d 14 (Wyo. 1969), *cert. denied,* 400 U.S. 845 (1970)	§ 7.31
E.M., *In re,* 137 Misc. 2d 197, 520 N.Y.S.2d 327 (Fam. Ct. 1987)	§ 4.10
E.P., *In re,* 167 Ill. App. 3d 534, 521 N.E.2d 603 (1988)	§§ 7.1, 7.57
Eslava v. State, 473 So. 2d 1143 (Ala. Crim. App. 1985)	§ 3.5
Estate of Ballard, *In re,* 210 Cal. App. 2d 799, 26 Cal. Rptr. 832 (1962)	§ 7.47
Estate of Hearst, *In re,* 67 Cal. App. 3d 777, 136 Cal. Rptr. 821 (1977)	§ 8.6
Estelle v. McGuire, 112 S. Ct. 475 (1991)	§§ 3.5, 3.9, 3.11, 3.12, 3.28, 3.29, 3.30, 4.17, 6.15, 6.17, 6.18
Everett v. State, 572 So. 2d 838 (Miss. 1990)	§§ 1.12, 1.16
Faleigh Fitkin-Paul Morgan Memorial Hosp. v. Anderson, 42 N.J. 421, 201 A.2d 537, *cert. denied,* 377 U.S. 985 (1964)	§ 3.17
Faretta v. California, 422 U.S. 806 (1975)	§ 8.9
Feist v. Feist, 236 Cal. App. 2d 433, 46 Cal. Rptr. 93 (1965)	§ 6.3
Fells v. State, 345 So. 2d 618 (Miss. 1977)	§ 7.26
Fitzgerald v. United States, 443 A.2d 1295 (D.C. 1982)	§§ 7.30, 7.31
Flanagan v. State, 586 So. 2d 1085 (Fla. Dist. Ct. App. 1991)	§§ 4.50, 6.18, 7.35, 7.39
Fleming v. State, 819 S.W.2d 237 (Tex. Ct. App. 1991)	§§ 7.35, 7.36
F.M. v. Old Cutler Presbyterian Church, Inc., 595 So. 2d 201 (Fla. Dist. Ct. App. 1992)	§ 1.12
Fortune v. Commonwealth, 416 S.E.2d 25 (Va. Ct. App. 1992)	§ 3.29
Fout v. State, 575 N.E.2d 340 (Ind. Ct. App. 1991)	§§ 3.28, 3.29
Frazier v. State, 195 Ga. App. 109, 393 S.E.2d 262 (1990)	§ 1.13
Freeman v. State, 681 P.2d 84 (Okla. Crim. App. 1984)	§ 6.17
Fricke v. State, 561 So. 2d 597 (Fla. Dist. Ct. App. 1990)	§ 7.46
Frisson v. State, 512 So. 2d 1092 (Fla. Dist. Ct. App. 1987)	§ 6.24
Frye v. United States, 293 F. 1013 (D.C. Cir. 1923)	§§ 3.5, 3.11, 3.15, 3.31, 4.18, 4.34
Fuhrman v. Fuhrman, 254 N.W.2d 97 (N.D. 1977)	§ 7.47

Case	*Book §*
Gale v. State, 792 P.2d 570 (Wyo. 1990)	§§ 4.45, 5.16
Gallagher v. Pequot Spring Water Co., 2 Conn. Cir. Ct. 354, 199 A.2d 172 (1963)	§ 7.47
Gannett Co. v. DePasquale, 443 U.S. 368 (1979)	§ 8.4
Garcia v. State, 629 S.W.2d 196 (Tex. Ct. App. 1982)	§ 7.56
Garcia v. Watkins, 604 F.2d 1297 (10th Cir. 1979)	§ 7.30
Garland v. Commonwealth, 8 Va. App. 189, 379 S.E.2d 146 (1989)	§ 7.31
Garrett v. Howden, 73 N.M. 307, 387 P.2d 874 (1963)	§ 7.29
Garza v. State, 828 S.W.2d 432 (Tex. Ct. App. 1992)	§ 7.46
Gault, *In re,* 387 U.S. 1 (1967)	§ 7.57
Geders v. United States, 425 U.S. 80 (1976)	§ 5.21
Geobel, *In re,* 26 Or. App. 251, 552 P.2d 281 (1976)	§ 3.19
George v. State, 306 Ark. 360, 813 S.W.2d 792 (1991)	§§ 7.30, 7.43, 7.46
Germany v. State, 235 Ga. 836, 221 S.E.2d 817 (1976)	§ 7.47
Gibbons v. State, 97 Nev. 299, 629 P.2d 1196 (1981)	§ 7.31
Gibbs v. State, 394 So. 2d 231 (Fla. Dist. Ct. App.), *aff'd,* 406 So. 2d 1113 (Fla. 1981)	§ 6.21
Gideon v. State, 721 P.2d 1336 (Okla. Crim. App. 1986)	§§ 3.8, 3.9, 3.11, 3.29
Giglio v. United States, 405 U.S. 150 (1972)	§ 5.21
Gillette v. United States, 401 U.S. 437, 91 S. Ct. 828 (1971)	§ 3.17
Gillion v. State, 573 So. 2d 810 (Fla. 1991)	§ 6.20
Glendening v. State, 536 So. 2d 212 (Fla. 1988), *cert. denied,* 492 U.S. 907 (1989)	§§ 4.37, 7.46, 8.8
Globe Newspaper Co. v. Superior Court, 457 U.S. 596 (1982)	§§ 5.23, 8.4, 8.5, 8.8
Globe Newspaper Co., *In re,* 729 F.2d 47 (1st Cir. 1984)	§ 8.6
Godfrey v. State, 258 Ga. 28, 365 S.E.2d 93, *on remand,* 187 Ga. App. 319, 370 S.E.2d 183 (1988)	§ 7.13
Goings v. United States, 377 F.2d 753 (8th Cir. 1967), *cert. denied,* 393 U.S. 883 (1968)	§ 5.13
Goldade v. State, 674 P.2d 721 (Wyo. 1983), *cert. denied,* 467 U.S. 1253 (1984)	§§ 7.35, 7.53
Goldberg v. Kelly, 397 U.S. 254 (1970)	§ 7.38
Goldhwaite v. Sheraton Restaurant, 154 Me. 214, 145 A.2d 362 (1958)	§ 7.47
Goldsberry v. United States, 598 A.2d 376 (D.C. 1991)	§ 7.53
Gonzales v. State, 818 S.W.2d 756 (Tex. Crim. App. 1991)	§ 8.8
Goodson v. State, 566 So. 2d 1142 (Miss. 1990)	§ 4.37
Goodwin v. State, 573 N.E.2d 895 (Ind. Ct. App. 1991)	§§ 1.12, 7.46
Goolsby v. State, 517 N.E.2d 54 (Ind. 1987)	§§ 2.15, 2.22, 7.30
Gotwald v. Gotwald, 768 S.W.2d 689 (Tenn. Ct. App. 1988)	§ 4.5
Gough v. General Box Co., 302 S.W.2d 884 (Mo. 1957)	§ 7.13
Government of Virgin Islands v. Edinborough, 625 F.2d 472 (3d Cir. 1980)	§ 8.2
Government of Virgin Islands v. Riley, 754 F. Supp. 61 (D.V.I. 1991)	§ 7.48

CASES

Case	*Book §*
Grand Jury Subpoena (Santarelli), *In re,* 740 F.2d 816 (11th Cir. 1984)	§ 1.12
Grantham v. State, 580 So. 2d 53 (Ala. Crim. App. 1991)	§§ 7.38, 7.51, 7.52
Griego v. State, 761 P.2d 973 (Wyo. 1988)	§§ 4.44, 4.45
Grier v. State, 257 Ga. 539, 361 S.E.2d 379 (1987)	§§ 3.13, 5.7
Griffin v. Griffin, 81 N.C. App. 665, 344 S.E.2d 828 (1986)	§§ 7.34, 7.47
Griffin v. State, 526 So. 2d 752 (Fla. Dist. Ct. App. 1988)	§§ 2.2, 2.15, 2.18, 2.19
Griffith v. State, 584 So. 2d 383 (Miss. 1991)	§ 7.48
Griggs v. Griggs, 707 S.W.2d 488 (Mo. Ct. App. 1986)	§ 1.18
Grodin v. Grodin, 102 Mich. App. 396, 301 N.W.2d 869 (1980)	§ 3.17
Gross v. Greer, 773 F.2d 116 (7th Cir. 1985)	§ 7.30
Haakanson v. State, 760 P.2d 1030 (Alaska Ct. App. 1988)	§ 4.50
Hagen, *In re,* 21 Wash. App. 169, 584 P.2d 446 (1978)	§ 3.25
Haggins v. Warden, 715 F.2d 1050 (6th Cir. 1983), *cert. denied,* 464 U.S. 1071 (1984)	§§ 7.30, 7.47
Hall v. State, 539 So. 2d 1338 (Miss. 1989)	§ 7.46
Hall v. State, 15 Ark. App. 309, 692 S.W.2d 769 (1985)	§§ 2.1, 2.18
Hambley v. State, 565 So. 2d 692 (Ala. Crim. App. 1990)	§ 1.1
Hamblin v. State, 268 Ark. 497, 597 S.W.2d 589 (1980)	§ 5.7
Hamling v. United States, 418 U.S. 87 (1974)	§ 1.1
Hancock v. State, 664 P.2d 1039 (Okla. Crim. App. 1983)	§ 6.22
Hanger v. United States, 398 F.2d 91 (8th Cir. 1968), *cert. denied,* 393 U.S. 119 (1969)	§ 7.24
Hardy v. Commonwealth, 719 S.W.2d 727 (Ky. 1986)	§ 5.7
Harrington v. California, 395 U.S. 250 (1969)	§ 7.54
Harris v. State, 257 Ga. 666, 362 S.E.2d 211 (1987)	§ 5.28
Harris, *Ex parte,* 461 So. 2d 1332 (Ala. 1984)	§ 2.1
Harvey v. State, 604 P.2d 586 (Alaska 1979)	§ 6.17
Harvey v. State, 579 So. 2d 22 (Ala. Crim. App. 1990)	§ 3.11
Harville v. State, 386 So. 2d 776 (Ala. Crim. App. 1980)	§ 7.30
Hauk v. State, 148 Ind. 238, 46 N.E. 127 (1897), *reh'g denied,* 148 Ind. 238, 47 N.E. 465, *overruled on other grounds by* White v. State, 234 Ind. 209, 125 N.E.2d 705 (1955)	§ 1.12
Haynes v. Commonwealth, 69 Va. (28 Gratt.) 942 (1877)	§ 7.31
Head v. State, 519 N.E.2d 151 (Ind. 1988)	§§ 2.14, 2.18, 4.44, 4.45
Heckathorne v. State, 697 S.W.2d 8 (Tex. Ct. App. 1985)	§§ 2.1, 2.14, 2.15, 2.18, 7.31
Heinemann's Appeal, 96 Pa. 112 (1880)	§ 3.17
Helvey v. Rednour, 86 Ill. App. 3d 154, 408 N.E.2d 17 (1980)	§ 3.20
Hendricks v. State, 554 N.E.2d 1140 (Ind. Ct. App.), *aff'd in part,* 562 N.E.2d 725 (Ind. 1990)	§ 5.21
Henry Vogt Mach. Co. v. Chamberlain, 279 S.W.2d 224 (Ky. 1955)	§ 7.49
Henson v. State, 535 N.E.2d 1189 (Ind. 1989)	§ 4.34
Hermanson v. State, 570 So. 2d 322 (Fla. Dist. Ct. App. 1990)	§ 3.17

Case	Book §
Hern v. State, 97 Nev. 529, 635 P.2d 278 (1981)	§ 3.28
Hernandez v. State, 643 S.W.2d 397 (Tex. Crim. App. 1982), *cert. denied,* 462 U.S. 1144 (1983)	§ 5.7
Hester v. Commonwealth, 734 S.W.2d 457 (Ky.), *cert. denied,* 484 U.S. 989 (1987)	§ 4.45
Hester v. State, 187 Ga. App. 873, 371 S.E.2d 684 (1988)	§§ 2.1, 2.15, 2.16, 2.18
Hewitt v. Grand Trunk W.R. Co., 123 Mich. App. 309, 333 N.W.2d 264 (1983)	§ 7.27
Hicks v. Hicks, 249 Cal. App. 2d 964, 58 Cal. Rptr. 63 (1967)	§ 6.3
Hicks v. Reese, 624 F. Supp. 1116 (W.D.N.C. 1986)	§ 6.19
Hicks v. State, 713 P.2d 18 (Okla. Crim. App. 1986)	§ 2.10
Hicks v. State, 175 Ga. App. 243, 333 S.E.2d 113 (1985)	§ 2.12
Hilburn v. State, 765 P.2d 1382 (Alaska Ct. App. 1988)	§ 5.7
Hildreth v. Key, 341 S.W.2d 601 (Mo. Ct. App. 1960)	§§ 2.1, 2.18
Hilyer v. Howat Concrete Co., 578 F.2d 422 (D.C. Cir. 1978)	§§ 7.27, 7.30
Hirst v. Gertzen, 676 F.2d 1252 (9th Cir. 1982)	§ 6.24
H.K., *In re,* 455 N.W.2d 529 (Minn. Ct. App. 1990)	§ 3.24
Hodges v. State, 524 N.E.2d 774 (Ind. 1988)	§§ 1.4, 2.1, 2.15, 2.18, 5.37, 6.21, 7.50
Hoener v. Bertinato, 67 N.J. Super. 517, 171 A.2d 140 (Juv. Dom. Rel. Ct. 1961)	§ 3.17
Holder v. State, 272 Ind. 52, 396 N.E.2d 112 (1979)	§ 5.16
Holesome v. State, 40 Wis. 2d 95, 161 N.W.2d 283 (1968)	§ 1.1
Holland v. State, 802 S.W.2d 696 (Tex. Crim. App. 1991)	§§ 7.31, 7.46
Hollenquest v. State, 394 So. 2d 385 (Ala. Crim. App. 1980) *cert. denied,* 394 So. 2d 389 (1981)	§ 7.31
Hopkins v. State, 579 N.E.2d 1297 (Ind. 1991)	§ 4.26
Hopper v. State, 489 N.E.2d 1209 (Ind. Ct. App.), *cert. denied,* 479 U.S. 992 (1986)	§ 7.30
Hosford v. State, 525 So. 2d 789 (Miss. 1988)	§ 7.50
Houston v. State, 531 So. 2d 598 (Miss. 1988)	§ 6.15
Houston Oxygen Co. v. Davis, 139 Tex. 1, 161 S.W.2d 474 (1942)	§ 7.27
Huddleston v. United States, 485 U.S. 681 (1988)	§§ 6.13, 6.15, 6.16, 6.18
Huerta v. State, 635 S.W.2d 847 (Tex. Ct. App. 1982)	§ 3.5
Huff v. White Motor Corp., 609 F.2d 286 (7th Cir. 1979)	§§ 7.43, 7.44
Huggins v. State, 184 Ga. App. 540, 362 S.E.2d 120 (1987)	§§ 2.16, 2.18
Hughes v. Detroit, G.H.& M. Ry., 65 Mich. 10, 31 N.W. 603 (1887)	§ 2.18
Hunter v. State, 172 Ind. App. 397, 360 N.E.2d 588, *cert. denied,* 434 U.S. 906 (1977)	§ 1.12
Hunter v. State, 194 Ga. App. 711, 391 S.E.2d 695 (1990)	§§ 2.18, 8.3
Idaho v. Wright, 110 S. Ct. 3139 (1990)	§§ 2.19, 4.5, 7.4, 7.23, 7.28, 7.42, 7.43, 7.44, 7.46, 7.49, 7.51, 7.53
Illinois v. Allen, 397 U.S. 337 (1970)	§§ 7.58, 8.13

CASES

Case	*Book §*
Ingram v. McQuiston, 261 N.C. 392, 134 S.E.2d 705 (1964)	§ 4.12
Inmon v. State, 585 So. 2d 261 (Ala. Crim. App. 1991)	§§ 6.14, 6.18, 7.31, 7.53
Ivy v. State, 522 So. 2d 740 (Miss. 1988)	§§ 2.3, 5.7, 8.14
J. Children, *In re,* 664 P.2d 1158 (Utah 1983)	§ 3.25
Jackson v. State, 239 Ala. 38, 193 So. 417 (1940)	§ 2.1
Jackson v. State, 290 Ark. 375, 720 S.W.2d 282 (1986)	§ 5.17
Jackson v. State, 198 Ga. App. 447, 402 S.E.2d 279 (1991)	§ 6.21
Jackson v. United States, 503 A.2d 1225 (D.C. 1986)	§ 5.17
Jaclyn P., *In re,* 578 N.Y.S.2d 252 (A.D. 1992)	§ 7.47
Jacobs, *In re,* 433 Mich. 24, 444 N.W.2d 789 (1989)	§ 3.22
Jacobson v. Massachusetts, 197 U.S. 11, 25 S. Ct. 358 (1905)	§ 3.17
Jager v. State, 748 P.2d 1172 (Alaska Ct. App. 1988)	§ 5.30
James A., *In re,* 505 A.2d 1386 (R.I. 1986)	§§ 7.35, 7.57
James B., *In re,* 166 Cal. App. 3d 934, 212 Cal. Rptr. 778 (1985)	§§ 3.11, 3.30
Jamie M., *In re,* 134 Cal. App. 3d 530, 184 Cal. Rptr. 778 (1982)	§ 3.21
Jamie V., *In re,* 111 A.D.2d 949, 490 N.Y.S.2d 45 (1985)	§ 3.24
J.C.O. v. Anderson, 734 P.2d 458 (Utah 1987)	§ 3.25
J.D.S., *In re,* 436 N.W.2d 342 (Iowa 1989)	§§ 7.56, 7.57, 8.8
Jean Marie W., *In re,* 559 A.2d 625 (R.I. 1989)	§§ 7.2, 7.3, 7.6, 7.8, 7.30, 7.35
Jefferson v. Griffin Spalding County Hosp. Auth., 247 Ga. 86, 274 S.E.2d 457 (1981)	§ 3.17
Jennette v. State, 197 Ga. App. 580, 398 S.E.2d 734 (1990)	§§ 4.45, 4.50, 5.9, 5.11, 6.21, 7.56
Jensen, *In re,* 54 Or. App. 1, 633 P.2d 1302 (1981)	§ 3.17
Jessica R., *In re,* 78 N.Y.2d 1031, 581 N.E.2d 1332, 576 N.Y.S.2d 77 (1991)	§ 5.16
Jessica Z., *In re,* 135 Misc. 2d 520, 515 N.Y.S.2d 370 (Fam. Ct. 1987)	§ 3.15
Jimmerson v. State, 190 Ga. App. 759, 380 S.E.2d 65 (1989)	§ 5.35
J.L.B., *In re,* 182 Mont. 100, 594 P.2d 1127 (1979)	§ 3.20
J.L.G., *In re,* 762 P.2d 42 (Wyo. 1988)	§ 7.38
Johns v. State, 181 Ga. App. 510, 352 S.E.2d 826 (1987)	§ 7.56
Johnson v. State, 259 Ga. 403, 383 S.E.2d 118 (1989)	§ 5.11
Johnson v. State, 525 So. 2d 809 (Miss. 1988)	§ 5.25
Johnson v. State, 292 Ark. 632, 732 S.W.2d 817 (1987)	§§ 4.13, 4.37
Johnson v. State, 484 N.E.2d 49 (Ind. Ct. App. 1985)	§ 2.1
Johnson v. State, 63 Md. App. 485, 492 A.2d 1343 (1985)	§ 7.49
Johnson v. United States, 333 U.S. 46 (1948)	§ 5.9
Johnston v. Earle, 313 F.2d 686 (9th Cir. 1962), *cert. denied,* 373 U.S. 910 (1963)	§ 5.11
Jonas v. State, 773 P.2d 960 (Alaska Ct. App. 1989)	§§ 2.22, 5.16
Jovann B., In re, 153 A.D.2d 858, 545 N.Y.S.2d 376 (1989)	§§ 3.19, 3.26

Case	*Book §*
J.R.B., *In re,* 715 P.2d 1170 (Alaska 1986)	§ 4.11
J.S. v. Commonwealth Dep't Pub. Welfare, 129 Pa. Commw. 382, 565 A.2d 862 (1989)	§ 3.2
J.S., *In re,* 140 Vt. 458, 438 A.2d 1125 (1981)	§ 8.5
J.V. v. State, 516 So. 2d 1133 (Fla. Dist. Ct. App. 1987)	§ 3.17
Kalafut v. Gruver, 239 Va. 278, 389 S.E.2d 681 (1990)	§ 3.17
Kauffmann v. Commonwealth, 8 Va. App. 400, 382 S.E.2d 279 (1989)	§§ 7.31, 7.33
Kehinde v. Commonwealth, 1 Va. App. 342, 338 S.E.2d 356 (1986)	§§ 2.12, 5.8
Keith R., *In re,* 123 Misc. 2d 617, 474 N.Y.S.2d 254 (Fam. Ct. 1984)	§ 3.18
Kelly v. Brown, 529 A.2d 271 (Del. Fam. Ct. 1987)	§ 1.19
Kelly v. Commonwealth, 8 Va. App. 359, 382 S.E.2d 270 (1989)	§ 3.32
Kelly v. State, 452 N.E.2d 907 (Ind. 1983)	§ 5.36
Kelly v. State, 197 Ga. App. 811, 399 S.E.2d 568 (1990)	§ 1.13
Kenney v. Lewis Revels Rare Coins, Inc., 741 F.2d 378 (11th Cir. 1984)	§ 7.7
Kent v. United States, 383 U.S. 541 (1966)	§ 5.25
Kentucky v. Stincer, 482 U.S. 730 (1987)	§§ 1.13, 2.18, 2.21, 7.50, 7.56, 7.57
Kern v. State, 237 Ind. 144, 144 N.E.2d 705 (1957)	§ 7.47
Kerr v. Caspari, 956 F.2d 788 (8th Cir. 1992)	§ 6.21
Kerry O., *In re,* 210 Cal. App. 3d 326, 258 Cal. Rptr. 448 (1989)	§§ 7.57, 7.58
K.H. v. Department of Health & Rehab. Servs., 527 So. 2d 230 (Fla. Dist. Ct. App. 1988)	§ 3.17
Kilgore v. State, 177 Ga. App. 656, 340 S.E.2d 640 (1986)	§ 7.30
Kipp v. State, 802 S.W.2d 804 (Tex. Ct. App. 1990)	§ 2.18
Kirkpatrick v. State, 747 S.W.2d 833 (Tex. Ct. App. 1987)	§ 4.45
K.M., *In re,* 149 Vt. 109, 539 A.2d 549 (1987)	§§ 3.16, 3.24
Kofford v. Flora, 744 P.2d 1343 (Utah 1987)	§ 4.17
Kosbruk v. State, 820 P.2d 1082 (Alaska Ct. App. 1991)	§§ 4.20, 7.18, 7.31
Koshman v. Superior Court, 111 Cal. App. 3d 294, 168 Cal. Rptr. 558 (1980)	§ 1.18
Krulewitch v. United States, 336 U.S. 440 (1949)	§ 7.54
K.S., *In re,* 737 P.2d 170 (Utah 1987)	§§ 3.24, 6.6
Lacey v. State, 803 P.2d 1364 (Wyo. 1990)	§ 7.22
Lancaster v. People, 200 Colo. 448, 615 P.2d 720 (1980)	§§ 2.19, 7.28, 7.29, 7.30, 7.44, 7.48, 7.49
Lantrip v. Commonwealth, 713 S.W.2d 816 (Ky. 1986)	§ 6.21
Larissa W., *In re,* 227 Cal. App. 3d 124, 277 Cal. Rptr. 802 (1991)	§ 3.30
Laubach v. Indus. Indem. Co., 286 Or. 217, 593 P.2d 1146 (1979)	§ 7.47
Lawrence v. State, 464 N.E.2d 923 (Ind. 1984)	§ 4.45
Lawrence v. State, 796 P.2d 1176 (Okla. Crim. App. 1990)	§ 4.45

CASES

Case	Book §
Lawson v. State, 377 So. 2d 1115 (Ala. Crim. App. 1979)	§ 7.31
Leatherwood v. State, 548 So. 2d 389 (Miss. 1989)	§§ 7.30, 7.45
Lee v. Illinois, 476 U.S. 530 (1986)	§§ 7.50, 7.54
Leif Z., *In re*, 105 Misc. 2d 973, 431 N.Y.S.2d 290 (Fam. Ct. 1980)	§ 3.18
Lewallen v. State, 199 Ga. App. 798, 406 S.E.2d 255 (1991)	§ 5.9
Lewin v. Jackson, 108 Ariz. 27, 492 P.2d 406 (1972)	§ 2.22
Lewis v. State, 161 Ga. App. 209, 288 S.E.2d 278 (1982)	§ 7.35
Leybourne v. Commonwealth, 222 Va. 374, 282 S.E.2d 12 (1981)	§ 7.31
Lickey v. State, 827 P.2d 824 (Nev. 1992)	§ 4.45
Limber v. State, 264 Ark. 479, 572 S.W.2d 402 (1978)	§§ 6.17, 6.18
Linda S., *In re*, 148 Misc. 2d 169, 560 N.Y.S.2d 181 (Fam. Ct. 1990)	§ 7.43
L.K.S., *In re*, 451 N.W.2d 819 (Iowa 1990)	§§ 2.18, 7.57
Logan v. State, 299 Ark. 266, 773 S.W.2d 413 (1989)	§ 2.18
Logan v. State, 300 Ark. 35, 776 S.W.2d 341 (1989)	§§ 2.1, 5.32
Long, *In re*, 313 N.W.2d 473 (Iowa 1981)	§ 7.57
Longfellow v. State, 803 P.2d 848 (Wyo. 1990)	§§ 3.28, 6.13
Lord Mohun's Trial, 12 How. St. Tr. 949 (1691)	§ 2.13
Loretta Lynn W., *In re*, 149 A.D.2d 928, 540 N.Y.S.2d 62 (1989)	§ 3.25
Love v. State, 64 Wis. 2d 432, 219 N.W.2d 294 (1974)	§ 7.30
Luce v. United States, 469 U.S. 38 (1984)	§ 5.21
Luck v. United States, 348 F.2d 763 (D.C. Cir. 1965)	§ 5.25
Lujan v. United States, 209 F.2d 190 (10th Cir. 1953)	§ 2.13
Lyle v. Koehler, 720 F.2d 426 (6th Cir. 1983)	§ 7.11
Lyles v. State, 412 So. 2d 458 (Fla. Dist. Ct. App. 1982)	§ 7.30
Lytle v. State, 816 P.2d 1082 (Nev. 1991)	§ 7.46
M.A. v. J.A., 781 S.W.2d 94 (Mo. Ct. App. 1989)	§ 3.18
Mackall v. Commonwealth, 236 Va. 240, 372 S.E.2d 759 (1988), *cert. denied,* 492 U.S. 925 (1989)	§§ 2.1, 2.10, 2.12, 2.18
Malinda S, *In re*, 51 Cal. 3d 368, 795 P.2d 1244, 272 Cal. Rptr. 787 (1990)	§§ 7.47, 7.57
Mancusi v. Stubbs, 408 U.S. 204 (1972)	§§ 7.48, 7.51, 7.52, 7.53, 7.55
Manocchio v. Moran, 919 F.2d 770 (1st Cir. 1990), *cert. denied,* 111 S. Ct. 1695 (1991)	§§ 7.39, 7.53
Maraziti, *In re*, 233 N.J. Super. 488, 559 A.2d 447 (1989)	§ 1.12
Marcum v. State, 299 Ark. 30, 771 S.W.2d 250 (1989)	§ 4.28
Marriage of Cavitt, *In re*, 564 S.W.2d 53 (Mo. Ct. App. 1978)	§ 7.47
Marriage of L.R., *In re*, 202 Ill. App. 3d 69, 559 N.E.2d 779 (1990)	§§ 7.30, 7.44
Marriage of Williams, *In re*, 303 N.W.2d 160 (Iowa 1981)	§ 7.47
Marroni v. Matey, 82 F.R.D. 371 (E.D. Pa. 1979)	§ 1.19
Martha, *In re*, 407 Mass. 319, 553 N.E.2d 902 (1990)	§ 7.56
Martin v. Commonwealth, 4 Va. App. 438, 358 S.E.2d 415 (1987)	§ 7.30

Case	*Book §*
Martin v. State, 747 P.2d 316 (Okla. Crim. App. 1987)	§ 8.7
Martin v. State, 584 S.W.2d 830 (Tenn. Ct. App. 1979)	§ 6.20
Martinez v. State, 822 S.W.2d 276 (Tex. Ct. App. 1991)	§ 5.15
Martinez v. State, 732 S.W.2d 401 (Tex. Ct. App. 1987)	§§ 2.1, 7.46
Mary S., *In re,* 186 Cal. App. 3d 414, 230 Cal. Rptr. 726 (1986)	§ 7.57
Maryland v. Craig, 110 S. Ct. 3157 (1990)	§§ 7.48, 7.49, 7.50, 7.51, 8.8
Mason v. State, 511 N.E.2d 487 (Ind. Ct. App. 1987)	§ 5.37
Mathews v. United States, 485 U.S. 58 (1988)	§ 3.29
Matthews v. Superior Court, 201 Cal. App. 3d 385, 247 Cal. Rptr. 226 (1988)	§§ 6.1, 6.22
Matthews, *In re,* 714 F.2d 223 (2d Cir. 1983)	§ 1.12
Mattox v. United States, 156 U.S. 237 (1895)	§§ 7.50, 7.51
Maynard v. State, 513 N.E.2d 641 (Ind. 1987)	§§ 2.15, 5.32, 6.21
M.C., *In re,* 391 N.W.2d 674 (S.D. 1986)	§ 1.17
MCA, Inc. v. Wilson, 425 F. Supp. 443 (S.D.N.Y. 1976), *aff'd and modified,* 677 F.2d 180 (2d Cir. 1981)	§ 7.27
McAdoo v. United States, 515 A.2d 412 (D.C. 1986)	§ 5.25
McAllister, *Ex parte,* 541 So. 2d 1104 (Ala. 1989)	§§ 2.9, 7.57
McCafferty v. Leapley, 944 F.2d 445 (8th Cir. 1991), *cert. denied,* 112 S. Ct. 1277 (1992)	§ 7.44
McCafferty v. Solem, 449 N.W.2d 590 (S.D. 1989)	§ 4.45
McCartney v. State, 262 Ga. 156, 414 S.E.2d 227 (1992)	§ 3.5
McCrary v. State, 176 Ga. App. 683, 337 S.E.2d 442 (1985)	§ 2.15
McCray v. Illinois, 386 U.S. 300 (1967)	§ 7.57
McEachern v. State, 474 N.E.2d 1034 (Ind. Ct. App. 1985)	§ 2.12
McFee v. State, 511 So. 2d 130 (Miss. 1987)	§ 6.20
McGowan v. State, 198 Ga. App. 575, 402 S.E.2d 328 (1991)	§ 6.21
McGuire v. State, 288 Ark. 388, 706 S.W.2d 360 (1986)	§§ 8.10, 8.11
McLean v. United States, 377 A.2d 74 (D.C. 1977)	§ 5.29
M.E., *In re,* 715 S.W.2d 572 (Mo. Ct. App. 1986)	§ 4.35
M.E. v. M.E.E., 715 S.W.2d 572 (Mo. Ct. App. 1986)	§ 7.8
Meeboer, *In re,* 134 Mich. App. 294, 350 N.W.2d 868 (1984)	§§ 7.30, 7.44
Menges v. Board of County Comm'rs, 290 Or. 251, 621 P.2d 562 (1980)	§ 7.47
M.H., *In re,* 745 S.W.2d 424 (Tex. Ct. App. 1988)	§ 3.19
M.H, *In re,* 367 N.W.2d 275 (Iowa Ct. App. 1985)	§ 6.6
Michael C., *In re,* 557 A.2d 1219 (R.I. 1989)	§ 7.57
Michael R., *In re,* 197 Cal. App. 3d 284, 242 Cal. Rptr. 814 (1987)	§ 6.6
Michaels v. Michaels, 767 F.2d 1185 (7th Cir. 1985), *cert. denied,* 474 U.S. 1057 (1986)	§ 7.27
Michelson v. United States, 335 U.S. 469 (1948)	§§ 6.1, 6.7, 6.8
Michigan v. Lucas, 111 S. Ct. 1743 (1991)	§ 5.28
Middlebrooks v. State, 253 Ga. 707, 324 S.E.2d 192 (1985)	§ 2.18

Case	Book §
Middleton v State, 194 Ga. App. 815, 392 S.E.2d 293 (1990)	§ 2.15
Miguel L., *In re,* 32 Cal. 3d 100, 649 P.2d 703, 185 Cal. Rptr. 120 (1982)	§ 7.47
Miller v. Basbas, 131 N.H. 332, 553 A.2d 299 (1988)	§ 1.19
Miller v. State, 575 N.E.2d 272 (Ind. 1991)	§ 4.11
Miller v. State, 531 N.E.2d 466 (Ind. 1988)	§ 7.46
Miller v. State, 105 Nev. 497, 779 P.2d 87 (1989)	§ 5.34
Miraglia v. Miraglia, 462 So. 2d 507 (Fla. Dist. Ct. App. 1984)	§ 1.18
Mitchell v. Commonwealth, 777 S.W.2d 930 (Ky. 1989)	§ 4.50
Mitchell v. Davis, 205 S.W.2d 812 (Tex. Civ. App. 1947)	§ 3.17
Mitchell v. State, 473 So. 2d 591 (Ala. Crim. App. 1985)	§§ 2.1, 2.18
M.L.S., *In re,* 234 Neb. 570, 452 N.W.2d 39 (1990)	§§ 2.1, 2.18
M.N.D. v. B.M.D., 356 N.W.2d 813 (Minn. Ct. App. 1984)	§§ 7.43, 7.44, 7.45
M.O., *In re,* 13 Kan. App. 2d 381, 770 P.2d 856 (1989)	§ 7.57
Moates v. State, 545 So. 2d 224 (Ala. Crim. App. 1989)	§ 2.9
Moll v. State, 351 N.W.2d 639 (Minn. Ct. App. 1984)	§ 2.18
Monn v. State, 811 P.2d 1004 (Wyo. 1991)	§§ 7.19, 7.20
Montana v. Imlay, No. 91-687 (U.S. 1992)	§ 4.47
Montgomery v. State, 810 S.W.2d 372 (Tex. Crim. App. 1990)	§§ 6.1, 6.13, 6.18, 6.21, 7.6
Montoya v. State, 822 P.2d 363 (Wyo. 1991)	§§ 4.28, 4.45
Moor v. State, 709 P.2d 498 (Alaska Ct. App. 1985)	§ 6.21
Moore v. State, 530 So. 2d 61 (Fla. Dist. Ct. App. 1988)	§ 3.29
Moore v. State, 703 S.W.2d 762 (Tex. Ct. App. 1985)	§ 5.17
Moore v. State, 26 Md. App. 556, 338 A.2d 344 (1975)	§ 7.49
Morgan v. Foretich, 846 F.2d 941 (4th Cir. 1988)	§§ 2.19, 7.1, 7.29, 7.30, 7.35, 7.36, 7.44, 7.45, 7.49
Morrison v. State, 252 S.W.2d 97 (Mo. Ct. App. 1952)	§ 3.17
Moser v. Moser, 82 S.D. 149, 143 N.W.2d 369 (1966)	§ 2.18
Moser, *In re,* 27 Or. App. 31, 554 P.2d 1022 (1976)	§ 1.17
Moss v. Ole South Real Estate, Inc., 933 F.2d 1300 (5th Cir. 1991)	§ 7.39
Mounce v. Commonwealth, 795 S.W.2d 375 (Ky. 1990)	§ 7.30
M.R., *In re,* 334 N.W.2d 848 (N.D. 1983)	§ 6.6
Murdoch v. Murdoch, 200 Neb. 429, 264 N.W.2d 183 (1978)	§ 7.47
Murray v. State, 770 P.2d 1131 (Alaska Ct. App. 1989)	§§ 4.8, 7.45
Murriel v. State, 515 So. 2d 952 (Miss. 1987)	§ 5.8
Mutual Life Ins. Co. v. Hillmon, 145 U.S. 285 (1892)	§§ 7.32, 7.34
M.V., *In re,* 742 P.2d 326 (Colo. 1987)	§§ 3.9, 3.11, 3.30
M.W., *In re,* 374 N.W.2d 889 (S.D. 1985)	§ 7.57
Nagle v. Hooks, 296 Md. 123, 460 A.2d 49 (1983)	§ 1.12
Nassau County Dep't of Social Servs. v. Steven K., 574 N.Y.S.2d 767 (A.D. 1991)	§ 7.47
N.C.K., *In re,* 411 N.W.2d 577 (Minn. Ct. App. 1987)	§ 3.21

Case	Book §
Nelson v. Farrey, 874 F.2d 1222 (7th Cir. 1989), *cert. denied,* 493 U.S. 1042 (1990)	§§ 7.44, 7.53
Nelson v. O'Neil, 402 U.S. 622 (1971)	§§ 7.51, 7.54
New York v. Ferber, 458 U.S. 747 (1982)	§ 8.8
Newbury v. State, 695 P.2d 531 (Okla. Crim. App. 1985)	§ 7.30
Newton v. State, 456 N.E.2d 736 (Ind. Ct. App. 1983)	§§ 5.7, 5.8
N.H., *In re,* 569 A.2d 1179 (D.C. 1990)	§ 1.17
Nicholson v. State, 579 So. 2d 816 (Fla. Dist. Ct. App. 1991)	§ 3.27
Nicole V., *In re,* 71 N.Y.2d 112, 518 N.E.2d 914, 524 N.Y.S.2d 19 (1987)	§§ 4.1, 4.10, 7.45
Nitz v. State, 720 P.2d 55 (Alaska Ct. App. 1986)	§§ 7.21, 7.23
Nixon v. Warner Communications, 435 U.S. 589 (1978)	§ 8.6
Niziolek v. Ashe, 694 F.2d 282 (1st Cir. 1982)	§ 5.23
Noel M., *In re,* 23 Conn. App. 410, 580 A.2d 996 (1990)	§§ 4.45, 7.23, 7.57
Noles v. State, 172 Ga. App. 228, 322 S.E.2d 910 (1984)	§ 2.1
Norma M., *In re,* 77 Cal. App. 3d 110, 143 Cal. Rptr. 412 (1978)	§ 6.6
Norris v. Gatts, 738 P.2d 344 (Alaska 1987)	§ 4.11
Nussdorf v. State, 526 So. 2d 174 (Fla. Dist. Ct. App. 1988)	§ 2.12
Nusunginya v. State, 730 P.2d 172 (Alaska Ct. App. 1986)	§ 7.23
Ochs v. Martinez, 789 S.W.2d 949 (Tex. Ct. App. 1990)	§ 4.45
O.E.P., *In re,* 654 P.2d 312 (Colo. 1982)	§ 7.30
Ohio v. Roberts, 448 U.S. 56 (1980)	§§ 7.48, 7.50, 7.51, 7.52, 7.53, 7.55, 7.56
Olden v. Kentucky, 488 U.S. 227 (1988)	§ 5.21
Oldham v. State, 467 N.E.2d 419 (Ind. Ct. App. 1984)	§ 2.18
Oldham v. State, 167 Tex. Crim. 644, 322 S.W.2d 616 (1959)	§ 7.49
Oldsen v. People, 732 P.2d 1132 (Colo. 1986)	§§ 7.35, 7.36, 7.44, 7.49
Orsini v. State, 281 Ark. 348, 665 S.W.2d 245 (1984), *cert. denied,* 111 S. Ct. 1093 (1991)	§ 6.19
Ortiz v. State, 188 Ga. App. 532, 374 S.E.2d 92 (1988)	§§ 8.3, 8.8
Owens v. State, 514 N.E.2d 1257 (Ind. 1987)	§§ 3.5, 4.21, 4.28
Page v. State, 274 Ind. 264, 410 N.E.2d 1304 (1980)	§§ 2.18, 5.16
Page v. Zordan, 564 So. 2d 500 (Fla. Dist. Ct. App. 1990)	§ 4.36
Pardo v. State, 596 So. 2d 665 (Fla. 1991)	§ 7.46
Parental Rights of P.P., *In re,* 648 P.2d 512 (Wyo. 1982)	§ 1.17
Park v. Huff, 493 F.2d 923 (1974), *withdrawn on other grounds,* 506 F.2d 849 (5th Cir.), *cert. denied,* 423 U.S. 824 (1975)	§ 7.11
Pasco, *In re,* 150 Mich. App. 816, 389 N.W.2d 188 (1986)	§ 6.6
Pavlovic, *In re,* 124 A.D.2d 732, 508 N.Y.S.2d 234	§ 3.25
Payne v. State, 21 Ark. App. 243, 731 S.W.2d 235 (1987)	§§ 3.29, 6.23
Peebles v. State, 305 Ark. 338, 808 S.W.2d 331 (1991)	§§ 3.5, 4.10
Peek v. State, 488 So. 2d 52 (Fla. 1986)	§ 6.24

CASES

Case	*Book §*
Peisach v. Antuna, 539 So. 2d 544 (Fla. Dist. Ct. App. 1989)	§ 1.18
Pendleton v. Commonwealth, 685 S.W.2d 549 (Ky. 1985)	§§ 2.1, 2.12, 2.18, 6.22, 8.1
Penelope B., *In re,* 104 Wash. 2d 643, 709 P.2d 1185 (1985)	§§ 4.35, 7.2, 7.12
Pennington v. State, 24 Ark. App. 70, 749 S.W.2d 680 (1988)	§§ 7.23, 7.30
Pennsylvania v. Ritchie, 480 U.S. 39 (1987)	§§ 1.13, 1.14, 1.15, 4.1, 5.1, 7.1
People v. Abair, 134 A.D.2d 743, 521 N.Y.S.2d 560 (1987)	§ 5.11
People v. Alfaro, 61 Cal. App. 3d 414, 132 Cal. Rptr. 356 (1976)	§ 7.31
People v. Amos, 163 Mich. App. 50, 414 N.W.2d 147 (1987)	§ 1.12
People v. Anita B., 592 N.E.2d 274 (Ill. Ct. App. 1992)	§ 7.44
People v. Arbo, 213 Ill. App. 3d 828, 572 N.E.2d 417 (1991)	§ 7.7
People v. Arenda, 416 Mich. 1, 330 N.W.2d 814 (1982)	§ 5.28
People v. Arguello, 737 P.2d 436 (Colo. Ct. App. 1987)	§ 7.48
People v. Armendariz, 37 Cal. 3d 573, 693 P.2d 243, 209 Cal. Rptr. 664 (1984)	§ 7.3
People v. Ashmus, 2 Cal. Rptr. 2d 112, 820 P.2d 214 (1991)	§ 4.22
People v. Baggett, 185 Ill. App. 3d 1007, 541 N.E.2d 1266 (1989)	§ 7.31
People v. Balle, 1992 WL 12591 (Ill. Ct. App. 1992)	§§ 3.28, 3.29
People v. Bashara, 677 P.2d 1376 (Colo. Ct. App. 1983)	§ 7.30
People v. Basir, 578 N.Y.S.2d 603 (A.D. 1992)	§§ 3.30, 6.18
People v. Bastien, 129 Ill. 2d 64, 541 N.E.2d 670 (1989)	§§ 7.51, 8.7, 8.8
People v. Battaglia, 156 Cal. App. 3d 1058, 203 Cal. Rptr. 370 (1984)	§ 1.16
People v. Beckley, 434 Mich. 691, 456 N.W.2d 391 (1990)	§§ 4.10, 4.32, 4.37, 4.44, 5.16
People v. Belasco, 125 Cal. App. 3d 974, 178 Cal. Rptr. 461 (1981), *cert. denied,* 456 U.S. 979 (1982)	§ 7.31
People v. Benjamin R., 103 A.D.2d 663, 481 N.Y.S.2d 827 (1984)	§ 4.44
People v. Bernal, 10 Cal. 66 (1858)	§ 2.2
People v. Bessettem, 564 N.Y.S.2d 605 (A.D. 1991)	§ 7.41
People v. Bianchino, 5 Cal. App. 633, 91 P. 112 (1907)	§ 7.31
People v. Bias, 170 Cal. App. 2d 502, 339 P.2d 204 (1959)	§ 7.24
People v. Bledsoe, 36 Cal. 3d 236, 681 P.2d 291, 203 Cal. Rptr. 450 (1984)	§§ 4.18, 4.34, 4.44
People v. Born, 156 Ill. App. 3d 584, 509 N.E.2d 125 (1987)	§§ 2.1, 2.18
People v. Bowers, 801 P.2d 511 (Colo. 1990)	§§ 7.1, 7.8, 7.44, 7.45, 7.46
People v. Bowker, 203 Cal. App. 3d 385, 249 Cal. Rptr. 886 (1988)	§§ 4.33, 4.44

Case	Book §
People v. Boyette, 201 Cal. App. 3d 1527, 247 Cal. Rptr. 795 (1988)	§§ 1.14, 8.14
People v. Branch, 158 Ill. App. 3d 338, 511 N.E.2d 872 (1987)	§ 7.31
People v. Breitweiser, 38 Ill. App. 3d 1066, 349 N.E.2d 454 (1976)	§ 2.18
People v. Brewer, 127 Ill. App. 3d 306, 468 N.E.2d 1242 (1984)	§§ 2.1, 2.12, 2.14, 2.15, 2.22, 5.16
People v. Broomfield, 163 A.D.2d 403, 558 N.Y.S.2d 126 (1990)	§ 7.20
People v. Brown, 214 Ill. App. 3d 836, 574 N.E.2d 190 (1991)	§ 6.24
People v. Brown, 199 Ill. App. 3d 860, 557 N.E.2d 611 (1990)	§§ 3.9, 3.28, 3.29, 6.13, 6.15, 6.17
People v. Brown, 170 Ill. App. 3d 273, 524 N.E.2d 742 (1988)	§ 7.30
People v. Buhrle, 744 P.2d 747 (Colo. 1987)	§ 7.41
People v. Bunyard, 45 Cal. 3d 1189, 756 P.2d 795, 249 Cal. Rptr. 71 (1988)	§ 7.3
People v. Burns, 118 Mich. App. 242, 324 N.W.2d 589 (1982)	§ 7.27
People v. Burrell-Hart, 192 Cal. App. 3d 593, 237 Cal. Rptr. 654 (1987)	§ 5.34
People v. Burton, 433 Mich. 268, 445 N.W.2d 133 (1989)	§§ 7.29, 7.30
People v. Burton, 55 Cal. 2d 328, 359 P.2d 433, 11 Cal. Rptr. 65 (1961)	§§ 2.18, 7.31
People v. Campos, 155 Ill. App. 3d 348, 507 N.E.2d 1342 (1987)	§ 2.18
People v. Caplan, 193 Cal. App. 3d 543, 238 Cal. Rptr. 478 (1987)	§ 1.14
People v. Cherry, 88 Ill. App. 3d 1048, 411 N.E.2d 61 (1980)	§§ 7.30, 7.49
People v. Cintron, 75 N.Y.2d 249, 551 N.E.2d 561, 552 N.Y.S.2d 68 (1990)	§ 8.8
People v. Coleman, 48 Cal. 3d 112, 768 P.2d 32, 255 Cal. Rptr. 813 (1989), cert. denied, 110 S. Ct. 1501 (1990)	§ 4.34
People v. Clark, 193 Cal. App. 3d 178, 238 Cal. Rptr. 230 (1987)	§ 7.31
People v. Clark, 6 Cal. App. 3d 658, 86 Cal. Rptr. 106 (1970)	§ 7.2
People v. Corbett, 656 P.2d 687 (Colo. 1983)	§ 1.16
People v. Crews, 38 Ill. 2d 331, 231 N.E.2d 451 (1967)	§ 3.28
People v. D.A.K., 198 Colo. 11, 596 P.2d 747 (1979)	§ 3.18
People v. Damen, 28 Ill. 2d 464, 193 N.E.2d 25 (1963)	§ 7.31
People v. Davis, 223 Ill. App. 3d 580, 585 N.E.2d 214 (1992)	§ 2.1
People v. Diefenderfer, 784 P.2d 741 (Colo. 1989)	§§ 4.5, 7.44, 7.45, 7.46, 7.48

CASES 379

Case	*Book §*
People v. District Court, 791 P.2d 682 (Colo. 1990)	§ 2.9
People v. District Court, 803 P.2d 193 (Colo. 1990)	§§ 3.13, 3.28
People v. District Court, 776 P.2d 1083 (Colo. 1989)	§§ 2.18, 2.19, 5.1, 7.1, 7.44, 7.45, 7.48
People v. District Court, 719 P.2d 722 (Colo. 1986)	§§ 1.14, 1.15, 7.56
People v. Dixon, 161 Mich. App. 388, 411 N.W.2d 760 (1987)	§ 1.12
People v. Draper, 150 Mich. App. 481, 389 N.W.2d 89 (1986)	§ 2.1
People v. Drumheller, 15 Ill. App. 3d 418, 304 N.E.2d 455 (1973)	§ 3.29
People v. Duell, 163 A.D. 866, 558 N.Y.S.2d 395 (1990)	§ 4.33
People v. Dunnahoo, 152 Cal. App. 3d 561, 199 Cal. Rptr. 796 (1984)	§ 4.44
People v. Edwards, 224 Ill. App. 3d 1017, 586 N.E.2d 1326 (1992)	§§ 2.1, 4.5, 4.50, 7.44
People v. Enoch, 189 Ill. App. 3d 535, 545 N.E.2d 429 (1989)	§ 5.9
People v. Esterline, 159 Ill. App. 3d 164, 512 N.E.2d 358 (1987)	§§ 6.18, 6.20, 6.24
People v. Estorga, 200 Colo. 78, 612 P.2d 520 (1980)	§ 8.14
People v. Exline, 775 P.2d 48 (Colo. Ct. App. 1988)	§ 1.14
People v. Fasy, 829 P.2d 1314 (Colo. 1992)	§ 4.44
People v. Fenner, 136 Mich. App. 45, 356 N.W.2d 1 (1984)	§ 7.30
People v. Fernandez, 138 A.D.2d 733, 526 N.Y.S.2d 547 (1988)	§ 2.16
People v. Figueroa, 134 Cal. 159, 66 P. 202 (1901)	§ 7.31
People v. Fisher, 169 Ill. App. 3d 785, 523 N.E.2d 368 (1988)	§ 7.30
People v. Flores, 168 Ill. App. 3d 284, 522 N.E.2d 708 (1988)	§§ 3.13, 3.14
People v. Foggy, 121 Ill. 2d 337, 521 N.E.2d 86, *cert. denied,* 486 U.S. 1047 (1988)	§§ 1.14, 1.15
People v. Ford, 139 Ill. App. 3d 894, 488 N.E.2d 573 (1985)	§ 2.14
People v. Freeman, 20 Cal. App. 3d 488, 97 Cal. Rptr. 717 (1971)	§ 7.20
People v. Gacho, 122 Ill. 2d 221, 522 N.E.2d 1146, *cert. denied,* 488 U.S. 910 (1988)	§ 7.30
People v. Gaffney, 769 P.2d 1081 (Colo. 1989)	§ 4.45
People v. Gage, 62 Mich. 271, 28 N.W. 835 (1886)	§ 7.31
People v. Garland, 152 Mich. App. 301, 393 N.W.2d 896 (1986)	§ 5.7
People v. Garrison, 166 Mich. App. 557, 420 N.W.2d 851 (1988)	§ 2.18
People v. Garvie, 148 Mich. App. 444, 384 N.W.2d 796 (1986)	§§ 5.8, 5.34
People v. Gil, 3 Cal. App. 4th 653, 4 Cal. Rptr. 2d 697 (1992)	§ 6.20

Case	Book §
People v. Gilbert, 7 Cal. Rptr. 660 (Ct. App. 1992)	§ 4.44
People v. Goebel, 161 Ill. App. 3d 113, 514 N.E.2d 60 (1987)	§ 6.18
People v. Gonzalez, 131 A.D.2d 873, 517 N.Y.S.2d 530 (1987)	§ 7.31
People v. Gordon, 738 P.2d 404 (Colo. Ct. App. 1987)	§§ 3.5, 3.6, 3.7, 3.9, 3.11
People v. Gould, 54 Cal. 2d 621, 354 P.2d 865, 7 Cal. Rptr. 273 (1960)	§ 7.26
People v. Gray, 568 N.E.2d 219 (Ill. Ct. App. 1991)	§ 5.36
People v. Gray, 187 Cal. App. 3d 213, 231 Cal. Rptr. 658 (1987)	§§ 4.33, 4.44
People v. Green, 209 Ill. App. 3d 233, 568 N.E.2d 92 (1991)	§ 3.32
People v. Guldbrandsen, 35 Cal. 2d 514, 218 P.2d 977 (1950)	§ 7.31
People v. Hackett, 421 Mich. 338, 365 N.W.2d 120 (1984)	§§ 5.28, 5.34
People v. Hackney, 183 Mich. App. 516, 455 N.W.2d 358 (1990)	§ 7.30
People v. Hampton, 746 P.2d 947 (Colo. 1987)	§§ 4.34, 4.44
People v. Harlan, 222 Cal. App. 3d 439, 271 Cal. Rptr. 653 (1990)	§§ 4.10, 5.17, 5.28
People v. Harp, 193 Ill. App. 3d 838, 550 N.E.2d 1163 (1990)	§ 4.34
People v. Harris, 132 A.D.2d 940, 518 N.Y.S.2d 269 (1987)	§ 5.34
People v. Harris, 158 Mich. App. 463, 404 N.W.2d 779 (1987)	§ 2.1
People v. Hayes, 139 Ill. 2d 89, 564 N.E.2d 803 (1990), *cert. denied,* 111 S. Ct. 1601 (1991)	§ 7.26
People v. Henson, 33 N.Y.2d 63, 304 N.E.2d 358, 349 N.Y.S.2d 657 (1973)	§§ 3.5, 3.9, 3.29, 3.30
People v. Hernandez, 88 Ill. App. 3d 698, 412 N.E.2d 572 (1980)	§ 7.31
People v. Herring, 135 Misc. 2d 487, 515 N.Y.S.2d 954 (1987)	§ 5.8
People v. Hickox, 197 Ill. App. 3d 205, 553 N.E.2d 1166 (1990)	§ 4.45
People v. Hicks, 183 Ill. App. 3d 636, 539 N.E.2d 756 (1989)	§ 5.9
People v. Holveck, 171 Ill. App. 3d 38, 524 N.E.2d 1073 (1988), *aff'd,* 141 Ill. 2d 84, 565 N.E.2d 919 (1990)	§§ 7.26, 8.4
People v. Hood, 1 Cal. 3d 444, 462 P.2d 370, 82 Cal. Rptr. 618 (1969)	§ 3.28
People v. Hubbell, 54 Cal. App. 2d 49, 128 P.2d 579 (1942)	§ 7.31
People v. Hudson, 198 Ill. App. 3d 915, 556 N.E.2d 640 (1990)	§§ 7.31, 7.35
People v. Hudy, 73 N.Y.2d 40, 535 N.E.2d 250, 538 N.Y.S.2d 197 (1988)	§ 5.21

Case	*Book §*
People v. Hughey, 194 Cal. App. 3d 1383, 240 Cal. Rptr. 269 (1987)	§ 7.29
People v. Hutson, 153 Ill. App. 3d 1073, 506 N.E.2d 779 (1987)	§ 5.8
People v. Iannone, 45 N.Y.2d 589, 384 N.E.2d 656, 412 N.Y.S.2d 110 (1978)	§ 1.4
People v. Jackson, 18 Cal. App. 3d 504, 95 Cal. Rptr. 919 (1971)	§§ 3.5, 3.8, 3.10, 3.30, 4.12
People v. Jensen, 747 P.2d 1247 (Colo. 1987)	§ 4.45
People v. Johnson, 118 Ill. 2d 501, 517 N.E.2d 1070 (1987)	§ 7.48
People v. Jones, 51 Cal. 3d 294, 792 P.2d 643, 270 Cal. Rptr. 611 (1990)	§§ 1.1, 1.3, 1.6, 1.7
People v. Jones, 155 Cal. App. 3d 653, 202 Cal. Rptr. 289 (1984)	§ 7.30
People v. Kahan, 15 N.Y.2d 311, 206 N.E.2d 333, 258 N.Y.S.2d 391 (1965)	§ 8.8
People v. Kasben, 158 Mich. App. 252, 404 N.W.2d 723 (1987)	§ 8.9
People v. Keindl, 68 N.Y.2d 410, 502 N.E.2d 577, 509 N.Y.S.2d 790 (1986)	§ 6.5
People v. Kelly, 17 Cal. 3d 24, 549 P.2d 1240, 130 Cal. Rptr. 144 (1976)	§ 4.18
People v. King, 41 Colo. App. 177, 581 P.2d 739 (1978)	§ 5.16
People v. Knapp, 139 A.D.2d 931, 527 N.Y.S.2d 914 (1988)	§§ 7.30, 7.49
People v. Knupp, 579 N.Y.S.2d 801 (A.D. 1992)	§ 4.37
People v. Kulakowski, 135 A.D.2d 1119, 523 N.Y.S.2d 238 (1987)	§ 7.44
People v. LaLone, 432 Mich. 103, 437 N.W.2d 611 (1989)	§§ 5.36, 7.35, 7.36
People v. Land, 178 Ill. App. 3d 251, 533 N.E.2d 57 (1988)	§ 4.28
People v. Landis, 593 N.E.2d 893 (Ill. App. Ct. 1992)	§ 7.45
People v. Larry, 162 Mich. App. 142, 412 N.W.2d 674 (1987)	§ 2.18
People v. Lendabarker, 215 Ill. App. 3d 540, 575 N.E.2d 568 (1991), *cert. denied,* 112 S. Ct. 1561 (1992)	§ 7.53
People v. Lewis, 69 N.Y.2d 321, 506 N.E.2d 915, 514 N.Y.S.2d 205 (1987)	§ 6.1
People v. Lewis, 147 Ill. App. 3d 249, 498 N.E.2d 1169 (1986), *cert. denied,* 482 U.S. 907 (1987)	§ 7.30
People v. Lobaito, 133 Mich. App. 547, 351 N.W.2d 233 (1984)	§ 1.12
People v. Luna, 204 Cal. App. 3d 726, 250 Cal. Rptr. 878 (1988)	§ 4.28
People v. Mateo, 73 N.Y.2d 928, 536 N.E.2d 1146, 539 N.Y.S.2d 727 (1989)	§ 8.5
People v. Matlock, 153 Mich. App. 171, 395 N.W.2d 274 (1986)	§§ 4.44, 4.45

Case	Book §
People v. Mayes, 66 Cal. 597, 6 P. 691 (1885)	§ 7.31
People v. McAlpin, 283 Cal. Rptr. 382, 812 P.2d 563 (1991)	§§ 4.40, 4.44, 4.50, 6.8
People v. McCarthy, 213 Ill. App. 3d 873, 572 N.E.2d 1219 (1991)	§§ 5.17, 6.20
People v. McClure, 779 P.2d 864 (Colo. 1989)	§§ 4.1, 5.1, 7.1, 7.46
People v. McDonald, 37 Cal. 3d 351, 690 P.2d 709, 208 Cal. Rptr. 236 (1984)	§ 4.18
People v. McNichols, 139 Ill. App. 3d 947, 487 N.E.2d 1252 (1986)	§§ 2.1, 7.30
People v. Meacham, 152 Cal. App. 3d 142, 199 Cal. Rptr. 586 (1984)	§ 7.31
People v. Meeboer, 181 Mich. App. 365, 449 N.W.2d 124 (1989), *aff'd,* 484 N.W.2d 621 (Mich. 1992)	§§ 7.35, 7.36
People v. Mendibles, 199 Cal. App. 3d 1277, 245 Cal. Rptr. 553 (1988)	§§ 4.12, 4.28
People v. Mikula, 84 Mich. App. 108, 269 N.W.2d 195 (1978)	§§ 5.29, 5.34
People v. Miller, 58 Ill. App. 3d 156, 373 N.E.2d 1077 (1978)	§ 7.49
People v. Mincey, 2 Cal. 4th 408, 827 P.2d 388, 6 Cal. Rptr. 2d (1992)	§§ 2.1, 2.12, 2.18, 3.2, 3.8, 3.28
People v. Morris, 61 N.Y.2d 290, 461 N.E.2d 1256, 473 N.Y.S.2d 769 (1984)	§§ 1.1, 1.3, 1.4
People v. Morton, 188 Ill. App. 3d 95, 543 N.E.2d 1366 (1989)	§ 7.31
People v. Nance, 118 A.D.2d 664, 500 N.Y.S.2d 13 (1986)	§ 3.30
People v. Naugle, 152 Mich. App. 227, 393 N.W.2d 592 (1986)	§ 1.3
People v. Nevitt, 135 Ill. 2d 423, 553 N.E.2d 368 (1990)	§§ 7.29, 7.30
People v. Newlun, 227 Cal. App. 3d 1590, 278 Cal. Rptr. 550, *cert. denied,* 112 S. Ct. 345 (1991)	§§ 1.1, 1.3, 1.7, 3.8
People v. Nicholl, 569 N.E.2d 604 (Ill. Ct. App. 1991)	§ 5.34
People v. Noble, 635 P.2d 203 (Colo. 1981)	§ 3.28
People v. Norfleet, 142 Mich. App. 745, 371 N.W.2d 438 (1985)	§§ 2.1, 2.14, 2.18
People v. Odom, 226 Cal. App. 3d 1028, 277 Cal. Rptr. 265 (1991)	§§ 3.28, 3.29
People v. Oldsen, 697 P.2d 787 (Colo. Ct. App. 1984), *aff'd,* 732 P.2d 1132 (Colo. 1986)	§ 7.35
People v. Oliver, 745 P.2d 222 (Colo. 1987)	§ 4.45
People v. O'Quinn, 109 Cal. App. 3d 219, 167 Cal. Rptr. 141 (1980), *cert. denied,* 450 U.S. 928 (1981)	§ 7.19
People v. Orduno, 80 Cal. App. 3d 738, 145 Cal. Rptr. 806 (1978), *cert. denied,* 439 U.S. 1074 (1979)	§§ 2.19, 7.31, 7.48, 7.49
People v. Ortega, 672 P.2d 215 (Colo. Ct. App. 1983)	§ 7.30
People v. Overton, 759 P.2d 772 (Colo. Ct. App. 1988)	§ 1.15
People v. Pack, 201 Cal. App. 3d 679, 248 Cal. Rptr. 240 (1988)	§ 1.14

Case	Book §
People v. Page, 166 A.D.2d 886, 560 N.Y.S.2d 546 (1990)	§ 4.44
People v. Panky, 82 Cal. App. 3d 772, 147 Cal. Rptr. 341 (1978)	§ 7.31
People v. Parks, 41 N.Y.2d 36, 359 N.E.2d 358, 390 N.Y.S.2d 848 (1976)	§§ 2.1, 2.16, 2.18
People v. Pendleton, 75 Ill. App. 3d 580, 394 N.E.2d 496 (1979)	§ 5.15
People v. Phillips, 122 Cal. App. 3d 69, 175 Cal. Rptr. 703 (1981)	§§ 3.15, 4.18, 6.14
People v. Pinta, 210 Ill. App. 3d 1071, 569 N.E.2d 1255 (1991)	§ 3.29
People v. Pitts, 223 Cal. App. 3d 606, 273 Cal. Rptr. 757 (1990)	§§ 4.28, 8.3
People v. Pluskis, 162 Ill. App. 3d 449, 515 N.E.2d 480 (1987)	§ 7.35
People v. Poindexter, 138 Mich. App. 322, 361 N.W.2d 346 (1984)	§ 5.25
People v. Polland, 589 N.E.2d 175 (Ill. App. Ct. 1992)	§ 4.52
People v. Puhl, 211 Ill. App. 3d 457, 570 N.E.2d 447 (1991)	§§ 2.1, 2.12, 4.10, 5.9, 6.20, 8.3
People v. Pullins, 145 Mich. App. 414, 378 N.W.2d 502 (1985)	§ 7.30
People v. Reber, 117 Cal. App. 3d 523, 223 Cal. Rptr. 139 (1986)	§§ 1.14, 1.15
People v. Renfro, 2 Cal. App. 4th 1626, 3 Cal. Rptr. 2d 909 (1992)	§ 4.37
People v. Rice, 709 P.2d 67 (Colo. Ct. App. 1985)	§ 5.33
People v. Ridgeway, 194 Ill. App. 3d 881, 551 N.E.2d 790 (1990)	§ 7.45
People v. Rippberger, 231 Cal. App. 3d 1667, 283 Cal. Rptr. 111 (1991)	§ 3.17
People v. Roark, 643 P.2d 756 (Colo. 1982)	§ 7.30
People v. Robertson, 168 Ill. App. 3d 132, 522 N.E.2d 239 (1988)	§ 7.31
People v. Robinson, 19 Cal. 40 (1861)	§ 7.13
People v. Robinson, 94 Ill. App. 3d 304, 418 N.E.2d 899 (1981)	§ 7.30
People v. Roscoe, 168 Cal. App. 3d 1093, 215 Cal. Rptr. 45 (1985)	§§ 4.37, 4.44
People v. Ross, 745 P.2d 277 (Colo. Ct. App. 1987)	§ 4.45
People v. Roy, 201 Ill. App. 3d 166, 558 N.E.2d 1208 (1990), *cert. denied*, 112 S. Ct. 965 (1992)	§§ 7.29, 7.30
People v. Sambo, 197 Ill. App. 3d 574, 554 N.E.2d 1080 (1990)	§§ 3.10, 7.18, 7.20, 8.3
People v. Sanchez, 208 Cal. App. 3d 721, 256 Cal. Rptr. 446, *cert. denied*, 493 U.S. 921 (1989)	§ 4.44
People v. Sandoval, 709 P.2d 90 (Colo. Ct. App. 1985)	§ 7.30
People v. Schmitt, 204 Ill. App. 3d 820, 562 N.E.2d 377 (1990)	§ 8.8

Case	Book §
People v. Schott, 145 Ill. 2d 188, 582 N.E.2d 690 (1991)	§ 5.17
People v. Serna, 738 P.2d 802 (Colo. Ct. App. 1987)	§ 7.46
People v. Server, 148 Ill. App. 3d 888, 499 N.E.2d 1019 (1986), *cert. denied,* 484 U.S. 842 (1987)	§ 5.7
People v. Sexton, 162 Ill. App. 3d 607, 515 N.E.2d 1359 (1987)	§§ 3.32, 7.35
People v. Sims, 110 A.D.2d 214, 494 N.Y.S.2d 114 (1985)	§§ 3.5, 3.8, 3.9, 3.13, 3.29
People v. Singer, 300 N.Y. 120, 89 N.E.2d 710 (1949)	§ 7.21
People v. Slavin, 66 Ill. App. 3d 525, 383 N.E.2d 1303 (1978)	§ 7.31
People v. Smallwood, 42 Cal. 3d 415, 722 P.2d 197, 228 Cal. Rptr. 913 (1986)	§ 6.13
People v. Smith, 104 A.D.2d 160, 481 N.Y.S.2d 879 (1984)	§ 7.13
People v. Snook, 745 P.2d 647 (Colo. 1987)	§ 4.45
People v. Stark, 213 Cal. App. 3d 107, 261 Cal. Rptr. 479 (1989)	§ 4.44
People v. Stewart, 181 Cal. App. 3d 300, 226 Cal. Rptr. 252 (1986)	§§ 6.22, 7.31
People v. Stoll, 49 Cal. 3d 1136, 783 P.2d 698, 265 Cal. Rptr. 111 (1989)	§§ 4.18, 4.50, 6.8
People v. Straight, 430 Mich. 418, 424 N.W.2d 257 (1988)	§§ 7.28, 7.30
People v. Stritzinger, 34 Cal. 3d 505, 668 P.2d 738, 194 Cal. Rptr. 431 (1983)	§§ 1.16, 7.48
People v. Stull, 127 Mich. App. 14, 338 N.W.2d 403 (1983)	§ 5.28
People v. Swist, 136 Cal. 520, 69 P. 223 (1902)	§ 7.31
People v. Taggart, 621 P.2d 1375 (Colo. 1981)	§ 6.17
People v. Taylor, 75 N.Y.2d 277, 552 N.E.2d 131, 552 N.Y.S.2d 883 (1990)	§§ 4.34, 4.44, 5.16
People v. Taylor, 66 Mich. App. 456, 239 N.W.2d 627 (1976)	§ 7.31
People v. Thomas, 770 P.2d 1324 (Colo. Ct. App. 1989), *aff'd in part and rev'd in part,* 803 P.2d 144 (Colo. 1990)	§ 8.8
People v. Thompson, 756 P.2d 353 (Colo. 1988)	§ 3.28
People v. Thornton, 11 Cal. 3d 738, 523 P.2d 267, 114 Cal. Rptr. 467 (1974), *cert. denied,* 420 U.S. 924 (1975)	§ 6.21
People v. Trimble, 7 Cal. Rptr. 2d 450 (Ct. App. 1992)	§ 7.30
People v. Turner, 193 Ill. App. 3d 152, 549 N.E.2d 1309 (1990)	§§ 3.8, 3.9, 3.12
People v. Tye, 141 Ill. 2d 1, 565 N.E.2d 931 (1990), *cert. denied,* 112 S. Ct. 112 (1991)	§§ 3.28, 3.29
People v. Tyrrell, 101 A.D.2d 946, 475 N.Y.S.2d 937 (1984)	§ 5.7
People v. Vandelinder, 163 A.D.2d 811, 558 N.Y.S.2d 343 (1990)	§§ 4.39, 5.3, 5.6
People v. Vasher, 167 Mich. App. 452, 423 N.W.2d 40 (1988)	§ 4.28

CASES

Case	*Book §*
People v. Wade, 43 Cal. 3d 366, 729 P.2d 239, 233 Cal. Rptr. 48 (1987), *cert. denied,* 488 U.S. 900 (1988)	§ 6.17
People v. Walkey, 177 Cal. App. 3d 268, 223 Cal. Rptr. 132 (1986)	§ 3.31
People v. Wall, 95 Cal. App. 3d 978, 157 Cal. Rptr. 587 (1979)	§ 5.34
People v. Ward, 207 Ill. App. 3d 365, 565 N.E.2d 740 (1991)	§ 7.45
People v. Watt, 579 N.Y.S.2d 429 (A.D. 1992)	§§ 1.3, 1.4
People v. Watts, 139 Ill. App. 3d 837, 487 N.E.2d 1077 (1985)	§ 7.30
People v. Wellman, 166 A.D.2d 302, 560 N.Y.S.2d 643 (1991)	§ 4.44
People v. Wheeler, 216 Ill. App. 3d 609, 575 N.E.2d 1326 (1992)	§ 4.50
People v. Wilkins, 134 Mich. App. 39, 349 N.W.2d 815 (1984)	§ 7.35
People v. Williams, 477 N.W.2d 877 (Mich. Ct. App. 1991)	§§ 5.28, 7.41
People v. Wilmot, 139 Cal. 103, 72 P. 838 (1903)	§ 7.31
People v. Wilson, 678 P.2d 1024 (Colo. Ct. App. 1983), *cert. denied,* 469 U.S. 843 (1984)	§§ 5.32, 5.34
People v. Winfield, 160 Ill. App. 3d 983, 513 N.E.2d 1032 (1987)	§ 7.20
People v. Woith, 126 Ill. App. 3d 817, 467 N.E.2d 614 (1984)	§ 7.30
People v. Wood, 743 P.2d 422 (Colo. 1987)	§ 7.46
People v. Zurak, 168 A.D.2d 196, 571 N.Y.S.2d 577 (1991), *cert. denied,* 112 S. Ct. 2276 (1992)	§ 7.31
People *ex rel.* D.L.E., 645 P.2d 271 (Colo. 1982)	§ 3.17
Perez v. State, 536 So. 2d 206 (Fla. 1988), *cert. denied,* 492 U.S. 923 (1989)	§§ 2.19, 7.45, 7.46, 7.48, 7.49
Perrin v. Anderson, 784 F.2d 1040 (10th Cir. 1986)	§ 6.7
Perry v. Fiumano, 61 A.D.2d 512, 403 N.Y.S.2d 382 (1978)	§ 1.18
Perry v. State, 586 So. 2d 242 (Ala. 1991)	§ 4.26
Petition of Catholic Charitable Bureau, *In re,* 395 Mass. 180, 479 N.E.2d 148 (1985)	§§ 3.19, 3.24
Petition of Catholic Charitable Bureau, *In re,* 392 Mass. 738, 467 N.E.2d 866 (1984)	§ 1.18
Petra B., *In re,* 216 Cal. App. 3d 1163, 265 Cal. Rptr. 342 (1989)	§ 3.17
Pfaff v. State, 830 P.2d 193 (Okla. Crim. App. 1992)	§ 8.7
P.H. v. State, 504 P.2d 837 (Alaska 1972)	§ 7.57
Phillip B., *In re,* 92 Cal. App. 3d 796, 156 Cal. Rptr. 48 (1979), *cert. denied,* 445 U.S. 949 (1980)	§ 3.17
Phillips v. Jackson, 615 P.2d 1228 (Utah 1980)	§ 4.19
Phillips v. State, 505 So. 2d 1075 (Ala. Crim. App. 1986)	§ 5.8
Phillips v. State, 173 Ga. App. 396, 326 S.E.2d 775 (1985)	§§ 2.1, 2.11, 2.12, 2.18

Case	Book §
Pittman v. State, 178 Ga. App. 693, 344 S.E.2d 511 (1986)	§ 5.8
Pittsburgh Action Against Rape, *In re*, 494 Pa. 15, 428 A.2d 126 (1981)	§ 5.34
Place v. Place, 129 N.H. 252, 525 A.2d 704 (1987)	§ 3.15
Plummer v. Ricker, 71 Vt. 114, 41 A. 1045 (1898)	§ 7.13
Pointer v. Texas, 380 U.S. 400 (1965)	§§ 7.50, 7.53, 7.55
Porter v. State, 308 Ark. 137, 823 S.W.2d 846 (1992)	§§ 3.8, 3.10, 3.11, 3.28, 3.29, 3.32
Posey v. United States, 41 A.2d 300 (D.C. 1945)	§ 2.14
Poteat v. United States, 330 A.2d 229 (D.C. 1974)	§ 7.57
Potter v. State, 410 N.W.2d 364 (Minn. Ct. App. 1987)	§ 4.44
Potts v. State, 427 So. 2d 822 (Fla. Dist. Ct. App. 1983)	§ 6.18
Powell v. Levitt, 640 F.2d 239 (9th Cir.), *cert. denied*, 454 U.S. 845 (1981)	§ 5.25
Powell v. State, 527 A.2d 276 (Del. 1987)	§ 4.45
Prater v. State, 307 Ark. 180, 820 S.W.2d 429 (1991)	§§ 4.18, 4.19, 4.26
Press-Enterprise Co. v. Superior Court, 478 U.S. 1 (1986)	§§ 5.23, 8.4, 8.5
Press-Enterprise Co. v. Superior Court, 464 U.S. 501 (1984)	§ 8.5
Prince v. Massachusetts, 321 U.S. 158 (1944)	§§ 3.17, 8.8
Provencal v. Provencal, 122 N.H. 793, 451 A.2d 374 (1982)	§ 1.12
Pryor v. State, 719 S.W.2d 628 (Tex. Ct. App. 1986), *cert. denied*, 485 U.S. 1036 (1988)	§ 5.8
Queen Caroline's Case, 2 Brod. & Bing. 284, 129 Eng. Rep. 976, 11 Eng. Ru. Cas. 183 (1820)	§ 7.18
R.A., *In re*, 225 Neb. 157, 403 N.W.2d 357 (1987)	§§ 3.25, 7.30
Ralph D., *In re*, 163 A.D.2d 752, 557 N.Y.S.2d 1003 (1990)	§§ 2.12, 2.16
Ralph M., *In re*, 211 Conn. 289, 559 A.2d 179 (1989)	§ 7.57
Ramirez v. State, 802 S.W.2d 674 (Tex. Crim. App. 1991)	§ 5.20
Ray v. State, 580 So. 2d 103 (Ala. Crim. App. 1991)	§§ 3.10, 3.11, 3.29, 3.32
Rayburn v. State, 194 Ga. App. 676, 391 S.E.2d 780, *cert. denied*, 111 S. Ct. 434 (1990)	§ 7.44
Redmond v. Baxley, 475 F. Supp. 1111 (E.D. Mich. 1979)	§ 7.24
Reece v. State, 192 Ga. App. 14, 383 S.E.2d 572 (1989)	§ 5.29
Renick v. Hays, 201 Ky. 192, 256 S.W. 26 (1923)	§ 2.13
Rex v. Brasier, Leach 199, 168 Eng. Rep. 202 (1770)	§ 2.2
Reyna v. State, 797 S.W.2d 189 (Tex. Ct. App. 1990)	§§ 2.1, 2.11, 2.18
Reynolds v. State, 575 N.E.2d 28 (Ind. Ct. App. 1991)	§ 6.21
Reynolds v. United States, 98 U.S. 145 (1878)	§ 3.17
Rhea v. State, 705 S.W.2d 165 (Tex. Ct. App. 1985)	§§ 2.1, 2.12
Riccardi v. Tampax, Inc., 113 A.D.2d 880, 493 N.Y.S.2d 798 (1985)	§ 1.12
Richard v. Tarzetti, 510 So. 2d 1361 (La. Ct. App. 1987)	§ 1.18
Richardson v. Marsh, 481 U.S. 200 (1987)	§§ 7.50, 7.54
Richardson v. State, 33 Ark. App. 128, 803 S.W.2d 557 (1991)	§§ 2.15, 2.18

Case	Book §
Richmond Newspapers, Inc. v. Virginia, 448 U.S. 555 (1980)	§ 8.5
Ricketts v. State, 488 A.2d 856 (Del. 1985)	§§ 2.1, 2.12, 2.14, 2.15, 2.18
Riffe, *In re,* 147 Mich. App. 658, 382 N.W.2d 842 (1985)	§ 3.19
Riley v. Goodman, 315 F.2d 232 (3d Cir. 1963)	§ 5.9
Rinesmith, *In re,* 144 Mich. App. 475, 376 N.W.2d 139 (1985)	§§ 4.35, 7.35
Ring v. Erickson, 1992 WL 155797 (8th Cir. 1992)	§ 7.36
R.J., *In re,* 436 N.W.2d 630 (Iowa 1989)	§ 3.23
R.L.R. v. State, 487 P.2d 27 (Alaska 1971)	§ 7.57
R.O. v. Pike County Dep't Human Resources, 578 So. 2d 1312 (Ala. Civ. App. 1990)	§§ 7.44, 7.57
Robert P., *In re,* 61 Cal. App. 3d 310, 132 Cal. Rptr. 5 (1976)	§ 6.5
Roberts v. Hollocher, 664 F.2d 200 (8th Cir. 1981)	§ 7.44
Roberts v. State, 87 Okla. Crim. 93, 194 P.2d 219 (1948)	§ 5.17
Robinson v. Shapiro, 484 F. Supp. 91 (S.D.N.Y. 1980), *aff'd,* 646 F.2d 734 (2d Cir. 1981)	§ 7.27
Robinson v. State, 453 N.E.2d 280 (Ind. 1983)	§ 3.28
Rodgers v. State, 261 Ga. 33, 401 S.E.2d 735 (1991)	§ 6.21
Roper v. Roper, 336 So. 2d 654 (Fla. Dist. Ct. App. 1976)	§ 1.18
Rosen v. United States, 245 U.S. 467 (1918)	§ 2.2
Ross v. Jones, 888 F.2d 548 (8th Cir. 1989)	§ 5.25
Ross, *In re,* 605 A.2d 524 (Vt. 1992)	§§ 4.45, 4.46
Rotolo v. United States, 404 F.2d 316 (5th Cir. 1968)	§ 5.7
Rouse v. State, 548 So. 2d 643 (Ala. Crim. App. 1989)	§ 7.48
R.R., *In re,* 79 N.J. 97, 398 A.2d 76 (1979)	§§ 2.1, 2.13, 2.14, 2.15, 2.16, 2.18, 5.7
R.S. v. Knighton, 125 N.J. 79, 592 A.2d 1157 (1991)	§ 7.36
Rubino v. Albany Medical Ctr., 126 Misc. 2d 204, 481 N.Y.S.2d 622 (Sup. Ct. 1984)	§ 1.12
Rubio v. Superior Court, 202 Cal. App. 3d 1343, 249 Cal. Rptr. 419 (1988)	§ 1.14
Russell v. State, 289 Ark. 533, 712 S.W.2d 916 (1986)	§ 4.37
Russell v. State, 572 So. 2d 940 (Fla. Dist. Ct. App. 1990)	§ 7.46
Russell v. State, 533 So. 2d 725 (Ala. Crim. App. 1988)	§ 1.14
Sampson, *In re,* 65 Misc. 2d 658, 317 N.Y.S.2d 641 (Fam. Ct. 1970), *aff'd,* 37 A.D.2d 668, 323 N.Y.S.2d 253 (1971), *aff'd,* 29 N.Y.2d 900, 278 N.E.2d 918, 328 N.Y.S.2d 686 (1972)	§ 3.17
San Bernardino County Dep't of Pub. Social Servs. v. Superior Court, 232 Cal. App. 3d 188, 283 Cal. Rptr. 332 (1991)	§ 8.5
Sanders v. State, 251 Ga. 70, 303 S.E.2d 13 (1983)	§ 3.31
Sanders v. State, 586 So. 2d 792 (Miss. 1991)	§ 7.30
Sanders v. State, 727 S.W.2d 670 (Tex. Ct. App. 1987)	§ 2.1
Sanderson v. State, 548 S.W.2d 337 (Tenn. Crim. App. 1976)	§ 6.20

Case	Book §
Santmier v. Santmier, 494 So. 2d 95 (Ala. Civ. App. 1986)	§ 1.18
Santosky v. Kramer, 455 U.S. 745 (1982)	§ 7.57
Sara M., *In re,* 194 Cal. App. 3d 585, 239 Cal. Rptr. 605 (1987)	§§ 4.18, 4.33
S.B., *In re,* 223 Mont. 36, 724 P.2d 168 (1986)	§ 3.19
Scadden v. State, 732 P.2d 1036 (Wyo. 1987)	§§ 4.44, 6.22
Scantling v. State, 271 Ark. 678, 609 S.W.2d 925 (1981)	§ 5.7
Scharf v. Attorney Gen., 597 F.2d 1240 (9th Cir. 1979)	§ 1.19
Schempp v. Reniker, 809 F.2d 541 (8th Cir. 1987)	§ 1.19
Schleret v. State, 311 N.W.2d 843 (Minn. 1981)	§§ 3.5, 3.9
Schmeltzer, *In re,* 175 Mich. App. 666, 438 N.W.2d 866 (1989)	§ 3.21
Scoggan v. State, 799 S.W.2d 679 (Tex. Crim. App. 1990)	§§ 4.41, 5.17
Scott v. United States, 412 A.2d 364 (D.C. 1980)	§ 5.7
Seales v. State, 581 So. 2d 1192 (Ala. 1991)	§ 4.28
Seering v. Department of Social Servs., 194 Cal. App. 3d 298, 239 Cal. Rptr. 422 (1987)	§§ 4.18, 4.37, 7.57
Seiferth, *In re,* 309 N.Y. 80, 127 N.E.2d 820 (1955)	§ 3.17
Senecal v. Drollette, 304 N.Y. 446, 108 N.E.2d 602 (1952)	§ 2.17
Shane T., *In re,* 115 Misc. 2d 161, 453 N.Y.S.2d 590 (Fam. Ct. 1982)	§ 3.18
Shannon v. State, 105 Nev. 782, 783 P.2d 942 (1989)	§§ 4.37, 4.50
Sharon H. v. Foster, 153 A.D.2d 627, 544 N.Y.S.2d 659 (1989)	§ 3.25
Shaver v. State, 199 Ga. App. 428, 405 S.E.2d 281 (1991)	§ 7.47
Sheldon v. State, 796 P.2d 831 (Alaska Ct. App. 1990)	§§ 4.5, 7.20
Shepard v. Purvine, 196 Or. 348, 248 P.2d 352 (1952)	§ 7.47
Shepard v. United States, 290 U.S. 96 (1933)	§ 7.34
Sherrick v. State, 157 Neb. 623, 61 N.W.2d 358 (1953)	§ 7.31
Shrock v. Goodell, 270 Or. 504, 528 P.2d 1048 (1974)	§ 5.23
Shunk v. Walker, 87 Md. App. 389, 589 A.2d 1303 (1991)	§ 7.47
Simek v. Superior Court, 117 Cal. App. 3d 169, 172 Cal. Rptr. 564 (1981)	§ 1.18
Singletary v. United States, 383 A.2d 1064 (D.C. 1978)	§ 7.57
Sipress v. State, 562 N.E.2d 758 (Ind. Ct. App. 1990)	§§ 3.13, 3.29
Sizemore v. State, 1992 WL 11627 (Ga. 1992)	§ 2.9
Skaggs v. State, 438 N.E.2d 301 (Ind. Ct. App. 1982)	§ 5.32
Slater v. Baker, 301 N.W.2d 315 (Minn. 1981)	§§ 7.22, 7.24, 7.25
Slater v. State, 575 So. 2d 1208 (Ala. Crim. App. 1990)	§ 7.41
Sledge v. State, 763 P.2d 1364 (Alaska Ct. App. 1988)	§ 1.14
Sloan v. State, 70 Md. App. 630, 522 A.2d 1364 (1987)	§ 3.31
Smith v. Illinois, 390 U.S. 129 (1968)	§ 7.56
Smith v. J.C. Penney Co., 269 Or. 643, 525 P.2d 1299 (1974)	§ 7.47
Smith v. State, 300 Ark. 330, 778 S.W.2d 947 (1989)	§ 5.25
Smith v. State, 538 So. 2d 66 (Fla. Dist. Ct. App. 1989)	§§ 7.21, 7.22, 7.23
Smith v. State, 259 Ga. 135, 377 S.E.2d 158, *cert. denied,* 493 U.S. 825 (1989)	§ 5.34
Smith v. State, 247 Ga. 511, 277 S.E.2d 53 (1981)	§ 2.1
Smith v. State, 100 Nev. 570, 688 P.2d 326 (1984)	§ 4.44

CASES 389

Case	*Book §*
Smith v. United States, 414 A.2d 1189 (D.C. 1980)	§ 2.1
Smith v. Whittier, 95 Cal. 279, 30 P. 529 (1892)	§ 7.31
Smith, *In re,* 128 Misc. 2d 976, 492 N.Y.S.2d 331 (Fam. Ct. 1985)	§ 3.17
Snyder v. Massachusetts, 291 U.S. 97 (1934)	§ 8.11
Soper v. State, 731 P.2d 587 (Alaska Ct. App. 1987)	§ 6.21
Sosebee v. State, 257 Ga. 298, 357 S.E.2d 562 (1987)	§ 7.46
Soto v. State, 736 S.W.2d 823 (Tex. Ct. App. 1987)	§ 2.18
Specht v. Jensen, 853 F.2d 805 (10th Cir. 1988)	§ 4.13
Spigarolo v. Meachum, 934 F.2d 19 (2d Cir. 1991)	§ 2.16
Spoerri v. State, 561 So. 2d 604 (Fla. Dist. Ct. App. 1990)	§ 8.12
Spollen's Trial, Ire. Pamphl. at 47 (1857)	§ 2.13
Sprayberry v. State, 174 Ga. App. 574, 330 S.E.2d 731 (1985)	§§ 2.12, 2.18
S.R., *In re,* 599 A.2d 364 (Vt. 1991)	§ 3.15
Stallnacker v. State, 19 Ark. App. 9, 715 S.W.2d 883 (1986)	§ 7.35
Stamps v. State, 107 Nev. 372, 812 P.2d 351 (1991)	§ 7.56
Stanger v. State, 545 N.E.2d 1105 (Ind. Ct. App. 1989)	§§ 7.50, 8.1, 8.3, 8.8
Starr v. Morsette, 236 N.W.2d 183 (N.D. 1975)	§ 7.27
State v. Abercrombie, 694 S.W.2d 268 (Mo. Ct. App. 1985)	§§ 3.8, 3.11, 3.28, 3.29
State v. Abraham, 107 Or. App. 212, 811 P.2d 658 (1991)	§ 4.45
State v. Adams, 544 A.2d 299 (Me. 1988)	§ 5.21
State v. A.D.M., 216 Mont. 419, 701 P.2d 999 (1985)	§ 2.12
State v. Aguallo, 318 N.C. 590, 350 S.E.2d 76 (1986)	§§ 4.45, 7.35, 7.39
State v. Albert, 13 Kan. App. 2d 671, 778 P.2d 386 (1989)	§ 8.8
State v. Alexander, 64 Wash. App. 147, 822 P.2d 1250 (1992)	§§ 4.45, 7.31
State v. Allen, 157 Ariz. 165, 755 P.2d 1153 (1988)	§§ 7.4, 7.30, 7.42, 7.44, 7.45, 7.48
State v. Allewalt, 308 Md. 89, 517 A.2d 741 (Ct. App. 1986)	§ 4.34
State v. Allison, 595 A.2d 1089 (N.H. 1991)	§§ 5.21, 5.23, 7.56
State v. Allred, 134 Ariz. 274, 655 P.2d 1326 (1982)	§§ 7.20, 7.47
State v. Altergott, 57 Haw. 492, 559 P.2d 728 (1977)	§ 7.25
State v. Anderson, 480 N.W.2d 727 (N.D. 1992)	§ 3.32
State v. Andrews, 707 P.2d 900 (Alaska Ct. App. 1985)	§ 4.8
State v. Anthony, 89 N.C. App. 93, 365 S.E.2d 195 (1988)	§§ 5.32, 5.34, 7.56
State v. Armstrong, 587 So. 2d 165 (La. Ct. App. 1991)	§ 4.50
State v. Armstrong, 453 So. 2d 1256 (La. Ct. App. 1984)	§ 2.12
State v. Asfour, 555 So. 2d 1280 (Fla. Dist. Ct. App. 1990)	§ 7.2
State v. Ayers, 369 S.E.2d 22 (W. Va. 1988)	§ 2.22
State v. Ayres, 236 Neb. 824, 464 N.W.2d 316 (1991)	§ 3.29
State v. Babayan, 106 Nev. 155, 787 P.2d 805 (1990)	§ 4.5
State v. Baca, 56 N.M. 236, 242 P.2d 1002 (1952)	§ 7.31
State v. Bailey, 89 N.C. App. 212, 365 S.E.2d 651 (1988)	§§ 1.14, 4.37, 4.44, 4.45
State v. Baker, 320 N.C. 104, 357 S.E.2d 340 (1987)	§§ 2.18, 4.28
State v. Baker, 46 Or. App. 79, 610 P.2d 840 (1980)	§ 7.31
State v. Baldwin, 571 S.W.2d 236 (Mo. 1978)	§ 5.17

Case | *Book §*

Case	Book §
State v. Barber, 13 Kan. App. 2d 224, 766 P.2d 1288 (1989)	§ 5.34
State v. Barber, 747 P.2d 436 (Utah Ct. App. 1987)	§ 7.30
State v. Barker, 178 W. Va. 736, 364 S.E.2d 264 (1987)	§ 8.2
State v. Baron, 58 N.C. App. 150, 292 S.E.2d 741 (1982)	§ 5.34
State v. Barrett, 299 S.C. 485, 386 S.E.2d 242 (1989)	§ 7.31
State v. Basker, 468 N.W.2d 413 (S.D. 1991)	§§ 1.1, 1.3, 3.28, 3.29, 6.18, 7.6
State v. Bass, 221 N.J. Super. 466, 535 A.2d 1 (1987)	§§ 7.22, 7.23, 7.30
State v. Batangan, 71 Haw. 552, 799 P.2d 48 (1990)	§ 4.45
State v. Bates, 784 P.2d 1126 (Utah 1989)	§§ 1.1, 1.3
State v. Baublits, 324 Mo. 1199, 27 S.W.2d 16 (1930)	§ 3.28
State v. Bauer, 146 Ariz. 134, 704 P.2d 264 (Ct. App. 1985)	§ 7.49
State v. Bauman, 98 Or. App. 316, 779 P.2d 185 (1989)	§§ 2.18, 7.35
State v. Bawdon, 386 N.W.2d 484 (S.D. 1986)	§§ 7.8, 7.30, 7.35
State v. Bean, 582 So. 2d 947 (La. Ct. App. 1991)	§ 7.30
State v. Beermann, 231 Neb. 380, 436 N.W.2d 499 (1989)	§§ 1.1, 1.3, 1.4
State v. Bellotti, 383 N.W.2d 308 (Minn. Ct. App. 1986)	§§ 7.35, 7.44, 7.45, 7.46, 7.48
State v. Benedict, 397 N.W.2d 337 (Minn. 1986)	§ 5.35
State v. Bennett, 549 So. 2d 398 (La. Ct. App. 1989)	§ 7.30
State v. Bennett, 36 Wash. App. 176, 672 P.2d 772 (1983)	§ 6.22
State v. Benny E., 110 N.M. 237, 794 P.2d 380 (Ct. App. 1990)	§§ 4.28, 5.7, 5.9, 8.8
State v. Benton, 759 S.W.2d 427 (Tenn. Crim. App. 1988)	§ 7.22
State v. Berry, 101 Ariz. 310, 419 P.2d 337 (1966)	§ 1.3
State v. Best, 89 S.D. 227, 232 N.W.2d 447 (1975)	§§ 3.5, 3.6, 3.7
State v. Bethune, 232 N.J. Super. 532, 557 A.2d 1025 (1989), *aff'd,* 121 N.J. 137, 578 A.2d 364 (1990)	§ 7.31
State v. Bingham, 116 Idaho 415, 776 P.2d 424 (1989)	§ 2.22
State v. Bishop, 63 Wash. App. 15, 816 P.2d 738 (1991)	§§ 7.19, 7.45, 7.46, 7.51, 7.56
State v. Black, 537 A.2d 1154 (Me. 1988)	§§ 4.10, 4.19, 4.37, 4.44, 8.8
State v. Black, 291 N.W.2d 208 (Minn. 1980)	§ 7.58
State v. Black, 109 Wash. 2d 336, 745 P.2d 12 (1987)	§ 4.34
State v. Blake, 157 Conn. 99, 249 A.2d 232 (1968)	§ 6.8
State v. Bloomstrom, 12 Wash. App. 416, 529 P.2d 1124 (1974)	§ 7.30
State v. Boisvert, 119 N.H. 174, 400 A.2d 48 (1979)	§ 5.16
State v. Bolden, 501 So. 2d 942 (La. Ct. App. 1987)	§ 3.11
State v. Bolton, 408 So. 2d 250 (La. 1981)	§ 5.7
State v. Bonello, 210 Conn. 51, 554 A.2d 277, *cert. denied,* 490 U.S. 1082 (1989)	§ 8.8
State v. Boodry, 96 Ariz. 259, 394 P.2d 196, *cert. denied,* 379 U.S. 949 (1964)	§§ 7.27, 7.29, 7.45
State v. Boston, 46 Ohio St. 3d 108, 545 N.E.2d 1220 (1989)	§§ 2.1, 4.28, 4.45, 7.26, 7.30, 7.35, 7.36, 7.48, 7.49

CASES

Case	Book §
State v. Bouchard, 31 Wash. App. 381, 639 P.2d 761 (1982)	§§ 7.30, 7.31
State v. Bounds, 71 Or. App. 744, 694 P.2d 566 (1985)	§ 7.48
State v. Boyer, 803 S.W.2d 132 (Mo. Ct. App. 1991)	§§ 7.44, 7.51
State v. Bratt, 250 Kan. 264, 824 P.2d 983 (1992)	§ 7.44
State v. Bridgman, 49 Vt. 202, 24 Am. Rep. 124 (1876)	§ 6.20
State v. Brodniak, 221 Mont. 212, 718 P.2d 322 (1986)	§ 4.34
State v. Brotherton, 384 N.W.2d 375 (Iowa 1986)	§§ 2.1, 2.12, 4.44, 4.45
State v. Brown, 400 N.W.2d 74 (Iowa Ct. App. 1986)	§ 2.1
State v. Brown, 220 Neb. 849, 374 N.W.2d 28 (1985)	§ 5.7
State v. Brown, 297 Or. 404, 687 P.2d 751 (1984)	§ 4.19
State v. Brown, 574 A.2d 745 (R.I. 1990)	§ 5.7
State v. Brown, 1992 WL 115567 (Tenn. 1992)	§§ 3.11, 3.12, 3.29
State v. Brown, 55 Wash. App. 738, 780 P.2d 880 (1989)	§ 1.6
State v. Bruce, 655 S.W.2d 66 (Mo. Ct. App. 1983)	§ 1.12
State v. Bruggeman, 161 Ariz. 508, 779 P.2d 823 (Ct. App. 1989)	§ 7.25
State v. Brunette, 501 A.2d 419 (Me. 1985)	§ 7.38
State v. Bryant, 828 P.2d 1121 (Wash. Ct. App. 1992)	§ 7.30
State v. Budis, 125 N.J. 519, 593 A.2d 784 (1991)	§§ 5.28, 5.35
State v. Buller, 484 N.W.2d 883 (S.D. 1992)	§ 7.44
State v. Bullock, 320 N.C. 780, 360 S.E.2d 689 (1987)	§ 7.35
State v. Bullock, 791 P.2d 155 (Utah 1989), *cert. denied*, 110 S. Ct. 3270 (1990)	§ 4.5
State v. Bult, 351 N.W.2d 731 (S.D. 1984)	§ 7.30
State v. Burns, 394 N.W.2d 495 (Minn. 1986)	§ 7.46
State v. Burns, 524 A.2d 564 (R.I. 1987)	§ 7.30
State v. Busch, 515 So. 2d 605 (La. Ct. App. 1987)	§§ 2.16, 2.18
State v. Burt, 546 So. 2d 931 (La. Ct. App. 1989)	§ 7.31
State v. Butcher, 165 W. Va. 522, 270 S.E.2d 156 (1980)	§§ 2.12, 2.19
State v. Butler, 256 Ga. 448, 349 S.E.2d 684 (1986)	§§ 4.13, 4.19 4.28
State v. Butler, 27 N.J. 560, 143 A.2d 530 (1958)	§§ 2.18, 2.22, 5.16
State v. Butler, 53 Wash. App. 214, 766 P.2d 505 (1989)	§ 7.35
State v. Byers, 102 Idaho 159, 627 P.2d 788 (1981)	§ 5.17
State v. Cabral, 122 R.I. 623, 410 A.2d 438 (1980)	§ 5.17
State v. Cain, 427 N.W.2d 5 (Minn. Ct. App. 1988)	§ 4.5
State v. Camele, 293 S.C. 302, 360 S.E.2d 307 (1987)	§ 2.18
State v. Campbell, 316 N.C. 168, 340 S.E.2d 474 (1986)	§ 3.13
State v. Campbell, 299 Or. 633, 705 P.2d 694 (1985)	§§ 2.18, 7.31, 7.48, 7.58
State v. Carlson, 311 Or. 201, 808 P.2d 1002 (1991)	§§ 7.28, 7.29
State v. Carlson, 61 Wash. App. 865, 812 P.2d 536 (1991)	§ 7.44
State v. Carpenter, 573 N.E.2d 1206 (Ohio Ct. App. 1989)	§ 4.22
State v. Carter, 572 S.W.2d 430 (Mo. 1978)	§ 2.18
State v. Carthan, 377 So. 2d 308 (La. 1979)	§ 5.7
State v. Carver, 380 N.W.2d 821 (Minn. Ct. App. 1986)	§§ 2.18, 5.17, 7.44, 7.45
State v. Catsam, 148 Vt. 366, 534 A.2d 184 (1987)	§§ 5.29, 6.22
State v. Cavallo, 88 N.J. 508, 443 A.2d 1020 (1982)	§§ 4.17, 4.18, 4.50
State v. Cermak, 350 N.W.2d 328 (Minn. 1984)	§ 2.1
State v. Cermak, 442 N.W.2d 822 (Minn. Ct. App. 1989)	§ 1.14
State v. Chandler, 324 N.C. 172, 376 S.E.2d 728 (1989)	§§ 5.7, 5.8, 7.48
State v. Chapin, 118 Wash. 2d 681, 826 P.2d 194 (1992)	§ 7.29

Case	Book §
State v. Chapple, 135 Ariz. 281, 660 P.2d 1208 (1983)	§ 4.13
State v. Charles, 398 S.E.2d 123 (W. Va. 1990)	§ 4.37
State v. Cherry, 154 N.J. Super. 157, 381 A.2d 49 (1977)	§ 7.31
State v. Chisholm, 250 Kan. 153, 825 P.2d 147 (1992)	§ 8.8
State v. Chisholm, 245 Kan. 145, 777 P.2d 753 (1989)	§ 8.8
State v. Christeson, 780 S.W.2d 119 (Mo. Ct. App. 1989)	§§ 3.29, 6.20, 6.22
State v. Church, 99 N.C. App. 647, 394 S.E.2d 468 (1990)	§§ 3.2, 3.9, 3.13
State v. Clark, 209 Mont. 473, 682 P.2d 1339 (1984)	§ 2.12
State v. Clarke, 343 N.W.2d 158 (Iowa 1984)	§ 5.35
State v. Clements, 244 Kan. 411, 770 P.2d 447 (1989)	§ 4.50
State v. Cleveland, 58 Wash. App. 634, 794 P.2d 546 (1990), *cert. denied,* 111 S. Ct. 1415 (1991)	§ 4.44
State v. Coe, 521 So. 2d 373 (Fla. Dist. Ct. App. 1988)	§ 5.16
State v. Coffelt, 33 Wash. 2d 106, 204 P.2d 521 (1949)	§ 1.3
State v. Coffey, 326 N.C. 268, 389 S.E.2d 48 (1990)	§ 6.13
State v. Collier, 23 Wash. 2d 678, 162 P.2d 267 (1945)	§ 2.12
State v. Conklin, 444 N.W.2d 268 (Minn. 1989)	§§ 7.44, 8.7, 8.8
State v. Conlogue, 474 A.2d 167 (Me. 1984)	§ 3.31
State v. Cook, 285 So. 2d 606 (La. Ct. App. 1986)	§ 2.18
State v. Cooley, 48 Wash. App. 286, 738 P.2d 705 (1987)	§ 7.44
State v. Cooper, 291 S.C. 351, 353 S.E.2d 451 (1987)	§ 7.50
State v. Coppola, 130 N.H. 148, 536 A.2d 1236 (1987), *cert. denied,* 493 U.S. 969 (1989)	§ 7.30
State v. Cousin, 136 Ariz. 83, 664 P.2d 233 (Ct. App. 1983)	§ 6.21
State v. Cox, 133 N.H. 261, 575 A.2d 1320 (1990)	§ 5.28
State v. Crandall, 120 N.J. 649, 577 A.2d 483 (1990)	§§ 8.8, 8.13
State v. Crane, 116 Wash. 315, 804 P.2d 10 (1991)	§ 1.6
State v. Crissman, 31 Ohio App. 2d 170, 287 N.E.2d 642 (1971)	§ 7.31
State v. Culkin, 791 S.W.2d 803 (Mo. Ct. App. 1990)	§ 5.8
State v. Cuvelier, 175 Conn. 100, 394 A.2d 185 (1978)	§ 7.47
State v. Dabkowski, 199 Conn. 193, 506 A.2d 118 (1986)	§ 7.31
State v. Dalphond, 133 N.H. 827, 585 A.2d 317 (1991)	§ 6.18
State v. D'Ambrosia, 212 Conn. 50, 561 A.2d 422 (1989), *cert. denied,* 493 U.S. 1063 (1990)	§§ 1.14, 5.21
State v. Dana, 422 N.W.2d 246 (Minn. 1988)	§§ 5.9, 7.46
State v. Daniels, 484 So. 2d 941 (La. Ct. App. 1986)	§ 8.12
State v. Daniels, 380 N.W.2d 777 (Minn. 1986)	§§ 2.19, 7.30
State v. Daniels, 222 Neb. 850, 388 N.W.2d 446 (1986)	§ 7.31
State v. Darby, 19 Conn. App. 445, 563 A.2d 710 (1989)	§ 8.8
State v. Davidson, 764 S.W.2d 731 (Mo. Ct. App. 1989)	§ 8.8
State v. Davis, 269 N.W.2d 434 (Iowa 1978)	§ 5.32
State v. Davis, 830 P.2d 1309 (Mont. 1992)	§§ 7.58, 8.3
State v. Davis, 422 N.W.2d 296 (Minn. Ct. App. 1988)	§ 4.44
State v. Davis, 229 N.J. Super. 66, 550 A.2d 1241 (1988)	§ 8.8
State v. D.B.S., 216 Mont. 234, 700 P.2d 630 (1985)	§§ 1.3, 2.1, 2.12, 2.18
State v. Dean, 589 A.2d 929 (Me. 1991)	§ 6.13
State v. DeBolt, 61 Wash. App. 58, 808 P.2d 794 (1991)	§§ 1.3, 7.31
State v. DeLawder, 28 Md. App. 212, 344 A.2d 446 (1975)	§ 5.36

Case	Book §
State v. Deleon, 813 P.2d 1382 (Haw. 1991)	§§ 3.1, 3.2
State v. DeLeonardo, 315 N.C. 762, 340 S.E.2d 350 (1986)	§§ 2.1, 2.12, 5.8, 6.22
State v. Denny, 296 N.W.2d 378 (Minn. 1980)	§ 5.9
State v. Doe, 105 Wash. 2d 889, 719 P.2d 554 (1986)	§§ 7.30, 7.44, 7.48
State v. Dollinger, 20 Conn. App. 530, 568 A.2d 1058 (1990)	§§ 7.3, 7.35
State v. Donnelly, 244 Mont. 371, 798 P.2d 89 (1990), *overruled on other grounds,* 813 P.2d 979 (Mont. 1991)	§ 4.37
State v. Doss, 522 So. 2d 1274 (La. Ct. App. 1988)	§ 2.18
State v. Douglas, 797 S.W.2d 532 (Mo. Ct. App. 1990)	§ 5.29
State v. D.R., 109 N.J. 348, 537 A.2d 667 (1988)	§§ 7.1, 7.28, 7.44
State v. D.R.H., 248 N.J. Super. 1, 589 A.2d 1353 (1990)	§ 1.13
State v. Drusch, 139 Wis. 2d 312, 407 N.W.2d 328 (Ct. App. 1987)	§ 7.48
State v. Dumlao, 3 Conn. App. 607, 491 A.2d 404 (1985)	§§ 3.5, 3.6, 3.30, 4.17
State v. Dunbar, 152 Vt. 399, 566 A.2d 970 (1989)	§ 8.3
State v. Duncan, 53 Ohio St. 2d 215, 373 N.E.2d 1234 (1978)	§ 7.31
State v. Dunn, 731 S.W.2d 297 (Mo. Ct. App. 1987)	§ 2.15
State v. Dupay, 405 N.W.2d 444 (Minn. Ct. App. 1987)	§ 6.22
State v. Durfee, 322 N.W.2d 778 (Minn. 1982)	§§ 3.5, 3.9, 3.30
State v. Dwyer, 143 Wis. 2d 448, 422 N.W.2d 121 (Ct. App. 1988), *aff'd,* 149 Wis. 2d 850, 440 N.W.2d 344 (1989)	§§ 2.3, 2.4, 2.12, 2.14, 2.16, 2.18, 7.30, 7.48, 7.56
State v. Eason, 402 S.E.2d 809 (N.C. 1991)	§ 2.1
State v. Eastham, 39 Ohio St. 3d 307, 530 N.E.2d 409 (1988)	§ 8.8
State v. Eaton, 244 Kan. 370, 769 P.2d 1157 (1989)	§§ 7.48, 8.8
State v. Edward Charles L., 183 W. Va. 641, 398 S.E.2d 123 (1990)	§§ 1.3, 6.13, 6.20, 6.21
State v. Edwards, 1992 WL 118977 (Minn. 1992)	§ 7.44
State v. Edwards, 785 S.W.2d 703 (Mo. Ct. App. 1990)	§ 4.38
State v. Eggert, 358 N.W.2d 156 (Minn. Ct. App. 1984)	§ 5.8
State v. Eiler, 234 Mont. 38, 762 P.2d 210 (1988)	§§ 2.1, 2.12, 2.14, 2.18
State v. Elbert, 1992 WL 67054 (Mo. Ct. App. 1992)	§§ 4.49, 4.50
State v. Eldredge, 773 P.2d 29 (Utah), *cert. denied,* 493 U.S. 814 (1989)	§§ 2.3, 2.4, 2.9, 2.17, 4.45
State v. Emmons, 528 A.2d 1266 (Me. 1987)	§§ 7.2, 7.6
State v. Erickson, 454 N.W.2d 624 (Minn. Ct. App. 1990)	§ 4.5
State v. Ester, 490 So. 2d 579 (La. Ct. App. 1986)	§ 5.11
State v. Estes, 99 N.C. App. 312, 393 S.E.2d 158 (1990)	§ 4.28
State v. Etheridge, 319 N.C. 34, 352 S.E.2d 673 (1987)	§ 6.26
State v. Evans, 802 S.W.2d 507 (Mo. 1991)	§§ 4.28, 5.8
State v. Evans, 594 A.2d 154 (N.H. 1991)	§§ 3.11, 3.28, 3.29
State v. Everett, 328 N.C. 72, 399 S.E.2d 305 (1991)	§ 1.3
State v. Fader, 358 N.W.2d 42 (Minn. 1984)	§ 7.30

Case	Book §
State v. Fagalde, 85 Wash. 2d 730, 539 P.2d 86 (1975)	§ 1.16
State v. Faircloth, 99 N.C. App. 685, 394 S.E.2d 198 (1990)	§ 6.18
State v. Farr, 558 So. 2d 437 (Fla. Dist. Ct. App. 1990)	§ 1.13
State v. Faucette, 326 N.C. 676, 392 S.E.2d 71 (1990)	§ 7.53
State v. Fawcett, 145 Wis. 2d 244, 426 N.W.2d 91 (Ct. App. 1988)	§§ 1.1, 1.3, 1.4, 1.5
State v. Fearing, 315 N.C. 167, 337 S.E.2d 551 (1985)	§ 7.35
State v. Feet, 481 So. 2d 667 (La. Ct. App. 1985)	§§ 2.1, 5.15
State v. Feltrop, 803 S.W.2d 1 (Mo.), *cert. denied*, 111 S. Ct. 2918 (1991)	§§ 2.1, 2.8, 2.10
State v. Ferguson, 5 Ohio St. 3d 160, 450 N.E.2d 265 (1983)	§ 4.28
State v. Ferguson, 100 Wash. 2d 131, 667 P.2d 68 (1983)	§ 7.31
State v. Fitzgerald, 382 N.W.2d 892 (Minn. Ct. App. 1986)	§ 2.1
State v. Fitzgerald, 778 S.W.2d 689 (Mo. Ct. App. 1989)	§§ 3.14, 3.29
State v. Fitzgerald, 39 Wash. App. 652, 694 P.2d 1117 (1985)	§ 7.35
State v. Fletcher, 322 N.C. 415, 368 S.E.2d 633 (1988)	§ 5.8
State v. Floody, 481 N.W.2d 242 (S.D. 1992)	§§ 1.1, 4.5, 4.45, 7.44
State v. Foell, 416 N.W.2d 45 (S.D. 1987)	§§ 7.46, 7.48
State v. Foley, 392 A.2d 1094 (Me. 1978)	§ 5.17
State v. Folley, 378 N.W.2d 21 (Minn. Ct. App. 1985)	§ 5.17
State v. Frey, 43 Wash. App. 605, 718 P.2d 846 (1986)	§ 7.45
State v. Friedrich, 135 Wis. 2d 1, 398 N.W.2d 763 (1987)	§§ 4.45, 6.14, 6.22
State v. Fritz, 44 S.D. 517, 184 N.W. 235 (1921)	§ 7.31
State v. Fulton, 742 P.2d 1208 (Utah 1987), *cert. denied*, 484 U.S. 1044 (1988)	§§ 2.3, 2.4
State v. Gallagher, 150 Vt. 341, 554 A.2d 221, *cert. denied*, 488 U.S. 995 (1988)	§ 7.44
State v. Galloway, 304 N.C. 485, 284 S.E.2d 509 (1981)	§ 4.28
State v. Galvan, 297 N.W.2d 344 (Iowa 1980)	§§ 7.30, 7.49
State v. Garfield, 34 Ohio App. 3d 300, 518 N.E.2d 568 (1986)	§ 4.44
State v. Garner, 116 Ariz. 443, 569 P.2d 1341 (1977)	§§ 2.19, 2.22
State v. Garza, 337 N.W.2d 823 (S.D. 1983)	§ 7.35
State v. Gettier, 438 N.W.2d 1 (Iowa 1989)	§ 4.34
State v. Gilbert, 109 Wis. 2d 501, 326 N.W.2d 744 (1982)	§ 7.48
State v. Gill, 806 S.W.2d 48 (Mo. Ct. App. 1991)	§ 7.44
State v. Gillette, 699, P.2d 626 (N.M. Ct. App. 1985)	§ 6.26
State v. Gilroy, 313 N.W.2d 513 (Iowa 1981)	§ 1.12
State v. Gitchel, 41 Wash. App. 820, 706 P.2d 1091 (1985)	§§ 2.1, 7.45, 7.48
State v. Goblirsch, 309 Minn. 401, 246 N.W.2d 12 (1976)	§ 3.31
State v. Gokey, 154 Vt. 129, 574 A.2d 766 (1990)	§§ 4.37, 4.44
State v. Gollon, 115 Wis. 2d 592, 340 N.W.2d 912 (Ct. App. 1983)	§§ 7.30, 7.48
State v. Gonzales, 219 Neb. 846, 366 N.W.2d 775 (1985)	§ 7.30
State v. Gordon, 463 So. 2d 665 (La. Ct. App. 1985)	§§ 2.18, 2.22
State v. Gordon, 316 N.C. 497, 342 S.E.2d 509 (1986)	§§ 2.1, 2.18
State v. Gorman, 229 Minn. 524, 40 N.W.2d 347 (1949)	§ 7.49

Case	Book §
State v. Goutro, 444 So. 2d 615 (La. 1984)	§ 2.1
State v. Gove, 148 Wis. 2d 936, 437 N.W.2d 218 (1989)	§§ 7.48, 7.58
State v. Grady, 183 N.W.2d 707 (Iowa 1971)	§ 7.31
State v. Graham, 59 Wash. App. 418, 798 P.2d 314 (1990)	§§ 4.34, 4.39, 4.44
State v. Granville, 304 Or. 424, 746 P.2d 715 (1987)	§ 1.14
State v. Gregory, 78 N.C. App. 565, 338 S.E.2d 110 (1985)	§ 7.35
State v. Grey, 256 N.W.2d 74 (Minn. 1977)	§ 7.57
State v. Gribble, 60 Wash. App. 374, 804 P.2d 634 (1991)	§§ 2.19, 4.28, 7.44, 7.45, 7.49
State v. Griffith, 45 Wash. App. 728, 727 P.2d 247 (1986)	§ 7.30
State v. Gross, 121 N.J. 1, 577 A.2d 806 (1990)	§ 7.20
State v. Guajardo, 605 A.2d 217 (N.H. 1992)	§ 8.4
State v. Guerin, 63 Wash. App. 117, 816 P.2d 1249 (1991)	§ 2.11
State v. Guy, 227 Neb. 610, 419 N.W.2d 152 (1988)	§§ 2.1, 2.10, 2.12, 2.18
State v. Hackett, 49 Or. App. 857, 621 P.2d 609 (1980)	§ 7.31
State v. Hadfield, 788 P.2d 506 (Utah 1990)	§ 4.5
State v. Hall, 406 N.W.2d 503 (Minn. 1987)	§ 4.44
State v. Hall, 330 N.C. 808, 412 S.E.2d 883 (1992)	§§ 4.34, 4.44
State v. Hall, 108 Or. App. 12, 814 P.2d 172 (1991)	§ 6.20
State v. Hamer, 188 Conn. 562, 452 A.2d 313 (1982)	§ 7.31
State v. Hamrick, 714 S.W.2d 566 (Mo. Ct. App. 1986)	§ 5.17
State v. Hancock, 109 Wash. 2d 760, 748 P.2d 611 (1988)	§ 7.20
State v. Hankins, 232 Neb. 608, 441 N.W.2d 854 (1989)	§§ 1.14, 3.32
State v. Hannah, 316 N.C. 362, 341 S.E.2d 514 (1986)	§ 5.7
State v. Hansen, 304 Or. 169, 743 P.2d 157 (1987)	§ 4.50
State v. Hanson, 286 Minn. 317, 176 N.W.2d 607 (1970)	§ 2.12
State v. Harper, 35 Wash. App. 855, 670 P.2d 296 (1983)	§§ 6.8, 7.23
State v. Harris, 247 Mont. 405, 808 P.2d 453 (1991)	§§ 7.36, 7.44
State v. Haseltine, 120 Wis. 2d 92, 352 N.W.2d 673 (Ct. App. 1984)	§ 4.37
State v. Hayes, 20 Conn. App. 737, 570 A.2d 716 (1990)	§ 6.13
State v. Hebert, 480 A.2d 742 (Me. 1984)	§ 7.35
State v. Helms, 322 N.C. 315, 367 S.E.2d 644 (1988)	§ 5.21
State v. Hernandez, 167 Ariz. 236, 805 P.2d 1057 (Ct. App. 1990)	§§ 3.5, 3.8, 3.9, 3.10, 3.11, 7.47
State v. Herrin, 562 So. 2d 1 (La. Ct. App. 1990)	§§ 2.18, 7.31, 7.44
State v. Hester, 801 S.W.2d 695 (Mo. 1991)	§§ 7.48, 7.50
State v. Hester, 114 Idaho 688, 760 P.2d 27 (1988)	§§ 4.37, 4.50
State v. Hewett, 93 N.C. App. 1, 376 S.E.2d 467 (1989)	§§ 5.8, 8.14
State v. Hibbs, 239 Mont. 308, 780 P.2d 182 (1989)	§§ 5.7, 7.22
State v. Hicks, 148 Vt. 459, 535 A.2d 776 (1987)	§ 4.44
State v. Hicks, 319 N.C. 84, 352 S.E.2d 424 (1987)	§ 4.28
State v. Higginbottom, 312 N.C. 760, 324 S.E.2d 834 (1985)	§§ 2.1, 2.15, 2.18, 5.7
State v. Higgins, 61 Ohio App. 3d 414, 572 N.E.2d 834 (1990)	§ 4.10
State v. Hightower, 376 N.W.2d 648 (Iowa Ct. App. 1985)	§ 8.4
State v. Hill, 59 Ohio App. 3d 31, 570 N.E.2d 1138 (1989)	§ 1.1
State v. Hoban, 738 S.W.2d 536 (Mo. Ct. App. 1987)	§§ 1.1, 1.3, 1.4 1.8

Case	Book §
State v. Holland, 346 N.W.2d 302 (S.D. 1984)	§§ 3.5, 6.17
State v. Holloway, 82 N.C. App. 586, 347 S.E.2d 72 (1986)	§ 4.45
State v. Hollywood, 67 Or. App. 546, 680 P.2d 655 (1984)	§§ 7.30, 7.42
State v. Hookfin, 476 So. 2d 481 (La. Ct. App. 1985)	§§ 5.13, 5.19
State v. Hoversten, 437 N.W.2d 240 (Iowa), *cert. denied,* 493 U.S. 875 (1989)	§ 8.8
State v. Howard, 405 A.2d 206 (Me. 1979)	§ 5.9
State v. Howard, 121 N.H. 53, 426 A.2d 457 (1981)	§§ 5.28, 5.30, 5.35
State v. Howie, 228 Mont. 497, 744 P.2d 156 (1987)	§ 2.18
State v. Hoyt, 806 P.2d 204 (Utah Ct. App. 1991)	§§ 1.1, 1.3
State v. Hubbard, 297 Or. 789, 688 P.2d 1311 (1984)	§ 5.23
State v. Hubbard, 601 P.2d 929 (Utah 1979)	§ 2.22
State v. Hudnall, 293 S.C. 97, 359 S.E.2d 59 (1987)	§§ 2.1, 2.18, 4.37
State v. Huey, 145 Ariz. 59, 699 P.2d 1290 (1985)	§ 4.34
State v. Hulbert, 481 N.W.2d 329 (Iowa 1992)	§ 4.5, 4.50
State v. Hunsaker, 39 Wash. App. 489, 693 P.2d 724 (1984)	§§ 2.1, 2.12, 2.18
State v. Hunt, 48 Wash. App. 840, 741 P.2d 566 (1987)	§§ 7.2, 7.48, 7.49
State v. Hunt, 8 Ariz. App. 514, 447 P.2d 896 (1968)	§ 6.5
State v. Hussey, 521 A.2d 278 (Me. 1987)	§§ 2.1, 2.12, 2.15
State v. Hutchins, 241 N.J. Super. 353, 575 A.2d 35 (1990)	§ 5.20
State v. Hyde, 735 S.W.2d 746 (Mo. Ct. App. 1987)	§ 7.56
State v. Infante, 596 A.2d 1289 (Vt. 1991)	§§ 1.1, 1.3
State v. Iorg, 801 P.2d 938 (Utah Ct. App. 1990)	§ 4.45
State v. Jackson, 239 Kan. 463, 721 P.2d 232 (1986)	§ 4.45
State v. Jackson, 82 Ohio App. 318, 81 N.E.2d 546 (1948)	§ 6.14
State v. Jackson, 46 Wash. App. 360, 730 P.2d 1361 (1986)	§ 6.8
State v. Jackson, 383 S.E.2d 79 (W. Va. 1989)	§ 4.34
State v. Jacques, 558 A.2d 706 (Me. 1989)	§ 5.35
State v. Jagielski, 161 Wis. 2d 67, 467 N.W.2d 196 (Ct. App. 1991)	§§ 5.35, 7.44
State v. Jalo, 27 Or. App. 845, 557 P.2d 1359 (1976)	§ 5.36
State v. James, 211 Conn. 555, 560 A.2d 426 (1989)	§§ 2.9, 8.14
State v. James, 819 P.2d 781 (Utah 1991)	§ 3.29
State v. Janes, 64 Wash. App. 134, 822 P.2d 1238 (1992)	§ 3.5
State v. Jano, 524 So. 2d 660 (Fla. 1988)	§§ 7.27, 7.30
State v. Jarzbek, 204 Conn. 683, 529 A.2d 1245 (1987), *cert. denied,* 484 U.S. 1061 (1988)	§§ 5.8, 8.8
State v. J.C.E., 235 Mont. 264, 767 P.2d 309 (1988)	§§ 5.1, 7.1, 7.35, 7.42, 7.44
State v. Jenkins, 326 N.W.2d 67 (N.D. 1982)	§ 5.7
State v. Jensen, 107 Or. App. 35, 810 P.2d 865 (1991)	§§ 7.30, 7.53
State v. Jensen, 141 Wis. 2d 333, 415 N.W.2d 519 (Ct. App. 1987), *aff'd,* 147 Wis. 2d 240, 432 N.W.2d 913 (1988)	§§ 4.9, 4.10, 4.32 4.37, 4.41, 4.44, 4.45
State v. Jerousek, 121 Ariz. 420, 590 P.2d 1366 (1979)	§ 5.7
State v. John C., 503 A.2d 1296 (Me. 1986)	§ 7.56
State v. Johns, 301 Or. 535, 725 P.2d 312 (1986)	§ 6.17

CASES

Case	Book §
State v. Johns, 615 P.2d 1260 (Utah 1980)	§ 5.28
State v. Johnson, 694 S.W.2d 490 (Mo. Ct. App. 1985)	§ 2.18
State v. Johnson, 105 N.C. App. 390, 413 S.E.2d 562 (1992)	§ 4.37
State v. Johnson, 135 Wis. 2d 453, 400 N.W.2d 502 (Ct. App. 1986)	§§ 3.5, 3.8, 3.9, 3.12, 3.29
State v. Jones, 204 Kan. 719, 466 P.2d 283 (1970)	§ 5.7
State v. Jones, 99 N.C. App. 412, 393 S.E.2d 585 (1990)	§ 4.45
State v. Jones, 89 N.C. App. 584, 367 S.E.2d 139 (1988)	§ 7.35
State v. Jones, 735 P.2d 399 (Utah Ct. App. 1987)	§ 6.5
State v. Jones, 59 Wash. App. 744, 801 P.2d 263 (1990)	§§ 3.5, 3.7, 3.8, 3.9, 3.10, 3.11
State v. Jones, 112 Wash. 2d 488, 772 P.2d 496 (1989)	§§ 4.1, 5.1, 7.1, 7.43, 7.44, 7.45, 7.46
State v. Jones, 362 S.E.2d 330 (W. Va. 1987)	§§ 2.12, 2.18, 7.30, 8.1
State v. J.Q., 599 A.2d 172 (N.J. Super.Ct. 1991), *cert. granted,* 606 A.2d 372 (N.J. 1992)	§§ 4.33, 4.37
State v. J.S., 222 N.J. Super. 247, 536 A.2d 769 (1988)	§ 7.31
State v. Jurgens, 424 N.W.2d 546 (Minn. Ct. App. 1988)	§§ 3.5, 3.6, 3.8
State v. Just, 184 Mont. 262, 602 P.2d 957 (1979)	§ 6.22
State v. Justiniano, 48 Wash. App. 572, 740 P.2d 872 (1987)	§§ 2.19, 7.45, 7.46, 7.48
State v. Kahey, 436 So. 2d 475 (La. 1983)	§ 5.7
State v. Kao, 245 Mont. 263, 800 P.2d 714 (1990)	§ 6.9
State v. Kelly, 554 A.2d 632 (R.I. 1989)	§ 1.14
State v. Kendrick, 239 Or. 512, 398 P.2d 471 (1965)	§ 7.30
State v. Kim, 318 N.C. 614, 350 S.E.2d 347 (1986)	§ 4.45
State v. King, 115 N.J. Super. 140, 278 A.2d 504 (1971)	§ 7.22
State v. Kinney, 35 Ohio App. 3d 84, 519 N.E.2d 1386 (1987)	§ 1.3
State v. Kivett, 321 N.C. 404, 364 S.E.2d 404 (1988)	§ 2.1
State v. Knapp, 45 N.H. 148 (1863)	§ 7.31
State v. Komurke, 560 So. 2d 986 (La. Ct. App. 1990)	§§ 4.5, 7.30, 7.31
State v. Kristich, 226 Or. 240, 359 P.2d 1106 (1961)	§§ 6.20, 6.21
State v. Kuone, 243 Kan. 218, 757 P.2d 289 (1988)	§§ 7.44, 7.45, 7.48
State v. LaChance, 524 S.W.2d 933 (Tenn. 1975)	§ 3.29
State v. Lafrance, 589 A.2d 43 (Me. 1991)	§§ 7.29, 7.30, 7.31
State v. Lairby, 699 P.2d 1187 (Utah 1984), *overturned on other grounds,* 793 P.2d 377 (1990)	§§ 2.1, 2.12, 2.12, 2.22, 5.16, 5.21
State v. Lanam, 444 N.W.2d 882 (Minn. Ct. App. 1989), *aff'd,* 459 N.W.2d 656 (Minn. 1990), *cert. denied,* 111 S. Ct. 693 (1991)	§§ 7.44, 7.48
State v. Lanter, 237 Kan. 309, 699 P.2d 503 (1985)	§ 7.46
State v. Lapage, 57 N.H. 245 (1876)	§§ 6.17, 6.18
State v. Larson, 472 N.W.2d 120 (Minn. 1991), *cert. denied,* 112 S. Ct. 965 (1992)	§§ 7.36, 7.53
State v. Lau, 409 N.W.2d 275 (Minn. Ct. App. 1987)	§ 2.1
State v. Le Clair, 83 Or. App. 121, 730 P.2d 609 (1986)	§ 5.34

Case *Book §*

State v. Leavitt, 49 Wash. App. 348, 743 P.2d 270 (1987), *aff'd,* 111 Wash. 2d 66, 758 P.2d 982 (1988) §§ 2.13, 7.46
State v. Lebel, 594 A.2d 91 (Me. 1991) § 6.8
State v. Lee, 9 Ohio App. 3d 282, 459 N.E.2d 910 (1983) § 5.8
State v. Lee, 88 Or. App. 556, 746 P.2d 242 (1988) § 6.18
State v. Leigh, 580 S.W.2d 536 (Mo. Ct. App. 1979) §§ 2.18, 5.7, 5.17
State v. Lewis, 4 Ohio App. 3d 275, 448 N.E.2d 487 (1982) § 5.7
State v. Lindner, 142 Wis. 2d 783, 419 N.W.2d 352 (Ct. App. 1987) §§ 7.22, 7.23, 7.30, 7.44, 7.48
State v. Lindsey, 149 Ariz. 472, 720 P.2d 73 (1986) §§ 4.9, 4.13, 4.44, 4.45
State v. Littlefield, 540 A.2d 777 (Me. 1988) § 7.23
State v. Loebach, 310 N.W.2d 58 (Minn. 1981) § 3.31
State v. Logan, 105 Or. App. 556, 806 P.2d 137 (1991) §§ 7.35, 7.36, 7.38
State v. Logue, 372 N.W.2d 151 (S.D. 1985) § 7.30
State v. Longuskie, 59 Wash. App. 838, 801 P.2d 1004 (1990) § 6.25
State v. Lopez, 170 Ariz. 112, 822 P.2d 465 (Ct. App. 1991) § 6.21
State v. Loss, 295 Minn. 271, 204 N.W.2d 404 (1973) § 3.31
State v. Loughton, 747 P.2d 426 (Utah 1987) §§ 2.9, 7.28, 7.46, 7.51
State v. Lounsbery, 74 Wash. 2d 659, 445 P.2d 1017 (1968) §§ 2.19, 7.49
State v. Lucero, 109 N.M. 298, 784 P.2d 1041 (Ct. App. 1989) §§ 7.22, 7.23
State v. Mace, 67 Or. App. 753, 681 P.2d 140 (1984) § 7.30
State v. Macias, 110 N.M. 246, 794 P.2d 389 (Ct. App. 1990) §§ 2.18, 4.28
State v. Madden, 15 Ohio App. 3d 130, 472 N.E.2d 1126 (1984) § 5.8
State v. Madison, 53 Wash. App. 754, 770 P.2d 662 (1989) §§ 4.44, 4.45
State v. Madsen, 772 S.W.2d 656 (Mo. 1989), *cert. denied,* 493 U.S. 1046 (1990) §§ 5.28, 5.32, 5.36
State v. Maestas, 92 N.M. 135, 584 P.2d 182 (Ct. App. 1978) § 7.27
State v. Mahurin, 799 S.W.2d 840 (Mo. 1990) § 3.28
State v. Makela, 1992 WL 137628 (Wash. Ct. App. 1992) § 4.44
State v. Maldonado, 13 Conn. App. 368, 536 A.2d 600 (1988) §§ 2.1, 2.18, 7.8, 7.35
State v. Mancine, 124 N.J. 232, 590 A.2d 1107 (1991) §§ 7.18, 7.20
State v. Manlove, 79 N.M. 189, 441 P.2d 229 (Ct. App. 1968) § 2.18
State v. Mannion, 19 Utah 505, 57 P. 542 (1899) § 8.3
State v. Marcum, 750 P.2d 599 (Utah 1988) §§ 1.1, 7.48
State v. Marks, 231 Kan. 645, 647 P.2d 1292 (1982) § 4.34
State v. Mateer, 383 N.W.2d 533 (Iowa 1986) § 7.30
State v. Matteson, 287 N.W.2d 408 (Minn. 1979) § 6.22
State v. Maule, 35 Wash. App. 287, 667 P.2d 96 (1983) § 3.31
State v. Mayes, 825 P.2d 1196 (Mont. 1992) § 7.44

CASES

Case	*Book §*
State v. Mayfield, 302 Or. 631, 733 P.2d 438 (1987)	§§ 4.35, 7.8
State v. McCafferty, 356 N.W.2d 159 (S.D. 1984), *cert. denied,* 476 U.S. 1172 (1986)	§§ 7.42, 7.44
State v. McCarthy, 589 A.2d 869 (Vt. 1991)	§ 6.8
State v. McClary, 207 Conn. 233, 541 A.2d 96 (1988)	§§ 3.5, 3.8, 3.11, 3.28, 3.30
State v. McCoy, 400 N.W.2d 807 (Minn. Ct. App. 1987)	§ 4.10
State v. McCoy, 366 S.E.2d 731 (W. Va. 1988)	§ 4.34
State v. McFarlin, 110 Ariz. 225, 517 P.2d 87 (1973)	§ 6.21
State v. McKay, 309 Or. 305, 787 P.2d 479 (1990)	§ 6.21
State v. McKinney, 50 Wash. App. 56, 747 P.2d 1113 (1987)	§§ 7.30, 7.44, 7.45
State v. McKnight, 820 P.2d 1279 (Mont. 1991)	§ 6.18
State v. McNeely, 314 N.C. 451, 333 S.E.2d 738 (1985)	§§ 2.1, 2.18
State v. McQuillen, 236 Kan. 161, 689 P.2d 822 (1984)	§ 4.34
State v. Medina, 245 Mont. 25, 798 P.2d 1032 (1990)	§ 6.22
State v. Menzies, 603 A.2d 419 (Conn. App. Ct. 1992)	§ 8.1
State v. Mercer, 34 Wash. App. 654, 663 P.2d 857 (1983)	§ 6.17
State v. Messamore, 2 Haw. App. 643, 639 P.2d 413 (1982)	§ 7.28
State v. Middleton, 294 Or. 427, 657 P.2d 1215 (1983)	§§ 4.9, 4.13, 4.44, 4.45
State v. Milbradt, 305 Or. 621, 756 P.2d 620 (1988)	§ 4.45
State v. Miller, 377 N.W.2d 506 (Minn. Ct. App. 1985)	§ 4.45
State v. Moats, 156 Wis. 2d 74, 457 N.W.2d 299 (1990)	§§ 5.34, 5.35, 7.30
State v. Moen, 309 Or. 45, 786 P.2d 111 (1990)	§§ 7.35, 7.36, 7.53
State v. Moore, 377 A.2d 1365 (Me. 1977)	§ 5.7
State v. Moore, 103 N.C. App. 87, 404 S.E.2d 695 (1991)	§ 4.28
State v. Moorison, 43 Wash. 2d 23, 259 P.2d 1105 (1953)	§ 2.18
State v. Moran, 151 Ariz. 378, 728 P.2d 248 (1986)	§§ 4.8, 4.10, 4.15, 4.37, 4.41, 4.44, 4.45, 7.20, 7.47
State v. Moran, 585 So. 2d 576 (La. Ct. App. 1991)	§ 7.31
State v. Morris, 825 P.2d 1051 (Haw. 1992)	§ 4.37, 4.45
State v. Morrison, 437 N.W.2d 422 (Minn. Ct. App.), *cert. denied,* 493 U.S. 858 (1989)	§§ 3.5, 3.9, 3.32, 7.38
State v. Morrison, 582 So. 2d 295 (La. Ct. App. 1991)	§ 3.28
State v. Mosby, 450 N.W.2d 629 (Minn. Ct. App. 1990)	§§ 2.16, 3.29, 6.20
State v. Moser, 82 S.D. 149, 143 N.W.2d 369 (1966)	§ 2.18
State v. Moton, 749 P.2d 639 (Utah 1988)	§ 7.56
State v. Moyer, 151 Ariz. 253, 727 P.2d 31 (Ct. App. 1986)	§§ 3.5, 3.7, 3.10, 3.13, 4.17
State v. Mulder, 29 Wash. App. 513, 629 P.2d 462 (1981)	§§ 3.5, 3.6, 3.8
State v. Muniz, 150 N.J. Super. 436, 375 A.2d 1234 (1977), *cert. denied,* 77 N.J. 473, 391 A.2d 488 (1978)	§§ 3.5, 3.14
State v. Murley, 35 Wash. 2d 233, 212 P.2d 801 (1949)	§ 7.31
State v. Murphy, 462 N.W.2d 715 (Iowa Ct. App. 1990)	§§ 7.19, 7.29
State v. Murray, 375 S.E.2d 405 (W. Va. 1988)	§ 5.24
State v. Myatt, 237 Kan. 17, 697 P.2d 836 (1985)	§§ 7.44, 7.46
State v. Myers, 382 N.W.2d 91 (Iowa 1986)	§ 4.45

Case   *Book §*

State v. Myers, 359 N.W.2d 604 (Minn. 1984)	§§ 4.44, 4.45, 5.17
State v. Naylor, 602 A.2d 187 (Me. 1992)	§§ 6.8, 7.31
State v. Nelson, 777 P.2d 479 (Utah 1989)	§ 7.42
State v. Nelson, 138 Wis. 2d 418, 406 N.W.2d 385 (1987)	§§ 7.35, 7.36, 7.44, 7.51
State v. Newman, 242 Mont. 315, 790 P.2d 971 (1990)	§ 2.11
State v. Nims, 357 N.W.2d 608 (Iowa 1984)	§ 2.1
State v. Noble, 342 So. 2d 170 (La. 1977)	§ 7.30
State v. Noltie, 116 Wash. 2d 831, 809 P.2d 190 (1991)	§§ 3.32, 4.28
State v. Norman, 61 Wash. App. 16, 808 P.2d 1159 (1991)	§ 3.17
State v. Norris, 101 N.C. App. 144, 398 S.E.2d 652 (1990)	§ 4.28
State v. Noyes, 596 A.2d 340 (Vt. 1991)	§ 4.44
State v. Ochoa, 576 So. 2d 854 (Fla. Dist. Ct. App. 1991)	§§ 7.36, 7.53
State v. Ogburne, 235 N.J. Super. 113, 561 A.2d 667 (1989)	§§ 5.32, 8.13
State v. Oliveira, 576 A.2d 111 (R.I. 1990)	§§ 5.34, 5.35
State v. Oliver, 158 Ariz. 22, 760 P.2d 1071 (1988)	§§ 5.24, 5.28, 5.29, 5.34, 5.35
State v. Oliver, 85 N.C. App. 1, 354 S.E.2d 527 (1987)	§§ 1.1, 1.3, 2.1, 2.12, 5.7
State v. Oliver, 161 Wis. 2d 140, 467 N.W.2d 211 (Ct. App. 1991)	§§ 7.44, 7.45
State v. O'Neill, 589 A.2d 999 (N.H. 1991)	§ 4.28
State v. Orona, 92 N.M. 450, 589 P.2d 1041 (1979)	§§ 5.7, 5.11, 5.13
State v. Ortlepp, 363 N.W.2d 39 (Minn. 1985)	§ 7.44
State v. Oslund, 469 N.W.2d 489 (Minn. Ct. App. 1991)	§§ 2.18, 4.7, 4.45, 7.44, 7.48
State v. Ostlund, 416 N.W.2d 755 (Minn. Ct. App. 1987)	§ 6.18
State v. Overshon, 741 S.W.2d 834 (Mo. Ct. App. 1987)	§ 2.18
State v. Pace, 187 Or. 498, 212 P.2d 755 (1949)	§ 6.21
State v. Padilla, 110 Wis. 2d 414, 329 N.W.2d 263 (Ct. App. 1982)	§ 7.30
State v. Pankow, 144 Wis. 2d 23, 422 N.W.2d 913 (Ct. App. 1988)	§ 3.5
State v. Parris, 219 Conn. 283, 592 A.2d 943 (1991)	§ 7.31
State v. Paster, 524 A.2d 587 (R.I. 1987)	§ 7.30
State v. Paulsen, 265 N.W.2d 581 (Iowa 1978)	§ 7.30
State v. Payton, 481 N.W.2d 325 (Iowa 1992)	§§ 4.44, 4.52
State v. Percy, 81 S.D. 519, 137 N.W.2d 888 (1965)	§ 7.30
State v. Percy, 149 Vt. 623, 548 A.2d 408 (1988)	§ 1.15
State v. Perry, 552 A.2d 545 (Me. 1989)	§ 1.15
State v. Perry, 95 N.M. 179, 619 P.2d 855 (Ct. App. 1980)	§ 7.27
State v. Person, 20 Conn. App. 115, 564 A.2d 626 (1989), *aff'd*, 215 Conn. 811, 568 A.2d 796 (1990), *cert. denied*, 111 S. Ct. 756 (1991)	§ 4.50
State v. Petrich, 101 Wash. 2d 566, 683 P.2d 173 (1984)	§§ 2.12, 4.44, 4.45
State v. Petry, 524 N.E.2d 1293 (Ind. Ct. App. 1988)	§ 7.45
State v. Pettis, 488 A.2d 704 (R.I. 1985)	§§ 2.1, 2.14, 2.18
State v. Pettit, 66 Or. App. 575, 675 P.2d 183 (1984)	§ 4.44
State v. Phelps, 215 Mont. 217, 696 P.2d 447 (1985)	§§ 1.9, 2.1, 2.12
State v. Philbrook, 525 A.2d 1047 (Me. 1987)	§ 2.22

CASES

Case	*Book §*
State v. Phillips, 328 N.C. 1, 399 S.E.2d 293, *cert. denied*, 111 S. Ct. 2804 (1991)	§§ 1.13, 1.15, 3.5, 3.7, 3.8, 3.9, 3.10, 3.30, 3.32, 6.24
State v. Pilkey, 776 S.W.2d 943 (Tenn. 1989), *cert. denied*, 494 U.S. 1032 (1990)	§§ 8.7, 8.8
State v. Pitts, 62 Wash. 2d 294, 382 P.2d 508 (1963)	§ 7.22
State v. Plant, 236 Neb. 317, 461 N.W.2d 253 (1990)	§§ 3.9, 7.30, 7.53
State v. Plymate, 216 Neb. 722, 345 N.W.2d 327 (1984)	§ 6.22
State v. Poehnelt, 150 Ariz. 136, 722 P.2d 304 (Ct. App. 1985)	§§ 3.5, 3.7, 3.29
State v. Pollard, 719 S.W.2d 38 (Mo. Ct. App. 1986)	§ 8.1
State v. Posten, 302 N.W.2d 638 (Minn. 1981)	§§ 7.13, 7.30, 8.2
State v. Presley, 542 So. 2d 1171 (La. Ct. App. 1989)	§ 8.8
State v. Price, 313 N.C. 297, 327 S.E.2d 863 (1985)	§§ 2.1, 2.18
State v. Przybylski, 48 Wash. App. 661, 739 P.2d 1203 (1987)	§§ 2.12, 2.18
State v. Pulizzano, 155 Wis. 2d 633, 456 N.W.2d 325 (1990)	§ 5.35
State v. Purro, 593 A.2d 450 (R.I. 1991)	§ 1.13
State v. Ramos, 553 A.2d 1059 (R.I. 1989)	§§ 1.13, 7.56
State v. Ramsey, 573 S.W.2d 720 (Mo. Ct. App. 1978)	§ 7.31
State v. Randolph, 190 Conn. 576, 462 A.2d 1011 (1983)	§ 7.7
State v. R.C., 494 So. 2d 1350 (La. Ct. App. 1986)	§ 7.48
State v. Red Feather, 205 Neb. 734, 289 N.W.2d 768 (1980)	§ 7.35
State v. Reeder, 105 N.C. App. 343, 413 S.E.2d 580 (1992)	§§ 4.37, 6.21
State v. Reinart, 440 N.W.2d 503 (N.D. 1989)	§ 5.29
State v. Renly, 111 Or. App. 453, 827 P.2d 1345 (1992)	§§ 4.52, 7.46, 7.53
State v. Resendez, 82 Or. App. 259, 728 P.2d 562 (1986)	§§ 7.23, 7.24
State v. Reser, 244 Kan. 306, 767 P.2d 1277 (1989)	§§ 4.10, 4.37
State v. R.H., 683 P.2d 269 (Alaska Ct. App. 1984)	§§ 1.16, 4.8
State v. Riddick, 315 N.C. 749, 340 S.E.2d 55 (1986)	§ 5.7
State v. Rimmasch, 775 P.2d 388 (Utah 1989)	§§ 4.17, 4.18, 4.19, 4.37, 4.45, 4.46
State v. Ritchey, 107 Ariz. 552, 490 P.2d 558 (1971)	§§ 7.30, 7.45
State v. Rivera, 139 Ariz. 409, 678 P.2d 1373 (1984)	§ 7.30
State v. Robbins, 709 P.2d 771 (Utah 1985)	§ 1.3
State v. Roberts, 25 Wash. App. 830, 611 P.2d 1297 (1980)	§ 5.21
State v. Robinson, 146 Wis. 2d 315, 431 N.W.2d 165 (1988)	§ 4.44
State v. Robinson, 44 Wash. App. 611, 722 P.2d 1379 (1986)	§§ 6.8, 7.30, 7.44, 5.45, 7.48, 7.51, 7.53
State v. Robinson, 153 Ariz. 191, 735 P.2d 801 (1987)	§§ 7.35, 7.36, 7.43, 7.44, 7.45, 7.46, 7.48
State v. Rogers, 213 Mont. 302, 692 P.2d 2 (1984)	§§ 2.1, 2.12, 2.18
State v. Rogers, 293 S.C. 505, 362 S.E.2d 7 (1987)	§§ 4.44, 8.8
State v. Roman, 248 N.J. Super. 144, 590 A.2d 686 (1991)	§ 7.48

Case *Book §*

State v. Romero, 94 N.M. 22, 606 P.2d 1116 (Ct. App. 1980) — § 5.16
State v. Roy, 151 Vt. 17, 557 A.2d 884 (1989) — § 1.15
State v. Roy, 140 Vt. 219, 436 A.2d 1090 (1981) — § 7.30
State v. Russell, 571 A.2d 229 (Me. 1990) — § 4.5
State v. R.W. 104 N.J. 14, 514 A.2d 1287 (1986) — §§ 2.18, 2.22
State v. Ryan, 103 Wash. 2d 165, 691 P.2d 197 (1984) — §§ 2.19, 7.31, 7.44, 7.45, 7.46, 7.48, 7.49
State v. Saccone, 7 N.J. Super. 263, 72 A.2d 923 (1950) — § 7.31
State v. Saldana, 324 N.W.2d 227 (Minn. 1982) — § 4.34
State v. Sammons, 47 Wash. App. 762, 737 P.2d 684 (1987) — § 7.46
State v. Sandberg, 406 N.W.2d 506 (Minn. 1987) — § 4.44
State v. Sanders, 691 S.W.2d 566 (Tenn. Crim. App. 1984) — § 7.31
State v. Santarelli, 98 Wash. 2d 358, 655 P.2d 697 (1982) — § 6.14
State v. Saraceno, 15 Conn. App. 222, 545 A.2d 1116 (1988) — § 7.31
State v. Schaal, 806 S.W.2d 659 (Mo. 1991), *cert. denied,* 112 S. Ct. 976 (1992) — § 7.50
State v. Scheffelman, 820 P.2d 1293 (Mont. 1991) — §§ 4.13, 4.32, 4.45, 7.22, 7.23
State v. Schmidt, 288 S.C. 301, 342 S.E.2d 401 (1986) — § 5.21
State v. Schoolcraft, 183 W. Va. 579, 396 S.E.2d 760 (1990) — § 1.1
State v. Schossow, 145 Ariz. 504, 703 P.2d 448 (1985) — §§ 2.1, 2.18
State v. Schultz, 88 N.C. App. 197, 362 S.E.2d 853 (1987), *aff'd,* 322 N.C. 467, 368 S.E.2d 386 (1988) — § 6.24
State v. Schwartzmiller, 107 Idaho 89, 685 P.2d 830 (1984) — § 5.25
State v. Schweider, 5 Wis. 2d 627, 94 N.W.2d 154 (1959) — § 2.18
State v. Segerberg, 131 Conn. 546, 41 A.2d 101 (1945) — §§ 2.1, 2.10
State v. Shaw, 149 Vt. 275, 542 A.2d 1106 (1987) — §§ 1.14, 5.9, 7.28, 7.30
State v. Shearer, 101 Or. App. 543, 792 P.2d 1215 (1990) — § 4.50
State v. Sheppard, 197 N.J. Super. 411, 484 A.2d 1330 (1984) — §§ 7.48, 8.8
State v. Siems, 535 S.W.2d 261 (Mo. Ct. App. 1976) — § 1.3
State v. Simmons, 52 N.J. 538, 247 A.2d 313 (1968), *cert. denied,* 395 U.S. 924 (1969) — § 7.49
State v. Singh, 586 S.W.2d 410 (Mo. Ct. App. 1979) — §§ 2.1, 2.18
State v. Slider, 38 Wash. App. 689, 688 P.2d 538 (1984) — §§ 7.30, 7.44
State v. Smith, 384 N.W.2d 546 (Minn. Ct. App. 1986) — §§ 7.44, 7.46
State v. Smith, 679 S.W.2d 899 (Mo. Ct. App. 1984) — §§ 2.1, 2.14, 2.18
State v. Smith, 206 Mont. 99, 670 P.2d 96 (1983) — § 1.13
State v. Smith, 315 N.C. 76, 337 S.E.2d 833 (1985) — §§ 7.30, 7.35
State v. Smith, 16 Utah 2d 374, 401 P.2d 445 (1965) — §§ 5.1, 7.1
State v. Sorenson, 143 Wis. 2d 226, 421 N.W.2d 77 (1988) — §§ 1.1, 1.4, 7.30, 7.35, 7.36, 7.42, 7.44, 7.45
State v. Soukup, 376 N.W.2d 498 (Minn. Ct. App. 1985) — § 7.45
State v. Spaulding, 313 N.W.2d 878 (Iowa 1981) — § 6.26

Case	*Book §*
State v. Speller, 102 N.C. App. 697, 404 S.E.2d 15 (1991)	§§ 4.35, 4.37
State v. Spigarolo, 210 Conn. 359, 556 A.2d 112, *cert. denied,* 493 U.S. 933 (1989)	§§ 4.10, 4.44, 8.8
State v. Stafford, 237 Iowa 780, 23 N.W.2d 832 (1946)	§ 7.30
State v. Stager, 329 N.C. 278, 406 S.E.2d 876 (1991)	§ 7.53
State v. Stange, 53 Wash. App. 638, 769 P.2d 823 (1989)	§ 7.44
State v. Stark, 470 N.W.2d 317 (Wis. Ct. App. 1991)	§ 1.3
State v. Stevens, 289 N.W.2d 592 (Iowa 1980)	§ 7.30
State v. Stevens, 238 N.W.2d 251 (N.D. 1975)	§§ 6.5, 6.17
State v. Stevens, 58 Wash. App. 478, 794 P.2d 38 (1990)	§§ 3.32, 4.30, 4.45, 7.13
State v. Strickland, 96 N.C. App. 642, 387 S.E.2d 62 (1990)	§ 4.37
State v. Strobel, 51 Ohio App. 3d 31, 554 N.E.2d 916 (1988)	§ 5.24
State v. Struss, 404 N.W.2d 811 (Minn. Ct. App. 1987)	§ 2.12
State v. Sullivan, 360 N.W.2d 418 (Minn. Ct. App. 1985), *cert. denied,* 484 U.S. 862 (1987)	§§ 2.1, 2.12, 2.22
State v. Sumowski, 794 S.W.2d 643 (Mo. 1990)	§ 3.8
State v. Suttles, 287 Or. 15, 597 P.2d 786 (1979)	§ 1.16
State v. Swan, 114 Wash. 2d 613, 790 P.2d 610 (1990), *cert. denied,* 111 S. Ct. 752 (1991)	§§ 7.45, 7.46
State v. Sypult, 304 Ark. 5, 800 S.W.2d 402 (1990)	§ 1.16
State v. Tanner, 675 P.2d 539 (Utah 1983)	§§ 3.5, 3.7, 3.8, 3.9, 4.17, 4.28, 6.17, 6.20
State v. Tavares, 590 A.2d 867 (R.I. 1991)	§ 7.39
State v. Taylor, 452 N.W.2d 605 (Iowa 1990)	§§ 3.11, 3.28
State v. Taylor, 562 A.2d 445 (R.I. 1989)	§ 8.8
State v. Taylor, 103 N.M. 189, 704 P.2d 443 (Ct. App. 1985)	§§ 2.1, 2.18, 7.42, 7.44, 7.45
State v. Teeter, 85 N.C. App. 624, 355 S.E.2d 804 (1987)	§ 6.22
State v. Thiel, 236 Mont. 63, 768 P.2d 343 (1989)	§ 1.14
State v. Thomas, 777 P.2d 445 (Utah 1989)	§§ 7.28, 7.30
State v. Thomas, 1 Wash. 2d 298, 95 P.2d 1036 (1939)	§ 5.19
State v. Thomas, 150 Wis. 2d 374, 442 N.W.2d 10, *cert. denied,* 110 S. Ct. 188 (1989)	§ 8.8
State v. Thompson, 503 A.2d 689 (Me. 1986)	§ 7.38
State v. Thompson, 430 N.W.2d 151 (Minn. 1988)	§§ 2.21, 8.13
State v. Thompson, 146 Ariz. 552, 707 P.2d 956 (Ct. App. 1985)	§ 7.35
State v. Tobin, 602 A.2d 528 (R.I. 1992)	§ 6.21
State v. Toennis, 52 Wash. App. 176, 758 P.2d 539 (1988)	§ 3.5
State v. Tolliver, 562 S.W.2d 714 (Mo. Ct. App. 1978)	§ 5.25
State v. Tomlinson, 33 Ohio App. 3d 278, 515 N.E.2d 963 (1986)	§ 5.32
State v. Tracy, 482 N.W.2d 675 (Iowa 1992)	§§ 7.20, 7.35
State v. Treadaway, 116 Ariz. 163, 568 P.2d 1061 (1977)	§ 6.21
State v. True, 438 A.2d 460 (Me. 1981)	§ 7.31
State v. Tucker, 165 Ariz. 340, 798 P.2d 1349 (Ct. App. 1990)	§ 4.36

Case Book §

State v. Tucker, 181 Conn. 406, 435 A.2d 986 (1980) § 6.17
State v. Turecek, 456 N.W.2d 219 (Iowa 1990) §§ 6.8, 7.20
State v. Turner, 33 Or. App. 157, 575 P.2d 1007 (1978) § 4.8
State v. Twist, 528 A.2d 1250 (Me. 1987) §§ 7.48, 8.8
State v. Twyford, 85 S.D. 522, 186 N.W.2d 545 (1971) § 7.31
State v. Van Hoff, 371 N.W.2d 180 (Iowa Ct. App.), *cert. denied*, 474 U.S. 1034 (1985) §§ 2.12, 2.14, 2.18
State v. Van Orman, 642 S.W.2d 636 (Mo. 1982) § 7.30
State v. Vanasse, 593 A.2d 58 (R.I. 1991) § 5.7
State v. Vega, 40 N.C. App. 326, 253 S.E.2d 94, *cert. denied*, 444 U.S. 968 (1979) § 3.28
State v. Verley, 106 Or. App. 751, 809 P.2d 723 (1991) §§ 7.2, 7.38
State v. Vess, 157 Ariz. 236, 756 P.2d 333 (Ct. App. 1988) § 8.8
State v. Vincent, 159 Ariz. 418, 768 P.2d 150 (1989) § 8.8
State v. Vines, 412 S.E.2d 156 (N.C. Ct. App. 1992) §§ 3.9, 3.13
State v. Vinzant, 200 La. 301, 7 So. 2d 917 (1942) § 3.28
State v. Vosika, 83 Or. App. 298, 731 P.2d 449, *on reconsideration*, 85 Or. App. 148, 735 P.2d 1273 (1987) §§ 2.18, 7.35
State v. Wagner, 30 Ohio App. 3d 261, 508 N.E.2d 164 (1986) §§ 7.8, 7.30
State v. Walker, 506 A.2d 1143 (Me. 1986) §§ 4.52, 5.16, 5.24
State v. Wallace, 37 Ohio St. 3d 87, 524 N.E.2d 466 (1988) §§ 7.28, 7.30, 7.49
State v. Walsh, 126 N.H. 610, 495 A.2d 1256 (1985) § 5.28
State v. Walton, 432 A.2d 1275 (Me. 1981) § 7.30
State v. Warford, 223 Neb. 368, 389 N.W.2d 575 (1986) §§ 8.7, 8.9, 8.12
State v. Warren, 304 Or. 428, 746 P.2d 711 (1987) § 1.14
State v. Warren, 55 Wash. App. 645, 779 P.2d 1159 (1989) § 7.46
State v. Watkins, 318 N.C. 498, 349 S.E.2d 564 (1986) § 5.8
State v. Watson, 484 So. 2d 870 (La. Ct. App. 1986) § 5.8
State v. Wattenbarger, 97 Or. App. 414, 776 P.2d 1292 (1989) § 5.36
State v. Watts, 675 P.2d 566 (Utah 1983) § 3.29
State v. Webb, 779 P.2d 1108 (Utah 1989) § 2.1
State v. Webb, 467 N.W.2d 108 (Wis.), *cert. denied*, 112 S. Ct. 249 (1991) § 8.4
State v. Weiler, 801 S.W.2d 417 (Mo. Ct. App. 1990), *cert. denied*, 112 S. Ct. 295 (1991) §§ 1.1, 2.22, 5.16, 5.35
State v. Weisenstein, 367 N.W.2d 201 (S.D. 1985) §§ 2.1, 2.12, 2.18, 5.7
State v. Wells, 423 A.2d 221 (Me. 1980) § 6.8
State v. Werner, 482 N.W.2d 286 (S.D. 1992) § 4.5
State v. West, 103 N.C. App. 1, 404 S.E.2d 191 (1991) §§ 3.27, 3.28, 3.29, 4.12, 6.13, 6.18
State v. Wetherbee, 594 A.2d 390 (Vt. 1991) §§ 4.37, 4.45
State v. White, 215 S.C. 450, 55 S.E.2d 785 (1949) § 7.47
State v. Whiteside, 400 N.W.2d 140 (Minn. Ct. App. 1987) § 4.44
State v. Wiklund, 546 So. 2d 250 (La. Ct. App. 1989) §§ 2.1, 2.18, 3.32
State v. Wilcox, 808 P.2d 1028 (Utah 1991) §§ 1.1, 1.3, 1.4, 1.5
State v. Wilkerson, 295 N.C. 559, 247 S.E.2d 905 (1978) §§ 3.5, 3.6, 3.7, 3.30

CASES

Case	Book §
State v. Williams, 451 N.W.2d 886 (Minn. Ct. App. 1990)	§§ 3.10, 3.13
State v. Williams, 729 S.W.2d 197 (Mo.), *cert. denied,* 484 U.S. 929 (1987)	§ 2.9
State v. Williams, 598 S.W.2d 830 (Tenn. Crim. App. 1980)	§ 7.30
State v. Willis, 370 N.W.2d 193 (S.D. 1985)	§ 6.26
State v. Willis, 735 S.W.2d 818 (Tenn. Crim. App. 1987)	§ 7.31
State v. Willoughby, 532 A.2d 1020 (Me. 1987)	§ 1.12
State v. Wilson, 199 Conn. 417, 513 A.2d 620 (1986)	§§ 6.17, 6.18
State v. Wilson, 247 Kan. 87, 795 P.2d 336 (1990)	§ 4.45
State v. Wilson, 156 Ohio St. 525, 103 N.E.2d 552 (1952)	§ 2.18
State v. Wingo, 403 S.E.2d 322 (S.C. Ct. App. 1991)	§ 1.1
State v. Winkler, 112 Idaho 917, 736 P.2d 1371 (Ct. App. 1987)	§ 5.32
State v. Woodburn, 559 A.2d 343 (Me. 1989)	§ 2.1
State v. Workman, 14 Ohio App. 3d 385, 471 N.E.2d 853 (1984)	§§ 2.1, 2.18
State v. Wright, 116 Idaho 382, 775 P.2d 1224 (1989), *aff'd,* 110 S. Ct. 3139 (1990)	§ 4.5
State v. Wright, 751 S.W.2d 48 (Mo. 1988)	§ 7.46
State v. Wright, 98 N.C. App. 658, 392 S.E.2d 125 (1990)	§ 5.29
State v. Wright, 97 Or. App. 401, 776 P.2d 1294 (1989)	§§ 5.28, 5.36
State v. Ybarra, 24 N.M. 413, 174 P. 212 (1918)	§ 2.14
State v. Yednock, 14 Conn. App. 333, 541 A.2d 887 (1988)	§ 7.48
State v. Young, 103 N.C. App. 415, 406 S.E.2d 3 (1991)	§ 1.3
State v. Young, 802 P.2d 829 (Wash. Ct. App. 1991)	§ 4.28
State v. Zihlavsky, 505 So. 2d 761 (La. Ct. App. 1987)	§ 6.20
State v, Zimmerman, 829 P.2d 861 (Idaho 1992)	§ 7.13
State v. Zybach, 308 Or. 96, 775 P.2d 318 (1989)	§ 6.13
State *ex rel.* Busch v. Busch, 776 S.W.2d 374 (Mo. 1989)	§ 3.23
State *ex rel.* Harris v. Schmidt, 69 Wis. 2d 668, 230 N.W.2d 890 (1975)	§ 7.30
State *ex rel.* Juvenile Dep't v. Karabetsis, 77 Or. App. 583, 713 P.2d 1075 (1986)	§ 7.31
State *ex rel.* Juvenile Dep't v. Randall, 96 Or. App. 673, 773 P.2d 1348 (1989)	§ 3.23
State *ex rel.* Pope v. Superior Ct., 113 Ariz. 22, 545 P.2d 946 (1976)	§ 5.29
State *ex rel.* Minor Male Child, 529 So. 2d 34 (La. Ct. App. 1988)	§§ 3.16, 3.19
State *ex rel.* K.A.W., 104 N.J. 112, 515 A.2d 1217 (1986)	§§ 1.1, 1.3, 1.4, 1.6
Stefanel Tyesha C., *In re,* 157 A.D.2d 322, 556 N.Y.S.2d 280 (1990)	§ 3.23
Stephan v. State, 810 P.2d 564 (Alaska Ct. App. 1991)	§ 4.8
Stephens v. State, 544 N.E.2d 137 (Ind. 1989)	§§ 5.28, 5.32
Steven S., *In re,* 126 Cal. App. 3d 23, 178 Cal. Rptr. 525 (1981)	§ 3.17
Stevens v. Bordenkircher, 746 F.2d 342 (6th Cir. 1984)	§ 5.21
Stevens v. Mirakian, 177 Va. 123, 12 S.E.2d 780 (1941)	§ 7.47

Case   *Book §*

Stevens v. People, 796 P.2d 946 (Colo. 1990)   § 7.46
Stewart v. State, 555 N.E.2d 121 (Ind. 1990)   § 4.45
Stewart v. State, 521 N.E.2d 675 (Ind. 1988)   §§ 1.1, 1.3
Stine v. State, 199 Ga. App. 898, 406 S.E.2d 292 (1991)   § 6.21
Strickland v. State, 550 So. 2d 1042 (Ala. Crim. App.
    1988), *aff'd,* 550 So. 2d 1054 (Ala. 1989)   § 8.7
Sullivan v. Minneapolis State Ry. Co., 161 Minn. 45, 200
    N.W. 922 (1924)   § 7.21
Sullivan v. Minnesota, 818 F.2d 664 (8th Cir.), *cert.*
    denied, 484 U.S. 862 (1987)   § 2.22
Swanigan v. Chicago Bd. Educ., 173 Ill. App. 3d 784, 527
    N.E.2d 1030 (1988)   §§ 2.12, 2.15, 2.18
Swift v. Swift, 64 F.R.D. 440 (E.D.N.Y. 1974)   § 2.22
Symposium on Science and the Rules of Evidence, 99
    F.R.D. 187 (1983)   § 4.9

Taft v. Taft, 388 Mass. 331, 446 N.E.2d 395 (1983)   § 3.17
Tanya P., *In re,* 120 Cal. App. 3d 66, 174 Cal. Rptr. 533
    (1981)   § 7.57
Taylor v. State, 727 P.2d 274 (Wyo. 1986)   § 8.7
Taylor v. State, 183 Ga. App. 314, 358 S.E.2d 845 (1987)   §§ 2.1, 2.15
Tennessee v. Street, 471 U.S. 409 (1985)   § 7.54
Terry W., *In re,* 59 Cal. App. 3d 745, 130 Cal. Rptr. 913
    (1976)   § 1.12
Tevlin v. People, 715 P.2d 338 (Colo. 1986)   § 4.45
T.H., *In re,* 561 So. 2d 904 (La. Ct. App. 1990)   § 3.13
Theresa J., *In re,* 158 A.D.2d 364, 551 N.Y.S.2d 219
    (1990)   § 3.23
Thomas v. Gunter, 962 F.2d 1477 (10th Cir. 1992)   §§ 7.58, 8.8
Thomas v. People, 803 P.2d 144 (Colo. 1990)   §§ 1.1, 1.4, 1.6, 8.8
Thomas v. State, 669 S.W.2d 420 (Tex. Ct. App. 1984)   § 6.8
Thomas v. State, 92 Wis. 2d 372, 284 N.W.2d 917 (1979)   § 7.23
Thompson v. State, 769 P.2d 997 (Alaska Ct. App. 1989)   §§ 4.45, 7.23, 7.45
Thompson v. State, 555 N.E.2d 1301 (Ind. Ct. App. 1990)   § 5.30
Thompson v. State, 468 So. 2d 852 (Miss. 1985)   § 5.7
Three Juveniles v. Commonwealth, 390 Mass. 357, 455
    N.E.2d 1203 (1983), *cert. denied,* 465 U.S. 1068 (1984)   § 1.12
Tibbetts v. State, 778 P.2d 925 (Okla. Crim. App. 1989)   § 5.29
Timmons v. State, 584 N.E.2d 1108 (Ind. 1992)   §§ 4.5, 7.2
Timsah v. General Motors Corp., 225 Kan. 305, 591 P.2d
    154 (1979)   § 7.7
Tingle v. State, 536 So. 2d 202 (Fla. 1988)   §§ 4.44, 4.45
Tissier v. State, 792 S.W.2d 120 (Tex. Ct. App. 1990)   § 7.35
Townsend v. State, 103 Nev. 113, 734 P.2d 705 (1987)   §§ 4.13, 4.37, 4.45
T.R., *In re,* 52 Ohio St. 3d 6, 556 N.E.2d 439, *cert. denied,*
    111 S. Ct. 386 (1990)   § 8.5
Trammel v. United States, 445 U.S. 40 (1980)   § 1.12
Travelers' Ins. Co. v. Mosley, 75 U.S. (8 Wall.) 397, 19 L.
    Ed. 437 (1869)   § 7.29
Travers v. State, 578 So. 2d 793 (Fla. Dist. Ct. App. 1991)   § 6.13

CASES

Case	Book §
Troy D., *In re,* 215 Cal. App. 3d 889, 263 Cal. Rtpr. 869 (1989)	§§ 1.17, 3.23
Tucker v. State, 264 Ark. 890, 575 S.W.2d 684 (1979)	§ 7.27
Tucker v. State, 564 A.2d 1110 (Del. 1989)	§ 7.48
20th Century Wear, Inc. v. Sanmark-Stardust, Inc., 747 F.2d 81 (2d Cir. 1984), *cert. denied,* 470 U.S. 1052 (1985)	§ 5.11
Uhl v. State, 479 S.W.2d 55 (Tex. Crim. App. 1972)	§ 5.7
United States v. Abel, 469 U.S. 45 (1984)	§ 5.21
United States v. Addonizio, 451 F.2d 49 (3d Cir. 1971), *cert. denied,* 405 U.S. 936 (1972)	§ 2.13
United States v. Alexander, 27 M.J. 834 (A.C.M.R. 1989)	§ 6.20
United States v. Alvarez, 584 F.2d 694 (5th Cir. 1978)	§ 7.47
United States v. Andrade, 788 F.2d 521 (8th Cir.), *cert. denied,* 479 U.S. 963 (1986)	§ 7.22
United States v. Armstrong, 33 M.J. 1011 (A.C.M.R. 1991)	§§ 7.35, 7.36
United States v. Arnold, 25 M.J. 129 (C.M.A. 1987), *cert. denied,* 484 U.S. 1060 (1988)	§ 7.30
United States v. Arruza, 26 M.J. 234 (C.M.A. 1988), *cert. denied,* 489 U.S. 1011 (1989)	§§ 4.45, 7.48
United States v. August, 21 M.J. 363 (C.M.A. 1986)	§ 4.50
United States v. Austin, 32 M.J. 757 (A.C.M.R.), *review granted in part,* 34 M.J. 19 (C.M.A. 1991)	§§ 4.4, 6.20
United States v. Austrew, 202 F. Supp. 816 (D. Md. 1962), *aff'd per curiam,* 317 F.2d 926 (4th Cir. 1963)	§ 7.41
United States v. Azure, 845 F.2d 1503 (8th Cir. 1988)	§§ 5.29, 5.34
United States v. Azure, 801 F.2d 336 (8th Cir. 1986)	§§ 4.9, 4.44, 4.45
United States v. Bahr, 33 M.J. 228 (C.M.A. 1991)	§ 5.21
United States v. Balano, 618 F.2d 624 (10th Cir. 1979), *cert. denied,* 449 U.S. 840 (1980)	§ 8.8
United States v. Balfany, 1992 WL 97006 (8th Cir. 1992)	§ 7.35
United States v. Barnard, 490 F.2d 907 (9th Cir. 1973), *cert. denied,* 416 U.S. 959 (1974)	§ 4.45
United States v. Barror, 23 M.J. 370 (C.M.A. 1987)	§§ 7.42, 7.44, 7.58
United States v. Bartlett, 633 F.2d 1184 (5th Cir.), *cert. denied,* 454 U.S. 820 (1981)	§ 5.9
United States v. Bartlett, 856 F.2d 1071 (8th Cir. 1988)	§ 5.34
United States v. Bear Ribs, 562 F.2d 563 (8th Cir.), *cert. denied,* 434 U.S. 974 (1977)	§ 8.14
United States v. Bear Runner, 574 F.2d 966 (8th Cir. 1978)	§ 5.17
United States v. Beckett, 22 M.J. 856 (A.F.C.M.R. 1986)	§ 5.29
United States v. Beckham, 789 F.2d 401 (6th Cir. 1986)	§ 8.6
United States v. Beechum, 555 F.2d 487 (5th Cir.), *reh'g granted,* 563 F.2d 782 (5th Cir. 1977), *vacated en banc,* 582 F.2d 898 (5th Cir. 1978), *cert. denied,* 440 U.S. 920 (1979)	§ 6.18
United States v. Begay, 937 F.2d 515 (10th Cir. 1991)	§§ 5.28, 5.29
United States v. Benn, 476 F.2d 1127 (D.C. Cir. 1972)	§§ 2.1, 2.22 5.16

Case	Book §
United States v. Benton, 637 F.2d 1052 (5th Cir. 1981)	§ 6.14
United States v. Berrio-Londono, 946 F.2d 158 (1st Cir. 1991), *cert. denied,* 112 S. Ct. 1223 (1992)	§ 7.56
United States v. Bey, 526 F.2d 851 (5th Cir.), *cert. denied,* 426 U.S. 937 (1976)	§ 7.47
United States v. Billingsley, 474 F.2d 63 (6th Cir.), *cert. denied,* 414 U.S. 819 (1973)	§ 6.3
United States v. Binder, 769 F.2d 595 (9th Cir. 1985), *cert. denied,* 484 U.S. 1073 (1988)	§ 8.8
United States v. Boise, 916 F.2d 497 (9th Cir. 1990), *cert. denied,* 111 S. Ct. 2057 (1991)	§§ 3.5, 3.8, 3.9, 3.11, 3.12, 3.28, 3.29, 3.30
United States v. Bostick, 33 M.J. 849 (A.C.M.R. 1991)	§ 4.45
United States v. Bowers, 660 F.2d 527 (5th Cir. 1981)	§§ 3.5, 3.32
United States v. Bradshaw, 690 F.2d 704 (9th Cir. 1982), *cert. denied,* 463 U.S. 1210 (1983)	§ 6.14
United States v. Brown, 770 F.2d 768 (9th Cir.), *cert. denied,* 474 U.S.1036 (1985)	§ 2.22
United States v. Brown, 608 F.2d 551 (5th Cir. 1979)	§ 6.17
United States v. Brown, 548 F.2d 1194 (5th Cir. 1977)	§ 7.41
United States v. Brown, 25 M.J. 867 (A.C.M.R. 1988)	§ 7.35
United States v. Button, 31 M.J. 897 (A.F.C.M.R. 1990), *aff'd,* 34 M.J. 139 (1992)	§ 7.20
United States v. Cardenas, 895 F.2d 1338 (11th Cir. 1990)	§ 4.52
United States v. Cardinal, 782 F.2d 34 (6th Cir.), *cert. denied,* 476 U.S. 1161 (1986)	§ 5.34
United States v. Carlson, 547 F.2d 1346 (8th Cir. 1976), *cert. denied,* 431 U.S. 914 (1977)	§§ 7.44, 7.58, 8.8
United States v. Carter, 26 M.J. 428 (C.M.A. 1988)	§ 4.34
United States v. Castillo, 29 M.J. 145 (C.M.A. 1989)	§§ 6.13, 6.20
United States v. Casamento, 887 F.2d 1141 (2d Cir. 1989), *cert. denied,* 493 U.S. 1081 (1990)	§ 7.52
United States v. Chapman, 866 F.2d 1326 (11th Cir.), *cert. denied,* 493 U.S. 932 (1989)	§ 7.48
United States v. Cherry, 938 F.2d 748 (7th Cir. 1991)	§§ 7.22, 7.23, 7.24, 7.35, 7.36
United States v. Ciro, 753 F.2d 248 (2d Cir.), *cert. denied,* 471 U.S. 1018 (1985)	§ 5.25
United States v. Clark, 15 M.J. 974 (A.C.M.R. 1983)	§ 6.20
United States v. Cokeley, 22 M.J. 225 (C.M.A. 1986)	§ 7.48
United States v. Conley, 503 F.2d 520 (8th Cir. 1974)	§ 5.11
United States v. Cottriee, 21 M.J. 535 (N.M.C.M.R. 1985)	§ 7.35
United States v. Cox, 18 M.J. 72 (C.M.A. 1984)	§ 4.28
United States v. Crayton, 17 M.J. 932 (A.F.C.M.R. 1984)	§ 7.44
United States v. Cree, 778 F.2d 474 (8th Cir. 1985)	§§ 7.42, 7.44, 7.45
United States v. Crockett, 21 M.J. 423 (C.M.A. 1986)	§ 7.48
United States v. Cuellar, 27 M.J. 50 (C.M.A. 1988), *cert. denied,* 493 U.S. 811 (1989)	§ 6.18
United States v. Curry, 31 M.J. 359 (C.M.A. 1990)	§§ 3.11, 3.28, 3.29
United States v. Dean, 31 M.J. 196 (C.M.A. 1990), *cert. denied,* 111 S. Ct. 1106 (1991)	§ 7.36

CASES

Case	Book §
United States v. Dejonge, 16 M.J. 974 (A.F.C.M.R. 1983)	§ 6.26
United States v. Deland, 22 M.J. 70 (C.M.A.), *cert. denied,* 479 U.S. 856 (1986)	§ 7.35
United States v. DeNoyer, 811 F.2d 436 (8th Cir. 1987)	§ 7.30
United States v. Deshotee, 15 M.J. 787 (A.C.M.R. 1983)	§ 5.17
United States v. Dildy, 39 F.R.D. 340 (D.C. 1966)	§ 2.22
United States v. Dorian, 803 F.2d 1439 (8th Cir. 1986)	§§ 7.44, 7.45
United States v. Dorsch, 34 M.J. 1042 (N.M.C.M.R. 1992)	§ 4.50
United States v. Downing, 753 F.2d 1224 (3d Cir. 1985)	§ 4.19
United States v. Dudding, 34 M.J. 975 (A.C.M.R. 1992)	§ 5.9
United States v. Eagle Thunder, 893 F.2d 950 (8th Cir. 1990)	§ 5.29
United States v. Ebens, 800 F.2d 1422 (6th Cir. 1986)	§ 7.15
United States v. Edens, 31 M.J. 267 (C.M.A. 1990)	§ 7.35, 7.36
United States v. Ellis, 935 F.2d 385 (1st Cir.), *cert. denied,* 112 S. Ct. 201 (1991)	§§ 7.8, 7.42, 7.44
United States v. Estrella, 21 M.J. 782 (A.C.M.R. 1986)	§ 7.41
United States v. Evans, 484 F.2d 1178 (2d Cir. 1973)	§ 2.17
United States v. Evans, 23 M.J. 665 (A.C.M.R. 1986)	§ 3.10
United States v. Farmer, 923 F.2d 1557 (11th Cir. 1991)	§§ 7.22, 7.23
United States v. Ferdinand, 29 M.J. 164 (C.M.A. 1989), *cert. denied,* 493 U.S. 1044 (1990)	§ 7.48
United States v. Ferguson, 14 M.J. 840 (A.C.M.R. 1982)	§ 5.36
United States v. Figueroa, 618 F.2d 934 (2d Cir. 1980)	§ 6.13
United States v. Fink, 32 M.J. 987 (A.C.M.R. 1991)	§§ 7.29, 7.30, 7.35, 7.51
United States v. Franks, 939 F.2d 600 (8th Cir. 1991)	§ 7.53
United States v. Frazier, 678 F. Supp. 499 (E.D. Pa.), *aff'd,* 806 F.2d 255 (3d Cir. 1986)	§ 7.42
United States v. Gagnon, 470 U.S. 522 (1985)	§§ 2.21, 8.13
United States v. Galloway, 963 F.2d 1388 (10th Cir. 1992)	§ 8.4
United States v. Gamble, 27 M.J. 298 (C.M.A. 1988)	§ 6.24
United States v. Gano, 560 F.2d 990 (10th Cir. 1977)	§ 6.22
United States v. Gans, 32 M.J. 412 (C.M.A. 1991)	§ 7.37
United States v. Garcia, 900 F.2d 571 (2d Cir.), *cert. denied,* 111 S. Ct. 169 (1990)	§ 4.52
United States v. Garcia-Rosa, 876 F.2d 209 (1st Cir. 1989)	§ 7.56
United States v. Geiss, 30 M.J. 678 (A.F.C.M.R. 1990)	§ 4.5
United States v. George, 960 F.2d 97 (9th Cir. 1992)	§§ 7.35, 7.53
United States v. Giambra, 33 M.J. 331 (C.M.A. 1991)	§§ 4.44, 7.42, 7.44
United States v. Gibson, 625 F.2d 887 (9th Cir. 1980)	§ 6.20
United States v. Gibson, 29 M.J. 379 (C.M.A.), *cert. denied,* 497 U.S. 907 (1990)	§ 7.51
United States v. Gillespie, 852 F.2d 475 (9th Cir. 1988)	§§ 4.35, 4.50
United States v. Gipson, 24 M.J. 246 (C.M.A. 1987)	§§ 4.18, 4.19
United States v. Gomez-Gallardo, 915 F.2d 553 (9th Cir. 1990)	§ 7.20
United States v. Gonsalves, 668 F.2d 73 (1st Cir.), *cert. denied,* 456 U.S. 909 (1982)	§ 6.23
United States v. Grady, 481 F.2d 1106 (D.C. Cir. 1973)	§ 6.17
United States v. Groce, 682 F.2d 1359 (11th Cir. 1982)	§ 7.11
United States v. Gunter, 631 F.2d 583 (8th Cir. 1980)	§ 7.57

Case *Book §*

United States v. Gutierrez, 696 F.2d 753 (10th Cir. 1982),
    cert. denied, 461 U.S. 909 (1983)   § 6.24
United States v. Hadley, 918 F.2d 848 (9th Cir. 1990),
    cert. granted, 112 S. Ct. 1261 (1992)   §§ 6.13, 6.15, 6.18
United States v. Hale, 422 U.S. 171 (1975)   §§ 7.18, 7.19
United States v. Harjak, 33 M.J. 577 (N.M.C.M.R. 1991)   § 7.44
United States v. Haro-Espinosa, 619 F.2d 789 (9th Cir.
    1979)   § 5.9
United States v. Harris, 761 F.2d 394 (7th Cir. 1985)   § 7.23
United States v. Harris, 661 F.2d 138 (10th Cir. 1981)   § 6.17
United States v. Harrison, 31 M.J. 330 (C.M.A. 1990)   §§ 4.37, 4.45
United States v. Harvey, 588 F.2d 1201 (8th Cir. 1978)   § 5.25
United States v. Haston, 24 M.J. 313 (C.M.A. 1987)   § 5.11
United States v. Herbert, 32 M.J. 707 (A.C.M.R. 1991)   § 6.18
United States v. Hershey, 20 M.J. 433 (C.M.A. 1985), *cert.*
    denied, 474 U.S. 1062 (1986)   § 8.4
United States v. Hicks, 24 M.J. 3 (C.M.A.), *cert. denied,*
    484 U.S. 827 (1987)   § 6.26
United States v. Hines, 23 M.J. 125 (C.M.A. 1986)   § 7.51
United States v. Hooks, 24 M.J. 713 (A.C.M.R. 1987)   § 6.8
United States v. Inadi, 475 U.S. 387 (1986)   §§ 7.48, 7.51, 7.52
United States v. Iron Shell, 633 F.2d 77 (8th Cir. 1980),
    cert. denied, 450 U.S. 1001 (1981)   §§ 5.7, 7.29, 7.30, 7.35, 7.36, 7.44, 7.47
United States v. Irwin, 30 M.J. 87 (C.M.A. 1990)   § 1.13
United States v. Jacobson, 785 F. Supp. 563 (E.D. Va. 1992)   § 8.5
United States v. Johnson, 15 M.J. 518 (A.C.M.R. 1982)   § 8.1
United States v. Jones, 766 F.2d 412 (9th Cir. 1985)   § 5.23
United States v. Jones, 683 F.2d 817 (4th Cir. 1982)   § 1.12
United States v. Jones, 663 F.2d 567 (5th Cir. 1981)   § 7.14
United States v. Jones, 26 M.J. 197 (C.M.A. 1988)   § 7.23
United States v. Kane, 944 F.2d 1406 (7th Cir. 1991)   § 7.20
United States v. Kasto, 584 F.2d 268 (8th Cir. 1978), *cert.*
    denied, 440 U.S. 930 (1979)   § 5.32
United States v. Keller, 145 F. Supp. 692 (D.N.J. 1956)   § 7.25
United States v. Kelly, 33 M.J. 878 (A.C.M.R. 1991)   § 5.31
United States v. King, 32 M.J. 709 (A.C.M.R.), *review*
    granted in part, 34 M.J. 23 (C.M.A. 1991)   § 4.9
United States v. King, 16 M.J. 990 (A.C.M.R. 1983)   §§ 6.18, 7.44
United States v. Langford, 15 M.J. 1090 (A.C.M.R. 1983)   § 7.19
United States v. Lara-Hernandez, 588 F.2d 272 (9th Cir.
    1978)   § 5.23
United States v. Lee, 455 U.S. 252, 102 S. Ct. 1051 (1982)   § 3.17
United States v. Lee, 28 M.J. 52 (C.M.A. 1989)   §§ 4.10, 4.44
United States v. Leggett, 326 F.2d 613 (4th Cir.), *cert.*
    denied, 377 U.S. 955 (1964)   § 8.2
United States v. Leight, 818 F.2d 1297 (7th Cir.), *cert.*
    denied, 489 U.S. 958 (1987)   §§ 6.17, 6.18
United States v. LeMere, 22 M.J. 61 (C.M.A. 1986)   §§ 7.29, 7.30
United States v. Leslie, 542 F.2d 285 (5th Cir. 1976)   § 7.20

CASES

Case	Book §
United States v. Lewis, 837 F.2d 415 (9th Cir.), *cert. denied,* 488 U.S. 923 (1988)	§ 6.18
United States v. Lingle, 27 M.J. 704 (A.F.C.M.R. 1988)	§ 7.35
United States v. Lips, 22 M.J. 679 (A.F.C.M.R. 1986)	§§ 4.44, 6.14, 7.31
United States v. Littlewind, 551 F.2d 244 (8th Cir. 1977)	§ 5.7
United States v. Lockwood, 23 M.J. 770 (A.F.C.M.R. 1987)	§ 7.44
United States v. Lopez, 328 F. Supp. 1077 (E.D.N.Y. 1971)	§ 7.57
United States v. Love, 592 F.2d 1022 (8th Cir. 1979)	§ 7.30
United States v. Lyons, 33 M.J. 543 (A.C.M.R. 1991)	§§ 7.29, 7.56
United States v. Maddox, 944 F.2d 1223 (6th Cir. 1991), *cert. denied,* 112 S. Ct. 948 (1992)	§ 6.23
United States v. Mahone, 537 F.2d 922 (7th Cir.), *cert. denied,* 429 U.S. 1025 (1976)	§ 5.25
United States v. Mann, 26 M.J. 1 (C.M.A.), *cert. denied,* 488 U.S. 824 (1988)	§ 6.18
United States v. Marzano, 149 F.2d 923 (2d Cir. 1945)	§ 5.9
United States v. McClaskey, 30 M.J. 188 (C.M.A. 1990)	§ 7.23
United States v. McCord, 509 F.2d 891 (7th Cir.), *cert. denied,* 423 U.S. 833 (1975)	§ 6.24
United States v. McDowell, 30 M.J. 796 (A.F.C.M.R. 1990)	§ 6.22
United States v. McKenney, 846 F.2d 528 (9th Cir. 1988)	§ 7.53
United States v. Merriweather, 22 M.J. 657 (A.C.M.R. 1986)	§§ 3.8, 6.13, 6.17
United States v. Miller, 32 M.J. 843 (N.M.C.M.R. 1991)	§§ 7.30, 7.35, 7.36, 7.44
United States v. Milliren, 31 M.J. 664 (A.F.C.M.R. 1990)	§ 4.28
United States v. Morano, 697 F.2d 923 (11th Cir. 1983)	§ 6.24
United States v. Morgan, 31 M.J. 43 (C.M.A. 1990), *cert. denied,* 111 S. Ct. 959 (1991)	§§ 2.12, 7.22, 7.23, 7.24
United States v. Morris, 24 M.J. 9 (1987)	§ 1.13
United States v. Munoz, 32 M.J. 359 (C.M.A.), *cert. denied,* 112 S. Ct. 437 (1991)	§ 6.22
United States v. Murdock, 290 U.S. 389 (1933)	§ 3.28
United States v. Muscato, 534 F. Supp. 969 (E.D.N.Y. 1982)	§ 7.16
United States v. Napier, 518 F.2d 316 (9th Cir.), *cert. denied,* 423 U.S. 895 (1975)	§§ 7.29, 7.30
United States v. Nelson, 25 M.J. 110 (C.M.A. 1987), *cert. denied,* 484 U.S. 1061 (1988)	§§ 4.37, 4.44, 7.35
United States v. Nez, 661 F.2d 1203 (10th Cir. 1981)	§ 5.35
United States v. Nick, 604 F.2d 1199 (9th Cir. 1979)	§§ 7.6, 7.30
United States v. Oates, 560 F.2d 45 (2d Cir. 1977)	§ 7.39
United States v. Orrico, 599 F.2d 113 (6th Cir. 1979)	§§ 7.20, 7.47
United States v. Orsburn, 31 M.J. 182 (C.M.A. 1990), *cert. denied,* 111 S. Ct. 1074 (1991)	§ 6.18
United States v. Ortiz, 33 M.J. 549 (A.C.M.R. 1991)	§ 6.22
United States v. Ostendorff, 371 F.2d 729 (4th Cir.), *cert. denied,* 386 U.S. 982 (1967)	§ 5.9
United States v. Owen, 24 M.J. 390 (C.M.A. 1987), *cert. denied,* 484 U.S. 1026 (1988)	§ 5.16

Case	Book §
United States v. Owens, 789 F.2d 750 (9th Cir. 1986), *cert. granted,* 479 U.S. 1084 (1987), rev'd, 484 U.S. 554 (1988)	§§ 7.19, 7.26, 7.37, 7.50, 7.51, 7.53, 7.56
United States v. Pacelli, 491 F.2d 1108 (2d Cir.), *cert. denied,* 419 U.S. 826 (1974)	§ 7.11
United States v. Palacios, 32 M.J. 1047 (A.C.M.R. 1991)	§§ 7.4, 7.44, 7.48
United States v. Palmer, 33 M.J. 7 (C.M.A. 1991)	§ 6.26
United States v. Pandozzi, 878 F.2d 1526 (1st Cir. 1989)	§ 5.25
United States v. Payne, 944 F.2d 1458 (9th Cir. 1991), *cert. denied,* 112 S. Ct. 1598 (1992)	§§ 7.15, 7.23
United States v. Pearson, 33 M.J. 913 (A.F.C.M.R. 1991)	§§ 7.29, 7.30
United States v. Penn, 647 F.2d 876 (9th Cir.), *cert. denied,* 449 U.S. 903 (1980)	§ 1.12
United States v. Peters, 754 F.2d 753 (7th Cir. 1985)	§ 8.6
United States v. Petersen, 24 M.J. 283 (C.M.A. 1987)	§ 4.45
United States v. Phillips, 599 F.2d 134 (6th Cir. 1979)	§ 6.1
United States v. Pickens, 17 M.J. 391 (C.M.A. 1984)	§ 5.32
United States v. Plenty Arrows, 946 F.2d 62 (8th Cir. 1991)	§ 4.28
United States v. Pollard, 34 M.J. 1008 (A.C.M.R. 1992)	§§ 7.30, 7.42, 7.43, 7.44
United States v. Portsmouth Paving Corp., 694 F.2d 312 (4th Cir. 1982)	§ 7.27
United States v. Posey, 611 F.2d 1389 (5th Cir. 1980)	§ 6.23
United States v. Proctor, 34 M.J. 549 A.F.C.M.R. 1992)	§ 6.18
United States v. Quarles, 25 M.J. 761 (N.M.C.M.R. 1987)	§ 7.44
United States v. Quick, 22 M.J. 722 (A.C.M.R. 1986), *aff'd,* 26 M.J. 460 (C.M.A. 1988)	§§ 7.43, 7.44, 7.45
United States v. Raffoul, 826 F.2d 218 (3d Cir. 1987)	§§ 8.5, 8.6
United States v. Rappy, 157 F.2d 964 (2d Cir. 1946), *cert. denied,* 329 U.S. 806 (1947)	§ 5.11
United States v. Rath, 27 M.J. 600 (A.C.M.R. 1988)	§§ 1.1, 4.37
United States v. Ray, 920 F.2d 562 (9th Cir. 1990), *cert. denied,* 111 S. Ct. 1084 (1991)	§ 7.53
United States v. Red Feather, 865 F.2d 169 (8th Cir. 1989)	§§ 7.21, 7.22, 7.23
United States v. Reece, 21 M.J. 736 (N.M.C.M.R. 1985)	§ 6.20
United States v. Renville, 779 F.2d 430 (8th Cir. 1985)	§§ 7.30, 7.35, 7.36, 7.42, 7.44
United States v. Reynolds, 715 F.2d 99 (3d Cir. 1983)	§ 7.11
United States v. Reynolds, 29 M.J. 105 (C.M.A. 1989)	§§ 4.34, 4.45, 6.18
United States v. Rhea, 33 M.J. 413 (C.M.A. 1991)	§ 6.14
United States v. Rhea, 1992 WL 110517 (A.F.C.M.R. 1992)	§ 6.26
United States v. Rodko, 34 M.J. 980 (A.C.M.R. 1992)	§ 7.18
United States v. Romey, 32 M.J. 180 (C.M.A.), *cert. denied,* 112 S. Ct. 337 (1991)	§§ 2.13, 8.1, 8.3
United States v. Rossbach, 701 F.2d 713 (8th Cir. 1983), *cert. denied,* 111 S. Ct. 83 (1990)	§ 5.7

CASES

Case	Book §
United States v. Ruffin, 12 M.J. 952 (A.F.C.M.R. 1982)	§ 7.48
United States v. Ryan, 21 M.J. 627 (A.C.M.R. 1985)	§ 5.17
United States v. Saenz, 747 F.2d 930 (5th Cir. 1984), *cert. denied,* 473 U.S. 906 (1985)	§ 2.18
United States v. St. Pierre, 812 F.2d 417 (8th Cir. 1987)	§ 4.50
United States v. Salim, 664 F. Supp. 682 (E.D.N.Y. 1987), *aff'd,* 855 F.2d 944 (2d Cir. 1988)	§ 7.53
United States v. Sargent, 33 M.J. 815 (A.C.M.R. 1991)	§ 6.26
United States v. Saul, 26 M.J. 568 (A.F.C.M.R. 1988)	§ 6.18
United States v. Saunders, 736 F. Supp. 698 (E.D. Va. 1990), *aff'd,* 943 F.2d 388 (4th Cir. 1991), *cert. denied,* 112 S. Ct. 1199 (1992)	§§ 5.28, 5.30, 5.31, 5.34
United States v. Savage, 30 M.J. 863 (N.M.C.M.R. 1990)	§ 4.44
United States v. Scofield, 33 M.J. 857 (A.C.M.R. 1991)	§ 3.2
United States v. Shaw, 824 F.2d 601 (8th Cir. 1987), *cert. denied,* 484 U.S. 1068 (1988)	§§ 5.29, 7.35, 7.42
United States v. Shaw, 701 F.2d 367 (5th Cir. 1983), *cert. denied,* 465 U.S. 1067 (1984)	§ 5.25
United States v. Sheets, 125 F.R.D. 172 (D. Utah 1989)	§ 7.7
United States v. Shipp, 409 F.2d 33 (4th Cir.), *cert. denied,* 396 U.S. 864 (1969)	§ 5.17
United States v. Silvas, 33 M.J. 135 (C.M.A. 1991)	§ 4.38
United States v. Simmons, 923 F.2d 934 (2d Cir.), *cert. denied,* 111 S. Ct. 2018 (1991)	§ 7.23
United States v. Smith, 776 F.2d 1104 (3d Cir. 1985)	§ 8.6
United States v. Smith, 303 F.2d 341 (4th Cir. 1962)	§ 5.17
United States v. Snipes, 18 M.J. 172 (C.M.A. 1984)	§ 4.37
United States v. Solomon, 490 F. Supp. 373 (S.D. Ga. 1980)	§ 6.24
United States v. Spotted War Bonnet, 933 F.2d 1471 (8th Cir. 1991), *cert. denied,* 112 S. Ct. 1187 (1992)	§§ 7.43, 7.56
United States v. Stamper, 766 F. Supp. 1396 (W.D.N.C. 1991), *aff'd,* 959 F.2d 231 (4th Cir. 1992)	§ 5.34
United States v. Stanley, 15 M.J. 949 (A.F.C.M.R. 1983)	§ 6.8
United States v. Stivers, 33 M.J. 715 (A.C.M.R. 1991)	§§ 7.44, 7.53
United States v. Suarez, 32 M.J. 767 (A.C.M.R. 1991)	§ 4.19
United States v. Szabo, 789 F.2d 1484 (10th Cir. 1986)	§ 7.58
United States v. Taylor, 32 M.J. 684 (A.F.C.M.R. 1991)	§ 4.44
United States v. Thompson, 31 M.J. 169 (C.M.A. 1990), *cert. denied,* 111 S. Ct. 956 (1991)	§ 8.3
United States v. Thompson, 708 F.2d 1294 (8th Cir. 1983)	§ 5.11
United States v. Tolppa, 25 M.J. 352 (C.M.A. 1987)	§§ 4.44, 4.45
United States v. Torniero, 735 F.2d 725 (2d Cir. 1984), *cert. denied,* 469 U.S. 1110 (1985)	§ 4.18
United States v. Tornowski, 29 M.J. 578 (A.F.C.M.R. 1989)	§ 7.36
United States v. Torres, 937 F.2d 1469 (9th Cir. 1991), *cert. denied,* 112 S. Ct. 886 (1992)	§§ 5.28, 5.29, 5.30, 7.56
United States v. Tu, 30 M.J. 587 (A.C.M.R. 1990)	§ 4.28

Case	Book §
United States v. Vachon, 869 F.2d 653 (1st Cir. 1989)	§ 4.52
United States v. Varelli, 407 F.2d 735 (7th Cir. 1969), cert. denied, 405 U.S. 1040 (1972)	§ 5.21
United States v. Vargas, 933 F.2d 701 (9th Cir. 1991)	§ 7.56
United States v. Vazquez, 857 F.2d 857 (1st Cir. 1988)	§ 7.53
United States v. Villalta, 662 F.2d 1205 (5th Cir. 1981), cert. denied, 456 U.S. 916 (1982)	§ 2.17
United States v. Watkins, 21 M.J. 224 (C.M.A.), cert. denied, 476 U.S. 1108 (1986)	§ 6.14
United States v. Weil, 561 F.2d 1109 (4th Cir. 1977)	§ 7.22
United States v. Welch, 25 M.J. 23 (C.M.A. 1987)	§§ 5.32, 7.35
United States v. Whitaker, 34 M.J. 822 (A.F.C.M.R. 1992)	§ 5.32
United States v. Whitney, 18 M.J. 700 (A.F.C.M.R. 1984)	§ 7.30
United States v. Whitson, 587 F.2d 948 (9th Cir. 1978)	§ 7.20
United States v. Williams, 816 F.2d 1527 (11th Cir. 1987)	§ 6.18
United States v. Williams, 1992 WL 121410 (A.F.C.M.R. 1992)	§ 6.26
United States v. Williams, 33 M.J. 754 (A.C.M.R. 1991)	§ 8.3
United States v. Williams, 25 M.J. 854 (A.F.C.M.R. 1988)	§ 4.28
United States v. Williamson, 26 M.J. 115 (C.M.A. 1988)	§§ 7.42, 7.44
United States v. Woods, 484 F.2d 127 (4th Cir. 1973), cert. denied, 415 U.S. 979 (1974)	§§ 6.17, 6.18
United States v. York, 933 F.2d 1343 (7th Cir.), cert. denied, 112 S. Ct. 321 (1991)	§§ 6.13, 6.15, 6.17
United States v. Zenni, 492 F. Supp. 464 (E.D. Ky. 1980)	§ 7.11
United States ex rel. Latimore v. Sielaff, 561 F.2d 691 (7th Cir. 1977), cert. denied, 434 U.S. 1076 (1978)	§ 8.4
Valenzuela-Gonzalez v. United States District Court, 915 F.2d 1276 (9th Cir. 1990)	§ 8.13
Vann v. State, 1992 WL 105295 (Ark. 1992)	§ 7.53
Vasko, In re, 238 A.D. 128, 263 N.Y.S. 552 (1933)	§ 3.17
Vasquez v. State, 819 S.W.2d 932 (Tex. Ct. App. 1991)	§ 4.44
Vasquez v. State, 814 S.W.2d 773 (Tex. Ct. App. 1991)	§§ 7.38, 7.39
Velez v. State, 762 P.2d 1297 (Alaska Ct. App. 1988)	§§ 6.1, 6.13, 6.21
Vera v. State, 709 S.W.2d 681 (Tex. Ct. App. 1986)	§§ 5.7, 5.8, 7.30, 7.31
Vernon v. State, 814 S.W.2d 845 (Tex. Ct. App. 1991)	§ 4.28
Waeltz v. Department Human Servs., 27 Ark. App. 167, 768 S.W.2d 41 (1989)	§§ 2.16, 3.32
Walden v. Sears, Roebuck & Co., 654 F.2d 443 (5th Cir. 1981)	§ 7.48
Walker v. Superior Court, 47 Cal. 3d 112, 763 P.2d 852, 253 Cal. Rptr. 1 (1988), cert. denied, 491 U.S. 905 (1989)	§ 3.17
Waller v. Georgia, 467 U.S. 39 (1984)	§§ 5.23, 8.4
Walton v. Elftman, 64 Ohio Misc. 45, 410 N.E.2d 1282 (1980)	§ 7.27
Ward v. State, 519 So. 2d 1082 (Fla. Dist. Ct. App. 1988)	§ 4.37

CASES

Case	Book §
Ward v. State, 186 Ga. App. 503, 368 S.E.2d 139 (1988)	§ 7.30
Warren v. United States, 436 A.2d 821 (D.C. 1981)	§ 7.48
Warren v. Waterville Urban Renewal Auth., 235 A.2d 295 (Me. 1967), *cert. denied,* 390 U.S. 1006 (1968)	§ 7.47
Washington Post Co., *In re,* 807 F.2d 383 (4th Cir. 1986)	§ 8.6
Watson v. State, 290 Ark. 484, 720 S.W.2d 310 (1986)	§§ 3.29, 3.32
Watson v. State, 512 N.E.2d 885 (Ind. Ct. App. 1987)	§ 2.18
W.C.L. v. People, 685 P.2d 176 (Colo. 1984)	§§ 7.35, 7.36
W.D.N., II, *In re,* 443 So. 2d 493 (Fla. Dist. Ct. App. 1984)	§ 6.6
Weatherford v. State, 561 So. 2d 629 (Fla. Dist. Ct. App. 1990)	§ 7.46
Weaver v. State, 271 Ark. 853, 612 S.W.2d 324 (Ct. App.), *cert. denied,* 452 U.S. 963 (1981)	§ 7.30
Welfare of J.A., *In re,* 417 N.W.2d 696 (Minn. Ct. App. 1988)	§ 1.17
Werner v. Kliewer, 238 Kan. 289, 710 P.2d 1250 (1985)	§ 1.18
West v. State, 290 Ark. 329, 719 S.W.2d 684 (1986)	§ 5.34
Westbrook v. State, 186 Ga. App. 493, 368 S.E.2d 131 (1988)	§ 2.1
Wetz v. State, 503 So. 2d 803 (Miss. 1987)	§ 3.32
Wheat v. State, 527 A.2d 269 (Del. 1987)	§§ 4.10, 4.41, 4.44, 4.45
Wheeler v. United States, 159 U.S. 523 (1895)	§§ 2.1, 2.2
Wheeler v. United States, 211 F.2d 19 (D.C. Cir. 1953), *cert. denied,* 347 U.S. 1019 (1954)	§ 5.19
White v. Illinois, 112 S. Ct. 736 (1992)	§§ 7.28, 7.35, 7.48, 7.51, 7.52, 7.53
White v. State, 234 Ind. 209, 125 N.E.2d 705 (1955)	§ 1.12
Wilcox v. United States, 425 F. Supp. 895 (D. Conn. 1975)	§ 7.57
Wildermuth v. State, 310 Md. 496, 530 A.2d 275 (1987)	§§ 7.48, 7.50, 8.5, 8.9, 8.13
Williams v. State, 539 So. 2d 1049 (Miss. 1989)	§ 5.8
Williamson v. Jones, 936 F.2d 1000 (8th Cir. 1991)	§§ 3.28, 3.29
Willner v. Committee on Character & Fitness, 373 U.S. 96 (1963)	§ 7.38
Wilson v. State, 515 So. 2d 1181 (Miss. 1987)	§ 1.3
Wilson v. State, 221 So. 2d 100 (Miss. 1969)	§ 2.18
Winfrey v. State, 293 Ark. 342, 738 S.W.2d 391 (1987)	§ 1.14
Wisconsin v. Yoder, 406 U.S. 205 (1972)	§ 3.17
Wise v. State, 546 So. 2d 1068 (Fla. Dist. Ct. App. 1989)	§§ 7.22, 7.23, 7.24
Wolf, *In re,* 231 N.J. Super. 365, 555 A.2d 722 (1989)	§ 7.57
Wong Sun v. United States, 371 U.S. 471 (1963)	§ 3.29
Woolridge v. State, 659 P.2d 943 (Okla. Crim. App. 1983)	§ 6.20
Wright v. Tatham, 7 Adolph. & E. 313, 112 Eng. Rep. 488 (Ex. Ch. 1837) (first appeal); 5 Cl. & Fin. 670, 47 Rev. Rep. 136 (H.L. 1838) (second appeal)	§§ 7.11, 7.12
W.W. Conner Co. v. McCollister & Campbell, Inc., 9 Wash. 2d 407, 115 P.2d 370 (1941)	§ 7.47
Wyatt v. State, 578 So. 2d 811 (Fla. Dist. Ct. App. 1991)	§ 4.50

Case   *Book §*

Zaal v. State, 326 Md. 54, 602 A.2d 1247 (1991)   §§ 1.14, 1.15
Zabel v. State, 765 P.2d 357 (Wyo. 1988)   § 4.45
Zappa, *In re,* 6 Kan. App. 2d 633, 631 P.2d 1245 (1981)   §§ 1.12, 1.17
Zariyasta S., *In re,* 158 A.D.2d 45, 557 N.Y.S.2d 895 (1990)   § 3.30
Ziegler v. Tarrant County Child Welfare Unit, 680 S.W.2d 674 (Tex. Ct. App. 1984)   § 7.38
Zuniga v. State, 811 S.W.2d 177 (Tex. Ct. App. 1991)   § 4.28

INDEX

ABDOMINAL INJURIES.
  See PHYSICAL ABUSE
ACCOMMODATING CHILD
  WITNESSES § 8.3
ACCUSATORY PLEADING
  Generally § 1.1
  Alibi defense §§ 1.3, 1.4
  Balancing approach to sufficiency § 1.4
  Date of offense §§ 1.1, 1.3
  Double Jeopardy § 1.5
  Investigation required to narrow time frame § 1.3
  Jury unanimity § 1.6
  Notice of charges § 1.1
  Number of abusive acts § 1.6
  "On or about" § 1.3
  Place of offense § 1.1
  Specific date and time not required §§ 1.1, 1.3
  Specific place of crime not required § 1.1
  Time, children's understanding of § 1.2
  Time of offense §§ 1.1, 1.3, 1.4
ADDRESS OF CHILD §§ 2.20, 5.21
ADMISSIBILITY.
  See COURT DETERMINES ADMISSIBILITY
ADMISSIONS.
  See HEARSAY
AFFIRMATION.
  See COMPETENCE
AGE, PROOF OF § 7.41
ALIBI DEFENSE §§ 1.3, 1.4
ANAL FINDINGS.
  See SEXUAL ABUSE
ANATOMICAL DOLLS
  Generally § 4.35
  Demonstrative evidence § 5.8
ATTACHMENT DISORDER.
  See FAILURE TO THRIVE

BACKLASH AGAINST CHILD
  PROTECTION § 5.16

BATTERED CHILD SYNDROME.
  See PHYSICAL ABUSE
BATTERING PARENT SYNDROME § 3.31
BIAS.
  See IMPEACHMENT
BITE MARKS.
  See PHYSICAL ABUSE
BRUISES.
  See PHYSICAL ABUSE
BURNS.
  See PHYSICAL ABUSE
BUSINESS RECORDS
  Generally § 7.38
  Firmly rooted § 7.53
  Multiple hearsay § 7.38

CATCHALL EXCEPTION.
  See RESIDUAL EXCEPTION
CHARACTER EVIDENCE
  Character evidence admissible § 6.7
  –Defendant's character § 6.8
  –Impeachment §§ 5.24, 6.7
  –Sex offense cases §§ 6.7, 6.21
  –Victim's character § 6.9
  Character evidence inadmissible § 6.1
  Character in issue §§ 6.2–6.6
  –Criminal litigation § 6.3
  –Divorce cases § 6.4
  –Juvenile court cases § 6.5
  –Parental rights, termination of § 6.6
  –Victim's character not in issue § 6.9
  Character witness
  –Impeachment of § 6.8
  –Impeachment with § 5.24
  –Opinion testimony § 6.8
  –Reputation testimony § 6.8
  Defendant's character
  –Physical abuse § 6.8
  –Sexual Abuse §§ 4.50, 6.8
  Depraved sexual propensity §§ 6.7, 6.21
  Distinguished from uncharged misconduct evidence § 6.12

CHARACTER EVIDENCE *(Continued)*
  Expert testimony § 4.50
  Habit § 6.10
  Identity of perpetrator § 3.30
  Impeachment §§ 5.24, 6.8
  Juvenile court cases § 6.5
  Physical abuse cases § 6.8
  Profile evidence. See EXPERT TESTIMONY
  Proof of character §§ 6.7, 6.8
  Sex offense cases §§ 6.8, 6.21
  Threats § 6.5
  Uncharged misconduct evidence §§ 6.11–6.12
  Untruthful character impeachment § 5.24
  Victim's character § 6.9
CHARACTER WITNESS.
  See CHARACTER EVIDENCE
CHEST INJURIES.
  See PHYSICAL ABUSE
CHILD DEVELOPMENT
  Children's understanding of legal system §§ 1.9–1.11
  Communication §§ 2.1, 2.12, 4.42
  –Interpreter § 2.13
  Date, proof of § 5.5
  Direct examination, establishing dates and times § 5.5
  Ecologically valid research § 4.5
  Egocentrism § 2.10
  Expert testimony regarding child development §§ 4.39, 4.44
  Honesty § 2.14
  Impeachment §§ 4.39–4.45
  Inconsistency §§ 1.10, 2.12, 4.42
  Intelligence § 2.1
  Language § 2.12
  Lying § 2.14
  Memory
  –Generally § 2.11
  –Competence §§ 2.1, 2.11
  –Deposition regarding memory § 1.19
  –Free recall § 2.11
  –Friendly interviewer, effect of § 2.11
  –Memory for repetitious events §§ 1.3, 1.6
  –Questions trigger memory § 2.11
  –Recognition memory § 2.11
  –Refreshing recollection §§ 5.5, 5.11
  –Repetitive events § 4.13
  –Stress, effect of § 2.11

CHILD DEVELOPMENT *(Continued)*
  Moral development § 2.14
  Observe, capacity to § 2.10
  Questions children can understand § 2.12
  Recess to reduce stress § 5.10
  Suggestibility
  –Generally § 4.5
  –Ambiguous events § 4.5
  –Authority figure § 4.5
  –Defense experts § 4.5
  –Ecologically valid research § 4.5
  –Lowering suggestibility § 4.5
  –Peripheral details § 4.5
  –Psychological research § 4.5
  Time, children's understanding of §§ 1.2, 2.12, 5.5
  Time, proof of § 5.5
  Truth and falsehood, understanding difference between §§ 2.1, 2.14, 2.20
CHILD HEARSAY EXCEPTION
  Generally § 7.46
  Competence of declarant § 2.19
  Corroboration § 7.46
  Not firmly rooted § 7.53
CHILD SEXUAL ABUSE ACCOMMODATION SYNDROME.
  See SYNDROMES
CIRCUMSTANTIAL EVIDENCE
  Intent, proof of § 3.29
  Sufficient for verdict § 3.5
CLOSING COURTROOM §§ 8.4–8.5
COACHING.
  See IMPEACHMENT
COERCION.
  See UNCHARGED MISCONDUCT EVIDENCE
COLLATERAL FACT RULE.
  See IMPEACHMENT
COLPOSCOPE § 4.27
COMMUNICATE, ABILITY TO
  Generally § 2.12
  Interpreters § 2.13
  Nonverbal communication § 2.12
  Questions children can answer § 2.12
COMPETENCE
  Alter decision regarding competence § 2.18
  Burden on party objecting to competence § 2.18
  Communicate § 2.12

COMPETENCE *(Continued)*
   Court determines competence §§ 2.1, 2.18
   Direct examination, supporting competence § 5.4
   Discovery of child's records §§ 1.13–1.15
   Discretion of court § 2.18
   Every person competent §§ 2.3–2.7, 2.9
   –Court controls order of witnesses § 2.7
   –Personal knowledge § 2.5
   –Prejudice by allowing testimony § 2.4
   Examination for competence
   –Attorneys may be allowed to question §§ 2.18, 2.20
   –Excluding defendant from examination § 2.21
   –Jury, presence of § 2.18
   –Location of examination § 2.18
   –Presumptive incompetence states § 2.8
   –Questioning child §§ 2.18, 2.20
   –Record of competency examination § 2.18
   –Suggested questions § 2.20
   Excluding defendant § 2.21
   Factual mistakes do not render incompetent § 2.12
   Fantasy, as related to competence §§ 2.14, 2.20
   Hearsay declarant, competence of §§ 2.19, 7.49
   Hesitance to answer questions does not render incompetent § 2.12
   Inconsistency does not render incompetent § 2.12
   Intelligence, threshold level of § 2.1
   –Mental retardation § 2.1
   Interpreter, use of § 2.13
   Memory §§ 2.1, 2.11, 2.17
   Mental Retardation § 2.1
   Moral development § 2.14
   No minimum age §§ 2.1, 2.2, 2.3
   Oath or affirmation §§ 2.3, 2.16
   –No particular form required § 2.16
   Obligation to tell truth. See Truth, understanding obligation to tell, this subject
   Observe, capacity to §§ 2.1 2.10
   Personal knowledge § 2.17
   Preliminary competency examination § 2.18
   Presumptive incompetence § 2.8

COMPETENCE *(Continued)*
   Psychological examination regarding competence § 2.22
   Punishment for false testimony § 2.15
   Reconsider decision regarding competence § 2.18
   Time, children's understanding of § 2.12
   Truth and falsehood, understanding difference between §§ 2.1, 2.14
   Truth, understanding obligation to tell §§ 1.11, 2.1, 2.14, 2.20
   Waiver of objection § 2.18
   When child must be competent § 2.19
CONFRONTATION CLAUSE
   Generally §§ 7.50–7.58
   Applicable proceedings § 7.57
   Co-defendants § 7.54
   Competency examination § 2.21
   Cross-examination, limits on § 7.56
   Discovery, relationship to § 1.13
   Elements of confrontation § 7.50
   Firmly rooted exceptions § 7.53
   Forfeiture §§ 7.58, 8.8
   Former testimony § 7.55
   Hearsay §§ 7.51–7.55
   Interview, no right to attend § 1.13
   Multiple defendant trials § 7.54
   Proceedings where confrontation applies § 7.57
   Recess during cross-examination § 5.10
   Reliability § 7.53
   Unavailable declarant § 7.52
   Video testimony §§ 8.7–8.13
   Waiver § 7.58
CONSCIOUSNESS OF GUILT
   Generally § 6.23
   Identity of perpetrator § 3.30
   Intent, proof of § 3.29
CONSENT § 6.26
CONSISTENCY.
   See CONSISTENT STATEMENTS and INCONSISTENT STATEMENTS
CONSISTENT STATEMENTS
   Bias § 7.23
   Contradiction § 7.22
   Control of admissibility § 7.23
   Fabrication § 7.23
   Firmly rooted § 7.53
   Hearsay §§ 7.21, 7.22
   Impeachment, relation to § 7.22
   Importance of § 7.21
   Improper influence § 7.23

CONSISTENT STATEMENTS
(Continued)
   Inconsistent statements § 7.24
   Memory lapse § 7.25
   Prior to motive to fabricate § 7.23
   "Recent" fabrication §§ 7.21, 7.22
   Rehabilitation § 7.21
CONSTRUCTIVE FORCE § 6.26
CONTROL OF QUESTIONING BY JUDGE
   Competency examination § 2.18
CONVICTION.
   See IMPEACHMENT
CORPORAL PUNISHMENT § 3.2
CORROBORATION
   Hearsay §§ 4.45–4.46
   Sex offense victim's testimony §§ 5.15–5.16
COURT DETERMINES ADMISSIBILITY
   Competence §§ 2.1, 2.18
   Expert testimony § 4.9
   Hearsay Chapter 7
   Qualifications of expert § 4.10
COURT RECORDS, ACCESS TO § 8.6
COURTROOM
   Altering to accommodate children § 8.3
   Closing §§ 8.4–8.5
CREDIBILITY.
   See EXPERT TESTIMONY
CRITERION BASED CONTENT ANALYSIS § 4.36
CROSS-EXAMINATION
   Address of witness § 5.21
   Expert witnesses §§ 5.22–5.23
   Expert witness's personal history of abuse § 5.23
   Leading questions § 5.22
   Learned treatise §§ 5.22, 7.40
   Limits on §§ 5.21, 7.56
   Preparing child for § 5.2
   Protecting child witnesses § 5.2
   Recess during § 5.10
   Specific instances of misconduct § 5.24
   –Limits on § 5.24
   Techniques § 5.22
   Untruthful character § 5.24
CURATIVE ADMISSIBILITY § 4.52
CUSTODY CASES
   Character in issue § 6.4
   Discovery § 1.18

CUSTODY CASES *(Continued)*
   Fabricated allegations of sexual abuse § 4.4
   Privileged information §§ 1.12–1.19
DATE OF OFFENSE.
   See ACCUSATORY PLEADING
DEATHS FROM CHILD ABUSE § 3.1
DEFENSES AND RESPONSES THERETO
   Alibi § 1.3
   Consciousness of guilt, undermines defense of accident § 3.29
   Corporal punishment, reasonable § 3.2, 3.29
   Physical abuse litigation § 3.3
   Sexual abuse cases §§ 4.3–4.8
   –Fabricated allegations § 4.4
   –Innocent conduct misinterpreted § 4.6
   –Interviewer used leading questions § 4.5
   –Leading questions during interviews § 4.5
   –Mistaken identity § 4.7
   –Statutory language § 4.8
   Suggestibility § 4.5
DELAY REPORTING ABUSE
   Direct examination explaining § 5.6
   Expert testimony explaining § 4.44
   Reasons for delay § 4.40
   Rehabilitation §§ 4.40, 4.44
   Uncharged misconduct evidence § 6.20
DEMONSTRATIVE EVIDENCE
   Generally § 5.8
   Anatomical pictures § 5.8
   Dolls § 5.8
DIAGNOSIS
   Battered child syndrome § 3.5
   Sexual abuse § 4.10
DIAGNOSIS OR TREATMENT EXCEPTION
   Generally § 7.35
   Children's understanding § 7.36
   Firmly rooted § 7.53
   Identity of perpetrator § 7.35
   Non-physicians § 7.35
   Rationales for exception § 7.36
   Testimonial competence § 7.36
DIFFICULT TO PROVE CHILD ABUSE § 5.1

INDEX

DIRECT EXAMINATION
    Generally §§ 5.2–5.17
    Competence, support for § 5.4
    Court, questioning by § 5.9
    Dates and times § 5.5
    Delay reporting abuse § 5.6
    Leading questions § 5.7
    Narrative testimony § 5.3
    Preparation § 5.2
    Psychological examination regarding credibility § 5.16
    Put child at ease § 5.3
    Recesses § 5.10
    Refreshing recollection § 5.11
    Repeating questions § 5.3
    While child not on stand § 5.15

DISCLOSURE OF ABUSE
    Described §§ 4.5, 4.41
    Inconsistency § 4.42
    Leading questions, need for § 4.5

DISCOVERY
    Generally §§ 1.12–1.19
    Civil litigation § 1.19
    Court-ordered psychological examination. See PSYCHOLOGICAL EXAMINATION
    Custody cases § 1.18
    Defense discovery §§ 1.13–1.15
    Deposition §§ 1.13, 1.19
    Juvenile court § 1.17
    Pretrial interviews § 1.13
    Privileged information § 1.12
    Prosecution discovery § 1.16
    Showing required for § 1.14

DIVORCE.
    See CUSTODY CASES

DNA FINGERPRINTING § 4.26

DOLLS.
    See ANATOMICAL DOLLS

DOUBLE JEOPARDY.
    See ACCUSATORY PLEADING

DRUG ABUSE.
    See NEGLECT

EDUCATIONAL NEGLECT.
    See NEGLECT

EXCITED UTTERANCE
    Generally §§ 7.28–7.30
    Competence of declarant §§ 2.19, 7.49
    Factors § 7.30
    Firmly rooted § 7.53
    First safe opportunity § 7.30

EXCITED UTTERANCE *(Continued)*
    Relate to event §§ 7.29–7.30
    Sleep § 7.13
    Startling event § 7.29

EXPERT TESTIMONY
    Admissibility of expert testimony § 4.9
    Ambivalence toward abuser §§ 4.43, 4.44
    Basis of expert testimony § 4.11
    –Inadmissible data may support opinion § 4.11
    –Physical abuse § 3.7
    Battered child syndrome § 3.5
    Court appointed expert § 4.51
    Court determines admissibility § 4.9
    Credibility, opinion on § 4.45
    Defense experts §§ 4.5, 4.50
    Degrees of expertise § 4.10
    Delay reporting abuse §§ 4.40, 4.44
    Discretion of court § 4.9
    Establishing number of abusive acts § 1.2
    Expert witness's personal history of abuse § 5.23
    Form of testimony § 4.12
    –Dissertation § 4.12
    –Hypothetical question § 4.12
    –Opinion § 4.12
    Guidelines for expert testimony § 4.44
    Hypothetical question § 4.12
    Inadmissible evidence can support expert opinion § 3.7
    Identity of perpetrator § 4.46
    Intent, proof of § 3.29
    Judge questioning expert § 5.9
    Means used to inflict injury §§ 3.8, 3.12
    Medical history §§ 3.7, 4.10
    Novel scientific principles. See NOVEL SCIENTIFIC EVIDENCE
    Opinion testimony § 4.12
    –Reasonable certainty standard § 4.12
    Parent's explanation, opinion regarding §§ 3.9, 4.21
    Penetration § 4.28
    Perpetrator
    –Identity of § 4.46
    –Penile plethysmograph § 4.49
    –Profile of perpetrator § 4.50
    –Psychological tests § 4.49
    Personal knowledge not required § 3.7
    Post-traumatic stress disorder §§ 4.2, 4.34, 4.37, 4.44

EXPERT TESTIMONY *(Continued)*
  Profile evidence. See Perpetrator, this subject
  Qualification of expert §§ 3.5, 4.10
  Recantation §§ 4.41, 4.44
  Rehabilitation §§ 4.39–4.44
  –Case law § 4.44
  Sexual abuse
  –Ambivalence toward abuser § 4.43
  –Behaviors commonly observed in abused children § 4.32
  –Child sexual abuse accommodation syndrome § 4.33
  –Credibility, direct opinion on § 4.45
  –Diagnosis §§ 4.10, 4.12, 4.20, 4.30–4.35
  –Distinction between substantive evidence and rehabilitation §§ 4.1, 4.29
  –Medical evidence §§ 4.20–4.28
  –Opinion child was abused § 4.13
  –Perpetrator, identity of § 4.46
  –Rape trauma syndrome § 4.34
  –Rehabilitation § 4.39–4.44
  –Rehabilitation vs. substantive evidence §§ 4.1, 4.29
  –Ultimate issues § 4.13
  Strength of testimony § 4.12
  Ultimate issue, testimony on §§ 3.7, 4.13
  When permissible § 4.44

FABRICATED ALLEGATIONS
  Custody litigation § 4.4
  Defense of § 4.4
  Misperception allegations § 4.4
  Research on § 4.4
  Unsubstantiated § 4.4
FAILURE TO PROTECT CHILD §§ 3.19, 3.28
FAILURE TO THRIVE § 3.19
FALLS.
  See PHYSICAL ABUSE
FANTASY IN CHILDREN.
  See COMPETENCE
FATAL CHILD ABUSE § 3.1
FIRMLY ROOTED EXCEPTIONS § 7.53
FORCE.
  See UNCHARGED MISCONDUCT EVIDENCE
FORMER TESTIMONY
  Confrontation clause § 7.55
  Firmly rooted § 7.53

FOSSA NAVICULARIS § 4.22
FRACTURES.
  See PHYSICAL ABUSE
FRESH COMPLAINT OF RAPE
  Generally § 7.31
  Competence of child §§ 2.19, 7.49
  Firmly rooted § 7.53
FREUD
  Impact on sexual abuse § 5.16
FRYE **TEST.**
  See NOVEL SCIENTIFIC EVIDENCE

GENETIC FINGERPRINTING § 4.26
GENITAL FINDINGS.
  See SEXUAL ABUSE
GUARDIAN AD LITEM
  Appointment of § 8.3
  Consent to interview § 1.13
  Exercise of child's privilege § 1.17
  Hearsay § 7.31

HABIT § 6.10
HEAD INJURY.
  See PHYSICAL ABUSE
HEARSAY
  Admissions
  –Consciousness of guilt as admission § 3.29
  Age, proof of § 7.41
  Artwork § 7.7
  Assertion §§ 7.2, 7.6
  Burden of proof § 7.5
  Competence of declarant §§ 2.19, 7.49
  Confrontation. See CONFRONTATION CLAUSE
  Consciousness of guilt not hearsay § 3.29
  Dangers of hearsay §§ 7.4, 7.17
  Definition § 7.2
  Dolls § 7.8
  Drawings § 7.7
  Effect on listener § 7.15
  Exceptions. See particular exceptions
  –Introduction § 7.17
  Expert testimony, hearsay as basis for § 4.11
  Expert witness, reliance on § 3.7
  Firmly rooted exceptions § 7.53
  Fresh complaint of rape. See FRESH COMPLAINT OF RAPE
  Grammatical structure §§ 7.2, 7.3
  Hearsay-on-hearsay § 7.38

INDEX

HEARSAY *(Continued)*
  Implied assertions §§ 7.10–7.12
  Interpreter, use of does not render child's statement hearsay § 2.13
  Introduction § 7.1
  Multiple hearsay § 7.38
  Nonhearsay use of statements §§ 7.6, 7.7, 7.8, 7.13–7.16
  Nonverbal conduct §§ 7.5, 7.8
  Out-of-court §§ 7.2, 7.3
  Personal knowledge requirement § 2.17
  Preliminary ruling § 7.5
  Reflex §§ 7.2, 7.3
  Refreshing recollection § 5.11
  Sexual arousal or gratification, proof of §§ 7.6, 7.14–7.15, 7.33
  Silence § 7.9
  Sleep talk as hearsay § 7.13
  Soliloquy §§ 7.2, 7.3
  Statement § 7.2
  Sufficiency of hearsay to support verdict § 7.47
  Truth of matter asserted §§ 7.2, 7.3, 7.6, 7.7
  Unavailability § 7.48
  Unique knowledge § 7.16
  Unusual sexual knowledge §§ 7.6–7.8
  Verbal acts § 7.14
  Videotape § 7.2
  Writings § 7.7
HISTORY
  Competence to testify § 2.2
  Sexual abuse § 5.16
HONESTY OF CHILDREN.
  See CHILD DEVELOPMENT and COMPETENCE
HYMEN
  Accidental injury § 4.22
  Described § 4.22
  Size of opening § 4.22

IDENTIFICATION, STATEMENT OF
  Generally § 7.26
  Firmly rooted § 7.53
IDENTITY OF PERPETRATOR
  Generally § 3.30
  Battered child syndrome § 3.30
  Character evidence § 3.30
  Diagnosis or treatment exception § 7.35
  Exclusive custody by defendant § 3.30
  Expert testimony regarding § 4.15
  Eyewitness testimony § 3.30

IDENTITY OF PERPETRATOR
  (Continued)
  Juvenile court § 3.30
  Out-of-court statement of identification §§ 3.30, 7.26
  Statement of identification § 7.26
  Uncharged misconduct evidence §§ 3.30, 6.24
IMPEACHMENT
  Address of child § 5.21
  Bias § 5.21
  –Collateral fact rule § 5.21
  –Foundation § 5.21
  Capacity, defects in § 5.27
  Character witness § 5.24
  Coaching § 5.21
  Collateral fact rule § 5.20
  Consistent statements §§ 7.21–7.25
  Contradiction
  –Generally § 5.26
  –Collateral fact rule §§ 5.20–5.26
  Conviction § 5.25
  –Collateral fact rule §§ 5.20–5.25
  –Juvenile court adjudications § 5.25
  –Status offenses § 5.25
  Delay reporting abuse § 4.40
  Developmental differences between children and adults §§ 4.39, 4.44
  Expert witnesses §§ 5.22–5.23
  Expert's personal history of abuse § 5.23
  Inconsistent statements. See INCONSISTENT STATEMENTS
  Learned treatises §§ 5.22, 7.40
  Prior inconsistent statements. See INCONSISTENT STATEMENTS
  Purpose of § 5.18
  Rape shield statutes. See RAPE SHIELD STATUTES
  Recantation § 4.41
  Specific instances of misconduct
  –Conduct probative of untruthfulness §§ 5.24, 6.7
  –Limits on § 5.24
  Untruthful character § 5.24
  Voucher rule § 5.19
INCONSISTENT STATEMENTS
  Caretakers' inconsistent explanations for child's injuries § 3.9
  Child development §§ 1.10, 2.12, 4.42
  Collateral fact rule §§ 5.20, 7.18
  Consciousness of guilt, proof of § 3.29

INCONSISTENT STATEMENTS *(Continued)*
  Defined § 7.19
  Developmentally inappropriate questions §§ 1.9–1.11, 2.12
  Firmly rooted § 7.53
  Foundation § 7.18
  Hearsay §§ 7.18, 7.19
  Inconsistent, what constitutes § 7.19
  Prior inconsistent statements §§ 7.18–7.20
  Reasons for §§ 2.12, 4.42
  Recantation § 7.20
  Sufficiency to support verdict §§ 7.20, 7.47
INDICTMENT.
  See ACCUSATORY PLEADING
INFORMATION.
  See ACCUSATORY PLEADING
INTELLIGENCE.
  See COMPETENCE
INTENT
  Generally §§ 3.28–3.29
  Circumstantial evidence § 3.29
  Consciousness of guilt § 3.29
  Discipline, intent to § 3.2
  Failure to protect child § 3.28
  General intent § 3.28
  Intent to kill § 3.28
  Knowledge § 3.28
  Malice § 3.28
  Manslaughter § 3.28
  Methods of proof § 3.29
  Nature of injuries, intent inferred from § 3.29
  Negligence, criminal § 3.28
  Omission, intent inferred from § 3.29
  Opinion proper from lay witness that defendant acted to gratify sexual desire § 3.29
  Premeditation § 3.28
  Proof of § 3.29
  Prosecutor's obligation to prove intent § 3.29
  Reckless § 3.28
  Sexual arousal or gratification, proof of §§ 3.28–3.29, 6.18, 6.21, 7.6, 7.14–7.15, 7.33
  Specific intent § 3.28
  Torture § 3.28
  Totality of circumstances § 3.29
  Uncharged misconduct evidence §§ 3.29, 6.15–6.18, 6.21

INTENT *(Continued)*
  Victim's testimony § 3.29
  Wanton § 3.28
  Willful § 3.28
INTERPRETER § 2.13
INTERVIEWS
  Anatomical dolls § 4.35
  Attack on interviewers § 4.5
  Cognitive interview § 4.5
  Defendant's right to attend § 1.13
  Discovery § 1.13
  Dolls § 4.35
  Leading questions during § 4.5
  Memory, effect on questioning §§ 2.11, 4.5
  Need to ask leading questions § 4.5
  Suggestibility § 4.5
  –Lowering suggestibility § 4.5
INVITED ERROR § 4.52

JUDGE
  Neutrality §§ 2.18, 5.9
  Questioning witness § 5.9
JUDICIAL NOTICE.
  See NOVEL SCIENTIFIC EVIDENCE
JURY
  Children's understanding of § 1.11
  Interaction with child § 5.15
  Invade province of. See ULTIMATE ISSUE, TESTIMONY ON
  Jurors' perceptions of children § 8.14
JUVENILE COURT
  Adjudication, impeachment with § 5.25
  Discovery § 1.17
  Identity of perpetrator § 3.30
  Res ipsa loquitur § 3.30
  Ultimate issue. See EXPERT TESTIMONY
  Unanimous verdict § 1.6

LANGUAGE DEVELOPMENT.
  See CHILD DEVELOPMENT
LAY WITNESSES
  Opinion rule §§ 4.13, 6.8
LEADING QUESTIONS
  Cross-examination § 5.22
  Direct examination § 5.7
  Interviews, leading questions during § 4.5
  Justification for § 4.5
  Refreshing recollection § 5.11

INDEX

LEARNED TREATISE
   Firmly rooted § 7.53
   Hearsay § 7.40
   Impeachment § 5.22
LIMITED ADMISSIBILITY
   Uncharged misconduct evidence § 6.18
LYING.
   See CHILD DEVELOPMENT

MATURE MINOR.
   See NEGLECT
MEDICAL CARE, DUTY TO PROVIDE.
   See NEGLECT
MEDICAL EVIDENCE.
   See PHYSICAL ABUSE and SEXUAL ABUSE
MEDICAL NEGLECT.
   See NEGLECT
MEMORY.
   See CHILD DEVELOPMENT
   Refreshing recollection §§ 5.5, 5.11
MENTAL RETARDATION.
   See COMPETENCE and NEGLECT
MINNESOTA MULTIPHASIC PERSONALITY INVENTORY § 4.49
MODUS OPERANDI.
   See UNCHARGED MISCONDUCT EVIDENCE
MORAL DEVELOPMENT.
   See CHILD DEVELOPMENT and COMPETENCE
MOTIVE.
   See UNCHARGED MISCONDUCT EVIDENCE
MULTIPLE HEARSAY § 7.38
MUNCHAUSEN SYNDROME BY PROXY § 3.15

NAME OF CHILD § 8.3
NEED FOR CHILDREN'S TESTIMONY § 2.2
NEGLECT
   Abandonment § 3.25
   Cultural differences § 3.16
   Drug abuse § 3.23
   Educational neglect § 3.26
   Failure to provide child's needs § 3.16
   General neglect § 3.24
   Mature minor, medical decisions of § 3.17
   Medical care, duty to provide § 3.17
   Medical neglect § 3.17
   Mentally retarded parent § 3.20

NEGLECT *(Continued)*
   Parens patriae § 3.17
   Poisoning § 3.27
   Psychiatrically impaired parent § 3.22
   Psychological maltreatment § 3.18
   Religious belief § 3.17
   Unborn children, neglect of §§ 3.17, 3.23
NEW TRIAL
   Recantation § 4.44
NONACCIDENTAL INJURY §§ 3.5–3.15
NONORGANIC FAILURE TO THRIVE.
   See FAILURE TO THRIVE
NOTICE OF CHARGES.
   See ACCUSATORY PLEADING
NOVEL SCIENTIFIC EVIDENCE
   Generally §§ 4.14–4.19
   Battered child syndrome not novel §§ 3.5, 4.17
   Colposcope not novel § 4.28
   Criterion based content analysis is novel § 4.36
   Frye test § 4.18
   Judicial notice §§ 4.17, 4.18
   Medical evidence of sexual abuse not novel § 4.28
   Munchausen syndrome by proxy not novel § 3.15
   Profile of perpetrator is novel § 4.50
   Psychological testimony that child was abused §§ 4.30–4.35
   Rape trauma syndrome § 4.34
   Relevance analysis § 4.19
   "Sex abuse legitimacy scale" is novel § 4.36
   Shaken infant syndrome not novel § 3.11
   Statement validity analysis is novel § 4.36

OATH.
   See COMPETENCE
OBSERVE.
   See COMPETENCE
OPINION TESTIMONY FROM LAY WITNESSES
   Lay opinion proper that defendant acted to gratify sexual desire § 3.29

PARAPHILIA § 4.48
PARENS PATRIAE.
   See NEGLECT

PARENTAL RIGHTS TERMINATION
    Character in issue § 6.6
    Discovery § 1.17
PAST RECOLLECTION RECORDED
    Generally § 7.37
    Distinguished from recollection refreshed § 5.11
    Firmly rooted § 7.53
PEDOPHILIA § 4.48
PENETRATION
    Circumstantial evidence § 4.28
    Cunnilingus does not require § 4.8
    Dolls as demonstrative evidence § 5.8
    Expert testimony on § 4.28
    Hymen § 4.22
PENILE PLETHYSMOGRAPH § 4.49
PERINEUM § 4.22
PERSONAL KNOWLEDGE
    Generally § 2.17
    Expert testimony, personal knowledge not required § 3.7
PHOTOGRAPHS
    Admissibility § 3.32
    Colposcopic § 4.28
    Refresh recollection with § 5.11
PHYSICAL ABUSE
    Abdominal injuries § 3.12
    Battered child syndrome § 3.5
    –Generally § 3.5
    –Identity of perpetrator, proof of § 3.30
    –Not necessary to prove that defendant caused injury § 3.5
    Bite marks § 3.10
    Bruises § 3.10
    Burns
    –Generally § 3.12
    –Cigarette burns § 3.12
    –Contact burns § 3.12
    –Doughnut burns § 3.12
    –Scalding water § 3.12
    –Splash burns § 3.12
    –Stocking and glove burns § 3.12
    Caretakers' explanations of injury § 3.9
    Character evidence § 6.8
    Chest injuries § 3.12
    Circumstantial evidence sufficient for verdict § 3.5
    Defendant's character § 6.8
    Defenses § 3.3
    Defined § 3.2
    Doctrine of chances § 6.17

PHYSICAL ABUSE *(Continued)*
    Expert testimony. See EXPERT TESTIMONY
    Falls § 3.10
    Fractures
    –Generally § 3.14
    –Rib § 3.12
    Head injury
    –Generally § 3.11
    –Falls causing head injury § 3.11
    –Shaken infant syndrome § 3.11
    –Shaking § 3.11
    –Subdural hematoma § 3.11
    Implausible explanation § 3.9
    Intent, proof of §§ 3.29, 6.15–6.18
    Means used to inflict injury §§ 3.8, 3.12
    Medical history § 3.7
    Prevalence § 3.1
    Shaking. See Head injury, this subject
    Subdural hematoma. See Head injury, this subject
    Uncharged misconduct evidence
    –Doctrine of chances § 6.17
    Intent §§ 6.15–6.18
PHYSICAL EXAMINATION OF CHILD
    Civil litigation § 1.19
    Discovery § 1.13
PLAN.
    See UNCHARGED MISCONDUCT EVIDENCE
PLETHYSMOGRAPHY § 4.49
POISONING § 3.27
PORNOGRAPHY
    Possession probative of intent § 6.18
POST-TRAUMATIC STRESS DISORDER §§ 4.2, 4.44
POSTERIOR FOSSA § 4.22
POSTERIOR FOURCHETTE § 4.22
PREJUDICIAL EVIDENCE.
    See UNFAIR PREJUDICE
PRELIMINARY COMPETENCE EXAMINATION BY COURT.
    See COMPETENCE
PRELIMINARY QUESTIONS
    Competence §§ 2.2, 2.18
    Consistent statements § 7.22
    Personal knowledge § 2.17
PREPARING CHILDREN FOR COURT
    Children's understanding of law §§ 1.9–1.11
    Suggestibility, techniques to lower § 4.5

INDEX

PRESENCE AT TRIAL, DEFENDANT'S RIGHT
    Competence examination § 2.21
    Constitutional right § 8.5
PRESENT SENSE IMPRESSION
    Generally § 7.27
    Competence of declarant § 2.19
    Firmly rooted § 7.53
PRESS ACCESS TO COURT RECORDS § 8.6
PRESS RIGHT TO ATTEND TRIAL § 8.5
PRIOR BAD ACTS.
    See UNCHARGED MISCONDUCT EVIDENCE
PRIOR CONSISTENT STATEMENTS.
    See CONSISTENT STATEMENTS
PRIOR INCONSISTENT STATEMENTS.
    See INCONSISTENT STATEMENTS
PRIVILEGE.
    See also DISCOVERY
    Generally § 1.12
    Custody cases § 1.18
    Defendant may not assert child's privilege § 1.12
    Defense discovery §§ 1.13–1.15
    Guardian ad litem exercises child's privilege § 1.17
    Holder, child as §§ 1.12, 1.17, 1.18
    Juvenile court discovery § 1.17
    Parent-child privilege § 1.12
    Patient-litigant exception §§ 1.12, 1.17, 1.18
    Prosecution discovery § 1.16
    Refreshing recollection, effect on § 5.11
    Reporting statute, effect of § 1.16
    Spousal privileges § 1.12, 1.16
    Third party present § 1.12
    Waiver §§ 1.12, 1.17
PROFILE EVIDENCE.
    See EXPERT TESTIMONY
PSYCHIATRICALLY DISABLED PARENT.
    See NEGLECT
PSYCHOLOGICAL EXAMINATION OF CHILD
    Civil litigation § 1.19
    Competence § 2.22
    Credibility § 5.16
    Custody cases § 1.18
    Discovery § 1.14–1.15

PSYCHOLOGICAL MALTREATMENT.
    See NEGLECT
PSYCHOLOGICAL RESEARCH
    Empirical validity § 4.5
    Peer reviewed journals § 4.5
    See CHILD DEVELOPMENT
PSYCHOLOGICAL TESTS
    Identity sex offender, no test § 4.49
PSYCHOSOCIAL DWARFISM § 3.19
PUBLIC RECORDS EXCEPTION
    Generally § 7.39
    Firmly rooted § 7.53
PUBLIC TRIAL § 8.4

QUESTIONS CHILDREN UNDERSTAND § 2.12

RAPE SHIELD STATUTES
    Generally §§ 5.28–5.37
    Bias § 5.36
    Child abuse litigation § 5.28
    Consent § 5.30
    Constitutional challenge § 5.28
    Contradiction § 5.33
    Credibility § 5.32
    Defendant's state of mind § 5.31
    Defendant's use of § 5.37
    False Allegations §§ 5.34, 5.35
    Fantasy § 5.35
    Injury, source of § 5.29
    Past sexual behavior defined § 5.28
    Prior false allegations § 5.34
    Purpose of § 5.28
    Semen, source of § 5.29
    Sexual behavior defined § 5.28
    Ulterior motive § 5.36
RAPE, FORCE REQUIRED FOR § 6.26
RAPE TRAUMA SYNDROME.
    See SYNDROMES
REACTIVE ATTACHMENT DISORDER § 3.19
RECANTATION
    Child sexual abuse accommodation syndrome § 4.33
    Expert testimony explaining § 4.44
    New trial § 4.44
    Reasons for § 4.41
    Rehabilitation §§ 4.41, 4.44
    Testifying, stress of § 5.10
RECESS
    Generally § 5.10

RECORDED RECOLLECTION.
  See PAST RECOLLECTION
    RECORDED
REDIRECT EXAMINATION § 5.3
REFRESHING RECOLLECTION
  Generally §§ 5.2, 5.5 5.11
  Date of offense § 5.5
  Distinguished from past recollection
    recorded § 5.11
  Foundation § 5.11
  Leading questions to refresh § 5.7
  Privileged records, refreshing with
    § 5.12
  Time of offense § 5.5
REHABILITATION
  Character witness § 5.24
  Children's credibility §§ 4.39–4.44
  Consistent statements § 7.21
  Expert testimony. See EXPERT
    TESTIMONY
  When permitted §§ 4.39–4.44, 5.20
RELIGIOUS BELIEF.
  See NEGLECT
REPORTING STATUTE
  False allegations § 4.4
  Juvenile court discovery § 1.17
  Prosecution discovery § 1.16
RESIDUAL EXCEPTION
  Generally §§ 7.42–7.45
  Competence of declarant § 2.19
  Corroboration § 7.45
  More probative than other evidence
    § 7.42
  Not firmly rooted § 7.53
  Reliability §§ 7.43–7.45
RES IPSA LOQUITUR § 3.30

SEMEN §§ 4.22, 5.29
SEQUESTRATION RULE § 8.2
"SEX ABUSE LEGITIMACY SCALE"
  § 4.36
SEXUAL ABUSE
  Age of victims § 4.2
  Anal findings. See Medical evidence,
    this subject
  Bruises § 3.8
  Character evidence §§ 4.50, 6.1–6.8,
    6.21
  –Depraved sexual propensity § 6.21
  Child sexual abuse accommodation
    syndrome § 4.33
  Colposcope §§ 4.27–4.28

SEXUAL ABUSE *(Continued)*
  Corroboration of victim's testimony
    §§ 5.16–5.17
  Criterion based content analysis § 4.36
  Defenses §§ 4.3–4.8
  Diagnosis §§ 4.10, 4.20, 4.31–4.35
  Difficult to prove § 4.1
  Freud, impact of § 5.16
  Genital findings. See MEDICAL
    EVIDENCE, this subject
  History §§ 4.21, 5.16
  Intent, proof of §§ 3.28, 6.15–6.18,
    7.14–7.15, 7.33
  Lack of medical evidence §§ 4.1, 4.20
  Leading questions § 4.5
  Medical evidence
  –Generally §§ 4.20–4.28
  –Accidents §§ 4.22–4.23
  –Admissibility § 4.28
  –Anal findings § 4.22
  –Boys, genital findings § 4.22
  –Genital findings §§ 4.22–4.23
  –History § 4.21
  –Hymen § 4.22
  –Nonabusive explanations § 4.23
  –Penetration § 4.28
  –Perineum § 4.22
  –Physical examination § 4.22
  –Post-traumatic stress disorder §§ 4.2,
    4.44
  –Posterior fourchette § 4.22
  –Posterior fossa § 4.22
  –Prevalence §§ 3.1, 4.2
  –Psychological damage caused by § 4.2
  –Sexually transmitted disease § 4.24
  Minnesota Multiphasic Personality
    Inventory § 4.49
  Penetration § 4.28
  Penile Plethysmograph § 4.49
  Psychological testimony
  –Base rates § 4.32
  –Behaviors commonly observed in
    abused children § 4.32
  –Case law § 4.37
  –Diagnosis §§ 4.10, 4.13, 4.20,
    4.29–4.30, 4.37
  –Opinion child was abused
    §§ 4.29–4.30, 4.37
  –Profile of perpetrator § 4.50
  –Rehabilitation §§ 4.39–4.44
  –Rehabilitation vs. substantive evidence
    §§ 4.10, 4.29

INDEX

SEXUAL ABUSE *(Continued)*
 –Sexualized behavior § 4.32
 –Substantive evidence of abuse §§ 4.30–4.37
 –Ultimate issues § 4.13
 Psychological tests § 4.49
 Rape trauma syndrome § 4.34
 Rehabilitation §§ 4.1, 4.39–4.44
 Semen § 4.22
 "Sex abuse legitimacy scale" § 4.36
 Sexual arousal, proof of §§ 3.16–3.17, 6.18, 6.21, 7.14–7.15, 7.33
 Statement validity analysis § 4.36
SEXUAL KNOWLEDGE
 Hearsay §§ 7.6, 7.7, 7.8, 7.44
SEXUALLY TRANSMITTED DISEASES § 4.24
SHAKING.
 See PHYSICAL ABUSE
SLEEP.
 See HEARSAY
STARVATION § 3.27
STATE OF MIND
 Generally §§ 7.32–7.34
 Civil litigation § 7.34
 Criminal litigation § 7.33
 Diary § 7.7
 Firmly rooted § 7.53
 Physical condition § 7.32
 Sleep statements § 7.13
STATEMENT VALIDITY ANALYSIS § 4.36
STATUS OFFENSES
 Impeachment for § 5.25
SUBDURAL HEMATOMA.
 See PHYSICAL ABUSE
SUBSTANTIAL EVIDENCE.
 See SUFFICIENCY OF EVIDENCE
SUFFICIENCY OF EVIDENCE
 Child's testimony as sufficient § 1.7
SUGGESTIBILITY.
 See CHILD DEVELOPMENT
SUPPORT PERSONS § 8.1
SYNDROMES
 Child sexual abuse accommodation syndrome § 4.33
 Post-traumatic stress disorder §§ 4.2, 4.44
 Rape trauma syndrome § 4.34
TELEVISION.
 See VIDEO TESTIMONY

TENDER YEARS EXCEPTION.
 See CHILD HEARSAY EXCEPTION
TERMINATION OF PARENTAL RIGHTS.
 See PARENTAL RIGHTS TERMINATION
TESTIMONIAL COMPETENCE.
 See COMPETENCE
THREATS
 Uncharged misconduct evidence § 6.26
 Video testimony § 8.8
TIME
 Accusatory pleading § 1.1
 Children's understanding of time § 1.2
 Child's testimony as sufficient evidence § 1.7
 Competence, relation to §§ 2.12, 2.20
 Time of offense §§ 1.1, 1.3
TORTURE § 3.28

ULTIMATE ISSUE, TESTIMONY ON.
 See EXPERT TESTIMONY
UNAVAILABILITY § 7.48
UNBORN CHILDREN.
 See NEGLECT
UNCHARGED MISCONDUCT EVIDENCE
 Admissibility, determination of § 6.13
 Attempts to prove intent § 6.19
 Capacity § 6.25
 Coercion § 6.26
 Consciousness of guilt § 6.23
 Constructive force § 6.26
 Distinguished from character evidence § 6.12
 Doctrine of chances § 6.17
 Entire picture § 6.20
 Force § 6.26
 Identity
 –Consciousness of guilt § 6.23
 –Modus operandi § 6.24
 –Motive § 6.14
 –Plan § 6.22
 Intent
 –Attempts § 6.19
 –Consciousness of guilt § 6.23
 –Doctrine of chances § 6.17
 –Intent on prior occasions § 6.18
 –Knowledge § 6.18
 –Motive §§ 6.14, 6.16
 –Plan §§ 6.15, 6.22

UNCHARGED MISCONDUCT
EVIDENCE *(Continued)*
–Pornography § 6.18
–Proof of § 6.13
–Sexual arousal or gratification §§ 3.28, 3.29, 6.18, 6.21
Limited admissibility § 6.18
Medical history, relevance of prior abuse § 3.7
Modus operandi § 6.24
Motive § 6.14, 6.16
Opportunity § 6.25
Permissible uses § 6.11
Plan § 6.22
–Defined § 6.22
–Spurious plan § 6.22
Pornography § 6.18
Proof of uncharged act § 6.13
Relationship of the parties § 6.20
Rule 404(b) is inclusive § 6.13
Threats § 6.26
Unfair prejudice § 6.13
Uses of § 6.11
UNFAIR PREJUDICE
Collateral facts, cross-examination on § 5.20
Competence § 2.4
Cross-examination on collateral facts § 5.20
Expert testimony based on inadmissible evidence §§ 3.7, 4.11
Expert testimony on credibility § 4.45
Limiting instruction § 3.7
Novel scientific evidence § 4.19
Specific instances of misconduct § 5.24
–Balancing §§ 6.11–6.12
–Character evidence § 6.7
–Defined §§ 6.11–6.12
–Factors considered §§ 6.11–6.12

UNFAIR PREJUDICE *(Continued)*
–Uncharged misconduct evidence § 6.13

VARIANCE § 1.1
VIDEOTAPE.
See VIDEO TESTIMONY
VIDEO TESTIMONY
Generally § 8.7
Compulsory Process § 8.11
Confrontation § 8.8
Counsel, assistance of § 8.9
Due process § 8.12
Hearsay §§ 7.2, 7.4
Jury § 8.10
Presence at trial § 8.13
VOUCHER RULE § 5.19

WAIVER
See also PRIVILEGE
Competence of child § 2.18
Confrontation right §§ 7.58, 8.13
Expert testimony on credibility § 4.45
Failure to object to variance in proof § 1.1
Personal knowledge § 2.17
See PRIVILEGE
WITNESSES, CHILDREN AS
Address, child's § 5.21
Character witness § 5.24
Cross-examination, preparing child for § 5.2
Direct examination §§ 5.2–5.12
Impeachment. See IMPEACHMENT
Preparation §§ 5.2, 5.8
Psychological examinations §§ 2.22, 5.16
Recess § 5.10
Visit to court § 5.2